SICILY

F. Mannino/Lara Pessina/MICHELIN

| **Editorial Director** | Cynthia Clayton Ochterbeck |

THE GREEN GUIDE SICILY

Editor	Jonathan P. Gilbert
Contributing Writer	Anna Melville-James
Production Manager	Natasha G. George
Cartography	Alain Baldet, Peter Wrenn
Photo Editors	Yoshimi Kanazawa
Proofreader	Alison Coupe, Rachel Mills
Layout & Design	John Higginbottom, Natasha G. George
Cover Design	Ute Weber, Laurent Muller

Contact Us:	The Green Guide
	Michelin Maps and Guides
	One Parkway South
	Greenville, SC 29615
	USA
	www.michelintravel.com
	michelin.guides@us.michelin.com
	Michelin Maps and Guides
	Hannay House
	39 Clarendon Road
	Watford, Herts WD17 1JA
	UK
	☎ (01923) 205 240
	www.ViaMichelin.com
	travelpubsales@uk.michelin.com

Special Sales:	For information regarding bulk sales,
	customized editions and premium sales,
	please contact our Customer Service
	Departments:

	USA	1-800-432-6277
	UK	(01923) 205 240
	Canada	1-800-361-8236

One Team…
A Commitment to Quality

There's just one reason our team is dedicated to producing quality travel publications—you, our reader.

Throughout our guides we offer **practical information**, **touring tips** and **suggestions** for finding the best places for a break.

Michelin driving tours help you hit the highlights and quickly absorb the best of the region. Our descriptive **walking tours** make you your own guide, armed with directions, maps and expert information.

We scout out the attractions, classify them with **star ratings**, and describe in detail what you will find when you visit them.

Michelin maps featured throughout the guide offer vibrant, detailed and easy-to-follow outlines of everything from close-up museum plans to international maps.

Places to stay and eat are always a big part of travel, so we research **hotels and restaurants** that we think convey the essence of the destination and arrange them by geographic area and price. We walk you through the best shopping districts and point you towards the host of entertainment and recreation possibilities available.

We **test**, **retest**, **check and recheck** to make sure that our guidebooks are truly just that: a personalized guide to help you make the most of your visit. And if you still want a speaking guide, we list local tour guides who will lead you on all the boat, bus, guided, historical, culinary, and other tours you shouldn't miss.

In short, we remove the guesswork involved with travel. After all, we want you to enjoy exploring with Michelin as much as we do.

The Michelin Green Guide Team

PLANNING YOUR TRIP

INTRODUCTION TO SICILY

Paola Ghirotti/Fototeca ENIT

CONTENTS

DISCOVERING SICILY (& CALABRIA)

B. Kaufmann/MICHELIN

HOW TO USE THIS GUIDE

PLANNING YOUR TRIP

The blue-tabbed PLANNING YOUR TRIP section at the front of the guide gives you **ideas for your trip** and **practical information** to help you organize it. You'll find tours, a host of breaks in the great outdoors, a calendar of events, information on shopping, sightseeing, kids' activities and more.

INTRODUCTION

The orange-tabbed INTRODUCTION section explores **Nature** from the beaches to the volcanoes. The **History** section spans from pre-Hellenistic times to contemporary Sicily and Calabria. The **Art and Culture** section covers architecture, art, literature, traditions and folklore, while **The Region Today** delves into modern Sicily and Calabria.

DISCOVERING

The green-tabbed DISCOVERING section features Sicily and Calabria's Principal

Sidebars

Throughout the guide you will find peach-colored text boxes (like this one), with lively anecdotes, detailed history, and background information.

Sights, arranged alphabetically by region, featuring the most interesting local **Sights**, **Walking Tours**, nearby **Excursions**, and detailed **Driving Tours**.

🛈 Contact information, 👓 admission charges, 🕐 hours of operation, and a host of other **visitor information** is given wherever possible. Admission prices shown are normally for a single adult.

STAR RATINGS★★★

Michelin has given star ratings for more than 100 years. If you're pressed for time, we recommend you visit the ★★★, or ★★ sights first:

★★★ Highly recommended
★★   Recommended
★   Interesting

Address Books - Where to Stay, Eat and more...

WHERE TO STAY

We've made a selection of hotels and arranged them by price category to fit all budgets (*see the Legend on the cover flap for an explanation of the price categories*). For the most part, we've selected accommodations based on their unique regional quality, their regional feel, as it were.

🕭 *See the back of the guide for an index to where to stay.*

🕭 *See the red-cover Michelin Guide Italy for more addresses.*

WHERE TO EAT

We thought you'd like to know the popular eating spots in Sicily and Calabria. So, we selected restaurants that capture the regional experience. We're not rating the quality of the food per se; as we did with the hotels, we selected restaurants for many towns and villages, categorized by price to appeal to all wallets.

🕭 *See the back of the guide for an index to where to eat.*

🕭 *See the red-cover Michelin Guide Italy for more addresses.*

MAPS

- Ⓐ **Principal Sights map** and **Driving Tours Map** on the cover.
- Ⓐ Detailed maps for **major cities** and **villages**, including **driving tour maps** and larger-scale maps for **walking tours**.

All maps in this guide are oriented north, unless otherwise indicated by a directional arrow. The term "Local Map" refers to a map within the chapter or Tourism Region. A complete list of the maps found in the guide appears at the back of this book, along with a comprehensive index.

Ⓑ *See the map Legend at the back of the guide for an explanation of map symbols.*

ORIENT PANELS

Vital statistics are given for each principal sight in the DISCOVERING section:

- Ⓘ **Information:** Tourist Office/Sight contact details.
- ▶ **Orient Yourself:** Geographic location of the sight with reference to surrounding boroughs, towns and roads.
- Ⓟ **Parking:** Where to park.
- Ⓐ **Don't Miss:** Unmissable things to do.
- Ⓞ **Organising Your Time:** Tips on organising your stay; what to see first, how long to spend there, crowd avoidance, market days and more.
- **Kids Especially for Kids:** Sights of particular interest to children.
- Ⓒ **Also See:** Nearby PRINCIPAL SIGHTS featured elsewhere in the guide.

SYMBOLS

Spa	**Spa Facilities**	🚌	**Tours**
Kids	**Interesting for Children**	Ⓟ	**On-site Parking**
Ⓒ	**Also See**	▶	**Directions**
Ⓘ	**Tourist Information**	✕	**On-site eating Facilities**
Ⓞ	**Hours of Operation**	⚠	**Camping Facilities**
Ⓞ	**Periods of Closure**	⚘	**Beaches**
⚮	**Closed to the Public**	☕	**Breakfast Included**
⊙	**Entry Fees**	Ⓐ	**A Bit of Advice**
🚫	**Credit Cards not Accepted**	Ⓐ	**Warning**
♿	**Wheelchair Accessible**		

Contact – Addresses, phone numbers, opening hours and prices published in this guide are accurate at the time of press. We welcome corrections and suggestions that may assist us in preparing the next edition. Please send your comments to:

UK
Michelin Maps and Guides
Hannay House
39 Clarendon Road
Watford, Herts WD17 1JA
travelpubsales@uk.michelin.com
www.michelin.co.uk

USA
Michelin Maps and Guides
Editorial Department
P.O. Box 19001
Greenville, SC 29602-9001
michelin.guides@us.michelin.com
www.michelintravel.com

Detail of a carretto, Sicilian cart
Lara Pessina/MICHELIN

MICHELIN DRIVING TOURS

Regional Driving Tours

A map of **Driving Tours** (*See pp10-11*) details these itineraries. The guidelines allow time to enjoy the scenery, visit key towns and sights, and make occasional unscheduled stops.

① ARCHAEOLOGICAL SITES AND ANTIQUITIES

500km/312mi (nine days, including three in Palermo and two in Agrigento)
After a few days in **Palermo**, follow the Golfo di Carini to **Segesta** to admire its Doric temple, and then to **Erice**, a spectacular medieval hill-top village. Return to A 29 junction and head south, stopping at the attractive small town of **Castelvetrano**, and then continuing to the Ancient Greek town of **Selinunte**. From here, take S 115 towards Agrigento, following the coast as far as the ruined city of **Eraclea Minoa** and its stunning beach, before continuing to the world-famous Valle dei Templi in **Agrigento**. Explore the pleasant historic centre and surrounding area for two days. Returning to Palermo, you cross the delightful mountain landscapes of the interior. Just before arriving in the city, take a brief diversion to the right

along the A 19 to visit the ruins of the Punic city of **Solunto**.

② SALTWORKS AND TUNA FISHERIES

150km/94mi (eight days, including four in the Egadi Islands)
For several days, explore the **Egadi Islands**, once home to the traditional tuna *mattanza* (a fishing ritual), then return to Trapani and visit this town. Continue south along the main road through the **saltpans** (*See VIA DEL SALE*) that lie between Trapani and Marsala. Spend at least half a day here visiting the Ancient Phoenician colony at **Mozia**. Next, head back to the main road and continue to **Marsala**, home to the famous dessert wine (vineyard tours are available). The town's Baglio Anselmi Archaeological Museum houses relics of a Punic ship. Continue southeast to **Mazara del Vallo**, a bustling port with a distinctly North-African feel. Return to Trapani before heading up to Erice, a delightful medieval hill-top town. The **Tonnara Bonagia** (tuna fishery) a few miles from Erice is also worthwhile.

③ REACH FOR THE HEIGHTS

250km/156mi (five days)
This tour explores some of the island's lesser-known sights, driving through the mountains and barren uplands. After visiting **Enna**, the highest provincial capital in Italy at 948m/3 109ft, take S 117 north, skirting past magnificently sited villages such as **Calascibetta** and **Leonforte**. This road takes you into the southern slopes of the Madonie mountains. After a visit to **Nicosia**, a picturesque town at an altitude of 700m/2 296ft, take S 120 west to **Gangi,** where stone houses line the narrow medieval streets. Climb to an altitude of 1 147m/3 762ft to **Petralia Soprana,** the highest village in the Madonie. Continue along S 120 to the A 19, following the motorway as far

Saltworks with a windmill in Trapani

J. Malburet/MICHELIN

as **Caltanissetta**. A minor road then leads to **Pietraperzia;** from here, pick up S 191 and continue as far as the famous **Villa Imperiale del Casale,** a splendid Roman villa renowned for its magnificent floor mosaics. **Piazza Armerina,** a small medieval town with an impressive cathedral surrounded by Baroque buildings, is located just a few miles from here. S 117 then wends through beautiful scenery as far as Enna, passing the **Lago di Pergusa** just outside town.

④ BAROQUE SICILY: DEMISE AND REVIVAL IN 1693

350km/219mi (nine days, including three in Siracusa)

The island's Baroque heritage includes monumental limestone buildings, finely worked gratings and splendid corbels adorned with fantastic and grotesque figures. Start in **Catania,** home to ancient ruins, and then follow the coast as far as **Siracusa**. Visit the archaeological site, the island of Ortygia and some of the city's splendid museums, finding time perhaps for a boat trip on the **River Ciane**. Leaving Siracusa, follow S 115 to **Noto**, a magnificent Baroque town. The road then continues to Ispica, famous for the nearby **Cava d'Ispica**, a 10km/6mi gorge dotted with underground dwellings and necropoli. Return to S 115 and follow signs to **Scicli**, another famous Baroque town. From here, return to **Modica**, renowned for its architecture and chocolate. Not far away stands **Ragusa**, whose lower town (Ibla) is fascinating for its Baroque *palazzi* built according to a medieval layout. From here, S 514 follows the western edges of the Iblei as far as **Grammichele**, a town with a regular plan centred on a hexagonal piazza. The tour then continues to **Caltagirone**, renowned for its fine ceramics, after which you join S 417 and return to Catania.

⑤ THE DEMONE VALLEY

400km/250mi (ten days, including four in the Aeolian Islands)

After spending time in **Catania**, take a trip up **Etna** (subject to volcanic conditions), believed by the ancient Greeks to house the forge worked by the giants of Hephaestus, the god of fire. Follow the volcano's eastern flank as far as **Linguaglossa**. Drive S 284 to **Randazzo**, a small town of black lava. Turn away from Etna, taking S 116 through beautiful mountain landscapes and down to **Capo d'Orlando**. Follow the coast road east, where resorts mingle with archaeological sites, such as the Roman villa at **Patti**, the Greek city of **Tyndaris** and the Roman villa of **Terme Vigliatore**. The road then comes to **Milazzo**, the main departure point for the **Aeolian Islands**, the mythological home of Aeolus, god of the winds. Explore these beautiful islands for a few days before returning to Sicily and visiting **Messina**. Continue along the Ionian coast as far as **Taormina**, the island's most famous sight, renowned for its magnificent Greek theatre with breathtaking views out to Etna and over the azure ocean. Continue along the coast to **Riviera dei Ciclopi** (☞*See ACIREALE)*; legend claims the *Faraglioni dei Ciclopi*, off the small port of **Aci Trezza**, were actually the large rocks that Polyphemus threw at Ulysses in the *Odyssey*.

⑥ GRAND TOUR OF SICILY

850km/530mi (15 days)

This tour highlights the island's most famous cultural and natural sights. After visiting **Palermo** and **Monreale**, head to the splendid Doric temple at **Segesta** and then continue south, following tour ① as far as **Agrigento**. From here, continue along the coast on S 115 to **Ragusa**, pausing at the archaeological museum in Gela. At Ragusa, join tour ④ until **Catania**. Continue to **Etna, Linguaglossa, Taormina, Messina** and the northeast coast, following tour ⑤ as far as **Capo d'Orlando**. Continue along the coast as far as **Cefalù**, returning to Palermo after visiting the Baroque villas in **Bagheria**.

Local Driving Tours

Listed below are driving tours within the *Discovering Sicily* section of the guide, which are not listed on the Driving Tours map.

ACIREALE – Other Aci in the Area: *15km/9mi*. Towns include Aci Catena and Aco Trezza.

AGRIGENTO – From Pircandello to Miinos (1 day): *90km/56mi round trip from Agrigento*. Drive alongside stunning beaches.

Toward Monte Sciani (1 day): *175km/109mi round trip*. See the Agrigento coast and Monte Sciani.

The hills around Naro (1 day): *90km/56mi round trip from Agrigento*. Including Baroque Naro and pretty Palma di Montechiaro.

CALTAGIRONE – Gli Iblei (2 days): *round trip of 160km/100mi, starting at Caltagirone and overnighting in Vizzini*. Through the villages of the Iblei Mountains.

CEFALÙ – Excursion Inland: *12km/7mi*. Follow signs to the *Santuariao di Gibilmann*a. A scenic road to the Santuario di Gibilmanna and Isnello.

ENNA – Along the hills north of Enna (1 day): *85km/53mi, plus 55km/34mi back to Enna*. Rolling hills between Enna and Catania, hilltop villages and panoramas.

ETNA – Three drives for differing perspectives of the iconic volcano.

From the coast to the southern slopes (half a day, excluding ascent): *45km/28mi from Acireale*.

The northeast flank (half a day, excluding ascent):: *60km/37mi starting from Linguaglossa*.

Circular tour of Etna (1 day): *155km/97mi round trip from Catania*.

GIBELLINA – The ruins of the 1968 earthquake (at least half a day): *60km/38mi*. Drive through the most affected areas, including towns and villages that were rebuilt.

MADONIE E NEBRODIE – Different scenic routes through the area, providing different sets of views.

The heart of the Madonie (1 day): *160km/100mi round trip starting from CEFALÙ*. Petralia Soprana and Sottana and Polizzi Generosa.

Between the Madonie and the Nebrodi (1 day): *180km/112mi round trip from Santo Stefano di Camastra*. Day includes Gangi and Sperlinga.

La Fiumara d'Arte (at least half a day): *80km/50mi, starting at Santo Stefano di Camastra*. Open-air gallery following the River Tusa.

A day in the Nebrodi Mountains (1 day): *200km/125mi*. Anticlock-wise offers great views of Etna,

The Eastern Nebrodi (half a day): *85kkm/53mi*. This tour snakes its way inland from Capo d'Orlando to Capo Calavà.

MESSINA – Capo Peloro (at least half a day): *70km/44mi*. Pano-ramic headland road winds past glorious beaches.

Ionian coast (1 day): *Messina to Taormina, 70km/44mi*.

MILAZZO – Capo di Milazzo: *8km/5mi by car*. This rocky spur includes Baia del Tono beach.

A day trip inland (1 day): *180km/112mi round trip from Milazzo*. Day includes stretches up the slopes of Monte Peloritani.

NOTO – Ruins and beautiful natural landscapes (1 day): *85km/53mi*. Day includes Cava Grande and the Riserva di Vendicari.

RAGUSA – Seaside (1 day): *110km/69mi from Ragusa, finishing in Comiso*.

SCIACCA – Valle del Belice and Valle del Sosio (1 day): *160km/100mi*. Tour starts around the shores of Lago Arancio and heads up to Prizzi.

SIRACUSA – Archaeological sites (1 day): *80km/50mi*.

TAORMINA – The Alcantra Valley (1 day): *60km/37mi*. Day includes a visit to the Gorges and taking the riverbed walk through the valley.

WHEN AND WHERE TO GO

When to Go

CLIMATE

In Giuseppe Lampedusa's 1958 novel *The Leopard,* the prince describes the Sicilian climate as "six months of 40°C (104°F) temperatures". Although the writer exaggerates, the southern coast and its immediate hinterland do indeed bake in summer. The northern and eastern shores, and the islands off Sicily enjoy milder climates, thanks to the coastal mountains that shield the hot African winds. The inland area has cooler summers and harsh winters. Catania is an exceptionally hot city, made more unpleasant by smog. July and August are the most uncomfortable months, while April, May, June, September and October offer pleasantly warm temperatures. Rainfall is scarce, but the centuries-old water shortage does not usually effect visitors, as most hotels have cisterns.

SEASONS

In **spring**, the weather is mild, crowds are smaller and rates lower. However, Etna is usually covered with snow and therefore inaccessible until early May, the sea is a little cool for swimming, and the offshore islands only welcome tourists from April or May to October. Most major festivals take place during the **Easter holidays**; book months in advance. **Summer** is the most popular period: all the tourist facilities are open, plus museums and monuments extend their hours. Disadvantages include the hordes and the heat, which is almost unbearable in some areas: the central inland region, the southern coast, Catania and Palermo. **Autumn** is a more pleasant time, offering similar conditions to spring. **Winter** is perfect for anyone planning a purely cultural trip, just check opening hours carefully. Be cautious driving inland, as the mountains can be wet and snowy.

Themed Tours

SICILIAN WINE ROUTES

Explore the area's major vineyards on itineraries designed by the Istituto Regionale della Vite e del Vino *(Via Libertà 66, Palermo; ☎091 62 78 111, Fax 091 34 78 70; www.vitevino.it).*

The Alcamo Route

Alcamo is a dry and fresh white table wine. This tour wends between Castellammare del Golfo, Scopello, Alcamo, Segesta and Calatafimi.

The Dessert Wine Routes

The Moscato *passito* is a rich, sweet, amber wine made from *zibibbo* grapes; Marsala is a darker and more famous blend (*See MARSALA*). The Marsala route passes through Erice, Trapani, Marsala, Salemi and Gibellina, while the Moscato trip covers Pantelleria island.

The Insolia Route

The Insolia (or Ansonica) grape variety – present in almost all Sicilian DOC *(Dominazione di Origine Controllata)* wines – adds a pleasant, fresh palate and floral aromas to the more robust white wines. This tour visits the wine-producing areas of the southern coast, stretching from Mazara del Vallo to Agrigento. Then it crosses inland to Palermo's outskirts, passing through Sambuca di Sicilia, Santa Margherita Belice and Monreale en route.

The Nero d'Avola and Cerasuolo di Vittoria Route

The Nero d'Avola (or Calabrese) grape variety is the basis of all the best Sicilian DOC reds. Blended with the frappato grape, it produces the Cerasuolo di Vittoria, an elegant wine with warm, harmonious tones. The route heads inland from Cefalù, crossing the island to Ragusa and passing through Castelbuono, Piazza Armerina, Caltagirone, Vittoria, Comiso, Ragusa and Modica.

Detail of the decorations in the cloisters, Monreale

The Moscato di Noto and Moscato di Siracusa Route

These two *moscati* wines have a sweet and harmonious palate and a delicate floral aroma. This tour explores the extreme southeast corner of Sicily, visiting Siracusa, Noto, Palazzolo Acreide and Pantalica.

The Etna Wine Route

The Etna vineyards produce red, white and rosé wines and were the first in Sicily to receive a DOC label. Trace their territory along the Ionian coast from Catania to Taormina, and then turn inland to the mountain.

The Malvasia delle Lipari

This ancient method dries grapes on reed mats, producing a delicate, fragrant wine. The tour explores the islands in the Aeolian archipelago.

Ideas For Your Visit

Given Sicily's size and rich heritage, you should spend at least one week there, although a two-week stay permits exploration of the offshore islands. However, below are a few suggestions for shorter breaks.

SHORT BREAKS (3-4 DAYS)

Highlights of Catania

One of the region's highlights is **Mount Etna**, combined with a stop at the delightful town of **Taormina**, and sunset on a beautiful beach. Spend

another day at **Siracusa** (Ortygia and the archaeological site), followed perhaps by a dusk excursion to **Noto** or **Ragusa Ibla**. Your third day's sightseeing should focus on the Valle dei Templi in **Agrigento**, easily combined with the magnificent **Villa Imperiale del Casale**, near Piazza Armerina.

Highlights of Palermo

Arriving at **Palermo** airport, you should first explore the capital city. On Day 2, admire the mosaic masterpieces in the cathedral at **Monreale**, followed by those in **Cefalù**, then retire to a beach in the late afternoon. Possible excursions for Day 3 include a day trip to the Valle dei Templi in **Agrigento**, or to the delightful town of **Erice**, stopping to admire the splendid Doric temple at **Segesta**.

The Ionian Coast

In addition to **Taormina** and its neighbouring seaside resorts, highlights include **Mount Etna**, the **Alcantara Valley, Catania** and **Siracusa**. Allow 1hr 30min to travel from Taormina to Siracusa (100km/62mi).

Outskirts of Palermo

Palermo is an excellent base. Spend one day exploring **Scopello** and the **Riserva dello Zingaro**, another visiting **Erice** and the **Via del Sale** between Trapani and Marsala, and a third following the suggested tour **inland from Palermo** (See PALERMO).

Agrigento, Temple of Heracles

A Few Days in the Mountains

Visitors based on the north coast at **Cefalù** or **Capo d'Orlando** can discover an unusual facet of Sicily by exploring the Alpine landscapes of the **Madonie e Nebrodi** (⟲See MADONIE E NEBRODI).

LONGER BREAKS (1-2 WEEKS)

This week-long introduction to the island includes two days in **Palermo**, **Monreale** and **Cefalù**, one day at **Segesta** and **Erice**, and one at the Valle dei Templi in **Agrigento**. Spend one day at the **Villa Imperiale del Casale** and the **Baroque towns** of Ragusa Ibla, Noto and Modica; the next in **Siracusa**; and the last visiting **Etna** and **Taormina**… with maybe even some time to relax on the beach.

The Tyrrenhian Coast – Start in the island's capital and chief sea port, **Palermo**. Take a day to explore the city. **The Historic Quarter** and vibrant area of **La Kalsa** are recommended. Beat the midday heat with visits to the Galleria regionale di Sicilia, Museo Archeologico Regionale or the fascinating, if macabre, 16C–20C interred friars at the Catacombe dei Cappuccini just outside the city. The next day, branch out from your Palermo base to **Monreale** and **Cefalù** to admire splendid cathedral frescoes and mosaics.

A morning visit to the ancient splendour of Segesta, with its splendid Doric Temple starts Day 3. In the afternoon, lose yourself inside the shady maze of **Erice**'s cobbled streets, dotted with churches and monasteries.

Mediterranean and Ionian Coasts

Head down to the Mediterranean coast and **Agrigento** on Day 4 to stroll through the **Valle dei Templi**. Feel the onward march of the ancient Romans the following day at the **Villa Imperiale del Casale**, with its superb mosaic floors. Arrive early to avoid crowds and high temperatures, then retire to the shady town squares of **Noto**, **Modica** or **Ragusa Ibla** in the afternoon to soak up their

Beach at Cefalù

B. Morandi/MICHELIN

Baroque beauty. Spend the next day in **Siracusa** admiring the immense Teatro Greco, before heading on to **Taormina**. There, either admire the views of **Mount Etna** from the Greek Theatre and then relax on the beach, or take an early morning trip to climb the volcano itself.

ISLAND HOPPING

The Aeolian Islands – The seven Aeolian islands are linked to each other, and to the mainland, by regular hydrofoil and ferry services. Highlights include the active volcanoes on **Stromboli** and **Vulcano**, the latter with its dramatic black lava beaches and healing mud. **Lipari**, the largest of the Aeolian islands , is fringed with spectacular beaches, such as the white pumice stretch at **Canneto**. On **Salina** the panoramic coastal road leads to beautiful coves such as that at Pollara. On **Filicudi** visit the Bronze Age village at **Capo Graziano**, while isolated **Alicudi** and tiny **Panarea** offer secluded traditional charm.

The Egadi Islands – Renowned for their wild coastal beauty, all three Egadi islands are easily reached from Trapani in under an hour. On **Favignana**, the tufa caves, once quarries, are now secret gardens. Offshore, take a boat trip out to the **Grotta Azzurra** and **Grotta dei Sospiri**. Divers and sunbathers also love the pristine bays of **Cala Rotonda** and **Cala Grande**. The tiny, hilly island of Levanzo is a peaceful haven, with a single road and hamlet, **Cala Dogana**. The island's highlight is the Grotta del Genovese, a two-hour walk away, with its Palaeolithic wall paintings. **Marettimo** has no hotels on it, although you can rent rooms. Visitors here come for the seclusion and beautiful walks, including those winding up the **Punta Troia**, topped with the ruins of a 17C Spanish castle.

Pantellaria – Explore the island's unique character at **Nika** with its cubic Arab-style houses, *dammuso* and traditional walled Pantelleria gardens filled with citrus trees. Inland, **La Montagna Grande** and **Monte Gibele** offer lovely walks and spectacular views. Other highlights include the ancient rock-hewn tombs at **Ghirlanda** and the natural cave sauna at **Grotta Benikula**.

Ustica – Surrounded by a Marine National Park, the small volcanic island of Ustica is popular with scuba divers. Highlights include the **Grotta dei Gamberi** and admiring Roman artefacts *in situ* along the sub-aqua archaeological trail off the **Punta Gavazzi** headland. Above water, boat trips around the coast are popular excursions.

The Pelagie Islands – The archipelago of Isole Pelagie comprises of the large island of **Lampedusa** and two smaller ones, **Linosa** and uninhabited **Lampione**. With their rocky volcanic coastlines, and desert interiors, the islands are primarily of interest for the superb diving and snorkelling around their shores.

LITERARY ROUTES

These itineraries celebrate the life and works of authors. Other projects include themed tours, known as "sentimental journeys". Led by a guide-cum-storyteller, these often include theatre performances. The group tours sometimes welcome individuals, if space permits (advance booking recommended). **Contact** Stefano D'Arrigo – Sedi a Reggio Calabria e Messina (Ganzirri-Capo Peloro); ☎090 53 167; Fax 090 57 28 038; ecos-med@me.nettuno.it.

Luigi Pirandello
This route links the towns between Agrigento and Porto Empedocle that have a connection with the Nobel Prize-winning playwright. **Contact** Il Cerchio, Via Ugo La Malfa a Monte 1, Agrigento; ☎0922 40 28 62; Fax 0922 55 40 37; www.parcopirandello.it.

Salvatore Quasimodo
Towns such as Modica (Salvatore Quasimodo's birthplace) and Roccalumera (between Messina and Taormina), whose Saracen tower inspired one of the poet's works, are included on this route. **Contact** Corso Umberto I, 242, Modica; ☎0932 75 38 64; www.quasimodo.it.

Leonardo Sciascia
This journey focuses on Racalmuto, Leonardo Sciascia's birthplace, and Caltanissetta, where he studied. **Contact** the Fondazione Leonardo Sciascia, Viale della Vittoria 3, Racalmuto; ☎0922 94 19 93; www.regalpetra.it.

Giuseppe Tomasi di Lampedusa
This route links Palermo, the birthplace of Giuseep Tomasi di Lampedusa; Santa Margherita Belice, where he spent much of his childhood and adolescence; and Palma di Montechiaro, the family's fief. **Contact** www.parcotomasi.it or Vicolo della Neve all'Alloro 2–5 (off Piazza Marina), Palermo; ☎091 61 60 796; Fax 091 61 00 618; Palazzo Ducale, Palma di Montechiaro; ☎0922 96 83 99; Fax 0922 96 82 57.

Giovanni Verga
This route wends its way between Catania, Aci Castello and Aci Trezza, home to the author Giovanni Verga and many of his characters. **Contact** Ghenea, Fantasticheria, via Arc. De Maria no 15, Aci Trezza; ☎328 68 55 328, Fax 095 71 16 638; www.museocasadelnespolo.it

Elio Vittorini
The main office is at Via S. Sebastiano 14, Siracusa; ☎0931 48 12 32.

KNOW BEFORE YOU GO

Useful Websites

The following sites offer information on Italian history and art, as well as trip-planning suggestions.

ITALY

- **www.enit.it**
  Italian tourist office
- **www.museionline.it**
  Italian museums
- **www.beniculturali.it**
  Government site detailing archaeology and culture.
- **www.trenitalia.com**
  State Railway

SICILY

- **www.regione.sicilia.it**
  Official regional portal
- **www.coloridisicilia.it**
  Photographs and culture
- **www.bestofsicily.com**
  English magazine on Sicily
- **www.parks.it**
  Natural parks and reserves.
- **www.wwf.it/sicilia**
  World Wildlife Fund, Sicily
- **www.festedisicilia.it**
  Festivals and events
- **www.insicilia.it**
  Tourism in Sicily
- **www.siciliano.it**
  Sicily search engine

SICILIAN PROVINCES

Agrigento: www.aaa-agrigento.it and www.lampedusa.to (Lampedusa)
Catania: www.turismo.catania.it, www.parcoetna.ct.it (Etna National Park)
Enna: www.apt-enna.com
Isole Eolie: www.portaledelleolie.it
Palermo: www.aapit.pa.it, www.arcidiocesi.palermo.it (churches), www.CEFALÙ-tour.pa.it (Cefalù)
Ragusa: www.ragusaturismo.it
Siracusa: www.apt-siracusa.it

Taormina: www.taormina-sicily.it
Trapani: www.apt.trapani.it, www.egaditourism.it (Egadi Islands)

Tourist Offices

INTERNATIONAL

CANADA
175 Bloor Street,
Suite 907, South Tower,
Toronto M4W 3R8
☎(416) 925 4882
www.italiantourism.com

UK
1 Princes Street,
London W1B 2AY
☎0207 408 1254;
Toll free from the UK and Ireland:
☎00800 00482542
www.italiantouristboard.co.uk

US - New York
630 Fifth Avenue,
Suite 1565, New York, NY, 10111
☎(212) 245 4822
www.italiantourism.com

US (LA)
12400 Wilshire Blvd., Suite 550,
Los Angeles, CA 90025
☎(310) 820 2977, 1898 or 1959
www.italiantourism.com

US (Chicago)
500 North Michigan Avenue,
Suite 2240, Chicago, IL 60611
☎(312) 644 0996
www.italiantourism.com

LOCAL TOURIST OFFICES

Italian State Tourist Office
Contact your country's ENIT bureau (Ente Nazionale Italiano per il Turismo) or visit www.enit.it.

Regional Tourist Offices

Local offices are listed near attractions, where applicable. Regional tourist information on Sicily is available from:

Assessorato Regionale del Turismo, delle Comunicazioni e dei Trasporti
Via Notarbartolo 9, 90141 Palermo
☎091 70 78 201
www.regione.sicilia.it

International Visitors

ITALIAN EMBASSIES ABROAD

For entry requirements and visas, ask the nearest Italian outpost.

Canada

275 Slater Street, 21st Floor, Ottawa, Ontario K1P 5H9
☎(613) 232 2401
Fax (613) 233 1484
www.ambottawa.esteri.it

UK

14 Three Kings Yard, London W1K 4EH
0207 312 2200
Fax 0207 312 2230
www.amblondra.esteri.it

US

3000 Whitehaven St, NW Washington, DC 20008
☎(202) 612 4400
Fax (202) 518 2151
www.ambwashingtondc.esteri.it

ITALIAN CONSULATES ABROAD

For language classes, cultural and tourist information contact:

Canada

3489 Drummond Street, Montreal, Quebec H3G 1X6
☎(514) 849 8351
Fax (514) 499 9471
www.consmontreal.esteri.it;
136 Beverley Street, Toronto, Ontario M5T 1Y5
☎(416) 977 1566
Fax (416) 977 1119
www.constoronto.esteri.it

UK - Edinburgh

32 Melville Street, Edinburgh EH3 7HW
☎(0131) 226 3631
Fax (0131) 226 6260
www.consedimburgo.esteri.it

UK - Manchester

Rodwell Tower, 111 Piccadilly, Manchester M1 2HY
☎(0161) 236 9024
Fax (0161) 236 5574
www.consmanchester.esteri.it

US

500 N Michigan Ave, Suite 1850, Chicago, IL, 60611
☎(312) 467 1550
Fax (312) 467 1335
www.conschicago.esteri.it

FOREIGN EMBASSIES AND CONSULATES IN ITALY

Australia

Via Antonio Bosio 5, 00161 Rome
☎06 85 27 21, Fax 06 85 27 23 00
www.italy.embassy.gov.au

Canada

Via Salaria 243, 00199 Rome
☎06 85 44 41, Fax 06 85 44 42 912
www.canada.it

Ireland

Piazza di Campitelli 3, 00186 Rome
☎06 69 79 121, Fax 06 679 2354
www.ambasciata-irlanda.it

UK (Palermo)

Via Cavour 121, Palermo
☎091 32 64 12, Fax 091 3804901
www.britain.it

UK (Rome)

Via XX Settembre 80A, Rome 00187
☎06 42 20 00 01
www.britain.it

USA (Palermo)

Via Vaccarini 1, 90143 Palermo
☎091 30 58 57
Fax 091 62 56 026

USA (Rome)

Via Veneto 119A, 00187 Rome
☎06 46 741
Fax 06 46 742 356
www.usembassy.it
http://rome.usembassy.gov;

ENTRY REQUIREMENTS

Passports
Americans, Australians, Canadians and Kiwis must carry a valid passport, as well as the British. Other EU citizens only need a national identity card. In case of loss or theft, report to the embassy or consulate and the police.

Visas
Entry visas are required for Australian, New Zealand, Canadian and US citizens (for a visit of more than three months). Apply to the Italian Consulate (visa issued same day; delay if submitted by mail). The US booklet **Your Trip Abroad** supplies information on visa requirements, customs regulations, medical care, etc. – available from the Superintendent of Documents, PO Box 37954; Pittsburgh, PA 15250-7954; ☎(202) 512 1800; Fax (202) 512 2104; www.access.gpo.gov.

CUSTOMS REGULATIONS

Since 1999, those travelling between European Union countries can no longer purchase "duty-free" goods. Visitors arriving from another EU country can import unlimited duty-paid goods for personal use. For more detailed information, request a free leaflet, **Duty Paid**, from HMRC National Advice Service (written enquiries section), Alexander House, Victoria Ave, Southend, Essex SS99 1BD; ☎0845 010 9000; www.hmrc.gov.uk. The US Customs Service offers a free publication **Know Before You Go** for US citizens: www.customs.gov.

Pets (Cats and Dogs)
Pets entering Italy from another country must have a Export Health Certificate and proof of rabies vaccination from a local veterinarian. To return to the UK, cats and dogs must have a 'pet passport' under The Pet Travel Scheme www.direct.gov.uk.

HEALTH

Medical facilities are excellent and most have English-speaking doctors.

Pharmacists can sometimes supply oral contraception and medicines for straightforward ailments like conjunctivitis (pink eye). More serious complaints and injuries can be treated at local hospital casualty departments *(pronto soccorso)*.

UK citizens should obtain an **EHIC (European Health Insurance Card)** before leaving home: www.ehic.org.uk; ☎0845 606 2030. This entitles the bearer to free or reduced-cost medical treatment in the state healthcare system when temporarily visiting an EU country. Separate travel and medical insurance is highly recommended. North Americans can contact the International Association for Medical Assistance to Travelers (IAMAT) ☎(716) 754 4883 or, in Canada, ☎(416) 652 0137; www.iamat.org for tips on travel, and lists of local, English-speaking doctors. The US Center for Disease Control and Prevention also advises on health hazards and food safety. ☎(800) 311 3435; www.cdc.gov

Accessibility

Many historic monuments do not have elevators, ramps or other facilities. Contact **CO.IN** (Consorzio Cooperative Integrate), Via Enrico Giglioni 54, Roma; ☎06 23 26 9231, Fax 06 232 69 231; www.coinsociale.it. English-language advice is also available at www.italiapertutti.it. Sights in the guide marked with the symbols ♿ have full or partial access for wheelchairs.

In the UK
Holiday Care Service ☎0845 124 9971; www.holidaycare.org.uk
RADAR (Royal Association for Disability and Rehabilitation) ☎020 7250 3222; www.radar.org.uk
In Italy
Accessible Italy ☎(378) 941 111; www.accessibleitaly.com
In the US
SATH (Society for the Advancement of Travel for the Handicapped) ☎(212) 447 7284; www.sath.org Alternative Leisure Co; ☎(781) 275 0023; www.alctrips.com

GETTING THERE AND GETTING AROUND

By Plane

As airport security and baggage regulations change frequently, it is always advisable to check the rules before you fly. Visit www.dft.gov.uk/airport security for more information about what to carry.

Several international carriers serve Palermo, Catania and Reggio Calabria on the mainland. Flights are more frequent in summer.

ALITALIA

Alitalia is Italy's national airline. It operates services to 27 domestic destinations, including Catania and Palermo, and 74 international destinations, including the UK, US and Canada.

UK

4 Portman Square, Marble Arch, London W1H 9PS; ☎0207 486 8432 or 08705 448 259; www.alitalia.co.uk

Ireland

4–5 Dawson Street, Dublin 2; ☎(01) 677 5171; Fax (01) 677 3373.

USA

666 Fifth Avenue, New York, NY 10103; ☎(212) 903 3300; 1 800 223 5730 (toll-free); www.alitaliausa.com

Italy

Viale Marchetti 111, 00148 Rome; ☎06 2222; www.alitalia.it

OTHER CARRIERS

- **Airone:** serves Mediterranean and Italian destinations. ☎199 20 70 80 (from Italy), 06 48 88 00 69 (from elsewhere); www.flyairone.it

- **Alpi Eagles:** internal flights only. ☎899 500 058 (from Italy) Fax 049 979 07 75 www.alpieagles.com
- **Meridiana:** links to Italian and European cities. ☎892 928 (from Italy), 0845 355 55 88 (from UK), 0789 52 682 (from elsewhere); www.meridiana.it
- **MyAir:** internal Italian flights only. ☎899 500 060 (from Italy), 20 73 65 15 97 (from elsewhere); www.myair.com
- **Ryanair:** flies Palermo to London Stansted and Trapani to Dublin ☎899 67 89 10 (from Italy), 0871 246 0000 (from UK), +353 1 249 7791 (from elsewhere) www.ryanair.com
- **easyJet:** flies Catania-Milan and Palermo-London Gatwick. ☎0905 821 0905 www.easyjet.com

DIRECT FROM THE USA

- **American Airlines** – www.aa.com
- **Continental Airlines** – www.continental.com
- **Delta Airlines** – www.delta.com
- **Eurofly** – www.eurofly.it
- **Northwest Airlines** – www.nwa.com
- **United Airlines** – www.ual.com
- **USAirways** – www.usairways.com

TOUR OPERATORS

- **Citalia** – ☎0208 686 0677 and 0870 909 7555; www.citalia.com
- **Italian Journeys** – ☎0207 373 8058; www.italianjourneys.com
- **Page and Moy Ltd** – ☎08708 334 012; www.page-moy.co.uk

AIRPORTS

Sicily's two main airports are **Falcone e Borsellino** (www.gesap.it) in

Palermo and **Fontanarossa** close to Catania; the latter is best for Taormina and Siracusa (www.aeroporto.catania. it). Tiny airports at **Trapani Birgi** and on the islands of **Pantelleria** and **Lampedusa** connect to the mainland and a few European hubs. Finally, consider flying into **Reggio Calabria**, on the "boot's toe" (www.sogas.it).

Airport Transfers
Falcoe e Borsellino is 35km/22mi from Palermo on the A 29 motorway. There is a taxi rank outside the arrivals terminal or call ☎091 225 455. By train, the Trinacria Express links the terminal directly with Palermo; www.trenitalia.it. Tickets €5. Airport buses to Palermo run every half hour and cost €5.30. Regular airport buses also run every 20 minutes between Catania and **Fontanarossa**.

By Ship

Ferries operate to Palermo from Genoa (20hr), Livorno (19hr), Civitavecchia (12hr), Naples (11hr) and Cagliari (13hr). Other routes include Trapani-Cagliari (10hr), Catania-Naples (10hr) and Messina-Salerno (8hr).
⌖ *See CATANIA, MESSINA, PALERMO and TRAPANI*

By Train

The rail network is limited in Sicily and doesn't cover the whole island. The main services operate along the coast, linking Messina–Siracusa (3hr), Messina–Palermo (3hr), Palermo-Agrigento (2hr) and Palermo–Trapani (2hr 30min). Services to the mountainous interior are infrequent. ☎89 20 21 (from Italy); www.trenitalia.com

The train operates via the Straits of Messina, with coaches loaded directly onto the ferry at Villa San Giovanni. Ticket prices are all inclusive. For information, apply to the **Ferrovie dello Stato** (Italian State Railways), ☎89 20 21 (from Italy); www.trenitalia.com

Getting off a ferry at Messina

By Coach/Bus

The coach network offers the best way of exploring the island for visitors without their own transport, offering regular services to many towns and cities. Contact the local tourist office (⌖*See the chapter headings in the* **Discovering Sicily** *section*).

Eurolines connects London's Victoria Coach Station and Italy: ☎08717 818181; www.eurolines.co.uk or www.nationalexpress.com. **Segesta Internazionale** runs buses between Rome, Palermo and Trapani. Journey time between Rome and Palermo is 12hr. ☎0935 565111; www.interbus.it (⌖*See PALERMO*)

By Car

The link between Sicily and the rest of Italy is provided by ferries and hydrofoils between Reggio Calabria or Villa San Giovanni and Messina. Ferrovie dello Stato (Italian State Railways) provide a car-ferry service from Villa San Giovanni (☎89 20 21; www.trenitalia. com). The crossing time depends on the ferry type (car-only or auto-train), and varies between 25–45min. Società Caronte also operates a service: ☎800 62 74 14, 0965 79 31 31 (toll-free in Italy); www.carontetourist.it. Because of the frequent service (every 20min), booking is not necessary.
From Reggio Calabria, foot passengers can board the ferry (☎89 20 21; www.

trenitalia.it) or hydrofoil (Ustica Lines, ☏0923 87 38 13, www.usticalines.it).

DRIVING IN SICILY

A car makes the island's remote stretches accessible. However, Palermo traffic is so chaotic that most visitors rely on shoe leather and public transport. Narrow, medieval streets in villages also make driving difficult. The **motorways** *(autostrade)* in Sicily do not cover the whole island. Stretches include Messina-Palermo (A 20), Palermo-Trapani-Mazara del Vallo (A 29); and Palermo-Enna-Catania (A 19).
Most major routes are free of charge. Roads to mountain settlements are usually stunning, but tend to be winding and therefore slower.

DRIVING LICENCE

EU citizens need a valid **national driving licence**. Visitors from other countries may want an **international driving licence**, which translates details. In the US, the American Automobile Association issues these: $18 for members and $20 for non-members. AAA National Headquarters ☏(407) 444 7000; www.aaa.com. Other documents required include the vehicle's current **log book** and a **green card** for insurance.

ROAD REGULATIONS

Traffic drives on the right and the **minimum age** is 18 years. **Seat belts** are mandatory in the front and back of the vehicle. Drivers must wear **shoes**. Carry spare lights and an emergency **red triangle** sign and a valid driving licence. Motorways *(autostrade)* and dual carriageways *(superstrade)* are indicated by green signs; ordinary roads by blue signs; tourist sights by yellow signs. Pay **motorway tolls** with cash, credit or **Viacard,** sold at motorway entrances and exits, in Autogrill restaurants and through ACI (Automobile Club Italiano) ☏803 116; www.aci.it

Speed Restrictions
- 50kph/31mph in built-up areas;
- 90-110kph/55-68mph on open country roads;
- 90/56 (600cc) – 130kph/80mph (excess of 1 000cc) on motorways, depending on engine capacity.

PARKING

The symbol 🅿 denotes car parks on the city maps and in this guide.
Do not leave valuable items in your car and pack all luggage out of sight.

MAPS AND PLANS

A list of Michelin maps helpful for navigating to Sicily and around the island appears in Maps and Plans at the back of this guide.

ROADSIDE ASSISTANCE

ACI (Automobile Club Italia)
☏803 116 (24-hour emergency service); www.aci.it

PETROL/GAS

Fuel is sold as *super* (4-star), *senza piombo* (unleaded 95 octane), *super plus* or *Euro plus* (unleaded 98 octane) or *gazolio* (diesel).
Manned petrol stations usually close noon–4pm and at night. Petrol can be bought 24 hours a day and on Sundays from automatic petrol pumps.

CAR RENTAL

The main car hire agencies have offices in cities and at the airports. Some tour operators offer "fly-drive" packages. Call (from Italy only):

- **Avis:** ☏199 100 133; www.avis.co.uk
- **Hertz:** ☏199 112 211, 0248 233 662 (from a mobile/cell); www.hertz.co.uk
- **Europcar:** ☏0870 607 5000 (UK), +44 1132 422 233 (international reservations); www.europcar.co.uk
- **Maggiore:** ☏848 867 067; www.maggiore.it

WHERE TO STAY AND EAT

Hotel and Restaurant recommendations are located in the Address Books throughout the **Discovering Sicily** section of the guide.
For coin ranges and for a description of the symbols used in the Address Books, see the Legend on the cover flap.

Where to Stay

For popular destinations, book well in advance, especially for trips in April to October. In general, prices dip from November to March, and many hotels offer discounts or weekend deals. For each establishment, the first figure refers to the price of a single room, the second figure to a double rate. Exceptions are highlighted (rural guesthouses, for example, which generally only have double rooms). Breakfast is usually included in the price, although this may not be the case in smaller hotels (in which cases, the cost of breakfast immediately follows the room rate).
Check the rates before booking and ask for confirmation in print.

HOTELS AND PENSIONI

Generally, the word **pensione** describes a small family-run hotel. Sometimes within a residential building, it offers simple, basic rooms, often without a private bathroom. Some pensioni do not accept credit cards.

RURAL ACCOMMODATION

Rural guesthouses – agriturismi – house visitors on farms and feed them the bounty of the land: olive oil, wine, honey, vegetables and meat. Extremely popular in Sicily, some properties rival the elegance of the best hotels – with prices to match. Catering options vary from breakfast to full board or an apartment kitchenette. We've selected agriturismi that sometimes accept one-night reservations. However, during high season,

expect a minimum stay (3–7 nights). Prices are only given when this formula is compulsory. Also, bear in mind that the rates are for double rooms (the only sort available in this genre). Solo travellers can request – but should never expect – discounts. Survey the following guides: Turismo Verde in Sicilia, published by the Consorzio Villaggio Globale (☎091 30 81 51); Vacanze e Natura, published by Associazione Terranostra (☎06 48 28 862; www.terranostra.it); Agriturismo e Vacanze Verdi, published by Associazione Agriturist (Corso Vittorio Emanuele 101, Rome; ☎06 68 52 342; Fax 06 68 52 424; www.agriturist. it); Guida all'Agriturismo, published by Demetra; and Vacanze Verdi published by Edagricole. Other interesting accommodation options are published in the Guida del Turismo alternativo (Sicilia occidentale and Sicilia orientale; in Italian only), available from bookshops and newsagents, or directly from the Sicilian Tourist Service, which provides an information and booking service (Piazza Don Bosco 6, Palermo; ☎091 36 15 67; Fax 091 63 72 482; www.stsitalia.it). Information is also available from **Turismo Verde**, Via Caio Mario 27 Rome; ☎06 36 11 051; www.turismoverde.it

BED AND BREAKFAST

In this varied category, the lines between hotel and B&B blur. Typically, hosts rent out their apartment, home or a few rooms. Minimum-stay requirements are common, credit cards are not. However, prices are competitive, especially given the cosiness and authenticity. Contact **Bed & Breakfast Italia**, Palazzo Sforza Cesarini, Corso Vittorio Emanuele II 282, 00186 Rome; ☎06 68 78 618; Fax/☎06 68 78 619; www. bbitalia.it, or **Bed & Breakfast Bon Voyage**, Via Procaccini 7, 20154 Milan; ☎02 33 11 814; Fax 02 33 13 009; www.bbbv.it.

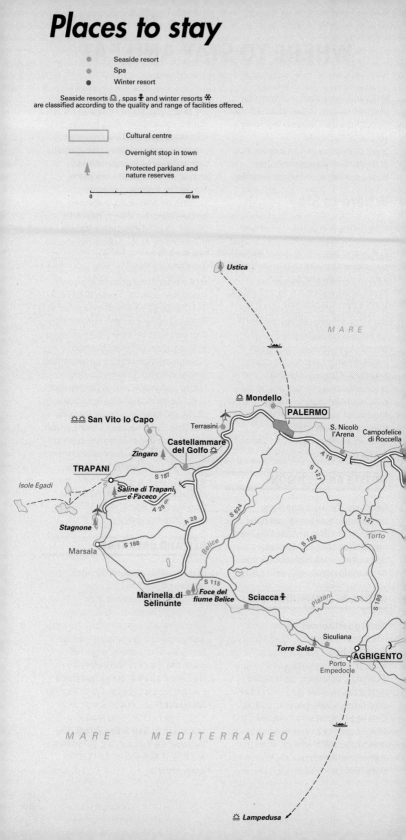

Places to stay

Seaside resort

Spa

Winter resort

Seaside resorts ♨, spas ✝ and winter resorts ❄
are classified according to the quality and range of facilities offered.

Cultural centre

Overnight stop in town

Protected parkland and
nature reserves

0   40 km

Ustica

MARE

♨ **Mondello**

PALERMO

♨♨ **San Vito lo Capo**

Terrasini

S. Nicolò
l'Arena

Campofelice
di Roccella

**Castellammare
del Golfo** ♨

Zingaro

TRAPANI

S 187

A 19

S 121

Isole Egadi

**Saline di Trapani
e' Paceco**

A 29 dir

S 624

S 121

Torto

A 29

Stagnone

Marsala

S 188

S 188

Belice

S 115

**Marinella di
Selinunte**

*Foce del
fiume Belice*

Sciacca ✝

Platani

S 169

Siculiana

Torre Salsa

AGRIGENTO

Porto
Empedocle

MARE   MEDITERRANEO

♨ *Lampedusa*

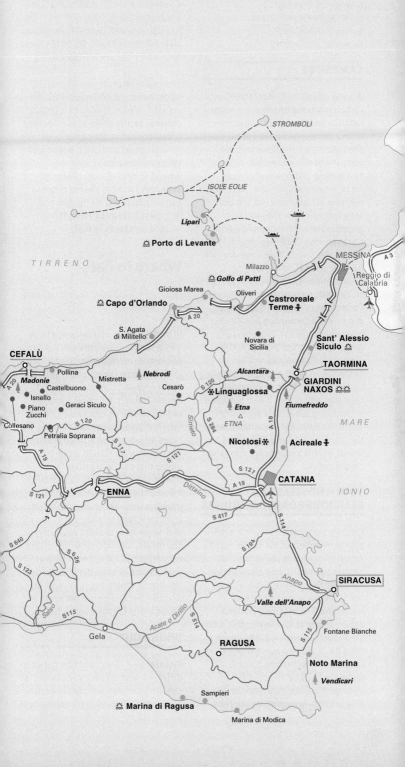

STROMBOLI

ISOLE EOLIE

Lipari

⚓ *Porto di Levante*

T I R R E N O

MESSINA

Milazzo

A 3

Reggio di Calabria

⚓ *Golfo di Patti*

Gioiosa Marea

Oliveri

Castroreale Terme ✚

⚓ Capo d'Orlando

A 20

S. Agata di Militello

Novara di Sicilia

Sant' Alessio Siculo ⚓

CEFALÙ

TAORMINA

Pollina

Alcantara

GIARDINI NAXOS ⚓⚓

A 20

Madonie

Mistretta

Nebrodi

S 120

Castelbuono

Cesarò

❋ *Linguaglossa*

Fiumefreddo

Isnello

Geraci Siculo

△ *Etna*

△ ETNA

S 284

MARE

Piano Zucchi

S 120

Simeto

A 18

Collesano

Nicolosi ❋

Acireale ✚

Petralia Soprana

A 19

S 117

S 121

S 121

Dittaino

CATANIA

ENNA

A 19

IONIO

S 121

S 640

S 6 26

S 417

S 19A

S 114

Anapo

SIRACUSA

S 123

Saso

S 115

Valle dell'Anapo

Acate o Dirillo

S 514

S 115

Fontane Bianche

Gela

RAGUSA

Noto Marina

Sampieri

Vendicari

⚓ Marina di Ragusa

Marina di Modica

See also:
- www.bedandbreakfast.it
- www.primitaly.it/bb
- www.bedebreakfast.it
- www.dolcecasa.it
- www.caffelletto.it

CAMPSITES

A good option for budget travellers, a camping ground usually has a restaurant, bar and food shop, sometimes even a disco or swimming pool. Some sites also rent bungalows and caravans. Prices shown are daily rates for two people, one tent and one car. An International Camping Carnet for caravans is useful, but not compulsory; buy one from the motoring organisations or the **Camping and Caravanning Club** (Greenfields House, Westwood Way, Coventry CV4 8JH, UK; ☎0845 130 7633; www.campingandcaravanningclub). co.uk. Request further details from the **Federazione Italiana del Campeggio e del Caravanning** (Via Vittorio Emanuele 11, 50041 Calenzano (FI); ☎055 88 23 91; fax 055 88 25 918; www.federcampeggio.it). The organisation offers a map of campsites and highlights those with special rates for cardholders. It also publishes an annual guide, *Campeggi e Villagi Turistici in Italia,* in collaboration with the Touring Club Italia (TCI). Local tourist boards also supply information on campsites.

YOUTH HOSTELS AND RELIGIOUS BOARDING HOUSES

Hostel accommodation is only available to members of the Youth Hostel Association. Join at any of the YHA hostels and renew your membership annually. Despite the name, all ages are welcome. In Italy, hostels are run by the **Associazione Italiana Alberghi per la Gioventù** (AIG), situated at Via Cavour 44, 00184 Rome; ☎06 48 71 152; www.ostellionline.org. **Case per ferie** (holiday homes), generally found in the big cities, offer simple – but clean and reasonably priced – accommodation. The

disadvantage is the curfew: visitors are expected to be back by 10.30pm. **Contact** the tourist offices and CITS, Centro Italiano Turismo Sociale, Associazione dell'Ospitalità Religiosa, viale del Monte Oppio 20, 00184 Rome ☎06 48 73 145; www.citsnet.it.

The map of Places to Stay (ⓒ See p24) recommends establishments for different kinds of trips. Those interested in **cultural centres** should look for the names framed in green. For brief trips, focused on art and cities, **overnight stops** are underlined in green. Among the many other **places to stay**, look for areas shaded in green (nature parks) and for the symbols ♦ **(spas)**, ⌂**(seaside resort)** and ❋ **(winter sports resort)**.

Where to Eat

ⓒ*see INTRODUCTION: The Island Today, Food and Wine.*

In Sicily, lunch is usually served from 1 to 2.30pm and dinner from 8.30pm. Booking is recommended, especially in high season. Dining out in Sicily is about enjoying the food, plain and simple. Nobody will mind if you just order a salad and a pasta dish, or ask for a first course as a main course. However, a traditional Sicilian feast starts with an antipasto, a pre-meal nibble that can be anything from stuffed artichoke hearts to sardines, followed by a first course, *il primo,* usually a soup. The meat or fish dish come next for *il secondo,* with salads and vegetables ordered separately. The meal is rounded off with a desert, either teeth-jangling sweet Sicilian concoctions, or more commonly fruit salad or ice cream. It's customary for a small cover charge per person to be added to the bill *(il conto)* for bread.

DINING OUT

Ristorante – The distinction between different restaurant types is not as obvious as it once was. But in general, a *ristorante* offers elegant cuisine and service in a relatively formal atmosphere. However, as this is Sicily, in many cases formal simply means extras such as tablecloths, waiters and a written menu. *Ristorante* are usually open for both lunch and dinner, the latter being the most popular.

Trattoria or osteria – Dining is a more relaxed, informal affair in a *trattoria*, many of which are family run. Those in smaller towns and villages will often only open for lunch. Here the emphasis is on hearty, unpretentious home cooking *(cucina casalinga)*. Written menus are often not available – instead, a waiter will describe the dishes of the day for you to choose from. If ordering these, enquire about the price before the bill arrives to avoid nasty shocks. Be wary of tourist menus, which limit choices. *Trattorias* used to almost exclusively serve house wine (by the carafe), but many now have extensive wine lists.

SNACKS

Bars, *pasticcerie* (pastry shops) and cafeterias offer a range of snacks and local specialities such as *arancini* (rice balls), *panelle* (fried chickpea pancakes) and slices of pizza. Alternatively, you may prefer to lunch on a dollop of sweet crushed ice *granita* or ice cream *(gelato)* traditionally eaten in a brioche. Sandwiches *(panini)* are a more filling option on the run. Most large towns will have sandwich bars, but in smaller villages grocers shops *(alimentari)* will usually make you one up on request. Fill your panini with Sicilian tastes such as tuna, anchovies, fresh plum tomatoes and artichokes.

TAKING A BREAK

Cafés and bars are ideal for a quick break in between sightseeing. In Italy, bars are used more as a pit stop for a morning espresso and *cornetto* (custard, jam or chocolate croissant) or a quick refreshing beer, than a place to sit all afternoon. Pay at the cash desk first, and then present your receipt to the barman. In both bars and cafés it's always cheaper to drink standing up

R. Mattes/MICHELIN

Summer evening on a terrace in Cefalù

at the counter, as the Sicilians do. The island's best cafés and bars are listed under **Taking a Break** in some of the sights' Address Books.

SPECIALITIES

Gelateria – Sicilian ice cream *(gelato)* is renowned, and beloved of locals who will stroll along in the evening promenade enjoying a cone *(un cono)*. Bars often sell ice cream, but for the widest choice of flavours head for the gelateria. A sign saying *produzione propria* means that the shop makes its own ice cream on site, usually a sign of quality.

Pizzeria – Sicilian pizza is some of the best in Italy; the authentic Italian wafer-thin crust, topped with a rich tomato sauce and a variety of toppings. Slices of tasty pizza-to-go are readily available from takeaway counters and bars. The best pizzas, however, are those in sit-down pizzeria restaurants. These are cooked to a bubbling, slightly charcoaled perfection in the traditional wood-burning ovens *(forno a legna)*. Classic Sicilian flavours to try on your pizza include oregano, capers, pecorino cheese and lots of anchovies.

AND DON'T FORGET THE MICHELIN GUIDE ITALIA

For a more exhaustive list of suggestions, please consult the *Michelin Guide Italia*. Establishments that offer particularly good dining value for money are marked with the **Bib Gourmand** symbols.

WHAT TO SEE AND DO

Outdoor Fun

Sicily is the ideal destination for outdoor activity enthusiasts, with plenty of opportunities for hiking, horse-riding, scuba-diving, canoeing, sailing, cycling and mountain biking. Explore options further with *La Guida del Turismo in Sicilia*, available in bookshops or from the publisher, Krea (Piazza Don Bosco, Palermo; ☎091 54 35 06; Fax 091 63 73 378; www.sikania.it). The same company produces a guide to nature reserves, *Le Riserve Naturali Orientate* (Italian only).

BIKING

Several disused railway lines in Sicily have been converted into cycle tracks. The **Agrigento-Castelvetrano** line runs alongside S 115 and passes through Realmonte, Eraclea Minoa and Sciacca.
The **Siracusa–Vizzini–Ragusa** line crosses the Iblei mountains, linking Pantalica, Palazzolo Acreide, Monterosso Almo, Vizzini and Chiaramonte Gulfi. The **Noto–Pachino** line runs parallel to S 19, passing through Noto Marina and Vendicari. For further information on cycling in Sicily, contact local tourist offices or the Comitato Regionale della Federazione Ciclistica Italiana, c/o Velodromo Paolo Borsellino, Via Lanza di Scalea, 90146 Palermo; ☎091 67 18 715; Fax 091 67 18 711; www.federciclismo.it.

Siciclando organises cycling tours of the island for individuals and groups. For further information, contact via Ppe di Pantelleria 37, 90146 Palermo, ☎091 754 1626, Fax 02 39 19 5454, www.siciclando.com

CANYONING

Information on canyoning in Sicily is available from the Associazione Italiana Canyoning, Sezione Sicilia (Signor Diego Leonardi), ☎095 70 81 995, www.canyoning.it, and from Etna Adventure, E. Longo 8, Zafferana Etnea, ☎329 91 88 187 or 347 58 29 748; www.etnaadventure.it

CAVING

Sicily has some cave-systems classed as natural reserves maintained by the Club Alpino Italiani (CAI), Via Petrella, 19, 20124 Milano; ☎02 20 57 231; www.cai.it; and by Legambiente, Comitato Regionale, Via Agrigento 67, Palermo ☎091 30 16 63; www. legambiente.com.
The main options are listed below:

Riserva Grotta di Carburangeli at Carini (Province of Palermo). Guided tours of the cave are organised by Legambiente, Corso Umberto I 64, Carini; ☎091 86 69797; www.parks. it/riserva.grotta.carburangeli.

Riserva Grotta di Santa Ninfa (Province of Trapani). Guided tours of the cave are organised by Legambiente, Via S. Anna 101, Santa Ninfa; ☎0924 62 376; www.parks.it/riserva. grotta.santa.ninfa.

Riserva Naturale Grotta Conza (Province of Palermo). Contact CAI Sicilia, via N. Garzilli 59, Palermo; ☎/Fax 091 32 26 89; palermo@cai.it.

M. Guillot/MICHELIN

Mount Etna

Riserva Naturale Monte Conca
(Province of Caltanissetta). Contact
CAI Sicilia, Corso Pietro Nenni 4,
Milena; ☎0934 93 32 54.

Riserva Naturale Grotta di Entella
at Contessa Entellina (Province of
Palermo). Contact CAI di Contrada
Bonfalcone, Monreale;
☎091 84 65 770.

For information on these and other
reserves being created, contact the
**Assessorato Regionale Territorio e
Ambiente**, Via La Malfa 169,Palermo;
☎091 75 42 071.

CIRCUMETNEA TOURIST TRAIN

Loop the volcano on the **Circumetnea**
train, which starts in Catania and
arrives in Riposto some five hours
later. The return trip to Catania is by
bus or train operated by Italian State
Railways. For further information,
contact Ferrovia Circumetnea, Via
Caronda 352A, Catania, ☎095 54 11
11; www.circumetnea.it.

ECOTOURISM

Both the WWF and Legambiente
run **wildlife reserves** in Sicily. The
WWF has reserves (Centri Recupero
Animali Selvatici) at Enna, Messina
and Alcamo, where it also breeds
endangered domestic animals (such as
local strains of hen, goat and donkey).
The group has marine turtle rescue
centres at various locations. Visitors
are welcome during annual field trips.
Contact the Sicilian branch of the
WWF (Delegazione Sicilia del WWF) at
Via E. Albanese 98, Palermo, ☎091 58
30 40; www.wwf.it/sicilia.
Legambiente also organises excursions to various wildlife reserves,
including one at Lampedusa (for the
protection and monitoring of marine
turtles) and another at Pantelleria: Via
Agrigento 67, Palermo,
☎091 30 16 63, Fax 091 62 64 139;
www.legambiente.com

GOLF

Golf courses on the island include
the Picchio Golf di Castiglione poised
between Etna and the sea: Via Nazionale, S.S. 120, 135, 95012 Rovittello,
Castiglione di Sicilia, near Catania;
☎0942 986 426, Fax 0942 986 323;
www.ilpicchiogolfresort.it.

HANG-GLIDING

Learn where to fly from Accademia
Siciliana Volo Libero, Via degli Astro-
nauti 14 trav. C, Altofonte (PA),
☎091 66 40 535; www.asvl.it.

HORSE-RIDING

Several *agriturismi* organise pony
trekking and horse-riding around the
island. For general information on
equestrian activities in Sicily, contact
the Federazione Italiana Turismo
Equestre, Comitato Regionale, Via
Marzabotto 1, Ragusa; ☎/Fax 0932 25
76 39; www.fiteec-ante.it.

SCUBA-DIVING

Much of the Sicilian coastline is
fringed by fascinating underwater
seascapes. The most exotic havens are
the islands offshore where the water
is particularly clear and the sea-life
especially varied. On Ustica, the
Riserva Naturale Marina organises sea-watching and diving trips,
special scuba-diving courses and the
opportunity of exploring underwater archaeology and photography.
For further information, contact the
Federazione Italiana Pesca Sportiva
Attivita Subacquea, Comitato Regionale Sicilia, Via Terrasanta 93, Palermo;
☎091 30 23 02; www.fipsas.it.

SKIING

The best place for skiing in Sicily is
obviously Etna. The two main resorts
are at Nicolosi and Piano Provenzana
(Linguaglossa), although much of the
infrastructure was badly damaged
during the most recent eruptions.

Skiing is also possible at Piano Battaglia (1 600m/5 248ft) in the Madonie.

WATER SPORTS

For details of **yacht charters**, contact specialist tour operators in your home country or the Federazione Italiana Vela, Via E. Albanese 7, Palermo; ☎091 34 28 20; www.federvela.it. Information on **canoeing** and **kayaking** is available from the Comitato Regionale Canoa-Cayak, Via Cannameli 9, 98030 Giardini Naxos; ☎/Fax 0942 50 250; www.canoalazio.com.

The most popular areas for **windsurfing** are Mondello, Cefalù, Capo d'Orlando, Marinello-Oliveri, Tremestieri (south of Messina), Scaletta, Catania, Portopalo, Marina di Ragusa, Agrigento, Pozziteddu (Capo Granitola, south of Campobello di Mazara) and Lo Stagnone. **Surfing** enthusiasts should make for Mondello, Aspra and Termini Imerese, while the best **kitesurfing** zones include Marina di Ragusa, Pozzallo and Scoglitti.
For more information: www.kite sicilia.it (kitesurfing), www.wind surfitalia.da.ru and www.shorebreak. it (windsurfing), and www.fuddittu.tk (kitesurfing and windsurfing).

Parks and Nature Reserves

REGIONAL PARKS

Sicily is home to a total of four Regional Parks. The **Parco delle Madonìe** and **Parco dei Nebrodi** lie inland between Palermo and Messina, and provide the perfect setting for excursions of varying length and difficulty (⌂ *See MADONIE E NEBRODI*). Another popular area for **walking** is the **Parco dell'Etna**, which has a number of hiking routes and nature trails (contact the park authorities for information on Etna, especially if you are planning to climb to the craters. We also recommend you book an authorized guide). The fourth park, the **Parco Fluviale dell'Alcantara**, home to the impressive gorges of the

same name, is located in the same area. Contact the Ente Parco Fluviale dell'Alcantara; ☎0942 98 99; www. parcoalcantara.it and www.parks.it.

REGIONAL NATURE RESERVES

Sicily has a number of regional nature reserves, including:

- **Cava Grande del Cassibile**
Spectacular natural canyon, stretching across the Hyblaean plateau to the coast and cradling a necropolis of 11–9 BC cave tombs.
⌂ *See NOTO*

- **Fiume Ciane e le Saline di Siracusa**
Habitat of lush vegetation that includes ancient ash trees, eucalyptus and a papyrus grove.
⌂ *See SIRACUSA*

- **Riserva Naturale di Fiume-freddo**
This river reserve supports an unusual variety of water loving plants, including papyrus.
⌂ *See ETNA*

- **Foce del Fiume Belice e Dune Limitrofe**
The wind-sculpted dunes and marshy terrain of this nature reserve on the River Belice attract species such as the Caretta-Caretta turtle.
⌂ *See CASTELVETRANO*

- **Riserva Naturale della Foce dell'Irminio,**
One of the last scrub forests in Sicily, full of interesting foliage shaped by high winds.
Near Marina di Ragusa. For information, contact ☎0932 67 51 11 (Provincia Regionale di Ragusa, Viale delFante 2, 97100 Ragusa)

- **Riserva Naturale Macalube di Aragona**
A volcanic hillside dotted with mud cones, a volcanic phenomenon that is known as *vulcanelli*.
⌂ *See AGRIGENTO*

Riserva Naturale Oasi del Simeto
Sand dune, marshland and wetland reserve for birds, located at the mouth of the River Simeto.
See ETNA

Oasi Faunistica di Vend"cari
Marshy coastline that provides a rare, and completely protected habitat for migratory species.
See NOTO

Riserva della Valle dell'Anapo
Stunning stretch of gorges and cliffs that combine natural and archaeological points of interest.
See PANTALICA

Riserva dello Zingaro
A variety of ecosystems within its 1600 hectares, from the ravines and caves of its calcerous coastline to the peak of Mt Speziale.
See Golfo di CASTELLAMMARE

Riserva Naturale Orientata Monte Pellegrino,
Reserve on the slopes of Monte Pellegrino, renowned for its birds of prey.
Run by Rangers d'Italia, Viale Diana, loc. Giusino, Palermo;
☎091 67 16 066

WWF NATURE RESERVES

The World Wildlife Fund manages the following reserves:

Riserva Naturale Orientata Capo Rama,
Birdwatching hotspot, with species such as kingfishers, kestrels, peregrine falcons and balckbirds. 2km/1.2mi from Terrasini.
For information, contact Via delle Rimembranze,16, 90049 Terrasini;
☎/Fax 091 86 85 187;

Saline di Trapani e Paceco
A large saltwater nature reserve habitat supporting many different species of birds.
See VIA DEL SALE

Riserva Naturale Integrale del Lago Preola e dei Gorghi Tondi,
Lake and wetland habitat a couple of miles southeast of Mazara del Vallo.
For information, contact Via F. Maccagnone, 2/a, 91026 Mazara del Vallo; ☎0923 93 40 55.

Riserva Naturale Orientata di Torre Salsa
Variety of habitats; dunes, cliffs, marshland and Mediterranean maquiz, inhabited by porcupines, birds of prey, waders, crows and sea birds.
See AGRIGENTO

Riserva Regionale di Isola Bella
Protected island nature reserve linked to the main shore by a narrow strip of land.
See TAORMINA

For further information, contact WWF Sezione Regionale Sicilia, Via E. Albanese 98, Palermo; ☎091 58 30 40; www.wwfsicilia.it

ORGANISATIONS

For a complete list of parks and reserves, log onto www.parks.it/regione.sicilia/index.html; or contact the **Assessorato Regionale Territorio e Ambiente,** Via La Malfa 169, Palermo; ☎091 75 42 071, or local CAI (Club Alpino Italiano) groups (www.cai.it). The main offices of this group in Sicily are located at:

Piazza Scammacca 1, Catania;
☎095 71 53 515

Via Natoli 20, Messina;
☎090 65 10 126

Via N. Garzilli 59, Palermo;
☎091 32 94 07

Via Maestranza 33, Siracusa;
☎0931 64 751

Spas

Sicily has been renowned for its hot springs since ancient times. The following resorts are listed by province:

Spa **Agrigento:**
The most important thermal town in this region is Sciacca, which has been renowned for its sulphurous waters for centuries.
Terme di Sciacca (*See SCIACCA*)
Terme di Acqua Pia, loc. Acque-Calde, **Montevago**; ☎0925 39 026;

Spa **Catania:**
The baths of Santa Caterina in Terme di Santa Venera are noted for their radioactive, sulphurous-composition, and traces of sodium bromide. (*See ACIREALE*)
www.terme.acireale.gte.it;

Spa **Messina:**
There are a number of spas in the area, most with a focus on thermal water and mud treatments. Fonte di Venere, Viale Stabilimento 85, **Terme Vigliatore**; ☎090 97 81 078; Terme di Giuseppe Marino, Via Roma 25; ☎0942 71 50 31 and Terme di Granata Cassibile, Via Crispi 1/13; ☎0942 71 50 29, both at **Alì Terme**; Terme di **Vulcano** (Aeolian Islands, *See Isole EOLIE*);

Spa **Palermo:**
Built on the ruins of a previous 17C baths, this spa offers inhalation, mud therapies, massage and thermal water treatments.
Terme di **Termini Imerese**, Piazza delle Terme 2; ☎091 81 13 557;

Spa **Trapani:**
The thermal waters at this spa have an alkaline and sulphurous composition said to aid dermatological and rheumatism ailments.
Terme di Gorga, contr. Gorga, **Calatafimi**; ☎0924 23 842.

Family holidays

Italians love children, which makes Sicily a wonderful place for a family holiday. Sicilians will go out of their way to make families comfortable and your *bambini* will have a fuss made of them wherever they go. Family dining in restaurants is the norm, and children generally stay up as late as everyone else – or fall asleep on a parent's lap. It's rare to find special children's menus, but restaurants will provide smaller versions of meals on request. It's not unusual to see children in bars either, usually running around happily outside, while parents have an *al fresco* drink. Hotels will put an extra cot in your room for a small charge.

Take the fierce Sicilian heat into account on holiday: cover children in sunblock at all times and make sure they drink plenty of water. Parents would also do well to follow the Sicilian habit of putting hats on children, and the use of a judicious siesta for everyone at the height of the heat in the middle of the day.
Take The Family –
www.takethefamily.com
Baby Goes 2 – ☎01273 230669;
www.babygoes2.com
Eurocamp – Fully-equipped camping sites in Italy. ☎0844 406 0402;
www.eurocamp.co.uk
Tots to Italy – ☎0870 458 5528;
www.totstoitaly.co.uk
Ciao Bambino! – ☎(510) 763 8484;
www.ciaobambino.com

Activities for Children Kids

Sights in the Discovering section of particular interest for children are marked by the Kids *symbol.*

A good time for families to visit is undoubtedly during Carnival or over the Easter holidays, when many of the island's towns and villages hold colourful, traditional festivals.
See Calendar of Events.

The following also hold special appeal for younger visitors:

Museo dei Pupi dell'Opra
(puppet museum) in Acireale
(*See ACIREALE*);
Museo del Giocattolo (Via Vittorio Emanuele 201, Catania), with its

collection of antique toys. ⏲*Open Tue–Sun 9am–7pm.* ✆*€3.50, children €2.* ☎*095 32 01 11;*

Etnaland, at the foot of Etna, with its exciting water park and prehistory theme park. A new amusement park is in progress to replace the zoo. ⏲*Park open 27 Jun–9 Sept, facilities open 10am–6pm (ticket offices opens 9am, closes 4pm).* ✆*Prices vary with the season and activities.* ☎*/Fax 095 79 13 334; www.etnaland.eu.*

Centro Studi sulle Tartarughe Marine at Linosa (⚲*See LINOSA);*

The **saltpans**, Museo del Sale (salt museum) and windmill in Nubia (⚲*See VIA DELSALE);*

Museo Internazionale delle Marionette in Palermo (⚲*See PALERMO).*

Calendar of Events

Following are just a few highlights in Sicily's social events. For a complete list, contact the APT (tourist information office) in the relevant area.
⚲*Festivals in towns marked * are also mentioned in the Discovering Sicily section of the guide.*

EASTER FESTIVALS

Easter week is one of the most evocative times to visit Sicily, with passion plays and dramatic processions throughout the island recalling the death and resurrection of Christ. These *via crucis* parades often involve floats held aloft by hooded members of local *confraternities* and watched by huge crowds. Book accommodation well in advance if you plan to visit at this time.

Alcamo
Good Friday procession.

Caltanissetta*
Good Friday procession of the Ancient Black Christ, with 16 groups of statues.

Castelvetrano
Good Friday procession.
Easter Sunday morning: Festa dell'Aurora, held here since 1860.

Enna*
Procession of floats carried by hooded members of the Confraternities on Good Friday.
www.enna-sicilia.it

Erice*
Processione dei Misteri held on Good Friday.
www.trapani-sicilia.it

A. Safina/Lara Pessina/MICHELIN

Processione dei Misteri, Trapani

Marsala*

Large Medieval Holy Week procession of the *Misteri,* accompanied by local musicians.

Messina*

Processione delle Barette: procession of wooden sculptures following the Stations of the Cross on Good Friday.

Piana degli Albanesi

During Holy Week, the inhabitants wear costumes embroidered with gold and silver thread. On Good Friday, choral concert and the Enkomia procession. On Easter Sunday, white doves are released, sprigs of rosemary thrown about and red-painted eggs exchanged.

Prizzi

Easter Sunday morning: *U n'contru – U ballu di diavula.* Villagers dance through the streets wearing terrifying iron masks and pretending to be devils collecting souls.

Ragusa*

Good Friday: *Processione e fiaccolata dei Misteri.* Statues of Christ and the Sorrowful Virgin from the city's churches are brought together in the Cathedral square and paraded through the streets. *www.comune.ragusa.it*

Scicli*

Procession of the Resurrected Christ on Easter Sunday. *www.comune.scicli.rg.it*

Trapani* *Processione dei Misteri* held on Good Friday afternoon and Saturday morning is one of the island's most famous processions – involving 17C and 18C religious statues. *www.comune.trapani.it/turismo*

OTHER FESTIVALS

6 JANUARY

Piana degli Albanesi

Festa della Teofania –Greek-Orthodox Epiphany.
🕯*See PALERMO*

20 JANUARY

Acireale*

Festa di San Sebastiano (St Sebastian). Annual parade of the float of San Sebastian through the streets.
🕯*See ACIREALE*

FIRST WEEK IN FEBRUARY (5 FEB)

Catania*

Festa di Sant'Agata. Procession of wooden floats, decorated with tableaux from the saint's life.
🕯*See CATANIA*

3 FEBRUARY

Salemi

Festa dei Pani di San Biagio – Festival of St Blaise held in the Rabato district. Small decorative loaves of bread are baked.
🕯*See GIBELLINA*

CARNIVAL WEEK, CULMINATING IN MARTEDÌ GRASSO (SHROVE TUESDAY)

Acireale*
Sciacca*
Termini Imerese*

Carnival with a parade of allegorical parade floats.
🕯*See ACIREALE and SCIACCA*

SATURDAY PRECEDING 19 MARCH

Scicli*

Cavalcata di San Giuseppe. Festival commemorating the flight of Joseph and Mary into Egypt.
🕯*See MODICA*

19 MARCH

Salemi

Festa di San Giuseppe (St Joseph's day) – *Cene di San Giuseppe,* with special dinners and votive loaves of bread baked.
🕯*See GIBELLINA*

END OF MAY

Scicli*
Festa della Battaglia delle Milizie.
A statue of Madonna on horseback
is carried in colourful procession
through the town.
See MODICA

LAST SUNDAY IN MAY

Ragusa*
Re-enactment of the martyrdom
of St George that ends with a
giant firework display.
See RAGUSA

14–15 JULY

Palermo*
"U fistinu", a festival for the city's
patron saint, Santa Rosalia, with
costumed parades, processions
and grand firework displays.
See PALERMO

24–25 JULY

Caltagirone*
Festa di San Giacomo with the
Luminaria. Festival in honour of
the town's patron saint. The steps
of Santa Maria del Monte are
decorated with small oil lamps.
See CALTAGIRONE

2–6 AUGUST

Cefalù*
Festa di San Salvatore:
Festival of the town's patron saint
includes a competition to balance
on a horizontal pole and reach a
statue of San Salvatore.
See CEFALÙ

14 AUGUST

Cefalù*
Madonna della Luce. Procession of
boats make their way from Kalura
to the old harbour and back.
See CEFALÙ

21–24 AUGUST

Lipari*
Festa di San Bartolomeo: Lively
festival that ends with a spectacular offshore firework display.
See ISOLE EOLIE

2 SEPTEMBER

Piana degli Albanesi
Festa della Madonna Odigitria.
Festival of Piana's patron saint,
with horse races and a brightly
costumed parade.
See PALERMO

7–8 SEPTEMBER

Mistretta*
Madonna della Luce: the Madonna
of Light festival centres on a
solemn procession of the
Madonna, flanked by the two
giants Kronos and Mytia.
See MADONIE E NEBRODI

NOVEMBER–JANUARY

Caltagirone*
Festa del Presepe: exhibition of terracotta Nativity figures and cribs
at different locations throughout
the town, celebrating the art and
tradition of the Nativity sculptors
that flourished here in the 18C.
See CALTAGIRONE

2 NOVEMBER

Palermo*
Festa dei Morti.
Children receive gifts and sweets
from their departed loved ones in
celebration of All Souls' Day.
See PALERMO

CULTURAL EVENTS

1–15 FEBRUARY

Agrigento*
Sagra del Mandorlo in fiore
(Almond-blossom Festival) and
International Folklore Festival.
See AGRIGENTO

MAY–JUNE

Siracusa*
Performances of classical drama
at the Greek theatre.
See SIRACUSA

JUNE–DECEMBER

Gibellina*
Orestiadi: theatre, music and film
festival held in the ruins of Gibellina. www.fondazione Orestiadi.it
See GIBELLINA

JULY–SEPTEMBER

Segesta*
Concerts and classical drama
at the Greek theatre.
See SEGESTA

Taormina*
Taormina Arte: theatre, music,
film and dance festival.
See TAORMINA

Tindari*
Tindari Estate: readings, music
and dance in the Greek theatre.
See GOLFO DI PATTI

END OF JULY

Marsala*
Marsala Jazz Festival.
See MARSALA

AUTUMN (VARIES YEARLY)

Monreale*
Settimana di Musica Sacra:
Festival of sacred music.
See MONREALE

UNESCO

"Our cultural and natural heritage are both irreplaceable sources of life and inspiration", insists the United Nations Educational, Scientific and Cultural Organization (UNESCO). This non-profit group has helped preserve locations since 1972.

More than 180 State Parties have joined in protecting over 800 sites "of outstanding universal value" on the World Heritage List. Representatives from 21
countries, assisted by technical organisations, annually evaluate proposals. A site
must be nominated by its home country. The protected cultural heritage may be
monuments (buildings, sculptures, archaeological structures, etc.) with unique
historical, artistic or scientific features; groups of buildings (such as religious
communities and ancient cities); or sites (human settlements and exceptional
landscapes), which are the combined works of man and the earth's beauty.

Sites may celebrate the stages of geological history or the development of
human cultures and creative genius. They may also honour significant ecological
processes, superlative natural phenomena or provide a habitat for threatened
species.

Well-known sites include: Australia's Great Barrier Reef (1981), India's Taj Mahal
and Peru's Macchu Pichu (1983), the Vatican City and the United States' Statue
of Liberty (1984), Canada's Rocky Mountain Parks (1984), Jordan's Petra (1985),
The Great Wall of China and Greece's Acropolis (1987), Russia's Kremlin and Red
Square (1990), England's Stonehenge (1986), Indonesia's Komodo National Park
and France's Banks of the Seine (1991), Cambodia's Angor Wat (1992) and Japan's
Hiroshima Peace Memorial (1996).

Italy's latest UNESCO sites are Tivoli's Villa Adriana (1999), Assisi's Basilica of San
Francesco and Other Franciscan Sites (2000), the City of Verona (2000), the Aeolian Islands (2000), Tivoli's Villa d'Este (2001), Southeastern Sicily's Late Baroque
Towns of the Val di Noto (2002), the Sacri Monti of Piedmont and Lombardy
(2003), Etruscan Necropolises of Cerveteri and Tarquinia (2004), Val d'Orcia
(2004), and Syracuse and the Rocky Necropolis of Pantalica (2005), Genoa:
Le Strade Nuove and the Palazzi dei Rolli (2006).

UNESCO
World Heritage Sites in Italy

Sites in Sicily are marked in bold.

18C Royal Palace at Caserta with the Park, the Aqueduct of Vanvitelli and San Leucio Complex

Assisi, the Basilica di San Francesco and other Franciscan sites

Botanical Garden, Padua

Castel del Monte

Cathedral, Torre Civica and Piazza Grande, Modena

Church and Dominican Convent of Santa Maria delle Grazie, with The Last Supper by Leonardo da Vinci, Milan

Cilento and Vallo di Diano National Park with the Archaeological Sites of Paestum and Velia and the Certosa di Padula

City of Vicenza and the Palladian Villas of the Veneto

Crespi d'Adda

Early Christian Monuments of Ravenna

Genoa: Le Strade Nuove and the Palazzi dei Rolli

Historic Centre of Florence

Historic Centre of Naples

Historic Centre of Pienza

Historic Centre of San Gimignano

Historic Centre of Siena

Historic Centre of Urbino

Late Baroque Towns of the Val di Noto (southeastern Sicily)

Portovenere, the Cinque Terre and the Islands (Palmaria, Tino and Tinetto)

Residences of the Royal House of Savoy, Piedmont

Rock Drawings, Valcamonica

Rome and the Holy See: historic centre of Rome, the properties of the Holy See which enjoy extraterritorial rights, and St Paul Without the Walls.

Su Nuraxi, Barumini

Teatro dell'Opera dei Pupi Siciliano (cultural tradition)

The Aeolian Islands

The Amalfi Coast

The Archaeological Site and Patriarchal Basilica of Aquileia

The Archaeological Site of Agrigento

The Archaeological Sites of Pompeii, Herculaneum and Torre Annunziata

The Renaissance City of Ferrara and the Po Delta

The Sassi (troglodyte dwellings) of Matera

The Trulli of Alberobello

Venice and its Lagoon Piazza del Duomo, Pisa

Verona

Villa Adriana and Villa d'Este, Tivoli

Villa Romana del Casale, Piazza Armerina

Almond-blossom festival in Agrigento

LATE NOVEMBER TO MID-DECEMBER

Palermo*
Festival di Morgana.
Performances by puppeteers
from around the world.
🍴*See PALERMO*

OTHER TRADITIONAL EVENTS

APRIL–MAY

Taormina*
Festa del Costume e del Carretto
Siciliano. Festival of traditional
Sicilian carts and local costume.
🍴*See TAORMINIA*

25 APRIL

Vizzini
Sagra della Ricotta.
Ricotta cheese festival.
🍴*See CALTAGIRONE*

THIRD SUNDAY IN MAY

Noto*
Primavera Barocca and the
Infiorata. Spring festival, culminat-
ing in a fragrant flower festival.
🍴*See NOTO*

12–14 AUGUST

Piazza Armerina*
Palio dei Normanni.
Re-enactment of the arrival of
Roger de Hauteville in the town,
followed by jousting competitions.
🍴*See PIAZZA ARMERINA*

14 AUGUST

Messina*
Passeggiata dei Giganti. Procession
of the Moor Grifone and Mata, the
legendary founder of the city.
🍴*See MESSINA*

Shopping

Souvenirs range from gastronomic
specialities to traditional handicrafts.

FOOD AND WINE

The area around Trapani and the
Egadi Islands (especially Favignana)
is well known for **tuna** specialities, as
well as fish roe and smoked swordfish. Pantelleria and Salina produce
excellent **capers**, while the **herbs** and
spices that form such an important
part of Sicilian cuisine can be found
in markets and grocery stores all over
the island. The most common include
oregano, wild fennel, pistachios (near
Bronte) and Sicilian saffron.

The Palermo region is famed for its delicious *paste reali* (colourful marzipan delicacies, which come in all shapes and sizes). Sweet specialities on the Ionian coast include the local *paste di mandorla* (almond pastries). The famous Sicilian crushed *ice granite* might be difficult to take home, but you can export a key ingredient: packets of almond paste (also used to make almond milk).

Numerous table **wines** stand out, especially Nero d'Avola, as well as Sicily's sweet wines: Moscato di Noto, Moscato Passito di Pantelleria, Marsala and Malvasia delle Lipari.

SOUVENIRS

One of the most typical crafts is **ceramic** work. The most important centres are Caltagirone, Santo Stefano di Camastra, Erice and Sciacca. The shops of these small towns display a fine array of vases, statuettes, crockery, ornaments and knick-knacks, as well as traditional containers for Sicilian *mostarda* (a caramel-like substance made from prickly-pear juice) and quince jam.

Apart from ceramics, plenty of other natural products and handicrafts evoke the island. These include carpets from the area around Erice; natural sponges from Lampedusa; and **papyrus** work (paper and cloth) from the Siracusa region. Finally, examine the Sicilian puppets and traditional carts, found at antique and second-hand shops, or, in Palermo, directly from the few remaining artisans.

Ceramic shop

Sightseeing

Information on admission times and charges for museums and monuments is given in the *Discovering Sicily* section of the guide.

Admission times and charges are liable to alteration without prior notice. Due to fluctuations in the cost of living and constant changes in opening times – as well as possible closures for restoration work – our information should merely serve as a guideline. Visitors are advised to confirm details.

The admission prices are for single adults with no concession; reductions for children, students, those over 60yrs old and large groups should be requested on site and should be endorsed with proof of ID. Special conditions often exist for groups, but arrangements should be made in advance. For EU citizens, many institutions provide free admission to visitors under 18 and over 65, and a 50% reduction for visitors under 25 years of age.

During **National Heritage Week** (Settimana dei Beni Culturali), which takes place at a different time each year, many sights don't charge admission. When custodians specially open museums, churches or other sites – or guide visitors – it is customary to leave a donation.

In summer, many museums and monuments close from 1 to 4pm.

MUSEUMS, GARDENS AND ARCHAEOLOGICAL SITES

Museums generally don't open on Mondays; otherwise ticket offices shut 30–60 minutes before closing. As this rule is strictly applied, it is almost impossible to enter a museum after this time. Many require use of the luggage deposit.

Taking photos with a flash is usually forbidden.

Archaeological sites generally close 1hr before dusk.

CHURCHES

Churches are usually open 8.30am–noon and 4–6pm, except during services. Exceptions are listed in the *Discovering Sicily* section of this guide. Notices outside a number of churches formally request visitors to dress in a manner deemed appropriate when entering a place of worship – this excludes sleeveless and low-cut tops, short miniskirts or skimpy shorts and bare feet.

Visitors are advised to visit churches in the morning, when the natural light provides better illumination of the works of art; also note that churches are occasionally forced to close in the afternoons due to lack of staff. Works of art are often illuminated by coin-operated lighting, so take change.

Books

The island has long fascinated both Italian and foreign authors. The suggestions below include translated works by famous Sicilians, as well as history books, mythology, biography and travel literature. For a wide selection of English and Italian books written about Sicily, log onto www.sicilybooks.it or www.siciliano.it/indexlibri.cfm.

FICTION

The Leopard – Giuseppe Lampedusa (Harvill Press 1996)
Little Novels of Sicily – Giovanni Verga, DH Lawrence (Steerforth Press 2000)
Sometimes the Soul: Two Novellas of Sicily – Gioia Timpanelli (WW Norton & Co 1998)
"Cavalleria Rusticana" and Other Stories – Giovanni Verga, H McWilliam (Penguin Books 1999)
Short Sicilian Novels – Giovanni Verga (Dedalus Ltd 1994)
The House by the Medlar Tree – Giovanni Verga (University of California Press 1983)
Il Giorno Della Civetta – Leonardo Sciascia, G Slowey (Ed) (St Martin's Press 1998)

BIOGRAPHY

Italian Journey – JW Goethe (Penguin Books 1970)
The Sicilian – M Puzo (Arrow 2000)
The Happy Ant-heap – Norman Lewis (Jonathan Cape 1998)
The Dark Princes of Palermo – Norman Lewis (Jonathan Cape 2000)
I Came, I Saw: an Autobiography – Norman Lewis (Picador 1996)
On Persephone's Island: A Sicilian Journal (Vintage Departures) – Mary Taylor Simeti (Vintage Books 1995)
Sicilian Lives – D Dolci (Writers and Readers 1982)

REFERENCE

The Greek Myths – R Graves (Penguin Books 1984)
Metamorphoses – Ovid, EJ Kenney (Ed), AD Melville (Trans) (Oxford Paperbacks 1998)
Odes – Pindar (Penguin Books 1901)
The Odyssey – Homer, R Fagles (Trans), B Knox (Intro) (Penguin Books 1997)
The Aeneid – Virgil, D West (Trans) (Penguin Books 1991)
The Normans in Sicily – John Julius Norwich (Penguin Books 1992)
The Sicilian Vespers – S Runciman (Cambridge University Press 1992)
The Norman Kingdom of Sicily – D Matthew (Cambridge University Press 1992)
The Golden Honeycomb – V Cronin, W Forman (Harvill Press 1992)
Walking in Sicily – Gillian Price (Cicerone Press 2000)
In Sicily – Norman Lewis (Jonathan Cape 2000)
The Honoured Society – Norman Lewis (Eland Books 1984)

Films

L'Avventura by Michelangelo Antonioni (1960). A portrait of three characters, set against the harsh Sicilian landscape.
Divorzio all'italiana by Pietro Germi (1962). A superb performance by

Marcello Mastroianni here met with international acclaim.

Il Mafioso by Alberto Lattuada (1962). A story of great cruelty, starring a masterful Alberto Sordi.

A ciascuno il suo by Elio Petri (1967). Based on Sciascia's novel, this film tells the story of an academic captured by the Mafia.

The Godfather by Francis Ford Coppola (1972). The first of the trilogy.

Cadaveri eccellenti by Francesco Rosi (1976). Obscure political plots are uncovered in this film, based on Sciascia's *Contesto*.

Il siciliano by Michael Cimino (1987). The story of the bandit Giuliano, based on Mario Puzo's novel.

Mery per sempre by Marco Risi (1989), set in Palermo Prison; and its sequel, *Ragazzi fuori* (1990).

Porte aperte by Gianni Amelio (1990). Based on a novel by Sciascia and inspired by a real-life event, this film explores the themes of crime and punishment.

Johnny Stecchino by Roberto Benigni (1991). Comedy about a naïve bus driver mistaken for a Mafiaboss.

Il giudice ragazzino by Alessandro di Robiland (1993). Last days of Assistant Public Prosecutor Livatino, killed by the Mafia in 1990.

Lo zio di Brooklyn by Ciprì and Maresco (1995). The first feature film by these two controversial directors, set in the Palermo suburbs.

La lupa by Gabriele Lavia (1997). Based on the play by Verga.

Sicilia! by Danèle Huillet and Jean-Marie Straub (1999). Based on *Conversazione in Sicilia* by Elio Vittorini, this black-and-white film follows a man returning to Sicily in search of his childhood.

I giudici by Ricky Tognazzi (1999). The story of Giovanni Falcone and Paolo Borsellino.

Malèna by Giuseppe Tornatore (2000). A young boy in provincial Sicily falls in love with Monica Bellucci at the beginning of WWII.

Placido Rizzotto by Pasquale Scimeca (2000). The story of the trade unionist Placido Rizzotto, killed in Corleone in 1948.

Il manoscritto del principe by Roberto Andò (2000). The experiences of Prince Giuseppe Tomasi di Lampedusa, recounted against the backdrop of 1950s Palermo.

Prime luci dell'alba by Lucio Gaudino (2000). Family problems force the main character of this film to examine his relationship with Sicily.-

Respiro by Emanuele Crialese (2002). This film, set amid the stunning scenery of Lampedusa, examines the breakdown of a young woman's sanity.

Angela by Roberta Torre (2002). This intense film, quite unlike the early work of this director, examines the life of a woman in the Mafia.

USEFUL WORDS & PHRASES

a destra	to the right	**ingresso**	entrance
a sinistra	to the left	**lavori in corso**	men at work
aperto	open	**neve**	snow
autostrada	motorway	**passaggio a livello**	level crossing
banchina	pavement	**passo**	pass
binario	(railway) platform	**pericolo**	danger
corso	boulevard	**piazza, largo**	square, place
discesa	descent	**piazzale**	esplanade
dogana	customs	**stazione**	station
fermata	(bus-) stop	**stretto**	narrow
fiume	river	**uscita**	exit, way out

viale	avenue
vietato	prohibited

PLACES AND THINGS TO SEE

abbazia, convento	abbey, monastery
affreschi	frescoes
arazzi	tapestries
arco	arch
biblioteca	library
cappella	chapel
casa	house
cascata	waterfall
castello	castle
chiesa	church
chiostro	cloisters
chiuso	closed
città	town
cortile	courtyard
dintorni	environs
duomo	cathedral
facciata	façade
funivia	cable car
giardini	gardens
gole	gorges
passeggiata	walk, promenade
piano	floor, storey
pinacoteca	picture gallery
pulpito	pulpit
quadro	picture
rocca	feudal castle
rovine, ruderi	ruins
sagrestia	sacristy
scala	stairway
scavi	excavations
seggiovia	chairlift
spiaggia	beach
tesoro	treasure
torre, torazzo	tower
vista	view

COMMON WORDS

yes, no	**si, no**
Sir	**Signore**
Madam	**Signora**
Miss	**Signorina**
please	**per favore**
thank you very much	**grazie tante**
excuse me	**mi scusi**
enough	**basta**
good morning	**buon giorno**
goodbye	**arrivederci**
how much?	**quanto?**
where? when?	**dove? quando?**
where is?	**dov'è?**

much, little	**molto, poco**
more, less	**più, meno**
all	**tutto, tutti**
large	**grande**
small	**piccolo**
dear	**caro**

NUMBERS

0	**zero**
1	**uno**
2	**due**
3	**tre**
4	**quattro**
5	**cinque**
6	**sei**
7	**sette**
8	**otto**
9	**nove**
10	**dieci**
11	**undici**
12	**dodici**
13	**tredici**
14	**quattordici**
15	**quindici**
16	**sedici**
17	**diciassette**
18	**diciotto**
19	**diciannove**
20	**venti**
30	**trenta**
40	**quaranta**
50	**cinquanta**
60	**sessanta**
70	**settanta**
80	**ottanta**
90	**novanta**
100	**cento**
1 000	**mille**
5 000	**cinquemila**
10 000	**diecimila**
1.00	**l'una**
1.15	**l'una e un quarto**
1.30	**un ora e mezzo**
1.45	**l'una e quaranta cinque**

TIME, DAYS OF THE WEEK AND SEASONS

morning	**mattina**
afternoon	**pomeriggio**
evening	**sera**
yesterday	**ieri**
today	**oggi**
tomorrow	**domani**
a week	**una settimana**

Monday	**lunedì**
Tuesday	**martedì**
Wednesday	**mercoledì**
Thursday	**giovedì**
Friday	**venerdì**
Saturday	**sabato**
Sunday	**domenica**
winter	**inverno**
spring	**primavera**
summer	**estate**
autumn/fall	**autunno**

USEFUL PHRASES

Do you speak English?
Parla inglese?
I don't understand
Non capisco
Please speak slowly
Parli piano per favore
Where are the toilets?
Dove sono i bagni?
At what time does the train/bus/plane leave?
A che ora parte il treno/l'autobus/l'aereo?
At what time does the train arrive?
A che ora arriva il treno ...?
What does it cost?
Quanto costa?
Where is the post office?
Dove è l'ufficio postale?
Where can I buy an English newspaper?
Dove posso comprare un giornale inglese?
Where can I change my money?
Dove posso cambiare i miei soldi?
May I pay with a credit card?
Posso pagare con una carta di credito?
the road to ...?
la strada per ...?
may one visit?
Si può visitare?
what time is it?
Che ora è?
I would like...
Desidero/vorrei...

GASTRONOMIC TERMS

Caffè corretto: *espresso* laced with brandy or *grappa*
Caffè decaffeinato (caffè "Hag"): decaffeinated coffee
Caffè latte: mainly hot milk, with a splash of coffee
Caffè lungo: coffee which is not quite as strong as *espresso*
Caffè macchiato: *espresso* with a splash of milk
Cannelloni: large pasta tubes filled with a meat or other sauce
Cappellini: very thin spaghetti
Cappuccino (or *cappuccio*): coffee topped with frothy milk and a dusting of cocoa
Cassata: ice cream containing chopped nuts and mixed dried fruit (similar to tutti-frutti)
Crema: vanilla (ice cream)
Farfalle: pasta bow-ties
Fettuccine: slightly narrower, Roman version of tagliatelle
Fior di latte: very creamy variety of ice cream
Fusilli: small pasta spirals
Gnocchi: tiny potato dumplings
Lasagne: sheets of pasta arranged in layers with tomato and meat sauce (or other) and cheese sauce, topped with Parmesan and baked
Maccheroni: small pasta tubes
Panino: type of sandwich (bread roll)
Panna: cream; similar to *fior di latte*
Prosciutto: cured ham
Ravioli: little pasta cushions, enclosing meat or spinach
Schiacciata: type of sandwich (on a pizza-type base)
Spaghetti: the great classic
Stracciatella: chocolate chip (ice cream)
Tagliatelle: long narrow pasta ribbons
Tiramisù: coffee-flavoured frozen gâteau *(semifreddo)*
Tortellini: small crescent-shaped pasta rolls filled with a meat or cheese stuffing, often served in a clear meat broth
Tramezzino: type of sandwich (on slices of bread)
Zabaglione: dessert made from egg yolks and Marsala wine
Zuppa inglese: trifle

BASIC INFORMATION

Business Hours

Shops - Most shops open Monday-Saturday from 8am–1pm and 3.30–7.30 or 8pm. Many supermarkets are closed on Wednesday afternoon.

Museums and galleries – Opening times in Sicily are dependent on the time of year, local and national holidays and closures for restoration work. If there's something you are particularly set on seeing it's worth telephoning ahead, either to the venue or the local tourist office, to check that it is open. Smaller museums open from 9am to 1pm, and some larger ones also open for a few hours in the afternoon. Open air sites usually open between 8–9am and close one hour before sunset.

Churches – Most Sicilian churches are open in the mornings between 8am and midday, which is the best time for sightseeing. Churches will usually open around 6–7pm as well, however this is the time when evening Mass is held and looking round should be done with sensitivity to this.

Communications

All forms of communication are well organised and widely available in Sicily, so you'll have no trouble keeping in touch. After many years in the cyber dark age, Italy has now fully embraced the internet, and you'll find Internet cafes in larger towns and cities, modem points in the rooms of many larger hotels and even WiFi connections. The Sicilian telephone service is organised by TELECOM ITALIA (formerly SIP), and public telephones are common, even though practically everyone owns a mobile phone in Italy. Telecom Italia offices also have public booths where the customer pays for units used (scatti) at the counter after the call. Italy has some of the highest phone tariffs in Europe, so save telephone calls until after 6.30pm to take advantage of cheaper rates. Rates are even lower between 10pm and 8am.

PHONE CARDS

Phone cards (schede telefoniche) are sold in denominations of €1, €2.50, €5 and €8 and are supplied by CIT offices and post offices, as well as tobacconists. Remove the top-corner tab before insertion. These prefixes quickly drain any phone card: 0338, 0335, 0339, 0349, 0347 and 0368.

AREA CODES

When making a call within Italy, the area code (e.g.: 091 for Palermo) is always used, both from outside and from within the city you are calling.

FOR INTERNATIONAL CALLS

For international calls dial 00 plus the following country codes:
61 for Australia
1 for Canada
64 for New Zealand
44 for the UK
1 for the USA
If calling from outside the country, the international code for Italy is 39. Dial the full area code, even when making an international call; for example, when calling Palermo from the UK, dial 00 39 091, followed by the correspondent's number. If you're on a budget, it's worth bearing in mind that international calls from Italy are markedly cheaper after 11pm.

USEFUL NUMBERS

(See also Emergencies, above)
☎176: International Directory Enquiries. Provides phone numbers outside of Italy in English and Italian. Calls to this number are subject to a charge.
☎170: Operator Assisted International Calls. This number is not toll-free either.

Electricity

The voltage is 220v, 50Hz; the sockets are for two-pin plugs. Most laptops and digital camera chargers have built-in convertors and only require an adaptor. Check carefully before trying hair dryers or shavers, however.

Emergencies

✚ ☎**113:** General emergency services (soccorso pubblico di emergenza). Calls are free.
✚ ☎**112:** Police (carabinieri); truly an emergency hotline. Calls are free.
✚ ☎**115:** Fire Brigade (vigili del fuoco). Calls are free.
✚ ☎**118:** Emergency Health Services (emergenza sanitaria). Calls are free.
✚ ☎**1515:** Forest Fire Service. Environmental emergencies. Calls are free.
✚ ☎**803 116:** Automobile Club d'Italia Emergency Breakdown Service. Calls are free.

Mail/Post

OPENING HOURS

Post offices are open 8am–1pm on weekdays and 8.30am–noon on Saturday. In cities and large towns opening hours may extend to 6 or 7pm, while those in smaller towns and villages will often close at the weekend. All post offices are closed on public holidays. Stamps are also sold at tobacconists (tabacchi), where queues are usually shorter. Tabacchi are identified by either a blue or black sign with a white T hanging outside.

STAMPS

Stamps for letters or postcards cost €0.45 to the EU, €0.56 elsewhere (posta ordinaria). The Italian postal service is notoriously slow and unreliable, so if a letter is urgent consider sending it by express service. Stamps cost €0.62 for postage within the EU, €0.80 outside (posta prioritaria).

Money

The unit of currency is the euro, which is issued in notes (€5, €10, €20, €50, €100, €200 and €500) and in coins (1 cent, 2 cents, 5 cents, 10 cents, 20 cents, 50 cents, €1 and €2). Correct change is something of a commodity in Sicily. Many bars, for example, are unable to break a €20 or €50 note. Keep a supply of small notes.

BANKS

Banks usually operate Monday to Friday, 8.30am–1.30pm and 3–4pm. Some are open downtown and in shopping centres on Saturday mornings; almost all close on Saturday afternoons, Sundays and holidays. Exchange bureaux in Sicily include post offices (except traveller's cheques), money-changers at railway stations and airports, and some hotel receptions (always on a rather stinging commission).

CREDIT CARDS

Payment by credit card is widespread in shops, hotels and restaurants and also some petrol stations. The Michelin Guide Italia and The Michelin Guide Main Cities of Europe indicate which ones are welcome at hotels and restaurants. Money may also be withdrawn from a bank, but could incur steep interest charges.

TAXES

In most cases VAT in Italy is 20%. EU non-resident travellers can get a VAT refund for goods intended for personal use that were purchased in Italy, where the overall value of goods exceeds €154.94. For information on how to claim a refund go to www.agenziadogane.it.

Newspapers

The main regional newspapers are *La Gazzetta del Sud* (the area around Messina), *La Sicilia* (Catania) and the *Giornale di Sicilia* (Palermo). Foreign newspapers are available in major cities and large towns.

Pharmacies

These are identified by a red and white or green neon cross. When closed, each pharmacy advertises competitors that are on duty and a list of doctors on call.

Public Holidays

A working day is *un giorno feriale; giorni festivi* and these include Saturdays, Sundays and eleven holidays. Public holidays are reverently observed in Sicily, so plan ahead and brace yourself for closed banks and shops, limited public transportation, and throngs on the roads and rails.

January 1	New Year
January 6	Epiphany
Easter Sunday and Monday	*lunedì dell'Angelo*
April 25	St Mark's Day and liberation in 1945
May 1	*Festa dei Lavoratori*
Sunday nearest June 2	Anniversary of the Republic
August 15	The Assumption – *Ferragosto*
November 1	*All Saints – Tutti i Santi*
December 8	Immaculate Conception
December 25 and 26	Christmas and St Stephen's Day

Reduced Rates

Visitors trying to keep costs down will find information on budget accommodation (*pensioni,* youth hostels, campsites, convents and monasteries) in the **Address Books** found in the *Discovering Sicily* sections of the guide (⮞ *Also see Where to Stay*).

BY AIR

Several airlines offer budget fares to Italy, although only Ryanair flies into Palermo from London Stansted. Prices vary according to how far in advance the booking is made. Virgin Express: www.virgin-express.com; BMI (British Midland): www.flybmi.com; Ryanair: www.ryanair.com; easyJet: www.easyjet.com Alitalia has various special offers for passengers buying their ticket one, two or three weeks before departure. The airline also offers special weekend rates for travellers departing on a Saturday and returning on a Sunday of the same weekend *(tipo corto)* and for the same type of ticket, but valid for a month *(tipo lungo)*.

BY TRAIN

InterRail
Italy honours the Eurail and Inter-rail passes (though a *supplemento,* an additional fee, may be charged for some services). An adult (26yrs+), 2nd-class, flexi five-day *InterRail Global Pass* (valid for ten days) costs €249. www.interrailnet.com.

Trenitalia
Trenitalia (www.trenitalia.it) offers the following discounts (see website for more details):
Amico: 50% discount on local trains, also applies to companion
Club Eurostar: 20% discount on first-class travel
Flexi: unlimited travel within 8, 15, 21 or 30 days
Prima: 20% discount on first-class travel
Rail Plus: 25% discount on international second-class travel

CONVERSION TABLES

Weights and Measures

1 kilogram (kg) 6.35 kilograms 0.45 kilograms	**2.2 pounds (lb)** 14 pounds 16 ounces (oz)	**2.2 pounds** 1 stone (st) 16 ounces	*To convert kilograms to pounds, multiply by 2.2*
1 metric ton (tn)	**1.1 tons**	**1.1 tons**	
1 litre (l) 3.79 litres 4.55 litres	**2.11 pints (pt)** 1 gallon (gal) 1.20 gallon	**1.76 pints** 0.83 gallon 1 gallon	*To convert litres to gallons, multiply by 0.26 (US) or 0.22 (UK)*
1 hectare (ha) **1 sq. kilometre (km²)**	**2.47 acres** 0.38 sq. miles (sq.mi.)	**2.47 acres** 0.38 sq. miles	*To convert hectares to acres, multiply by 2.4*
1 centimetre (cm) **1 metre (m)**	**0.39 inches (in)** 3.28 feet (ft) or 39.37 inches or 1.09 yards (yd)	**0.39 inches**	*To convert metres to feet, multiply by 3.28; for kilometres to miles, multiply by 0.6*
1 kilometre (km)	**0.62 miles (mi)**	**0.62 miles**	

Clothing

Women					Men			
		35	4	2½			40	7½	7

Sizes often vary depending on the designer. These equivalents are given for guidance only.

Speed

KPH	10	30	50	70	80	90	100	110	120	130
MPH	6	19	31	43	50	56	62	68	75	81

Temperature

Celsius (°C)	0°	5°	10°	15°	20°	25°	30°	40°	60°	80°	100°
Fahrenheit (°F)	32°	41°	50°	59°	68°	77°	86°	104°	140°	176°	212°

To convert Celsius into Fahrenheit, multiply °C by 9, divide by 5, and add 32.
To convert Fahrenheit into Celsius, subtract 32 from °F, multiply by 5, and divide by 9.
NB: Conversion factors on this page are approximate.

Women Shoes: 35 4 2½ / 36 5 3½ / 37 6 4½ / 38 7 5½ / 39 8 6½ / 40 9 7½ / 41 10 8½
Dresses & suits: 36 6 8 / 38 8 10 / 40 10 12 / 42 12 14 / 44 14 16 / 46 16 18
Blouses & sweaters: 36 06 30 / 38 08 32 / 40 10 34 / 42 12 36 / 44 14 38 / 46 16 40
Men Shoes: 40 7½ 7 / 41 8½ 8 / 42 9½ 9 / 43 10½ 10 / 44 11½ 11 / 45 12½ 12 / 46 13½ 13
Suits: 46 36 36 / 48 38 38 / 50 40 40 / 52 42 42 / 54 44 44 / 56 46 48
Shirts: 37 14½ 14½ / 38 15 15 / 39 15½ 15½ / 40 15¾ 15¾ / 41 16 16 / 42 16½ 16½

DISCOUNTS FOR UNDER-26

By Train
The **Carta Verde Railplus** (€40, valid for a year; www.trenitalia.it) gives young people a 25% discount on first- or second-class international ticket prices on routes connecting any two of the countries taking part in the RAILPLUS offer (www.railplus.com). The ticket is non-transferable.

DISCOUNTS FOR SENIOR CITIZENS

By Train
For travellers over 60 years of age, the **Carta d'Argento** (€30, valid for a year) offers the same discounts and conditions as the Carta Verde (⟲see above).

DISCOUNTS FOR FAMILIES AND SMALL GROUPS

By Train
Children aged 4–12 travel at half-price. Those younger travel free, but share a seat with a family member. Easter, Christmas and summer holidays may invalidate these offers. Limited availability. www.trenitalia.it.

By Air
Some airlines offer discounts for families as long as they meet certain criteria. Check with your airline before booking flights in order not to miss out on any potential discount. ⟲See Getting There and Getting Around for details of airlines flying to Sicily.

Smoking

Since 2005 it has been illegal to light up inside any hotel, bar, restaurant or public building – or on public transport throughout Italy, including Sicily. On-the-spot fines of up to €270 can be imposed on offenders.

All Sicilian hotel rooms are now, therefore, effectively non-smoking. However, Italy is still a nation with a smoker's psyche, and those wanting an after-dinner cigarette can find solace at tables in the outdoor dining areas of restaurants. These areas are common and open for much of the year thanks to Sicily's warm al fresco climate.

Tobacconists
Besides smoking products, tabacchi sell postcards, stamps, confectionery, phone cards, public transport tickets, lottery tickets and such like. The shops – sometimes inside bars – are instantly recognizable by the white "T" on a blue or black sign.

Time

The time in Italy is usually the same as in the rest of mainland Europe (one hour ahead of the United Kingdom) and changes during the last weekend of March and of October, between summer time (ora legale) and winter time (ora solare).

Tipping

Leaving a token of your gratitude for good service is welcome in Sicily. Service is generally included in restaurant bills, but a couple of coins in the dish over this is appreciated. If no service charge has been included in your bill then it's customary to leave 10%. If you're having a drink standing at the bar it's a nice gesture to leave the copper-coloured change from your order. Seated drinkers should put 40–50 cents in the saucer if the service has been friendly. Tipping for taxi drivers ranges from rounding up your fare to 10% on top, depending on how your feel about the journey.

For the best little places, follow the leader.

Looking for the latest news on today's best hotels and restaurants? Pick up the Michelin Guide and look for the Bib Gourmand and Bib Hotel symbols. With 45,000 addresses in Europe, in every category and price range, the perfect place to dine or stay is never far away.

A better way forward

Tuna fishing in Favignana, Isole Egadi
Paola Ghirotti/Fototeca ENIT

INTRODUCTION TO SICILY

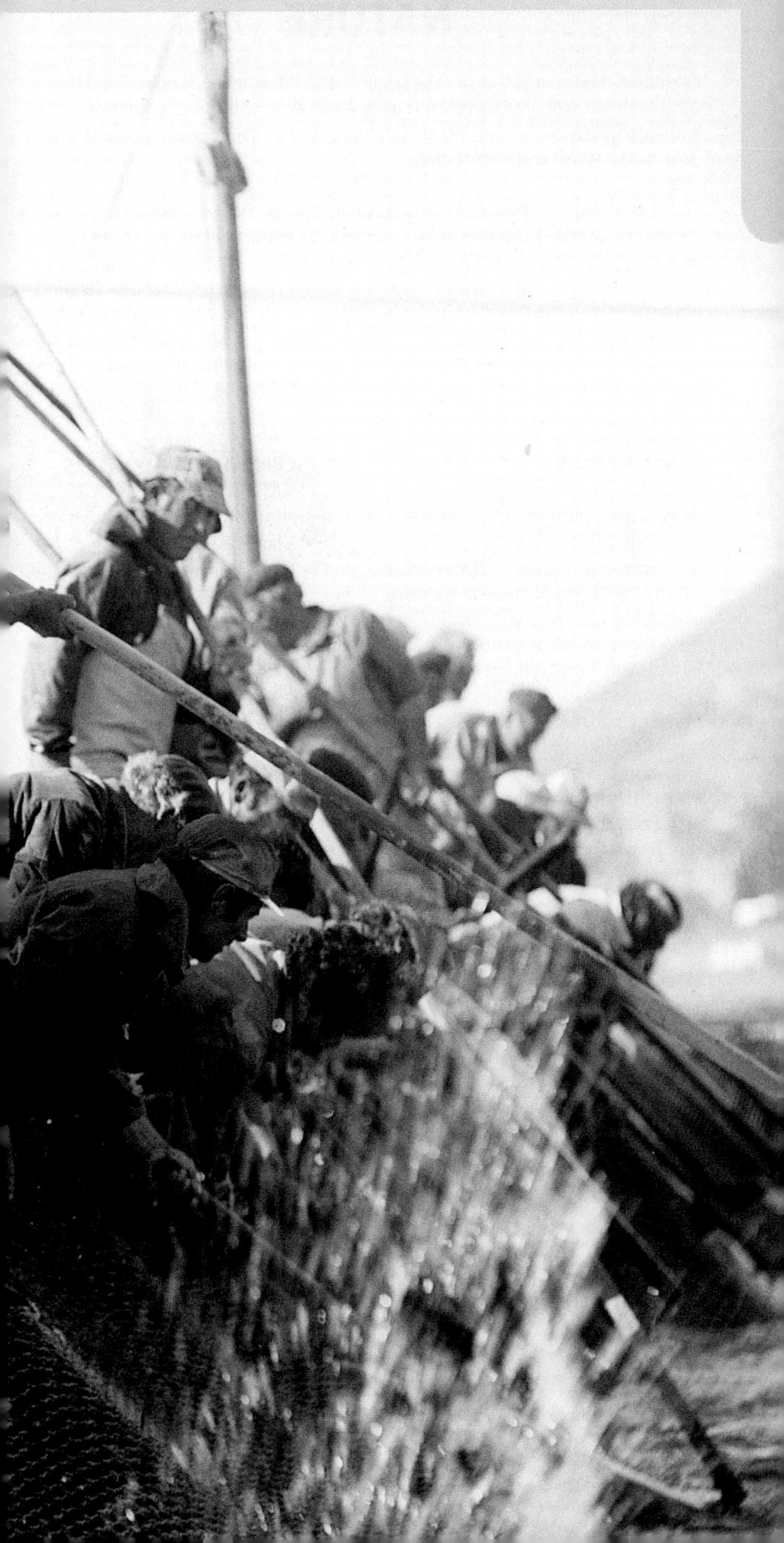

NATURE

Emerald pastures unfurl above the sparkling Mediterranean, while prickly pears cling to slopes scorched by volcanic lava. White almond blossoms dot the terrain like snowflakes. Sicily – among all Italy's provinces – lives closest to nature in all its beauty, power and profundity.

The seasons bring myriad colours and changes to the Sicilian landscape: the yellow broom, mimosa and sweetly scented orange blossom of spring; the red poppies, bougainvillea and green meadows of early summer; and the early autumn ochre-coloured earth burned by the relentless sun. On this island of beaches and mountains, you can travel from the heights of magnificent Mount Etna (Sicily's highest peak at over 3 000m/10 000ft and the highest volcano in Europe) to a secluded, sandy bay on the coast in just a few miles. Best of all, its wild scenery is tempered with all the *dolce vita* comforts at which Italians excel.

Landscape

Sicily is the largest island of the Mediterranean (25 709sq km/9 926sq mi). It is separated from the Italian peninsula by the Straits of Messina – a mere 3km/1.8mi at the widest point – and from Africa, about 140km/87mi away, by the Sicily Canal. The island is more or less triangular in shape, its long sides fronting on to the Tyrrhenian Sea in the north and the Sicily Canal in the south. The short side fringes the Ionian Sea to the east. Under Muslim occupation, the island was divided into three large "valleys" or provinces: the **Val di Mazara** to the west, **Val Demone** to the northeast and the **Val di Noto** in the southeast.

Harbour at Cefalù

B. Morandi/MICHELIN

AN ISLAND AMONG ISLANDS

The region of Sicily includes many minor islands: off the northern coast, in the Tyrrhenian Sea, are the Aeolian or Lipari Islands (northeast) and Ustica (northwest); the Egadi lie to the west, close to the Trapanese Coast. To the south, in the Sicily Canal, lie Pantelleria and the Pelagian Islands, including Lampedusa (which is 113km/70mi from Tunisia and 205km/128mi from the Sicilian coast). **Ferdinandea Island** (originally claimed by the British as Graham Island and by the French as Ile de Giulia) is a tiny outcrop that surfaced off Sciacca's coast in 1831, only to sink again a few months later; it now lies 7m/22ft below sea level.

SANDY BEACHES AND ROCKY CLIFFS

The Sicilian coastline stretches over some 1 000km/621mi. The northern or Tyrrhenian flank extends from Cape Peloro, near Messina, to Cape Lilibeo in the vicinity of Marsala: here the rocks are uniformly high and protrude jaggedly out into the sea.

By contrast, the short western coast between Trapani and Marsala is flat and dotted with saltpans. The southern shoreline remains flat and mainly sandy all the way out to Capo Passero, the far southwestern spur of the island. Resorts like Mazzara del Vallo, Sciacca and Gela dominate the broad bay with

Sicily's hilly landscape with olive trees

B. Kaufmann/MICHELIN

the same name that lies between Licata and Marina di Ragusa.

The eastern coast facing the Ionian Sea is low-lying at first, shaped into a succession of three broad sweeps: the Gulf of Noto, the Gulf of Augusta and the great Gulf of Catania, which provides Sicily's largest plain with a sea front. North of Catania, the shoreline to Messina consists once more of high cliffs broken by a series of craggy inlets. As Etna's tall black lava flows give way to the Peloritani Mountain limestone (an extension of the Calabrian Apennines), a number of huge, steep cliffs plunge down to the sea, endowing the landscape with matchless beauty , especially at Taormina and Acireale.

MOUNTAINS AND VALLEYS

The Sicilian land mass is predominantly hilly (62% of the surface area); 24% is mountainous, with the remainder (14%) classified as plain or lowland. The highest outcrop is Etna, with an altitude of 3 323m/10 902ft. This mountain dominates the skyline from almost every viewpoint on the island. North of Etna, separated from the Alcantara Valley, rise the precipitous heights of Sicily's principal mountain range, which runs some 200km/124mi parallel to the Tyrrhenian Coast. The **Appennino Siculo** fall into three distinctive sections. The western portion constitutes the **Monti Peloritani**, which lie between Messina and Patti; the highest peak is Montagna Grande (1 374m/4 507ft). This relief does not rise to any great altitude; in contrast with a steeply angular and craggy profile, its lower slopes have been eroded by powerful streams. The range extends westwards with the **Monti Nebrodi**: these have gentler slopes and rounded, densely wooded summits, which culminate in Monte Soro (1 847m/6 060ft). West of the Nebrodi come the **Madonie**; these include several high peaks, such as Carbonara (1 979m/6 491ft), the second highest summit on the island. The vast area between Termini Imerese and the Trapanese consists of a gently undulating hills and broad valleys. This is rudely broken by three minor massifs: the **Monti Termini Imerese, Monti di Palermo** and **Monti di Trapani** .

The south is a vast open region of arid upland (often called the *solfiferi* or *solfataras* after the high levels of sulphur deposits in the area), which stretches from Marsala to Caltanissetta. The only mountains in the area are the **Sicani Mountains** behind Agrigento and the **Monti Erei** to the east of Caltanissetta. In the southwestern corner of the island are the massive calcareous (limestone) Monti Iblei, rising to 1 000m/3 300ft.

Sicily's largest expanse of lowland plain is the **Piana di Catania** which extends from the southern lower slopes of Etna to the foothills of the Iblei range. Crisscrossed by large rivers, the plain is renowned for being especially fertile and is intensively farmed (citrus, fruit and market gardening).

RIVERS AND LAKES

Sicily's lack of water has been a major problem throughout its history. The land here has limited permeability, rainfall is erratic and water distribution is poorly managed. Although numerous, the rivers that run into the Tyrrhenian Sea are short and flow quickly to the sea.

The aquifer of the southern slopes feeds a more extensive system of sunken wells, natural springs and sluggish rivers. The rivers Gornalunga, Dittaino and Simeto irrigate the fertile plain of Catania before flowing into the Ionian.

Sicily has almost no natural lakes (except Lago di Pergusa); however, man-made reservoirs nestle among the mountains. Brackish ponds – known as **bivieri** or **pantani** – form behind the dunes along the shore. A few survive on the southeastern coast of the island and near Capo Peloro.

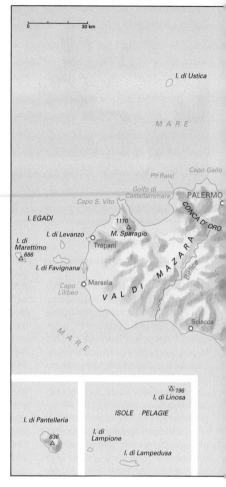

Volcanoes

According to mythology, Sicily's underworld was inhabited by Hephaestus, the god of fire, and his team of giant blacksmiths, who worked the forge that made the weapons of the gods. The Ancient Greeks attributed the volcano's rumblings to the underground anvil and forge, while eruptions from Mount Etna were furnace sparks.

VOLCANOLOGY

Volcanic Activity

Traditionally, there are four types of volcanic explosion: Plinian, Hawaiian, Strombolian and Vulcanian. The last two types take their names from the volcanoes on the Aeolian Islands, where the phenomena were first observed.

The Strombolian, peculiar to the volcano on Stromboli, has phases of persistent, moderate explosions, followed by periods of idleness.

Large gas build-ups suddenly release – like a pressure cooker.

Such eruptions can project tall fountains of lava up to several hundred metres.

First observed on the island of Vulcano in 1888, **hydrovolcanic**, or Vulcanian, eruptions expel lava and pyroclastics (solid fragments suspended in clouds of dense gas reaching exceptionally high temperatures) down the volcano's slopes at speeds that can reach up to 300m/330yd per second.

Volcanic Fallout

Volcanoes belch three types of matter: lava, pyroclastics and gas (including smoke, steam and chemical vapours). **Lava** consists of magma, which flows and folds around any obstacles, cooling quickly into glassy smooth stone like obsidian. In contrast to this, viscous lava sludges overground with difficulty, breaking into blocks. Both types appear on Etna, as well as lava tunnels in the gorges of the Alcantara and at the Faraglioni dei Ciclopi.

By-products of explosive eruptions are generally classified as **pyroclastics**. The blast lifts rock fragments from the immediate environment, crystals (solidified particles in the magma or granite) and **juvenile** formations or tuff (consolidated volcanic fragments and solidified magma), which include various types of ash, lapilli and volcanic bombs, depending on size. Should the discharge cool rapidly, it solidifies into a dense formation such as obsidian or lava glass; should it cool slowly, trapped gases can bubble out, imparting a distinctive sponge-like appearance as in the case of pumice and scoria.

Eruptions also release great quantities of volcanic vapour, indeed, sometimes only this material spouts. Both Etna and Vulcano have intensively active vents or fumeroles that expel hot **gases** like carbon, hydrogen and sulphur.

©Henri Faure/iStockphoto.com

Bocca nova crator, Mount Etna

VOLCANIC AREAS OF SICILY

Aeolian Islands

A volcanic fault, a result of the collision between ocean crust and continental crust, arcs some 200km/124mi in a semicircle and comprises eight separate islands (the seven Aeolians, plus Ustica) and many submerged volcanoes. The still active **Stromboli**, in fact, was created by 100 000 years of volcanic layers. According to classical mythology, the Aeolian islands were the home of Aeolus, ruler of the winds, who forecast the weather by interpreting the shape of the cloud rising from Stromboli. The more prosaic explanation for the cloud's shape is found in the influence of atmospheric pressure on it. Today the active craters, which vary in number and position, emerge at about 700m/2 300ft up the Sciara del Fuoco. At a distance of 1.5km/1mi off the northeastern coast of Stromboli sits **Strombolicchio:** the

outcrop stands over 40m/130ft high and is all that remains of the volcano's original core.

Etna

Mount Etna (also known as *Muncibeddu* in Sicilian dialect, and *Mongibello* in Italian) is Europe's largest active volcano, and one of the most active in the world, being in an almost constant state of eruption. It rises to a height of over 3 300m/10 900ft from a base diameter of about 40km/25mi, with rich, fertile volcano soils on its lower slopes supporting vineyards and extensive agricultural production. The volcano's activity started 600 000 years ago, following movement between the tectonic plates: this released magma through the ocean floor into the Aci Castello area and provoked surges of lava that settled near present-day Patern. During the past 100 000 years, the activity has shifted westwards. The mountain's present

Zeus and Typhon

In his *Metamorphoses,* Ovid recounts the struggle between Zeus and the giant Typhon (or Typhoeus), in which the god overcomes the giant by crushing him with the island of Sicily: "Because Typhon dared to covet the divine throne, his gigantic limbs were crushed under the vast land mass of Sicily. The giant often fights and struggles to release himself, but his right hand is held down by Peloro, his left by Pachino, his legs are weighed down by Lilibeo and his head by Etna. Typhon lies helpless under this great weight, furiously kicking sand and vomiting flames from his mouth."

profile is largely the result of an explosion about 14 000 years ago, when the Cratere Ellittico (or elliptical crater) came into being. Etna's summit comprises four active craters: (Cratere di Sud-Est, Bocca Nuova, Voragine, Cratere di Nord-Est). Eruptions also occur periodically on the flanks of the volcano, due to some 300 vents that range in diameter from small holes to larger craters.

Sicily Canal

The Sicily Canal harbours two volcanic islands, Pantelleria and Linosa, and many submarine outcrops (also known as seamounts). A rift between the continental shelves of Sicily and Tunisia is the genesis of all this excitement. Its most recent landscaping efforts include the emergence of the small island of Ferdinandea, some 50km/31mi northeast of Pantelleria, in 1831. This was the fifth time the island mass had risen above the waves since volcanic activity was first documented here, around the time of the First Punic War. Its reappearance sparked a territorial dispute over its sovereignty. However, before the issue of ownership could be resolved the island disappeared again, slipping below the water just five months later, where it remains today, lying some 7m/22ft below the surface. There was also significant activity in 1891, on the sea bed approximately 7km/4mi northwest of Pantelleria. In 2006, scientists identified these fissures as one giant underwater volcano. Named in honour of the Greek

Fruits on a strawberry tree

philosopher Empedocles, it has a base larger than the city of Rome.

Flora and Fauna

The mild climate of Sicily nurtures a fairly typical range of Mediterranean flora. The most common species found include **myrtle** *(Myrtus)*, **strawberry tree** *(Arbutus)*, **lentisk** *(Pistacia lentiscus)* and **tree spurge** *(Euphorbia dendroides)* – a bush that grows to a height of 1.5m/5ft. In springtime, sun-drenched hillsides are set ablaze by yellow flowering, sweet-smelling broom bushes *(Ginestra cinera)*. These species alternate with such imports as the evergreen, river-bed loving **oleander** *(Nerium)*; the **carob tree** *(Ceratonia)* that produces toffee-brown bean pods, populating the landscape around Ragusa; the formally erect gum or **eucalyptus** with its weeping branches and aromatic leaves; the tall pyramidal **maritime pine** *(Pinus pinaster)*; and the majestic **stone or umbrella pine** *(Pinus pinea)*. The bastard **olive** *(Olea oleaster)* grows everywhere: this spiny shrub produces rather mean, less fleshy fruits than its cultivated cousin.

Large tracts of land are devoted to **vineyards**, groves of **olive trees** *(Olea)* that contort with age and **citrus trees** (lemons; sweet, blood and Seville oranges; mandarins. Note: here "*giardino*" describes a citrus grove and not an ornamental garden, as elsewhere in Italy).

Delicate volcanic flowers

Prickly pears

G. Bludzin/MICHELIN

In the more arid areas thorny plants are common, such as various varieties of thistle (Silybum), **palms** and **dwarf**

palms – a perennial typical of the Zingaro area (so much so that it has been chosen as the symbol of the nature reserve). A broad range of succulent plants encompass the huge **agave** or **century plant**, **cactuses** and the ubiquitous **prickly pears** (Opuntia – known locally as *Fico d'India*).

The first signs of spring, heralded by meadows of wild garlic and oxalis, stir the **almond trees** (especially around Agrigento) into injecting clouds of white blossom into the landscape. Next comes the fluffy yellow mimosa and the sweet-smelling, crisp white **orange blossom**, from which bees produce a particularly fragrant honey. Soon the pinks and reds of the **oleanders** and **hibiscus** mark the advent of summer. They are joined by the garishly purple, puce and magenta **bougainvilleas** and the intensely perfumed **jasmine**, which blinks open its starry flowers all over the main island – but most especially in Pantelleria and the Aeolian Islands. Through the summer, stone walls sprout cascades of round-leafed **caper plants**. Chefs pinch the buds long before the exquisite, pinkish white flowers can flourish.

Each region has its local flora, such as the **cork plantations** near Niscemi (inland from Gela), **papyrus** plants along the River Ciane (just outside Siracusa) and the **ash tree manna** grown in the Castelbuono area of the Madonie.

Agave

After a long period of vegetation – lasting up to 50 years – the agave plant produces a long stem. Shaped like a candelabra, it can grow to a height of 6-8m/20-26ft.

Highly scented flowers blossom along this stem, just before the plant dies. Legend compares the agave plant with a young girl, who having waited years to get married, dies a year after her wedding.

Box of Sicilian lemons

M. Magni/MICHELIN

J. Malburet/MICHELIN

HISTORY

In the 14C BC, the Mediterranean was crucial to the history of man: in the words of Plato, people flocked to its coasts "like frogs around a pond". Sicily lies in the centre of this sea and consequently became a natural intersection of many cultures and civilisations. The island attracted navigators from the East and over the centuries its coastline was transfigured by myth and poetry.

Ancient Greeks

Legends about the Greeks in Sicily date back to the 8C BC. Angry at a failed sacrifice in his honour, Neptune caused a shipwreck off the eastern coast of Sicily. The sole survivor took refuge in the vast bay that extends between Capo Taormina and Capo Schisò. Struck by the island's beauty, he persuaded others to found a colony there.

HISTORY AND SOCIAL PHENOMENA

Contacts between Sicily and the Hellenistic world go back to the dawn of Greek civilisation: numerous archaeological artefacts testify to thriving maritime centres along the eastern and southern Sicilian coast trading with Crete and Mycenae from the middle of the 2nd millennium BC. Colonisation only began when living conditions within Ancient Greece became untenable: famine followed civil war and unrest from the new "social class", drawn from restless second sons, who could not inherit land.

Foundations

Various small groups of Hellenes took part in colonising Sicily. The pioneers were the Ionians: in 735 BC, they settled near Capo Schis and founded Naxos, then Leontinoi, Catane and Zancle (now Messina).
Almost simultaneously, Dorians founded Syracuse; meanwhile, colonists from Megara settled at Megara Hyblaea.
At the beginning of the 7C BC, Rhodians and Cretans arrived and founded Gela on the south coast. This first phase of expansion involved sites with abundant fresh water that were easily accessible from the sea, yet with space to expand inland.

Founders

Each expedition, comprised predominantly – but not exclusively – of men. Before scouting sites, the leader (*oikistes*) would travel to Delphi and ask the gods where to found the colony. This role had great power and prestige. He transferred the holy flame and the lifeblood of the religious cult from the metropolis to the satellite colonies. Advised by surveyors, engineers and soothsayers, he presided over the construction of the citadel and the public buildings and over the administration of justice. The leader was also responsible for ensuring fair practice when the draw for plots of land took place. His decisions were considered sacred. Upon death, he was honoured almost like a deity.

Colony

The founder would establish the new city's institutions. Each colony (*apoikia* in Greek meaning "new family") was completely independent. Despite Corinth's vain attempts to maintain control, its satellites forcefully embraced autonomy as independent entities. In this way, Akragas (Agrigento) was able to develop excellent trading relations with Carthage, which officially was hostile to Greece. Zancle and Reggio blockaded the Straits of Messina and demanded that Greek ships pay harbour taxes. The colonists lost their rights of citizenship in their city of origin and acquired the equivalent status in their new home. Restrictions on religious practices were kept in place, as was the option of "exchanging" citizenship of one city with the resident of another by mutual consent. The colonies were not only independent from their motherland, but also from each other. All grew quickly, thanks to flourishing trade links and fertile territories. A sharp increase in

SCALA

Olympus by Luigi Sabatelli, Sala dell'Iliade in Palazzo Pitti, Florence

population, partly from births and partly from immigration, sparked secondary settlement farther inland.

The Greeks and Indigenous Populations

Relations with the indigenous peoples were extremely varied. In some cases, the rapport inspired commercial and religious exchanges. These coastal Hellenic settlements barely disturbed the pre-existing communities. Yet when the Greeks spread inland, strife began. Eventually, open conflict led to the systematic extermination of villages as happened during the great revolt by the indigenous population that gripped the eastern part of the island sometime in the mid-5C. With defeat came obligations to pay tributes and, in some cases, enforced conditions of slavery. In Syracuse, the descendants of the indigenous people (the Cilliri) were constrained to cultivating the land of their overlords (Gamòroi), who were descended from the ancient colonists. The Greek settlers were known as the **Siceliots**. These peo-

ple, armed and endowed with sophisticated technology, rapidly imposed their civilisation upon Sicily: between the 6C BC and the 5C BC, they managed to completely hellenise the territories they held.

Economy

Prosperity depended not only on the natural fertility of the Sicilian land, but on good farming practices. Grafts improved the yields of wild plants. Colonists adapted common wheat for intensive cultivation, planted almond trees and pomegranates and bred animals selectively. The cities reclaimed land where possible, most notably at Camarina and Selinus, under the direction of Empedocles. Besides their success at arable farming and careful husbandry, the Western Greeks amassed fortunes through commerce, trading with the motherland, as well as Spain, southern Italy and North Africa. They imported fine ceramics, perfumes and metals against timber, wheat and wool. Soon the Siceliot cities needed their own

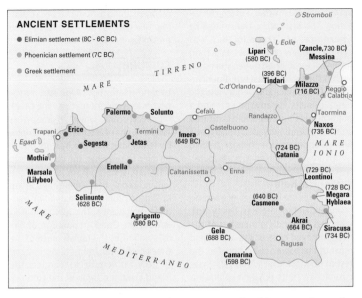

ANCIENT SETTLEMENTS

● Elimian settlement (8C - 6C BC)
● Phoenician settlement (7C BC)
● Greek settlement

△ Stromboli

I. Eolie

Lipari (580 BC)

(Zancle, 730 BC)
Messina

TIRRENO

MARE

C.d'Orlando

(396 BC) Tindari

Milazzo (716 BC)

Reggio di Calabria

Palermo   Solunto   Cefalù

Randazzo

Taormina

Trapani   Erice

I. Egadi

Termini   Imera (649 BC)

Castelbuono

Naxos (735 BC)

Segesta   Jetas

MARE IONIO

Mothia

Entella

(724 BC) Catania

Caltanissetta   Enna

(729 BC) Leontinoi

Marsala (Lilybeo)

Selinunte (628 BC)

(728 BC) Megara Hyblaea

MARE

Agrigento (580 BC)

(640 BC) Casmene

Akrai (664 BC)

Siracusa (734 BC)

Gela (688 BC)

Ragusa

MEDITERRANEO

Camarina (598 BC)

currencies. The earliest coins were of silver – later they introduced gold and bronze.

Political Evolution

To qualify for citizenship, individuals were required to own a piece of land and have a fixed abode. In reality, many of the Greeks would have earned their living as skilled craftsmen, fishermen, traders and collectors of customs duties. At least one-third of the population must have worked on large-scale construction projects, be it as a woodcutter supplying timber or a painter decorating.

Many more lived from one day to the next without a roof over their heads or permanent employment. In the space of a few years, therefore, the very inequalities that the colonists thought they had escaped by leaving Greece had become issues of contention. The aristocracy, together with the owners of the best land, hoarded power. They repressed the new moneyed classes of businessmen and those who owned no land. To deal with the continual crises provoked by economic rivalry and internal social pressures, some cities tried to correct the balance by replacing the oral legal

B. Kaufmann/MICHELIN

Theatre at Segesta

system of oaths with a written constitution. The first codex, transcribed by **Charondas of Catane** (6C BC), was copied by many other cities, including Athens. It established duties and rights within the family; prescribed punishments for violence and perjury and the death penalty for anyone entering a political meeting armed; and instituted a sort of citizens' jury, decreeing that a fine – proportional to earnings – be paid by anyone who refused to participate.

Tyrannical Rule

Tyranny was the other way of averting economic and social crises. The **tyrant**, who was generally a member of the new moneyed class or the army, held most of the power and delegated the rest to his most loyal supporters. Syracuse achieved its greatest splendour and managed to impose its authority throughout the island first under **Gelon** and then **Hieron I**. The other Siceliot cities, desperate to salvage their independence, sought assistance from Carthage or Athens, but to no avail. Meanwhile, the civil strife continued to split the Greek communities and the Carthaginian threat was growing. After a period of anarchy, **Timoleon**, who had arrived from Corinth to assist the colonies, succeeded in restoring democracy and peace to Sicily. Upon his death, the Greeks began to quarrel once more among themselves and with the Carthaginians. Finally, in the second half of the 3C BC, the citizens of Messina

(Zancle) turned to Rome for help, opening their gates to the Imperial city and precipitating her conquest of Sicily.

CULTURE

Legend relates how **Alpheus**, a river god, was wandering across the Greek region of Arcadia, when he came across Arethusa, one of Artemis' water nymphs. He fell in love with the nymph, but as he tried to seize her, she changed into a stream, slipping from him into the Ionian Sea only to re-emerge as a spring in Siracusa. Alpheus pursued her, mingling their waters. This myth, diffused among the Greek population of Sicily, symbolises the transference of the Greek civilisation from the motherland to Sicily. Far from being marginal, the island attracted some of the culture's most illustrious figures. It also succoured native geniuses, who became famous throughout the Hellenic world.

According to some scholars, Greek culture should be indebted to Sicily for one of its fundamental masterpieces, the *Odyssey*. Many of Ulysses' adventures were unequivocally set in the Island of the Sun, the name used by **Homer** to describe Sicily, so obviously that Apollodorus defined the *Odyssey* as a kind of "journey around Sicily." Many of the places can be identified with Sicily *(see the Ulysses in Sicily map, below)*: the Aeolian Islands are the kingdom of Aeolus and the "errant rocks" mentioned by Circe in Book XII are the Faraglioni rocks between Lipari and Vulcano; Scylla and Charybdis personify the impetuous currents in the Straits of Messina; the port at which Ulysses' companions steal the flocks of the Sun is Messina; the Sirens (according to the Sicilian interpretation of the work) waited for sailors in the seas around Capo Peloro; the Cyclops' cave was inside Mount Etna; and the rocks thrown by Polyphemus landed in the sea in front of Aci Trezza. Lastly, the Lestrigoni,

ULYSSES IN SICILY

the giant cannibals of Book X, lived near Lentini, while the Lotus Eaters (Book IX) lived between Agrigento and Camarina.

Tyrannical Patrons

According to Aristotle, comedy in its classical form was invented by the Megareans of Greece and Sicily. Undoubtedly both **Epicharmus** and **Phormis**, the two earliest identifiable authors of comedies engaged at the court of Gelon, were Sicilian. Interestingly, the tyrants were noted for being generous patrons, summoning to their courts the best poets of the time.

Among the illustrious guests was the poet **Simonides**, famous as a writer of epigrams and funeral laments. He dedicated many verses to Sicily, telling how Hephaestus and Demeter disputed possession of the island, because of its fire and abundant wheat harvests. The simultaneous presence of poets of a certain renown also generated bitter rivalries: for years, **Bacchylides** and **Pindar** contested Hieron's favours, as they exalted his success at the games. At the height of his achievement, the great tragedian **Aeschylus** was based at the court of Hieron.

To celebrate the conquest and re-naming of the city of Aetna (later Catania), he arranged performances of *The Women of Etna* (now lost) and *The Persians*. Pindar marked the occasion by composing his Pythian Odes. **Theocritus** (c. 300–260 BC), meanwhile, was a native of Syracuse; he is attributed with inventing pastoral poetry.

Philosophy

Two of the most interesting pre-Socratic thinkers were born in Sicily: **Empedocles** came from Agrigento and **Gorgias** from Leontinoi. Empedocles (c. 500– c 430 BC) is a complex figure: a mystic, miracle worker, doctor and student of natural philosophy. He also founded a school of medicine that regarded the heart as the seat of life, an idea taken up by Aristotle. He taught that all matter was composed of four elements (earth, water, air and fire). These – regulated by the two universal forces harmony and discord (love and hate) – gave rise to the

whole cosmos. According to legend, he jumped into one of the fiery craters of Mount Etna to persuade his fellow citizens that he had been summoned by the gods. Gorgias (483–375 BC) responded to a different cultural climate, one of sophism (false argument), that aimed at satisfying the requirements of the emerging democracy, with particular emphasis on moral and political issues. He became an orator of considerable renown, especially in Athens, where he was acclaimed a "master of wisdom."

The first great philosopher of mathematical harmony was Pythagoras. His doctrines were widespread in Sicily, particularly in Agrigento and Catania. The **School of Pythagoras** was established at Croton in the 6C–5C BC. The group had much political clout and suggested a new aristocracy be drawn from business- and tradesmen.

Sicily was also the setting envisaged by **Plato** for his Utopian state, ruled by philosophers, as contemplated in the *Republic*.

The philosopher visited Syracuse in 388–387 BC; when the tyrant became suspicious of the Athenian, he incarcerated Plato as a slave on the island of Aegina. He later returned to Sicily after Dionysius II had succeeded his father; to begin with, Plato appears to have found Dionysius II the better disciple, that is, until Dion was sent into exile and Plato was detained as a prisoner.

Science and History

Archimedes (first half of the 3C BC) was the one person in the Greek world capable of consolidating the theoretical and practical aspects of scientific knowledge at that time. Besides his important discoveries in the fields of mathematics, geometry and naval engineering, his name is associated with the invention of war machines. His weapons of mass destruction convinced the Romans that they battled gods.

Diodorus Siculus, born at Agyrion in the 1C BC, was the author of a universal history of 40 volumes entitled *Biblioteca*. He traced Greek history from the mythical era to contemporary times; this still constitutes a valuable source for scholars.

RELIGION

Religion touched upon everything in the life of a Greek: he or she saw every event, be it of major or minor importance, as a possible manifestation of the divine.

In no way, however, was the religion in the least dogmatic. Indeed, on coming into contact with another people, the Greeks welcomed their gods to the Olympic pantheon, or assimilated them with their own deities.

The Greek gods, who personified the forces of nature or some moral quality, had human personalities and shapes. The Greeks turned to a deity for protection and favour. Prayers were usually accompanied by an offering (libations of milk or wine, sweets, cakes or fresh produce). In the event of more demanding requests, an animal might be sacrificed; parts were then burnt on the altar, while the rest was divided between the priest and the faithful. However, festivals were the most important public ceremonies. These included literary and poetry competitions, sporting events including organised games like the Olympics.

Each part of Greece was especially devoted to a particular deity. Colonists transferred these traditions to the new land. They created new holidays too, like founding-anniversary banquets.

Metope of Temple C at Selinunte showing Heracles dragging the thieving Cercopes, National Archaeological Museum, Palermo

© 1990 Photo Scala, Florence/National Archaeological Museum, Palermo

Three important figures

Among all the different gods and heroes venerated, the most significant are **Demeter**, regarded as the protector of Sicily, and **Heracles**. Sometimes the Greeks embraced local cults and rites, like the hot spring nymphs at Termini Imerese or the **Palici** brothers.

Demeter, the goddess who embodies the earth's fertility, was the object of a cult prevalent especially in Ionian Greece and therefore in **Sicily**. Here, the mother-protector became a more complex deity. The Greek colonists adapted her story to Sicily, rooting it with specific geographical allusions. In it, **Persephone**, daughter of Zeus and Demeter, was gathering flowers near the Lake of Pergusa. Hades (Pluto), the king of the Underworld, fell in love and carried her off. For nine days, Demeter wandered over Sicily in search of her lost daughter. Near Trapani, she dropped her sickle: the origin of the curved headland behind the town. One night, as she scoured the slopes of Etna by the light of flaming pine trees, she believed the lupins were mocking her quest. From that day forth, the flowers lost their sweetness and became bitter. Frustrated, Demeter inflicted a terrible drought. Men and animals died by the hundreds. This prompted her brother Zeus to intervene. He told Hades to release Persephone, provided she had eaten nothing in the Underworld. But

Statue of a goddess restored as Demeter, Museo Pio-Clementino, Vatican

© 2003 Photo Scala, Florence/Museo Pio-Clementino, Vatican

The Greek Gods in Sicily

Acis: god of the river of the same name and lover of Galatea (💧*see ACIREALE*).

Aeolus: son of Poseidon, god of the winds and lord of the Aeolian Islands.

Alpheus: god of the river of the same name in the Peloponnese. He fell in love with the water-nymph, Arethusa, and followed her to Sicily (💧*see SIRACUSA*).

Aphrodite (Venus): goddess of love and wife of Hephaestus, much worshipped in Erice.

Charybdis: a monster who inhabited the Sicilian shore of the Straits of Messina. Three times a day the monster swallowed huge amounts of water, creating dangerous whirlpools, including one which trapped Ulysses' ship.

Cocalus: Sicilian king who offered refuge to Dedalus; the latter was pursued by Minos after helping Theseus to escape from Minos' labyrinth.

Demeter (Ceres): goddess of the harvest who fought with Hephaestus for control of Sicily.

Eryx: son of Aphrodite and Butes (or Poseidon). He challenged Heracles and was killed by him.

Etna: a Sicilian nymph who intervened in the dispute between Demeter and Hephaestus over the possession of Sicily. One legend recounts that the Palici were born from her union with Hephaestus.

Galatea: a nymph who was loved by the monster Polyphemus and was in love with Acis (💧*see ACIREALE*).

Giants: son of Gaia (the Earth) and Uranus, enemies of the Olympic gods, and particularly of Zeus and Athena.

Hades (Pluto): brother of Zeus; lord of the kingdom of the dead. He abducted Demeter's daughter, Proserpina, on the banks of Lake Pergusa.

Helios: god of the sun. He owned a herd of cattle in Sicily, some of which were eaten by Ulysses' companions, thus incurring the wrath of the god.

Hephaestus: god of fire and lord of the volcanoes, in which he worked with his helpers, the Cyclops.

Heracles: a hero during his earthly life and a god after his death. One of his 12 Labours, that of the cattle of Geryon, took place in Sicily.

Palici: twin sons of Zeus and the muse Thalia or, according to another tradition, of Hephaestus and Etna, born in the waters of Lake Naftia, near Palagonia.

Persephone (Proserpina): goddess of the Underworld and wife of Hades.

Typhon: a giant who fought with Zeus and Athena. He escaped by crossing the Sicilian sea, then was crushed when Zeus hurled Sicily on top of him.

before she departed, Hades forced her to eat a few pomegranate seeds as a symbol of fidelity. Thus Persephone was destined to spend a third of the year with him and the remainder with her mother on earth. The story explains the cycle of seasons.

The second deity to enjoy special status was **Heracles**. This probably stems from another older myth, involving a Phoenician deity who shared many elements with the Greek hero.

The legend claims Heracles was born to Zeus and a mortal woman, Alcmena. He had to undertake 12 labours in order to assuage a dreadful deed and become

a god. According to tradition, Sicilians were the first to recognise his divinity. Heracles came to the island during his tenth labour, when he crossed the Straits of Messina pursuing a bull belonging to Geryon.

Almost every little place on the island claims a visitation: Erice was where he wrestled and killed the son of Aphrodite and Butes, the king who shared his name with the town; at Syracuse he is said to have instituted a sacred festival near the Gorge of Cyane.

Agiro first honoured him as a god; thus he created a lake outside the city walls and raised two sanctuaries there.

The Siceliot House

The Archaic houses were fairly simple affairs: rectangular sun-dried brick buildings with bases of dry pebbles stood inside a walled plot. Flat tiles covered the sloping gable roof. In the courtyard were stored tools and those great terracotta jars for provisions; it also served as a communal area where the family gathered, ate and received visitors. The terrace was used for drying fruit, as a place to sit and talk, pray and sleep. Among the foundations, a talisman was hidden, sometimes a bone or a votive object, to ensure the house remained sturdy and solid. Often it was sprinkled with the blood of a young animal, as were the threshold, the architrave and the door-jambs. In time, the houses became more sophisticated: a raised floor was added, complete with a stairway supported by a portico. The largest of the rooms – facing onto the portico and connected to the kitchen – hosted gatherings, for it was here that the men met for their *symposia*.

The **Palici** rank among Sicily's own ancient divinities, whom the Greeks later appropriated by adopting them as the twin sons of Zeus and the muse, Thalia. The cult's centre was Naftia, a small lake with bubbling sulphurous waters in the Plain of Catania, near Palagonia. The myth relates how Thalia, fearing the wrath of Hera, hid underground. The birth of the divine twins caused the waters of the lake to bubble and steam. Beside the sanctuary dedicated to the Palici, the Greeks swore solemn oaths and enacted a ritual in the lake.

If tablets bearing written agreements sank, this was interpreted as a sign of perjury, which the Palici punished with blinding. According to another tradition, the Palici were the children of Hephaestus, the god of fire, and Etna, the nymph who intervened in the struggle between the god and Demeter for control of Sicily.

In general, the Siceliots were hugely sensitive to the indigenous cults, especially the worship of the dead and of the chthonic gods of the Underworld.

Mysteries

Mystery rites were also particularly widespread in Sicily. These religious practices provided answers to the inexplicable and soothed worries about facing death. The Mysteries promised to purify celebrants through an initiation and thus ensure happiness in the afterlife.

One of the most famous cults, the Eleusinian Mysteries, revolved around Demeter and Persephone.

ART

Architecture: Civil and Military

The oldest ruins date to the end of the 6C BC. Presumably, military emplacements existed here from the 8C, when the various cities rivalled one another before the rise of tyrants.

Fortresses and Fortifications – Under the tyrants, buildings were fortified with local materials: in the east, lava was common, as at **Naxos** and **Lipari.** In the absence of suitable stone, walls were sun-dried brick with a base of broken stones, or pebbles and clay.

Only a few forts have survived. These citadels ensured the defence of a city, its roads and other means of access.

Urban planning – Almost on arrival, the Greek settlers organised the area into a rational system. They designated some as places of worship, others for public buildings and as residential quarters. Generally Sicilian cities conformed to the urban planning theories outlined by **Hippodamus of Miletus,** the 5C BC Greek philosopher and surveyor. He advocated a city on a rectangular street plan, centred around two axes: the *cardo* (or *stenopos,* in Greek) that ran from north to south and the *decumanus maximus* (*plateia* in Greek) that bisected it from east to west. Smaller streets ran parallel to both. A precise set of buildings and zones was then constructed, such as the *agora,* the main square and the centre of public life, the *pritaneo,* which stood beside the *agora* and was the setting for a range of civic activities, the *ekklesiasterion*, a secular public building reserved for the people's assembly *(ekklesia)*, the most famous example of which can be seen at Agrigento, and the *bouleutérion*, where the citizen's council *(boulé)* met. The temples, sometimes outside the city limits, were often surrounded by other sacred buildings, which could include porticoes, votive monuments, gymnasia and theatres.

Walls usually fortified the urban area; beyond lay the agricultural land, subdivided into family plots, and a burial ground.

All the Greek cities and, sometimes even the villages, were supplied with reservoirs for water and aqueducts, the most famous being that built by the architect Phaeax at Akragas (Agrigento), and the extremely complex one at Syracuse.

Architecture:
Sacred and Religious

There are two forms of sacred building: the **temple** and the theatre. Usually located outside the city, they were designed to be visible from a distance.

Temples – From the 8C BC, Greek colonists brought cults and gods to Sicily, transforming the island into what is now regarded as one of the most extraordinary open-air museums of "severe style " Doric temples. The heart of the building comprised the **naos** *(cella)*, an oblong chamber that housed a statue of the

god. Temples normally faced east, so that the statue could be illuminated by the rising sun, the source of all life. Before the *naos* was the **pronaos** (a kind of antechamber), while behind stood the **opisthodomos** which served as a treasury. A **peristyle**, or colonnade, surrounded the building.

The temple was founded on a stepped base; onto the last step **(stylobate)** were erected the **columns**, which rose to support the **architrave**. A sloping roof covered the building.

First conceived in the Peloponnese, the **Doric style** spread to mainland Greece and consequently to its colonies, including Sicily.

The Doric order, which combines majesty with sobriety, comprises a base-less column shaft indented with 20 vertical grooves or flutes (as from the 5C) that sits directly on the stylobate. The entablature consists of a plain architrave, the upper section of which comprises a frieze articulated by **metopes** (generally panels sculpted with shallow relief) and **triglyphs** (rectangular projections ornamented with two deep vertical grooves in the centre flanked by a narrower one at each edge).

In the 6C BC, almost all the temples built in Sicily were peripteral (that is, surrounded by a line of columns) and hexastyle (six-columned front elevation); although some examples have more than six front columns, such as Temple G at Selinunte.

Temple at Selinunte

M. Guillot/MICHELIN

As a result of its simplicity of structure and perfect harmony of proportion, the temple was long considered to be the architectural prototype of ideal beauty. Building designers corrected for the human eye's distortion: the central section of the architrave, which appeared to sag slightly, was fractionally raised to restore an impression of perfect balance. The outer columns of the façades were slightly inclined inwards, thereby countering the natural tendency to lean outwards. Finally, they cut a slight bulge into columns, so they wouldn't appear to taper absurdly (particularly in large buildings, such as the Temple of Concord at Agrigento and the temples at Selinunte and Segesta).

When compared with the architecture of mainland Greece, the temples of Magna Graecia and Sicily are more monumental, pay more attention to spatial effect and have abundant decoration. Sculptures crown the prominent features, in some cases those elements with no structural function – on the **tympanum** of a pediment, for example, or above the **metopes** of the architrave and on the edges of roofs.

Theatres – Beside most of the Greek sanctuaries, there was a theatre where Dionysian celebrations were held (in honour of Dionysus, the god of wine) with hymns called "dithyrambs," from which Greek tragedy later derived.

Built first of wood and then, from the 4C BC, in stone, a theatre would comprise a **cavea** (koilon) – a series of tiered ledges arranged in a semicircle, the first row being reserved for priests and dignitar-ies. Access was from the base by means of side entrances (parodos); one passage (diazoma) led through to the central section, another up to the top rows of seating. The **orchestra** consisted of a circular area where the chorus and actors, wearing masks corresponding to their roles, took their places around the altar of Dionysus. Behind the orchestra stood the **proscenium**, a construction similar to a portico which served as backdrop scenery, and the skéné which at once fulfilled three functions, namely stage

B. Kaufmann/MICHELIN

The white marble Ephebus of Motya, now on display in the Joseph Whitaker Museum near where it was found, clearly demonstrates the evolution of the Ionic style: this 1.81m/5.93ft youth is dressed in a long tunic of soft, figure-hugging linen, which flatters the muscular body of the athlete.

Pithos: used for storing grain

Amphora: stored and transported oil and wine

Pelike: container for oil

Crater: container for wine

Hydria: container for water.

scenery, backstage and a storage area. During the Hellenistic period, the *skéné* came to be reserved for actors. Given that these complexes are generally set in the most splendid landscape, on the slope of a hill or a mountain, the natural scenery (particularly spectacular at Taormina and Segesta) provided the perfect background for productions. The *skéné*, almost always raised onto a platform, dominated the circular orchestra, where sacrifices were also sometimes made.

Sculpture

According to authors such as Diodorus Siculus (1C BC historian) and Pausanias (Greek traveller of the 2C AD), Sicily had established an artistic heritage even before she was colonised.

During colonisation, indigenous artistic taste and aesthetics were affected by Greek influences, leading to the gradual erosion and eventual extinction of a purely "Sicilian" style. In such a way, the island succumbed to the three chronological phases of Greek art: the Archaic, Classic and Hellenistic eras.

The scarcity of marble – and the particular Sicilian taste for pictorial and chiaroscuro effects – resulted in limestone and sandstone constructions predominantly. Clay was widely used in the pediments and acroteri of the temples, as well as for votive statues.

Archaic (8C–5C BC) – This phase coincides with the production of the first large, rather wooden, hieratic figures which, in the 6C BC, gave rise to two distinctive forms: the *kouros* – the young

The discovery of the bronze ram at Castello Maniace (on display at the Palermo Archaeological Museum) betrays the major impact of Greek aesthetics, notably their canons of beauty, on a city such as Syracuse.

male nude – and the *koré* – the young female equivalent, though modestly dressed in a tunic.

The statue of the **Ephebus of Agrigento** is one excellent example of Late Archaic sculpture: it suggests the sculptor was striving to conform to a predetermined aesthetic type, although its basic sense of balance has yet to be perfected (the right leg appears extremely rigid, while the outstretched arms seem set too far away from the body).

As far as Archaic sculptural ornament used to adorn temples is concerned, two examples are to be found in Sicily: the polychrome winged **Gorgon** that once ornamented the pediment of the Athenaion in Syracuse and the six **metopes of Selinunte**, now displayed in the archaeological museum at Palermo.

Oinochoe: a jug for wine

Kantharos: a tall goblet

Kylix: a drinking cup

Rhyton: a cup shaped like a horn or an animal's head

Lekythos: a vase for ointment

Classic (5C–3C BC) – The Ionic style of sculpture, which appeared in Sicily from the 6C BC onwards, is characterised by a better portrayal of individual features and a greater sense of realism and sensitivity, now free of the severe rigidity of the earlier phase, as shown in the famous Ephebus of Motya.

Hellenistic (3C–1C BC) – During this phase, sculpture becomes yet more expressive and oriental. Deities are portrayed with more realism, with human – rather than ideal – features and in a less formal state of dress (Aphrodite, the goddess of beauty and love, is often shown in a pleated, flowing shift nonchalantly revealing her glorious nudity). Sculpture from this period is highly expressive in emotion, physical strength and movement.

The terracotta **theatrical masks** in the Archaeological Museum on Lipari (over 250 examples) portray a great range and subtlety of expressions.

Mainly they were inspired by Greek tragedy, which became widespread in Sicily from the 3C BC. 🔊 *See ISOLE EOILE: Limari.*

Painting and Pottery

Greeks considered painting the most noble and eloquent form of artistic expression, described by the poet Simonides (5C BC) as "mute poetry". Unfortunately, examples are rare, because of the pigments' fragility and vulnerability to weather conditions. Large easel paintings, extolled by original sources, can be partially reconstructed from vase painting renditions.

"This is the light of the great Constance, who, from the second gale of Swabia, produced the third, which was also the last."
– Dante Alighieri,
The Divine Comedy, Paradise III
(Oxford University Press)

Styles – Vases with **black figures** on a red or pale yellow background date from the Archaic and early Classic phase. The artists scratched away the black paint with a steel-tipped instrument. The most common subjects were from mythology or everyday life; sometimes geometric or abstract motifs appeared, especially on the early vases.

Red-figure vases appear in southern Italy towards the latter half of the 5C BC, earlier than in Greece, where this style became prevalent from 480 BC. In this case, the black paint forms a background, with the figures in brick red colour with touches of black and white. This inverted technique, allowing greater freedom of expression, was a revolutionary discovery; designs acquired softer lines and contours than those graffitied with a sharp steel point. The choice of subjects, however, does not change a great deal. Among the most beautiful examples of imported Attic vases are the magnificent two-handled craters from Agrigento (5C BC).

Sicilian School of Poetry

Literature developed in Frederick's court, the *Magna Curia*, as an elegant pastime for aristocrats, princes and high officials. The Sicilian poets modelled their subject matter and style on the Provençal troubadour poetry of courtly love: the sort of loving service that man, as a servant, dedicates to a Madonna. The language was a refined Sicilian, stripped of any colloquialisms, enriched instead with Latin and Provençal phraseology. Strictly literary, it excluded any form of realism, which influenced Italian lyric poetry as a whole. Among the Sicilian School poets ranked several sovereigns: Frederick II, his sons Henry, Frederick, Manfred and Enzo king of Sardinia, all wrote poetry. Other notable exponents of the genre include the court notary **Giacomo da Lentini**, who is regarded as the inventor of the sonnet, **Pier della Vigna** (mentioned by Dante in Inferno, Canto XIII v 25) and **Cielo d'Alcamo**, author of the famous dialogue-poem *Rosa Fresca Aulentissima*. With the decline of the *Magna Curia*, the Sicilian School's golden age came to an end.

The Codex Astensis: Frederick II granting privileges to the town of Asti

Archivio Municipale di Asti/SCALA

Frederick II

THE LIFE OF FREDERICK II

On 27 January 1186, Costanza d'Altavilla, heiress to the throne of Sicily, married Henry VI of Swabia, son of Frederick I Barbarossa and heir to the Holy Roman Empire, with great pomp and ceremony in Milan. Aged 31, Costanza had long passed the normal age for matrimony and was 11 years older than her husband. The couple were married for eight years before producing an heir. On 26 December 1194, Costanza went into labour at Jesi and decided to birth the infant under a canvas in the city's main square, possibly to dispel doubts cast on her maternity at such an advanced age. In 1197, aged 32, Henry died of a fever caught while hunting on Mount Etna. His wife died the following year, but before doing so entrusted their son Frederick to Pope Innocent III, who had the child crowned king of Sicily in 1198. For political and dynastic reasons, Frederick had a difficult, lonely childhood in Palermo. Left to his own devices, he would haunt the poorer districts of the city, mixing with people of all religions and walks of life. These cosmopolitan experiences influenced the future emperor's broad view of life and grand political projects. Back in the court, Frederick's education

The Four Wives of Frederick II

1209: Constance of Aragon, mother of Henry VII, who rebelled against his father. Constance died in 1222.

1225: Isabella of Brienne, heiress to the throne of Jerusalem. She bore Frederick two children: Conrad IV and Margherita. Isabella died in 1228.

1235: Elizabeth of England, sister of Henry III of England and mother of Henry. She died in 1241.

1250: Bianca Lancia. Just before his death, Frederick II married the woman with whom he had enjoyed a relationship for many years. She was the mother of his favourite son, Manfred, of Costanza and, possibly, of Violante.

was worthy of his lineage: he possessed an enquiring mind, loved nature and culture, studied Latin and the natural sciences and deepened his knowledge of the Arab classics and Islamic culture.

In 1215, Pope Innocent III excommunicated Otto IV, Emperor of the Holy Roman Empire, crowning Frederick II emperor in his place.

Frederick travelled to Germany and only returned to Sicily in 1220. In 1227 he was excommunicated by Pope Honorius III and in 1229, having completed the "Crusade of the Excommunicants", he declared himself king of Jerusalem. The following year the Pope withdrew the excommunication.

After years of conflict with the Pope and two excommunications, Frederick died in the Castello di Fiorentino on 13 December 1250 and was buried in Palermo Cathedral.

A PRODIGIOUS TALENT

Frederick II was a man of many talents. A skilful statesman, commander and legislator, he loved the arts and sciences and was the author of a famous treatise on falconry entitled *De arte venandi cum avibus*. His character combined the medieval holiness of his imperial role and a remarkably modern eclecticism. His court was a meeting place for scholars from all fields, including writers, mathematicians, astronomers, doctors and musicians. Frederick was responsible for the foundation of the University of Naples, the development of the Salerno Medical School, where a Chair of Anatomy was created, and the birth of the School of Sicilian Poetry.

Dante affirms Frederick's fame as a man of culture, describing the emperor as "a great logician and scholar". Credited as a lover of wisdom and patron of the arts, Frederick II showed considerable open-mindedness in his political dealings. His greatest wish was to be regarded as the "emperor of recent times", summoned with a mission to restore the golden age of justice on earth. This legendary vision conflicts with the accusations made by the papal curia, which tended to regard Frederick as the Antichrist mentioned in the Bible.

Time Line

PREHELLENISTIC SICILY

The Greek historian Dionysius of Halicarnassus chronicled how ancient expeditions embarked in the East, setting sail for the Italian peninsula and Sicily. Archaeology provides more concrete proof. Evidence of Mycenaean visits has been found at Thapsos and Panarea (pottery incised with Linear B script: the Mycenaean syllabic alphabet).

1270-650 BC – Late Bronze Age: the Greeks seem to have brought iron and a higher level of material civilisation. The Athenian historian Thucydides recorded this colonisation and described the island's indigenous peoples: the **Siculi** and the **Sicani**. The former resided in eastern and central southern Sicily, inland from Syracuse. The origins of the western Siculi should, perhaps, be traced back to the Italian peninsula, given commonalities with the mainland's Apennine culture. The Sicani seem not to conform with Indo-European people, but rather to be of Iberian origin.

The **Elimi**, founders of Erice (Eryx) and Segesta, seem to belong to the ancient family of Mediterranean and pre-Indo-European peoples. Various evidence suggests contact with the East (like the cult of Aphrodite Ericina) and a rapid Hellenisation of this people (the Doric temple at Segesta).

Phoenicians from Carthage settled at Solunto, Panormus (modern Palermo) and Mozia (Motya) in the northwestern part of the island, where the foundations of Lilybaeum (modern Marsala) – an impregnable stronghold and the fulcrum of Carthaginian military power – were later laid.

SIKELÍA:
SICILY UNDER THE GREEKS

775 BC – Establishment of the trading colony of Pithecusa on Ischia; the first Hellenistic settlement near mainland Italy.

735 – The first Hellenistic settlement, Naxos, is created in Sicily, securing trade routes through the Straits of Messina. The Corinthians found Syracuse (Siracusa) in 734.

730-700 – The Chalcidians found Catana, Leontinoi and Zancle (now Messina); the Megarians found Megara Hyblaea.

688 – Colonists from Rhodes and Crete found Gela, the same city that seized Akragas (Agrigento) in 580.

598 – Foundation of Camarina.

491 – Gelon becomes the tyrant of Gela. In 488, he wins the chariot race at Olympia – and thus great prestige.

480-479 – The Greeks in Sicily face hostility from the Carthaginians and the Etruscans.

485 – Gelon becomes Syracuse's tyrant.

480 – Battle of Himera: the Syracusans defeat the Carthaginians.

474 – Hieron, tyrant of Syracuse, wins a decisive naval victory at Cumae over the Etruscans. Catania, on the Ionian coast, is occupied by Dorian colonists and subjugated to the rule of Hieron's son.

465 – The tyrant Thrasybulus is expelled and Syracuse is ruled by a moderate democracy.

453 – Rebellion of Ducetius: the Siculi towns form a confederation. The uprising dies in 450.

414 – Athenians besiege Syracuse. The Spartan Gylippus comes to the town's rescue.

413 – The Athenian hold over Sicily is broken. During the war, Athens loses 50 000 men (including 12 000 ordinary citizens) and more than 200 triremes.

409 – Carthaginians attack and destroy Selinunte and Himera.

406 – The general Dionysius I seizes power in Syracuse. Over the ensuing years, he secures a vast dominion including a large portion of southern Italy and the Adriatic coast (he conquers Croton and founds Ancona).

Archaeological Museum, Syracuse/SCALA Syracuse/SCALA

Syracusan coins

392 – Peace between the Carthaginians and Dionysius I.

367 – Death of Dionysius I.

347 – Dionysius II, exiled previously by Dion – a family relative and fellow adherent of Plato – returns to Syracuse.

344 – The mother city of Corinth sends 700 soldiers to Syracuse led by Timoleon, who defeats the Carthaginians at the battle of River Crimisus (341).

316 – Agathocles, a man of modest origins, heads a revolt against the barons and seizes power in Syracuse.

310 – The Carthaginians defeat Agathocles at Ecnomus. Soon after, he lands in Africa at the head of 14 000 men bent on wreaking vengeance on Carthage.

289 – Death of Agathocles. In the same year, the Mamertini, mercenaries of Campanian origin, seize Messina.

280 – Pyrrhus, king of Epirus in Greece, tries in vain to unite Sicily between 278 and 275.

269 – Hieron II, formerly one of Pyrrhus' officers, declares himself *basileus* (king) of Syracuse after a victory over the Mamertini.

264-241 – First Punic War.

SICILY UNDER THE ROMANS

Ruled by a praetor and two quaestors, Sicily was of prime importance to Rome (not least for the large tributes it paid).

The island continued to be of economic importance, despite two devastating slave rebellions and Syracuse's disastrous revolt (and subsequent sacking). Sicily possessed many large estates, which, in turn, provided the Roman aristocracy with elegant residences. In many cases, these villas became centres of literary patronage and recreation for the ennobled Romans.

227 BC – Sicily is made a province.
218-201 – Second Punic War. In 211, after a long siege, Consul Marcellus sacks Syracuse for rebelling against Rome.
149-146 – Third Punic War and final destruction of Carthage.
138-131 – First slave revolt in Sicily led by the Syrian slave, Eunus.
104-99 – Second slave revolt led by the slave Trifon.
70 – Several towns accuse Verres, Sicily's praetor, of embezzlement. The great orator Cicero leads their legal defence.
48 – Battle of Pharsalus: Caesar's troops defeat Pompey's.
44 – Pompey's son, Sextus Pompeius, controls Sardinia, Corsica and Sicily with his fleets. In 36 BC, he is defeated by Vipsanius Agrippa, one of Octavian's admirals.
31 – Battle of Actium: Octavian (later Augustus) becomes sole ruler of Rome.

2C AD – Spread of Christianity on the island.
468 – Gaiseric, King of the Vandals in Africa, conquers the island.

ARABIC SICILY

Sicily benefited from almost two centuries of Muslim domination. A magnificent and highly original Arab-Norman style of architecture evolved, along with a unique literary tradition and a predilection for scholarship (here Plato's *Dialogues* were first translated in the 11C). This autonomous culture has proved to vital to all European history.

AD 491 – Theodoric's Ostrogoths assume control of the island: its administration is re-organised according to Imperial standards. The Roman Church extends its land holding.
535 – The Eastern Roman Empire annexes Sicily at the start of the Gothic-Byzantine war.
652 – First Arab incursions.
663 – For political reasons, the Byzantine basileus Constans II takes up residence in Sicily.
725 – Iconoclastic crisis: Sicily remains faithful to the cult of images.
827 – The Arabs land at Mazara. The invaders (mostly Berbers and Persians) conquer Palermo and make it their capital.

Linguistic Traces of the Arabs in Sicily

Traces of the Arab presence in Sicily can be found in the language of the island, especially in place names. Names of towns and villages that have evolved from Arabic include Calascibetta, Calatafimi, Caltabellotta, Caltagirone, Caltanissetta and Caltavuturo, all of which derive from the word *kalat,* meaning castle; Marsala from *marsa* (port); Mongibello, Gibellina and Gibilmanna from *gebel* (mountain); Modica from *mudiqah* (narrowing in the road); Racalmuto and Regalbuto from *rahal* (hamlet); and Sciacca from *shaqqah* (fissure, referring to the caves at Monte Kronio). The most common Italian words to have derived from Arabic are *albicocca* (apricot), *alcool, algebra* (from *al giabr,* meaning transport), *arancia* (orange), *bizzeffe* (galore, from *bizzef,* meaning many), *calibro* (gauge, from *qalib,* the measurement used for shoes), *carciofo* (artichoke), *cifra* (figure) and *zero* (both from *sifr,* meaning empty), *cotone* (cotton), *dogana* (customs), *limone* (lemon), *magazzino* (warehouse), *melanzana* (aubergine), *ragazzo* (boy, from *raqqas,* meaning messenger), *taccuino* (notebook, from *taquim,* meaning proper order), *tazza* (cup), *tariffa* (tariff), *zafferano* (saffron), *zecca* (mint, from *sikka,* meaning coin) and *zucchero* (sugar).

842-59 – Messina, Modica, Ragusa and Enna fall. Only the northeast resists effectively, with Byzantine assistance.

878 – Syracuse, the ancient capital, is stormed and destroyed.

902 – Fall of Taormina, the last Byzantine stronghold in Sicily.

948-1040 – The island is ruled by the Emirs of the Kalbite dynasty.

The arrival of the Arabs split the political and economic status quo in Sicily. The indigenous people and invaders collaborated profitably in the west. However, the area around Syracuse never fully accepted Arab dominion, even if their arrival sealed the demise of the decadent ancient metropolis and of eastern Sicily, where the Greek language and culture still prevailed. The northeast, which maintained its Christian solidarity, offered fierce resistance.

Palermo came to symbolise Arab-Sicilian civilisation. It was densely populated (estimated at 300 000 inhabitants) and wealthy, with bands of sprawling suburbs and small farms. Some 300 mosques and as many *madrasa* (Koranic schools) were instituted. The Emir was advised by an assembly *(giama'a)*, drawn from the local aristocracy. Land was divided into small plots, thus benefiting the new rulers; intensive and more sophisticated farming methods were imposed (including irrigation channels known as *qanat*) and new cash crops were introduced such as cotton, flax, sugar cane, rice, citrus fruits, henna, nuts and dates.

Culture also flourished, encouraged by links with Islam from around the Mediterranean (Andalucia in the case of literature, the Maghreb and Egypt in the case of science). The perfect expression of this cross-fertilisation is the splendid Arabic literature from the court at Palermo. Ibn Hamdis, in his melancholy farewell to Sicily, wrote: *"a land to which the dove lent its collar, clothed by the peacock from its many-coloured mantle of feathers"*.

1061 – The Normans land in Sicily. During the next 30 years, Christianity struggles to reaffirm itself across the island and drive out Islamic culture.

SICILY UNDER THE NORMANS

The "men of the north", having set out from their homes in Scandinavia, had settled in what is now Normandy by 911. Some of these fierce warriors fought as mercenaries in Italy's south, where disputes raged among Roman popes, Lombard dukes of Benevento and Salerno, Arabs in Sicily and Byzantines in Apulia and Calabria.

Through the Treaty of Melfi (1059), the Normans not only became vassals of the Pope, they also secured feudal rights over southern Italy. One, a certain Robert Guiscard ("the Sly"), acquired the title of Duke of Apulia and promptly subdued Bari and Salerno.

His brother **Count Roger** (1031–1101) set about conquering Sicily, marching into Palermo in 1072. The last Arab stronghold, Noto, did not capitulate until 1091, when Roger won the coveted title of Papal Legate, making him the Holy See's representative on the island.

1130 – Roger II (1095–1154) succeeds his father Roger I in 1101; the title of King of Sicily and Duke of Campania is conferred upon him by the Antipope Anacletus II; this position is sanctioned nine years later by Pope Innocent II.

Mosaic depicting Christ crowning Roger II, La Martorana, Palermo

©Urban/Wikimedia Commons

Roger II extended his kingdom as far as Tronto, adding Capua, Amalfi and Naples; he maintained his capital at Palermo. The feudal system spread through Sicily, though the government's administration remained complex, reflecting its Byzantine origins.

In ecclesiastical circles, special prerogatives were given to the Norman sovereigns nominated as Papal Legates by Pope Urban II: their prime objective was to eradicate Islam and to resist corruption from the (Greco-Byzantine) Eastern Church. Meanwhile, the Arab influence persisted at Roger II's court at Palermo: there, the geographer **al-Idrisi** constructed a large silver planisphere and wrote his geographical treatise, entitled *Kitab-Rugiar,* or *The Book of Roger.*

1147 – Incursions by the Norman fleet in the Byzantine Empire: Corfu, Thessalonika and Thebes are sacked; numerous craftsmen skilled in working with silk are deported to Sicily.

1154 – **William I** (1120–66) succeeds his father Roger II. While engaged in conflict with Frederick Barbarossa, he must also confront a rebellion from his barons, which he succeeds in quelling in 1156.

1166 – **William II** (1153–89), William I's son, is crowned king. By supporting the Pope and the northern towns in their struggle against Barbarossa, he is also able to attack the declining Byzantine Empire. He is hailed a champion of the Third Crusade against Saladin: in fact, Norman troops were committed to rescuing Tripoli.

He designates his aunt Costanza as his heir; she is betrothed to Henry, the eldest son of Barbarossa; thus the Swabian dynasty can claim legitimate rights to the throne of Sicily.

SWABIANS AND ANGEVINS

1186– The marriage of the future Emperor Henry VI (Barbarossa's son) to Costanza d'Altavilla is celebrated.

1190-97 – Henry VI of Swabia (1165–97) is made Emperor and King of Sicily. 1198 – Innocent III is elected Pope. Costanza has her young son Frederick crowned king of Sicily.

1209 – Frederick marries Costanza of Aragon.

1214 – Innocent III excommunicates Emperor Otto of Brunswick and nominates Frederick II in his place. Frederick arrives in Germany; he does not return to Sicily until 1220.

1228 – Exhorted by Pope Gregory IX, Frederick leaves for the Holy Land, where he reaches a peaceful agreement with the Sultan. In 1229, he is crowned king of Jerusalem.

1231 – Frederick II issues the *Constitutions of Melfi,* a code of law designed for a centralised state, that is operational outside the jurisdiction of the feudal lords.

1250 – Death of Frederick II.

1250-54 – Conradin IV (1228–54) succeeds his father Frederick II and is crowned Emperor, despite the rivalry with **Manfred** (1232–66), Frederick's son and heir, who was "fair and well-made and of gentle aspect" *(The Divine Comedy).*

1265 – Pope Clement IV summons the Christian princes to rally against Manfred; the French, led by Charles of Anjou, rise.

1266 – Battle of Benevento: Manfred is defeated and killed.

1268 – Defeat of the Ghibellines (supporters of the Empire) at Tagliacozzo; Conradin, the 15-year-old Swabian heir, is beheaded in Naples. The **Guelphs of Anjou** secure rule of southern Italy.

SICILIAN VESPERS AND THE ARAGONESE (1282–1416)

1282 – A revolt against the ruling Angevins by the **Sicilian Vespers** breaks out in Palermo.

Museo di Capodimonte, Naples/SCALA

Detail of Sicilian Vesper by Domenico Morelli

Corleone and Messina, the seat of the Angevin viceroy at that time, also rise to join the cause. Nobles appeal to **Peter III of Aragon** (1239–85) for help.

1285 – Charles dies in 1285, before he is able to return to Sicily.

1296 – **Frederick of Aragon** concedes the right for an annual assembly of the barons.

1302 – Peace of Caltabellotta ends the war: Frederick of Aragon, Peter's son, is declared King of Trinacria (avoiding the name "Sicily") provided that, at his death, the kingdom returns to Robert of Anjou. The pact was broken and the Norman kingdom splits.

1425-42 – **Alfonso V of Aragon** (1396–1458) intervenes against the Angevins in Naples. The island and the mainland are again united under one king.

MODERN SICILY

1492 – Sicily expels Jews from Salemi and Palermo.

1497 – The *Tribunale di Sant'Uffizio*, the Spanish Inquisition, is introduced to Sicily

1556 – Parliament – which only has advisory power – is nonetheless revered. Three *Brazos* or Chambers host the clergy, the 72 barons, military leaders and town representatives.

1570 – A great Christian fleet rallies at Messina and recruits crews from Calabria and Sicily. In 1571, it famously triumphs over the Turks at Lepanto.

1624 – Plague ravages Palermo. The miraculous discovery of

Museo del Risorgimento, Roma/SCALA

The Thousand's landing at Marsala in 1860

Santa Rosalia's bones helps, according to popular belief, to assuage the epidemic. Henceforth, the saint is acclaimed a patron of the city.

1647 – Revolt in Palermo, coinciding with the insurrection in Naples. The anti-Spanish uprising is spearheaded by two commoners, Nino de la Pelosa and Giuseppe d'Alessi, but the rebellion is quickly suppressed. In 1674, Messina also rises up against the Spanish, with help from the king of France. The town is brutally recaptured in 1678.

1693 – A terrible earthquake shakes southeastern Sicily.

1713 – The Treaty of Utrecht assigns Sicily to Savoy; **Victor Amadeus**, the new king, visits.

1718-20 – Spain recaptures Sardinia and threatens Naples and Palermo. The British sink the Spanish fleet at Capo Passero. The Habsburg emperor trades Sardinia to Savoy and assumes control of Sicily.

1733 – The Scottish writer Patrick Brydone publishes his *Tour through Sicily and Malta*.

1735 – The coronation of **Charles Bourbon** (1716–88) in Palermo.

1781-86 – Caracciolo is viceroy of the island: a number of reforms are promised with the aim of increasing his powerbase. The Inquisition is abolished.

The Sicilian Statute

On 15 May 1946, a royal decree promulgated a law on Sicilian autonomy. On 26 February 1948, the Constituent Assembly turns the Statute of Sicily into law, in accordance with provisions under Article 116 of the Italian Constitution listing the specifications and conditions for autonomous rule as granted to five Italian regions. The regional statute provides for a regional council, known as the Parliament, composed of 90 members. The Parliament elects a regional committee *(Giunta Regionale)* and a president from among its members by a majority consensus. The president has the right to sit in with the Council of Ministers in Rome during debates on issues affecting Sicily. The Parliament can approve legislation for the island, its powers, sanctioned by Article 117 of the Italian Constitution, being fairly extensive. Special delegations from the Council of State and the State Audit Court sit permanently in Palermo so as to ensure a certain degree of administrative decentralisation.

1794 – Leblanc's discovery of how to isolate sodium carbonate (soda or soda ash) revolutionises several industrial processes: the price of sulphur becomes competitive. From 1790, Sicilian citrus fruits are exported on a large scale across Europe. In 1814, English-owned distilleries in Marsala begin producing a sherry-like wine.

1806 – British troops are stationed in Sicily to provide protection from the armies of Napoleon Bonaparte. These contribute to the economic prosperity.

1812 – With help from Britain's representative in Sicily, Lord Bentinck, reforms are implemented for a more liberal constitution that abolishes feudal rights.

1816 – Creation of the Kingdom of Two Sicilies: the kingdoms of Naples and Palermo are unified and the Sicilian flag is abolished.

1840 – The issue of water and its illegally controlled distribution comes to a head. Smuggling also get out of hand.

1847 – An investigation reveals that half of the island's woodland has been destroyed over the past 100 years, resulting in the climate becoming drier. Francesco Ferrara's *Letter from Malta* proposes Sicilian autonomy within a federation of Italian states.

1848-49 – Insurrections in Palermo and across Sicily.

1860 – In April, there is rioting in Palermo, provoked by agents from the north. The Thousand are sent to Sicily, headed by Garibaldi (👈 *see MARSALA*). On 21 October, a plebiscite sanctions the island's union with the Kingdom of Italy.

1866 – Revolt in Palermo as a result of the acute economic situation (15 000 unemployed). In the end, the Italian fleet bombards the city, while 4000 soldiers quash the riots.

1886 – The Jacini report on the state of Italian agriculture reveals that the island is heading towards a food shortage, aggravated by a rise in population. Between 1880 and 1914, about 1.5 million Sicilians leave, with the majority heading for the United States.

1893 – The Notarbartolo scandal surrounding the director of the Banca d'Italia breaks out; he is assassinated after denouncing political and financial malpractice.

1894 – A poor harvest, coupled with the inequalities in the distribution of ecclesiastical land, provoke disorder and insurrection rallied by the supporters of the *Fasci di Lavoratori*. Sicilian Francesco Crispi forms a new government and imposes martial law.

1908 – Earthquake in Messina causing over 60 000 fatalities.

1911 – Population census: 58% of Sicilians are illiterate.

1925 – Fascist government extends the "battle of wheat" to Sicily. **Mori**, nicknamed the "Iron Chief of Police" because of his

House in Messina severely damaged by the earthquake on 28th December 1908

UPPA/Photoshot

anti-Mafia efforts, becomes Palermo's Chief of Police.

SICILY IN THE 20C

1940 – The government announces agricultural reforms, impeded by the outbreak of war.

1943 – American and British troops – **Operation Husky** under Eisenhower's command – seize Licata and Augusta. On 22 July, Palermo falls, then Messina. On 3 September, at Cassibile, near Siracusa, emissaries of the Badoglio government sign the armistice with the Allied delegations.

1947 – Many Sicilians dream of the island being annexed to the United States. In the elections, the separatists receive less than ten per cent of the vote and seek to take up arms. **Salvatore Giuliano**, in hiding since 1943, is nominated colonel of EVIS (the Voluntary Army for Sicilian Independence). On 1 May, 1947, his men fire on a group of demonstrating farmers at Portella delle Ginestre, killing 12. National indignation is high. Giuliano is found dead on 5 July, 1950, at Castelvetrano, in mysterious circumstances.
The separatists disappear from the political scene with the elections of 1951.

1950 – Agricultural reforms are implemented: some 115 000ha/ 284 000 acres are reallocated to over 18 000 farmers.

1951-75 – A million Sicilians emigrate to northern Italy and Europe.

1953 – Crude oil is discovered at Ragusa and Gela; in 1966, eight million barrels are extracted.

1958 – A terrorist bomb shatters the headquarters of the Palermo daily newspaper *L'Ora*, following its allusion to the power of the Mafia.

1968 – A disastrous earthquake affects the Belice Valley.

1973-76 – The Parliamentary Anti-Mafia Commission begins work.

27 June 1980 – An Italia DC9 flying from Bologna to Palermo crashes off the coast of Ustica, killing 81.

3 September 1982 – The Palermo Chief of Police, General Carlo Alberto Dalla Chiesa, his wife and a police escort are killed in a terrorist attack.

1986 – During the American-Libyan crisis, the Libyans launch missiles targeted at Lampedusa.

1987 – End of the major court case held in Palermo against the Mafia, with 19 people sentenced to life imprisonment.

1992 – 12 March: the politician Salvo Lima is murdered in Palermo. 23 May: Giovanni Falcone, Director of Penal Affairs at the Ministry of Justice, is killed by an explosive device placed at a motorway crossing near Capaci. His wife and three members of his police escort also die in the blast. 19 July: in Via D'Amelio in Palermo, a car bomb kills Judge Paolo Borsellino and four police. In September, the Mafia boss Giovanni Madonìa is arrested.

1993 – Mafia boss Salvatore Riina, head of the Corleonesi, is arrested in Palermo.

1996 – The dome and a large section of the nave of the cathedral of Noto collapse.

1997 – The Teatro Massimo in Palermo reopens after 20+ years.

THE NEW MILLENNIUM

2001-2002 – Etna continues to make its destructive presence felt, with eruptions destroying the cable car and part of the base station at Rifugio Sapienza on the southern slopes of the volcano, as well as buildings and the pine forest of Piano Provenzana on the northern slopes. In December 2002, part of the

© Amet Jean Pierre/Corbis Sygma

Tree in memory of Giovanni Falcone on via Notarbartolo, Palermo

Sciara del Fuoco breaks away from the Stromboli volcano, causing an impressive tidal wave.

2002 – March: 1 000 migrants, mainly Kurds, land in Sicily – the largest group yet. Police arrest 30 farmers for diverting a river, as the drought intensifies.

2003 – January: the entire island of Stromboli evacuates, as eruption threats rise. March: Police arrest crime boss Salvatore Rinella in Palermo.

2004 – June: Sicily rehabilitates property seized in Mafia raids as tourist destinations.

2005 – Immigration issues continue, as do anti-Mafia raids. Salvatore Cuffaro, the head of Sicily's regional government, stands trial for leaking police secrets to organized crime.

2006 – Cuffaro is re-elected, as his trial continues. Scientists identify a giant underwater volcano off Sicily's southern coast. Named after the Greek philosopher, Empedocles, it has a base larger than Rome. October: Italy scraps plans to build the world's longest single-span suspension bridge across the Messina Straits.

Changing Face of the Mafia

The roots of the organized crime structure synonymous with Italy's deep south, rest in its rural landscapes. Once considered feudal folk heroes standing against Sicily's tyrannical overlords, the Mafia tide took a less 'righteous' turn in the early 20C with the emergence of organized crime nurtured through traditions and values inextricable from Sicilian society These principles were mafia with a small m – a perverted shorthand for family, honour, solidarity, silence. The biggest Sicilian Mafia boss at this time was Don Vito Cascio Ferro, who had links with the Black Hand, a growing immigrant Mafiosi organization in America. Mussolini's anti-Mafia campaigns in WWII responded to the power that organized crime was beginning to exhibit. Il Duce wanted to clear a path for unchallenged Facist leadership, and employed Cesare Mori as prefect of Palermo to put some 11 000 Mafia in prison (often on little or no evidence) – but the triumph was short lived. Following the end of the war, they were set free by an Anglo-American administration. The flood of Mafiosi back onto the scene, coupled with the general municipal upheaval of Italy's reconstruction, led to an explosion of crime in the south.

© Stringer/Italy/Reuters/Corbis

Town of Corleone

Key Mafia figures such as Don Calogero Vizzini and Lucky Luciano were part of a vanguard of Mafiosi who now took organized crime away from its rural roots and into the cities – real estate, protection money (known as *pizzo*) and construction – and even transatlantically, as abilities to control the growing heroin trade began to determine power within the Mafia structure. Government investigations in the 1960s prompted a new wave of activity, the targeting of state officials – and indeed anyone threatening the Cosa Nostra in any way, in a sustained campaign of intimidation. In 1982, police General Dalla Chiesa began investigating Sicily's construction industry, his intense scrutiny threatening to expose the full extent of corruption in high ranking political circles – the so called Third Level. Dalla Chiesa was gunned down three months later in Palermo. The onset of the super-trials or *Maxiprocessi*, in the 1980s, used information from former Mafia member Tommaso Buscetta to convict over 350 members of the Mafia. Layers of social infiltration by the Cosa Nostra continued to peel away as further testimonies from *pentiti*, Mafiosi turned police informants, began to implicate the highest levels of government. Those called into question included former prime minister, Guilio Andreotti, who was acquitted in 1999. Silvio Berlusconi also faced allegations of Mafia money laundering in 1998, and was also acquitted. Even though high-profile arrests continue to be made, Giovanni Brusca of the Corleone famly in 1996 and most recently, in 2008 former Sicilian President Salvatore Cuffaro (🌀*see Government*), violence and corruption continues, and *pizzo* continues to be paid by a high proportion of small businesses in Sicily.

However, the bloodbath of the 80s and 90s has declined for now, thanks in part to popular culture and media, such as television, destroying the stranglehold of silence around the Mafia, and, some might say, a softening of the fierce, fearless approach that previous anti-Mafia crusaders took – and paid the price for.

The super-trials or 'Maxiprocessi'

In 1982, Tommaso Buscetta, a disillusioned Mafioso, broke the Mafia's sacred code of silence, the omerta, and turned police informant, sparking the so-called super-trials. The biggest of these trials, in 1986, lasted 18 months and dealt a devastating blow to organized crime syndicates. Buscetta's information on the inner workings and hierarchies of the Cosa Nostra and his testimony helped judges Giovanni Falcone and Paolo Borsellino convict 357 Mafiosi. Nineteen were given life sentences, the sentences of the other 338 totalled 2 065 years. Both judges were later assassinated by Mafia car bombs in the early 1990s.

ART AND CULTURE

Architecture

Thermal baths

VILLA DEL CASALE
Plan of the thermal baths (3C-4C AD) and hypocaust

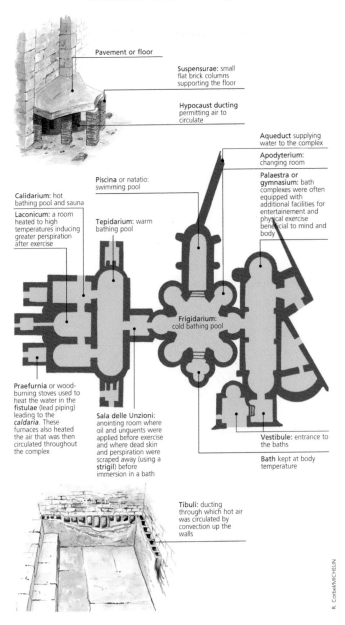

Pavement or floor

Suspensurae: small flat brick columns supporting the floor

Hypocaust ducting permitting air to circulate

Aqueduct supplying water to the complex

Apodyterium: changing room

Palaestra or gymnasium: bath complexes were often equipped with additional facilities for entertainement and physical exercise beneficial to mind and body

Piscina or natatio: swimming pool

Calidarium: hot bathing pool and sauna

Laconicum: a room heated to high temperatures inducing greater perspiration after exercise

Tepidarium: warm bathing pool

Frigidarium: cold bathing pool

Praefurnia or wood-burning stoves used to heat the water in the fistulae (lead piping) leading to the caldaria. These furnaces also heated the air that was then circulated throughout the complex

Sala delle Unzioni: anointing room where oil and unguents were applied before exercise and where dead skin and perspiration were scraped away (using a strigil) before immersion in a bath

Vestibule: entrance to the baths

Bath kept at body temperature

Tibuli: ducting through which hot air was circulated by convection up the walls

R. Corbel/MICHELIN

Religious architecture

RAGUSA IBLA – Duomo di San Giorgio (18C)

Latin cross floor plan with transepts

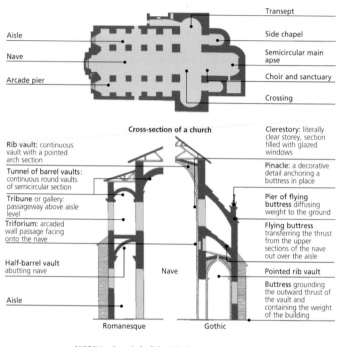

Transept

Aisle

Side chapel

Nave

Semicircular main apse

Arcade pier

Choir and sanctuary

Crossing

Cross-section of a church

Rib vault: continuous vault with a pointed arch section

Clerestory: literally clear storey, section filled with glazed windows

Tunnel of barrel vaults: continuous round vaults of semicircular section

Pinacle: a decorative detail anchoring a buttress in place

Tribune or **gallery:** passageway above aisle level

Pier of flying buttress diffusing weight to the ground

Triforium: arcaded wall passage facing onto the nave

Flying buttress transferring the thrust from the upper sections of the nave out over the aisle

Half-barrel vault abutting nave

Pointed rib vault

Nave

Aisle

Buttress grounding the outward thrust of the vault and containing the weight of the building

Romanesque

Gothic

NICOSIA – Cattedrale di San Nicolò: main doorway (14C)

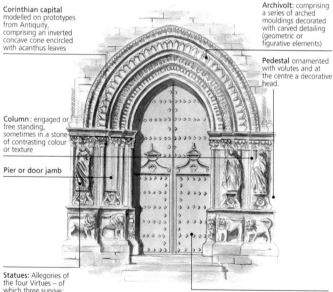

Corinthian capital modelled on prototypes from Antiquity, comprising an inverted concave cone encircled with acanthus leaves

Archivolt: comprising a series of arched mouldings decorated with carved detailing (geometric or figurative elements)

Pedestal ornamented with volutes and at the centre a decorative head.

Column: engaged or free standing, sometimes in a stone of contrasting colour or texture

Pier or **door jamb**

Statues: Allegories of the four Virtues – of which three survive: Prudence, Justice and Temperance

Door panel

R. Corbel/MICHELIN

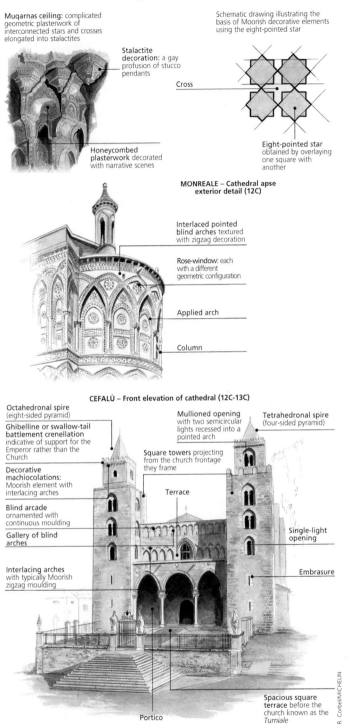

PALERMO – Cappella Palatina: celling detail (12C)

Muqarnas ceiling: complicated geometric plasterwork of interconnected stars and crosses elongated into stalactites

Schematic drawing illustrating the basis of Moorish decorative elements using the eight-pointed star

Stalactite decoration: a gay profusion of stucco pendants

Cross

Honeycombed plasterwork decorated with narrative scenes

Eight-pointed star obtained by overlaying one square with another

MONREALE – Cathedral apse exterior detail (12C)

Interlaced pointed blind arches textured with zigzag decoration

Rose-window: each with a different geometric configuration

Applied arch

Column

CEFALÙ – Front elevation of cathedral (12C-13C)

Octahedronal spire (eight-sided pyramid)

Ghibelline or swallow-tail battlement crenellation indicative of support for the Emperor rather than the Church

Decorative machiocolations: Moorish element with interlacing arches

Blind arcade ornamented with continuous moulding

Gallery of blind arches

Interlacing arches with typically Moorish zigzag moulding

Mullioned opening with two semicircular lights recessed into a pointed arch

Square towers projecting from the church frontage they frame

Terrace

Tetrahedronal spire (four-sided pyramid)

Single-light opening

Embrasure

Spacious square terrace before the church known as the *Turniale*

Portico

R. Corbel/MICHELIN

85

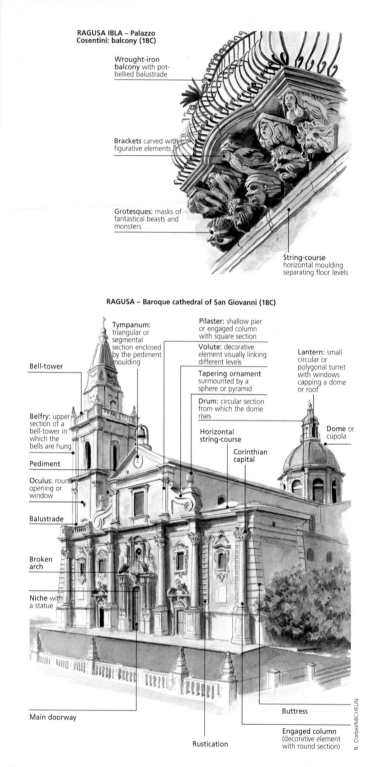

RAGUSA IBLA – Palazzo Cosentini: balcony (18C)

Wrought-iron balcony with pot-bellied balustrade

Brackets carved with figurative elements

Grotesques: masks of fantastical beasts and monsters

String-course horizontal moulding separating floor levels

RAGUSA – Baroque cathedral of San Giovanni (18C)

Bell-tower

Tympanum: triangular or segmental section enclosed by the pediment moulding

Pilaster: shallow pier or engaged column with square section

Volute: decorative element visually linking different levels

Tapering ornament surmounted by a sphere or pyramid

Lantern: small circular or polygonal turret with windows capping a dome or roof

Belfry: upper section of a bell-tower in which the bells are hung

Drum: circular section from which the dome rises

Horizontal string-course

Corinthian capital

Dome or cupola

Pediment

Oculus: round opening or window

Balustrade

Broken arch

Niche with a statue

Main doorway

Buttress

Rustication

Engaged column (decorative element with round section)

R. Corbel/MICHELIN

86

CASTELBUONO – Cappella di Sant'Anna (Castello dei Ventimiglia) (1683)

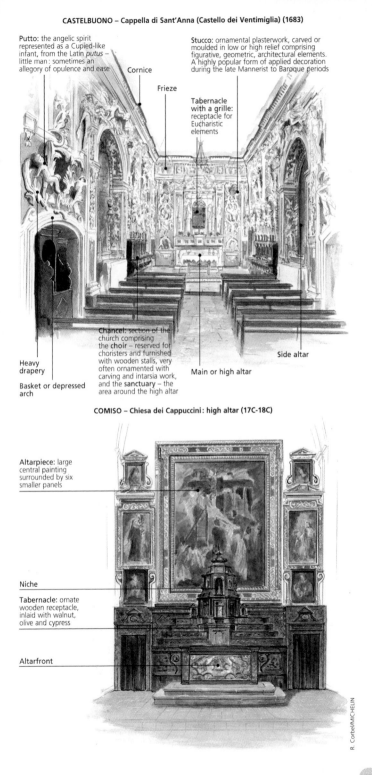

Putto: the angelic spirit represented as a Cupied-like infant, from the Latin *putus* – little man : sometimes an allegory of opulence and ease

Cornice

Frieze

Stucco: ornamental plasterwork, carved or moulded in low or high relief comprising figurative, geometric, architectural elements. A highly popular form of applied decoration during the late Mannerist to Baroque periods

Tabernacle with a grille: receptacle for Eucharistic elements

Chancel: section of the church comprising the **choir** – reserved for choristers and furnished with wooden stalls, very often ornamented with carving and intarsia work, and the **sanctuary** – the area around the high altar

Side altar

Main or high altar

Heavy drapery

Basket or depressed arch

COMISO – Chiesa dei Cappuccini : high altar (17C-18C)

Altarpiece: large central painting surrounded by six smaller panels

Niche

Tabernacle: ornate wooden receptacle, inlaid with walnut, olive and cypress

Altarfront

R. Corbel/MICHELIN

Civil and military buildings

Sicilian stronghold or *baglio*

Complex of buildings arranged around a central courtyard, including living quarters and workshops. In some cases the complex includes a small private chapel. Fortifications are integrated for defensive purposes. Examples located in rural positions were often used as grain depositories and for storing farm equipment; those located by the sea were inhabited by fishing communities (especially tuna fishermen) and included areas reserved for processing the fish and for repairing boats. At Marsala these *bagli* served as wineries (hence by implication, an actual cellar). Today most of these complexes have been transformed into museums or hotels.

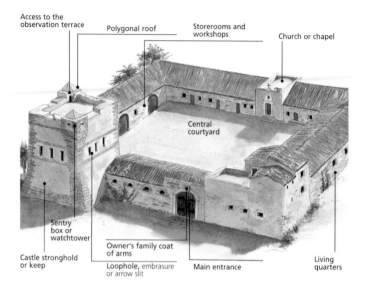

Access to the observation terrace

Polygonal roof

Storerooms and workshops

Church or chapel

Central courtyard

Sentry box or watchtower

Castle stronghold or keep

Owner's family coat of arms

Loophole, embrasure or arrow slit

Main entrance

Living quarters

CATANIA – Castello Ursino (1239-50)

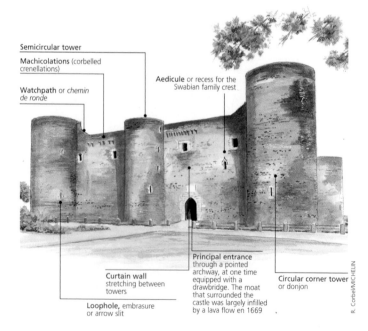

Semicircular tower

Machicolations (corbelled crenellations)

Watchpath or *chemin de ronde*

Aedicule or recess for the Swabian family crest

Curtain wall stretching between towers

Loophole, embrasure or arrow slit

Principal entrance through a pointed archway, at one time equipped with a drawbridge. The moat that surrounded the castle was largely infilled by a lava flow en 1669

Circular corner tower or donjon

R. Corbel/MICHELIN

Architectural Terms

Altarpiece (or ancona): a large painting or sculpture adorning an altar.

Ambulatory: extension of the aisles around the chancel for processions.

Antefix: a carved ornament at the end of the eaves of a roof to hide the joint between the tiles.

Antependium: a covering hung over the front of an altar.

Apse: a semicircular or polygonal end of a church behind the altar; the outer section is known as the chevet.

Apsidiole: small chapel opening onto the ambulatory of a Romanesque or Gothic church.

Architrave: the lowermost horizontal division of a Classical entablature sitting directly on the column capital and supporting the frieze.

Archivolt: arch moulding over an arcade or upper section of a doorway.

Arcosolium: a tomb found in numerous catacombs, which was built in the wall and surmounted by a niche.

Atlas figure or telamon: a sculptured figure of a man used as a column (the female equivalent is called a caryatid). In Sicily, the most famous are the telamons of the Temple of Olympian Zeus at Agrigento.

Bay: any of a number of principal divisions or spatial units of a building (or part of a building like an aisle of a church) contained within two or four vertical supports (piers, columns, pilasters).

Bouleuterion: meeting place for the town council *(boulé).*

Buttress: external support of a wall, which counterbalances the thrust of the vaults and arches.

Capital: the upper end of a column, pillar or pier crowning the shaft and taking the weight of the entablature or architrave. There are three Classical orders: Doric (✆ *see illustration in the section on Greek Art)*; Ionic, with a scroll-like ornament – the Composite has the Ionic scrolls and acanthus leaf ornament; and the Corinthian, ringed with burgeoning acanthus leaves, especially popular in the 16C and 17C for Baroque buildings. The abacus sits between the capital and the architrave; the structure beneath the abacus is the echinus.

Cardo: one of the main axes of the town plan as recommended by the Classical surveyor Hippodamus of Miletus, normally orientated north–south; the Greek equivalent is the stenopos.

Cathedra: the high-backed throne of a bishop, in Gothic style.

Chiaramonte: an architectural style characterised by two- or three-light windows surmounted by arches with tracery or polychrome geometric decoration.

Ciborium: a canopy (baldaquin) over an altar.

Corbel (or truss): a triangular bracket, usually made of wood, supporting a roof.

Counter-façade: the internal wall of church façade.

Cross (church plan): churches are usually built either in the plan of a Greek cross, with four arms of equal length, or a Latin cross, with one arm longer than the other three.

Crypt: an underground chamber or vault usually beneath a church, often used as a mortuary, burial place or for displaying holy relics. Sometimes it was a small chapel or church in its own right.

Decumanus: a major thoroughfare bisecting a Classical town plan, running on a complementary axis to the cardo, orientated east–west; the Greek equivalent is the plateia.

Dosseret: supplementary capital in the shape of the base of an upturned pyramid, often decorated, set above a column capital to receive the thrust of the arch.

Ekklesiasterion: a meeting place for popular assemblies *(ekklesia).*

Entablature: in certain buildings, the section at the top of a colonnade consisting of three parts: the architrave (flat section resting on the capitals of a colonnade), the frieze (decorated with carvings) and the cornice (projecting top section).

Exedra: the section in the back of Roman basilicas containing seats; by extension, curved niche or semicircular recess outside.

Fresco: a wall painting applied to wet plaster.

Ghimberga: a triangular Gothic pediment adorning a portal.

Hypocaust: an underground heating system used in Antiquity, whereby floors were raised on a series of small brick columns, enabling hot air to circulate underneath.

Intrados: the inner surface of an arch or vault.

Jamb or pier: a pillar flanking a doorway or window and supporting the arch above.

Keep: the tower stronghold of a castle, usually situated in the centre of a well-protected area.

Keystone: the topmost stone in an arch or vault.

Lantern: a turret with windows on top of a dome.

Lesene (or Lombard strips): a decorative band of pilasters joined at the top by an arched frieze.

Matroneo: the gallery reserved for women in palaeo-Christian and Romanesque churches.

Merlon: part of a crowning parapet between two crenellations. There are two types of merlons: Ghibelline (swallow-tailed), symbolising civil, Imperial power, and Guelf (rectangular), symbolising religious, Papal power.

Modillion: a small console supporting a cornice.

Moulding: an ornamental shaped band which projects from the wall.

Ogive: a pointed arch.

Opus signinum: floor covering obtained by mixing fragments of terracotta and other small pieces of rubble with lime. It is sometimes decorated with marble or stone cobbles.

Overhang: an overhanging or corbelled upper storey.

Ovolo moulding: an egg-shaped ornament incorporated into the entablature.

Palazzo: Italian for town house or square building (housing commercial offices, for example) subtly different in connotation from the word "palace". In the Renaissance, the ground floor was usually reserved for storage or commercial activities, the first floor or *piano nobile* comprised the main apartments, and the second floor *(alto piano)* was allocated to children and domestic staff.

Pantocrator: a hieratic figure of Christ with his hand raised in blessing, often depicted in the apse of palaeo-Christian churches.

Pendentive: the spherical triangular panel that provides the transition from a square or polygonal base (at a crossing) to a circular dome.

Peristyle: the range of columns surrounding a Classical building or courtyard.

Pilaster strip: a structural column partially set into a wall.

Pluteus: a decorated balustrade made from various materials, separating the chancel from the rest of the church.

Polyptych: a painted or carved work consisting of more than three folding leaves or panels (diptych: 2 panels; triptych: 3 panels).

Predella: the base of an altarpiece, divided into small panels.

Pulpit: an elevated dais from which sermons are preached in the nave of a church.

Pyx: a cylindrical box made of ivory or glazed copper for jewels or the Eucharistic host.

Raceme: ornamental vine motif with tendrils, leaves and stylised fruits.

Relief: high relief *(altorilievo)* is a sculptural term describing the modelled forms that project from the background by at least half their depth (halfway between shallow relief and sculpture in the round). Low relief *(bassorilievo)* projects only very slightly from the background (also known as bas relief).

Retable: a large and ornate altarpiece divided into several painted or carved panels, especially common in Spain after the 14C.

Rib: a projecting moulding or band on the underside of a dome or vault, which may be structural or ornamental.

Rustication: the facing of a building that exaggeratedly replicates dressed stonework, raised or otherwise from the mortar joints. Rustication was used in the Renaissance to consolidate the impression of impregnability on the ground floor of a palazzo.

Splay: a surface of a wall that forms an oblique angle to the main surface of a doorway or window opening.

Squinch: an alternative to a pendentive comprising a compound number of miniature strainer arches, often intricately decorated with Moorish plasterwork.

Tambour: a circular or polygonal structure supporting a dome.

Trompe l'oeil: two-dimensional painted decoration giving the three-dimensional illusion of relief and perspective.

Vault: an arched structure of stone or brick forming a ceiling or roof over a hall, room, bay or other wholly or partly enclosed space. **Barrel vault** – a vault with a semicircular cross section. **Groin vault** (or cross vault) – formed by the perpendicular intersection of two vaults. **Bowl-shaped vault** – a spherical vault enclosing a semicircular apse.

Vaulting cell: one of the four segments of the cross vault.

Window cross: a stone or wooden post which divides the opening of a window or door. The vertical posts are known as mullions.

Art

From the period of Greek colonisation to the present day, Sicilian creativity has never been idle. The complex history of this island – fashioned and formed by a number of foreign peoples and cultures, isolated by the sea – in part explains the unique and varied nature of Sicilian expression over the centuries.

ROMAN ART

Vestiges from Roman times are fewer and less impressive than those from the Greek period, largely because the Romans showed comparatively little interest in Sicily. Once the threat of a Carthaginian invasion receded, the island lost its strategic importance and became prized exclusively as a "Roman granary". This allowed the enriched native land owners to build splendid villas by the sea – as the ruins at Patti, near Tyndaris, testify. Not until the end of the 3C AD, during the reign of Diocletian, did Sicily become sought after by the Roman aristocracy, who acquired large tracts of land on the island.

During seven centuries of occupation (3C BC–5C AD), Rome did not endow Sicily with any prestigious monuments other than the odd functional public building (amphitheatres, public baths) and the foundations for a comprehensive road system.

Architecture

Unlike the Greeks, the Romans knew about cement and how to use it effectively. They erected walls, vaults and columns using casements filled with small bricks, and then poured concrete into them. Finishing touches were added in the form of marble facings (or high-quality stone) or, for the interiors, ably applied stucco that suggested splendid stone walls.

Civil architecture – During this period, **Greek theatres**, like the ones at **Taormina** and **Catania**, underwent considerable transformation. The circular orchestra (reserved for the chorus) was reduced to a semicircle, while a stage wall was added for the special effects machinery. The theatre provided a venue both for circus entertainment and combat with wild animals; to protect the spectators, a wall was constructed along the bottom of the cavea (part of which can still be seen at Taormina). Roman monuments of special interest include the amphitheatres at **Siracusa** and Catania; the odeons at Taormina and Catania, and, finally, the Naumachie of Taormina (now badly damaged), which consists of a large-scale brick-built gymnasium (122m/400ft long) ornamented with niches. Besides these complexes dedicated to sport and entertainment, the Romans left nothing of value in terms of civic architecture. The fine basilica at Tyndaris suggests that the Romans introduced the art of vaulting to Sicily

Interior of the Martorana, Palermo

G. Bludzin/MICHELIN

(for it was unknown to the Greek civil engineers), and more significantly, to settlements removed from the major urban centres. Vestiges of **public baths complexes** (*terme*), largely dating from the Imperial period, are preserved at Catania, Taormina, Comiso, Solunto and Tindari. Traces of fora have been found at Taormina, Catania, Siracusa and Tindari.

Domestic architecture – The Romano-Sicilian house closely resembles its Hellenistic counterpart. The peristyle town house was introduced towards the close of the 3C–2C BC (Morgantina). The most elegant homes, however, were the country villas, the most typical example being the magnificent **Villa Imperiale del Casale** near Piazza Armerina. Here, private bath facilities indicate this was a highly sophisticated and luxurious house; it is particularly renowned for its splendid floor mosaics.

BYZANTINE ART

Archaeological excavation undertaken in Palermo and Siracusa has uncovered complete cemeteries on the outskirts, dating from Late Antiquity, when the Romans imposed Christianity on Sicily. The **catacombs** preserve traces of painted decoration – most particularly those at Siracusa (4C–5C AD) – and pro-vide the earliest examples of Christian art in Sicily. Gradually islanders were coerced into erecting churches, modelled on the Roman **prototype basilica**: this consisted of a simple rectangular building, articulated by columns into three aisles, with a central nave terminated by a single apse. The other, more striking solution, was to incorporate a church around a pagan Antique temple – as with the Temple of Concord at Agrigento and the Temple of Athena at Siracusa. The walls of the cella were cut away to make arcades and the outer colonnade was infilled with masonry.

In AD 535, as a result of the Byzantine conquest, links between the Church of Sicily and the Exarchate of Ravenna were reinforced. In 751 when Ravenna fell to the Lombards, this allegiance was transferred to Constantinople. Interestingly enough, the rift dividing the Roman and Byzantine Churches as a result of Pope Gregory II's opposition to Emperor Leo III's Iconoclast movement in 725–26 had serious repercussions in Sicily.

The ban on the cult of holy icons imposed by the Byzantine Emperor prompted crowds of refugees to seek asylum in Sicily, where the icon continued to be venerated. Whole monastic communities and groups of skilled craftsmen found sanctuary and set about applying their trades, notably in the art of mosaic.

This prosperous period gave rise to the building of numerous shrines (including the ones at Cava d'Ispica and Pantalica) and the institution of troglodyte settlements hewn into the bedrock (almost all now destroyed). Small, centrally planned, square (typically Byzantine) churches appeared. A few examples survive in the eastern part of the island, north and east of Etna (☾ *see TAORMINA: Castiglione di Sicilia*), in the vicinity of Noto and around Siracusa. Other Byzantine monuments were completely transformed, dismembered or converted to another use through the ensuing centuries.

ARABO-NORMAN ART

Arab Occupation

The Muslim conquest began in 827 in the area of Trapani. During their two-and-a-half centuries of sovereignty, the Arabs transformed the appearance of Sicily. They shifted their power base from Siracusa to Palermo, altering the countryside with irrigation and eastern crops. Most dramatically, they introduced new architectural forms. They were prolific builders and sensitive planners, ever conscious of a building's relationship with its natural setting: palaces, mosques and minarets stood among gardens and fountains. In terms of design, their acute sense of line and elegance was applied to sophisticated decorative schemes. Human figures gave way to geometric and arabesque forms, house interiors were transformed with coloured ceramic tiles, while ceilings were encrusted with rich plaster decorations *(muqarnas)*.

Alas, no important monument survives intact from the Arab occupation. Indeed, most of their splendid buildings disappeared with the arrival of the Normans, who appropriated, rebuilt and redecorated them. A few examples of Arab craftsmanship survive, as do a number

of intricate networks of irregular streets tucked away in cities like Palermo.

Norman Eclecticism

The Arabo-Norman style combines elements from Islamic, Romanesque (introduced by Franco-Norman Benedictine monks) and Byzantine art. Much of its wealth is rooted in the Norman sovereigns' desire to copy the splendour of Byzantium, a city they yearned to conquer. The new Sicilian master builders channelled their creative power into monuments of incomparable beauty. From the end of the 11C and throughout the next century, large churches were conceived by architect-monks, mainly from the Benedictine and Augustinian orders, whether Greek, French or Latin (from mainland Italy). Designs were modelled on Classical prototypes: a transept was incorporated in a basilica giving it a Latin- or Greek-cross plan, towers were erected to house bells, a doorway was inserted in the front elevation, the presbytery was often crowned with a dome. At the same time, these edifices were given the latest contemporary decoration: Byzantine mosaics laid by Orthodox (Greek) artists and Moorish features (horseshoe arches, arabesque and honeycomb ornament). The mixture of these three styles is quite unique.

Byzantine influence – The Eastern elements incorporated into religious architecture include the square centralised plan, adapted in turn to the Greek cross, roofed with intersecting barrel vaults (Church of the Martorana,

Story of Samson sculpted on the cloisters of Monreale Cathedral (12C)

G. Bludzin/MICHELIN

San Nicolò at Mazara del Vallo, or Santissima Trinita di Delia at Castelvetrano). Elsewhere, the intersection is vaulted with the typical Sicilian Byzantine dome rising from a polygonal drum. Even the capitals reflect an Arabo-Norman style adapted from the Byzantine, by incorporating a dosseret between the capital and the impost of the arch (Monreale Cathedral).

The reason for the lack of Byzantine sculptures of humans is threefold: firstly, the Christians wished to distance themselves from pagan statuary; secondly, the Iconoclastic movement forbade the veneration of anything that might be construed as an idol; and, lastly, the Islamic influence. They also adapted the techniques; stone was no longer worked just on the surface, but in the round, drilling tiny holes and fretting effects that resembled stone lace.

The Byzantine artists' richest and most effective medium was the mosaic. This they applied to immense areas, animating them with figures and decorative motifs, upgrading the art form to monumental proportions. Apart from the Martorana, which fully conforms to Byzantine canons, the iconography and presentation of subject matter were adapted in Sicilian churches. At Cefalù, Monreale and the Cappella Palatina in Palermo, Christ Pantocrator fills the top of the vault above the apse; in Greek Byzantine churches, he would always be in the dome. Finally, the Norman kings had themselves depicted in areas traditionally reserved for saints, with the symbols of the basilei (Byzantine emperors), as a way of asserting their power.

Islamic influence – The Arabs brought new building methods and decorative know-how that enabled them to create masterpieces. In architecture, they introduced the horse-shoe (or Moorish) arch: the upper part of this arch is semi-circular, although it can be pointed at its apex, but comes in at the base to form a horseshoe shape. The interior of Arab buildings were often encrusted with stalactite plasterwork decoration called **muqarnas**; this in turn was painted, carved and textured into overhanging honeycombs. The interior decoration of Monreale Cathedral, the Palatine Chapel, the Zisa and Cuba *palazzi* are splendid testimonies to the influence of Islam. The Arab predilection for elaborate ornament featured in the serrated edge to the cornice with merlons of San Cataldo in Palermo – an elegant base for the three pink domes. They also brought an alternative view of proportion and volume, as indicated by the squat domes of San Giovanni degli Eremiti.

Romanesque influence – The most typical elements of the Romanesque style are the Latin-cross plan and the façade framed by massive towers, features that were devised by the Benedictine monks, most notably at Cluny, for the buildings they planned on a massive and monumental scale. On the whole, the religious buildings did not allocate much space to Norman sculpture (primarily geometric motifs on small arches and other decorative details – like strips of small leaves and ovolo moulding – applied to the dosserets of capitals). Their inclination towards stylisation touched representations of animals and plants which are reduced to simple palmettes or rather thin, flat, rigid-looking flowerless species (reeds and rushes). A handful of monuments, including the cloisters at Monreale, preserve some most splendid

D. Boggini/MICHELIN

Cloisters, Monreale Cathedral

Palazzo della Zisa, Palermo

figurative capitals relating historical and biblical scenes, founded in the Romanesque tradition.

Arabo-Norman Creativity

Although many buildings conformed to a clearly defined influence, some combinations of styles became models and prototypes for other art forms promoted during the rule of the Altavilla (de Hauteville) dynasty.

Religious Buildings – The undisputed masterpiece of this Sicilian Norman School is the Palatine Chapel (Cappella Palatina) in Palermo. Here elements of Romanesque art – an extended plan comprising nave, side aisles and narrow windows through which light suffuses – are married with the Moorish love for sumptuous decoration (notable in the ceiling), calligraphy (various Arabic inscriptions) and structural design (pointed arches). All this merges with the monumental splendour of Byzantine art (dome pendentives, gold-background mosaics, marble wall facing, and inlaid floors). The chapel demonstrates how the centrally planned Byzantine choir is superimposed onto the wooden-vaulted Latin basilica nave (set at a lower level). This became a new prototype, subsequently used at Monreale.

Secular buildings – Besides the odd large castle a in strategic position – Palermo, Castellammare and Messina – the Norman kings built various palaces for rest and recreation. At the end of the Altavilla (de Hauteville) rule, there were nine such residences in Sicily; today only the **Zisa** and **Cuba** *palazzi* in Palermo survive. These splendid houses are surrounded by large gardens ornamented with expanses of water.

The interior space divided into two main areas: the *iwan* (a room with three exedras) and an open courtyard containing one or more fountains and surrounded by porticoes. The first of these two distinctive areas originated in Abbasid Persia, the second in Fatimid Egypt. Together, they appear in Sicily sometime in the 12C, imported via the Maghreb (North Africa), which then extended as far as the coasts of modern Tunisia, and was under Sicilian rule.

The decoration is also largely drawn from Islamic art: herringboned marble or brick cover the floors, Moorish-motif mosaics face the walls. Finally, the ceilings and arches are encrusted with carved and painted muqarnas.

GOTHIC ART

For two centuries, between the 13C and the 15C, Sicily suffered political instability under a succession of sovereigns: the Swabians (1189–1266), Angevins (1266–82), and the House of Aragon. All appreciated the Gothic style on a grand scale – not the case on the mainland.

©Photo Scala, Florence/Luciano Romano

Courtyard, Palazzo Abatellis

Swabian military constructions – Henry VI, and more particularly **Frederick II** who enjoyed a longer reign (1208–50), preserved the numerous religious and civil buildings erected by the Normans. They also built fortresses designed by northern master masons, who introduced the Gothic style. From this era date the castles at Siracusa (Castello Maniace), Catania (Castello Ursino) and Augusta, as well as the fortifications of the castle at Enna (eight imposing towers survive). These buildings conform to a highly geometric ground plan (square centrepiece defended with angle, and sometimes lateral, towers), doorways and windows set into pointed arches, austerely bare walls pierced with embrasures, that rise to battlements and, finally, quadripartite vaulted casements.

14C: Chiaramonte style – The great feudal dynasties in power during the 14C, most especially the Chiaramonte, demonstrated a real talent for the construction of town houses and churches. The Palermo residence, Palazzo Chiaramonte, provided a model for future *palazzi*: the façade is extremely refined, the windows set into decorative pointed arches are unique and quite wonderful, the roof line is crested with merlons. The Chiaramonte style is characterised by two-or three-light windows surmounted by arches with tracery or polychrome geometric decoration. The Chiaramonte, who maintained their supremacy throughout the 14C as the royal power base declined, sponsored many new buildings and restored others: from Mussomeli to Racalmuto, Montechiaro to Favara, they are responsible for at least 10 castles and palazzi.

15C: Catalan Gothic – Catalan Gothic flourished easily in Sicily because of the Spanish viceroys' influence from the late 14C, under the rule of the House of Aragon. This more sober form of Gothic is characterised by elongated forms, a marked tendency towards breadth of space over height (particularly in the religious context), and ample windows alternating with bare flat wall surfaces. Typical examples include the Palazzo Santo Stefano and Palazzo Corvaja at Taormina and the main doorway of Palermo Cathedral. At the end of the 15C, **Matteo Carnelivari** probably best epitomises the new influence, mixing Catalan features with Byzantine, Arab and Norman elements. Carnelivari designed Palazzo Abatellis and Palazzo Ajutamicristo, and probably the Church of Santa Maria della Catena in Palermo.

Sculpture and painting – Only non-Sicilian artists achieved any renown in these two fields at this time: sculptors were summoned from Tuscany, particularly from Pisa. **Nino Pisano** completed a graceful Annunziata for the cathedral in Trapani, a place that attracted a large number of sculptors to its marble quarries from the 14C. Bonaiuto Pisano carved the eagle that stands above the gateway of Palazzo Sclafani in Palermo.

In painting, **Antonio Veneziano** (trained in Venice, worked in Florence), Gera da Pisa, and various Spanish artists such as **Guerau Janer** also worked in Sicily for a time. At the end of the 15C, some painters became so successful that they settled in Sicily, among them **Nicolò di Maggio** (from Siena) who worked particularly in Palermo.

RENAISSANCE AND MANNERISM

Because the Aragonese court favoured the Spanish Gothic style, the Renaissance and Mannerism that spread from Italy to the rest of Europe did not have a great impact on Sicily. It fell to artists trained by the great Tuscan masters to introduce the principles to Sicily.

Painting – In the 15C, Sicily started to show an interest in the new Renaissance movement, prompted by the work of **Antonello da Messina**. Although his life and career have long been a mystery, this artist remains the most famous Sicilian painter. Born in Messina in 1430; he was in Naples, possibly engaged as a pupil to the workshop of Colantonio, in 1450. There he would most certainly have seen Flemish painting. In 1475–76, Antonello was in Venice, where he must have encountered Giovanni Bellini and Piero della Francesca.

Antonello's supreme reputation, however, is founded on his mastery of the Van Eycks' exacting oil-painting techniques. His mature style combines the detail so typical of Flemish art with the breadth of form upheld by the Italian Schools. Indeed, his works all are static in composition, explore texture, and demonstrate an almost perfect tonal unity in terms of colour.

His works found in Sicily include an *Annunciation* in Siracusa's Palazzo Bellomo, *Polyptych of St Gregory* in the Messina's Museo Regionale, and the *Portrait of an Unknown Man* in Cefalù's Museo Mandralisca. These are among the most notable works of the Renaissance to be preserved in Sicily.

During the first half of the 16C, the painters **Cesare da Sesto, Polidoro da Caravaggio** and Vincenzo da Pavia played their part in spreading the Mannerist style prevalent in Tuscany and Rome.

Simone de Wobreck meanwhile, who lived in Sicily until 1557, introduced the basic elements of Flemish Mannerism.

Sculpture – In the second half of the 15C, sculpture was completely revitalised by a range of Italian artists, notably **Francesco Laurana** and Domenico Gagini. The sculptor and engraver Laurana spent five years in Sicily (1466–71). He worked at the Cappella Mastrantonio in the Church of San Francesco and produced the bust of Eleonora of Aragon in Palermo's Palazzo Abatellis. Other paintings include a *Madonna and Child* in Noto's Church of the Crocifisso, another in the Church of the Immacolata in Palazzolo Acreide and a third in the museum at Messina.

Gagini, who was born into a family of Italian sculptors and architects from Lake Lugano, moved south and settled in Sicily. There he practised his art in association with his son **Antonello**, who was born in Palermo in 1478. Their workshop flourished in the capital, producing

Portrait of an Unknown Man by Antonello da Messina

Museo Mandralisca, Cefalù/SCALA

works that satisfied the contemporary predilection for elegant, refined forms in Carrara marble, rather than travertine. Domenico's style and technique were continued by his descendants (including his son Giandomenico), sculptors and goldsmiths who achieved fame up to the mid-17C. Numerous Sicilian churches preserve splendid statues executed by the Gagini, although their very proliferation has aroused accusations of their work being repetitive and therefore considered of a lesser value.

Mannerism exercised its influence on sculpture in the 16C largely thanks to such artists as the Florentine **Angelo Montorsoli** (1505–63), who was working in Messina around 1547–57. The fact that he had collaborated with Michelangelo in Florence and Rome gave Montorsoli a certain cachet. His work demonstrates a shift from the Renaissance style to a Michelangelesque Mannerism. The works that survive include the Fontana di Orione (1547–50) in Messina, which is regarded as one of the greatest masterpieces of the 16C.

BAROQUE

During the 16C, the Spanish authorities asserted their influence in the arts. They imposed the values promoted by the Counter-Reformation (resulting from the Council of Trent, 1545), before choosing to sponsor an elaborate, exuberant form of the Baroque that was more typically Spanish than Italian.

Counter-Reformation – Sicily soon succumbed to the power and influence of the Society of Jesus (later known as the Jesuits), founded in 1540 by the Spaniard St Ignatius Loyola (1491–1556). Modelled on the Chiesa del Gesù in Rome, the **Jesuit** churches in Sicily were designed with the same features. The one broad nave is devoid of any element that might restrict the congregation's view of the main altar and obstruct or deflect the words of the preacher from reaching all of the faithful. The solemnity, authority, opulence and luminosity of the internal space is in keeping with the exterior: the main body of the church, so tall and wide, is screened by a central bay; the lateral chapels which open directly off the nave are screened by a lower bay. The bare surfaces that lent a dignity to the Renaissance buildings are here textured with features that vary in weight and depth: engaged columns at ground level give way to superficial pilasters above as sharp contrasts effectively dissolve into lightness (the Church of Sant'Ignazio all'Olivella in Palermo is a good example of this style).

The painting of the **Counter-Reformation** revives a predilection for those images rejected by Protestantism, subjects such as the Virgin Mary, the dogma of the Eucharist and the veneration of saints. Painting follows the examples of Michelangelo and Raphael, although in Sicily the practitioners of this style, like Vincenzo degli Azani, are few and lesser known.

Politics and style – The Baroque which in Spain reached its apogee in the second half of the 17C, was quickly assimilated by the Sicilians, for they had enjoyed and appreciated the opulent use of marble and gilding since Arab and Byzantine tastes had prevailed in previous centuries. This movement placed great importance on detail, producing finely worked wrought-iron railings and gates, balcony brackets carved with the most original grotesques, and imaginative designs interpreted in polychrome panels of *pietra dura*.

Grotesque Baroque decoration on a balcony in Scicli

G. Bludzin/MICHELIN

San Giorgio di Modica

G. Bludzin/MICHELIN

At the beginning of the 17C, the Spanish viceroy's administration launched an ambitious building programme. They founded some 100 new towns to reorganise and then develop their extensive territories. The earthquake of 1669, followed by a more devastating one in 1693, destroyed almost all the southeastern part of the island. The rebuilding of the towns was immediately initiated under the combined direction of the local authorities, the aristocracy, town planners (Fra' Michele la Ferla, Fra' Angelo Italia) and architects (Vaccarini, Ittar, Vermexio, Palma and Gagliardi). The earthquake laid bare a great expanse of land stretching from Catania to Siracusa, damaging Avola, Noto, Scicli, Modica, Ragusa, Vittoria, Lentini and Grammichele. As a result, Sicilian Baroque is concentrated in this swathe and around Palermo (Bagheria, Trapani), being the seat of power.

Architecture – The majority of the Baroque architects had trained in Rome. They therefore modelled their ideas on Roman interpretations of the Baroque, sometimes exaggerating their iconographic forms, volumes and subject matter for sculptural effect. The delicate relationship between the fragility of life and the forces of nature was translated into an art form far removed from any quest for beauty. The grotesque, excess, death, suffering and even ugliness (decrepitude of old age, poverty and physical deformity) underlie the expressions of exuberance that ornament every surface at this time. Contorted form proved an ideal vehicle for expressing movement through façades or an internal decorative scheme.

Giovanni Battista Vaccarini (1702–69) served his apprenticeship in Rome under Carlo Fontana, through whom he absorbed the ingenuity of the tormented Borromini. On his return to Sicily around 1730, Vaccarini settled in Catania and devoted the next 30 years of his life to rebuilding the city. His undoubted masterpiece is the Church of St Agatha, which is elliptical in shape and has a restless and undulating façade inspired by Borromini's oval Church of San Carlo alle Quattro Fontane in Rome.

Even **Palermo** bristles with buildings modelled on prototypes in Rome. Most of these were built by one of the city's most highly regarded architects, **Giacomo Amato** (1643–1732), who came from Palermo and was trained in Rome. He uses decorative elements borrowed from 16C Roman architecture; characteristic examples include the Church of Santa Teresa alla Kalsa (1686), the Church of the Pietà that rises through two imposing storeys articulated with columns (1689), the Church of the Santissimo Salvatore with its oval dome, as well as numerous private *palazzi*. The monument that best epitomises the urban Baroque style in Palermo is the Quattro Canti junction faced with four interacting façades and fountains.

Noto had to be completely rebuilt following the 1693 earthquake. Thus it exemplifies the Baroque homogeneity in Sicilian cities, largely as a result of being conceived as a vast theatre. The author of this exceptional ensemble is presumed to be the enigmatic **Rosario Gagliardi**, about whom little is known other than his year and place of birth (Siracusa, 1680) and death (Noto, 1726). This man, the greatest Baroque architect of Sicily, exerted his considerable impact on this small area around Noto and its two neighbouring towns: Ragusa and Modica. In **Ragusa**, he is responsible for the churches of San Giuseppe and San Giorgio; in **Modica**, he designed the magnificent Church of San Giorgio with its distinctive slender bell tower.

The most evocative Sicilian Baroque villas are to be found at **Bagheria**, about 18km/11mi east of Palermo. One of the most remarkable of these refined residential buildings, endowed with luxuriously furnished halls and gardens populated with statuary, is the Villa Palagonia, famous for its wildly extravagant interior decoration. The villa became a symbol of the absurd, renowned throughout Europe during the Age of Enlightenment, long before Goethe's famous visit in 1787 (see BAGHERIA).

Sculpture and applied decoration – Baroque sculpture and decoration is characterised by rich ornamentation. Altarpieces are provided with carved marble panels and contained among twisted columns; cornices and pediments are crested with figures of angels. Ranking high among his many fellow artist-craftsmen, **Giacomo Serpotta** (1652–1732) excelled at using marble, stucco and polychrome decoration.

After training in Rome, Serpotta returned to his home town Palermo to work on an equestrian statue of Charles II of Spain. He then embarked on a long career there as a decorator specialising in stucco. The Oratory of San Lorenzo, the Oratory of Santa Cita and the Oratory of the Rosary at San Domenico are encrusted throughout with figures and swirling curlicues in bold relief, executed with an exquisite attention to detail. The other church interiors on which Serpotta worked include La Gancia, and Il Carmine. Later in life, he was engaged on the decoration of the Church of San Francesco d'Assisi and that of Sant'Agostino (with pupils), which contains a number of narrative panels in shallow relief that illustrate a rare degree of virtuosity. While Serpotta is regarded as the greatest exponent of Sicilian Baroque sculpture, he is also considered to be a precursor of the characteristic forms of Rococo.

Baroque painting – Baroque painters were predominantly engaged in experimenting with perspective and trompe l'oeil, constructing complex compositions on diagonal axes around swirling gestures. Their most common subjects were narrative scenes from the Bible or mythology. The most representative adherent of this movement was **Caravaggio**. Michelangelo Merisi (1573–1610), known as Caravaggio after his birthplace near Bergamo, began his career in Rome alongside Cavaliere d'Arpino in 1588. Thanks to his temper and bad behaviour, Caravaggio was forced to flee the city in 1605, making for Naples, Malta and then Sicily. Venturing to the extremes of every artistic convention, Caravaggio perfected a highly personal style using low-life figures to animate his pictures. He heightened the drama with bold contrasts of light and shadow, the technique known as "chiaroscuro". While in Sicily, he executed a number of important works, notably the *Burial of St Lucy* (1609, in Palazzo Bellomo in Siracusa), *The Adoration of the Shepherds* and *The Resurrection of Lazarus* (in the Messina museum).

These paintings fired the imagination of many subsequent artists, namely Alfonso Rodriguez (1578–1648) and **Pietro Novelli** (1603–47). Novelli was also influenced by the Dutch painter **Anthony Van Dyck**, who, during a sojourn in Palermo in 1624, painted *The Madonna of the Rosary* for the oratory in the Church of San Domenico.

18C TO THE PRESENT DAY

Neoclassicism – The Classical revival started in the mid-18C and was fed by the passion for Ancient Greek and Roman architecture, following the discovery and excavation of Herculaneum, Pompeii and Paestum. In the graphic arts, this movement was translated into depictions of Romantic ruins and topographical views that met with great success. One of the most successful of the neoclassical sculptors was **Ignazio Marabitti** (Palermo 1719–97), who trained in Rome under Filippo della Valle. Works by this artist include the altarpiece of St Ignatius commissioned for the Church of Sant'Agata al Collegio in Caltanissetta. In Palermo, the native-born **Venanzio Marvuglia** (1729–1814) met with moderate success: a pupil of Vanvitelli in Rome, he was responsible for enlarging the Church of San Martino delle Scale, the Oratory of Sant'Ignazio dell'Olivella (Palermo) and the villa for the Prince of Belmonte. Marvuglia's predominantly Classical style is sometimes touched with the exotic, as the Chinese pavilion in the park of La Favorita in Palermo testifies.

Naturalism – Although sharing with many other contemporary Italian artists a keenness to portray reality, the sculptor **Domenico Trentacoste** (b. Palermo, 1859, d. Florence, 1933) still cannot be regarded as a true exponent of Naturalism. Fascinated first by 15C exponents, Trentacoste then turned to Rodin, whom he encountered in Paris in around 1880, before gradually concentrating on popular painting, mythological subjects, portraiture and nude painting (*Little Faun* in the Galleria E. Restivo in Palermo). **Ettore Ximenes** (b. Palermo, 1855, d. Rome, 1926) trained first in Palermo and then in Naples under Domenico Morelli.

Stile Liberty – The Art Nouveau style, already well established in Europe, appeared in Italy at the turn of the 20C. Its main impact was on the decorative arts; its most distinctive feature, the serpentine line, insinuated itself into figurative depictions, wrought-iron

*Photo Scala, Florence

Sculpture by Ignazio Marabitti in Villa Giulia, Palermo

work, and furniture. The best exponent in Sicily is the architect **Ernesto Basile** (b. Palermo, 1857, d. 1932), son of **Giovanni Basile** (designer of the Teatro Massimo in Palermo), who turned to the Art Nouveau style after studying forms of Arabo-Norman and Renaissance design. Examples of his work from this period include the decoration of Villa Igiea (today the five-star *Hilton Hotel Villa Igiea Palermo*), notably the wonderful floral decoration of the dining room, Caffè Ferraglia in Rome, and various villas in Palermo, such as Villino Florio. He also worked on designing soft furnishings, fabrics and furniture.

Palermo's **Villa Malfitano**, once owned by the Whitakers, a prominent English family, epitomises the success and effectiveness of the Stile Liberty in Sicily.

Contemporary art – Although Sicily has not given rise to an international movement, it has nurtured several interesting personalities.

The painter **Fausto Pirandello** (1889–1975), the son of the famous writer, was mainly interested in Cubist painting (Braque in particular). Later he balanced the abstract and figurative.

> *Without Sicily, Italy leaves no image in the soul: it is the key to everything.*
>
> – *Italian Journey*, JW von Goethe

The Neo-Realist painter **Renato Guttuso** (1912–87) studied Classics in Palermo, before moving to Rome and then Milan. There he affirmed his political position as clearly anti-Fascist. During these years he turned to Realist art. His paintings are characterised by a flattened perspective and by form that has been refracted into geometric shapes – reminiscent of Picasso. Yet his subjects always reflect his social predicament. From 1958 onwards, Guttuso was influenced by Expressionism. The result is a new painting style: the realism that pervaded his subject matter is now imbued with emotion, movement is suggested by the use of strong colour and boldly decisive line.

Among contemporary Sicilian artists, mention should be made of various sculptors. **Pietro Consagra,** who came from Mazara del Vallo (1920–2005), studied in Palermo before going to Rome where he came into contact with abstract art. He experimented with different materials, honing them to produce the finest end result.

The sculptor **Emilio Greco** (b. Catania, 1913, d. Rome, 1995) sought that elusive harmony and equilibrium, drawing inspiration from Greek, Etruscan, Roman and Renaissance art. One of his favourite subjects was the female body; other concepts and ideas explored are associated with religion (the bronze doors of Orvieto Cathedral and the monument to Pope John XXIII for St Peter's Basilica in Rome).

Finally, **Salvatore Fiume** (1915–97), also known as Giocondo, was active in various media, including sculpture, film and painting. The latter range from ideal depictions of nature to flat portrayals of everyday life (such as women at a market). Clearly, he was influenced by the various cultures and civilisations that history imprinted on Sicily. In later life, Fiume devoted himself to religious art, illustrating biblical texts for the Catholic publisher Edizioni Paoline.

The Grand Tour

During the reign of the English Queen Elizabeth I (1533–1603), the concept of a "Grand Tour" of the Continent first became popular. The medieval style pilgrimages by noblemen had been decried by the likes of Erasmus. Now, excursions were for education and pleasure *(utilitas et verits):* Venice, Milan, Verona, Florence and Rome, of course, were the compulsory ports of call. But after Elizabeth I's excommunication and aggressive actions against Spain, Protestant travellers would have been wary of journeying south to Naples and Sicily, then under the dominion of the Spaniards and their Catholic Inquisition. Slowly the Papacy endeavoured to woo the English. Aristocrats sojourned at leisure in Italy (the Earl of Leicester's son, Sir Robert Dudley, was in Florence; Earl Arundel spent time in Padua); Inigo Jones (1573–1652) reported on the delights of Classical and Palladian architecture. Finally, after the Restoration (1660) of Charles II, the frontiers were opened once more.

The **Age of Sensibility** exalted Italy as the cradle of civilisation. Instructive journeys completed the education of young intellectuals. They travelled to the Continent, visiting places endowed with rich artistic heritage and cultural fervour. Richard Boyle, then Lord Burlington (1684–1753), and Robert Adam (1728–92) followed in the wake of Jones to study the antique monuments.

As the **Age of Reason** dawned, still Rome and its academic institutions attracted ambitious young artists to study, muse and enjoy life without responsibility. After the Seven Years' War (1756–63), the Grand Tour became institutionalised: now not only the British **(Sir William Hamilton, Gavin Hamilton, Benjamin West)** came, but also the French, the Germans and the Dutch. Visitors extended their tours to Naples and the south following the exciting discovery and excavation of Pompeii (1740s) and the neighbouring Herculaneum (1750s). This provided a genuine and "scientific" view of Roman life, buried intact beneath layers of volcanic debris since the eruption of Vesuvius in AD 79, as had been described by Pliny the Younger. Scholars and tourists alike extended their travels to take in Paestum (documented by two other Englishmen,

John Berkenhout and **Thomas Major**, in 1767–68). Before long, Sicily was also included in the itinerary. But these discoveries not only encouraged interest in things Roman relevant to Neoclassicism and the Greek Revival, they also precipitated an ever greater fascination for the latent power of volcanoes. This is encapsulated by Sir William Hamilton (Plenipotentiary at the Court of Naples 1764–1800) in his book *Observations on Mount Vesuvius, Mount Etna and other Volcanos* (1773).

Napoleon's invasion of Italy (1796) interrupted all forms of travel across the Continent. When peace was restored, the grandness of the tours evaporated. After 1815, Thomas Cook began operating his package tours and visitors urged the Italians to rise against their Austrian occupiers. Yet all the while, Italy provided a safe haven for those fleeing trouble at home, most especially those young and of a Romantic disposition (Byron, Shelley, Browning).

ENGLISHMEN ABROAD

The first English traveller to compile a journal of his travels abroad is **Sir Thomas Hoby** (1530–66), who set out from England in June 1549 and travelled to Padua, Florence, Rome, Naples, Calabria and Sicily. **John Dryden, Jr.** travelled the Mediterranean in the early 18C (*A Voyage to Sicily and Malta* was published in 1776).

In 1770, the Scotsman **Patrick Brydone** visited the island: his impressions are contained in the entertaining letters that form his *Journey to Sicily and Malta* (published 1773), which library records prove to be the most popular book of the late 18C. The first thing that strikes him is the port of Messina, a harbour enclosed by a sickle-shaped tongue of land protecting it from all the winds. Here reality combines immediately with myth, in which the terrible monsters of Scylla and Charybdis lurk in the underground caves on either side of the Straits of Messina. The luxuriant vegetation also catches the traveller's eye, alongside the more everyday crops of vines, olives and wheat, which alternate with flowers, bushes and prickly pears. Ever present in the background stands the menacing form of Etna, smouldering benignly – the ultimate "curiosity" in this southern region. Then Taormina, and the first leap into the classical past, and Etna looms up again, a sleeping giant, but ever vigilant and ready to prove its great power: "in the centre... we could just see the summit of the mountain raising its proud head, vomiting clouds of smoke."

For travellers, Etna acts as a powerful magnet: the very antithesis of the peace and serenity of the past inspired by the Greek ruins of Girgenti (Agrigento). It symbolises life in the form of fire and heat, an uncontrollable, unpredictable phenomenon. The fact that it is visible

Taormina (1876) by W. J. Ferguson

from a long way off seems almost to endow it with the inevitability of something that man cannot control, like life and death. Brydone journeys on towards the larger towns on the island: Catania, Siracusa, Agrigento and the "beautiful, elegant" Palermo, to which pages and pages of description are devoted.

In Brydone's footsteps followed **Henry Swinburne**, urged on by the other writer's "lies" and "nonsensical froth"; he published his travels in four volumes entitled *Travels in the Two Sicilies in the Years 1777, 1778, 1779 and 1780*. These, along with the Brydone account, were soon translated into French and German. **Johann Wolfgang von Goethe** (1749–1832) used Brydone and JH Von Riedesel's Reise (1771) when he undertook his Italian journey, writing his own *Italienische Reise* (1786-88).

As descriptions were penned, draughtsmen and painters flocked to the island, eager to depict the natural landscape, the topography of the cities and views, the ruins and the people. Towards the end of the century, Sicily became the key destination for anyone undertaking the Grand Tour: it was the gateway of things classical, but also a natural treasure trove of rare features that could not be found elsewhere.

TRAVELLING DIARY

The diary was the traveller's faithful companion. In it, he would transcribe impressions, musings, pleasures and discomforts (Goethe's descriptions of seasickness, for example) in an informal letter to himself or a close friend. What is remarkable is how perceptive these observations are, touching upon technical and scientific details, curious facts, encounters, and images of a Sicily that has changed profoundly since. Yet the portraits of the people, their kindness and hospitality are true for all time.

Literature

Sicilian literature has evolved in a curious way: nowhere has dialect been used as a literary language for such a long time and in such an uncompromising

way as on this island. In fact, it has given rise to two linguistically different parallel streams, often present in the same author: one form being written in Italian, the other in the Sicilian dialect.

The Sicilian School of Poetry's golden age came to an end with the decline of the Magna Curia of Frederick II. During the 14C–15C, poetry was modelled on Tuscan literature; then it faded gradually, overshadowed by a more popular genre in local dialect.

HUMANISM AND THE RENAISSANCE

The discovery of Classical texts, in particular the understanding of Ancient Greek which underpinned the emergence of Humanism, resounded strongly in Sicily. Noto, Palermo, Siracusa, Catania and Messina became leading cultural centres. The latter instituted a school for Greek, which achieved international acclaim largely thanks to the teachings of **Costantino Lascaris**.

The 16C saw a resurgence in the use of Sicilian. Local patriotism and pride swelled, as publishers debuted the first Sicilian-Latin dictionaries and a grammar for the regional dialect. As far as poetry is concerned, the preponderance of the Petrarchan style found expression in dialect through Antonio Veneziano (1543–93). He was in prison with Cervantes in Algiers and was the author of two volumes of poems entitled *Celia*.

17C–18C

In keeping with the general mood of the Baroque, the 17C witnessed an upsurge of interest and development in the theatre, largely generated by the tragedies of **Ortensio Scammacca** and by comedies both in Italian and in dialect.

In the course of the 18C, the Age of Enlightenment made its presence felt, as expressed in the *History of Sicily* written by the abbot **G Battista Caruso** (1673–1724) and the *History of Sicilian Literature* edited by **Antonio Mongitore** (1663–1743). Philosophical reflection inspired various other literary genres: Cartesian thought was voiced by **Tommaso Campailla** (1668–1740), who wrote a philosophical poem entitled *Adamo, ovvero il mondo é creato (Adam, or How the World was Created)*. Leibniz, meanwhile, was exalted by **Tommaso Natale** in *La filosofia Leibniziana (The Philosophy of Leibniz)*. Rousseau's precepts on the Noble Savage and the relationship between morality and the environment were promoted by the great poet, **Giovanni Meli** (1740–1815), in his bucolic contemplations *La bucolica* and philosophical satires clearly influenced by the Enlightenment *L'origini du lu munnu, Don Chisciotti e Sanciu Panza*.

19C

Romanticism encouraged the writing of lengthy histories and research into the origins of regional culture and tradition. **Michele Amari** (1806–89) initiated a new period of history criticism with his *La guerra del Vespro siciliano (War of the Sicilian Vespers)* and *Storia dei Musulmani di Sicilia (History of the Muslims in Sicily)*. **Giuseppe Pitré** (1841–1916) studied folklore, thereby raising the life and traditions of Sicilians to a level worthy of historical consideration.

Realism was formulated as a reaction to Romanticism and became widespread in Sicily towards the close of the 19C. Early foundations were laid by the Positivist poetry of **Mario Rapisardi** (1844–1912); reinforcements came from the accomplished theorist, **Luigi Capuana** (1839–1915). He argued that art should embrace a sense of real life and examine the contemporary world and the laws of nature so as to document human life. His masterpieces – *Giacinta* and *Il Marchese di Roccaverdina* – reflect these values; furthermore they portray reality in an impersonal way. Even **Giovanni Verga** (1830–1922), after the Late Romantic tone of his earliest work, shows a move towards Realist poetry. His masterpiece – *I Malavoglia*, intended as the first part of a cycle of novels entitled *I Vinti (The Conquered)* – was followed by just one sequel *(Mastro Don Gesualdo)*. Verga's main theme concentrates on the description of the real Sicily, with the destiny of the humble folk portrayed objectively, yet compassionately. He uses a sombre writing style and a language which, when compared to the Italian mainstream, succeeds in mimicking the cadences and rhythms of the spoken vernacular. Other adherents of the Realist School include **Federico de Roberto** (1861–1927) – author of *I Vicerè (The Viceroys)* and *L'Illusione (The illusion)* – and the poets **Giuseppe Aurelio Costanzo** (1843–1913) and **Giovanni Alfredo Cesareo** (1861–1937).

20C

Modern Italian literature is indebted to Sicily for one of its greatest protagonists: the 1934 Nobel Prize winner **Luigi Pirandello** (1867–1946). His early work as a poet and novelist lies in the Realist vein. Later works explore the theme of isolation, painting the individual at sea in a society that is foreign to him *(Il fu Mattia Pascal, Novelle per un anno)*. This idea found its most poignant expression on stage; Pirandello's masterpieces include *Liolà, Pensaci Giacomino! (Think about it, Giacomino), Così é (se vi pare) – That's How It Is (If You Like)* and *Sei personaggi in cerca di autore (Six Characters in Search of an Author)*.

Another figure central to the history of Italian culture is the philosopher **Giovanni Gentile** (1875–1944), who, as Minister for Education in the Fascist government, promoted the reform of the Italian education system. On the opposing political front, **Concetto Marchesi** (1878–1957) published studies on the history of Latin literature that are still regarded as classics today.

The decadence of the Sicilian aristocracy during the Risorgimento is poignantly, if bitterly, portrayed in *Il Gattopardo (The Leopard)*, the novel by **Prince Giuseppe Tomasi di Lampedusa** (1896–1957), published posthumously. The satirical and grotesque storyteller **Vitaliano Brancati** attacked myths of eroticism and sexual conceit in his novels *(Don Giovanni in Sicilia, Il bell'Antonio* and *Paolo il Caldo)*. **Elio Vittorini** (1908–66) played a fundamental role in spreading awareness of contemporary American literature and in revitalising the Italian narrative tradition in the neo-Realist convention *(Conversazione in Sicilia, Uomini e no)*. The rough-and-ready style more often associated with police inquiries animates the novels of **Leonardo Sciascia** (1921–89), which include *Il giorno della civetta (The Day of the Owl)*, *Todo modo*, and *Candido ovvero un sogno fatto in Sicilia (Candido, or a Sicilian Dream)*. **Gesualdo Bufalino** (1920–96) is a huge literary personality, having emerged at the age of 60 with *Diceria dell'untore*. Both critics and the public alike acclaimed his prose, poetry, memoirs and criticism *(Argo il cieco, Il Guerrin Meschino)*. The baroque prose of **Vincenzo Consolo** (b. 1933) is full of precise reflections on history. The detective novels of **Andrea Camilleri** (1925), based on the fictitious character of police superintendent Montalbano, have enjoyed great success both in Italy and abroad. His novels are infused with musical language, rich with Sicilian expressions and vocabulary.

Other works in this genre include the novels of Santo Piazzese (Palermo, 1948), which are based in Sicily's capital city.

As far as poetry is concerned, **Salvatore Quasimodo** (1901–68), awarded the Nobel Prize for Literature in 1959, occupies a position of prime importance. His later work sought to draw attention to political and social issues *(Ed é subito sera, La terra impareggiabile, Dare e avere)*. Less well known, but nevertheless of interest, is the metaphorical poetry of **Lucio Piccolo** (1903–69), cousin of Tomasi di Lampedusa and author of *Canti Barocchi and Plumelia*. A great sense of social commitment is voiced in the poetry of **Ignazio Buttitta** (1899–1997), who demonstrated once again that dialect was the best vehicle for expressing the thoughts and emotions of the Sicilian people *(Lu pani si chiama pani, La peddi nova)*.

Cinema

Many famous directors have attempted to create a portrait of Sicily on film. This complex, stunningly beautiful island is inhabited by a proud, hospitable people who, despite a certain reserve, are happy to extend warmth and generosity in equal measure. Here the conspiracy of silence known as "omertà" exists along-

side an equally ardent will to fight this silence. Transcribing all these characteristic traits into art is no simple task.

The first great masterpieces were based on the classics: **Luchino Visconti** turned to Verga to make such films as *La Terra Trema (The Ground Trembles)* in 1948 based on his book *I Malavoglia*, and to Tomasi di Lampedusa for **Il Gattopardo** *(The Leopard)* in 1963 from the book of the same name. He was determined to capture reality in all its different guises, while peppering it with the local colour and poetry. Thus Visconti selected his main cast from amateur actors living in a typical community, such as Aci Trezza, who spoke in dialect. Secondly, he chose a historical epic that was respected and established in its own right, set in the magnificent, yet already decadent Palermo of the late 19C. Then he illuminated it all with sparkling performances by Claudia Cardinale, Burt Lancaster, and Alain Delon.

In the same vein is the sad and agonising story related in **Stromboli terra di Dio** (1949). This strong portrait of a woman, filmed against a background of untamed nature, was directed by **Roberto Rossellini** and starred Ingrid Bergmann. Films about the Mafia are a case apart. Since the making of the films-cum-denunciations – **In nome della legge** (In the Name of the Law), directed by Pietro Germi (1949) and **Salvatore Giuliano** directed by Francesco Rosi (1961) – the subject matter and circumstances quickly transformed into an entire genre, which for Italian viewers compares well with the popular spaghetti western elsewhere. This in turn generated a veritable industry of Mafia family epics with the inevitable shoot-outs, clashes, and use of broad Sicilian dialect.

These films were distributed all over the world, giving a somewhat negative impression of the island. However, also belonging to this genre are films of social importance, such as **I cento passi** *(One hundred steps)* directed by Tullio Giordana (best screenplay in the 2000 Venice Film Festival), which skilfully recounts the story of the journalist Peppino Impastato, who was killed in 1978 after many years fighting the Mafia.

A very different Sicily appears on the cinema screen: a Sicily that is mournful, but veined with humour, emerges in the magnificent tales retold in **Kaos** *(Chaos)*, made in 1984 by the **Taviani brothers**, based on novels by Pirandello (brilliant performances by Franco Franchi and Ciccio Ingrassia in *La Giara)*. A poetic view is portrayed in Michael Radford's **Il Postino** *(The Postman)* made in 1994 and starring Massimo Troisi, and in Giuseppe Tornatore's **Nuovo Cinema Paradiso** (1989), which received an Oscar for Best Foreign Film in 1990. An ironic Sicily "– in search of its lost tranquillity" –is shown in the Isole episode (about the Aeolian Islands) in *Caro Diario* (1993) by Nanni Moretti and in the funny *Tano da Morire* (1997), a musical about the Mafia, by Roberta Torre. In 2000, Bagheria-born director Giuseppe Tornatore scored a European hit with *Malèna*, starring Monica Bellucci.

Sicilian Puppets

The fate of puppets and marionettes in Italy took an upward turn in the 16C, when the aristocracy took an interest in marionettes. The spread to a wider, paying audience came about in the 18C. But it was not until the mid-19C that the puppet show became a genre, complete with shiny armour, swords and agile movements in fight scenes.

Sicilian puppet masters weave their stories around bandits, saints and Shakespearean heroes, as well as local vignettes. The favourite source of subject matter is the popular **picaresque stories of chivalry**, from the **Carolingian cycle**, in particular. The puppeteers prepare a text that follows the basic lines of the plot, and then exaggerate clashes between the paladins and infidels, as the fight is always the culmination of the show.

The puppeteers' arrival was always awaited with great anticipation, most especially by the less fortunate classes, and no one would dream of missing a single performance. This is why the puppeteers would break up the story into episodes and present them in series that might last several months. Each performance had to include at least one fight (such was the explanation for having to adapt the historical facts).

The puppet master also prepared various boards with panels summarising the salient elements of the story. The board, displayed outside the theatre, would act as an advertisement for the evening and also summarise for the public the story so far. In 2001, Sicilian puppet theatre was declared a masterpiece of oral tradition by UNESCO.

©Photo Scala, Florence/Museo Etnografico Siciliano Pitre', Palermo

Sicilian puppet theatre with puppets

> "We are puppets, Signor Fifì! Divine spirit enters us and makes us puppets.
> I'm a puppet, you're a puppet, everyone's a puppet."
> – Luigi Pirandello, *The Cap with the Jingle Bells*

PRINCIPAL CHARACTERS

The most famous protagonists were the paladins (courtly peers) of France who, under the leadership of Charlemagne, spent their lives fighting the infidels. The show hinged on predetermined values and sentiments: there were "goodies" (the paladins), "baddies" (the infidels) and traitors, such as **Gano di Magonza**. The audience participates in the show and takes the sides of one character or another. At one time puppet performances were followed so closely that the audience would immediately recognise the characters. The easiest markers are the shields: Orlando's shield has a cross, while Rinaldo and Bradamante carry shields bearing a lion.

PERFORMANCE

The show has three main elements: the puppet who acts on stage; the master who remains off-stage, pulls the strings and voices several characters at a time; and the music. The latter emphasises the most dramatic moments, particularly when there is a duel – the sound of clashing swords must be accompanied by the frenzied strains of a mechanical pianola or wind instruments. Stunt puppets even pull off special effects: one might lose its head or be torn asunder, only to be magically restored to one piece in the next show, or a witch might need to take on a disguise, turning from a pretty, angelic face to a death mask.

TWO TRADITIONS

Puppets are made of wood and are jointed with metal hinges (the warriors, at least); their manipulation is controlled by lengths of wire connected to the head and right hand. The embossed armour is usually made of bronze or copper. There are two main schools: Palermo and Catania (associated with the school of Acireale), which builds puppets to different criteria.

The Palermo puppet is around 80cm–1m/2.5–3.25ft in height, weighs 8kg/18lb, has flexible knees and can draw and sheathe its sword. Its relative lightness makes it easy to manoeuvre: the puppet moves with extreme agility, reacting quickly and suddenly to provocation, and seemingly jumping about on stage to drive home or avoid blows during a duel.

Palermo puppets are moved from the side, and the puppet master has to stretch out his arm to reach the centre of the stage. The Catania puppet measures 1.4m/4.6ft in height and weighs between 16 and 20kg/35–44lb. Its knees are rigid (partly because supporting such a weight for any length of time would be a mean feat) and its sword is always drawn, ready to parry blows. The Acireale puppet has the same features as the Catania puppet, but the height (1.2m/4ft) and the weight (15–18kg/33–40lb) are different.

The puppets from Catania and Acireale, are heavier, have longer wires and are controlled from above: the puppet master standing on a manoeuvring bench (in the case of the Acireale puppets), 1.9m/6.25ft high.

Music

POPULAR SICILIAN MUSIC

At the very mention of this island's name, anyone with a keen ear for music recalls the *siciliana*, an ancient shepherds' dance. This was transcribed in pieces of the 17C and 18C. Traditional dance music features the straight reed pipe (*fiscalettu* or *friscaleddu*), and the *marranzanu*, a mouth harp.

Popular music includes songs *alla carrittera* – literally "of the cart-driver", and those sung by the *cantastorie* – modern equivalents of minstrels who travel from with a guitar and a board illustrating their story. The most famous of these was Ciccio Busacca (1926–1984).

THE ISLAND TODAY

Myth

OVERVIEW

A legend tells of three nymphs who travelled around the world to collect its best produce. Coming across a sea of extraordinary beauty, they dropped their flowers and fruit into it. From the waters rose the land mass of Sicily – with its three headlands of Capo Peloro, Capo Passero and Capo Lilibeo – the jewel-casket of all the world's beauty. This myth attempts to explain the origins of the harmoniously shaped triangular island, known as *Triskeles* (three legs) to the Greeks and *Triquetra* (three peaks) to the Romans. The evocative symbol of the island is the Trinakria, a figure with three legs running around a Medusa's head.

Trinakria

B. Kaufmann/MICHELIN

THEN AND NOW

Beauty is certainly the first element that strikes visitors to Sicily. This feature is ever present in the island's clear seas, blue sky and grandiose mountains framing the coast. There is little subtlety in the scenery here: stunning natural landscapes offer bright colours, fragrant scents and unforgettable views. The region has been inhabited by many different peoples over the centuries: the Greeks established colonies here that were later developed by the Romans; the Arabs created magnificent buildings and gardens, subsequently converted into splendid palaces by the Normans; and the French and Spanish introduced the severe Gothic and exuberant Baroque styles. Sicily was dominated by foreign rulers until 1860, when Garibaldi and his troops landed near Marsala, paving the way for the unification of Italy.

Three thousand years of tumultuous history have endowed Sicily with its complex character, best expressed through the island's varied and fascinating art. The human and social mosaic here is

G. Bludzin/MICHELIN

> *"Climb aboard this triangular ark of stone floating upon the waves of millennia… And keep a smattering of Greek to hand, lest you encounter Aphrodite, the goddess of love, emerging from the sea and eager to exchange a few words…"*
>
> – Gesualdo Bufalino, *La luce e il lutto (The Light and the Struggle)*

even more challenging. Media coverage focuses all too often on Mafia-related crime, and Sicilians are often frustrated by the portrayal of their homeland. And yet Sicily has many facets, as the title *La luce e il lutto* (The Light and the Struggle), a collection of essays by the Sicilian writer Gesualdo Bufalino, suggests. The traditional images of Sicily are sunshine, blue skies, warm sea, Greek temples, the Mafia and southern Mediterranean vegetation. But visitors willing to look beyond will discover a proud, hospitable people and a rich, vibrant culture.

island is playing an increasingly prominent part in the Sicilian economy. This has been immeasurably aided by the growth of transport companies and vast improvements to the road system over the past decade. Refined petroleum, from petroleum fields in the southeast, natural gas and sulphur (traditionally a Sicilian industry at the sulphur mines in Caltanissetta) make up the bulk of the island's modern industries. Sicily's other major industry is tourism, which brings an important influx of foreign currency to the island through the summer months.

Economy

Sicily's economy is relatively underdeveloped compared with the rest of Italy, and its unemployment rate is the highest in the country. Agriculture is the primary economic activity on the island, which has been historically long coveted for its fertile land and long, hot growing season. However, the land is divided between a large amount of smallholdings, with the result that incomes are relatively low across the board. The main crops are oranges and lemons, peaches, pears, figs, almonds, salt from Trapani and grapes as well as barley, corn and wheat, particularly around Enna where durum wheat is grown for pasta and bread. Sicily's farms also produce and export a significant amount of dairy products including ricotta and Pecorino cheeses. Other agricultural industries are wine, from Malvasia, Marsala, Donna Fugata and Regaleali, balsamic vinegar, olive oil, bottled water from Geraci and honey. On the coast, the fishing industry still flourishes, providing important tuna and sardine fisheries, as well as catches of swordfish, octopus, squid, prawns and sea bream for domestic consumption. Away from the farms and orchards, industrial development on the

Government

Sicily became an autonomous region in 1946 under the new Italian constitution, with its own parliament and elected President. Sicilian politics is hung on the framework of a presidential representative democracy, in which the President of Regional Government *(Presidente della Regione)* is the head of government *(Giunta Regionale)* and also of a multi-party system. The Sicilian Regional Assembly *(Assemblea Regionale Siciliana, ARS)* is elected for a five-year term and, along with the President, has legislative power. However, if a vote of no confidence is registered in the President, or he or she resigns or dies, a new election is triggered. The last regional election in Sicily was held on 13–14 April 2008. This followed the resignation of President Salavatore Cuffaro as a result of his conviction on charges of aiding the Mafia and committing breaches of confidentiality, something to which he pleaded not guilty. Investigations into Cuffaro, whose first presidential term was in 1991, had been running since 2003. Despite this shadow, Cuffaro managed to be re-elected President of Sicily in the 2006 regional election, beating Rita Borsellino, the sister of the

Mafia-executed judge, Paolo Borsellino. In January 2008 Cuffaro was given a five-year prison sentence and suspended from all public offices for the period. The subsequent election was fought by Anna Finocchiaro for the centre-left and Raffaele Lombardo for the centre-right. Lombardo won by a landslide, 65.3%, becoming the new President of Sicily, with Finocchiaro gaining just 30.4% of the votes.

Population

Historically, Sicily has been one of the more populated of Italy's regions, and today it has the fourth highest regional population in the country. However, the relatively extensive size of the region – which includes the Aeolian islands – means that its population density is only slightly higher than the national average. Population density is highest around the coastal areas, where the bulk of tourism and industry are also concentrated, while the inland zone, dominated by agriculture, is relatively uninhabited. This is also partly due to a trend in migration of workers from the countryside to the cities, where earning potential is higher. The most densely populated areas are around Palermo and Catania, along the coastal areas between Catania and Messina, Siracusa and around Agrigento. The high grounds of the island – Etna, the Iblei, Erei mountains and the Sicilian Apennines – have the lowest population density of all, so much so that a few hours drive may offer almost complete solitude out of season.

Festivals and Traditions

By combining pagan rites, holy days allowed by the Christian Church and local festivals, the Sicilians ensure that lavish celebrations are high points in their social calendars.

The most important festivals are Easter, Carnival and the feast days of local saints. Other highlights include the *Palio dei Normanni*, which commemorates Roger II's delivery of Piazza Armerina; events derived from pagan rites, such as Gangi's *Sagra della Spiga* with a procession dedicated to the ancient goddess Demeter (Ceres); and festivals linked to a celebration of nature, such as Agrigento's *Sagra del Mandorlo in fiore* (celebrating the blossoming of the almond trees) and Vizzini's *Sagra della Ricotta*, both of which fête the advent of spring.

Festa della Vara, Messina

Lara Pessina/MICHELIN

A devil in the festival at Prizzi

PATRON SAINTS

The most spectacular festivals in honour of patron saints are those held in the large towns. In Palermo, *U fistinu*, dedicated to Santa Rosalia, lasts for six action-packed days.

In Catania, the citizens honour St Agatha, whose relics, contained in a precious silver bust of the saint set with enamels and jewels, are processed for three days by the *nudi* – men dressed in simple jute sacks to commemorate the night in 1126 when citizens poured onto the streets, eagerly jumping out of bed without taking the time to get dressed as the relics were brought back to the city from Constantinople.

In Siracusa, eyes of wax, silver and bronze are fixed to the litter of St Lucy in grateful acknowledgement of grace received from the saint, the protector of all things optical. In Messina, the most spectacular festival is held on 15 August, when thousands pull an enormous statue representing the Assumption of the Virgin Mary to the cathedral, where it remains for two days guarded by 14 young girls dressed in white.

This *Festa della Vergine* is celebrated alongside the anniversary of the arrival of Count Roger: the sacred mixes with the profane in an inseparable cocktail of religious devotion, high spirits, social occasion and entertainment.

EASTER

Easter is certainly the most eagerly awaited festival in Sicily. In almost every town and small village, enormous effort is invested in preparing for the processions and the celebrations of a rite that has changed little through the centuries. Processions move the sacred element – a representation of a holy figure – through the streets of the town, stopping here and there to re-enact the Madonna's desperate search for her son, the Crucifixion and the events of the Passion. The most poignant elements fall between the Thursday before Easter and Easter Sunday (the discovery of the empty tomb as evidence of the Resurrection), although these can be more protracted, as is the case with the celebrations held at **Trapani**. There, the evenings leading up to the Good Friday grand procession are devoted to the *discese delle Vergini*. At sunset, representatives of each and every *ceto* of the town (associations roughly comparable to the medieval trade guilds) bear on their shoulders the image of their patron Madonna (Madre dei Massari, Madre Pietà del Popolo) and carry her down to the old part of town by candlelight. The men compete to be chosen as bearers. The icon sways along, stopping at wayside crosses, shrines and churches, but also outside the houses and workplaces of people who have

Elaborate headgear for the festival

offered a donation. In so doing, it is almost as though the Madonna is paying homage to the people who worship her. The elegant *palazzi* open their doors and gracious inner courtyards to visitors, to the crowd, and to the band, who at intervals interrupt the silence with a burst of music. On Good Friday, 20 figurative groups are continuously borne aloft round the town over a period of 20 hours: in a meaningful and symbolic succession of day, night and day (from early afternoon on the Friday through the night to Saturday morning) the faithful are reminded of, and share in, the emotional endurance and physical pain suffered by the Madonna and by Christ in His Passion. An equally evocative occasion is the procession through Caltanissetta of 16 groups of statues.

In **Marsala** the re-enactment of the Passion is assigned to real men and women. At **Enna**, the celebrations reach their climax on Good Friday, when hooded members of the confraternities process through the streets to the town centre carrying the two heavy statues of the dead Christ and the *Addolorata* (Our Lady of Sorrows). The processions meet at the cathedral and together undertake an exhausting journey that lasts throughout the night. The whole event is then repeated on the Sunday, but with one fundamental difference: this time, the meeting between the Madonna and the Resurrected Christ takes place in a happy, festive atmosphere. A rather unusual rite takes place in **Prizzi** on the Sunday morning. It is called the **Uballu di diavula:** devils – dressed in red, with goatskins slung across their shoulders, their faces covered by horrible tin masks – run through the streets of the town rattling iron chains. Another masked figure, dressed in yellow and armed with a wooden crossbow, represents Death. Anyone hit is carried off to the bar (identified as hell), where he pays for a complete round of drinks. The devils jump around, uttering threats, trying to avert the Madonna from meeting the Resurrected Christ. The scene repeats several times, until at last the two angels accompanying the Madonna strike them to the ground. Only Death cannot be touched, spared partly in recognition of human mortality and partly because Christ has already overcome it. At **Terrasini**, the festival of **li schietti** (eligible bachelors) is more profane: young men prove their virility by lifting orange trees.

In addition to staging elaborate re-enactments, some places bedeck the streets with spectacular decorations. At San Biagio Platani, for example, locals build grand triumphal arches and ornament them with sculptures made of bread.

Food and Drink

Talk of food in Sicily is like talking about the weather in England – it is fundamental to life itself. Each region has its own dishes and each community sings the praises of their home-grown vegetables and fragrant herbs, which impart flavour, texture and colour to the local cuisine. The island's eternal links with the sea are also clearly evident, with myriad fish dishes.

Sicilian cuisine relies on an abundance of strongly flavoured basic ingredients (fennel, for example), which are blended and fused with the ruddiest sun-blushed tomatoes, the most gleaming rich aubergines (eggplants), delicate courgettes (zucchini) and freshest tuna. The food is a natural extension of the local landscape. It forms an integral part of the gastronomic culture of the Mediterranean, halfway between Greece and North Africa, Spain and Ancient Phoenicia (the Middle East). Just as the landscapes of the coast and the hinterland are radically different, so their cuisine

Tomatos being dried under the Sicilian sun

Arancine Di Riso (Deep-Fried Rice Balls)

©G. Melfi/Wikimedia Commons

400g/1lb rice, 1/2 small packet of saffron, 150g/6oz minced veal, 1/2 peeled tomato, 100g/4oz shelled peas, six eggs, 75g/3oz fresh caciocavallo cheese, 100g/4oz butter, 1/2 onion, 300g/12oz flour, 300g/12oz breadcrumbs. Serves four.

Boil the rice until it has a crunchy, *al dente* texture and then mix it with the saffron, three eggs and half the butter. Leave to cool. Parboil the peas, drain and brown in the remaining butter. In a separate pan, gently fry the chopped onion. Add the meat, peeled tomato, salt and pepper. Cover and cook over a low heat. Once the meat sauce is ready, mix with the peas. To make the *arancini* balls, take some of the rice mixture and make into a shell shape, then pour in some of the meat sauce. Add a slice of cheese and cover with more of the rice, making a ball. Whisk the remaining eggs and add a little salt. Roll the rice ball in the flour, then in the egg mixture and finally the breadcrumbs. Fry in plenty of sunflower oil and serve hot.

is quite distinctive. Imagine, therefore, Sicily's gastronomy as a palette of paints, with strong colours and subtle hints. 🍴*See food terms in Useful Words and Phrases.*

TYPICAL MEDITERRANEAN CUISINE

As with all simple culinary traditions, the most popular single-course meal is often the tastiest. Pasta, prepared with seasonal vegetables and local olive oil, is the main staple. *Pasta con le sarde*, originally a Palermo dish using freshly caught sardines, is now common across the whole island. Pasta cooked predominantly with vegetables is more typical of the inland areas; more elaborate preparations include types of *pasta al forno* (baked pasta) such as *pasta 'ncaciata* from Messina, and Catania's *pasta alla Norma* (cooked with tomatoes, aubergines and salty ricotta cheese).

However, before pasta was invented, bread was the mainstay of the diet. The many Sicilian varieties have always been accompanied by oil, oregano and tomatoes, resulting in the widespread dish *pane cunzato,* eaten hot from the oven. The more unusual *pane ca' meusa* is a toasted roll spread with a meat paste, often sold on the streets of Palermo.

The central part of the island is dominated by farming habits and the cuisine consequently uses a great deal of fresh vegetables. The aubergine (eggplant) is an important ingredient and forms the basis of a whole range of delicious dishes, culminating in the glorious *parmigiana* (baked aubergine with ricotta, a touch of tomato sauce and occasionally a sprig of basil). Sheep milk plays an important role in the hills (providing the fresh and salted cheese known as *ricotta fresca* and *ricotta salata*). Meat is usually reserved for special occasions, when *castrato* (castrated ram) is roasted. Grilling is the most common preparation otherwise. Pork is also popular.

J.Malburet/MICHELIN

Pasta alla Norma

The eastern flank of the island preserves Greek cooking methods. The west, meanwhile, is marked by an Arab influence and by courtly practices. The cuisine is more elaborate, refined and full of unexpected contrasts. In an analogy with the landscape, the simple austerity of the Greek temples is replaced here with a sophistication imparted by a *Thousand and One Nights,* such as is prevalent in Moorish Palermo.

The *caponata di melanzane* is an example of the different approach to vegetables (cooked aubergine, tomato, onion, olives, celery and capers, served cold in a sweet-sour sauce). *Falsomagro* is a large roll of meat stuffed with ham, cheese and eggs. This demonstrates the chefs; ingenuity with meat, as does *involtini alla primavera* (rissoles made with breadcrumbs, sultanas, pine nuts, cheese, bay leaves and onion). *Sarde a beccafico* (sardines fried with breadcrumbs, lemon juice and pine nuts) do likewise for fish. The complexity of these dishes displays wealth.

On the other hand, road-side shops sell food that has just been fried or cooked in the oven. And stalls vend all kinds of dishes around the clock (*sfinciuni* and *panelle* to name but two).

The Arabs introduced citrus fruits, sugar, cinnamon and saffron, as well as rice to Sicily. Rice recipes vary from the risottos of northern Italy; take *arancine*, for instance, (deep-fried rice balls filled with meat ragout and peas, or ham and cheese), a sort of symbol of the island's traditional cuisine.

Fish abounds, as do the different ways of cooking it. Tuna has always occupied a prime position, possibly because of the ritual associated with its catch and killing; sardines and anchovies appear everywhere, while *pesce spada* (swordfish) is more common around Messina. Fish prepared with onions, olives, capers and tomatoes *(alla ghiotta)* is an unusual speciality. Around Trapani, the *cuscusu* is the island's version of the Moroccan dish, where fish replaces meat.

SWEET DELICACIES

Sicily's cake and pastry-making tradition deserves special attention. Daily, its

Cannoli

fragrance lingers, mixed with the pungence of crushed herbs (rosemary, wild fennel, oregano, basil, thyme) growing throughout the countryside.

Convent sweetmeats, like the brightly coloured *frutta martorana,* named after the convent in Palermo where they originated, have become popular throughout the island. Cannoli, *cassate, pignoccata, biancomangiare* and the traditional *gelo di mellone* (watermelon jelly) are the most common, but each province has its own particular specialities.

The area produces *gelato* and *granite,* which are not merely products of great craftsmanship and culinary pride but smack of habits and rites of another era. In summer, it is nearly compulsory to offer guests a coffee-, lemon- or almond-flavoured *granita* when they arrive, often served with a warm brioche. Literature even mentions such sophisticated delights as a jasmine *granita,* consumed by the Piccolo barons in their Cala Novella refuge.

WINES

Sicily's wines were once regarded as *vini da taglio,* padding to boost the alcohol content of other blends. Today, Sicilian table wines and DOC *(denominazione di origine controllata)* vintages – such as Alcamo, Nero d'Avola, Etna Rosso, il Corvo and Regaleali – are delights.

In addition to the famous **Marsala**, dessert wines made here include Moscato di Noto, Passito di Pantelleria and Malvasia di Lipari. *For a description of wine routes in Sicily, see Planning Your Trip: Themed Tours.*

Caccamo
B. Kaufmann/MICHELIN

ACIREALE

POPULATION: 51 532.

The spectacular Pizza Duomo anchors this Baroque city, erected following 1693's earthquakes. Among its elegant shops stand many gelaterie, serving the renowned local ice cream. Acireale is also famous for its ancient hotsprings, extravagant carnival and puppet theatre.

🛈 **Information:** Corso Umberto 179. ☎095 60 45 21. www.acirealeturismo.it.

▸ **Orient Yourself:** Acireale is accessible via the A 18 motorway (Acireale exit) or along S 114 coast road. The historic centre and Piazza Duomo are clearly signposted.

🅿 **Parking:** A number of car parks (fee) are located around Piazza Duomo.

🏵 **Don't Miss:** A granita or gelato in Piazza Duomo; the view from the terrace of the Villa Belvedere.

🕐 **Organising Your Time:** Set aside a half day, or more if it's carnival season.

Kids **Especially for Kids:** Museo dei Pupi dell'Opra (puppet museum).

🕭 **Also See:** CATANIA; ETNA; GIARDINI NAXOS; TAORMINA.

Basilica dei Santi Pietro e Paolo

B. Kaufmann/MICHELIN

Address Book

A Bit of History

Acis and Galatea – The sea nymph Galatea fell in love with the shepherd Acis. Unfortunately, she also caught the eye of Polyphemus, the gigantic Cyclops and arch enemy of Odysseus (Ulysses). Rejected, the monstrous creature left the caves of Mount Etna to kill his rival. Zeus took pity and transformed her lover into a river (the modern Akis), which flows to Galatea's realm, the sea, and reunites the pair forever.

Another legend claims his dismembered body became the nine Aci towns: Aci Bonaccorsi, Aci Castello, Aci Catena, Aci Platani, Acireale, Aci San Filippo, Aci Sant'Antonio, Aci Santa Lucia and Aci Trezza. This particular stretch of coastline is also known as the Riviera dei Ciclopi (Cyclops' Coast).

Walking Tour

The main hub of the town is Piazza Duomo. Corso Umberto I extends to the north, Via Vittorio Emanuele to the south, lined by fine buildings, shops and *gelaterie*.

Piazza Duomo★★

The square once had the name Piazza del Cinque d'Oro (Golden Five), a reference to the playing-card configuration of its flower beds. This finely proportioned space is enclosed by Baroque buildings: the **Duomo**, the **Basilica dei Santi Pietro e Paolo** (17C–18C), and the **Palazzo Comunale** (1659) graced with elegant wrought-iron **balconies**★. Slightly back, at the beginning of Via Davì, sits the splendid 17C **Palazzo Modò**; the façade still bears the name of the theatre, the Eldorado, that occupied the premises in the early 20C.

Duomo

The cathedral is dedicated to the Annunciation and Santa Venera. Its two-tone neo-Gothic façade was designed by GBF Basile (1825–91), the architect of the Teatro Massimo in Palermo and father of the more famous Ernesto Basile, master of the Liberty style. Standing between two campanili with majolica spires, the front is ornamented by a fine 17C portal.

▸ *From Piazza Duomo take Via Settimo, then Via Vittorio Emanuele.*

Basilica di San Sebastiano

A statue-topped balustrade crowns the **Baroque façade**★, which consists of a harmonious combination of columns, pilasters, niches and volutes, drawn together within a frieze of angels. Inside, the transept and chancel contain frescoes by P Vasta depicting episodes from the life of St Sebastian, the town's patron saint.

▸ *From Piazza Duomo take Via Cavour (in front of the square).*

Piazza San Domenico

Open 10am–1pm (Tue and Thu 4.30pm –7.30pm). Closed Mon. ☎095 76 34 516.
The fine Baroque façade of **San Domenico** dominates one side of the tiny piazza, also overlooked by **Palazzo Musmeci** (17C) with its elegant wrought-iron balconies and Rococo windows.
Farther along the right hand road is the **Biblioteca Zelantea**, the town library, annexed with an **art gallery**. Here reside the plaster model for the statue of Acis and Galatea (now in the gardens of the Villa Comunale) by Rosario Anastasi, and a bust of **Julius Caesar** (1C BC).

▸ *From Piazza Duomo continue to the end of Corso Umberto I.*

Villa Belvedere

The lovely, peaceful gardens, complete with a panoramic terrace, provide a magnificent **view**★ of Mount Etna and the sea. Here also is the statue of **Acis and Galatea**.

Terme di Santa Venera

Open Mon–Fri 9am–1pm, 1.30pm– 5.30pm by appointment (at least two days in advance). Closed Sat, Sun and holidays. ☎€2. ☎095 60 12 50. www. terme.acireale.gte.it.
To the south of the town, entrance off S 114. The neo-Classical baths complex dates back to 1873. Acireale quickly became a renowned spa town, whose visitors included Wagner and the royal family. The baths of Santa Caterina, which opened in 1987, are known for their radioactive, sulphurous water with traces of sodium bromide. Their source-spring lies about 3km/2mi inland, south

of Acireale, in the district of Reitana. There, the remains of the **Roman Baths of Santa Venera al Pozzo** have been discovered: including two barrel-vaulted rooms, presumably a **tepidarium** and **caldarium**.

Excursions

Grotta del Presepe di Santa Maria della Neve

From S 114 to Messina, turn right at the traffic lights by the Villa Belvedere towards Santa Maria la Scala.
The church of Santa Maria della Neve is on your left.
The Grotto of the Crib, adjacent to the church, is a winding lava ravine, a refuge for bandits and fishermen until the 18C. In 1752, the first nativity scene featured 32 life-size figures with wax faces, dressed in sumptuous clothes (most especially the Magi). Group visits only in summer, winter visits on request. ☎095 60 56 33.

▸ *Follow the same road as far as the coast.*

Santa Maria della Scala

This picturesque village, which grew up around the 17C parish church, has an attractive little harbour.

▸ *Return to S 114 and continue towards Catania, take the left fork for Capo Mulinit. About 100m/330ft along this road lies the Museo dei Pupi dell'Opra (Via Nazionale per Catania, 193–195).*

Driving Tour

Other Aci in the Area

Approximately 15km/9mi.

Aci Catena

Aci Catena, along with Aci San Filippo, is almost an extension of Acireale. The little town, which owes its name to the cult of the *Madonna della Catena* (Madonna of the Chain), centres on the charming square, Piano Umberto.

Giovanni Verga

The little harbour of Aci Trezza, bathed in sunshine and dotted with multicoloured boats hauled up onto the beach, seems inhabited by the ghosts of fictitious characters created by the Italian author Verga. How easy to imagine Maruzzi and the other members of the Malavoglia family waiting here anxiously on the shore, ceaselessly searching the horizon, alas in vain, for the Provvidenza with its cargo of lupins. How appropriate, therefore, that Aci Trezza should have been used by Luchino Visconti in 1948 to shoot his film *La Terra Trema (The Ground Trembles)*, based as it was on Verga's novel I Malavoglia. An organisation based in Aci Trezza organises tours to the **Parco Letterario Giovanni Verga** (a route that links places mentioned in the works of Verga, which winds between Catania, Aci Castello and Aci Trezza), as well as boat trips entitled *"In the footsteps of the Provvidenza"*.

Aci San Filippo

At the heart of the hamlet stands the church, ornamented with an 18C façade and a campanile with a lava base.

▷ *From Aci San Filippo return to S 114 and continue towards Catania.*

Aci Trezza

This small fishing town is dominated, on the seaward side, by the **Rocks of the Cyclops**★ (Faraglioni dei Ciclopi). The treacherous, jagged black lava rises from crystal-clear waters. The Odyssey relates that these were the rocks hurled by Polyphemus against Ulysses. Next to these rocks sits the **island of Lachea**, now a biology research station run by the University of Catania.

▷ *Continue along S 114.*

Aci Castello

This seaside village is on a stretch of coastline dotted with lemon trees (hence the area's other nickname **Riviera dei Limoni**), agaves and palms.

Castle★

The Norman fortress, built of black lava, stands on a rocky spur. This place has been fortified since Roman times, when it accommodated the Rocca Saturnia (Saturnia Fortress). Under the Bourbons (1787), the castle was a prison.

From the top there is a marvellous **view**★ of the **Faraglioni dei Ciclopi** and the island of **Lachea**. The castle houses a small museum. ◐*Open Jun–Sept 9am–1pm, 4pm–8pm; Oct–Apr 9am–1.30pm, 3pm–5pm;* ✆€1.50; ☎095 73 71 506.

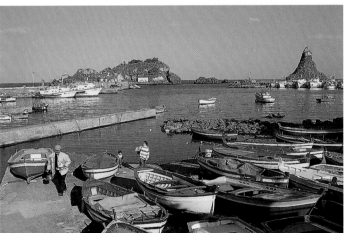

Harbour, Aci Trezza

B. Kaufmann/MICHELIN

AGRIGENTO ★★★

POPULATION: 58 853

Although Agrigento is best known for its archaeological site, it is also worth exploring the historic city centre, which has a wealth of impressive buildings and monuments. Almond trees surround this town and bloom in January and February, when locals celebrate the Sagra del Mandorlo in Fiore (Almond Blossom Festival). Sunset is the best time to approach Agrigento, as the last rays illuminate the pastel houses and the Temple of Heracles.

- **Information:** Via Cesare Battisti 15; ☎0922 20 454. Viale della Vittoria 255; ☎0922 40 13 52; www.agrigentoweb.it.
- **Orient Yourself:** The archaeological site is situated in the lower part of Agrigento, facing the sea, while the modern urban centre is perched on the slope.
- **Parking:** The archaeological area has two car parks: one in the temple area, the other near the archaeological museum. In the city centre, visitors can park in Piazza Vittorio Emanuele, east of the old town, which is crossed by a busy shopping street, Via Atenea.
- **Don't Miss:** The temple and garden of Kolymbetra at the site; the sarcophagus of Hippolytus and Phaedra in San Nicola Church; the Ephebus of Arrgriento in the museum; sweets from the abbey of San Spirito, the church of Santa Maria dei Greci.
- **Organising Your Time:** Because of the hot summers, and the many steps in the historical centre, visit in early morning or late afternoon, when the warm tufa stone takes on an attractive golden hue.
- **Also See:** CALTANISSETTA; GELA; LAMPEDUSA; SCIACCA.

A Bit of History

Story of Akragas – The **site**★★ has been inhabited since prehistoric times, but was not a proper town until 580BC, when settlers arrived from Rhodes and Crete. Under the tyrant **Phalaris** (570–554 BC), the city was fortified and organised politically. The ancients believed he tortured his enemies by roasting them alive inside a hollow bronze bull. Hated by his people, Phalaris was publicly stoned to death.

The city reached its golden age under the tyrant **Theron** (488–472 BC), who, among other things, forbade human sacrifices. Economic stability was matched with political strength: the Temple of Zeus was built, literature and the performing arts flourished.

The philosopher Empedocles (c. 492–432 BC) advocated a moderate form of democracy, which lasted for some time. In 406 BC, Akragas suffered a crushing defeat at the hands of the Carthaginians, who all but destroyed it. **Timoleon**, a mercenary general from Corinth, rebuilt with improved urban planning (visible still in the ruins of the Greco-Roman quarter). In 210 BC, Romans besieged and conquered the city, changing its name to Agrigentum.

Vicissitudes of Girgenti – With the fall of the Roman Empire, the city passed first to the Byzantines, then into Arab hands (9C). They built a new centre higher up (at the heart of what is now the modern town), calling it **Girgenti**, which became the capital of the Berber kingdom.

Normans conquered it in 1087, prompting a new phase of prosperity and power, which helped repel the frequent Saracen attacks.

After a turbulent period, when the population gradually declined, Girgenti enjoyed a change in fortune, most notably in the 18C when the centre was shifted from Via Duomo to Via Atenea. In 1860, the inhabitants, dissatisfied like the rest of the island with Bourbon misrule, enthusiastically supported Garibaldi's mission.

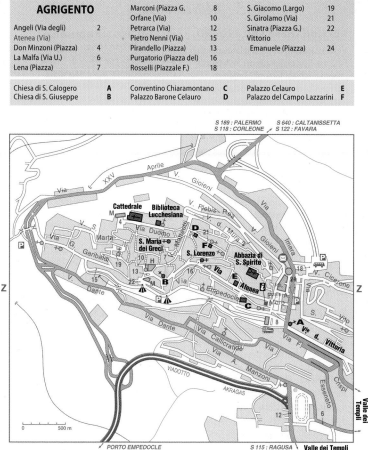

During the Second World War, Agrigento suffered a number of air raids.

Two famous sons – Agrigento has nurtured famous personalities, both in antiquity and in more recent times. Among the most renowned are the philosopher **Empedocles** (5C BC), who leapt into Etna's crater to prove his divine powers (supposedly the volcano spit back his shoes, turned to bronze).

In the 20C, **Luigi Pirandello**, the playwright and novelist, was born in the small village of Caos.

Enthusiasts should visit the **Biblioteca Luigi Pirandello** at 120 Via Regione Sicilia, which also contains a vast selection of works by other Sicilian authors.

La Valle Dei Templi★★★ (Valley of the Temples)

Tour: half a day. Archaeological site: Open 8.30am–dusk (the site often stays open until 11pm in summer). Museo Archeologico: Open 9am–7pm; closed Mon, and the afternoon of Sun and public hols. Antiquaria: Open 9am–1pm; closed Mon, and the afternoon of Sun and public hols. €6 archaeological site; €10 combined ticket with the Museo Archeologico and Antiquaria. ☎0922 62 16 11 or 0922 62 16 620.

The monuments are grouped in two areas: the first (the lower agora, to the south) includes the temples, the Giardino della Kolymbetra, the antiquaria and the palaeo-Christian necropolises;

Address Book

GETTING THERE AND AROUND

Visitors arriving by air will land at either Falcone-Borsellino airport in Palermo (approximately 150km/93mi from Agrigento) or at Fontanarossa airport in Catania (approximately 160km/100mi). Bus services operate between Agrigento and the other main cities in Sicily, as well as to Porto Empedocle (the port for ferries to Lampedusa); the bus terminal is situated in Piazza Rosselli. For train enthusiasts, the only comfortable option is the Palermo-Agrigento service (approx. 2hr). Agrigento Centrale railway station (not to be confused with Agrigento Bassa) is in Piazza Marconi. This square is also the departure point for shuttle buses to the archaeological area and the beaches in San Leone.

For coin ranges, see the Legend on the cover flap.

WHERE TO STAY

Alternative accommodation options to Agrigento include San Leone, a seaside resort 7km/4mi from the city with a wide choice of hotels and restaurants, and Villaggio Mosè, 4km/2.5mi east of the Valley of the Temples, on S 115.

Camping Nettuno – *Via Lacco Ameno 3, San Leone, 7km/4mi S of Agrigento.* ☎0922 41 62 68. www.geocities. com/campingnettuno. After a day in the Valley of the Temples, this campsite is an inexpensive, but pleasant, outdoor option.

Hotel Akragas – *Viale Emporium 16/18, San Leone, 4km/2.5mi S of Agrigento.* ☎0922 41 40 82. www.hotel akragas.net. 15 rooms. ⌐. This family-run hotel offers simple, well-appointed rooms and a renowned restaurant serving traditional Sicilian cuisine.

Fattoria Mosè – *Via Pascal 4, Villaggio Mos, 4km/2.5mi SE of Agrigento on S 115.* ☎0922 60 61 115. www.fattoria mose.com. Closed Nov–Feb. 24 rooms. Not far from the sea and the Valley of the Temples, this farm has a number of comfortable houses for rent, all equipped with a kitchen area and an outdoor sitting area. There is a room in the restored olive mill available for business visitors.

Oasi 2000 Bed & Breakfast – *Via Atenea 45 (first floor), Agrigento.* ☎0922 27 645. Fax 178 22 61 714. oasi2000ag@libero.it. 5 rooms. ⌐. This comfortable family guesthouse in the city centre has five attractive bedrooms decorated with antique furniture and parquet floors.

Hotel Villa Athena – *Via Passeggiata 33, Agrigento.* ☎0922 59 62 88. www.athenahotels.com. 40 rooms. ⌐. *Restaurant* ⌐. This restored 18C villa is surrounded by a delightful garden of citrus trees. The hotel has spacious, comfortable rooms, a terrace and a view of the Temple of Concord.

WHERE TO EAT

Kókalos – *Via Cavaleri Magazzeni 3, Agrigento (Valle dei Templi).* ☎0922 60 64 27. www.ristorante-kokalos.com. *Booking recommended.* This rustic restaurant, ideally placed for the archaeological site, serves pizzas and typical regional dishes. Good wine list.

Leon d'Oro – *Via Emporium 102, San Leone, 7km/4mi S of Agrigento.* ☎0922 41 44 00. Closed Mon. Situated in the seaside resort of San Leone, this renowned family-run restaurant also has an excellent wine list, as one owner is a professional sommelier. Local dishes and fresh fish are served in two warmly decorated rooms.

Trattoria dei Templi – *Via Panoramica dei Templi 15, Agrigento.* ☎0922 40 31 10. Closed Sun (Jul–Aug), Fri (Sept–Jun) and 10–20 Jan. After the site, why not stop in this friendly trattoria where traditional Sicilian fish dishes are served in rustic surroundings?

Kalo's – *Piazza San Calogero, Agrigento.* ☎0922 26 389. Closed Sun and at lunchtime Nov–Jan. This simple, well-kept restaurant is not far from the station. Mainly meat and fish.

LOCAL SPECIALITIES

The Benedictine nuns of the **Abbazia di Santo Spirito**, in Via S. Spirito *(see Walking Tour)*, make exquisite almond sweetmeats and the famous *cuscusu* – a semolina pudding, sweetened with chocolate and pistachio nuts (available by advance order only).

SHOWS

Stoai – *Via Cavaleri Magazzeni 1, Valle dei Templi. ☎0922 60 66 23. www.lestoai.it*. The atmosphere of the former covered market survives in this multimedia environment, which hosts the artisan's market, as well as a theatre show (by reservation only).

FESTIVALS

Sagra del Mandorlo in Fiore – This almond blossom festival is the highlight of the year in Agrigento. It takes place during the first ten days

of February, at the same time as the International Folklore Festival.

Festa di San Calogero – The Feast of San Calogero is celebrated from the first to the second Sunday in July.

Festa degli Archi di Pasqua (*Festival of the Easter Arches*). If you can take the Driving Tour to Monti Sicani over the Easter period, make sure you stop at **San Biagio Platani**, where this festival is celebrated. The inhabitants of the town, divided into two brotherhoods, erect spectacular reed arches decorated with citrus fruit, dates and various types of bread, which are then exhibited along Corso Umberto I.

---

the second (the upper agora, to the north) comprises the archaeological museum, the Chiesa di San Nicola, the Oratorio di Falaride and the Greco-Roman quarter. *The description below starts with the Temple of Zeus. However, visitors with plenty of time should begin at the Antiquarium di Villa Aurea, which provides a comprehensive introduction to the site.*

▶ *To walk from one area to the other, visitors can either follow the busy main road or a quieter route within the park.*
🅿 *Car parks are located near the Temple of Zeus and the archaeological museum. Ticket offices stand at both entrances.*

Stretched along the ridge – inappropriately called the "valley" – and nestling to its south are the 5C BC temples. Burnt by the Carthaginians in 406 BC, the buildings were restored by the Romans (1C BC) in their original Doric style. Their subsequent disrepair is due to either to seismic activity or destructive Christians, egged on by the Emperor of the Eastern Empire, Theodosius (4C). The only one intact is the Temple of Concord, which, in the 6C, was converted into a church. During the Middle Ages, masons removed stones to use for other buildings. In particular, the Temple of Zeus, known locally as the Giant's Quarry, provided material for the church of San

Nicola and the 18C part of the jetty at Porto Empedocle.

All the buildings face east, respecting the Classical criterion (both Greek and Roman) that the rising sun illuminate the deity's statue. Built of limestone tufa, the temples provide a particularly impressive sight at dawn, and even more so at sunset, when they blush a warm gold.

Sacrificial Altar

Just beyond the entrance, on the right, are the remains of an enormous altar. As many as 100 oxen could be sacrificed here at one time. The Italian word *ecatombe*, which today means "disaster", comes from the Greek "100 (*hecatòn*) oxen (*bôus*)".

Tempio di Zeus Olimpico (Giove)★

Razed to the ground, the Temple of Zeus (Jupiter) was re-erected following the victory over the Carthaginians at Himera (in about 480 BC). One of the largest temples built in ancient times, it stood 113m/371ft long by 36m/118ft wide, and may never have been completed. The entablature was supported by half-columns 20m/66ft high, which probably alternated with giant male caryatids (atlantes or **telamons**); an example hulks in the local archaeological museum *(see below)*. A reproduction stands in the middle of the temple, giving some idea of the vast scale. Some

The temple of the Dioscuri

B. Kaufmann/MICHELIN

blocks still bear the marks of lifting: deep U-shaped incisions through which a crane's rope was threaded.

Tempio di Castore e Polluce o dei Dioscuri★★

The Temple of Castor and Pollux (or of the Dioscuri) is the veritable symbol of Agrigento. Built during the last decades of the 5C BC, it is dedicated to the twins born to Leda and Zeus while transformed into a swan.

Four columns and part of the entablature are all that remain of the temple, which was reconstructed in the 19C.

Under one edge of the cornice is a rosette, one of the typical decorative motifs used.

On the right are the remains of what was probably a sanctuary to the chthonic deities: Persephone (Proserpina), queen of the underworld, and her mother, Demeter (Ceres), the goddess of corn and fertility and patroness of agriculture. On the site are a **square altar**, probably used for sacrificing piglets,

Sicilian Gardens

Here the term "garden" means a citrus grove, rather than flower-beds and ornamental plants.

and another, **round one**, with a sacred well in the centre.

In the distance, last in the imaginary line, is the **Temple of Hephaistus** (Vulcan), of which little remains.

According to legend, the god of fire and the arts had a forge under Etna where he fashioned thunderbolts for Zeus, assisted by the Cyclops.

Giardino della Kolymbetra★

Open Jul–Sept 10am–7pm; Apr–Jun 10am–6pm; rest of the year 10am–5pm. Closed Mon, 7–31 Jan. €2. 335 12 29 042 (mobile phone).

This 5-ha/12-acre "basin," dug by Carthaginian prisoners and used as a fish-breeding pond, grew into a fertile grove of fruit and citrus trees. After years of neglect, the Kolymbetra – now restored and managed by the Italian Foundation for the Environment (Fondo per l'Ambiente Italiano) – is planted with olives, prickly pear, poplar, willow, mulberry, orange, lemon and mandarin trees. A pleasant area for a stroll.

▶ *Retrace your steps, leave the fenced area and follow Via dei Templi, on the other side of the road, on the right.*

Tempio di Eracle (Ercole)★★

Conforming to the Archaic Doric style, the Temple of Heracles (Hercules) is the earliest of the group.

The remains reveal how elegant this structure must have been. Today, a line of eight tapering columns stand re-erected.

South of the temple can be seen the mistakenly named **Tomba di Terone** *(also visible from the Caltagirone road)*. The monument was not the tomb of the tyrant Theron; in fact, it honours Roman soldiers killed during the Second Punic War. Made of tufa, it is slightly pyramidal and probably once had a pointed roof. The high base supports a second order with false doors and Ionic columns at the corners.

Continuing along the path, observe the cartwheel **ruts**, eroded deep into the mud by water.

Antiquarium multimediale della Valle dei Templi (Villa Aurea)

This multimedia museum inhabits the former residence of Sir Alexander Hardcastle, a passionate patron of archaeology, who financed the re-erection of the columns of the Temple of Heracles. The museum greatly enhances any visit to the Valley of the Temples.

Necropoli paleocristiana

The palaeo-Christian necropolis is beneath the road, dug into the bed rock, not far from the ancient city walls. The tombs include loculi (cells or chambers for corpse or urn) and arcosolia (arched cavities like niches), as were often found in catacombs.

Before the Temple of Concord there is another group of tombs on the right.

Tempio della Concordia★★★

The Temple of Concord is one of the best-preserved ancient temples, providing a glimpse of the elegance and majestic symmetry of these buildings. The reason it has survived intact is due to its transformation into a church in the 6C AD.

Inside the colonnade, the original arches through the cella walls of the classical temple can still be made out.

Scholars date the structure to around 430BC, but don't know what god it honored (the name "Concord" comes from a Latin inscription found in the vicinity). The temple shows the architectural refinement known as "optical correction". The columns taper, curve and slant, tricking the eye; an observer at a certain distance sees a perfectly straight image.

Antiquarium di Agrigento Paleocristiana e Bizantina (Casa Pace)

Turn back through the town, stopping perhaps to consult the various information boards: one in particular explains how the Temple of Concord was transformed into a basilica.

Antiquarium Iconografico della Collina dei Templi (Casa Barbadoro)

⊶ Closed for restoration at the time of going to press. ☎0922 62 11 or 0922 62 16 620.

In this modern, but sympathetically designed, building is a series of drawings, engravings and prints of the Valley of the Temples as seen by travellers undertaking the Grand Tour.

Tempio di Hera Lacinia (Giunone)★★

Atop the hill, the Temple of Hera Lacinia (Juno) honored the protectress of matrimony and childbirth. The name "Lacinia" derives from an erroneous association with the sanctuary of the

Tempio della Concordia

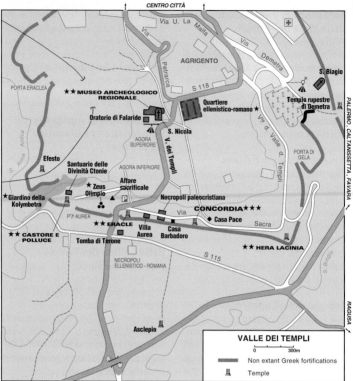

CENTRO CITTÀ

VALLE DEI TEMPLI

0   300m

Non extant Greek fortifications

Temple

same name on the Lacinian promontory near Crotone.

The temple preserves its colonnade (though not in perfect condition), which was partially re-erected in the early 1900s. Built about the mid-5C BC, it was set ablaze by the Carthaginians in 406 BC (scorch marks are still visible on the walls of the *cella*). To the east is the altar of the temple while, at the back of the building (beside the steps), there is a cistern.

▸ *From the Antiquarium di Casa Pace, a small road leads up the Collina di San Nicola, crossing fields of prickly pear, pistachio and olive trees.*
As you approach the hilltop, continue straight towards a group of ruins, passing under a bridge.
The path leads to the Greco-Roman Quarter (entry ticket required).

Greco-Roman Quarter★

This extensive complex contains the vestiges of houses with fragments of ancient pavements bearing geometric or figurative motifs *(protected by roofing and plexiglass)*. The streets follow the rules of the Greek town planner Hippodamus of Miletus: broad parallel avenues *(decumani)* bisected at right angles by secondary roads *(cardini)*.

Chiesa di San Nicola

🕐*Open 10am–12.30pm.* 💶*Donations welcome.* ☎*0922 59 64 80.*
Built of tufa, the Church of St Nicholas was erected in the 13C by Cistercian monks in a transitional Romanesque to Gothic style. They took the stone blocks from the Giant's Quarry, as the ruined Temple of Zeus was known. The façade is dominated by two imposing reinforcing buttresses (added in the 16C), which flank a beautiful pointed-arched doorway.
The interior is enclosed within a single barrel-vaulted nave. Four chapels open off the south side. The second contains the famous 3C **sarcophagus of Hippolytus and Phaedra**★ (Goethe was

particularly smitten with it). Inspired by Greek prototypes, all four sides are sculpted in high relief. The compositions are animated by clean flowing lines and the figures are endowed with delicate features that are set in gentle expressions. The subject is the tragic story of Phaedra's unrequited love for her stepson Hippolytus, who was banished and killed by crazed horses, thanks to the false accusation that he had tried to seduce her.

Above the altar is a fine 15C wooden crucifix, nicknamed *il Signore della Nave* (Lord of the Ship). This crucifix inspired Pirandello's short story of the same name, included in his anthology *Novelle per un Anno*.

From the terrace before the church, there is a beautiful **view**⋆ over the Valley of the Temples.

Oratorio di Falaride

According to legend, the oratory occupies the site of the palace built by the tyrant Phalaris, hence its name. The present monument was probably a small Greco-Roman temple, converted in Norman times.

Next to the oratory are the remains of an Ekklesiasterion, a small amphitheatre used for political meetings (from the Greek *ekklesia* – meeting), identified as an ancient agora (market place or place of assembly).

Museo Archeologico Regionale★★

Partially housed in the old monastery of San Nicola, the museum contains finds from the province of Agrigento. *Panels provide information on the most important exhibits.*

Pre-Greek conquest – Among the prize exhibits is a fine two-handled cup with a very tall base, decorated with geometric patterns; its shape may stem from the custom of eating seated on the ground with the cup at chest level. Others of note include a small, elegant Mycenaean amphora, the mould of a **patera** with six animals (oxen) in relief, and two signet rings, again bearing animals. The most interesting, meanwhile, is a **dinos** (sacrificial vase) depicting the triskelos (literally "three legs"), the symbol of Sicily.

Colonisation – The superb collection of **Attic vases**⋆ *(Room 3, exhibited in two parallel corridors)* consists mainly of black-figure and red-figure ware, including the *cratere di Dionisio* (or cup of Bacchus): the god of wine, dressed in flowing robes, holds a sprig of ivy in his hand, and has a leopard-skin draped over his arm. Among the other vessels, look for a *krater* with a white background, with a bold depiction of the proud figure of Perseus on the point of liberating Andromeda from her chains.

This section also contains a large number of votive statues, theatrical masks, moulds and other terracotta figures found during the excavations of the temples. A lower level of this section is filled by the massive figure of **Atlas**⋆ from the Temple of Zeus, the only one to survive of the 38 male caryatids that once adorned the building. On the left, in a case, are the heads of another three such powerful figures, one of which has well-preserved facial features.

The **Ephebus of Agrigento**⋆⋆ *(Room 10)* consists of a marble statue of a young man (5C BC), found in a cistern near the Temple of Demeter, which was transferred during the Norman period to the Church of San Biagio *(see below)*. Archaeologists believe it depicts a local Olympic victor.

The Ephebus of Agrigento

B. Kaufmann/MICHELIN

Telamons and Atlantes (Or Atlas Figures)

These imposing giants from Agrigento, more often referred to as atlantes, are sometimes called Telamons (*Telamone* in Italian) after the Latin word derived by the Romans from the Greek, *Telamo(n)* which indicated their function: to carry or bear the structure. Their supporting role is accentuated by their position, with arms bent back to balance the weight upon their shoulders. The more common term alludes to the mythological figure Atlas, the giant and leader of the Titans who struggled against the gods of Olympus and was condemned by Zeus to support the weight of the sky on his head. When the earth was discovered to be spherical, he was often shown bearing the terrestrial globe on his shoulders.

Other archaeological finds – Artefacts retrieved from various other sites in the province include sarcophagi, prehistoric remains and the magnificent krater from **Gela**★★ (Room 15), attributed to the Painter of the Niobids. The upper half depicts a centauromachia (battle between Centaurs and Lapiths), while the lower section shows scenes from battles between the Greeks and the Amazons.

Visitors may wish to finish their tour of Ancient Agrigento with a visit to the Chiesa di San Biagio and the Tempio di Asclepio, both some distance from the other ancient monuments.

Chiesa di San Biagio

P *There is space to park in front of the cemetery. The church is on the left, reached by a path.*
The 13C Norman church stands on the remains of a **Greek temple** dedicated to Demeter. Just below is another more rudimentary **temple** to her (the inaccessible *Tempio Rupestre di Demetra*), which bears witness to the popularity of the goddess in ancient Sicily.

Tempio di Asclepio (Esculapio)

Just beyond the Tomb of Theron, on the road to Caltanissetta. Look out for a sign (although obscured) on the right.
The ruins of this 5C BC temple sprawl in the middle of the countryside. It was dedicated to Asclepius (Aesculapius), the Greek god of medicine.
The interior, it is thought, harboured a beautiful statue of the god Apollo by the Greek sculptor Myron.

Walking Tour

The broad **Viale della Vittoria**, shaded by trees, provides beautiful views of the Valley of the Temples and leads to a square in front of the station. On the right stands the 16C **Church of San Calogero**, dedicated to a saint who is particularly venerated in this area. The façade has a fine doorway with a pointed arch.
A little farther on is Piazza Aldo Moro, where the lovely **Via Atenea** begins. Along this thoroughfare are to be found: on the right **Palazzo Celauro** (best admired from the street of the same name) where Goethe stayed when on his Grand Tour and, on the left, the Franciscan Church of the Immacolata (Blessed Virgin), altered in the 18C.
To the right of the church, beyond the gate, can be seen the façade of the 14C **Conventino Chiaramontano**, so called because of the style of the portal between the two-light windows.
Return to Via Atenea and continue to Piazza del Purgatorio, which is overlooked by the splendid façade of 18C **San Lorenzo**★ (⊙*Open Mon–Sat 10am –1pm, 5pm–8pm; Sun and public hols by appointment; ⊛€1.50; ☎0922 40 18 10; www.sanlore.it*) its golden ochre tufa contrasting dramatically with the whiteness of the doorway, ornamented with twisted columns.
The **interior** contains stuccoes by Serpotta and a painting by Guido Reni.
Nearby, level with Via Bac Bac, stands San Giuseppe, a **church** dedicated to St Joseph.

In Piazza Pirandello is the town hall, formerly a Dominican monastery (17C) and an adjacent church with a fine Baroque façade overlooking an elegant flight of steps. Set back, on the left side of the church, is the bell tower.

▸ *From Via Atenea, take Via Porcello, follow the steps up Salita di Santo Spirito.*

Abbazia di Santo Spirito★

🕐*Open Mon–Fri 8am–1pm, 3pm–6pm; Sat 9am–1pm.* 🕐*Closed Sun.* ⊚⊚*€2.50.* ☎*0922 59 03 71.*

The church and its dependent convent date from the 13C. Sadly, the state of the buildings is gradually deteriorating. The church façade has a fine Gothic doorway with a rose window above.

The Baroque interior consists of a single nave. On the walls are four high **reliefs** attributed to Giacomo Serpotta: *The Nativity* and *The Adoration of the Magi* on the right, *The Flight into Egypt* and *The Presentation of Jesus at the Temple* on the left.

To the right of the façade is a doorway into the **cloisters**, leading under two of the great buttresses supporting the church.

The beautiful **entrance**★ to the chapterhouse of the monastery consists of an elegant doorway through a pointed arch, flanked by highly decorative Arabo-Norman two-light windows.

The monastery is also home to the **Museo di Santo Spirito**, housing a collection of everyday objects relating to rural life, and works by Francesco Lojacono from Palermo (1841–1915).

Via San Girolamo

This street is lined with elegant *palazzi*: of note is the façade of the 19C **Palazzo del Campo-Lazzarini** at no 14 (opposite Santa Maria del Soccorso) and that of the 18C **Palazzo Barone Celauro** at no 86.

Biblioteca Lucchesiana

🕐*Open Fri, 9am–1.30pm by appointment.* ☎*0922 22 217.*

The library, founded in 1765 by Bishop Lucchesi Palli, contains more than 45 000

TAKING A BREAK

Before leaving the Abbazia di Santo Spirito, make sure you try the excellent confectionery made by the nuns here *(ring the bell to the right of the cloisters; also see Address Book).*

ancient books and manuscripts. The central hall, dominated by a statue of the bishop, is lined with beautiful wooden shelving. Books on profane subjects are kept to the left of the statue, while religious texts are on the right.

This division is echoed by the two sculpted wooden figures behind the statue: on the left is a woman meditating, on the right, a woman holding a mirror, symbolising the search for truth in the inner self.

Cathedral

The side of the cathedral facing onto Via del Duomo still bears traces of the Noman original (notably the 11C windows). The main church was rebuilt in the 13C–14C, and remodelled in the 17C; it was then restored after a landslide in 1966.

A broad double stairway leads up to the main door, marked by a tympanum, flanked by pairs of pilasters.

On the right stands the unfinished bell tower (1470), which on the south side is articulated with four blind arches in the shape of an inverted ship's keel, and a series of pointed arches above.

Inside★, the nave has a beautiful **wooden ceiling**★ with tie-beams decorated with figures of the saints, painted in the 16C.

The section beyond the triumphal arch is coffered (18C); the great two-headed eagle in the centre is the symbol of the Royal House of Aragon.

The Baroque exuberance of the choir, with its angels and golden garlands, contrasts dramatically with the sobriety of the nave.

Santa Maria dei Greci

The 14C church, dedicated to St Mary of the Greeks, was built on the foundations of a temple to Athena (5C BC).

M. Guillot/MICHELIN

Pirandello's Pine before the storm in 1997

Driving Tours

From Pirandello to Minos along stunning beaches

▶ *90km/56mi round trip from Agrigento – allow one day. From Agrigento, head 6km/4mi W on the Porto Empedocle road (S 115). Turn left after Morandi viaduct.*

Il Caos

In the Villaseta district. 🚶⏰*Open 9am–1pm, 4pm–7pm.* 🎫*€2.* ☎*0922 51 18 26. www.regione.sicilia.it.*

This village, on the outskirts of Agrigento, was the birthplace of **Luigi Pirandello**, whose **house** stands alone in the middle of the countryside.

The first floor is open to the public. A short film documents his most salient moments, including the Nobel

---

Ritorno (La Via)

A solitary house set amid my native countryside: up here, on this plateau of blue clay, to which the submissive bitter African sea sends a fervour of foam, I see you always, from afar, if I think of that moment in which my life opened up minutely to the immense, vain world: this, this, I say, was where I set out along the path of life.

Luigi Pirandello in *Zampogna*, Rome 1901

Prize award ceremony and the author's funeral. Pirandello last visited the house in 1934, but only from a distance, as it had been sold. The rooms contain written and illustrative material pertaining to the writer and Marta Abba, the actress to whom he became very close in the latter period of his life. On display also is a 5C BC Greek krater, which once held his ashes. A small path to the right of the house leads to a **pine tree** (damaged in the storm of November 1997). At its foot are buried Pirandello's ashes. Beyond, lies the sea.

▶ *Continue along S 115 to Sciacca. From Porto Empedocle, follow signs to Madison Hotel.*

Scala dei Turchi★★

▶ *Turn left into the Discesa Maiata (the Scala dei Turchi is signposted), which leads along the beach to the rock (10min on foot). Alternatively, follow the road for a further 300m/330yd until you come to an electricity transformer hut on the left. A small path to the left of the hut leads down to the sea. Arriving from Realmonte, the rock is visible once you have passed the Madison Hotel.*

This impressive white rock (made of marl, a mixture of clay and limestone, smoothed by erosion) has gently sloping steps *(scala)* and is a popular place for sunbathing. Narrow, winding, wave-like formations scar the other side.

The name refers to the local legend that Saracen pirates once scaled the rock, after anchoring in the bay.

▶ *Continue along S 115 as far as Siculiana Marina, then follow the road to Montallegro for approximately 2km/1.2mi.*

Riserva Naturale Orientata di Torre Salsa

The reserve is closed Nov–Feb.
🔭*For guided tours, contact the WWF* ☎*0922 81 82 20. www.ftorresalsa.it.*

This World Wildlife Fund reserve covers a wide variety of habitats (dunes, cliffs,

M. Magni/MICHELIN

Spectacular Scala dei Turchi

marshland and Mediterranean maquis) inhabited by porcupines, crows, birds of prey, waders and sea birds. The reserve also has a delightful beach of fine sand, made all the more spectacular by the intense blue of the Mediterranean.

Eraclea Minoa

The remains of the Greek city Heraclea Minoa enjoy a magnificent **setting**★★ on the edge of a lonely hill with a fine view of the sea, at the beginning of Capo Bianco. At its feet, the coast opens into a broad bay, lined with a long **beach**★★ of the whitest sand (*from S 115 follow signs to Montallegro-Bovo Marina and Montallegro Marina; a small road on the right leads to the sea*). Before the excavations, on the right, are white "dunes" of marl sculpted by the wind.

The city was probably founded in the 6C BC by Greek colonists from Selinus (now Selinunte).

Sometime in the 3C BC, the town passed into the hands of the Romans; thereafter it embarked upon a series of wars and was gradually abandoned. By the 1C BC it was deserted.

Serious excavation began here in 1950, uncovering the **remains** of rough brick houses, some still containing fragments of mosaic and, most excitingly, a **theatre** built of a very friable stone. This, inevitably, is not well preserved.

A small **antiquarium** (⊙*open 9am–1hr before dusk;* ⬤€2; ☎*0922 84 60 05*) collects together various objects found for the most part in the necropoli.

Toward Monti Sicani

175km/109mi round trip from Agrigento – allow one day.

This tour wends its way up through **magnificent scenery**★★ from the Agrigento coast to the slopes of Monti Sicani, offering delightful views of hills, woods, mountains and meadows. In the spring, the area is an explosion of red poppies and yellow broom.

▶ *Take S 189 to Palermo and exit at Aragona.*

Vulcanelli di Macalube★

At the entrance to Aragona, follow signs to Macalube. Turn left at the roundabout, then left again at the next junction and follow the tarmacked road that ends in a clearing. 🅿 *Park here and then follow the middle path that heads up to the top of a small hill (on the right). For information, contact Legambiente-Uffici della Riserva, Via Salvatore La Rosa 53, Aragona.* ☎*0922 69 92 10. www.macalife.it.*

This hill is dotted with a myriad mud cones, known as *vulcanelli* (literally, small volcanoes), because of the cold, whiteish slime that they expel. This process is a sedimentary, gaseous volcanic phenomenon.

▶ *Return to Aragona and take the road to Sant'Angelo Muxaro.*

Sant'Angelo Muxaro

Sant'Angelo clings to a craggy mountainside. Some believe this was the capital of the ancient kingdom of Cocalus, that mythical king who received Daedalus on his flight from Minos. The 18C front elevation of the Chiesa Matrice is divided into three sections by strongly accented pilaster strips framing the three doorways, and rectangular windows above.

Grotta del Principe

By the side of the road, just outside town. Leave the car on the verge so that it does not obstruct the traffic. Although the distance is short, the going is rough. The Prince's Cavern is a proto-historic tomb (9C BC) consisting of two circular chambers. The first, the larger of the two with a domed ceiling, comprised the atrium for the actual burial chamber.

▷ *Take the road to Alessandria della Rocca.*

The road winds its way uphill through delightful rolling countryside.

Bivona

At the centre of Bivona stands a lovely **Arabo-Norman archway**, all that remains of the former Chiesa Matrice. A little farther on, **Palazzo Marchese Greco** preserves its fine, though damaged, façade ornamented with wrought-iron balconies and elegant Baroque stonework.

▷ *From Bivona take the road to Santo Stefano Quisquina, then continue to Castronuovo di Sicilia.*

The road *(attractive, but in poor condition)* skirting the **Lago di Fanaco** passes through beautiful **mountain scenery**★ of meadows, thick woodland, flowers and rocky outcrops.

Castronuovo di Sicilia

The little piazza is overlooked by the Chiesa Madre della Santissima Trinita (1404) and its fine bell tower. From the centre, an attractive paved street leads up to the Chiesa di San Vitale and the castle ruins. A **viewpoint**★

at the top of the village offers a magnificent panorama of the surrounding countryside.

▷ *From here, the tour heads along S 189 to Agrigento before turning left to Mussomeli. Alternatively, visitors can follow the 'Hills Around Naro' tour described below.*

Mussomeli

Mussomeli crams onto the bare hillside, in a place high enough to enjoy a scenic position.

The houses jostle one another, apparently cowering below the watchful gaze of the **Castello Manfredonico**, which perches on its lonely rock outcrop. The centre is marked by the tall front elevation of the Chiesa Matrice (altered in the 17C), which peeps over the rooftops. Some way below stands the 16C white limestone Santuario della Madonna dei Miracoli with its attractively arranged doorway set between two spiral columns and broken pediment.

▷ *Head back along S 189 to Agrigento. At Comitini, you can either carry on to Agrigento or join the tour described below.*

The Hills Around Naro

90km/56mi, starting and finishing in Agrigento – allow one day. Take S 640, then turn right towards Favara.

Favara

A town of Arab origin, Favara reached its apogee under the powerful Chiaramonte family (13C–14C), who oversaw the building of the massive castle. Piazza dei Vespri is dominated by the imposing façade of the 18C Chiesa Madre, its tall dome resting gently on a ring of arches.

▷ *Return to S 640. After 7km/4mi, turn left to Racalmuto.*

Racalmuto

Racalmuto was once an important centre for sulphur extraction. In the centre stand the remains of the **Chiaramonte castle**, marked by two large towers.

▷ *Follow signs to Canicattì.*
  Just before the village, take the
  turn-off to the right to Naro.

Naro★

The many Baroque buildings testify to the prosperous history of the town, which was probably founded by the Greeks.

The historical centre – Via Dante, the town's central axis, is lined with elegant Baroque buildings. At the western end, Piazza Padre Favara is overlooked by the Chiesa di San Agostino and its adjacent Augustinian monastery, a powerful influence in the 18C. On the left-hand side of Via Dante stands the **Chiesa di San Nicolò di Bari**, preceded by a flight of steps and with a fine early Sicilian Baroque façade (17C–18C).

Another church, the **Chiesa Madre**, is immediately visible on the left. This church, built in the 17C by the Jesuits, became the town's main one when the Duomo began to crumble (1867).

At the same time, many of the furnishings and works of art were transferred here from the abandoned cathedral, including the carved wooden sacristy furniture.

A right turn after the Chiesa Madre leads into the attractive **Piazza Garibaldi**, enclosed on all sides by gracious buildings. Among the most notable of these is the **façade★** of the **Chiesa di San Francesco**, founded in the 13C, but restored four centuries later. The adjacent former Franciscan monastery has attractive cloisters overlooked by municipal offices.

▷ *From Piazza Garibaldi take Corso*
  Vittorio Emanuele and turn left
  into Via Cannizzaro.

The **Chiesa di Santa Caterina**, which was built in 1366 and altered in the 18C, has subsequently been restored to its original appearance. A bold linearity pervades the interior arrangement, relieved in part by a highly decorative Chiaramonte archway.

Returning to Via Dante, pass the elaborate Baroque façade of the **Chiesa del Santissimo Salvatore** on your left.

Leonardo Sciascia

Racalmuto is known as the birthplace of **Leonardo Sciascia (1921–89)**, the Sicilian writer and astute commentator who spent much of his life here and who is buried in the town's small cemetery. Much of Sciascia's inspiration came from this harsh, dry and sun-scorched landscape, and from the toil of living and working here. In works such as *The Day of the Owl* and *To Each His Own*, the writer constantly explores themes that have their roots in Sicily and Sicilian identity. A **literary park** in Racalmuto (☾*See RACALMUTO*) is dedicated to the writer.

▷ *From Piazza Cavour turn*
  left into Via Archeologica.

The **Norman Duomo** (12C–13C) stands on the right-hand side of the street. All that remains is a ruin, although fragments of the Chiaramonte doorway still grace the front. The **castle** silhouette can be seen farther along the street.

▷ *Retrace your steps to Piazza*
  Cavour and walk to the end of
  Viale Umberto I.

Santuario di San Calogero

Piazza Roma. From this church there are lovely **views** over the Valle del Paradiso. Inside, against the wall of the stair-

Doorway of the Chiesa del Santissimo Salvatore

Minos, Daedalus and Cocalus

In mythology, **Minos** reigned over Crete and the islands of the Aegean. Poseidon sent him a magnificent bull for sacrifice, but the king substituted another animal. Angered, the Sea God inspired Queen Pasiphaë with an unnatural passion for the bull. She asked Daedelus to construct her a hollow cow, then hid inside, and coupled with the Cretan Bull.

Subsequently, she bore the Minotaur. Daedelus built the Labyrinth to conceal and contain the monstrous creature with a human body and a bull's head. On discovering Daedelus' treachery, Minos imprisoned him and his son Icarus in the Labyrinth. Pasiphaë released them and Daedelus made wings to escape to Sicily (Icarus flew too close to the sun, melted his wings, and plummeted to his death).

Every ninth year, Minos sent the beast seven Athenian youths and seven maidens. When the third tribute was due, Theseus volunteered himself. Minos' daughter Ariadne fell in love with the hero. She gave him a sword to kill the monster and a ball of silk to retrace his path through the impenetrable maze.

Daedelus is said to have taken refuge with Cocalus, the king of Sicily, who killed Minos to protect his guest. In fact, the kingdom of Cocalus was situated on the banks of the River Platani, with a capital called Camico, now identified by some as being the modern Sant'Angelo Muxaro, by others as Caltabellotta.

way down to the crypt, is a remarkable **Wounded Christ**★ in pink marble, its dark veins suggestive of blood. The crypt is built around the cave where San Calogero, the patron saint of Naro, supposedly lived. The black statue is processed on 18 June, his feast day.

Catacombe paleocristiane

In the contrada Canale, south of the town. This catacomb comprises passageways lined with niches and shallow hollows containing grave goods. The main underground chamber or hypogeum is the Grotta delle Meraviglie (Cave of Marvels), which extends 20m/66ft.

Castellazzo di Camastra

2km/1.2mi S along the road to Palma. This small ruined castle perches on an isolated rocky outcrop. According to local folklore, this is where Cocalus lived while ruling over his mythical kingdom, hence the popular epithet **Reggia di Cocalo**.

▷ *Follow S 410 as far as Palma di Montechiaro.*

Palma di Montechiaro

The town was founded in 1637 by the twins Carlo and Giulio Tomasi, one of whose descendants, **Giuseppe Tomasi di Lampedusa** (1896–1957) wrote the novel *The Leopard*, published posthu-

mously in 1958. Luchino Visconti based his film on this book, which charts the decline of an aristocratic family from Palermo between 1860 and 1910.

Standing atop a long flight of steps, the **Chiesa Madre** has a Baroque façade, built in white limestone, framed by two bell towers with onion domes.

Set to one side of the great stairway up to the church is **Palazzo Tomasi**. The building is often referred to as the "palace of the holy duke," in reference to Giulio Tomasi's nickname. The duke had a strong religious vocation and converted the palace into a monastery.

Castello di Montechiaro

8km/5mi SW along the road to Marina di Palma, then right towards Capreria. High upon a sea crag (magnificent **view**★ of the coast), the 14C castle has a bleak, proud quality about it. In 1863, its name was incorporated into that of the nearby town of Palma.

▷ *Head back to S 115 to return to Agrigento.*

TAKING A BREAK

Make sure that you try the delicious confectionery made by the nuns of the Benedictine convent next to Palazzo Tomasi.

VILLE DI BAGHERIA

POPULATION: 54 164

Bagheria is renowned for its numerous Baroque villas built from the 17C onwards by wealthy Palermitan aristocrats as their summer residences. Unfortunately, they are all closed to the public, except the famous Villa Palagonia.

- **Information:** Villa Palagonia ☎091 93 20 88. www.villapalagonia.it.
- ▶ **Orient Yourself:** Bagheria, situated approximately 15km/9mi from Palermo, can be reached along the A 19 motorway (Bagheria exit), along S 113 or by train (the railway station is located close to Villa Cattolica). For easy access to the monuments, enter along S 113, which leads into Corso Butera and then the main street, Corso Umberto.
- **Don't Miss:** The "monsters" of Villa Palagonia that scandalised Goethe.
- **Also See:** CEFALÙ; MONREALE; PALERMO; SOLUNTO; TERMINI IMERESE.

Sights

Villa Palagonìa★

The entrance is at the rear, which faces onto Piazza Garibaldi, at the end of the main street, Corso Umberto I. ◯*Open Apr–Oct 9am–1pm, 4pm–7pm; Nov–Mar 9am–1pm, 3.30pm–5.30pm.* ⊜€4. ☎091 93 20 88. www.villapalagonia.it.

This most celebrated of Bagheria villas, built in 1715, is a building of unusual shape: the façade is concave, while the rear is convex. The house was constructed by Prince Gravina's father, but it was the prince's idea to add the exuberant **sculptural decoration**★. Goethe considered the building a monstrosity. But this arrangement, consisting of 60 crude, often monstrous tufa statues, has provoked various esoteric interpretations. They include mythological figures, musicians, soldiers, dragons and grotesque beasts creating a surreal atmosphere. Curiously, the statues are facing the villa and not, as was usual, the outside world to keep evil spirits at bay. The result is an insight into the mind of the prince, who aimed to surprise, if not frighten, his guests. This eccentricity runs through the villa's rooms. The great oval entrance hall, painted with trompe l'oeil frescoes illustrating four of the twelve Labours of Heracles, leads into the distorted Hall of Mirrors.

Villa Butera

This stands at the southern end of Corso Butera. The villa was built in the second half of the 17C by Prince Branciforti di Raccuia. Although now in a sad state of repair, it preserves an imposing tufa doorway to the piano nobile.

Villa Cattolica

Via Consolare 9 (S 113). From the motorway, cross Bagheria following the signs to Aspra. ♿◯*Open Tue–Sun 9.30am–6pm* ◯*Closed Mon, national hols.* ⊜€4.50. ☎091 94 39 02.

This massive, square building, built in 1736 by Giuseppe Bonanni Filangeri, Prince of Cattolica, houses the **Civica Galleria d'Arte Moderna e Contemporanea Renato Guttuso**. This modern art gallery exhibits works by native son Guttoso and other artists close to him. The villa gardens harbour the **tomb** of the painter, designed by his friend, Giacomo Manzù.

Sculptural decoration, Villa Palagonìa

M. Magni/MICHELIN

CALTAGIRONE ★

POPULATION: 39 166

Ceramics pervade this city – not only in shops and homes, but as embellishments on bridges, balustrades, facades and balconies. The art is nearly as old as the ancient city itself.

- ☐ **Information:** Palazzo Libertini ☎0933 53 809 and Via Duomo 7 ☎0933 34 191; www.comune.caltagirone.ct.it.
- ▶ **Orient Yourself:** Most of the major monuments are in the upper town, best explored on foot.
- ☐ **Parking:** Lots stand along the ringroads to the east and west of the town.
- ☺ **Don't Miss:** La Villa Comunale, la Scala di S. Maria del Monte, the Gli Iblei Driving Tour or the sweets made in Militello.
- ☐ **Organising Your Time:** Plan a half day. The Luminaria festival is 24–25 July.
- **Kids Especially for Kids:** Buscemi's eight-fold museum of the mountain people.
- ☺ **Also See:** CATANIA; COMISO; GELA; PIAZZA ARMERINA; RAGUSA; VILLA IMPERIALE DEL CASALE.

A Bit of History

City of Earthenware Potteries

The reason behind it all rests in the area's inexhaustible deposits of clay. The manufacture of terracotta potteries evolved into tableware, then the industry took over the town. Local shapes gave way to Greek influences (as trade increased), production improved, becoming more efficient and more precise with the introduction of the wheel (by the Cretans in about 1000 BC). The critical turning point, however, was the 9C arrival of the Arabs, who brought Eastern designs and, more importantly, glazing techniques, which rendered objects impermeable to water. The dominant colours were blue, green and yellow. The significance of the Arab contribution is honoured in the town's name which, according to the most intriguing hypothesis, might be derived from the Moorish word for *castle* or *fortress of vases*.

With Spanish domination, tastes and demands changed. The painted decoration was predominantly monochrome (blue or brown) and comprised organic designs or the coats of arms of some noble family or religious order. The town enjoyed a period of notable prosperity as a result of other industries, such as honey production.

The artisans organised themselves into confraternities, which, in turn, helped to build workshops in the town's southern quarter. In addition to ceramic table and kitchenwares, Caltagirone established a reputation for making tiles and ornamental plaques for domes, floors, church and *palazzo* facades. Of all the great artists to work here during the 16C and 17C, the Gagini brothers and Natale Bonajuti are perhaps the most renowned. With the arrival of the 19C there began a period of decline, arrested in part by the production of figurines often used in Nativity scenes. In the second half of the century, this art form reached new heights of excellence in the hands of such experts as Bongiovanni and Vaccaro.

The art of clay-working – The techniques used here have remained unchanged for centuries. The ductile clay mixture is worked wet, by hand, using a potter's wheel. Otherwise it is turned into a liquid and cast in a mould. The object is then left and placed in an oven to dry at a very high temperature. After firing, it is ready for use.

Decorating techniques are many, including carving, graffito design or moulding made with stones, shells or other objects on the unbaked article. Colour may be applied at various stages for different effects (before or after firing, following a second firing, or cold). The simplest product is the porous reddish terracotta, typical of objects made in antiquity. The

Address Book

For coin ranges, see the Legend on the cover flap.

WHERE TO STAY

CALTAGIRONE

Albergo La Scala 2 – *Piazza Umberto I 1, Caltagirone.* ☎*0933 51 552. 6 rooms.* The owners of the La Scala restaurant have simple, but well-kept rooms, without private bathrooms.

Pomara – *Via Vittorio Veneto 84, San Michele di Ganzaria, 14km/9mi NW of Caltagirone on S 124.* ☎*0933 97 69 76. www.hotelpomara.com. 40 rooms.* A rural retreat within easy distance of a town, between Caltagirone and Piazza Armerina. The family-run hotel has a swimming pool, spacious rooms and classical decor.

WHERE TO EAT

CALTAGIRONE

La Scala – *Scala di S. Maria del Monte 8, Caltagirone.* ☎*0933 57 781.* This atmospheric restaurant is housed in a beautiful 18C building, just to the right of the famous steps to Santa Maria del Monte.

CHIARAMONTE GULFI

Majore – *Via Martiri Ungheresi 12, Chiaramonte Gulfi.* ☎*0932 92 80 19. Closed Mon and Jul.* This hundred-year-old restaurant only serves dishes made from pork, as a sign on the wall testifies (*"qui si magnifica il porco"*). The food here is beautifully presented and reasonably priced.

MILITELLO IN VAL DI CATANIA

U' Trappitu – *Via Principe Branciforte 125, Militello in Val di Catania.* ☎*095 81 14 47. Closed Mon.* This trattoria is in an old oil mill (*"trappitu"*) dating from 1927. Carefully restored, it retains many original features such as oil presses and millstones.

PALAZZOLO ACREIDE

Valentino – *Via Galeno, on the corner of Ronco Pisacane 125, Palazzolo Acreide.* ☎*0931 88 18 40.* This pleasant restaurant is situated in the centre of an attractive small town, whose origins date back to the Ancient Greeks. Both the atmosphere and the food served here are simple in style.

SHOPPING

Glazed earthenware is on sale in countless shops in the town centre and on either side of the **Scala di Santa Maria del Monte**. In general, the further up the steps you climb, the lower the prices. For an overview, head for the Mostra Mercato Permanente in Via Vittorio Emanuele, which displays work by the town's craftsmen. *b0933 56 444.*

The seasonal specialities in the sweets line associated with Militello range from the cassatelline – made with ground almonds, chocolate and cinnamon; the mastrazzuoli – Christmas tidbits made with almonds, cinnamon and vermouth; to the mostarda – concocted from semolina or wine must, boiled with prickly-pear extract (available around the second or third Sunday in October, for the Sagra della Mostarda).

FESTIVALS

La Luminaria – Festa di San Giacomo – This festival in honour of San Giacomo, the town's patron saint, is the highlight of the summer in Caltagirone. On the 24 and 25 July, the steps of Santa Maria del Monte are decorated with small oil lamps, known as *coppi*.

Festa del Presepe – The art of the *figurinai* – sculptors who created small terracotta statues for Nativity scenes (*presepe* in Italian) – flourished in Caltagirone until the end of the 18C. This old tradition is celebrated from November to January, with exhibitions of different cribs held throughout the town.

first *maiolica* (terracotta decorated with enamel) appeared in the 16C. Porcelain is produced from a different type of clay, a white paste known as kaolin, usually with a glazed finish.

Walking Tour

Via Roma, Caltagirone's main street, bisects the town, cutting towards the famous steps to Santa Maria del Monte,

Bandstand, Villa Comunale

M. Magni/MICHELIN

and continuing on up to the church entrance. Its way is lined with some of the town's most interesting buildings, many with maiolica decoration. Near its start, on the left, begins the elegant balustraded enclosure of the Villa Comunale (a public garden) and the Teatrino (housing the Ceramics Museum).

Villa Comunale★

This wonderful garden was designed in the late 19C by GB Basile, who modelled it on classic English landscapes. The edge along Via Roma is marked by an ornamental balustrade topped with vases bearing disturbingly devilish faces. These alternate with bright green pine cones and maiolica lamp standards. Shaded pathways open into secluded spaces, ornamented by ceramic sculptures, figures and fountains. A delightful **bandstand** is decorated with Moorish elements and glazed panels of maiolica.

Beyond the Museo della Ceramica on the right-hand side of Via Roma is the splendid 18C balcony-cum-terrace of **Casa Ventimiglia**. Beyond the **Tondo Vecchio**, the curved stone and brick building, sits the remarkable façade (on the right) of **San Francesco d'Assisi;** this overlooks the maiolica bridge, also named after St Francis, which carries the road into the very heart of the town. Beyond the little Church of **Sant'Agata**, the seat of the ceramicists' confraternity, stands an austere prison block that was built under Bourbon rule.

Carcere Borbonico

The prison, an imposing square sandstone building, has been greatly improved by recent restoration. It was designed in the late 18C by the Sicilian architect Natale Bonajuto. Now it houses the town's small municipal museum.

Piazza Umberto I

The most prominent building to face onto the square is the **Duomo di San Giuliano**, a great Baroque edifice that has been subjected to much remodelling. The most drastic change replaced the whole front in the early 1900s. It comes into view from the steps below Santa Maria del Monte, at the foot of which, on the left, stands **Palazzo Senatorio** with the courtyard, **Corte Capitaniale**, behind. This is a fine example of early civic architecture (1601) by one of the Gaginis.

To the right, a stairway leads up to the **Chiesa del Gesù**, which is home to a Deposition by Filippo Paladini (third chapel on the left). Behind it nestles the **Chiesa di Santa Chiara** with its elegant façade attributed to **Rosario Gagliardi** (18C) and, beyond again, the early 20C Officina Elettrica, the façade of which was designed by **Ernesto Basile**.

▶ *Return to Piazza Umberto I.*

Scala di Santa Maria del Monte★

This long flight of steps acts as a conjunction between the old town (at the top), which accommodated the seat of religious authority in the 17C, and the new town, where the municipal administrative offices were located. On either side of this axis lie the old quarters of San Giorgio and San Giacomo; both conceal some fine buildings among their narrow streets (⊙ *See below*). The 142 lava stair treads are complemented by highly decorative multicoloured maiolica tile uprights, echoing Moorish, Norman, Spanish, Baroque and contemporary influence. Once a year, the stairway is brought to life by a multitude of small flickering coloured candles. This fabulous spectacle takes place on the nights of San Giacomo, 24 and 25 July. Presiding atop the steps is **Santa**

Maria del Monte, formerly the town's main church and headquarters of the religious authorities. The altar is graced with the lovely Conadomini Madonna, a 13C painting on panel.

San Giorgio and San Giacomo quarters

Via L Sturzo, leading off to the right from the foot of the steps, has a number of fine buildings. These include **Palazzo della Magnolia** (no 74), which is ornamented with exuberant and elaborate terracotta decoration by Enrico Vella. Just beyond the *palazzo* are two 19C churches: **San Domenico** and **Santissimo Salvatore**. The latter contains the mausoleum of the politician Don Luigi Sturzo, and a *Madonna and Child* by **Antonello Gagini**. At the far end of Via Sturzo stands the **Chiesa di San Giorgio** (11C–13C); home to the panel painting of the **Mystery of the Trinity**★, attributed to the Flemish artist Rogier van der Weyden.

The logical extension of Via Sturzo, on the opposite side of the steps, is Via Vittorio Emanuele. This leads to the **Basilica di San Giacomo**, dedicated to the town's patron saint, housing a Gagini silver casket containing the relics of the saint.

On The Edge Of Town

A stroll through the typical back streets of the old quarters on the periphery of town reveals various unexpected surprises, such as the splendid neo-Gothic façade of the **Chiesa di San Pietro**, complete with maiolica decoration.

Chiesa dei Cappuccini

Open 9am–noon, 3.30pm–7pm. €1.50. 0933 21 753.

The Capuchin church on the eastern edge of the town contains a lovely altarpiece by Filippo Paladini, which depicts the Hodegetria Madonna (an icon representing the Virgin as a Guide or Instructress pointing to the Way of Redemption, said to have been painted by St Luke). On the nave's left side is a Deposition by Fra' Semplice da Verona, which has an interesting play of perspective. Additional paintings are displayed in the local art gallery next to the church, with works drawn from the 16C to the present day. There is access from here to the crypt, where an unusual arrangement of figures re-enact different scenes from the life of Christ.

Visit

Museo della Ceramica

Via Giardino Pubblico.

Open 9am–6.30pm. €3. 0933 58 418. www.regione.sicilia.it/beniculturali.

The **Teatrino**, an unusual 18C building decorated with maiolica tiles, houses this interesting museum. The impor-

Scala di Santa Maria del Monte

G. Bludzin/MICHELIN

tance of moulded clay is exemplified by an elegant 5C BC **krater**★ showing a potter at his wheel, working as he is watched by a young apprentice.

The 17C is particularly well represented, with *albarello* jars (apothecaries' jars) – painted in shades of yellow, blue and green – and amphorae and vases.

Museo Civico
Via Roma 10.
🕐 *Open 9.30am–1.30pm, 4pm–7pm.*
🕐 *Closed Mon, Wed and Thu afternoons.*
💶 *€2.60.* ☎ *0933 31 590. www.comune. caltagirone.ct.it.*

The second floor displays a permanent exhibition of contemporary work in maiolica. One room displays the gilded wood and silver litter of San Giacomo (late 16C), which still featured in processions up until 1966: note the caryatids' delicate facial features.

The third room is devoted to the Vaccaro family: two generations of painters active during the 19C; Mario's *Little Girl Praying* is especially evocative.

The first floor holds the municipal art gallery containing works by Sicilian painters.

Driving Tours

Gli Iblei★

▶ *The round trip of approx 160km/100mi can be completed over two days, starting at Caltagirone and overnighting in Vizzini. From Caltagirone follow signs to Ragusa and Grammichele along S 124.*

The southeastern corner of Sicily is dominated by the Iblei mountains, which encircle and protect Ragusa. The little mountain villages have retained their rural aspect, living in close harmony with the fertile land that has sustained them for centuries.

▶ *Follow S 124 as far as a junction where both roads are signposted to Grammichele; take the left-hand fork.*

The road provides wonderful **views**★★ over the vast agricultural plain that is intensely cultivated with cereal crops. Beyond the hills which, according to Tomasi di Lampedusa, evoke *un mare bruscamente pietrificato* (a suddenly petrified sea), looms the dark majestic form of Mount Etna.

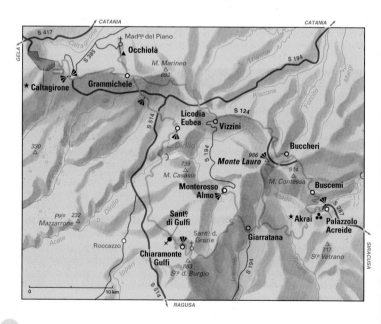

©Guido Alberto Rossi/Tips Images

Aerial view of Grammichele

Grammichele

The development of Grammichele can be traced back to 1693, when a terrible earthquake shattered the southeastern section of Sicily.

The new town was laid out according to a singular plan, centred around a hexagonal piazza and six radial axes passing through the centre of each side. A series of orthogonal streets were then arranged in concentric hexagons around the central space.

The buildings overlooking the piazza include the Chiesa Madre and the town hall; the latter, in turn, houses the municipal **museum** (first floor)(🕐*Open 9am–12.30pm, 4pm–7pm (Tue and Thu 3pm–6.30pm).* ✆€1.50. ☎0933 85 92 29).

Occhiolà

Ufficio Parco Archeologico Occhiolà, piazza Morello, Grammichele, ☎*0933 94 48 55.*

Occhiolà is situated about 3km/1.8mi from Grammichele along the road to Catania, near a road-maintenance building before a tight bend.

A stone on the left bearing an inscription marks the beginning of the road to the site where the old town stood, enjoying a **scenic position**.

▶ *From Grammichele, travel the road up to Licodia Eubea (11km/7mi) and enjoy a series of wonderful* **views**★★ *over the plain below.*

Licodia Eubea

This hamlet, occupying a panoramic situation at the head of the River Dirillo, was probably built upon the ancient ruins of Euboia, founded by the colonists of Leontinoi in about 7C BC. It comprises several 18C churches and **Palazzo Vassallo** *(Via Mugnos, at the end of Via Umberto, on the right)*, a formal Baroque building with a doorway flanked by columns and a balcony laden with masks and volutes. From the atmospheric ruins of the medieval castle a sweeping **view**★ extends over the valley.

▶ *Backtrack to the Lago di Licodia (or Dirillo) turn-off and head towards the lake.*

Follow the old road to Chiaramonte Gulfi for approximately 10km/6mi through a lovely stretch of **mountain scenery**★. A little farther on, the **Lago Dirillo** dam comes into view on the left.

▶ *Near a bend, just before a road-maintenance* casa cantoniera *(on the right), turn left (the road to the right leads to Vittoria and Chiaramonte Gulfi).*

Santuario di Gulfi

Before the 1693 earthquake, a village occupied this broad site, now home only to the sanctuary of Gulfi. The sanctuary was built in the 18C on the spot where it is said yoked oxen transporting a statue

The Iblei landscape, with its typical drystone walls

of the Madonna "emerged from the sea" knelt down. The story is illustrated inside by four painted medallions, which also relate how the statue of the *Salvatore* (Saviour) wound up in Chiaramonte.

▶ *Continue along the road for approximately 4km/2.5mi.*

Chiaramonte Gulfi

The Greek town of Akrillai, renamed "Gulfi" by the Arabs, was razed to the ground in 1296 and immediately rebuilt by Manfred Chiaramonte, after whom it was renamed. Although much of the fabric was destroyed by the 1693 earthquake, the hamlet preserves its medieval organisation. The *Arco dell'Annunziata*, an ancient gateway to the old town, is the only fragment to survive from the Chiaramonte era (14C). Among the principal Baroque buildings, look out for San Giovanni (at the top of the hill) and the **Chiesa Madre**. The main street, Corso Umberto I, is lined with 18C and 19C *palazzi*, At its western extremity, you'll find the Villa Comunale (town hall), from which a magnificent **view** opens out over the valley.

The 16C **Palazzo Montesano** on via Montesano (Open 10.30am–12.30pm, 3.30pm–6pm. ☎0932 71 12 18.) houses a museum showcasing ethnic instruments, art nouveau works (including those by Lalique and Basilie) and olive oil, one of the town's principal products.

In the higher part of town, the Santuario delle Grazie sits surrounded by pine trees

Drystone Walling

An ever-present reminder of human impact on the rural landscape are the ribbons of drystone walling that extend in all directions: small, low-lying yet resistant courses of stone, no more than a metre high, enclose the cultivated fields. Interestingly, the very nature of these walls reflects the geological formation of the Iblei. For, just as with the bed rock, the surface layer of limestone is impermeable: where this layer is damaged by erosion or fracture, water will penetrate through the underlying layers causing them to crumble and disintegrate into lumps; in the most extreme cases, this can produce whole canyons. The broken lumps of rock litter the ground, requiring farmers to remove them before they can sow their fields: the walls are conceived as a way of re-using the stones so laboriously gathered which, instead of being heaped in a pile, are employed as building materials. However, this is no haphazard pastime but a skilled art learned from master-craftsmen known in the vernacular as *mastri ri mura a siccu*. The walls segregate different land holdings and enable flocks to graze unsupervised; they also support terraced land.

(picnic facilities) and an all-encompassing **view**★ over Chiaramonte and Etna. Legend claims the local people offered up their prayers to the Madonna for salvation from the plague in 1576, whereupon a spring of clear water emerged here. The road to Monterosso Almo (*20km/12.5mi*) snakes its way among gentle slopes covered with cultivated fields enclosed by **drystone walls**, an ever-present feature of the Iblei landscape. These transfer geometric figures onto the green fields, endowing the scenery with a sense of order and distorted perspective.

Monterosso Almo

The Church of **San Giovanni** lends its name to the piazza here: together they provide a focal point for the upper part of this agricultural town. The front elevation of the church, attributed to **Vincenzo Sinatra**, rises through columns to culminate in a bell tower. In the lower neighbourhood stands a church to rival San Giovanni, this time honouring **Sant'Antonio** (also known as *Santuario di Maria Santissima Addolorata*). The same square is graced with the neo-Gothic **Chiesa Madre**, and the elegant Palazzo Zacco.

▶ *Follow S 194 for 7km/4mi.*

Giarratana

Three monuments constitute the artistic heritage of this hamlet: the late-Renaissance Chiesa Madre, and two Baroque churches dedicated to San Bartolomeo and Sant'Antonio Abate. An onion festival, the *Sagra della Cipolla*, is held every August in Giarratana.

▶ *From Giarratana, either continue to Palazzolo or shorten the tour by turning left to Buccheri and following the winding road that leads to the top of* **Monte Lauro**.

The road (*10km/6mi*) that wends its way up the mountain through intense patches of colour provided by red valerian (*Centranthus ruber*), dark green carobs and pines, provides glorious **views**★ over the high plateau.

▶ *To get to Palazzolo from Giarratana, follow the main road for 14km/9mi, then turn right towards the site of Ancient Akrai.*

Akrai★

 ⊙*Open 9am–until one hour before dusk.* ⊛€2. ☎0931 87 66 02.
Akrai was founded in 664 BC as a defensive outpost of Syracuse. At the top of the hill, where the acropolis once stood, is the orchestra from an ancient white stone theatre.
The **bouleuterion**, a stepped meeting-area, lies to the right. Near the gate is a section of the old *plateia* (main east-west road), paved with large slabs of lava stone.

The small theatre at Akrai

B. Kaufmann/MICHELIN

Christians converted two old Greek quarries next to the theatre into catacombs and troglodyte dwellings. Near the entrance to the **Intagliatella**, the narrower of the pair, on the right, there is a evocative low relief of a hero banqueting *(right)* and sacrificing *(left)*.

Excavation of the area along the fence has uncovered vestiges of a residential quarter and an ancient circular building, probably a temple, built in Roman times. Walk the track that skirts the archaeological site to enjoy a lovely **view**★ over the surrounding valley.

I Santoni

1km/0.6mi from the archaeological site.
Tucked in a small valley nearby, a dozen 3C BC rock-hewn figures testify to the existence in Sicily of a cult of Oriental origin.

The main sculpture represents the **goddess Cybele** (Demeter), seated between two lions, or standing surrounded by smaller figures. No II is one of the best-preserved and represents the Dioscuri – Castor and Pollux on horseback on either side. No VIII shows the goddess seated.

Palazzolo Acreide

Palazzolo was largely rebuilt in the 18C and has a superlative spread of Baroque buildings lining its main thoroughfares: Corso Vittorio Emanuele and Via Carlo Alberto, which intersect at Piazza del Popolo. The square is dominated by the majestic, elevated facade of **San Sebastiano**. At the western end of the *corso* stands the **Chiesa dell'Immacolata** with its convex frontage, in which is preserved a delicate *Madonna and Child* by **Francesco Laurana**. Via Carlo Alberto passes between a series of *palazzi* with wonderful Baroque details. One of the streets off to the right *(Via Machiavelli)* leads to the **Casa-Museo dell'etnologo Antonino Uccello** (🕐*Open 9am–1pm, 3.30pm–7pm;* ☎*0931 88 14 99)* a *palazzo* once owned by Baron Ferla and later turned into a house-museum by another owner, the ethnologist Antonio Uccello.

At the end of the street, turn right onto Piazza Umberto I where the Church of **San Paolo** is situated.

The striking frontage, possibly designed by **Vincenzo Sinatra**, rises through three tiers of rounded arches and Corinthian columns. The top storey comprises the bell tower.

Follow Via dell'Annunziata out of the piazza to the church of the same name; its facade, which remains incomplete, has an interesting **doorway**★ flanked by spiral columns.

Return along Via dell'Annunziata and turn left down Via Garibaldi to take a look at **Palazzo Iudica** (at nos 123–131) and its amazingly long balcony supported by brackets carved with monsters, fantastical figures, masks and other elements so typical of the Baroque period.

▸ *The road to Buscemi (9km/5.5mi) provides a succession of wonderful* **views**★.

Buscemi

This little farming hamlet accommodates an unusual and intriguingly interesting museum dedicated to rural craftsmanship: **I Luoghi del Lavoro Contadinoa**. The various venues, eight in all, are scattered throughout the town: each is dedicated to recapturing the life and work of the Iblei mountain people. These include the blacksmith's forge, the oil press (where some of the scenes of the film *La Lupa* by Gabriele Lavia were shot), a farmstead, the houses of a farm labourer *(lo Jurnataru)*, cobbler and carpenter, and a wine press.

Seeds and Diamonds

One of the most commonly recurring elements in the Iblei landscape is the **carob tree**, a large evergreen growing, often in isolation, in the middle of a field. The broad growth of characteristically shiny dark green leaves provides deep shade. Its beans, which can be used as a thickener or as an alternative to coffee when ground into powder, or as animal feed, once had a nobler use: the fact that their weight is always consistent, meant that they came to be used as units of measurement for precious stones; the term "carat" derives from the Arabic name for the carob, *Qirat*.

A room attached to this last venue contains a small film library. The tour finishes with the watermill (*Mulino ad acqua Santa Lucia*), situated in the valley of mills *(valle dei mulini)* at Palazzolo Acreide. The mill now houses a small museum, the **Museo della Maccina del Grano** (⏰*Open 9am–1pm; ⌖€5 for the "Luoghi del Lavoro Contadino", €3 for the mill and minibus there (reservation necessary);* ☎*0931 87 85 28; www.museobuscemi.org).*

A number of Baroque monuments line the streets, including the lovely façade of the Chiesa Madre, the curvilinear elevation of Sant'Antonio da Padova e San Sebastiano, as well as various other hidden corners of town, notably the farmers' quarter scattered with low stone houses. Immediately after rejoining the main road, glance up at the rock face below the town, to see the Siculi excavated tombs (12C–13C BC).

▷ *After 6km/4mi, the road reaches Buccheri.*

Buccheri

Perched at a height of 820m/2 689ft, this hamlet boasts a church dedicated to Mary Magdalen with a lovely façade (18C) articulated by two tiers of columns and pilasters. Another honours St Anthony Abbot with a front elevation that rises in one sweep to a tall tower, exaggerated by a long, steep staircase up to the door.

▷ *Continue to Vizzini.*

Vizzini

Vizzini was used by the novelist **Giovanni Verga** as a backdrop for several of his books, including *La Lupa (The She-Wolf)*, *La Cavalleria Rusticana* (on which Mascagni based his famous opera), and *The Story of Mastro Don Gesualdo.*
Vizzini has grown up around Piazza Umberto I, where the Palazzo Verga and the Palazzo Municipale are located. Alongside the town hall rises a flight of steps, the **Salita Marineo**, decorated with maiolica tiles featuring geometric and floral designs arranged around a central medallion painted with views of buildings in Vizzini. This scheme, com-

Vizzini: Ricotta Festival

G. Iacono/Lara Pessina/MICHELIN

pleted in 1996, echoes a similar stairway to Santa Maria del Monte at Caltagirone (⌖*See CALTAGIRONE).* The Chiesa Madre preserves a Norman-Gothic doorway *(right side)*, a lonely vestige of the original church that survived the 1693 earthquake.

The town's Baroque constructions include the beautiful frontage of **San Sebastiano**. The church of **Santa Maria di Gesù** contains a *Madonna and Child* by **Antonello Gagini**.

> From Vizzini, either take the old road to Caltagirone and Grammichele (S 214 for 30km/19mi), or follow the tour described below.

Beyond the Northern Slopes of the Iblei

Tour: 100km/62mi from Caltagirone or 75km/47mi from the end of the tour described above (Vizzini) – allow one day. See above for the Caltagirone-Grammichele section of the tour.

> After Grammichele, follow S 124 for approximately 10km/6mi as far as the turn-off to the left for Militello in Val di Catania (25km/15mi E of Grammichele).

Militello in Val di Catania

The Baroque town of Militello is largely indebted to Joan of Austria (1573–1630), Charles V's granddaughter, for its prosperity. When she married Francesco Branciforte, she brought a sophisticated culture and aesthetic sensibility here. Militello was transformed into an aristocratic court. As a result, the streets of the old town centre offer up a multitude of fine Baroque buildings.

Start at Piazza del Municipio, home to the **Monastero Benedettino** (1614–41), an imposing Benedictine monastery (now used as the town hall), which has a highly decorative frontage. The main **facade** of the **church** next door is ornamented with rusticated window surrounds, a common feature peculiar to the Militello style of Baroque. Inside, it contains Sebastiano Conca's painting of *The Last Communion of St Benedict* (third chapel on the left) and a fine set of carved wooden choir stalls depicting the Mysteries and scenes from the life of St Benedict (1734).

> Continue along Via Umberto, past the Palazzo Reforgiato, to Piazza V. Emanuele.

Museo di San Nicolò

Open summer Wed–Mon 9am–1pm, 5pm–8pm; Rest of the year 9am–1pm, 4pm–7pm. Closed Tue. €2.50. 095 81 12 51.

The museum is housed in the undercrofts of the Chiesa Madre, built in 1721. The objects are displayed in a fabulous **arrangement**★ so as to enhance their beauty and heighten their impact. The last rooms are devoted to pictures: an altarpiece *Annunciation* by Francesco Franzetto (1552), a strongly lit Caravaggesque *Attack on San Carlo Borromeo* by the Tuscan painter Filippo Paladini (1612), and a gentle treatment of the *Immacolata* by Vaccaro.

The Church of **Santa Maria alla Catena** on Piazza Vittorio Emanuele was rebuilt in 1652. Its fine **interior**★ is encrusted with lovely **stuccowork** by artists from Acireale; scenes from the Joyful Mysteries adorn the upper tier, while the lower tier harbours various Sicilian saints surrounded by cherubs, festoons and cornucopias. The overall effect is completed by an elegant coffered wooden ceiling that dates from 1661.

> Turn left onto Via Umberto. Beyond the attractive concave façade of the Chiesa del Santissimo Sacramento al Circolo, lies Piazza Maria Santissima della Stella.

Maria Santissima della Stella

This church, with its fine doorway and spiral columns, was erected between 1722 and 1741. Inside, it preserves a magnificent glazed terracotta **Nativity altarpiece**★ (1487) by the Florentine master **Andrea della Robbia**. The **Treasury** contains a fine late-15C altarpiece with scenes from the life of St Peter by the Maestro della Croce of Piazza Armerina, and the Portrait of Pietro Speciale, a shallow relief by **Francesco Laurana**.

Palazzo Majorana, one of the few buildings dating from the 16C, extends along the same side of the square beside the church. Note its heavily rusticated cornerstones bearing carved lions.

> At the far end of the palazzo, turn left, then immediately right for Santa Maria la Vetere up ahead.

Chiesa di Santa Maria la Vetere

Most of the church collapsed following the earthquake of 1693, leaving only the wall of the south aisle intact. Above the front's 16C porch sits a lunette enclosing shallow reliefs. The overall **impact**★ is heightened by the splendid position of the church, nestling in its green valley, right on the edge of town.

▶ *Pass back through the town gate and turn immediately left for the Chiesa dei Santissimi Angeli Custodi.*

The **Chiesa dei Santissimi Angeli Custodi** contains a wonderful maiolica **floor**★, laid with tiles from Caltagirone (1785). ☎095 65 53 29.

▶ *Return the way you have come and turn left so as to skirt around the ruins of the Branciforte castle (comprising of a round tower and sections of stone wall), pass through the town gate – Porta della Terra – and reach the piazza beyond.*

At the centre of what once constituted the castle courtyard sits a fountain: **Fontana della Ninfa Zizza** was built in 1607 to commemorate the construction of Militello's first aqueduct.

▶ *Continue on to Scordia (11km/7mi NE).*

Scordia

Scordia is built on a rectilinear town plan, arranged around the palazzo of the Branciforte family, who were the lords of the town during the 17C. The main square, Piazza Umberto, is enclosed by many noble *palazzi* and a church with a lofty front elevation. The 18C **Santa Maria Maggiore** has an interesting façade incorporating a belltower.

▶ *Continue on to Palagonia (12km/7.5mi NW).*

S 385 picks its way through rolling **landscape**★ past the endless lush groves of lemon and orange trees for which the area is famous, and the small rocky hills known as *Coste* to the south.

Palagonia

Siculi legend explains that their gods the **Palici**, were born from the bubbling sulphurous waters of the **Laghetto di Naftia**. Thus locals erected a temple to honour them close by on the shore. Nowadays, the lake is rather prosaically masked from view by natural gas pumping rigs. The name Palagonia is strongly associated with the area's production of superbly juicy blood oranges.

▶ *Follow S 385 from Palagonia towards Catania; take the right fork signposted for Contrada Croce. After 4.5km/3mi, as the road curves to the right, look out for a track on the left barricaded by a metal barrier.*

Eremo di Santa Febronia

A 15min walk up the track, the evocative little hermitage is named after Santa Febronia. It's known locally as *a' Santuzza*, because the saint's relics are brought here each year in a great procession from nearby Palagonia. The small retreat, carved out of the rock, is Byzantine in date (7C). Inside, the apse contains a fine, albeit slightly damaged, fresco of Christ flanked by the Madonna and an angel.

▶ *Take S 385 to Caltagirone. After 8km/5mi, turn left to Mineo.*

Mineo

The place where the writer Luigi Capuana (1839–1915) was born has been identified as the ancient town of Mene, founded by Ducetius, the king of the Siculi. The town's main gateway is the **Porta Adinolfo**, which dates from the 18C. Beside it sits the Jesuit College, and beyond this lies the shady main square and the **Chiesa del Collegio**.
At the top of the town, next to the Church of Santa Maria, lie the ruins of a castle.

▶ *Retrace your steps to S 385, from where the views on the return journey to Caltagirone (25km/15mi) are particularly impressive.*

CALTANISSETTA

POPULATION: 61 000

In the heart of the Sicily, between soft hills and valleys, stands this city on a plateau of 568m/1 863ft, which offers an immense panorama. This historic town once boomed with the sulphur industry, now eclipsed.

- **Information:** Viale Conte Testasecca 21. ☎0934 21 089. www.amicomune.it.
- ▶ **Orient Yourself:** Caltanissetta is a difficult town for motorists, as a result of poor signposts and frequent road works.
- **Parking:** Explore the narrow streets of the town on foot.
- **Don't Miss:** The historic town centre including the lovely cathedral.
- **Organising Your Time:** Several hours will be enough for this small town.
- **Especially for Kids:** The sea horse and monsters on the Fontana del Tritone.
- **Also See:** AGRIGENTO; ENNA; PIAZZA ARMERINA; VILLA IMPERIALE DEL CASALE.

A Bit of History

Caltanissetta started out as a small Greek town, before succumbing to the same fate endured by the rest of Sicily and succumbing to one domination after another. It enjoyed its greatest prosperity in the early 1900s, when the extraction of local sulphur deposits was at its height. Caltanissetta was the leading sulphur exporter, at one point responsible for four-fifths of the world's production. Fierce competition from America, however, soon forced all the sulphur mines in the area to close.

Walking Tour

The historic town centre clusters around **Piazza Garibaldi** at the junction of the town's two main thoroughfares, Corso Umberto and Corso Vittorio Emanuele. Grouped around the square are the town hall (in the former Carmelite convent), the cathedral, the **Chiesa di San Sebastiano** with its baroque frontage which, like Sant'Agata (at the end of Corso Umberto) and Santa Croce (at the end of Corso Vittorio Emanuele), is painted dark red, in marked contrast with the natural stone colour of the other architecture. In the centre sits the **Fontana del Tritone** (1956) by the local sculptor Michele Tripisciano, based on a 19C model. The bronze sculpture consists of a seahorse being held back by a triton, while under threat from two winged monsters. Beyond the town hall in Salita Matteotti, stands the 17C **Palazzo Moncada**, which although never completed, has a façade with intriguing carved corbels of human and animal figures.

Cathedral

The cathedral was erected in the late 16C. Its interior frescoes are by the Flemish painter Guglielmo Borremans (1720). The alternation of painted panels and stucco decoration combine to produce a dramatic impact. The 17C wooden figure of St Michael (1615) is by the Sicilian sculptor Stefano Li Volsi *(chapel to the right of the choir)*. The gilded wooden organ in the choir was built in 1601.

Sant'Agata al Collegio

The 17C church has a composite front elevation fashioned in natural stone, red plasterwork and marble (doorway). Inside, it displays elaborate inlaid polychrome marble decoration, and a beautiful marble altarpiece carved by **Ignazio Marabitti**.

To the east of Piazza Garibaldi stretches the *Quartiere degli Angeli*, which preserves its medieval layout. At its centre stands **San Domenico** (⟲open daily, 4pm–5.30pm; ☎0934 25 104) a church with a fine Baroque façade enthusiastically decorated by undulating panels. The painting inside of the *Madonna of the Rosary* is by Filippo Paladini.

Address Book

For coin ranges, see the Legend on the cover flap.

WHERE TO STAY

Hotel Plaza – *Via Gaetani 5, Caltanissetta. ☎0934 58 38 77. Fax 0934 58 38 77. www.hotelplazacaltanissetta. it. 33 rooms. ☞.* After a day's sightseeing in Caltanissetta and its surrounding area, enjoy a relaxing stay in this central hotel. Spacious and comfortable, with modern furnishings.

WHERE TO EAT

Legumerie le Fontanelle – *Via Pietro Leone 45, contrada Fontanelle, 2km/1.2mi NW of Caltanissetta. ☎934 59 24 37.* This small restaurant is part of a farm riding centre. With its rural-style decor, rustic feel and simple local dishes featuring meat and vegetables, it has the atmosphere of a typical trattoria.

Duomo – *Piazza Garibaldi 3, Caltanissetta. ☎0934 58 23 31. Closed Sun, Mon lunchtime and in Aug. Booking recommended.* This simply decorated restaurant situated near the Duomo offers a wide selection of quintessential local dishes. The menu has been created with an emphasis on delicious and innovative regional cuisine.

FESTIVALS

The town is notorious for its extravagant celebrations of **Holy Week:** when, on the Thursday evening, groups of 19C statues arranged in tableaux representing scenes from the Mysteries of the Passion (the Deposition composition is particularly powerful), made by Neapolitan craftsmen, are processed through the streets. On Good Friday, the statue of a Black Christ is carried in procession across town. Outside Holy Week, these figures are kept in the **Chiesa di Pio X** in Via Colajanni.

Visit

Museo Archeologico

☛*At the time of publication, the museum was moving to Abbazia di S. Spirito, in via S. Spirito 57.* ☎0934 50 42 40.

The museum highlights the indigenous civilisation and Hellenistic influences. Finds from the Greek necropolis at **Gibil-Gabib** include an unusual small clay cask from 4C BC, later used as a funerary urn. Other exhibits, such as a *strigil* (the tool used by athletes to scrape away oil, sweat and dead skin as illustrated in a mosaic at Villa Imperiale del Casale), were discovered at the Greek necropolis at **Vassallaggi**.

Among the objects found in the Greek settlement of Sabucina, note the small-scale terracotta model of a **temple**★; the votive object dating from the 6C BC; two large basins (one on a high pedestal) for holding drink or oil; and the *krater* bearing a painting of the god Hephaestus, seated in his forge, hammering out hot iron (6C–5C BC).

Finds from the site at **Dessueri**, include a fine set of "teapots" used for boiling opium (indigenous culture, 13C BC) and an Attic *kylix* showing Heracles armed with a club.

Excursions

Abbazia di Santo Spirito

3km/2mi NE on S 122 to Enna.
The abbey – founded by Roger I (11C) and consecrated in 1153 – is Romanesque in style. It has three typically Norman apses ornamented by decorative blind arcading. Inside, it has a lovely 15C wooden crucifix and an early Romanesque baptismal font, decorated with stylised palmettes.

Archaeological Sites Around Caltanissetta

The archaeological excavations undertaken (and still in progress) in the Province of Caltanissetta are open to the public, even though they can be extremely difficult to find and are rarely visited.

Sabucina

Signposted off the main Enna road, 12km/7mi E of Caltanissetta.
Here, traces of an early hut settlement (12C BC) have been brought to light by excavations, together with elements from the subsequent phase (7C BC) in the local civilisation. A section of wall dating from the 5C or 4C BC has also been found.

Vassallaggi

From Caltanissetta, take S 640 towards San Cataldo. Follow to the junction with Serradifalco signed to the left and San Cataldo to the right:
☺*The sign (pointing right) for the excavations is wrong; the correct direction is straight on. After a few metres, a small tarred road branches right, passing through a gate, which is usually open (information panel); follow the road until it degenerates into a dirt track (farm on the left). A green fence on the left delineates the excavated site.*
An ongoing dig has so far uncovered an ancient settlement, probably 5C Greek, spread out over five hills. The area includes a sacred precinct dedicated to gods of the underworld. This is surrounded by some 50 or so dependent buildings that were used by the officiators of the cult. Artefacts from the site have been moved to the Museo Archeologico in Caltanissetta. Finely painted urns and vases that were uncovered in its necropolis are now preserved in the museums at Gela and Agrigento.

Gibil-Gabel

6km/4mi S of Caltanissetta.
This preserves the ruins of a Sicani town and necropolis.

CAPO D'ORLANDO ☼

POPULATION: 12 871

As one of the more important seaside resorts on the northern coastline, this pleasant town offers beautiful pebbled and rocky beaches, along with the delightful Lido San Gregorio to the east.

- 🗎 **Information:** Via Volta 11. ☎0941 90 33 29. www.aastcapodorlando.it.
- ▶ **Orient Yourself:** Capo d'Orlando is a good base for trips to the Nebrodi, while little more than 60km/37mi separate it from Randazzo, on Mount Etna.
- ⊛ **Don't Miss:** In summer, daily excursions are organised to the Aeolian Islands.
- 🕐 **Organising Your Time:** Lounge on the beach for a day. In summer, good music abounds, especially during the International Blues Festival.
- ⚲ **Also See:** CEFALÙ; Isole EOLIE; ETNA; MADONIE E NEBRODI; MILAZZO; Golfo di PATTI.

Walking Tour

The centre of the town falls between Via Piave, which is lined by smart shops, and the promenade that parallels the beautiful beach.
At the promontory tip is a purpose-built **viewpoint**★ accessed up a flight of stairs. It overlooks the ruins of the castle of Orlando and the 17C **Santuario di Maria Santissima di Capo d'Orlando**, where pilgrims flock each year on the 22 October.

Driving Tours

Along the Coast from Capo d'Orlando to Capo Calavà

Approximately 20km/12.5mi along S 113 in the direction of Messina.

Following the coast beyond the cape towards San Gregorio, the road offers beautiful **views**★ of the blue sea and coast, dotted with rocks and small, characterful seaside resorts.

Terme di Bagnoli

🕐*Open Apr–Sept, 9am–7pm; rest of the year, 9am–2pm.* ☎*0941 95 54 01.*

On the outskirts of Capo d'Orlando at San Gregorio are the remains of a bathing complex attached to an Imperial-era Roman villa. They include the **frigidarium** (marked 1-2-3), the **tepidarium** (marked 4) and the **caldarium** (marked 5 and 6). In rooms 4, 5 and 6 are fragments of mosaics displaying geometric decoration.

Villa Piccolo di Calanovella

Marked by the 109km/68mi distance marker on S 113 between Messina and Palermo.

♿ 🕐 *Open daily, 9am–noon, and 4.30pm–6pm, Wed–Fri.* 🕐*Closed Sat in summer and national hols.* ☞*€3.* ☎*0941 95 70 29. www.fondazionepiccolo.it.*

In keeping with the wishes of the last members of the Piccolo family, a museum-foundation was set up in the late 19C villa, where they had lived since the 1930s. The Piccolos were an artistic family: in particular, Lucio (who died in 1969), an acclaimed poet, and Casimiro, an enthusiastic painter and photographer, and scholar of the occult. They were often visited by their cousin **Giuseppe di Lampedusa**, drawn by the limpid peace and quiet of the villa, who wrote a large part of his masterpiece *(The Leopard)* here. In the room he once used is one of his letters to the Piccolo family, as is the bed in which he slept. This is ornamented by a beautiful ivory and mother-of-pearl bedhead depicting the Baptism of John (made by Trapani craftsmen in the 17C).

Elsewhere in the villa a series of fantastical **watercolours**★ by Casimiro Piccolo line the walls. He enjoyed painting scenes from a fairy-tale world suffused

Il Gran Visir by Casimiro Piccolo

Fondazione "Famiglia Piccolo di Calanovella"

with light and populated with amiable gnomes, elves, fairies and butterflies. Before leaving, take a stroll under the pergolas in the villa gardens and seek out the **canine graveyard** for the family pets.

Brolo

A flourishing port until the late 17C and now a seaside resort, the town has a fine medieval castle (private) built by the Lancia family in the 15C.

▸ *Beyond Brolo, turn right at the next junction for Piràino.*

Piràino

Stretched strategically along the spine of a hill, Piraino retains much of its medieval form and is scattered with religious buildings. Its legendary origins (supposedly it was founded by the Cyclops Piracmon) are probably rooted in the discovery of large bones in several nearby caves. All the **churches** are strung along the main street of the town (🕐*Open Jun–Aug 10am–noon, 6pm–8pm; Sept–May 10am–noon only; when churches are closed, contact the tourist office for the key;* ☎*0941 58 14 07).*

The Legend of Capo d'Orlando

The history of Capo d'Orlando is intertwined with the legend of its foundation at the time of the Trojan War by Agathyrsus, the son of Aeolus. The legend also relates how the ancient settlement of Agathyrnis came to be renamed Capo d'Orlando by Charlemagne, who passing through these lands on a pilgrimage to the Holy Land, decided to call the place after his heroic paladin.

In 1299, the town witnessed the pivotal naval battle between James and Frederick of Aragon over the throne of Sicily.

Address Book

For coin ranges, see the Legend on the cover flap.

WHERE TO STAY

Nuovo Hotel Faro – *Via Libertà 7, Capo d'Orlando.* ☎*0941 90 24 66. www. nuovohotelfaro.com. 30 rooms.* As its name suggests ("lighthouse" in Italian), this family-run hotel is situated near a beacon. The communal areas are simple, but pleasant, and although the bedrooms are not the most modern, they are clean and well kept. The biggest draw is the location – the beach is only a stone's throw away.

Hotel La Tartaruga – *Lido San Gregorio, Capo d'Orlando, 2km/1.2mi E of Capo d'Orlando.* ☎*0941 95 54 21. www. hoteltartaruga.it. Closed Mon (restaurant) and in Nov. 53 rooms.* Situated in the heart of the tourist area, 2km/1.2mi from Capo d'Orlando, this hotel occupies an imposing building overlooking the beach. Comfortable, modern rooms and a swimming pool. The adjoining restaurant is renowned for its fresh fish.

WHERE TO EAT

Trattoria La Tettoia – *Contrada Certari 80, Capo d'Orlando, 2.5km/1.5mi S of Capo d'Orlando on S 116.* ☎*0941 90 21 46. Closed Mon (except Jul–Sept).* This family-run trattoria has a friendly, informal atmosphere; genuine regional cuisine; and a panoramic terrace that's delightful in the summer.

Il Gabbiano – *Via Trazzera Marina 146, Capo d'Orlando.* ☎*0941 90 20 66. Closed Tue.* Unanimously considered to be the best pizzeria in the area, this simple, well-run restaurant also has a spacious veranda.

Bontempo "Il ristorante" – *Via Fiumara 38, Naso, From S 113 to Milazzo, turn right to Sinagra just before Ponte Naso.* ☎*0941 96 11 88. www. bontempoilristorante.com. Closed Mon (Nov).* This restaurant is housed in a modern, white building surrounded by greenery, 10km/6mi to the southeast of Capo d'Orlando. It has three spacious dining rooms and serves a range of local dishes.

FESTIVALS

Vita e paesaggio di Capo d'Orlando
Since 1955, the town has hosted a summer competition, backed by the Messina painter Giuseppe Migneco, on the theme of the life and countryside of Capo d'Orlando. Successful artists from Italy and abroad are commissioned to come and paint; once the prize has been awarded, some of the works are acquired by the municipal art gallery.

Capo d'Orlando in blues –
For information on this summer festival of Blues music, contact the Cross Road Club/Associazione Siciliana Musica Blues, Via Consolare Antica 623, Capo d'Orlando; ☎*0941 95 72 35.*

The **Chiesa del Rosario**, the easternmost, dedicated to the Madonna of the Rosary, was rebuilt in 1635, while retaining its 16C campanile. Inside, it has a fine coffered wooden **ceiling** set with Byzantine-Norman rosettes, and an unusual wooden **high altar** painted with floral motifs (first half of the 17C) decorated with wooden medallions representing the Mysteries of the Rosary. The wooden figures in the centre of the altar represent the Madonna with saints.

Farther along is the **Chiesa della Catena**, erected in the latter half of the 17C, where the first elections were held after the Unification of Italy. It contains some fine Byzantine-type **frescoes** from

another church, the Chiesa della Badia. Beyond is Piazza del Baglio, named after the complex of low-level workers' houses and workshops arranged around the **Palazzo Ducale**, built by the Lancia family (15C–16C).

Proceeding westwards, the high road passes the beautifully preserved **Torre Saracena** or *Torrazza* (10C). From its terrace extends a magnificent **view**★ across the rooftops and beyond to Capo d'Orlando. The tower was part of a defensive chain system that would have transmitted signals from the 16C **Torre delle Ciavole** on the coast, via the **Guardiola** situated to the north of the town, to the *Torrazza*.

On the western edge of town is **Santa Caterina d'Alessandria**, the church dedicated to St Catherine of Alexandria, built in the 16C, but altered in the 17C. Inside, the wooden altar is decorated with floral motifs. A low relief to the right of the altar depicts St Catherine of Alexandria overcoming the infidel.

▶ *Turn back towards the coast.*

Note, on your left, the **Torre delle Ciavole** (*See above*).

▶ *Continue on to the small seaside resort of* **Gioiosa Marea** *and follow the signs for San Filippo Armo and*

San Leonardo (about 9km/5.5mi) to Gioiosa Guardia.

Rovine di Gioiosa Guardia

The ruins of this medieval town, abandoned by its inhabitants in the 18C for Gioiosa Marea, are situated at 800m/2 625ft above sea level and surrounded by a romantic landscape. The idyllic serenity of the place is enhanced by the splendid **view**★.

▶ *Return to the coast.*

A little farther on is **Capo Calavà**, a spectacular rocky spur.

CARINI

POPULATION: 25 752

A road curves up to this graceful town, poised between a hill and gulf. Legend holds that the town was originally built by Daedalus, who called it Hyccara in memory of his son Icarus, while history shows it was razed by the Athenians and rebuilt by the Phoenicians. Later, its imposing medieval castle shadowed the tragic fate of Baroness Laura Lanza and her lover.

- **Information:** Corso Umberto I, 9044 Carini. ☎091 861 11 11. www.comune.carini.pa.it.
- ▶ **Orient Yourself:** Carini, situated slightly inland from the bay of the same name, lies some 20km/12.5mi from Palermo.
- **Parking:** Good bus services operate between the two towns.
- **Don't Miss:** The red cliff of Terrasini.
- **Organising Your Time:** Three hours is enough to see this small town at a leisurely pace.
- **Also See:** Golfo di CASTELLAMMARE; MONREALE; PALERMO.

Walking Tour

Corso Umberto I, Carini's main street, begins just beyond a belvedere presenting sweeping views over the coast. From here, a horseshoe-shaped flight of shallow steps makes its way up past the town's medieval water fountain to a 12C archway and beyond to the old part of the town, threaded by narrow streets, and the castle.

Castle
Open 9am–1pm, 3pm–7pm. Closed Mon. €2. ☎091 88 15 666. www.comune. carini.pa.it.

The ancient Norman fortress-cum-castle has foundations dating back to the 10C, and is the setting for a famous and dramatic Sicilian story of thwarted love. Here, in 1563, **Baronessa di Carini** was killed by her father for having an affair while betrothed. The tragic episode was later immortalised in a anonymous contemporary poem, now one of the most famous verses in Sicily's lyrical canon and is a favourite subject of traditional ballad singers.
The building has now decayed to a rather dilapidated state, but still houses some worthwhile sights. On the ground floor is the **Salone delle Derrate** (Vict-

A Bit of History

Carini claims to have legendary origins. Allegedly, it was founded by Daedalus who called it Hyccara in memory of his son Icarus; history then records how the town came to be destroyed by the Athenians in 415 BC, rebuilt by the Phoenicians and, after the Roman conquest, became a stipendiary town of the Empire. With time came changes in fortune: the town was assimilated into the feudal holdings of the most powerful Chiaramonte dynasty, before passing to the Moncada (14C) and, finally in the 15C to the La Grua-Talamanca, in whose hands it remains today.

uals Hall), this was later transformed into a library, with its two elegant 15C stone arches springing from a single solid pier. On the floor above, the **Salone delle Feste** has a wonderful 15C coffered wooden **ceiling**, heavy with Catalan Gothic decorative pendentives.

▶ *Return to Corso Umberto I.*

Opposite the fountain stands the **Chiesa di San Vincenzo**. The space is bisected by a wrought-iron grille (segregating the area reserved for the nuns from the adjacent convent) and decorated with white and gold neo-Classical stucco festoons, delightful cherubs and grotesques.

Corso Umberto I opens out into **Piazza del Duomo**, overlooked by two churches: San Vito on the right and the Chiesa Madre on the left.

Chiesa Madre

🕐*Open by appointment 9am–1pm, 3pm –7pm (same admission times for other churches in the town). ☎091 86 11 341 or 091 86 11 339.*

Although subjected to considerable alteration in the 18C, the church preserves a loggia on its right side and a series of interesting maiolica panels depicting the *Crucifixion, Assumption, St Rosalia* and *St Vitus* (1715). **Inside**, the church houses a prized *Adoration of the Magi* by Alessandro Allori (1578), an eminent Tuscan painter who came to prominence at the Medici court.

In the chapel dedicated to the Crucifixion sits an exquisite 17C wooden Christ with a crown of silver on cross of agate. The statue is set above a grandiose altar, which is flanked by stucco statues by Procopio Serpotta.

Oratorio del Santissimo Sacramento

The oratory beside the Chiesa Madre dates from the mid-16C. Its interior is a glorious profusion of **stucco decoration**★★ (18C) by the Trapani artist Vincenzo Messina. He depicted life-size allegories (Faith, Charity, Strength and Penitence on the left; Hope, Justice, Divine Grace and the Roman Catholic Church on the right).

Elsewhere, surfaces are encrusted with other Serpotta-like elements: cherubs, heavy garlands of flowers and fruit, heraldic coats of arms and grotesques.

A Tale of Love and Tragedy

1563: Laura Lanza, the beautiful young daughter of the Count of Mussomeli, although betrothed to Don Vincenzo La Grua, falls in love with Ludovico Vernagallo, who reciprocates her love. Despite every effort by the girl's father to put an end to the affair, nothing will quell the passion of the two young lovers. Finding an accomplice in her nurse, the girl devises a plan with her lover, enabling them to marry in secret and run away together. The appointed day arrives: 4 December. Laura and Ludovico pronounce their vows of reciprocal fidelity before a chaplain, when Laura's enraged father bursts in on the scene. The two clandestine lovers are put to death, thereby salvaging the family's honour. The story is hushed up, no-one is punished, yet with time, the incident was assimilated into the colourful anthology of romance popularly celebrated in ballad and song.

Chiesa di Santa Maria degli Angeli

Behind the Chiesa Madre, in Via Curreri.
This church once belonged to the Capuchin monastery; a ring of side chapels radiate from the nave, each one embellished with intricate intarsia. Pride of place in the elaborate Rococo chapel of the Crucifixion, among the various small reliquaries, is a lovely wooden **Crucifix** by the Capuchin Fra' Benedetto Valenza (1737), who also worked on the overall decor.

Chiesa degli Agonizzanti

Via Roma.
This church, completed in 1643, is richly decorated inside with white and gold **stucco**★: playful cherubs, eagles, garlands of flowers and fruit encircle a number of frescoed panels about Mary, which culminate in the ceiling *(Apotheosis of the Virgin)*. Along the side walls, about half way, there are frescoes depicting the Death of Joseph and the Madonna.

Excursions

Terrasini

15km/9mi W.
The main area of this seaside resort comprises a nice sandy strip, edged by small trattorias with outdoor tables and upmarket hotels. The bay curls before a lofty red **cliff**★, which intermittently shelters little beaches and delightful little rocky creeks that are well worth exploring on a hot day.

Museo Civico

The Palazzo D'Aumale,
Lungomare Peppino Impastato.
🕐*Open 9am–1pm, 3pm–6.30pm.* 🚫*Closed Mon–Tue and Sun afternoon.* 🎫*€5.* ☎*091 88 10 990.www.regione.sicilia.it/beni culturali/museodaumale.*
Terrasini harbours an interesting local **museum**, although its presentation doesn't quite match the quality of the collections. These comprise three departments, the most significant being the **natural history** section *(Via Cala Rossa, 8)*. This comprises, among other things, the rich Orlando collection of

Red cliffs at Terrasini

birds with species ranging from crows, nocturnal birds, storks and raptors to those approaching extinction or considered rare, such as the griffon vulture, golden eagle and capercaillie. In the archaeological department *(in Piazza Falcone e Borsellino)* there are displays of artefacts retrieved from shipwrecks found in the seas off Terrasini.

Festa di li schietti

The Saturday before Easter, all the eligible young men *(schietti)* of the town go out and cut a bitter-orange tree *(melangolo)*. They trim and tidy the top into a round shape and decorate it with coloured ribbons and bells *(ciancianieddi)*. The dressed result, which must weigh at least 50kg/110lb, is then carried into the town. On Sunday morning, each tree is blessed in the piazza before the main church. After the service and urged on by the local populace, each young man carries his tree to the house of his chosen love; there he must demonstrate his strength by balancing the tree on his palm for as long as possible. This local festival has lost much of its importance today. Once it constituted a veritable test of virility: if the young man should fail to lift his heavy offering or, indeed, should fail to hold it long enough, the engagement might, literally, be broken off.

GOLFO DI CASTELLAMMARE ★★

This splendid gulf is characterized by soft hills, dominated to the west by the imposing size of the Mount Còfano, best seen from the promontory on Capo San Vito. In addition to the splendid coastal landscapes, the region offers castles, tuna fisheries and archaeological zones.

🛈 **Information:** Via Savoia 57, San Vito lo Capo. ☎0923 97 24 64. www.sanvitoweb.com.

▶ **Orient Yourself:** The Golfo di Castellammare stretches from Capo San Vito to Capo Rama. A scenic road follows the coast as far as Scopello, then heads inland at the Riserva dello Zingaro to rejoin the coast at Capo San Vito.

☺ **Don't Miss:** Scopello's tuna fishery, the reserve of Zingaro, the Grotta Mangiapane.

🕓 **Organising Your Time:** The summer months, barring August, are most pleasant. September sees the Cous Cous festival at Capo San Vito.

🧒 **Especially for Kids:** Boat tours at the Zingaro Reserve and the Grotta Mangiapane, especially at Christmas, when it stages a live Nativity.

👶 **Also See:** CARINI; ERICE; MONREALE; PALERMO; SEGESTA.

Visit

Castellammare del Golfo ⚓

Set in the beautiful bay of the same name, this town, now a popular seaside resort, was once the main port and principal trading post for the ancient cities of Segesta and Erice.

In the centre of the town stands the **medieval castle**. After Castellammare del Golfo, the road winds its way up a ruggedly bleak mountainside, providing glorious **views**★.

Scopello

The road leads onwards to Scopello, a small hamlet on the sea dominated by its 18C *baglio* (a large, fortified building), which faces onto the central piazza. After a bend, a dirt road on the right leads down to the old tuna fishery (accessible on foot).

La Tonnara

The tuna fishery, now disused, testifies to an activity that once flourished in these fish-rich waters. Out of season, the place

Old tuna fishery

M. Guillot/MICHELIN

takes on an atmosphere all of its own as silence reigns among the abandoned buildings, and the net weights sit impassively aside. In the summer, by contrast, the place bustles with sun-seekers and bathers. From here there is a wonderful **view**★ of the monolithic rocks (*i faraglioni*), that recall their more famous cousins off the island of Capri.

Riserva Naturale dello Zingaro★ Kids

The nature reserve between Scopello and San Vito lo Capo can be accessed from either of these two places. For information on admission times and prices, call ☏0924 35 108 or 800 11 66 16 (toll-free number). www.riservazingaro.it.

This, Sicily's first nature reserve, measures some 7km/4mi in length and covers approximately 1 650ha/4 076 acres. The main track follows the coastline high above the sea offering spectacular **views**★ down over the successive creeks, bays, beaches (many of which are accessible), sheer cliffs and rocky headlands. These, seen together, provide a gloriously unspoilt view of Sicily. The wonderful, lush Mediterranean vegetation (some 700 species) occasionally allows patches of red bedrock to show through. This provides a striking contrast of warm colour, offset by the deep green fronds of dwarf palms and the softer shades of green added by shiny laurel bushes, matt agave spikes and tender asphodels. Other equally attractive paths meander inland. As the scenery alters, so too does the vegetation until, at last, it is largely dominated by tumbling capers and flowering ash.

The reserve maintains a number of nooks and crannies that provide sheltered burrows and nesting sites for a variety of animals (including small predators) and, more particularly, birds (with 39 different species documented including Peregrine falcons, Bonelli's eagles and kestrels).

The Zingaro Nature Reserve also preserves important marks made by early man here. Neolithic and Mesolithic settlements have been uncovered near the Grotta dell'Uzzo, while vestiges of rural settlements, consisting of some 20 well-preserved houses, are at Baglio Cusenza.

Other settlements have been found at la Tonnarella dell'Uzzo.

▶ *As there is no coast road from Scopello to San Vito lo Capo, you will need to retrace your steps for a couple of kilometres before turning right towards Castelluzzo.*

After Castelluzzo the road offers some splendid **views**★ of the Golfo del Cofano. To the left, note one of the many 16C watchtowers that punctuate this area. The road then continues on past an attractive, characteristically cube-like, little chapel, dedicated to Santa Crescenzia (16C).

San Vito lo Capo ♨♙

San Vito is a well-known seaside resort, noted in particular for its beautiful coastline. This opens into a bay lined with wonderful beaches that are lapped by waves of blues and greens, from aquamarine to navy.

The small whitewashed town, which developed in the 18C, clusters around the **Chiesa Madre**, which is square and massive in profile. It's a constant reminder of its early beginnings as a Saracen fortress. Inside, it used to preserve a small church dedicated to San Vito (erected over the site where the saint is supposed to have lived), but this became too small to accommodate the many pilgrims that visited it, and so it was enlarged until it actually incorporated the very building which once harboured it.

Capo San Vito e Golfo del Còfano

Leaving San Vito to the east and heading beyond the Punta di Solanto, a scenic road provides views to the left of the old, and now abandoned, tuna fishery **(Tonnara del Secco)**, and continues as far as the solitary **Torre dell'Impiso** (*visible on the return trip*). The Riserva dello Zingaro starts at the end of the road.

▶ *Return to San Vito and take the road to Castelluzzo. Once past Castelluzzo, turn right to Custonaci and head up the hill on the road to the right.*

Address Book

For coin ranges, see the Legend on the cover flap.

WHERE TO STAY

CASTELLAMMARE DEL GOLFO

Arabesque Agriturismo – *Loc. Manostalla, Balestrate, 10km/6mi E of Castellammare; take the Balestrate exit on A 29.* ☎091 87 87 755. www. agriturismoarabesque.com. This beautiful guesthouse is situated among vineyards and olive trees, just 2km/1.2mi from the coast. Facilities include a swimming pool, children's games, boules and table tennis. Mountain bikes are also available to explore the surrounding countryside.

Hotel Punta Nord Est – *Viale Leonardo da Vinci 57, Castellammare del Golfo.* ☎0924 30 511. Fax 0924 30 713. www.puntanordest.com. 58 rooms. This hotel on the seafront has private access to a small beach. The interior is tastefully decorated in pale colours and the rooms are well appointed, light and spacious.

SAN VITO LO CAPO

El Bahira Campeggio – *Località Salinella, Bahira, 4km/2.5mi S of San Vito Lo Capo.* ☎0923 97 25 77. www.elbahira. it. This campsite offers a good range of sports and leisure facilities. The site is divided into separate sections for tents, campervans and caravans, and also has chalets and small apartments for rent.

La Pineta Campeggio – *Via Del Secco 88, San Vito Lo Capo.* ☎0923 97 28 18. www.campinglapineta.it. Closed Nov. As well as providing plentiful space for tents on grass under the shady pines, this campsite has around 40 rooms available.

L'Agave – *Via Nino Bixio 35, San Vito Lo Capo.* ☎0923 92 10 88. www. lagave.net. Closed Nov. 10 rooms. Although this small hotel has only 10 rooms, plans are underway to extend its capacity. Enjoy a quiet, relaxing stay in this modern establishment with good service and facilities.

Al Tair Hotel – *Via Duca degli Abruzzi 83, San Vito Lo Capo.* ☎0923 97 25 33. www.hotelaltair.it. Closed Nov–Feb. 9 rooms. A recently opened

hotel with a very pleasant atmosphere. The decor has made good use of different types of marble and the stylish bedrooms are decorated with Tunisian tables and furnishings. Breakfast is served outside in the small garden.

Halimeda – *Via Generale Arimondi 100, San Vito Lo Capo.* ☎0923 97 23 99. www.hotelhalimeda.com. 9 rooms. This small hotel has been recently renovated in a highly original style by its young, dynamic management team. Despite their simplicity, the rooms still have lots of character. An attractive veranda roof-garden is also open to guests in summer.

SCOPELLO

Tranchina – *Via A. Diaz 7, Scopello.* ☎0924 54 10 99. 10 rooms. Right in the heart of the town, this friendly, well-maintained family-run hotel has 10 individually-decorated rooms adorned with wooden furniture. Excellent cuisine.

WHERE TO EAT

CASTELLAMMARE DEL GOLFO

Al Madarig – *Piazza Petrolo 7, Castellammare del Golfo.* ☎0924 33 533. www.almadarig.com. 33 rooms. This atmospheric restaurant facing the sea is housed in some of the carefully restored old warehouses around the port. It serves local cuisine on tables outside during the summer and also has a number of simple, yet spacious guest rooms.

SAN VITO LO CAPO

Gnà Sara – *Via Duca degli Abruzzi 8, San Vito Lo Capo.* ☎0923 9743 08. www.gnasara.com. Closed Mon (except Jun–Sept) and in Nov. Situated in a street parallel to the town's main thoroughfare, this restaurant is renowned for its generous portions of good quality fish. Meals are served on comfortable tables with linen tablecloths either in the rustic dining room or on the summer veranda.

Da Alfredo – *Contrada Valanga 3, San Vito Lo Capo, 1km/6mi S of San Vito Lo Capo.* ☎0923 97 23 66. Closed Mon (except mid-Jun–Sept) and 20 Oct–20

Nov. A splendid terrace-cum-garden, friendly atmosphere, a delightful shady arbour and a menu full of traditional Sicilian cuisine make up the main features of this pleasant restaurant.

SCOPELLO

◎◉**Il Baglio** – *Via Baglio Isonzo 4, Scopello.* ☎*0924 54 12 00. Closed Mon and Nov–Feb.* This restaurant, housed in the 13C Baglio Isonzo, has an attractive courtyard with wooden tables, as well as a smart interior dining room. The menu includes traditional fish dishes and wood-fired pizza.

FESTIVALS

Festa di Maria Santissima del Soccorso – The festival of the patron saint of Castellammare del Golfo is celebrated from 19–21 August with a procession to the sea, during which thousands of small candles are floated on the water.

Couscous Fest – In September every year, a festival celebrating Mediterranean food and wine is held at San Vito Lo Capo, along with concerts of ethnic music and other cultural events. *www.sanvitocouscous.com*

TOURS

Boat trips to the Riserva dello Zingaro – [Kids] Two boats offer trips from San Vito Lo Capo: the *Leonardo da Vinci* (☎0924 34 222) and the *Nautilus* (☎0347 57 66 391). The latter has a glass bottom, which allows visitors of all ages to admire the myriad colourful underwater life without the need for a snorkel and mask.

Monte Còfano

The towering limestone peak and the bay that surrounds it, now a nature reserve, make for a magnificent **sight**★, as the steep pinky-red cliffs extending skywards are mirrored in the mirror calm sea. A number of quarries are gouged into the rocky flank, from which the marble known as *Perlato di Sicilia,* is extracted. This is a startlingly white stone in comparison with the other natural rock of the area, which is brownish. The grotto known as the **Grotta Mangiapane** (in the vicinity of Scurati) nestles not far from the quarries (*follow the signs*). Inside, it shelters a tiny rural hamlet, which is enchantingly complete with chapel and cobbled street. The endearing charm of this abandoned village, with its vaguely Mexican air (especially because of the square, mud-coloured houses), is especially poignant at Christmas, when it stages a live Nativity.

Excursions

Alcamo

About 11km/6.5mi S of Castellammare del Golfo.

The name of the town is suggestive of the 13C poet **Cielo d'Alcamo,** author of a well-known work entitled *Rosa Fresca Aulentissima (The Fresh Fragrant Rose),* one of the earliest texts to be written in

Capo San Vito

Italian. The town lies in the heartland of the renowned Alcamo Doc wine region, and one glance at the landscape, striated by lush vineyards, is likely to prompt more basic – though no less pleasant – associations with the local dry white wine, which bears the town's name.

The town's churches contain works by members of the **Gagini** family (16C) and by Giacomo Serpotta, one of the Sicilian masters of the Baroque.

The main works are to be found in Santa Oliva, San Francesco d'Assisi, San Salvatore and the imposing **Chiesa Madre**, the principal church, which also has a fine 15C chapel. Overlooking Piazza Repubblica, which has been laid out with gardens, is the **Castello dei Conti di Modica**.

The castle, built for the Counts of Modica in the 14C, is rhomboid in shape and has two rectangular and two round towers. Gothic two-light windows pierce the northern side, while inside there is a regional enoteca and a nicely laid out wine museum, detailing the wine making process.

CASTELVETRANO

POPULATION: 30 448

This pleasant agricultural area – dominated by olive farming – is home to the famous bronze statue, the **Ephebus of Selinunte**. Elegant churches and architecture grace the town's centre.

- **Information:** Piazza Generale Cascino. ☎0924 90 91 28. www.comune.castelvetrano.tp.it.
- **Orient Yourself:** The first sight of the town, situated some 10km/6mi from Selinunte and the coast, is the large glass hospital, and beyond, the old town.
- **Don't Miss:** S. Trinità di Delia, an Anglo-Norman church, and the Ephebus.
- **Especially for Kids:** The Trinità lake, dunes and turtles at the Belice reserve.
- **Also See:** MAZARA DEL VALLO; SCIACCA; Antica città di SELINUNTE.

Walking Tour

The focal centre of Castelvetrano hinges on two adjacent squares, **Piazza Umberto I** and **Piazza Garibaldi**. The town's major monuments cluster in this area.

Piazza Garibaldi
The square is lined with fine buildings such as the town's main church and the **Chiesa del Purgatorio** (now an auditorium). The latter has elaborate details, drawn from a transitional late Mannerist-Baroque style. Next in line sits the 19C **Teatro Selinus**, which preserves its original stage.

Chiesa Madre
Castelvetrano's principal church dates, in its present form, from the 16C. The front elevation rises through two storeys; a pair of pilasters ornamented with garlands flank the entrance at ground level, the upper section is pierced by a rose window.

The glorious **stucco decoration**★ adorning the triumphal arch is attributed to **Gaspare Serpotta** (17C, father of the more famous Giacomo): a host of angels bearing festoons and garlands interact with others brandishing musical instruments.

The same elements are applied to the transept arch, albeit in a more restrained fashion.

Piazza Umberto I
This delightful little piazza lies to the left of the church, providing a clear view of the bell tower, which is hidden from the front. Gracing the square is a lovely fountain, the 17C **Fontana della Ninfa**, erected to celebrate the restitution of an aqueduct.

In the nearby Piazza Regina Margherita, overlooking a pleasant municipal garden, is the stark façade of **San Domenico** (15C). Now a secondary school, it once was attached to a convent and thus contains cloisters *(entrance to the right of the church)*. Opposite sits the 16C Church of **San Giovanni** and its massive bell tower.

Visit

Museo Selinuntino
Via Garibaldi.
🕐 *Open 9am–1pm, 3pm–6pm (except Sun).* ▨ *€2.50.* ☎ *0924 90 49 32.*
The 16C palazzo, once home to the Majo family, now accommodates a museum for artefacts recovered from Selinunte. The well-presented displays are arranged around the prize exhibit: an elegant bronze statue of a young man (c. 460 BC), known as the **Ephebus of Selinunte**★.
In a side niche nestles a lovely *Madonna and Child* by **Francesco Laurana** and his workshop, from the Church of the Annunziata. The museum also includes displays of religious objects and reliefs by the contemporary artist Giuseppe Lo Sciuto.

Excursions

Santa Trinità di Delia★
4km/2.4mi W: follow directions from Piazza Umberto I. The church is part of the Baglio Trinità farm complex. Contact Signore Stefano Saporito for the key. ☎ *0924 90 42 31.*
This enchanting Arabo-Norman church (12C) conforms to a Greek-cross plan with three apses projecting on one side; it is capped by a pink dome. The exterior walls are pierced by single-light windows screened with perforated stone panels. Inside, the dome hovers above pendentives – a typically Moorish element – supported by four marble columns with Corinthian capitals. A few metres from the church, on the opposite side of the road, extends the **Trinità forestry estate**, a lush area of eucalyptus, palm trees and pines. This

Santa Trinità di Delia

B. Kaufmann/MICHELIN

ideal picnic spot overlooks an attractive **man-made lake**.

Riserva Naturale Foce del Fiume Belice e Dune Limitrofe
12km/7.5mi S, between Marinella di Selinunte and Porto Palo di Menfi.
🐾 *For guided tours, contact Via Vivaldi 100, Marinella di Selinunte.* ☎ *0924 46 042. www.parks.it/riserva.foce.fiume.belice/.*
The dunes crisply sculpted by the wind make this natural reserve at the mouth of the River Belice particularly evocative. The welcoming marsh-like terrain attracts a number of species of birds to the area, as well as the Caretta-Caretta turtle (ℰ*See LAMPEDUSA*).

CATANIA

POPULATION: 307 774

Risen many times from the ashes of eruptions, war, earthquakes and other events, Catania is the city of Etna. Its character is intertwined with the volcano's: its dominant colour is the black of lava, used to construct monuments, houses and other edifices. The home town of Vincenzo Bellini and Giovanni Verga is an elegant and bustling city, animated by industry, including high technology. In fact, some call this the Silicon Valley of Sicily.

- **Information:** Via Cimarosa 10. ☎ 095 73 06 211. www.turismo.catania.it.
- **Orient Yourself:** The Viale Regina Margherita hosts the impressive old mansions. Flanked by the best shops, Via Etnea runs past the Piazza del Duomo, Piazza dell'Universita, Piazza Stesicoro, before arriving at Villa Bellini.
- **Parking:** The undisciplined traffic makes exploring on foot preferable. The port has a large underground parking lot; other sites dot the city.
- **Don't Miss:** Piazza Duomo and its elephant obelisk, Palazzo Biscari, the lovely gardens of the Villa Bellini, a break at the bookstore cafe Tertulia.
- **Organising Your Time:** Catania is one of the hottest cities in Italy, with summer temperatures often exceeding 40°C/104°F, and is therefore best visited early in the morning or later in the evening.
- **Especially for Kids:** The Circumetnea railway that circles Mount Etna from Catania, the summertime steam train and whalewatching.
- **Also See:** ACIREALE; CALTAGIRONE; ETNA; GIARDINI NAXOS; SIRACUSA; TAORMINA.

A Bit of History

When the town planner William Light was designing the city of Adelaide in 1836, he adopted the layout of Catania, which he had visited a few years previously. Fortunately, the chaotic traffic conditions were less easy to export. If you drive there, park and explore the pleasant city centre in a more relaxed manner on foot. *Catania is the departure point for the "Circular Tour of Etna."* See *ETNA: Driving Tours.* Katane, founded by Greek colonists around 724 BC, flourished during the Roman period, as many surviving monuments testify. The 17C saw its most tragic historical chapter, when lava flowed into the streets from volcanic vents near Nicolosi. Roughly 20 years later, a terrible earthquake destroyed most of the buildings. But the city rose from the rubble and its new plan dazzled with wide streets, piazzas and monuments. The main force behind the change was the architect **Giovanni Battista Vaccarini** (1702–68). Baroque swallowed ancient in this rebuilding process. Thus the theatre, odeon and amphitheatre are all hidden behind or beneath 18C *palazzi.*

Walking Tour

Piazza Del Duomo

This square is the centre of town, surrounded by an elegant Baroque ensemble designed by Vaccarini. In the middle stands the **Fontana dell'Elefante**, the symbol of Catania. On the south side of the square, offset by the Chierici and Pardo *palazzi* behind, sits the more delicate Fontana dell'Amenano.
The star is the Duomo façade, flanked to the right by the Bishop's Palace and Porta Uzeda and, to the left, by the attractive front of the Badia di Sant'Agata. The square's north side belongs almost entirely to the **Palazzo Senatorio** or **Palazzo degli Elefanti** (now the town hall), another Vaccarini creation.

Fontana dell'Elefante

This fountain, recalling Bellini's famous obelisk-bearing monument in Rome's Piazza Minerva, is the symbol of Catania and was conceived by Vaccarini in 1735. The lava elephant sculpture dates from the Roman period and bears an Egyptian obelisk celebrating the cult of

Isis (the Mother goddess, who became the centre of a popular Greco-Roman mystery cult), as well as the emblem of St Agatha.

Duomo★

🕐 *Open 7am–noon, 4pm–7pm.* ☎095 32 00 44.

The cathedral is dedicated to St Agatha, the patron saint of the city; it was erected in the late 11C by the Norman king Roger I, and rebuilt after the earthquake of 1693. The **façade**★ is considered one of Vaccarini's masterpieces.

Farther along Via Vittorio Emanuele II, the tall Norman lava apses can be admired from the courtyard of the Bishop's Palace. Its solid outward appearance, relieved in part by the tall, single, narrow, slit-like openings that underlines its origin as a fortified church. The remains of Roman baths, the **Terme Achilliane** *(accessible through a trap-door)*, can be seen to the right of the entrance outside the church.

Interior

Restoration of the floor has revealed several column bases from the original Norman church. Against the second pilaster on the right, in the nave, stands the funerary monument of Bellini. He died at home in Puteaux, near Paris, where he was originally buried. The transepts both contain chapels, segregated from the crossing by a glorious Renaissance archway. The chapel to the right, dedicated to the Madonna, contains the sarcophagus of Constanza, wife of Frederick III of Aragon, who died in 1363.

The southern chapel is dedicated to St Agatha: this, although Renaissance in spirit, is encrusted with gilded stucco decoration that verges on the over-exaggerated. The elaborate Spanish doorway leads through to the reliquary and treasury of the saint.

The sacristy has a large fresco (badly damaged) showing a fairly accurate topographical view of Catania before 1669. To the right of the Duomo, the Seminario now houses the Museo Diocesano di Catania.

Fontana dell'Elefante

J. Malburet/MICHELIN

Badia di Sant'Agata★

The church beside the Duomo contributes to the overall splendour of the piazza.

The serpentine lines of the **façade**★ are contained by a cornice that emphasises the ground level with a triangular pediment at the centre.

This is another example of Vaccarini's mastery in design.

Vito Arcomano/Fototeca ENIT

Duomo

Address Book

GETTING THERE AND AROUND

Getting to Catania – Fontanarossa **airport** is 7km/4.5mi to the south of Catania (☎095 72 39 111; www. aeroporto.catania.it). The Alibus links the airport with the city centre and the railway station (departures every 20min from 5pm to midnight); the ticket is the same price as on the city buses. The **bus** terminal is in Piazza Giovanni XXIII, also home to the main **train** station.

Catania has good rail connections with Messina (2hr) and Siracusa (1hr 30min); the service to and from Palermo (just over 3hr) is less frequent.

TTT Lines runs a **ferry** between Catania and Naples(about 10 hrs); ☎800 915365 (toll-free in Italy), 095 73 40 211; www.tttlines.it.

City buses – These are operated by AMT (Azienda Municipale Trasporti), Via Plebiscito 747; ☎095 73 60 111; www. amt.ct.it A ticket costs €0.80 and is valid for 90min; a day pass costs €2.

For coin ranges, see the Legend on the cover flap.

WHERE TO STAY

Jonio Campeggio – *Via Villini a Mare 2, Catania, From Corso Italia take Via Messina.* ☎095 49 11 39. *www. jonioeventi.it.* This campsite, offering a relaxed alternative to the town's more traditional hotels, has bungalows for rent in addition to pitches for tents.

Villaggio Turistico Europeo – *Viale Kennedy 9, 6km/4mi S of Catania on S 114.* ☎095 59 10 26. *www.villaggio europeo.it. Closed 10 Oct–20 Apr.* This campsite, in a tranquil, beautifully rural setting by the sea, is just a few miles from Catania. Tent pitches and small bungalows are available.

Agorà Hostel – *Piazza Currò 6, Catania.* ☎095 72 33 010. *www. agorahostel.com.* This reasonably priced hostel is situated in a 19C building fronting an old square close to the fish market. It offers two doubles, rooms with bunk beds and a number of communal areas.

Bed & Breakfast Casa Mia – *Via D'Annunzio 48 (second floor, with lift), Catania.* ☎095 44 56 82. www.bbcasa-mia.com. 6 rooms. This central B&B has six well-appointed rooms with wrought-iron beds and dark wooden furniture, as well as an attractive lounge with comfortable armchairs and sofas. Pleasant accommodation at a reasonable price.

Hotel La Vecchia Palma – *Via Etnea 668, Catania.* ☎095 43 20 25. www.lavecchiapalma.com. 11 rooms. This family-run, art nouveau-style hotel has spacious rooms that offer modern facilities, but retain their original decor.

Il Gelso Bianco – *Misterbianco – 8km/5mi SW of Catania on the Catania-Palermo A19 motorway.* ☎095 71 81 159. www.gelsobianco.it. 91 rooms. Conveniently situated near the motorway to Palermo, this hotel is suitable for business clients, conference delegates and tourists. A lovely garden and swimming pool in the summer months.

WHERE TO EAT

Midday options include the city centre bars, which sell sandwiches and one-course lunches, and the trattorias near the fish market (behind Piazza Duomo).

Cantine del Cugno Mezzano – *Via Museo Biscari 8, Catania.* ☎095 71 58 710. cantinecugno@tin.it. Closed Sun, Mon at lunchtime, 10–28 Aug, and lunchtime 15 May–15 Oct. This young, fashionable restaurant, housed in an 18C palazzo in the centre of Catania, serves fine, modern cuisine accompanied by a good selection of wine. The decor is rustic, with large wooden tables.

La Lampara – *Via Pasubio 49, Catania.* ☎095 38 32 37. Closed Wed. A simple, family-run restaurant, where the son is the chef and the father the maitre de. The cuisine here is traditional, based on fresh fish and seafood.

Metrò – *Via Crociferi 76, Catania.* ☎095 32 20 98. Closed Sat at lunchtime, Sun, Easter, 1 May and 25 Dec. This modern restaurant-cum-wine bar near Villa Ceremi serves regional dishes. A pleasant outdoor setting in summer.

🍷🍷🍷🍷**La Siciliana** – *Viale Marco Polo 52/A, Catania.* ☎*095 37 64 00. lasiciliana@tiscalinet.it. Closed Sun evening, evenings of public hols. Booking recommended.* This renowned local restaurant is well worth a visit for its traditional Sicilian cuisine served in a rustic setting. The patio is superb to sit out on in summer.

TAKING A BREAK

Al Caprice – *Via Etnea 28–34, Catania.* ☎*095 32 05 55. Closed Mon.* This traditional-style café, situated in the city centre not far from the cathedral, is perhaps the most typical in Catania with its pleasant old-world atmosphere.

Caffè-Pasticceria Savia – *Via Etnea 302–304, Catania.* ☎*095 31 69 19. Closed Mon.* Opened in 1897, opposite the entrance to Villa Bellini, this café is popular with locals and tourists alike, who sample the wide range of sweet and savoury snacks on offer.

Chiosco Vezzosi – *Piazza Vittorio Emanuele, Catania.* This *chiosco* (kiosk) serves a range of healthy and refreshing snacks, such as inexpensive fruit salads and freshly squeezed juices, made from lemons, melons and peaches.

Enoteca Regionale di Sicilia – *Viale Africa 31, Catania.* ☎*095 74 62 210. Open 8.30am–1pm, 4.30pm–8pm. Closed Mon.* The full force of the Sicilian sun can be tasted in the island's wines. This bar has a good selection, as well as tasting options.

Focacceria Turi Finocchiaro – *Via Euplio Reina 13, Catania.* ☎*095 71 53 573. Open from 7pm. Closed Wed.* This establishment has been serving excellent, home-made Sicilian cuisine – such as meat from the rotisserie and delicious fish and seafood dishes – since 1900. Tables inside and out. A real gastronomic treat.

Pasticceria Spinella – *Via Etnea 300, Catania.* ☎*095 32 72 47.* Opposite the Villa Bellini, this is one of the best-known pasticcerie in Catania, dating back to 1930. The elegant atmosphere, excellent service and high-quality produce ensure that this remains one of the busiest cafes in town.

SHOPPING

Tertulia – *Via Michele Rapisardi 1–3, Catania.* ☎*095 71 52 603.* This modern bookshop-café offers a relaxed atmosphere and a good selection of books.

ENTERTAINMENT

Le Ciminiere – *Viale Africa 2 (at the Eastern end of Via Umberto I), Catania.* ☎*095 73 49 911.* The town's old sulphur refinery, abandoned after the Second World War, has been transformed into a venue for cultural events, such as art exhibitions, music concerts and theatre shows. There are also plans to house a puppet theatre, the Teatro Stabile dell'Opera dei Pupi, in the building.

FESTIVALS

Festa di Sant' Agata – During the Festival of St Agatha, from 3–5 February, the bust and reliquary of this patron saint of Catania are paraded through the city to scenes of great jubilation.

OUTDOOR FUN

The sea – Il Lido di Plaja, south of the city, is Catania's beach. The River Simeto delivers golden sand here. North, after Le Ciminiere, is the old neighbourhood of San Giovanni li Cuti with a beach of black sand and lava chunks.

In search of dolphins – 🧒 The Società Whalewatching boats leave from the ports of Catania, Aci Trezza and Riposto. ☎*347 40 86 749 or 335 40 72 88; www.whalewatch.it*

Steam train – 🧒 Operates Jul–Sept. Departs from Catania Centrale to Militello, Vizzini, Grammichele, Caltagirone, Castiglione and Randazzo.

TOURS

By bus – The circular bus route 410 passes the main sights and points of interest. Services run by appointment only. For further information, contact ☎*095 73 60 111.*

Guided tours – Catania's tourist office (APT di Catania) organises tours at 9am Fri–Sun, starting in Largo Paisiello. Themes include Literature and Cinema, Homage to Vincenzo Bellini, From the Birth of the City to the Baroque Period, and Sacred Itineraries. For information and reservations, call ☎*095 73 06 211. www.turismo.catania.it.*

The Liotru of Catania

Locals refer to the elephant in Piazza Duomo as the **Liotru**, which is local dialect for "**Eliodoro**," the name of a learned 8C necromancer from Catania. Legends claim he rode an elephant after bringing it to life. Over the centuries, the magician's name has been adopted for the statue of his steed.

During prehistoric times, dwarf elephants did inhabit Sicily – the Museo Archeologico Paolo Orsi in Siracusa houses models – so perhaps the story isn't entirely fantastical. Some scholars even connect the cyclops of Homeric legend with pachyderms (where the trunk is interpreted as the third eye).

Fontana dell'Amenano

The fountain is named after the river that supplies it on its way past a few of the principal monuments from the Roman period (the theatre and baths or *Terme della Rotonda*). Locally, the fountain is called *"acqua a lenzuolo,"* because the cascade of water resembles a fine veil. The open area behind is Piazza Alonzo di Benedetto, where a bustling and picturesque **fish market** takes place each morning. The covered section once housed the military guard for the **Porta Carlo V**, part of the city's 16C fortifications. Its main frontage can still be seen from Piazza Pardo.

The Surrounding Quarter

In the stretch of Via Vittorio Emanuele II behind the Duomo nestle a number of important sights. A small square on the right harbours the lovely church of **San Placido** with its gently undulating façade by **Stefano Ittar** (1769). Opposite the right side of the church (Via Museo Biscari) is its former convent. The courtyard *(access from Via Landolina)* preserves remains of the 15C **Palazzo Platamone**. Original features include a decorative balcony in coloured stone, adorned by a series of pointed arches. The courtyard is now used as a venue for concerts and theatre performances.

Palazzo Biscari★

Via Museo Biscari. Guided tours only *(20min) by appointment.* ☎*095 71 52 508. www.palazzobiscari.com.*

This is the finest civic building in the city. Erected after the devastating earthquake of 1693, the palazzo reached its greatest splendour about 60 years later, thanks to Ignazio Biscari. He was a man of eclectic interests, and an impassioned lover of art, literature and archaeology. The entrance to the *palazzo (Via Museo Biscari)* is through an elaborate portal. Inside is a splendid room with frescoes by Sebastiano Lo Monaco, complemented with stuccowork, gilded mouldings and mirrors. The ceiling's centre opens into an oval dome, complete with gallery. Musicians once played here, so the notes seemed to descend from the heavens. A pretty spiral staircase provides access to the little platform, where an admirable view extends over the terrace.

Lavish **decorations**★★ adorn the south wing, in particular: figures and volutes, cherubs and racemes fill the window frames, relieving the sombreness of the dark façade.

Via Crociferi★

▷ *Begin at Piazza San Francesco with its monumental church dedicated to St Francis, and turn down the lovely Via Crociferi.*

Via Crociferi is regarded as Catania's Baroque street *par excellence*. The magnificent buildings along either side, particularly in the first section, impart a graciousness that is quite unique. Through the gateway, **Arco di San Benedetto**, are the Badia Grande and its diminutive Badia Piccola. On the left two churches dedicated to **San Benedetto** and **San Francesco Borgia** are aligned; between the two runs a narrow street with **Palazzo Asmundo** at the far end.

Farther along Via Crociferi on the left, stands a former Jesuit residence that now accommodates the Istituto d'Arte. The first courtyard, attributed to Vaccarini, is graced with a fine two-tiered portico: the same bay elevation has also been used in the University courtyard in Piazza dell'Università. It is also laid with a striking black and white cobbled pavement.

The elegant, curvilinear **façade**★ of **San Giuliano** on the right was probably designed by Vaccarini. Above the elaborate altar of agate and other semi-precious stones sits a 14C painted wooden Crucifix.

▸ *Turn left into Via dei Gesuiti.*

San Nicolò l'Arena

The Benedictine Order, one of the richest and most powerful in the city, built a grandiose monastery (16C–17C) and an imposing **church** alongside, although the façade was never completed. Inside the huge and starkly bare church, there is a lovely 18C organ case behind the altar. The meridian line was laid into the transept floor in 1841; this catches the sunlight precisely at 13 minutes past midday (at one time, this occurred dead on noon).

Monastery★

The present building dates from the 18C. The eye-catching doorway on the left of the church provides access to the courtyard, from where the east and south sides of the building, designed by Antonino Amato, may be admired. The opulent **decoration** recalls that of the contemporary Palazzo Biscari. The first cloisters surround a small neo-Gothic arcaded courtyard with maiolica. The monastery now accommodates the University's Faculty of Arts and preserves the magnificent **Sala Vaccarini**.

▸ *Return to Via Crociferi.*

The street terminates at the gates of Villa Cerami, now the seat of the Faculty of Jurisprudence.

▸ *Head towards Corso Vittorio Emanuele. Perhaps continue with visits to the Museo Belliniano,*

Museo Emilio Greco, Teatro Antico and Casa di Verga (see Visit).

Via Etnea★

Catania's best shops and boutiques flank this straight, 3km/1.8mi long thoroughfare, which runs through Piazza del Duomo, Piazza dell'Universita, Piazza Stesicoro, before arriving at last in front of Villa Bellini, Catania's lovely flower-filled public gardens.

Piazza dell'Università

Elegant *palazzi* surround the square piazza on all sides. On the right stands Vaccarini's **Palazzo Sangiuliano**; on the left, the **University**, arranged around an attractive courtyard surrounded by a portico with a loggia above. In the evening, the piazza is illuminated by four splendid lamps (1957), produced by a sculptor from Catania.

Farther down the street rises the lovely concave frontage of the **Collegiata** (Santa Maria della Consolazione) designed by **Stefano Ittar** (18C). A short distance beyond, on the left, comes the gracious **Palazzo San Demetrio** (17C–18C).

On the right, along Via Antonio di S. Giuliano, stands the richly decorated **Palazzo Manganelli**. Luchino Viscon-

---

CATANIA DURING THE ROMAN PERIOD

Visitors particularly interested in Roman remains can request to be taken by a theatre custodian to visit the **Terme della Rotonda** *(Via della Rotonda)*; little survives of these baths, however, other than a single circular domed chamber that was converted into a church in Byzantine times (6C). Access may also be arranged to the **Terme dell'Indirizzo** *(Piazza Currò)*, a more extensive baths complex comprising at least 10 domed rooms. Here the wood-stoked burner that provided heating is clearly visible as are sections of rectangular hot-air ducting.

Guided tours run by the staff of the Ancient Theatre; contact the theatre in advance ☎095 74 72 111.

Elaborate decor of Palazzo Biscari

B. Kaufmann/MICHELIN

ti's *The Leopard* – based on the famous novel by Tomasi di Lampedusa– filmed here. Returning to Via Etnea, just inside the entrance to the next church, the 18C **San Michele Arcangelo**, a double marble staircase climbs up to two Baroque stoups with angels drawing aside a marble drape to reveal the basin.

Piazza Stesicoro
To visit, contact the Ancient Theatre in advance ☎095 74 72 111.
The ruin in the middle of the square is all that survives of an enormous **Roman amphitheatre** (105m/344ft by 125m/410ft), whose arena was the Empire's second largest, after the Colosseum. Most traces are beneath the piazza and the surrounding Baroque buildings.

San Biagio
(Sant'Agata alla Fornace)
🕐*Open Mon–Sat, 5pm–7pm; Sun and public hols, 9am–1pm.* ☎095 71 59 360.
The 18C building stands upon the foundations of a chapel dedicated to the patron saint of Catania. In Roman times, the town's lime kilns were concentrated here.
A chapel within the church (far right) preserves the *carcara* (kiln or furnace), where Agatha supposedly died. Tradition claims the Church of **Sant'Agata**

in Carcere, behind Piazza Stesicoro, was built on the site of her imprisonment in 251.

Villa Bellini★
The large, luxuriant park is thick with exotic plants. From the top of the hill (where a kiosk stands), there is a beautiful view over the city and out towards Mount Etna.

Santa Maria del Gesù
Although built in 1465, this church has undergone considerable alterations. From the original survives the Cappella Paternò, complete with Renaissance archway surmounted by a lunette, inset with a Pietà by **Antonello Gagini**. He is also the author of the Madonna and Child (second altar on the right).

Visit

Teatro Antico and Odeona
Corso Vittorio Emanuele II 260.
🕐*Open 9am–1.30pm, 3pm–7pm.* ⊜€3.
☎095 71 50 405.
The theatre's design dates from the Roman era. However, scholars suggest it occupies the site of an older Greek structure. Built of lava stone, its tiered seats would have seated 7 000. As far back as Norman times, the theatre's marble

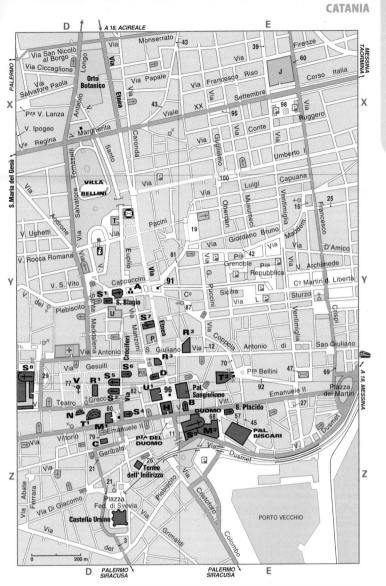

CATANIA

Angelo Custode (Via)	DZ	3	Conte di Torino (Via)	EY	25	Giuffrida (Via Vincenzo)	EX	39

Angelo Custode (Via) — DZ 3
Androne (Via) — DY
Archimede (Via) — EY
Bellini (Piazza) — EY
Benedetto (Piazza A. d.) — DZ 11
Biondi (Via) — EY 12
Bovio (Piazza G.) — EY 15
Bruno (Via G.) — EY
Cappuccini (Via) — DY
Capuana (Via L.) — EY
Carlo Alberto (Piazza) — EY 19
Caronda (Via) — DX
Castello Ursino (Via) — DZ 21
Ciccaglione (Via) — DX
Colombo (Via C.) — DEZ

Conte di Torino (Via) — EY 25
Conte Ruggero (Via) — EX
Coppola (Via) — EY
Crispi (Via F.) — EXY
Crociferi (Via) — DYZ
Currò (Piazza) — DZ 26
Cutelli (Piazza) — EZ 27
D'Amico (Via) — EY
Dante (Piazza) — DY 29
Duomo (Piazza d.) — DZ
Dusmet (Via) — EZ
Etnea (Via) — DXY
Ferrara (Via A.) — DZ
Firenze (Via) — EX
Garibaldi (Via) — DZ
Gesuiti (Via) — DY
Giacomo (Via d.) — DZ

Giuffrida (Via Vincenzo) — EX 39
Grenoble (Piazza) — EY
Grimaldi (Via) — DEZ
Guardie (Piazza delle) — EY 42
Imbriani (Via M. R.) — DEX 43
Ipogeo (Via) — DX
Italia (Corso) — EX
Landolina (Via) — EZ 45
Lanza (Piazza V.) — DX
Longo (Via A.) — DX
Lupo (Piazza Pietro) — EY 47
Maddem (Via) — EY
Manzoni (Via) — DY
Martiri (Piazza d.) — EZ
Martiri della
  Libertà (Corso) — EY
Monserrato (Via) — DX

Museo Biscari (Via)	EZ	57	Rocca Romana (Via)	DY		Stesicoro (Piazza)	DY	91
Musumeci (Via)	EXY		Rotonda (Via d.)	DYZ	77	Sturzo (Via)	EY	
Oberdan (Via G.)	EXY		S. Anna (Via)	DZ	79	Svevia (Piazza F. d.)	DZ	
Orlando (Via Vitt. E.)	EX	60	S. Eupilio (Via)	DXY		Teatro Greco (Via)	DZ	
Pacini (Via)	DY		S. Francesco d'Assisi			Teatro Massimo (Via)	EYZ	92
Paola (Via S.)	DX		(Piazza)	DZ	80	Tomaselli (Via S.)	DXY	
Papale (Via)	DX		S. Gaetano alle Grotte			Trento (Piazza)	EX	95
Plebiscito (Via d.)	DY		(Via)	DEY	81	Ughetti (Via)	DY	
Porticello (Via)	EZ	68	S. Giuliano (Via A. d.)	DEY		Umberto I (Via)	DEX	
Puccini (Via G.	EY		S. Giuseppe al			Università (Piazza dell')	DZ	96
Rabbordone (Via)	EY	69	Duomo (Via)	DZ	82	Ventimiglia (Via)	EXY	
Rapisardi (Via Michele	EY	70	S. Maddalena (Via)	DY		Verga (Piazza)	EX	98
Regina			S. Nicolò al Borgo (Via)	DX		V. Emanuele II (Via)	DEZ	
Margherita (Viale)	DX		S. Vito (Via)	DY		V. Emanuele III (Piazza)	EY	100
Repubblica (Piazza)	EY		Sicilia (Corso)	DEY		XX Settembre (Viale)	DEX	
Riso (Via F.)	EX		Spirito Santo (Piazza)	EY	87			

Anfiteatro	DY	A	Palazzo Biscari	EZ		S. Michele Arcangelo	DY	S⁷
Badia di S. Agata	EZ	B	Palazzo Manganelli	EY		S. Nicolò l'Arena	DY	S⁸
Casa di Verga	DZ	C	R2 Palazzo S. Demetrio	DY	R³	S. Placido	EZ	
Castello Ursino	DZ		Palazzo Sangiuliano	DEZ		Seminario		
Collegiata	DY	D	Palazzo Senatorio			Arcivescovile	EZ	S³
Duomo	EZ		o degli Elefanti	DZ	H	Teatro Antico	DZ	T¹
Museo Belliniano	DZ	M¹	S. Agata al Carcere	DY	S¹	Teatro Bellini	EY	T²
Museo Diocesano	EZ	M²	S. Benedetto	DZ	S²	Terme dell'Indirizzo	DZ	
Museo Emilio Greco	DZ	M	S. Biagio	DY		Terme della Rotonda	DZ	V
Odeon	DZ	N	S. Francesco	DZ	S⁴	Università	DZ	U¹
Orto Botanico	DX		S. Francesco Borgia	DYZ	S⁵	Villa Bellini	DXY	
Palazzo Asmundo	DZ	R¹	S. Giuliano	DY	S⁶			

slabs were recycled into the cathedral, while houses and a street occupied the theatre structure.

Next door stands an **odeon**, although this is later in date. It served as a more intimate context for musical shows, poetry readings and orations.

A small **antiquarium**, exhibits materials and fragments that were discovered during excavation work.

Casa di Verga

Via Sant'Anna 8.
🕐*Open Tue–Sat, 9am–1.30pm.* 🕐*Closed public hols.* 🎟️€2. ☎095 71 50 598.

The little house where the writer **Giovanni Verga** (1840–1922) spent many years is preserved much as he left it. His study's bookcases contain writers such as Capuana, D'Annunzio and Deledda.

Castello Ursino

🔒*Closed for work on the north passage at the time of going to press. Piazza Federico di Svevia.* ☎095 34 58 30.

Frederick II of Swabia erected this austere, solid-looking castle on the seafront in the 13C, however a great river of lava extended the shore in 1669. The castle is supposedly named after a Roman consul

A Composer of Genius

Vincenzo Bellini, the creator of *La sonnambula*, *Norma* and *I puritani*, was a Romantic composer who dedicated himself to his works with "the passion that is so characteristic of genius, convinced that a large part of success depends on the choice of an interesting theme, warm expressive tones and a contrast of passions". He is commemorated in Catania's opera house, the *Teatro Bellini*, inaugurated with a production of his *Norma* in 1890. The acoustics of its beautiful auditorium are among the best in the world.

Lara Pessina/MICHELIN

St Agatha

Agatha was a wealthy, Christian noblewomen from Catania who lived in the city during the 3C. A victim of religious persecution and the unwelcome attentions of the Consul Quilianus, she was thrown into prison and tortured (her breasts were cut off) with red-hot pokers and coals. She died on 5 February 251. The following year, the saint's veil was said to have saved Catania from a flow of lava, after which Agatha became the city's patron saint. During the festival in her honour, celebrated on 3–5 February, the city's streets are thronged with noisy and colourful crowds, bearing witness to her continuing popularity. She is even remembered in one of the local specialities, the *minni di Sant' Agata* (*minni* is Sicilian dialect for breasts); these small cakes covered with frosted icing and topped with a cherry recall the martyrdom of the saint.

(Arsinius), or possibly after the Orsini, the famous Roman family that sought refuge here in the Middle Ages.

The castle is square in plan; it has a large round tower at each corner and two additional towers.

Pinacoteca

The art gallery principally showcases southern Italian artists from the 15C to the 19C. Notable works include a polyptych with the *Virgin Enthroned with St Anthony and St Francis* by **Antonello de Saliba** (15C), a pupil of Antonello da Messina. Among the pictures influenced by Caravaggio's strong use of chiaroscuro and theatrical gesture is the expressive *St Christopher* by **Pietro Novelli**. There are two beautiful studies by **Michele Rapisardi**, an artist from Catania, who was prominent in the 19C. One prefigured his depiction of the Sicilian Vespers, the other is a sketched *Head of the Mad Ophelia* – a haunting image of a woman's hypnotic stare. Examples by another Catanese artist, Giuseppe Sciuti, include a *Widow* – an expression of infinite sadness. Before leaving, cast an eye over the *Pastorello Malato (The Ailing Shepherd-boy)*, a delicate watercolour by Guzzone, and the vivid paintings by Lorenzo Loiacono.

Museo Belliniano

⊶*Closed for restoration at time of going to press. Piazza S. Francesco 3. For more information, call* ☎*095 71 50 535.* The house where the composer **Vincenzo Bellini** (1801–35) was born now displays relevant documents, mementoes and portraits of the com-

poser, together with a harpsichord and a spinet that once belonged to his grandfather. The last room contains various autographed original scores.

Museo Diocesano

⊶*Closed for restoration at time of going to press.* ☎*095 28 16 35. www.museodiocesicatania.it.*

The Diocesan Museum houses a collection of paintings, ornaments and vestments belonging to the cathedral and the diocese, as well as the **Vara di Sant'Agata** – the float that was used to carry the saint's bust and reliquary during processions. A panoramic terrace accessed from the museum has fine views of Porta Uzeda.

Museo Emilio Greco

Piazza S. Francesco d'Assisi 3.
🕐*Open daily, 9am–1pm (also 3pm–6pm Tue and Thu).* 🕐*Closed public hols.* ☎*095 31 76 54.*

This archive-cum-museum houses the complete **graphic output**★ of the native-born artist Emilio Greco (1913–95), who achieved particular fame as a sculptor. The subjects, for the most part are female heads and nudes, and amply illustrate his perceptive predilection for Hellenistic art.

Orto Botanico

Entrance in Via Longo.
🕐*Open daily except Sun, 8.30am–1.30pm.* 🕐*Closed national hols.* ☎*800 90 11 42. www.dipbot.unict.it.*

The botanical gardens were laid out in the 1950s with various indigenous as well as exotic varieties.

CEFALÙ

POPULATION: 13 757

The Greek "Kephaloidion" (head) is a charming fishing village, now courting visitors, who, in turn, respond eagerly to its charms, from the cathedral to the unparalleled natural setting, as well as the numerous wine bars.

- **Information**: Piazza Duomo. ☎0921 92 41 30. www.comune.cefalu.pa.it and www.cefalu.it.
- ▶ **Orient Yourself:** The town clusters on the west side of the majestic outcrop.
- **Parking:** The motorway exit leads easily to Via Roma, where you can park, then head towards Via Matteotti and Corso Ruggero on foot.
- **Don't Miss:** The cathedral and its mosaics, *Portait of an Unknown Man* by Antonello da Messina at the Museo Mandralisca, a stroll on the lungomare.
- **Organising Your Time:** In the summer months take your time. Otherwise, plan a half day for the town. Summit excursions are best in the morning.
- **Especially for Kids:** Puppet shows at Corte delle Stelle.
- **Also See:** BAGHERIA; CAPO D'ORLANDO; MADONIE E NEBRODI; PALERMO; SOLUNTO; TERMINI IMERESE.

Visit

Arriving from Palermo, visitors catch their first **sight**★★ of the town from a distance, with the impressive bulk of the cathedral set against the Rocca. Cefalù is an excellent base for excursions into the Madonie. Cefalù is the departure point for a tour through the Madonie (*See MADONIE E NEBRODI*).

Duomo★★

Open 8am–noon, 3.30pm–7pm (5pm winter). ☎0921 92 20 21.

The gold-coloured cathedral, a Romanesque jewel set behind a series of palm trees, appears to merge with the limestone hillside called La Rocca behind. It was built by the Norman **King Roger II** between 1131 and 1240, following a vow during a near-shipwreck.

Towers frame the Moorish-style facade, divided into two storeys by the portico, rebuilt in the 15C by the Lombard architect Ambrogio da Como.

The upper section is beautifully ornamented with blind arcading. The central doorway, known as the **King's Gate**

View of Cefalù from the sea

H. Champollion/ B. Juge/MICHELIN

B. Kaufmann/MICHELIN

Christ Pantocrator in the apse, Duomo

(*Porta dei Re*), served at one time as the main entrance.

Interior

The church, with a Latin-cross floor plan, consists of a single nave flanked by aisles, subdivided by columns with fine **capitals**★ carved in the Sicilian Arabo-Norman style.

The fabulous **mosaics**★★ (1148), executed in a spectacular array of colours (emerald green in particular) on a gold background, adorn the chancel. The eye is immediately attracted to the huge majestic image of the **Christ Pantocrator** gazing down from the apse, his right hand raised in benediction. His left holds a text from *St John's Gospel* (Chapter 8, verse 12): "I am the light of the world: he who followeth me shall not walk in darkness, but shall have the light of life."

Below, on three different levels, the Virgin, attended by four Archangels and the twelve Apostles, is imbued with sensitivity and gentleness unusual to poker-faced Byzantine art.

The side walls of the choir are covered with more mosaics dating from the late 13C, depicting prophets, saints and patriarchs; the angels in the vault date from the same period.

The stained-glass windows designed by Michele Canzoneri depict biblical themes and date from the 1990s; they bathe the interior of the church in evocative coloured light.

Walking Tour

Piazza del Duomo, stretching below the cathedral, is enclosed with ranges of splendid *palazzi*: Palazzo Piraino (on the corner of Corso Ruggero) with its late 16C portal, the medieval Palazzo Maria with a Gothic portal, possibly once a royal residence and, to the left of the cathedral, the 17C Palazzo Vescovile or Bishop's Palace.

Corso Ruggero

Cefalù's main street, lined with a wide range of boutiques, overlies the ancient Roman *decumanus,* which bisects the town on a north-south axis. The two resulting halves are quite different: to the west lies the medieval quarter, a labyrinth of narrow streets dotted with steps, arches and narrow passageways; to the east, a network of regular streets at right angles.

From Piazza Duomo, take the left road. Farther along on the left, stands the **Chiesa del Purgatorio** (formerly Santo Stefano Protomartire), its front graced by an elegant double staircase leading up to a Baroque doorway. Just inside is the sarcophagus of Baron Mandralisca (⏱*For information on admission times, call* ☎*0921 92 20 21*).

Osterio Magno★

On the right of the *corso* stands the residence of King Roger, later the property

Address Book

GETTING THERE AND AROUND

Buses runs from Palermo to Cefalù (the terminal is in front of the railway station). The **train** takes just over 1hr. Train connections are less frequent from Messina and the journey takes approximately 3hr. The railway station is about 10min walk from Corso Ruggero, following Via Aldo Moro and Via Matteotti. **Boats** leave Cefalù for the Aeolian islands (approx. 90min); for further information, contact Aliscafi SNAV, Corso Ruggero 82, ☎0921 42 15 95; Aliscafi SNAV; www.snav.it. In summer, hydrofoils speed to the Aeolian Islands (2 hrs); Ustica Lines, ☎0923 87 38 13 and 0909 889 949; www.usticalines.it.

For coin ranges, see the Legend on the cover flap.

WHERE TO STAY

Hotel Baia del Capitano – S 113, Località Mazzaforno, 5km/3mi E of Cefalù on S 113. ☎0921 42 00 03. www.baiadelcapitano.it.   Closed in Jan and Feb.   48 rooms. . This attractive, recently restored hotel offers guests spacious rooms, a swimming pool, access to a delightful cliff and a quiet location surrounded by Mediterranean vegetation.

WHERE TO EAT

La Botte – *Via Veterani 6, Cefalù.* ☎0921 42 43 15. Closed Mon and in Jan. This centrally located, family-run trattoria serves fresh, traditional Sicilian cuisine in a simple, rustic atmosphere.

Porticciolo – *Via C.O. di Bordonaro 66, Cefalù.* ☎0921 92 19 81. al.porticciolo@libero.it. Closed Wed. Booking recommended. In the heart of the small town, this pleasant, well-run restaurant is decorated in traditional style, with colourful furnishings. It serves fish and seafood, as well as pizza, the local speciality.

TAKING A BREAK

Bar del Molo – *Piazza Marina 4–5, Cefalù.* ☎0921 42 23 39. This popular bar with a splendid terrace enjoys lovely views of the surrounding area.

Bar Duomo – *Piazza Duomo 19, Cefalù.* ☎0921 42 11 64. Situated close to the town's magnificent cathedral, this bar is well known for its excellent ice cream.

Pasticceria-Gelateria Pietro Serio – *Via Giuseppe Giglio 29 (at the intersection with Via A. Moro, the continuation of Via Matteotti), Cefalù.* ☎0921 42 22 93. Open 7am–1pm, 3pm–10pm. Closed Wed. This recommended pasticceria serves a range of cakes, pastries and traditional confectionery.

GOING OUT

Le Petit Tonneau – *Via V. Emanuele 49, Cefalù.* ☎0921 42 14 47. This excellent rustic-style wine bar overlooking the marina in the medieval heart of Cefalù has a pleasant balcony, plus a good list of Sicilian and Italian vintages.

SHOPPING

A Lumera – *Corso Ruggero 180, Cefalù.* ☎0921 92 18 01. This shop sells a range of traditional Sicilian ceramics, famed for their quality and beauty. The selection includes the shop's own range of ceramics, plus items from Sciacca, Caltagirone and Santo Stefano di Camastra.

ENTERTAINMENT

Teatro dei Pupi a Cefalù – *Corso Ruggero 92, Cefalù.* ☎0921 92 38 82. Shows at 6pm and 9pm. Closed Fri. The Girolamo Cuticchio puppet company from Palermo recounts the extraordinary exploits of Orlando, Rinaldo and Carlo Magno (Charlemagne) in this splendid theatre.

FESTIVALS

Festa di San Salvatore – The festival of Cefalù's patron saint is held from 2–6 August and includes the 'nntinna 'a mari. During this competition volunteers must crawl along a horizontal pole suspended above the water in order to reach the statue of the Saviour (the event starts at 5pm on 6 August).

Madonna della Luce – On 14 August a procession of boats makes its way from Kalura to the old harbour and back.

of the Ventimiglia family, comprising two parts dating from different periods. The older, two-coloured part of lava and gold-coloured stone faces onto Via Amendola and has two elegant **two-light windows;** it dates from the 13C. The adjoining square tower, on the corner of Corso Ruggero, built in the 14C, has a fine three-light window set into an elaborate Chiaramonte-style arch. The palace, now completely restored, is used for temporary exhibitions.

Corso Ruggero leads into **Piazza Garibaldi**, site of one of the town's four gates. Facing the piazza is the Baroque Church of **Santa Maria alla Catena** (Saint Mary of the Chain). Its bell tower incorporates bits of the ancient megalithic town walls.

▸ *From Piazza Garibaldi, take Via Spinuzza and then Via Vittorio Emanuele.*

A little farther along on the left is the medieval **wash house**, known by the locals as *u ciumi* – meaning "the river" – used until comparatively recently. The road ends in Piazza Marina; just before, note **Porta Pescara** on the left. This is the only surviving medieval gateway of the original four, and currently has a display of fishing equipment.

Turn right into Via Ortolano di Bordonaro. Towards the end of the road, a street to the left leads directly into Piazza Crispi where the **Chiesa della Idria** (Church of the Hydria) stands, flanked by the Bastion of Cape Marchiafava with its sweeping view.

Retrace your steps and continue as far as Via Porpora, where there is a tower with a postern (an opening that allowed only one person to pass at a time). Behind Via Giudecca the ruins of ancient fortifications can still be seen.

Return to Piazza Duomo and take the picturesque **Via Mandralisca**, leading to the museum of the same name. Set into the paving (towards the beginning of the street before Piazza del Duomo) is the Cefalù coat of arms: three fishes with a loaf of bread, all symbols of Christianity, while also referring to the town's economic resources.

Visit

Museo Mandralisca
Via Mandralisca 13.
🕓*Open Apr–Sept, 9am–11pm (7pm winter).* ⊷€5. ☎0921 42 15 47. *www.museo mandralisca.it.*

The museum was founded at the request of one of Cefalù's most generous benefactors, Baron Enrico Piraino di Mandralisca, a 19C art collector. The museum houses a collection of coins and medals; a series of paintings including **Antonello da Messina's** wonderful **Portrait of an Unknown Man**★ from c. 1470; and archaeological artefacts, including an unusual bell-shaped *krater* depicting a tuna seller (4C BC).

Excursion

La Rocca
20min to the Temple of Diana;
another 40min to the top.
A path leads uphill from Corso Ruggero and Via dei Saraceni to the summit. The first part of the route leads past ancient crenellated walls before rising steeply. During summer, this stretch is best tackled in the early morning or at dusk. From such height, the magnificent **view**★★ pans across from Capo d'Orlando to Palermo. On a good day the Aeolian Islands are visible. Finds on this rocky outcrop confirm it to have accommodated the earliest settlements in the area, with evidence from different periods in history including the ruins of an Ancient Greek megalithic building, popularly called the **Temple of Diana**. On the top are the remains of a 12C–13C castle, recently restored.

Christian Symbols

The Greek word for fish, *Ichthys*, is composed of the initial letters of the Greek words *Iesoùs Christòs Theoù Hyiòs Sotr*, which translates as "Jesus Christ, Son of God, Saviour." This is why the image of a fish is often used as a symbol of Christ.

Driving Tour

Excursion Inland 60km/37mi.

▶ *From Cefalù, follow signs to the Santuario di Gibilmanna, 12km/7mi along an attractive scenic road.*

Santuario di Gibilmanna

🕐 *Open 8am–1pm, 3pm–7pm (5.30pm winter).* ☎ *0921 42 18 35.*

The **sanctuary**, dedicated to the Madonna, is perched high on the Pizzo San Angelo 800m/2 600ft above sea level, surrounded by oak and chestnut woods. Its name refers to its position (from the Arabic *Jebel*, a mountain) and the old tradition, now obsolete, of making manna. Of ancient origins – founded at the behest of Gregory the Great in the 6C – it passed into the hands of the Capuchin Friars Minor in 1535. The present building is the result of numerous remodelling, especially in the Baroque period. The façade was rebuilt in 1907. The shrine is the object of a devout pilgrimage on 8 September, the festival of the Madonna.

The building adjacent to the monastery, once used as a stable and guest rooms, has been converted into an interesting **museum** about the Capuchin Friars of the Demone Valley. Of particular interest are a polyptych by Fra' Feliciano (at the time he was Domenico Guargena), a 16C alabaster rosary belonging to Fra' Giuliano da Placia and a small 18C reed organ.

Down in the catacombs there are rare reliquaries in painted tin or wood made by the friars.

▶ *Return to the road and continue for a further 10km/6mi.*

Isnello

This little holiday resort, the starting-point for many walks into the surrounding area, stands in a spectacular **position**★ clinging to the rock amid a gorge of high limestone walls. Its narrow streets have a typical medieval layout. Take the road back towards the sanctuary; at the junction (signposted to Piano delle Fate), turn left to continue along the panoramic road. This leads through two small villages, **Gratteri**, the centre of which preserves a medieval feel, and **Lascari**, before continuing on down to the coast and Cefalù.

COMISO

POPULATION: 29 000

Originally a Greek settlement, Comiso was destroyed by the Romans. Monasteries revived the area in Byzantine times; prosperity continued under the Normans and Aragonese. After an earthquake in 1693 shattered its architecture, Comiso rebuilt in a Spanish Baroque style. During the Cold War, the town housed American missiles, not removed until 1991.

🛈 **Information:** Via Cap Bocchieri 33, 97100 Ragusa. ☎ 0932 621 421. www.comune.comiso.rg.it.

▶ **Orient Yourself:** Comiso stands on the lower western slopes of the Iblei. As a result, many of the streets in the town are quite steep.

😊 **Don't Miss:** The great Naselli chapel in the Chiesa di San Francesco.

🕯 **Also See:** CALTAGIRONE; GELA; Cava d'ISPICA; MODICA; NOTO; RAGUSA.

Walking Tour

Piazza Fonte di Diana

The central square is graced with a neo-Classical **fountain** dedicated to the goddess Diana. Excavations that were carried out in the little street directly opposite have revealed parts of the **Ancient baths:** an octagonal caldarium, and a nymphaeum with a black and white mosaic featuring Neptune surrounded by nereids (2C AD).

Piazza delle Erbe

🕐*Open Mon–Sat, 8am–1pm.* 🕐*Closed Sun and national hols.* ☎*0932 86 40 38.*
The main building overlooking the square is the town's principal church, dedicated to **Santa Maria delle Stelle**. Its front elevation rises through three tiers of Doric, Ionic and Corinthian pilasters. The square also harbours the neo-Classical **covered market** (1871): this houses the **Museo Civico di Storia Naturale** with its collection of cetaceans (whales and other such mammals) and sea turtles, and the **Biblioteca di Bufalino**, a library endowed by the author (who died in 1966) for his native town and refuge.

Chiesa dell'Annunziata

The elegant neo-Classical front elevation of this church, raised high above an unusual flight of steps, comprises two levels linked by a single element: the palm leaf. The airy light interior, ornamented with white, blue and gold stucco decoration, contains two paintings by Salvatore Fiume *(in the chancel)*.

Chiesa di San Francesco (dell'Immacolata)

This Renaissance church contains the great **Naselli Chapel;** this rises from a square ground plan to an octagon, then a ribbed dome.
Against the wall stands the funerary monument of Baldassare Naselli, surmounted by a small shrine, both by the Gagini. At the back of the church, there is a lovely 17C gallery, painted with fruit and flowers.

Piazza San Biagio

The square is graced with the **Chiesa di San Biagio**, a Byzantine church (buttresses) that was rebuilt in the 18C, and the **Castello Aragonese**.

Chiesa dei Cappuccini

In the southern part of the town.
🕐*Open 9am–10am.* ☎*0932 72 25 21.*
The building dates from 1616. Inside, there is a fine intarsia (inlaid wood) **altar**★ and a delicate little statue of the Madonna (18C). The mortuary chapel preserves the mummified remains of various religious and illustrious men.

Gesualdo Bufalino

The elaborate and expressive writing of Gesualdo Bufalino, born in Comiso in 1920, first came to public attention in 1981, with the publication of the author's first novel, *Diceria dell'untore*, which was awarded the Premio Campiello. An intense period of literary activity followed until 1996, when the writer was killed in a car accident. Some of Bufalino's best works include the collection of poetry *L'amaro miele*, and the novels *Argo il cieco ovvero i sogni della memoria* and *Le menzogne della notte*.

Excursions

Vittoria

6km/3.6mi W.
The town – founded in the 17C at the wishes of Countess Vittoria Colonna, after whom it is named – was partly spared by the 1693 earthquake. The straight, perpendicular streets are scattered with elegant Liberty-style *palazzi*. The centre is the Piazza del Popolo, where **Santa Maria delle Grazie** stands with its harmoniously facade and the neo-Classical municipal theatre. In Via Cancellieri, leading off the piazza, are a number of fine buildings: note the Liberty-style **Palazzo Carfì-Manfré** (no 71) and the Venetian Gothic **Palazzo Traìna** (nos 108–116).
Via Cavour provides access to the town's main church and the museum. **San Giovanni Battista** (1695) has a distinctively linear front with three entrances and two small lateral domes. The interior is richly decorated with neo-Classical stucco friezes picked out in white, pale and dark blue and gold. The **Museo Civico** (🕐*Open Tue–Sat 9am–1pm, 4pm–7.30pm; Sun 9am–1pm only;* 🕐*Closed Mon and Sun 4pm–7.30pm;* ⊜*€2;* ☎*0932 72 25 21)* is accommodated in the countess's castle, completed in 1785 on much earlier foundations. The well-restored rooms continue to reflect the fact that they were used as a prison until 1950. The small museum collects together old machinery for producing

special theatrical effects (wind and hail-producing apparatus), a selection of traditional farming tools, and various ornithological specimens.

The WWI **concentration camp** located just outside the town centre in Via Garibaldi primarily held Hungarian soldiers (who were on excellent terms with the locals); one of the dormitory blocks now contains **Museo Storico Italo-Ungherese** (◷*Open Mon–Sat, 8.30am–1pm;* ◷*Closed Sun and public hols;* ☎*0932 86 59 94).*

Acate
Approx. 15km/9mi NW.

In the past, the little town was called Biscari; its modern name probably comes from the word for agate, a semi-precious stone found locally.

For generations, it belonged to the princes of Paterno-Castello, hence the massive residence in the town centre. It is also worth seeking out the town's main church (Chiesa Madre) and San Vincenzo, which claims to preserve the martyred saint's relics.

ISOLE EGADI ★
POPULATION: 4 000

The *Odyssey* dubbed the ancient Aegates "islands of the goats". This tiny archipelago stands near Trapani and is renowned for its wild aspect, coastal beauty and the limpid sea that embraces it all.

- **Information:** Favignana Largo Marina 14 ☎0923 92 21 21 and Piazza Matrice 8 ☎0923 92 16 47. www.egadiweb.it.
- **Orient Yourself:** Favignana, the largest of the three islands and the most accessible, is popular with holidaymakers. Levanzo, the smallest island, and Marettimo, the most inaccessible, have fewer traditional tourist facilities and appeal to visitors looking for a simpler holiday, surrounded by peaceful landscapes.
- **Don't Miss:** The quarries of Favignana, the superb cave paintings in the Genovese grotto on Levanzo and sea caves of Maretimo.
- **Organising Your Time:** Avoid August, when all Italy goes on holiday. In May and June, crowds fill Favignana for the tuna rituals. A small ferry connects this island to Levanzo (10–25min) and to Marettimo (30min–2hr).
- **Especially for Kids:** Sandy beaches at Cala Azzurra and Lido Burrone.
- **Also See:** TRAPANI; MARSALA.

A Bit of History

The islands have been inhabited since prehistoric times (Levanzo and Favignana may even have been part of the main island in the Palaeolithic era). Here the treaty ending the First Punic War (241 BC) was signed, when Carthage assigned Sicily to the Roman Empire. After changing hands many times over the centuries, the islands were sold in 1640 to the Pallavicino-Rusconi family. The Florios purchased them in 1874.

Sights

Favignana ★

The nearest of the Egadis to the Sicilian mainland, this island is often referred to as *La Farfalla* on account of its shape, lik-

Address Book

GETTING THERE AND AROUND

Several hydrofoil and ferry services (especially during the summer) operate every day out of Trapani and Marsala (20–60min by hydrofoil and 1hr by ferry). For information contact: **Siremar**, ☎091 74 93 111 (from Italian land lines) or 081 017 1998 (from mobile phones); www.siremar.it; or **Ustica Lines**, Via Amm. Staiti 23, Trapani, ☎0923 22 200, www.usticalines.it. The same company runs services between Trapani-Favignana-Levanzo-Ustica-Naples. The Favignana-Naples crossing takes approximately 6hr.

For coin ranges, see the Legend on the cover flap.

WHERE TO STAY

In addition to several traditional hotels, a number of **rooms** are also available for rent (apply to the Pro Loco for names and addresses).

FAVIGNANA

Camping Villaggio Egad – *Contrada Arena, Favignana.* ☎*0923 92 15 55. Closed Oct–Apr.* This beautiful campsite just one kilometre from the centre of Favignana is surrounded by pine, eucalyptus, acacia and oleander. A number of small apartments with modern bathrooms and kitchens are also available for rent.

Egadi Hotel – *Via Colombo 17, Favignana.* ☎*0923 92 12 32. www. albergoegadi.it. Closed Oct–mid-Apr. 12 rooms.* ⌣. This hotel is one of the best known and most popular on the island. The staff here are friendly and helpful and the rooms simple, attractive and well maintained.

L'Oasi Villaggio – *Contrada Camaro 32, Favignana.* ☎*0923 92 16 35. diamonik@libero.it. Closed Oct–mid-Apr. 25 rooms.* ⌣. This family-run hotel is located in a peaceful setting within close proximity to the town centre. The recently renovated rooms are comfortable, well-appointed and are arranged around a garden with tropical plants, pines and other Mediterranean vegetation.

Aegusa Hotel – *Via Garibaldi 11/17, Favignana.* ☎*0923 92 24 30. www. aegusahotel.it. Closed end Oct–Mar. 28 rooms.* ⌣. The Aegusa hotel has bright, airy rooms with simple wicker furniture and a friendly, sunny holiday atmosphere. The restaurant, set in a pleasant garden-courtyard, offers a reasonably priced menu, with a wide selection of great fish dishes and traditional cuisine.

WHERE TO EAT

FAVIGNANA

La Bettola – *Via Nicotera 47, Favignana.* ☎*0923 92 19 88. Closed Thu (winter) and Jan.* ⌐. This typical trattoria serves traditional Egadian cuisine using fresh, local ingredients. The ambience is simple and typical of the islands.

MARETTIMO

Il Timone – *Via Garibaldi 18, Marettimo.* ☎*0923 92 31 42. www. marettimonline.it/mangiare.html. Closed mid-Oct–Mar.* ⌐.*Booking recommended.* Situated down a narrow typical street in Marettimo, this simple restaurant, with its striking blue and white decor, serves delicious fresh fish and hand-made pasta. Perfect for visitors looking for genuine Sicilian cuisine.

SHOPPING

Favignana's most popular specialities are the edible kind: *bottarga* (dried tuna-fish roe) and *bresaola* (cured or smoked) tuna and swordfish.

OUTDOOR FUN

Mopeds and bicycles – The two most convenient ways of exploring the island are by bicycle or moped, and both can be hired here: cycling is especially popular on this flat and easy terrain.

A. Safina/Lara Pessina/MICHELIN

Diving and snorkelling – The best areas for diving and snorkelling are Punta Marsala, Secca del Toro, the submerged cave between Cala Rotonda and Scoglio Corrente, and the rocks off Punta Fanfalo and Punta Ferro.

TOURS

The Pro Loco of Favignana (Piazza Matrice 8, ☎0923 92 16 47, www.egadiweb.it) arranges guided tours of the tuna fishery and other excursions.

ened to a butterfly. Its proper name is, in fact, derived from *favonio*, the prevalent local wind. In times past, the principle profession here was tuna fishing, and the **mattanza** (the traditional, but cruel, ritual of systematically killing the tuna trapped in the nets, known as the *camera della morte* – "room of death").

Favignana covers an area of about 20km2/8sq mi. The west "wing" is dominated by **Montagna Grossa**, which, despite its name, rises to a mere 302m/991ft. The eastern part, on the other hand, is flatter and harbours the island's main town. The jagged coastline is interrupted, here and there, with short stretches of sandy beach.

Tufa caves

Quarrying was the island's secondary source of employment. Once cut, the blocks were transported elsewhere in Sicily and exported to North Africa. These quarries, a characteristic feature of the island's eastern flank, give the landscape a disturbing quality. Great, gaping, rectangular, stepped cavities mar the cliffs.

These are often overgrown, used as rubbish tips, or transformed into secret small gardens, sheltered from the marauding winds. Along the east coast, some sites have been partly flooded by waves, leaving behind small geometric pools of water. The most spectacular quarries are those grouped around Scalo Cavallo, Cala Rossa and Bue Marino.

La Mattanza

The complex and ritual method of catching tuna follows – or rather used to follow – very precise rules, timings and strictly disciplined practices. These were established by the **Rais**, the head of the tuna fishermen and, at one time, also the head of the village: a sort of shaman who specified when it should begin and what procedure should be followed. The methods date back to ancient times, indeed possibly even to the Phoenicians. However, it was not until Arab domination that the most fundamental elements of the "rite" were firmly established. For the *mattanza* was a ritual, complete with propitiatory songs (the *scialome*), concluding in a cruel struggle with these powerful creatures at very close quarters. The outcome, however, was a foregone conclusion and rarely, if ever, in the tuna's favour.

In late spring, the tuna collect in great shoals off the west coast of Sicily where the conditions are conducive to breeding. The fishing boats laid the nets in a long corridor, which the tuna were forced to follow. The last nets were dropped like barriers to form antechambers, thus averting the risk of overloading and tearing the nets, and losing fish. Beyond these antechambers was laid the *camera della morte* – the "room of death" –an enclosure of tougher netting, often closed along the bottom. When an appropriate number of fish arrived, the Rais ordered the *mattanza* to begin. The tuna, exhausted from escape-attempts and panicked, injured each other in the press. One by one they were speared or hooked and heaved aboard.

The term *mattanza* comes from the Spanish word "matar", to kill, which derives from the Latin *mactare*, meaning to glorify, or immolate.

Favignana città

The main town of the island, indeed, of the archipelago, is built around a small port that nestles in a large bay. On the skyline, perched up on its very own hill, sits the **Fort of Santa Caterina** (now under military control), which began life as an ancient Saracen warning station. This was rebuilt by the Norman King Roger II, and subsequently enlarged before serving as a prison under Bourbon rule (1794–1860).

Down by the seafront, Favignana boasts two buildings endowed by the **Florio** family, a wealthy dynasty involved in the production and export of Marsala wine, before it developed any financial interests in tuna fishing. These comprise the **Palazzo Florio**, built in 1876, and the great **tonnara** or tuna fishery, now abandoned (plans are afoot to redevelop). For information, contact the tourist office, ☎0923 92 16 47.

The little town centres around two piazzas: Europa and Madrice, linked by the main street, where the passeggiata (evening stroll) is enacted. On the northeastern edge of town lies the district of San Nicola (behind the cemetery), which preserves vestiges of the past: there is no access to this area, however, as long as it remains private property.

Bathing and beaches★

There are two main beaches: a small sandy bay south of the town, below the lighthouse, in **Cala Azzurra** and, to the southwest, the popular, and more inviting, broad sandy stretch known as the **Lido Burrone** Kids . A bus runs there hourly. The rocky bays on this side of the island are more exciting and thrilling to visit, notably those under the towering tufa cliffs at the spectacular **Cala Rossa★** and **Cala del Bue Marino** nearby. Once these were quarries; deep in the grottoes; where the roof has not fallen in, there still remains a network of long, dark and mysterious passages.

The other half of the island harbours lovely bays as the **Cala Rotonda**, where local legend has it Odysseus was washed up after doing battle with the Cyclops, **Cala Grande** and Punta Ferro, which doubles as a popular area for diving.

The caves

The west side of the mountain slopes into the sea, forming a number of evocative caves and grottoes. Each calm summer morning, the local fishermen vie with each other to whisk visitors to see the most picturesque: Grotta Azzurra (Azure Grotto), Grotta dei Sospiri (The Grotto of Sighs, which sounds its laments in winter), and Grotta degli Innamorati (Lovers' Grotto), so named because of two identical rocks standing side by side deep against the back wall.

Levanzo★

Tiny Levanzo (pronounced with an emphasis on the first syllable) has a surface area of 6km2/2sq mi, and undulates with pastoral charm and goats and sheep grazing quietly on the sides of its many hills. The tallest of these, Pizzo del Monaco (278m/912ft), tumbles its jaggedly rocky skirts down into the sea; a particularly beautiful section of the southwest coast.

Only one road bisects the island from south to north, making it a veritable haven of peace and serenity. The northern part of the island consists of a succession of sheer drops, rocky outcrops and secluded little creeks. Between Levanzo and the coast of Sicily lie two minute islets, **Maraone** and **Formica** (on which there are the remains of an old tuna fishery).

Cala Dogana

The only hamlet on Levanzo is little more than a clutch of houses overlooking a bay of the clearest water on the south side of the island. From here, a well-kept path snakes to the bays of the southwestern coast, each tightly embracing its own miniature pebbled beach, as far as the Faraglione (a large rock). Beyond this you'll find a rocky path that leads north up the coast to the Grotta del Genovese.

Grotta del Genovese★

Accessible on foot (approximately 2hr there and back), by jeep and then on foot along a steep slope, or by sea. To visit the cave, contact Signore Castiglione, Via Calvario, Levanzo.

M. Retano/Lara Pessina/MICHELIN

Levanzo

☎*0923 92 40 32 or 339 74 18 800 (mobile).*

Discovered in 1949, this excavated hollow in the side of a tall cliff bears the marks of prehistoric man. Vestiges of wall-painting here have been identified as dating from the Upper Palaeolithic era, while the incised drawings may be from the Neolithic period. The *graffiti*, now located behind glass near the entrance, completed when the island was still attached to the island of Sicily, represent bison and a **deer**★★ of the most pleasing proportions, elegance and foreshortening. The charcoal and animal fat paintings represent early attempts at fishing (stylised representations of both tuna and dolphins are discernible), animal husbandry (a woman leads a cow with a halter) and ritual images of men dancing and women with wide hips. These evocative paintings are comparable with the Franco-Cantabrian cave paintings of Lascaux in southwest France (♨ *See The Green Guide Dordogne Berry Limousin*) and Altamira in Spain (♨ *See The Green Guide Spain*).

Marettimo★

A steep rocky mountain with great limestone cliffs that plunge down into the sea define Marettimo is the most remote island of the Egadi group. It welcomes only the more curious visitors, who arrive at its tiny harbour knowing that there are no hotels there. The only accommodation available is that offered by local fishermen and consists of simple, rented rooms *(either log on to www.marettimoresidence.it or contact the Pro Loco in Favignana for addresses of available accommodation).*

At the foot of the mountain nestles the hamlet of Marettimo, a compact collection of square flat-roofed white houses and terraces interspersed with splashes of colourful bougainvillea, collected around the miniature harbour. Behind the Scalo Nuovo (the main dock) stands the Scalo Vecchio reserved for the local fishermen. To one side, extends **Punta Troia**, topped with ruins of a Spanish castle (17C) that served as a prison until 1844. A series of rugged paths (manageable most easily astride a donkey) lead to the remote and wild uplands.

Boat Trip Around the Island★★

In the harbour, many local fishermen offer excursions to the numerous caves that hide among the precipitous cliffs along the coast. The most striking include the **Grotta del Cammello**, sheltering a small pebble beach, **Grotta del Tuono** (Cave of Thunder), Grotta Perciata and the **Grotta del Presepio**, likened to a Nativity scene. Many will leave you in a cove to swim and come back to pick you up later on request for an extra fee. The island's beautifully clean and clear waters teem with underwater interest and are also popular with both snorkellers and divers alike.

ENNA

POPULATION: 28 625

Situated on a beautiful plateau in the centre of the island, Enna is called the "lookout of Sicily" and is the highest capital of an Italian province at 948m/3 110ft. One of the oldest towns on the island, it was founded by the Sicani, long before the Greeks, the town's main attractions are the 13C Lombard Castle, built by Frederick II, and a plethora of churches.

- **Information:** Via Roma 413. ☎0935 52 82 28. www.comune.enna.it.
- ▶ **Orient Yourself:** The road in is narrow and winding, especially the last stretch. In town, the Via Roma is the main thoroughfare.
- **Parking:** Park in the upper town.
- **Don't Miss:** The cathedral, Lombard castle and view from the Pisana tower.
- **Organising Your Time:** Allow one day to see the town fully.
- **Also See:** CALTANISSETTA; PIAZZA ARMERINA; VILLA IMPERIALE DEL CASALE.

A Bit of History

The origins of Enna date to prehistoric times. Its elevated position, so easily defensible, made it especially desirable. It was probably inhabited by the Sicani, defending against Siculi advances. There subsequently developed a Greek, and then later, a Roman town; in 135 BC the First Slave War erupted here, prompted by the Syrian slave Euno, before spreading across the island and lasting for seven long years.

After the Roman conquest, Enna fell in the 6C, only to be absorbed into the Byzantine dominion (as did all the rest of Sicily).

Arabs took the city in the 9C. Enter the Normans, who made it the political and cultural stronghold of their kingdom, followed by the Swabians, the Angevins and the Aragonese. Here Frederick II took the title of King of Trinacria (the ancient name for Sicily) in 1314, and convened parliament in 1324. Subsequently, the town followed the vicissitudes of the rest of the island, rebelling against the Bourbons and supporting Garibaldi. In 1927, the ancient name of Enna was restored under Mussolini.

Mythology – In ancient times, the cult of **Demeter** (Ceres to the Romans), earth mother and goddess of fertility, was especially important here. Furthermore, according to the Greek myths, it was on the shores of nearby Lake Pergusa, that the God of the Underworld abducted her daughter Persephone (Proserpina).

Walking Tour

Bring a jumper or jacket, as it's generally cooler here than it is on the coast.

Town Centre

The axis of the town is marked by the **Via Roma**, which starts near the Castello di Lombardia. After a sharp turn, it leads downhill to the Torre di Federico. Along this principal thoroughfare are most of the monuments and points of interest.

Castello di Lombardi★★

Open 8am–8pm. ☎0935 52 82 28.
Situated uppermost on the plateau, the **castle** looks out over the town and the valley, including the Rocca di Cerere (Fortress of Ceres), where a temple to Demeter may have stood. This site has been fortified since earliest times because of its strategic position. Under Norman dominion, the castle was reinforced. It was made habitable by Frederick II of Aragon, who added a number of rooms that rendered it suitable for court life. Indeed, he intended it as his summer residence: it was here that he was crowned King of Trinacria and, in 1324, convocated the Sicilian parliament. The name of the castle dates from this same period, linked to the presence of a garri-

Address Book

For coin ranges, see the Legend on the cover flap.

WHERE TO STAY

Sicilia – *Piazza Colaianni 7, Enna.* ☎*0935 50 08 50. www.hotelsicilia enna.it. 76 rooms.* The Sicilia is a modern hotel in the heart of this attractive town, which caters for both tourists and business visitors. The rooms have been recently renovated and the communal areas are spacious and attractive. A comfortable hotel with good service.

WHERE TO EAT

Tiffany – *Via Roma 467, Enna.* ☎*0935 50 13 68. Closed Thu.* This small, reasonably priced restaurant, considered one of the best pizzerias in the centre of Enna, has a particularly warm and friendly atmosphere.

Centrale – *Piazza VI Dicembre 9, Enna.* ☎*0935 50 09 63. www.ristorante centrale.net. Closed Sat (except Jul–Sept).* As the name suggests, this family-run restaurant is downtown. It offers a good choice of local fish and meat dishes, under high ceilings.

TAKING A BREAK

Bar del Duomo – *Piazza Mazzini 1, Enna.* ☎*0935 24 205.* This popular bar, located just in front of the cathedral, serves a good selection of typical Sicilian cakes, savoury specialities and excellent ice cream.

Caffè Roma – *Via Roma 312, Enna.* ☎*0935 50 12 12. Open 8am–11pm. Closed Tue.* The Caffè Roma was founded in 1921 and has long been a firm favourite with locals. Rustic decor and exposed stone provide the backdrop for excellent sweets and savouries.

FESTIVALS

Settimana Santa – During the traditional Holy Week festival the confraternities of Enna take part in a hooded and cloaked procession through the town.

For additional suggestions, see PIAZZA ARMERINA: Address Book.

---

son of Lombard soldiers posted there to defend it. The ground plan of the castle, which is roughly pentagonal, hugs the tortuous lie of the land. Of the original 20 towers, only six survive (some only in part).

The most interesting and complete is the one called *La Pisana* or *Torre delle Aquile* (The Pisan Tower or Tower of the Eagles), topped by Guelph crenellations. From the top, a breathtaking **view**★★★ stretches over the best part of the Sicilian mountain ranges, Mount Etna and Calascibetta.

Just outside the castle precincts, in the direction of the Fortress of Ceres, stands the statue of **Euno**, a memorial to the slave who began the Slave War.

Rocca di Cerere

From the top of the hill, where the Fortress of Ceres – a temple dedicated to the fertility goddess – once stood, extends an all-encompassing **view**★★, that spreads out to include Calascibetta opposite, and Enna itself.

Duomo

Although largely rebuilt in the Baroque style in the 16C and 17C, the cathedral has retained its Gothic apses. Its front, preceded by a dramatic staircase, rises above a portico to a bell tower through the three Classical orders. The 16C south door, named after San Martino, has a marble relief panel depicting St Martin and the Pauper; this balances the Porta Santa, adjacent, which is Gothic. The **interior**★ is divided into nave and aisles by columns of black basalt, each with finely sculpted bases and capitals (note, in particular, the reliefs incorporating allegorical creatures, *putti*, serpents and two-headed gargoyles on the second column on the right and the corresponding column on the left, which are considered to be by **Giandomenico Gagini**). The 16C woodwork is especially fine. The coffered **ceiling**★ is finely inlaid, and graced at the end of each beam by unusual winged figures. At the end of the aisles, the organ loft and choir gallery have elegant inlaid and painted wooden balustrading, and niches containing statues of Christ and the twelve Apostles. Behind the high altar, the wooden choir stalls display scenes from the Old and New Testaments. Above the altar hangs a fine 15C Christ on the Cross with, on the reverse, a painting of the Resurrection: this is called the Christ of the Three Faces because Christ's expression appears to alter depending on the angle from which the painting is contemplated.

San Michele Arcangelo

Erected in 1658, probably on the site of an old mosque, the church of the Archangel Michael has a blockish square façade and an elliptical plan with radiating side chapels.

Follow Via Polizzi out of the square and turn right into Via del Salvatore to **San Salvatore**, an old Basilian church remodelled in the 16C, and has recently been restored.

Continue to Piazza Colajanni, which is bordered by fine buildings, including the **Palazzo Pollicarini** and the Church of Santa Chiara.

Santa Chiara

⏱*For information on admission times, call ☎0935 26 119.*

The Church of St Clare, now a memorial to fallen soldiers, has a single nave. The tiled floor is set with two panels: *The Triumph of Christianity over Islam* and *The Advent of Steam Navigation*.

Farther along Via Roma is **San Giuseppe**, with its lovely (though rather dilapidated) Baroque façade, complete with bell tower.

▷ *From Piazza Coppola, turn left into Via Candrilli.*

Campanile di San Giovanni Battista

The elegant bell tower of John the Baptist, with its round-headed arches in the upper storey, is all that remains of the church of the same name.

▷ *Return to Via Roma.*

The Confraternities

One peculiarity of the residents of Enna is the fact that they are divided into confraternities, each having its "spiritual *contrada* or quarter." Every confraternity has its own hierarchy of officers, church and traditional costume, all of which are fiercely and proudly defended by its adherents. The most important popular event is the **Processione della Settimana Santa**, a week-long festival beginning on Palm Sunday when the Collegio dei Rettori (a council of governors) processes to the Duomo to begin celebrations in adoration of the Holy Eucharist. In turn, delegations from each confraternity leave their own churches and converge on the cathedral, followed by bands playing funeral marches. At noon on the Wednesday of Holy Week, the church bells are removed

J. Malburet/MICHELIN

and the *troccola*, a special mechanical instrument made of wood, is sounded. The real and proper procession takes place on the evening of Good Friday: hundreds of representatives from the various confraternities, hooded and cloaked in mantles of different colours, process through the streets bearing first the Dead Christ, followed by Our Lady of Sorrows, on their shoulders. On Easter Sunday, the two statues are carried back to their respective churches.

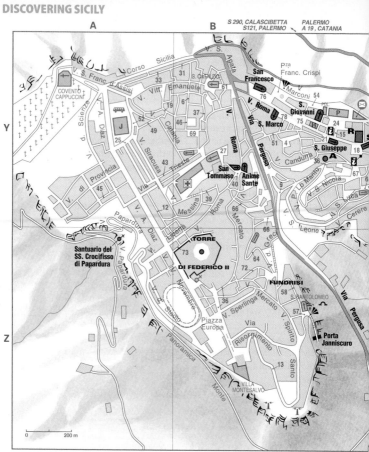

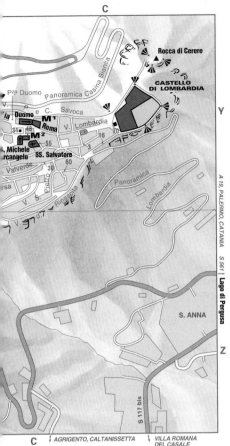

S. Bartolomeo (Piazza)	BZ		S. Nicola (Via)	BY		Stadio (Via d.)	ABZ
57S. Bartolomeo (Via)	BZ	58	S. Pietro (Via)	CY	S.	Studio (Via)	BZ	72
S. Biagio (Via)	CY	60	Sofia (Piazza)	BY	67	Torre di Federico (Via)	BZ	73
S. Cataldo (Piazza)	BY	61	Salvatore (Via)	CY	69	Trieste (Via)	ABY
S. Francesco			Savarese Nino (Viale)	CY	70	Umberto I (Piazza)	BY	75
d'Assisi (Via)	AY		Savoca (Viale P. e C.)	CY		Valverde (Via)	CY
S. Giorgio (Piazza)	BY	63	Scienze (Via d.)	AY		VI Dicembre (Piazza)	BY	78
S. Leonardo (Via)	BYZ	64	Sicilia (Cso)	ABY		V. Emanuele (Piazza)	BY	76
S. Leone (Via)	BY		Siracusa (Via)	AY		V. Emanuele (Via)	ABY
S. Luca (Via)	BCY		Sperlinga (Via)	BZ			
S. Matteo (Via)	BY	66	Spirito Santo (Via)	BZ			

Anime Sante	BY		Palazzo Pollicarini	BY	R	S. Tommaso	BY	
Campanile di			Porta Janniscuro	BZ		SS. Salvatore	CY	
S. Giovanni Battista	BY	A	Rocca di Cerere	CY		Santuario del SS.		
Castello di Lombardia	CY		S. Chiara	BY	S	Crocifisso di Papardura	AZ	
Duomo	CY		S. Francesco	BY		Torre di Federico II	BZ	
Fundrisi	BZ		S. Giovanni	BY			
Museo Alessi	CY	M	S. Giuseppe	BY			
Museo Archeologico			S. Marco	BY			
Varisano	CY	M	S. Michele Arcangelo	CY			

Frederick's Towers

Frederick II, the Swabian King of Sicily, gave a considerable boost to civic building in the south of Italy. This architecture is characterised by rigorous geometry: buildings rise from a square base, imitating the form of the Roman *castrum*. This shape also appears in the Islamic world, with cylindrical or square towers at the corners and one cylindrical or polygonal tower in the centre *(see the castle at Augusta or Maniace Castle at Siracusa)*. Through time, the *octagonal* ground plan evolved and was applied to the one here, at Enna. This choice of plan is in accordance with the mind of medieval man, fascinated as he was by precise geometry and the symbolic significance of such forms. The square – symbolising the Earth and humankind – contrasts with the circle, which symbolised the divine and the heavens. At that time, the octagon represented mediation, the fusion of the two.

San Giovanni

Originally built in the Romanesque style, the Church of St John has been remodelled, decorated with stucco and completely restored in 1967. Inside is an unusual font: the base is Roman, the central section is a Byzantine capital made of red marble, the carved basin is medieval (14C).

San Marco

This church, dating from the 17C, was erected on the site of an old synagogue, in what was Enna's Jewish quarter. **Inside**, the spacious hall church is decorated with fine stuccoes of cherubs, garlands of flowers, fruit and shells by Gabriele de Blanco da Licodia (1705). It is also worth noting the inlaid wooden women's gallery.

Almost directly opposite the belvedere in Piazza Francesco Crispi, there extends a fabulous **view**★ of Calascibetta, Lake Nicoletti and the Lombardy Castle on the right.

The fountain in the garden is graced with a bronze copy of Bernini's *Rape of Persephone*.

Further along is a monumental church dedicated to St Francis (**San Francesco**). Right on the bend of the road is another, San Cataldo, with a square façade. Via Roma continues to Piazza Neglia, onto which faces the **Chiesa delle Anime Sante** (All Souls) – with a fine Baroque limestone doorway – and the 15C **San Tomaso**, with its lovely gallery and campanile, intended and used (around the 10C) as a watchtower.

▶ *Continue along Via Roma.*

Torre di Federico★

At one time, Enna might have been called the city of towers. Their proliferation is explained by the defensive and strategic role of the town. Many have disappeared, many have been incorporated into churches as bell towers; only a few survive as free-standing towers today. A case in point is the octagonal tower named after Frederick II of Swabia, which occupies pride of place in a small public park.

▶ *This tour can be continued through the Fundrisi Quarter.*

Quartiere Fundrisi

About halfway along Via Mercato.

In 1396, King Martin of Aragon quelled the revolt on the island and razed several of the small towns near Castrogiovanni, as it was then, to the ground. The inhabitants of the town called Fundr were transferred here and, over the centuries, created an independent community. A walk through the narrow streets, all up and down, among the typical single-storey houses with their distinctive galleries (especially along Via San Bartolomeo), is particularly recommended. From here or Piazzetta San Bartolomeo, which takes its name from the church that presides over the scene, extend various **prospects**★ across the northeastern part of the town. A short way below the piazza, stands **Porta Janniscuru**, the only gate to survive of the five that once served the city, and, adjacent to this, the Grotta della Guardiola (literally translated as the "Cave of the Guardroom"), perhaps a cult site long before the foundation of the town. Continuing on an axis with Via Mercato, Via Spirito Santo leads to a church of the same name, enjoying a splendid position, perched on a rocky spur over a vertical drop.

Visit

Museo Alessi
Entrance at the back of the Duomo.
o━ *Closed for restoration at time of going to press.*
In 1862, the museum was created to house the impressive collections of Canon Alessi, which include 17C and 18C sacred vestments embroidered with gold thread and coral (in the basement). There are a selection of **paintings** *(on the upper floor)*, notably a gentle Madonna and Child by an unknown 15C Flemish painter, a 16C *Pietà* with the symbols of the Passion, and two panels with John the Baptist and St John the Evangelist from a 16C polyptych attributed to Il Panormita.
Displayed on the first floor is a canvas by Giuseppe Salerno (known locally as the Lame Man of Gangi) depicting the *Madonna delle Grazie*, together with the glorious **treasures** from the Chiesa Madre. The latter consists of sacred relics, a fabulous Madonna's **crown**★ exquisitely enamelled and engraved (17C), a magnificent 17C **pelican jewel**★ – symbol of the Sacrifice of the Resurrection for Eternal Life – and the monumental **processional monstrance**★ engraved with the spires of a Gothic cathedral, attributed to Paolo Gili (1536–38).

Museo Archeologico Varisano
Piazza Mazzini.
🕐*Open daily 8am–7pm.* 🚫*Closed Mon, Sat and Sun.* ✆€2. ☎0935 24 720.
On display are the archaeological finds, mainly rendered in terracotta, recovered from the various necropoli at Calascibetta, Capodarso, Pergusa, Cozzo Matrice and Rossomanno.

▶ *Take Via Libertà after the crossroads with Viale Diaz; turn right down a*

minor road marked with the Stations of the Cross.

Santuario del SS Crocifisso di Papardura
🕐*Open Mon–Sat 3.30pm–6.30pm, Sun 10.30am–noon.* ☎0935 37 626.
The Sanctuary of the Holy Crucifix of Papardura incorporates the cave where, in 1659, an image of the Crucifix was found painted on a stone slab. This has been attributed as the work of Basilian monks and can now be seen on the high altar. Inside, the fine **stuccoes** initiated in 1696 by Giuseppe and Giacomo Serpotta, were completed in 1699 by another artist, who also executed the statues of the Apostles. Note also the high altar silver **façade**★ made by a craftsman from Messina (17C).

Driving Tours

Among the Hills North of Enna

85km/53mi, plus 55km/34mi back to Enna – allow one day.

▶ *Leave Enna as indicated on the plan and follow directions for Calascibetta (4km/2.5mi N).*

This tour runs through the gently rolling hills that separate Enna from Catania, passing old hill-top villages and providing stunning **panoramic views**★.

Calascibetta
Benefiting from a glorious **setting**★ that consists of a natural amphitheatre nestled in a rocky hollow on the side of a hill, this little town was probably founded during the Arab occupation. The **Chiesa Madre**, founded in the 14C, was completely rebuilt following a 17C earthquake. Inside, the nave is divided from its aisles by stone columns, which rise from bases bearing carvings of monstrous figures to support the arcades of pointed arches. To the left of the entrance is a fine 16C font. The **Norman tower** (11C), standing beside the ruined church of San Pietro, is ornamented with a shallow relief

The spectacular setting of Calascibetta

in stone. From the piazza on the left extends a marvellous **view**★★, with Enna on the right (where the castle and belvedere can be seen quite clearly) and the Lago di Pergusa below.

Leaving the town in the direction of Villapriolo, the road passes the rock-cut tombs of the **necropolis of Realmese** (4C BC).

▶ *Return to the crossroads and take the left turning (S 121) for Leonforte (20km/12mi NE of Calascibetta).*

Leonforte

The town perches on a hump enjoying a superb **position**★. The monumental silhouette of Palazzo Branciforte is discernible from a distance, a powerful reminder that the town was founded in the 17C by Nicola Placido Branciforte. The palazzo, dating from 1611, runs along one side of the enormous piazza of the same name. Of particular interest is the lovely fountain or **Granfonte** (1651), built by the Branciforte family: constructed of gold-coloured stone it comprises 24 spouts.

▶ *Backtrack, and at the fork, turn left for Assoro (6km/4mi E of Leonforte).*

Assoro

At a height of 850m/2 800ft, the town is grouped around the little Piazza Umberto I, which is attractively paved, has a central fountain and a lovely **belvedere-terrace**★. Beyond the ele-

gant archway linking Palazzo Valguarnera to the town's main church, is another little square with viewing terrace, which opens out before the Chiesa Madre, or **Basilica di San Leone** (To visit, contact the priest ☎0935 66 72 78). The church, founded in 1186, has been subjected to major alterations: first in the late 14C and again in the 18C. It consists of a nave and aisles and has a doorway on the south side. The **interior**★, enclosed by a fine ribbed vault, is particularly attractive on account of its compactness and profuse gilded Baroque **stucco decoration**. The spiral columns were in fact embellished with their climbing plant ornament in the 18C, at the same time as the pelican *(right)* and the phoenix *(left)* were added above the apses. These emblems allude to the Sacrifice of the Crucifixion and the Resurrection of Christ: the first represents the bird which, according to myth, plucked flesh from its own breast to feed its young, while the second fabulous creature, having burnt itself to ashes, emerged rejuvenated.

A **wooden tie-beam ceiling**, painted and ornamented with arabesques (1490) spans the main body of the church; the attractive wrought-iron chapel **gates** (15C) are also worthy of note.

▶ *Beyond the town, follow the road past San Giorgio which intersects S 121 again at Nissoria. Turn right towards Agira (17km/10mi E of Assoro).*

Agira

Spread over the slopes of Monte Teja, at a height of 650m/2 130ft, the town is overshadowed by the silhouette of the **castle**, which towers above it. Built under Swabian rule, this defensive outpost appears to have played an active role in various struggles between the Angevins and the Aragonese and, later, between the Aragonese and the Chiaramonte. From the ruins, there is a beautiful **view**★ over Lago di Pozzillo.

Abbazia San Filippo

🕒 *Open 7.30am–11.30am and 4pm–7pm.* ☎*0935 69 10 08.*
This abbey is the town's most important religious building. It dates in its present form from the late 18C and early 19C (the front was completely rebuilt in 1928). **Inside**, it is decorated with gilded stuccowork; among the works of art is a dramatic wooden Crucifix by Fra' Umile da Petralia *(over the high altar)*, wooden choir stalls depicting scenes from the life of St Philip by Nicola Bagnasco (1818–22).

▶ *Continue along S 121 for 14km/9mi.*

Regalbuto

Coming from Agira, you see the Baroque pink stone facade of Santa Maria La Croce (1744), graced with columns crowned by an elegant pediment. Turning left into Via Ingrassia, immediately on the left-hand side is the Jesuit school and, just beyond it, the Liberty-style Palazzo Compagnini. A little farther, the town's main square provides a broad open space before the Chiesa Madre (1760), from which to survey the monumental Baroque façades of the church dedicated to St Basil assembled from a miscellany of features, articulated by pilasters.

▶ *From S 121, a narrow road winds to Centùripe (21km/13mi SE of Regalbuto).*

Centùripe

This little town, surrounded by olive groves and orange orchards, today seems rather off the beaten track. Historically however, it was once a highly-prized and strategic outpost nestled between the plain of Catania and the mountains inland. This explains why, particularly in Roman times, Centùripe was quite wealthy (in 70 BC, Cicero described it as one of the most prosperous towns in Sicily). Today the town is focused around a central piazza, and a terrace nearby from which there are superlative views. Elsewhere, the **Tempio degli Augustali** (1C–2C AD) is a rectangular building raised above a colonnaded street (alongside the new archaeological museum). The two monumental tombs with towers are known as *la Dogana* (with only the upper floor visible) and "the castle of Conradin." Down a cobbled side street on the far

---

Town and Monastery

The story of Agira, home of the ancient historian Diodorus Siculus (90–20 BC), echoes the pattern in fortune of the Basilian monastery of San Filippo, which was founded by a Syrian monk some time between the 5C and 6C AD, and which quickly rose to become an important centre of culture and religion. It came to particular prominence when, during the Norman occupation, the resident community was joined by a group of monks from Jerusalem who were forced into exile by the wrath of Saladin. The monastery also prospered on account of the enormous income generated by its immense holdings throughout Europe. In 1537, Emperor Charles V conceded the title of *città demaniale* upon Agira, providing it with a special "royal" status complete with privileges that included the right to administrate its own civil and penal justice system. The town's decline began in 1625 when King Philip IV of Spain, in a desperate effort to boost the dwindling finances of the monarchy, decided to sell the town to Genoese merchants: faced with the threat of losing their freedom, the citizens of Agira offered to raise the enormous sum required themselves.

northwestern side of the town, in the *contrada* of Bagni, sit the ruins of a **nymphaeum**, hanging above the ravine of the river.

Finally, the vast majority of artefacts recovered from the 8C BC to the Middle Ages are displayed in the **Museo Archeologico** (*Via SS Crocifisso*), (🕐*Open daily, 9am–7pm;* 🕐*closed Mon and national hols;* 👛*€2.60;* ☎*0935 91 94 40)* including the statues from the Tempio degli Augustali, representing various emperors and members of their families.

Highlights are a fine head of the Emperor Hadrian which, given its immense size, must have belonged to a statue at least 4m high; two splendid **funerary urns**★ belonging to the Scribonii family (almost certainly imported from Rome); locally produced pottery (3C–1C BC), and an impressive collection of theatrical masks.

▶ *To return to Enna from Centùripe, continue in the direction of Catenanuova and take the motorway (55km/34mi).*

Natural History, Archaeology and Sulphur

Approximately 130km/81mi – allow one day.

▶ *Leave Enna as indicated on the plan and follow directions for Pergusa (9km/5.5mi S).*

The waters of **Lago di Pergusa**, are set between a group of mountains in the Erei chain and are an important migratory stop for many bird species. Now disfigured by the most important motor-racing track in Southern Italy, the *Autodromo di Pergusa*, the lake's shores once had a more romantic legend – as the backdrop for a Greek mythological story: the abduction of **Persephone** by Hades, Lord of the Underworld.

▶ *At the next junction, turn left towards Valguarnera (18km/11mi SE of Pergusa).*

Parco minerario Floristella-Grottacalda
Flagged along the roadside.

A sulphur mine until 1984, the park documents an important industry.

A dirt track leads to a large open area and the *palazzina* Pennisi, a small building erected by the barons of Floristella, who were the long-standing owners of the mine since workings began around 1750. The small white hillocks are the *calcheroni*, round pits lined with inert material, where sulphur was separated from its slag of impurities.

After 1860, domed Gill furnaces replaced the *calcheroni*. Opposite is a sort of gallery with arcades and narrow slits, from which the molten sulphur would flow down to the collection point. There it was allowed to solidify in wooden trapezoidal moulds so as to produce 50–60kg/110–130lb blocks. On the far right is the oldest section of the mine, where the shaft-steps used by miners and *carusi* – the young boys employed

Persephone and Hades

Legend describes how the daughter of Demeter and Zeus was once playing here with her companions the ocean nymphs, when her eye was caught by a particularly beautiful narcissus. As she reached out to pick it, the earth gave way, forming a great abyss from which, with due majesty, **Hades** and his immortal horses emerged. The god forced her to mount his golden chariot before disappearing with her, near Syracuse, by the Cyane Fountain (🍂*See SIRACUSA*), down into the Underworld. Her distraught mother, hearing her daughter's piercing cries, set about searching for her. After wandering relentlessly, she finally succeeded in discovering where the girl had been taken and arranged to see her. Before allowing his bride to see Demeter, Hades (or Pluto, as he is also known) made her eat some pomegranate seeds, thus binding her to him for the winter months.

to carry the ore up to the surface in wooden structures on their backs – can still be seen.

Valguarnera

This small town was inextricably associated until only a few years ago with sulphur mining. It has a 17C church with an overpowering Baroque front made of limestone.

▶ *Return in the direction of Piazza Armerina (18km/11mi S of Valguarnera).*

The road winds through a beautiful **valley**★ with gently sloping hills, covered in springtime by a veil of emerald green.

Piazza Armerina ⟲ *See PIAZZA ARMERINA.*

Imperial Villa of Casale★★★
⟲ *See Villa Imperiale del CASALE.*

▶ *Proceed along S 191 towards Caltanissetta to the fork signposted on the left for Barrafranca (21km/13mi W of Piazza Armerina).*

Barrafranca

At one time called Convicino (its current name dates from the 16C), Barrafranca simply consists of a collection of ochre-coloured houses clustered on the gentle slopes of a hill.

The entrance into the town is along Via Vittorio Emanuele, which is flanked on either side by elegant town houses, including Palazzo Satariano and Palazzo Mattina. The **Chiesa Madre** (18C) has a bare brick façade and a bell tower crowned with a small dome covered with polychrome tiles.

The **Benedictine Monastery** in Piazza Messina is now virtually in ruins; just beyond it stand a large, eye-catching 18C building that once housed small shops (**i Putieddi**) and the **Chiesa della Maria Santissima della Stella**, marked by its tall campanile topped with a maiolica spire.

Return to the town's main street, Corso Garibaldi, which leads into Piazza

dell'Itria; taking pride of place here is the 16C church with its façade and bell tower of brick.

▶ *From here it is possible to continue towards Pietraperzia (10km/6mi) or make a detour (14km/9mi) via Mazzarino.*

Mazzarino

This medieval hamlet largely developed as a result of the Branciforte family. The main features are collected along the main street Corso Vittorio Emanuele. Alongside the Chiesa Madre sits Palazzo Branciforti (17C) and the contemporary Carmelite church. Just outside the little town, perched on top of a small hill lie the ruins of the **castle** with its solid, impenetrable round keep.

▶ *Take S 191 to Barrafranca and continue as far as Pietraperzia.*

Pietraperzia

Here, too, the dominant colour of the stone is ochre. The ruins of the Norman castle overlook the valley of the River Salso. On entering the town, you see in Piazza Matteotti the 16C Chiesa del Rosario and, opposite, the fine neo-Gothic Palazzo Tortorici. The 19C **Chiesa Madre** (⟲ *For information on admission times, call ☎0943 40 16 83)* has a square façade crowned with a squat pediment. Inside, hanging above the main altar, is the lovely *Madonna and Child* painted by Filippo Paladini.

Also of interest in passing is the **Palazzo del Governatore** (17C) with its elegant square balcony ornamented with brackets provided by grotesque figures.

▶ *From Pietraperzia the road continues to Caltanissetta (approximately 15km/9mi).*

Caltanissetta ⟲ *See CALTANISSETTA.*

▶ *From Caltanissetta, return to Enna via S 117bis, a road providing fine views over the countryside (33km/20mi).*

ISOLE EOLIE ★★★

POPULATION: 12 000

These seven sisters punctuate the sapphire sea of the northeast coast of Sicily. All are of exceptional interest for their volcanic nature, their beauty, their light and their climate.

The "home of the winds" in mythology, this archipelago has weather extremes even in summer, ranging from still and hot to stormy. The Greek ruins at Lipari attract visitors, but the main draws are sun, sand and sea. Rocky shores shelter rich aquatic life: anemones, sponges, algae, crustaceans and molluscs, as well as flying fish, turtles and hammerhead sharks. Boat trips provide good views of the indented coastlines, hidden coves and bays.

- **Information:** Corso Vittorio Emanuele 202, Lipari ☎090 98 80 095. Via Levante 4, Vulcano (Jul–Sept) ☎090 98 80 095. www.aasteolie.info.
- ▶ **Orient Yourself:** The two most remote islands, Filicudi and Alicudi, are wild and untamed; Salina is secluded and isolated; Lipari and Panarea are popular with tourists. Vulcano and Stromboli are active volcanoes that frequently spout fire, ash and stone.
- **Don't Miss:** The castle, archaeological museum, boat trips and belvedere Quattrocchi on Lipari; the crater, black beaches and healing mud on Vulcano; the volcano and night-time boat trips on Stromboli; Pollara beach at Salina; the bay of Cala Junco on Panarea.
- **Organising Your Time:** Plan several days to explore the stunning string of islands. Summer is the best season, barring August. Inter-island trips can take 10 minutes or four hours, depending on transport mode and the itinerary.
- **Especially for Kids:** Beaches at Cave di Pomice a Porticello and Canneto.
- **Also See:** MESSINA; REGGIO CALABRIA.

A Bit of History

The Greek myths ascribe the islands to **Aeolus**, the son of Poseidon, whom Zeus made guardian of the winds. He ruled over an island encircled by walls of bronze. The hero **Odysseus** (Ulysses) sheltered on the Aeolians temporarily during his travels, where he met the monster Polyphemus.

The history of these islands is lost in the mists of time, when tectonic plates moved to create a great chasm in the Tyrrhenian Sea. The released magma hardened into a great volcanic outcrop, some 1 000m–3 000m (3 000ft–10 000ft) from the ocean floor, of which only a minute proportion emerges above the water. According to the most recent theories, this happened during the Pleistocene Era, just under a million years ago. The first islands formed were Panarea, Filicudi and Alicudi. The youngest are those active today: Vulcano and Stromboli. Each successive eruption over the millennia added different phenomena: from pumice, a material so light that it floats on water, to the great streams of black obsidian, a glassy and friable material that was made into cutting tools by ancient people.

The islands' sparse population subsists on fishing, farming (especially vines and harvesting of capers for salting), quarrying pumice (as on Lipari, although this is a dying trade), and most particularly, albeit for a short season, from tourism.

Visit

Lipari ★

This is the largest and most densely populated of the Aeolian Islands. Its physical relief, with areas of gentle lowland, encouraged a number of towns. Inhabited since antiquity, when it was

©Danin Tulic/iStockphoto.com

Island of Lipari

famous for obsidian, the island has enjoyed several periods of great prosperity, interrupted by frequent incursions and attacks. In 1544, the Turk **Kaireddin Barbarossa** razed **Porto delle Genti** (a small hamlet near Lipari), killing or deporting most of the population as slaves to Africa.

The main moorings are in the town of Lipari, served by two ports: the charming and constantly bustling Marina Corta is used by the hydrofoils and by smaller craft, and Marina Lunga, where the ferries moor (its also the site of the town's bus terminal).

From here it is easy to reach the island's other towns: Canneto, Acquacalda, Quattropiani and Pianoconte. The best way to explore is by car or moped. **Boat trips**★★ leaving from Marina Corta to Canneto survey the roughly hewn, indented coastline of the southwestern corner of the island.

Città di Lipari★

Lipari is also the name of the main town on the island. At its crest is a fortified citadel and, behind, the former Franciscan monastery that now accommodates the town hall. Two bays sprawl far below. **Marina Corta** is watched over by a little church dedicated to the souls in Purgatory – **'Anime del Purgatorio'** (once isolated on a rock, but now linked to the mainland) – and by the 17C **Chiesa di San Giuseppe**. Marina Lunga is the larger of the two inlets. The lower town

or *città bassa* provides the perfect backdrop for the traditional *passeggiata* or early evening stroll.

Castle★

Head up to the castle from Piazza Mazzini. The citadel was constructed on a Greek acropolis before being surrounded by walls (13C); it was reinforced by Emperor Charles V (16C) after the town was sacked by Barbarossa. Approach from Piazza Mazzini, by the most ancient route. Beyond the Spanish fortifications and the Greek tower (4C BC) with its great medieval portcullis (12C–13C) lies the heart of the citadel. On the right is a church, Santa Caterina, and beyond it, an **archaeological area** spanning the Bronze Age (Capo Graziano culture) through to Hellenistic and ancient Roman times. Behind sits the **Chiesetta dell'Addolorata** and the 18C **Chiesa dell'Immacolata**. To the left of these, in the centre, stands the cathedral

---

Pumice

White and sponge-like, light enough to float on water, pumice stone is used in pharmaceutical processes, cosmetics (it has delicately abrasive properties), buildings (to make earthquake-proof breeze-blocks) and most recently for stone-washed jeans and denim. The pumice from Lipari is of particularly high quality.

Address Book

GETTING THERE AND AROUND

The Aeolian islands are linked to the mainland by hydrofoil (aliscafo) and ferry (traghetto). On average, the hydrofoil (foot-passengers only) costs twice as much and takes half the time. Ferries run regularly from **Milazzo** on the main island (1hr 30min–4hr) and are operated by Siremar; the same agency also runs a hydrofoil service (40min–2hr 45min). SNAV also operates a daily hydrofoil service from **Messina**, **Reggio Calabria**, Palermo (Jun–Sept), and **Cefalù** (Jun–Sept only; not daily). Ferries (14hr; twice a week) and hydrofoils (4hr, Jun–Sept) also leave from Naples. The former are operated by Siremar and the latter by SNAV. For information and reservations, contact: **Siremar** (Gruppo Tirrenia); ☎091 74 93 111 (from Italy) or 081 017 1998 (from mobiles and abroad); www.siremar.it. **SNAV**, Stazione Marittima, Napoli; ☎081 42 85 555, www.snav.it. For information on additional services, contact **N.G.I**, ☎0800 25 00 00 or 090 92 84 091; www.ngi-spa.it

VISITOR INFORMATION

Banking facilities – Banks are available on Lipari, Vulcano (in Porto di Levante) and Salina (in Malfa). Visitors should note that the only cashpoint facilities in the Aeolians are on Lipari, in Corso Vittorio Emanuele, and that credit cards are NOT universally accepted in the islands.

Post offices – Corso Vittorio Emanuele 207, Lipari; Via Risorgimento 130, Santa Maria di Salina; Via Roma, Stromboli.

🪙For coin ranges, see the Legend on the cover flap.

WHERE TO STAY

In addition to traditional hotels, more moderately priced accommodation is available in rented rooms and flats (contact the tourist office for a detailed list of what's available).

ALICUDI E FILICUDI

⊜⊜**Hotel Ericusa** – Via Regina Elena, Alicudi. ☎090 98 89 902. www.alicudi hotel.it. Closed Oct–May. 20 rooms. ⌸. The only restaurant and accommoda-

tion option on the island, this small, simple hotel is situated right on the beach. Ideal for visitors in search of sun, sea and solitude, the rooms at the Ericusa each have their own private entrance. The restaurant serves freshly caught fish, accompanied by simple salads or local vegetables.

⊜⊜**Hotel La Canna** – Contrada Rosa, Filicudi. ☎090 98 89 956. www. lacannahotel.it. 8 double rooms. ⌸€7.50. This typical hotel, built in keeping with its surrounding environment, enjoys an excellent location overlooking the port and the sea. The two rooms both have small sun terraces, and offer the perfect romantic hideaway for newly-weds. Facilities here include an attractive pool and sun terrace.

LIPARI

⊜**Baia Unci Campeggio** – Via Marina Garibaldi, Loc. Canneto, Lipari. ☎090 98 11 909. www.baiaunci.com. Closed mid-Oct–mid-Mar. ⌸. For visitors who enjoy the outdoors, this campsite is ideally placed by the sea, in one of Lipari's delightful bays. Fully equipped with modern facilities, the campsite also has a beach where deckchairs, parasols and boats are available for rent.

⊜⊜**Hotel Oriente** – Via Marconi 35, Lipari. ☎090 98 11 493. www.hotelorientelipari.com. Closed Nov–Easter. 32 rooms. ⌸. This small, family-run hotel in the centre has simple rooms and a pleasant garden. The owner's interest in ethnography is reflected in his large collection of traditional Aeolian artefacts.

⊜⊜⊜**Hotel Poseidon** – Via Ausonia 7, Lipari. ☎090 98 12 876. www.hotelposeidonlipari.com. Closed Nov–Feb.18 rooms. ⌸. This central hotel is built in typical Mediterranean style with vivid blue and white tones. The fully equipped rooms are spotless, with modern, practical furnishings. Service is polite and there's a pleasant sun terrace.

⊜⊜⊜**Villa Augustus** – Via Ausonia 16, Lipari. ☎090 98 11 232. www.villaaugustus.it. Closed Nov–Feb. 34 rooms. ⌸. Hidden among the alleyways of the historical centre, this hotel is situated in an old patrician villa, with a pleasant reception area, spacious lounge and well-appointed rooms. Breakfast is served on an attractive patio brimming over with plants and flowers.

SALINA

Tre Pini Campeggio – *Via Rotabile 1, Loc. Leni, Salina. ☎090 98 0155. www. trepini.com. Closed Nov–Mar.* This campsite is located on the southern side of the island, among olive groves that provide welcome shade for tents and caravans. The site also has bungalows for rent.

Hotel Santa Isabel – *Via Scalo 12, Malfa, Salina. 4.5km/3mi NE of Pollara beach. ☎090 98 44 018. www.santaisabel.it. Closed Nov–Apr. 10 rooms.* The Santa Isabel enjoys a delightful panoramic location, with an attractive terrace overlooking the beach and the inviting crystal-clear waters of the Mediterranean. The rooms are spacious, each with its own small lounge area and mezzanine. The restaurant serves a varied choice of fish dishes and local cuisine.

STROMBOLI

Locanda del Barbablù – *Via Vittorio Emanuele 17/19, Stromboli. ☎090 98 61 18. www.barbablu.it. Closed at lunchtime (Nov–Feb). 6 rooms.* This inn has six pleasant rooms, decorated in a successful fusion of modern, arte povera and period styles. The menu offers a wide selection of typical Aeolian dishes.

VULCANO

Campeggio Togo Togo – *Via Porto Levante, Vulcano. ☎090 98 52 303. www.campingvulcano.it. Closed Oct–Mar.* The perfect compromise for visitors who are on a tight budget, but don't want to miss the splendours of Vulcano. The bungalows, tents and pitches here have a delightful setting either among trees or by the sea, lined by black sandy beaches.

Hotel Conti – *Loc. Porto Ponente, Vulcano. ☎090 98 52 012. www.contivulano.it. Closed 21 Oct–Apr. 67 rooms.* This Mediterranean-style hotel is situated near the thermal

baths. Housed in a number of different buildings, the rooms are simply furnished and all have their own private entrance. All lie just a stone's throw from the famous black sandy beaches.

Hotel Orsa Maggiore – *Via Porto Ponente, Vulcano. ☎090 98 52 018. www.orsamaggiorehotel. com. Closed Nov–Mar. 25 rooms.* A delightful garden and a refreshing swimming pool are two of the highlights of this recently renovated dazzling white hotel. Situated near the port, the hotel has comfortable communal areas and simple, but well-maintained rooms. The hotel restaurant specialises in fish dishes.

WHERE TO EAT

LIPARI

La Ginestra – *Loc. Pianoconte, 5km/3mi NW of Lipari. ☎090 98 22 285.* Fish and antipasti are displayed in the dining room and meals are generally served on the covered terrace.

Filippino – *Piazza Municipio, Lipari. ☎090 98 11 002. www.filippino. it. Closed Mon (except Jun–Sept), mid-Nov–mid-Dec. Compulsory 12% service charge.* This long-established restaurant is renowned throughout Sicily for its wonderful fish, which is prepared according to traditional recipes. It has a relaxed atmosphere, friendly service and a delightful view of Piazza della Rocca.

E Pulera – *Via Isa Conti, Lipari. ☎090 98 11 158. Closed lunchtime and Nov–May. Booking recommended. Compulsory 12% service charge.* E Pulera has a garden for dining. In July and August, a menu of typical Aeolian dishes is accompanied by music and folk dancing.

SALINA

Da Franco – *Via Belvedere 8, Loc. Santa Marina Salina, Salina. ☎090 98 43 287. Closed third week in Dec.* This simple restaurant is easy to find in the upper part of the village. Its delightful terrace and veranda with wonderful views is the setting for cuisine that relies heavily on the sea.

STROMBOLI

🥢🥢**Punta Lena** – *Via Marina, Loc. Ficogrande, Stromboli.* ☎*090 98 62 04. Closed Nov–Mar.* The Punta Lena is renowned for its high-quality fresh fish and delicious seafood specialities served under an arbour with magnificent sea views.

VULCANO

🥢🥢**Don Piricuddu** – *Via Lentia 33, Vulcano.* ☎*090 98 80 221. www.donpiri-cuddu.it. Closed Tue, end Oct–mid-Apr. Booking recommended.* This restaurant has a friendly atmosphere and efficient service. Fresh fish dishes are served in the dining room or on a long terrace overlooking the village.

🥢🥢**Il Diavolo dei Polli** – *Loc. Cardo, Vulcano.* ☎*090 98 53 034. Closed Nov. Booking recommended.* This family-run establishment has a spacious dining room adorned with decorative plates and maritime paintings. The restaurant serves specialities from the Aeolian interior, which are beautifully presented and presented with great attention to detail.

TAKING A BREAK

Bar Ritrovo Remigio – *Via Vulcano 1, Porto Levante, Vulcano.* ☎*090 98 52 085.* This café offers an enticing selection of typical local specialities such as cannoli, cassate and granite, as well as delicious profiteroles.

Pasticceria Subba – *Corso Vittorio Emanuele 92, Lipari.* ☎*090 98 11 352.* Since 1930, this *pasticceria* has been making fabulous cakes and pastries, such as *cannoli* (filled with ricotta cheese), *cassate* (brimming with candied fruit), *pasta paradiso* (almond cake with fine strips of citron peel), *nacatuli* (puff pastry made with Malvasia wine filled with almond paste and mandarin juice), as well as delicious ice cream.

SHOPPING

The famous *Malvasia delle Lipari* is a strong, sweet, golden wine made from grapes that have been left to wither on the vine. Its smooth, aromatic flavour makes it an excellent dessert wine. The DOC-endorsed variety, produced only on the islands, must bear the words *"Malvasia delle Lipari"* in full.

OUTDOOR FUN

Diving – To rent snorkel or scuba gear, take a guided dive or join a PADI course, contact the Diving Center La Gorgonia, Salita San Giuseppe, Lipari; ☎090 98 12 616; mobile 335 57 17 567; www. lagorgoniadiving.it

Mud therapy on Vulcano – Vulcano's muds are renowned for their rich sulphurous content and special mud treatments are recommended for people with rheumatic ailments and dermatological conditions (greasy skin, acne, psoriasis). Mud baths are NOT recommended for expectant mothers or people suffering from tumours or with fevers, heart conditions, osteoporosis, gastrointestinal upsets, diabetes and hyperthyroidis. If you have any doubt as to whether you should have a mud treatment consult a doctor beforehand. Recommendations for use are short immersions (never more than 20min at a time), taken in the coolest hours of the day, and then followed by a hot shower. Do not apply mud to the eyes. In the event of mud getting into the eyes, rinse them out liberally with fresh water. If you develop any ailments as a result of the mud, consult a doctor.

FESTIVALS

Festa di San Bartolomeo – The festival of St Bartholomew is held on Lipari from 21–24 August, finishing at Marina Corta with a magnificent display of fireworks set off from the sea.

TOURS

SNAV and **Siremar** operate regular services between the islands. Departure times are usually posted up at the port.

G. Bludzin/Michelin

Grocery shop in Lipari

Taranto Navigazione runs mini-cruises day and night, with departures from Milazzo, Capo d'Orlando, Patti and Vulcano. Contact Tar.Nav., Via dei Mille 40, Milazzo; ☎090 92 23 617; www.minicrociere.com

Boat trips – The easiest and most congenial way to explore the islands is by rubber dinghy. However, given the exorbitant cost of hiring one, there is always the option of joining an excursion to Stromboli from Lipari or Vulcano (from the other islands, the boats are smaller and the services less frequent). Even at night, the "Strombolian explosions" can be watched from the sea. Tours also leave from Filicudi and Alicudi, Panarea and Salina. The trips usually take in all the islands; they sometimes include stops for swimming and for brief visits to the main towns. Excursions can last a whole day (departing around 9am and returning between 5pm and 7pm) or half a day (departing early afternoon and returning late in the evening, as for the Stromboli evening trip).

On land – The best way to explore the islands is to rent a bicycle or moped. Contact the tourist office for info.

Excursions on Stromboli – Visitors to the volcano are charged a tax of €3 and must be accompanied by a guide (ensure the leader is qualified). Contact the CAI-AGAI, Porto di Scari e Piazza San Vincenzo, Stromboli. ☎090 98 62 11. Another option is Magmatrek, Via Vittorio Emanuele, ☎090 98 65 768, www.magmatrek.it.

---

dedicated to the patron saint of the Aeolian Islands, **San Bartolomeo**. Medieval in plan, it was rebuilt under Spanish rule; the facade is 19C.

Museo Archeologico Eoliano★★
Via del Castello.
&。☉*Open daily 9am–1pm, 3pm–7pm.* ☞€6. ☎090 98 80 174.www.regione.sicilia.it.
Housed in several of the castle buildings, the exhibits of this excellent museum rang from prehistoric to classical times. The museum is laid out chronologically, and special displays also explore marine archaeology and vulcanology. Most of the artefacts have been recovered from excavations since 1949.

The **prehistory of Lipari** dedicates a room entirely to obsidian. The glass-like volcanic stone was highly prized for its strength and razor-sharp cutting edge; although fragile, it was crafted into tools and exported widely in antiquity.

The Capo Graziano culture (1800–1400 BC), which takes its name from a site on Filicudi, and the ensuing Capo Milazzese culture from Panarea mark a particularly prosperous period for the islands *(Rooms V and VI)*. The large Mycenean vases – probably traded here for raw materials – support this notion. The following period (13C–9C BC), known as the Ausonian, is classified according to various criteria: there are many one-handled bowls with horn-shaped appendages (probably to ward off evil spirits) which, later on, evolved into stylised forms of animal heads *(Rooms VII–IX)*. The buildings opposite contain rooms devoted to the prehistory of the smaller islands and to **vulcanology** *(building on the left)*.

The chronological displays continue in the building to the north of the cathedral. The **reconstruction of the Bronze Age necropolis★** (12C BC) compares burial techniques and is quite interesting. Trading vessels often sought shelter in rough weather, but not all made harbour intact. The museum displays cargo from some 20 trading shipwrecks, including **amphorae★**. Among the fine examples of **red-figure ware★** there is a highly unusual scene (360 BC): a naked acrobat balances in a handstand before Dionysus and two comic actors with exaggerated features. The same case contains three vases by the **"painter of Adrastus"** (king of Argos).

The cult of Dionysus, god not only of wine but also of the theatre and celestial bliss, explains the inclusion among the grave goods recovered from votive pits of **statuettes of actors** and **theatrical masks**. The museum has an extremely rich, varied and early **collection★★** of such objects *(Room XXIII)*, which is quite

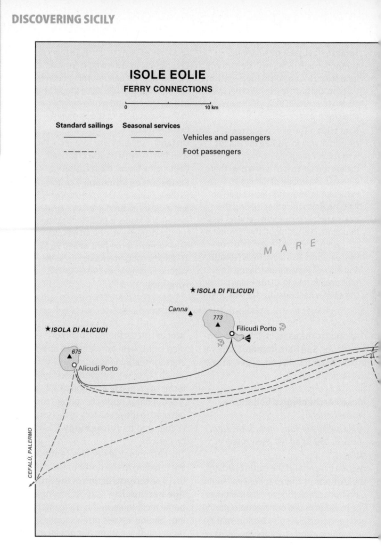

ISOLE EOLIE
FERRY CONNECTIONS

0   10 km

Standard sailings   Seasonal services

       Vehicles and passengers

       Foot passengers

M A R E

★ ISOLA DI FILICUDI

Canna ▲

773 ▲

Filicudi Porto

★ ISOLA DI ALICUDI

675 ▲

Alicudi Porto

CEFALÙ, PALERMO

unique. The figures, some happy, some sombre, are particularly charming and set out in their own scaled-down theatrical sets. Among the masks are those used in productions of plays by Euripides, Sophocles and Aristophanes.

Parco Archeologico
On the far side of the citadel on the right.
In the archaeological gardens are aligned numerous sarcophagi. From the terrace there is a lovely **view**★ over the little Church of the Lost Souls, jutting out into the sea opposite Marina Corta, and Vulcano.

Driving Tour
27km/17mi round trip.

▶ *Set out from Lipari town in the direction of Canneto, to the north along the coastal road.*

Canneto
This small town is a favourite access point for the **white beaches**★ Kids, reached by a footpath. The brilliance of the sand, and, in particular, of the clear sea is due to the high content of pumice dust in it. From the harbour of Canneto, it is possible to visit the pumice quarries near Porticello. *To get to the white*

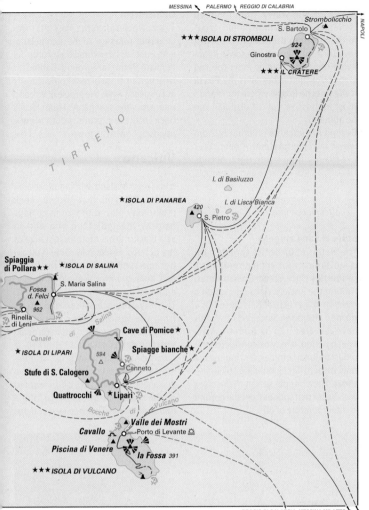

MESSINA   PALERMO   REGGIO DI CALABRIA

NAPOLI

Strombolicchio

S. Bartolo

★★★ ISOLA DI STROMBOLI

924

Ginostra

★★★ IL CRATERE

T I R R E N O

I. di Basiluzzo

★ ISOLA DI PANAREA

I. di Lisca Bianca

420

S. Pietro

Spiaggia
di Pollara ★★

★ ISOLA DI SALINA

S. Maria Salina

Fossa
d. Felci

962

Rinella
di Leni

Canale   di   Salina

Cave di Pomice ★

Spiagge bianche ★

★ ISOLA DI LIPARI

594

Canneto

Stufe di S. Calogero

Quattrocchi   ★ Lipari

Bocche   di   Vulcano

Valle dei Mostri

Cavallo   Porto di Levante

Piscina di Venere

la Fossa   391

★★★ ISOLA DI VULCANO

REGGIO DI CALABRIA, MESSINA, MILAZZO

beaches and quarries by boat, contact the fishermen at the harbour. The return time should be arranged directly with the fisherman. The trip can also be made by bus from Canneto and Marina Piccola; ask to be dropped by the only factory still in operation (5min by foot).

Cave di Pomice a Porticello★   Kids

This lovely bay is lined by a mass of pumice quarries and workshops; all, save the last and most northern, are now abandoned. Waste resulting from the extraction and working of the stone accumulates naturally along the shore in mounds of very fine white sand, which hardens with time. On the beach lie small fragments of black obsidian. The **scene**★★ is strangely compelling: the sea is the palest tinges of blue, as clear as glass (revealing the pumice-lined sea-bed), old wooden jetties stand still and empty. One of the bathers' favourite pastimes is to climb the white mounds and cover themselves with pumice dust to smooth their skin. The keenest can then emulate the children in the scene from *Chaos* (the film directed by the Taviani brothers), who hurled themselves down the mounds, roly-poly fashion, straight into the sea (however, the sea is now about a metre away).

At sunset, the **view**★ from the road is dramatic as the white pumice pyramids in **Campo Bianco** catch the last rays: for a split second, the scene might evoke thoughts of alpine snow-covered slopes. A little farther on is the **Fossa delle Rocche Rosse**, where the island's most impressive flow of obsidian can be admired.

Beyond **Acquacalda** is Puntazze, from where a wonderful **view**★★ opens over five islands: from left to right, Alicudi, Filicudi, Salina, Panarea and Stromboli.

▶ *Turn right immediately after Pianoconte.*

Stufe di San Calogero

The waters of these hot springs have been famous for their therapeutic properties since Greco-Roman times. Among the ancient ruins (alongside a modern spa which, alas, is closed) is a **domed chamber**. Since recent studies have revealed it to be from the Mycenean period, it may be considered the oldest thermal complex, and indeed the only Ancient Greek building still in use today. Here people splash themselves with water that springs from the ground at a temperature of 60°C.

Quattrocchi

This viewpoint offers the most spectacular **panoramas**★★ in the archipelago, with Punta di Jacopo and then Punta del Perciato in the foreground. Behind sit treacherous crags of rock known locally as *faraglioni*, while the profile of Vulcano interrupts the skyline. As Lipari looms back into the picture, a fine **view**★ opens out onto the town.

Vulcano★★★

It was on this island, with a surface area of 21km2/8sq mi, that Ancient Greek mythology placed the forge of Hephaestus, the god of fire who worked as a blacksmith with the assistance of the Cyclops. His Roman name (Vulcan) became synonymous with the island and, indeed, with vulcanology: the scientific study of volcanoes.

The very existence of the island results from the fusion of four volcanoes: the largest and most dominant peak, **Vulcano della Fossa**, is a 391m/1 282ft mountain of reddish rock; it is also the most active. Beside it sits the diminutive Vulcanello (123m/403ft), which erupted on the north side in 183 BC, to form a round peninsula. The peculiar way these

Sulphurous vapours of Vulcano

M. Andreini/Lara Pessina/MICHELIN

volcanoes behave – spewing acid lava and setting off a series of explosions until the plug is catapulted skywards, thereby releasing large incandescent masses of molten rock – has been classified as **Vulcanian**.

Although the last eruption occurred in 1890, Vulcano is still active; even today, phenomena continue to occur, including: fumaroles (steam plumes) and sulphurous mud, highly prized for its therapeutic properties. The jagged shoreline resembles tentacles plunging into the sea. The rock's hue ranges from red to yellow ochre. Together with desolate, lonely scenery, all this endows the island with a strangely unnerving, yet outstanding, beauty.

Porto di Levante e Porto di Ponente

The main town of the island nestles midway between these two ports, and borrows both their names. A compact place full of small shops, it is furnished with contemporary sculptures made of lava (*Hephaestus and Pandora's Box* at the harbour and *Aeolus at Rest* in the main square).

Ascent to the Crater★★★

Allow 2hr. From end of main road leading out of Levante.

The crater path is at the road's terminus outside Porto di Levante. As the track gently climbs the mountainside in a series of broad zig-zags, it provides fabulous **views**★★★ of the archipelago in the foreground and the Vulcanello peninsula. Lipari lies opposite, on the left is Salina – recognisable by its two humps – while in the distance sits Filicudi (on a clear day Alicudi may also be visible). Off to the right, surrounded by its flock of islets, sits Panarea, with Stromboli some way beyond. The higher the path climbs, the stronger the smell of sulphur, accompanied by the occasional cloud of steam. At the top, the **sight**★★★ is unforgettable: the Cratere della Fossa's huge bowl stretches below, its southern rim blurred by clouds of boiling sulphurous vapours.

These fumaroles escape from cracks in the crust with a whistle. The rock is stained yellow ochre and red by the fumes that condense into the most delicate crystals while still hot.

A **tour of the crater**★★★ (about 30min) permits an exploration of the southern part of the island and, from the highest point, stunning **views**★★★ of the archipelago stretch out.

Beaches★

Beware of being scalded in the steam vents.

There are two beaches near the main town: black beaches **(spiagge nere)** – so called because of the dark lava sand – line the lovely bay of Porto di Ponente, although these tend to become very crowded in summer. The other **(spiaggia delle Fumarole)** has waters that can reach very high temperatures, heated by bubbles of sulphurous steam.

The Ascent to the Crater

As the eruptions at night are particularly exciting, hike up the mountain in the late afternoon and return in the evening (don't forget to take a flashlight) or the following morning. Allow three hours for the climb up and two hours for the descent. Although the climb is not particularly taxing, it is not recommended for those who suffer from heart problems, asthma or vertigo and should not be undertaken by the faint-hearted, especially in rare cases of bad weather. **Qualified guides** are available on Stromboli; they offer guided walks of the island and afternoon or evening excursions to the crater.

For the ascent, be sure to bring sturdy shoes, a flashlight, a light jacket, water, a pair of long trousers, a spare T-shirt and, if opting to stay the night, a good sleeping-bag and heavier clothing to wear at the top, where the temperature can drop quite dramatically. Though this excursion can be completed year-round, the best time is in late spring when the weather is mild and temperatures are not too high. A night excursion during the summer months can also be very rewarding.

On the opposite side of the island is the remote, and therefore less frequented, **spiaggia del Gelso** (Mulberry Beach), accessible by sea, by bus from Porto del Levante (*check timetables as services are highly restricted*), or by car along the road from Porto Levante to Vulcano Piano that forks for Gelso and CapoGrillo.

Grotta del Cavallo e la piscina di Venere

Departures by boat from the black beaches. Take a swimming costume for Venus' Pool.

The boat skirts around Vulcanello, with its so-called Valley of Monsters, before circumnavigating the most jagged part of the coast. It stops at this glorious grotto, named after the sea horses that once lived here. On the left is Venus' Pool, a shallow pool of the clearest water and an idyllic place for an unforgettable swim. *(Those who wish to stay for a few hours can go with one of the early boat trips, which run fairly regularly throughout the day, and return on one of the later ones; check with the fisherman for details.)*

I fanghi★

Mud is one of Vulcano's specialities. Leaving the port on the right, behind a rock of incredible colours ranging through every shade of yellow to red, there is a natural pool, the **Laghetto di Fanghi**, sitting in what looks like a pale moonscape, The pool itself contains sulphurous mud with renowned therapeutic properties for skin and circulation, if not for the putrid smell that lingers in the air.

La Valle dei Mostri

On Vulcanello.

A trip at dawn or sunset is particularly recommended when the evocative shapes of the rocks, caught by the sun's rays, are at their most eerie and impressive. The Valley of Monsters consists of a downwards slope of black sand dotted with blocks of lava. These strange shapes suggest prehistoric animals, monsters and wild beasts (including a bear reared up on its hind legs, and a crouching lion).

Capo Grillo

Approx 10km/6mi from Porto Levante.

The local road to Vulcano Piano and beyond to the cape, offers a variety of prospects of Lipari and the great crater. From the promontory, there is a splendid **view**★ of the archipelago.

Stromboli★★★

This island-volcano possesses a sombre, disquieting beauty: the coastline of steep crags is forbidding. The almost total lack of roads, the untamed scenery and, most particularly, the volcano – that methodically makes its presence felt with outbursts of fire and brimstone – all have a strange and awesome power of attraction.

Rossellini's 1950 film *Stromboli, terra di Dio* (Stromboli, Land of God) highlighted the difficulties of living in such a elemental place. The volcano plays the main role, while the island is portrayed as the most fascinating and atmospheric of all the Aeolians.

There are two villages: on the northeastern slopes, surrounded by a green mantle, stand the small square white houses of **San Vincenzo** (where the landing stage is located).

On the southwestern side is **Ginostra**, which consists of a huddle of about 30 houses clinging to the rock, in desperate isolation. It has no roads, just a mule-track that winds along the side of the hill. The town is accessible by sea (although not all year around) via the smallest port in the world.

The arid, precipitous northern flank, which separates the two villages, is the most impressive, scarred by the *Sciara del Fuoco* – down which the burning lava flows each time the volcano decides to erupt. On 30 December 2002, new vents opened in the volcano and a huge section of the mountain fell into the sea, causing a tidal wave that engulfed boats and houses, fortunately without any loss of life.

Opposite San Vincenzo is the tiny islet of **Strombolicchio**, a single spur of rock, resembling a horse's head and topped by a lighthouse.

© Danin Tulic/Dreamstime.com

View of Stromboli from the sea

The Crater★★★

The hike up to the crater of Stromboli makes for a unique and fascinating experience. The route itself is beautiful, opening up unforgettable **views**★★ in all directions, before emerging at the top of one of the very few active volcanoes in the world. The crater comprises five vents. A certain feeling of restlessness pervades the place. This atmosphere is charged and heightened by what is going on some few hundred metres away, as with each explosion, incandescent stones are thrust skywards. The spectacle more than compensates for the steep and arduous climb.

Ascent

5hr round trip. From the ferry jetty at San Vincenzo, head for the village centre and follow the tarred road to San Bartolo. Before long, the typical white houses dwindle away and a mule-track begins *(follow the signs)*, at first paved with slabs of lava and then, after a few bends, degenerating into a well-worn footpath. After 20min, it reaches an observation point called Punta Labronzo (there are refreshments available here, and a good view of the craters); beyond this point, the real climb then begins. From here, the path picks through the lush vegetation; meandering upward at a moderate incline to its end at a ledge (*be careful of going to close to the edge*). Here there is a magnificent **view**★★ of the **Sciara del Fuoco** – the great black slope where lava chunks crash from crater to the sea. The footpath is reduced to a steep track that is cut deeply into the side of the mountain. This veritable trench, excavated by water erosion, leads to a reddish lava section, where care should be taken in the awkward scramble upwards. After the next easy bit, a fine view opens to the left, taking in the town and Strombolicchio, now almost 700m/2 300ft below. At this point, the path climbs onto a broad, steep and sandy ridge up to the summit. Level with the craters, safely tucked behind low semicircular walls, are the first eruption-viewing points. At this altitude, the craters appear between intermittent clouds of vapour. A final stretch of ridge leads to the highest point and the observation point closest to the crater vents. On a day blessed with a favourable light wind, the view from here can be truly exceptional, providing an unforgettable **experience**★★★.

Evening Boat Trip★★★

A night time excursion is perhaps the most dramatic introduction to the island. Under normal conditions, the rocky Sciara del Fuoco makes for an impressive sight; at night the impact is exaggerated a hundredfold. The volcanic eruptions thrust fountains of luminous stones into the black night sky with incredible regularity in nature's most magnificent firework display (in daylight, the emissions merely look grey).

M. Magni/MICHELIN

The cliffs at Pollara

Salina☆

Recognisable by its distinctive two-humped volcanic profile (hence Didyme, its name in antiquity, meaning "twins"), this island is remote and lonely, despite its central location in the archipelago. At one time it comprised six volcanoes, but four have since disappeared. Their historic eruptions have, however, left Salina with a welcome legacy – some of the most fertile soil in the islands. Salina itself derives its modern name from the salt works (a small lake) – now abandoned – at Lingua, a small town situated on the south coast.

Today, the island is renowned for two specialities: capers that are gathered locally, and the famous sweet and strong golden-coloured wine *Malvasia delle Lipari*, made from the island's grapes. Both the carpet of vines that carry the Malvasia grapes and the profusion of caper flowers give the island a fecund feel.

There are two landing stages: **Santa Maria Salina** and the smaller **Rinella di Leni** (where there is also a campsite that gets extremely crowded during the second and third week of August).

Trips Inland

By car or moped (available from small car-hire firms on the island). There is also a local bus service: timetables are displayed at the port of Santa Maria Salina.

A panoramic road offering many **views**☆ of the jagged coastline links the harbour with the island's other hamlets. From the main town, **Santa Maria Salina**, the road heads northwards, past Capo Faro, on its way to Malfa. The coast road climbs above Punta del Perciato, a beautiful natural arc visible only from the sea or from the beach a little farther on at **Pollara**. Before descending to this stunning beach, peep through the vegetation for a glimpse of the house *(private)* where parts of the film *Il Postino* (The Postman) were made: it was here that the meetings between Neruda (Philippe Noiret) and the postman (Massimo Troisi) took place.

Spiaggia di Pollara★★

There are two paths down to this beautiful bay: one leads to a small anchorage enclosed by its own miniature shoreline of rocks. The other provides access to a broad beach overshadowed by a striking white semicircular cliff wall, a desolate remnant of a crater.

On the way back to Malfa, the road forks inland to **Valdichiesa**, where a popular pilgrimage site – the sanctuary dedicated to the Madonna del Terzito – is located, and **Rinella di Leni**.

Fossa delle Felcia

Nestling inside the dormant crater of the taller of Salina's two mountains is a beautiful fern wood (known as *Fossa delle Felci*). This protected nature reserve is accessible on foot *(about 2hr at a leisurely pace)* by a path from the Santuario della Madonna del Terzito in Valdichiesa. There is a second track that runs from Santa Maria Salina.

Panarea ☆

The smallest Aeolian Island rises to its highest point with **Punta del Corvo** (420m/1 378ft high), the western flank of which plunges almost vertically down into the sea. The gentler slopes on the eastern side accommodate Panarea's small resident community, before terminating in a high black lava coastline, skirted by small pebbled beaches.
The island was settled by the Romans, but archaeological evidence dates back to Mycenaean inhabitants and beyond. In the southeast, around **Punta Milazzese**, lie the remains of a prehistoric village set high above the bay of Cala Junco.
Around the island are scattered islets and rocks, the most notable of which are the dreaded *formiche*. Hidden just below the surface, they are responsible for a large number of shipwrecks along this coastline since antiquity.

Filicudi ☆

Steep slopes and a rocky coastline, for the most part of basalt, determine the nature of this small island, which consists of a group of craters: the highest being the **Monte Fossa delle Felci** (773m/2 535ft), traversed by a few faintly cut paths. About 250 souls reside here, mainly in three sleepy hamlets.
From the island's landing stage at **Filicudi Porto**, it is simple to reach the **prehistoric village** situated on the promontory of **Capo Graziano** *(about 40min there and back)*. This contains the remains of about 25 roughly oval huts. The settlement dates from the Bronze Age and was transferred from its original site closer to the shore for better defence *(See also the Archaeological Museum at Lipari, where the finds from this site are displayed)*. From here, there is a beautiful **view**☆ of the bay, the summit of Fossa delle Felci and Alicudi (in the distance on the left).

If approaching by sea, stop at the huge cave called **Grotta del Bue Marino**, whose lava red walls are barely visible in the pitch-black interior.
The tall volcanic chimney-stack formation *(faraglioni)* just offshore is known as **la Canna** (stick or cane) on account of its shape.

Alicudi ☆

Alicudi is the most isolated of the Aeolian Islands: it consists of a round cone covered with purple heather (hence its ancient name, "Ericusa").
Tombs from the 9C were uncovered here by archaeologists in 1904, but there is little else to suggest that the island was permanently settled in ancient times – one possible suggestion that it was used purely as a burial ground by some of the other Aeolian islands. Today it is inhabited by no more than 140 people, living a remote way of life that has remained virtually unchanged for centuries. Here, with the bustle of mainland Italy a world away life continues at an easy pace – there are no real navigable roads, instead the network around the island consists of variously challenging volcanic stone paths. Walking – along with mules (invariably overloaded with people and their burdens) – are the only real ways to get around.
A single village, **Alicudi Porto**, groups together one small church and a handful of white and pastel-coloured houses at the foot of the mountain; its slopes rise up past the **Timpone delle Femmine**, fissures in the rock where local women used to hide from pirates, to the **Filo d'Arpa** (literally, Harp String), the indentation of an ancient crater.
The rather taxing hike up to this point rewards you with a **magnificent view**☆ out over coastline that drops precipitously to the sea, pockmarked with caves on the way *(follow the footpath as it snakes its way from Chiesa di San Bartolo up through the cultivated terraces. The walk takes about 1hr 45min to the summit and back at a brisk pace. There is little shade on this walk, so take a sunhat, plenty of water and sunscreen with you during the summer months)*.

ERICE

POPULATION: 29 367

An unforgettable site★★★ crowns a triangular plateau at 751m/2 463ft. Defended by bastions and walls, the city is a maze of cobbled narrow lanes; some so narrow they allow the passage of just one person at a time.

In summer, Erice blossoms with bright sunshine. Light overflows the alleys, and panoramas reveal the valley and the sea. Come winter, clouds muffle the city, which seems to rejoin its mythical roots. The medieval atmosphere, the fresh air, the beautiful woods that girdle it, the tranquillity and the local handicrafts render it unmissable.

- **Information:** Via Vito Carvini, Erice. ☎0923 86 90 25. www.comune.erice.tp.it.
- **Orient Yourself:** On fine days, the two roads that climb up to the town offer magnificent views across the plain and out to sea; the road to the north, overlooking Monte Cofano, is the easier of the two.
- **Parking:** Near Porta Trapani.
- **Don't Miss:** The view, walking the narrow alleys of the centro storico, the sweets of Maria Grammatico.
- **Organising Your Time:** Allow half a day.
- **Also See:** MARSALA; SEGESTA; TRAPANI; VIA DEL SALE.

A Bit of History

The history of Erice is lost among folklore and superstition. The name is the one given by Eryx, the mythical hero and king of the Elimi, to the mountain upon which the temple to his mother, Venus Erycina (later associated with the cult of Aphrodite), was built.

The origins of the town are also linked with **Aeneas**. In Virgil's narrative, he came ashore at the foot of the mountain to perform the funeral of his father Anchises. Having lost several ships in a fire, he was forced to abandon a number of companions, who founded the town.

Another major mythological figure associated with Erice is **Heracles**. The hero landed in this part of Sicily on his way back to Greece, having stolen the cattle of Geryon (one of the legendary Twelve Labours). During his sojourn, he killed the Elimian king. He left, warning that one of his descendants, Dorieus, would later take over as ruler.

In antiquity, Erice was famous for its temple where, in succession, the Phoenicians worshipped Astarte, the Greeks venerated Aphrodite, and the Romans celebrated Venus.

Mount Eryx served as a point of reference for sailors: at night, a large fire turned the sacred precinct into a guiding beacon.

Walking Tour

This small walled mountain town takes the shape of a perfect equilateral triangle, whose symbolism has provoked mystery and endless argument; it is bounded by the Castello di Venere (southeastern axis) and the Chiesa Madre (southwestern side).

Exactly in the centre of the triangle is the Church of St Peter. Around it lies an intricate maze of narrow streets, each cobbled with polished, rectangular stones and including some alleys so narrow that only one person can pass at a time. A wander through this atmospheric web provides unexpected glimpses of Erice's churches and monasteries, of which there are over 60, scattered through the town. As you walk, explore the small shops tucked down side streets, selling some of the local handicrafts that still flourish here, including colourful ceramics, tapestries and almond-paste sweets (*dolci di badia*).

Address Book

GETTING THERE AND AROUND

A.S.T. buses (☎0923 23 222) run between Trapani (Piazza Malta) and Erice. Journey time is approx 30–60min. *For coin ranges, see the Legend on the cover flap.*

WHERE TO STAY

Ostello per la Gioventù – *Viale delle Pinete, Erice.* ☎0923 86 91 44. *www. ostellionline.org. Closed Nov. . 52 beds. . Open from July to September*, this youth hostel has space for up to 100 guests in the splendid old town.

Azienda Agricola Pizzolungo – *Contrada S. Cusumano, Erice Casa Santa.* ☎0923 56 37 10. *www.pizzolungo. it. . Apartments.* A rustic and romantic atmosphere awaits guests at this 19C farmhouse, which is surrounded by a luxuriant garden and is only a few metres from the sea. The hotel has 2-, 4- and 6-bedded apartments, each equipped with a kitchen.

Hotel La Pineta – *Viale N. Nasi, Erice.* ☎0923 86 01 27. *www.lapinetadierice. com. 23 rooms.* The hotel's attractive stone bungalows, many of which have small terraces, have been built in the tranquil surroundings of a cool pine forest. Comfortable accommodation with modern furnishings.

VALDERICE

Hotel Baglio Santacroce – *2km/1.2mi E of Valderice on S 187 (Km 12).* ☎0923 89 11 11. *www.bagliosantacroce.it. 24 rooms. .* This 17C farmhouse has been transformed into a delightful small hotel in a bucolic setting with magnificent views of the Golfo di Cornino. The rooms are quite small, but are embellished with wood beam ceilings and tiled floors.

WHERE TO EAT

Belvedere San Nicola – *Contrada San Nicola, Erice* – ☎0923 86 01 24 – *www.pippocatalano.it. 10 rooms* – – . This restaurant, close to the old town walls, enjoys beautiful views of Trapani and the sea from its large terrace. Ten rooms welcome guests.

Monte San Giuliano – *Vicolo San Rocco 7, Erice* – ☎0923 86 95 95 – *www.montesangiuliano.it – Closed Mon, 6–25 Jan and 2–17 Nov – Booking recommended.* This fine restaurant located in the heart of Erice specialises in local cuisine. Meals from a broad menu are served either in pleasant, rustic dining rooms or under a pretty arbour in a cool inner courtyard.

TAKING A BREAK

Maria Grammatico – *Via Vittorio Emanuele 14.* ☎0923 86 93 90. *Via Guarnotta 1.* ☎0923 86 97 77. Signora Maria's 15 years spent in a convent introduced her to the secrets of delicious pastries. Her specialities include almond and marzipan cakes, *buccellati* (stuffed with dried figs, almonds, walnuts and sultanas), genovesi, and orange and chocolate *palline*.

FESTIVALS

Good Friday – 18C wooden figures are borne aloft in procession through the town during the traditional Good Friday *Processione dei Misteri.*

Settimana di Musica Medievale e Rinascimentale – Concerts are held in Erice's churches during the Medieval and Renaissance Music Festival, which takes place annually at the end of July.

Chiesa Matrice★

The town's main church is situated near **Porta di Trapani**, built by the Normans over 8C fortifications like most of the town's other gates and walls. The Chiesa Matrice itself was built in the 14C, again reusing stone, this time from the Temple of Venus. Its massive form and merlon-topped walls suggest it was a church-fortress. The facade is graced with a fine rose window (replicating the original), now partly concealed by the Gothic porch that was added a century later. Inside, the rather austere, gloomy interior was extensively remodelled in the 19C; its main draw is a lovely *Madonna*

Narrow street of Erice

and Child, said to have been painted by Francesco Laurana.

Bell tower

The lonely tower left of the church was originally a watchtower. The first level has simple narrow slits, while the upper section is graced with fine two-light Chiaramonte-style windows. The town hall on Piazza Umberto I houses the Museo Cordici. Further along, on the right of the piazza, is Via Cordici, leading into the picturesque Piazza San Domenico, a harmonious confection of elegant palazzi.

Elimo-Punic Walls★

The Elimini built a mighty wall (8C–6C BC) around the northeastern flank of the town – the only section open to possible attack. Massive blocks characterise the most ancient stone courses.

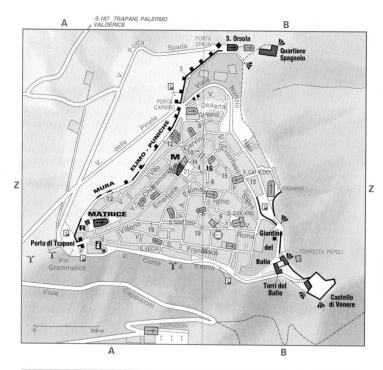

ERICE								
Addolorata (Viale d.)	AZ	3	S. Cataldo (Piazza)	BZ	13	Museo Cordici	AZ	M
Cordici (V.)	ABZ	4	S. Cataldo (Via)	BZ	15	Torre Campanaria	AZ	R
Giudaica (Via)	ABZ	6	S. Domenico (Piazza)	BZ	16			
Guarnott (Via G. F.)	BZ		S. Giuliano(Piazza)	BZ	18			
Guarrasi (Via)	ABZ	10	Salerno (Via Gen. G.)	ABZ	19			
Rabata (Via)	AZ	12	Umberto I (Piazza)	AZ	21			
			Vittorio Emanuele (Via)	AZ				

The skyline was punctuated with look-out towers, steep stairways provided access to the *chemin-de-ronde,* while small openings allowed residents to come and go freely and supplies to be imported. The best-preserved walls run along Via dell'Addolorata, from Porta Carmine to Porta Spada.

Santa Orsola

This church, built in 1413, preserves its original Gothic rib-vaulting down the nave. The 18C Mystery figures, representing the Stations of the Cross, are kept here when not being processed around the town on Good Friday before the Easter celebrations.

Quartiere Spagnolo

From the top of the so-called Spanish Quarter building, initiated in the 17C, but never completed, there is a marvellous view over the bay of Monte Cofano and the area beyond, and down towards the tuna fishery at Bonagìa.

Giardino del Balio

The lovely public gardens centre around the Castello di Venere and the Torri di Balio: the Norman defences. The glorious **view**★★★ embraces Monte Cofano, Trapani, the Egadi Islands, and on a clear day it's even possible to catch a distant watercolour glimpse of Cap Bon some 170km/106mi away in Tunisia.

Castello di Venere

Covered in a veil of ivy, the 12C Venus' Castle crowns the mountain that sits at the easternmost corner of the town. This was originally the site of an ancient temple to Venus Erycina, goddess of fertility, so large it was used as a landmark by sailors off the coast.

Erycina eventually became completely associated with the goddess of love, Aphrodite, especially after Rome dedicated a temple to her (217 BC). The temple subsequently fell into decay, and centuries later when Count Roger conquered Erice, the Normans were ordered to clear all traces of the pagan ruins. In its place they built a fortress, surrounded by great walls that incorporated chunks of the original stones from the temple.

The towers (**Torri del Balio**) would once have been accessible from the castle by a drawbridge. This elevation provides a perfect **viewpoint**★★★ out over the Egadi Islands.

Visit

Museo Cordici

Piazza Umberto I. Open Mon–Fri, 8.30am–1.30pm (also Mon–Thu 2.30pm–5.30pm). ⏲*Closed national hols.* ☎*0923 86 00 48.* Accommodated inside the town hall is the local museum, which houses finds from Neolithic, Punic, Greek and Roman culture. The museum has an interesting and varied collection for its size, which includes jewellery, bronze statues, terracotta and marble sculptures. Notable exhibits include Antonello Gagini's sculpture of the Annunciation (1525) from the Chiesa del Carmine, a fine head of Aphrodite dating from the 4C and, on the first floor, beyond the library, a small marble **head of a woman**, modelled on a Greek original.

Excursion

Tonnara di Bonagìa

Approx 13km/8mi N. ⏲*To visit the tuna fishery, contact the Hotel Tonnara a few days in advance.* ☎*0923 43 11 11. Drive down to Valderice and continue towards Tonnara (from the main Valderice road, turn left at the supermarket). At Bonagìa, follow signs for the Tonnara (tuna fishery), while looking out for its distinctive tower.* The 17C tuna fishery (now an attractive hotel complex), was once a simple self-contained village. Clustered around a large courtyard were the fishermen's houses, as well as facilities for cleaning and processing the tuna, the boathouse and a small chapel. The Saracen tower now houses the **Museo della Tonnara**, a small museum displaying tools and equipment from the tuna industry. On the second floor, a scale model shows the long net corridors that the tuna navigated before reaching the *camera della morte* (death chamber). Here the traditional, but brutal ritual of the *mattanza* (kill or slaughter) took place.

ETNA★★★

The "mountain of mountains" is the highest summit of Sicily. Cloaked in snow during winter, Etna, still active, is one of greatest European volcanos. Its height, continuously modified from the eruptions, is around 3350m/11 000 ft. Etna is one of the island's points of greater interest, not only for the evocative volcanic displays, but also for the excursions by bicycle, ski, horse, car or train (the Circumetnea circles the mountain's base). The area also has a grand cultural tradition, which stretches to the culinary arts: Etna wine, pistachio nuts of Bronte, the honey of Zafferana Etnea, the strawberries of Maletto, fragrant granite and warm brioche.

- **Information:** Catania: APT, Via Cimarosa 10, ☎095 73 06 211, www.apt.catania.it. Nicolosi: Azienda di Soggiorno e Turismo, Via Vittorio Emanuele, ☎095 91 44 88, www.aast-nicolosi.it. Linguaglossa: Pro Loco, Piazza Annunziata 7, ☎095 64 30 94. Zafferana Etnea, Pro Loco, Piazza Luigi Sturzo 3, ☎095 70 82 825.
- **Orient Yourself:** Etna can be explored from the southern or northern slopes of the volcano. The two routes offer contrasting views and landscapes: the route up the southern side to Rifugio Sapienza passes through a barren, black and desert-like environment, while that on the northern side via Piano Provenzana winds its way through a lush larch forest.
- **Parking:** Park at the Rifugio Sapienza for trips to both sides of the volcano.
- **Organising Your Time:** The best time for a volcano trip is summer, when the roads are accessible. Climb early in the morning.
- **Also See:** ACIREALE; CAPO D'ORLANDO; CATANIA; GIARDINI NAXOS; TAORMINA.

A Bit of History

The volcano and its story – Etna evolved as a result of submarine eruptions during the Quaternary Era (c. 500 000 years ago), at the same time that the plain of Catania was formed, originally as a broad bay. Etna erupted regularly during Antiquity – at least 135 times. In 1669, however, the most cataclysmic disaster occurred. A lower vent expelled a river of lava. As it flowed to the sea, it devastated part of Catania. Violent eruptions took place in 1910 leading to 23 additional craters being formed; in 1917 a fountain of lava spurted 800m/2 500ft into the air. In 1923, outpourings of molten lava

View of Etna from the sea in winter

H. Champollion /MICHELIN

Address Book

For coin ranges, see the Legend on the cover flap.

WHERE TO STAY

NICOLOSI

Ostello Etna – *Via della Quercia 7, Nicolosi.* ☎095 791 4686. *www.ostellionline.org.* . The village of Nicolosi perches on the volcano slopes. The room rate includes entrance to the Museo Vulcanologico, which is housed in the hostel.

Hotel Corsaro – *Loc. Piazza Cantoniera, Etna Sud, Nicolosi.* ☎095 91 41 22. *www.hotelcorsaro.it. Closed 15 Nov–24 Dec. 20 rooms.* . If you'd like a contrast to Sicily's coastal scenery, then this comfortable hotel situated at an altitude of 2 000m/6 560ft is the perfect choice. Popular with skiers and walkers, it has 20 pleasant rooms and a good restaurant.

RANDAZZO

Agriturismo L'Antica Vigna – *Loc. Monteguardi, 3km/1.8mi E of Randazzo on S 284.* ☎095 92 40 03. . *10 rooms.* . At the foot of Mount Etna, this family-run farm-guesthouse serves regional dishes made from organic home-grown produce.

TRECASTAGNI

Bed & Breakfast Il Vigneto – *Via Zappalà 1, Trecastagni.* ☎095 78 01 029. *www.ilvignetobeb.net.* . *3 rooms.* Surrounded by greenery, this large villa offers bed and breakfast accommodation in period-style rooms with antiques. (*Two-night minimum.*)

ZAFFERANA ETNEA

Hotel Airone – *Via Cassone 67, Zafferana Etnea.* ☎095 70 81 819. *www.hotel-airone.it. Closed 2 Nov–15 Dec. 60 rooms.* . An elegant and friendly mountain hotel with modern, comfortable rooms and magnificent views that extend out as far as the coast. Famous guests at the hotel, which was founded in the 1930s, have included the Italian writer Vitaliano Brancati.

WHERE TO EAT

RANDAZZO

Fa Veneziano – *Via Romano 8, Randazzo.* ☎095 79 91 353. *Closed Sun evening and Mon.* Elegant but friendly, this restaurant serves regional dishes, with emphasis on the mushrooms that are plentiful in this area.

TRECASTAGNI

Villa Taverna – *Corso Colombo 42, Trecastagni.* ☎095 78 06 458. *Closed Mon, at lunchtime during the week and evenings on Sun and public hols.* . Go back in time in this highly original restaurant, where the decor evokes a typical district of Catania's old town.

EXCURSIONS

ASCENT TO THE SUMMIT

Unpredictable and ongoing eruptions undermine any permanent infrastructure (roads, ski runs, ropeways, refuges). Favourite or recommended itineraries, therefore, should be considered as temporary and subject to being closed at short notice. At the start of the season (normally in May), shorter walks that stop well below the top are organised. When the highest sections are cleared of snow, it's possible to reach 3 000m/10 000ft. High summer is the best time, especially in the early morning. At any altitude, temperatures can plummet here. Carry a thick fleece, a light jacket and appropriate footwear (preferably waterproof hiking boots). You can rent jackets and boots locally. Sunglasses and sunscreen are also wise.

On Foot – Opportunities abound for both short and long excursions (the longest and most complex being the **Grande Traversata Etnea**: five days of trekking, with daily 12–15km/ 7–9mi hikes), and marked nature trails.

By Car – For the less agile, see the volcano via a **circular tour of Etna**, either by car or train. The rail line starts in Catania, loops the mountain, and stops at Riposto (approximately 5hr); returning to Catania by bus or train. For information, apply to the Ferrovia Circumetnea, Via Caronia 352/A, Catania; ☎095 54 12 50; www.circumetnea.it.

stayed hot for more than 18 months; and in 1928, the volcano destroyed the village of Mascali. More recently, a 2001 blast swept away key components of the cable car, reaching as far as the boundary of Rifugio Sapienza.

The black lava around the craters dates from recent eruptions; lichens grow on the older grey stone. The presence of both and, sometimes, their distressing effects (blocked roads and ruined buildings) demonstrate the volcano's constant activity.

Etna has four maws: the southeastern crater that began suppurating in 1978, the immense **central crater**, the northeastern crater at the highest point, which has been dormant since 1971, and the *Bocca Nuova* (literally the 'New Mouth'), most active lately. ⓒ *See Introduction: Volcanoes in Sicily.*

National Park – The protected area, designated a National Park in 1987, covers some 59 000ha/145 730 acres. The mountain consists of an enormous black cone, visible up to 250km/155mi away. The extremely fertile lower slopes are heavily cultivated with dense groves of oranges, mandarins, lemons, olives, agaves and prickly pears, as well as bananas, eucalyptus, palm trees, maritime (parasol) pines. Vineyards here produce the excellent red, rosé and white *Etna* wines. Probably the most common of the wild plants is *Euphorbia dendroides* (tree spurge). Above 500m/1 640ft, plantations of hazelnuts, almonds, pistachio and chestnuts give way to oaks, beeches, birches and pines, especially around Linguaglossa. The landscape at this altitude is also characterised by a local variety of broom.

At 2 100m/6 900ft, the desolate landscape sustains desert-like plants like *Astragalus aetnensis* (a local variety of milk-vetch), a small prickly bush often found alongside violet, groundsel and other flowers that populate the slopes of the secondary craters. Higher up, snow and, for a long time after an eruption, hot lava prevent any type of macroscopic vegetation from growing: this comprises the "volcanic desert."

Etna also harbours colonies of small mammals (porcupine, fox, wild cat, weasel, marten and dormouse), birds (kestrel, buzzard, chaffinch, woodpecker and hoopoe), a few reptiles, including the asp viper, and a large variety of butterflies, including the Eastern orange tip (*Anthocharis damone,* more commonly known in Italy as the *Aurora dell'Etna*).

Visit

The Volcano

As the volcano is still active, the landscape constantly evolves. Contact the local tourist office to find out which side of the mountain is currently the most

The lunar landscape of the Crateri Silvestri

M.Magni/MICHELIN

Ascent of Etna

The ascent of Etna was difficult, but the view from the top was worth all the effort: "no imagination in the world has had the courage to depict such a marvellous sight. There is nowhere on the surface of the globe that can combine so many striking, sublimely beautiful details… The summit… is situated on the edge of a bottomless chasm, as old as the world itself, and it often erupts cascades of fire, thrusting up incandescent stones with a roar that shakes the whole island."

From *Journey to Sicily and Malta* by Patrick Brydone (1773)

interesting. The delightful village of **Zafferana Etnea** is a good base for trips to either side of the volcano; because of its altitude of 600m/1 950ft, it has the advantage of offering magnificent views of the coast from Acireale to Taormina.

South side★★★

Four-wheel drive excursions operate daily (weather permitting) from the week before Easter to the end of Oct, 9am–4pm. Duration: approximately 2hr there and back.
€42.50, including guide. For further information, contact Funivia dell'Etna, Piazza V. Emanuele 45, Nicolosi; ☎095 91 11 58 or 095 91 41 41.

From **Nicolosi**✳ and **Zafferana Etnea** two beautiful roads wind up to **Rifugio Sapienza** (1 910m/6 262ft), the starting-point for all expeditions to the crater. The **route**★★ runs through an unnerving and alien landscape, dominated by black lava and relieved occasionally by a white patch of snow or pink and yellow bursts of flower in spring. Arriving from Zafferana, just before the refuge, a sign points to the **Crateri Silvestri**, craters formed in 1892, reached by a short walk through a lunar landscape.

Following the 2001–02 eruptions, which seriously damaged parts of the cable car, you must drive or hike *(allow 4hr for the ascent)* to the summit. Funivia dell'Etna runs four-wheel drive vehicles from Rifugio Sapienza to around 2 700m/8 850ft. The last stretch is purely pedestrian. *Visitors are strongly advised to avoid the central vent.*

The **Valle del Bove** – a vast sunken area, split with great crevasses and chasms – extends to the southeast of the central crater. This area is prone to violent eruptions, some of which are highly dangerous, precipitating lava flows that on occasion have reached the towns below.

At the time of going to press the Valle del Bove can be reached on foot (1hr there and back from the arrival area for four-wheel drive vehicles). The walk is fairly strenuous and walking boots are essential. Ask local guides for directions.

North side★★★

Four-wheel drive excursions with a guide operate May–Oct, 9am–4pm (weather permitting), from Piano Provenzana. Duration: approximately 2hr there and back. €37, including a guide. To book a trip and arrange a time, contact S.T.A.R. a few days in advance. ☎095 37 13 33.

The guided ascent to the craters can be made either on foot or by four-wheel drive. Visitors can leave their car at Piano Provenzana, badly damaged in 2002. A new observatory stands at 2 750m/9 020ft with a magnificent **view**★★. A shuttle bus runs to 3 000m/ 9 840ft before abandoning hikers to the final leg and those awesome puffing vents. The route may vary, depending on current volcanic activity.

TREKKING

Hiking, downhill skiing trips and visits to the extraordinary **volcanic caves** dotted around Etna are organised on request by local mountain guides. *For further information, contact the Gruppo Guide Alpine Etna Sud, Via Etnea 49, Nicolosi; ☎095 79 14 755 and, for the northern side of the volcano, S.T.A.R., Via Santangelo Fulci 40, Catania; ☎095 37 13 33, or Albergo Le Betulle at Piano Provenzana, Linguaglossa; ☎095 64 34 30.*

On the downwards return journey, stop at 2 400m/7 900ft and take a moment to examine the craters that were the cause of the 1809 eruption.

Driving Tours

1 From the Coast to the Southern Slopes

45km/28mi drive from Acireale: allow half a day (excluding the summit ascent).

On the bleaker, southern slopes, concretions of black lava form a lunar-like **landscape**★★. Little towns ring the edge. All have one feature in common: the dark lava stone that paves the streets and ornaments the buildings.

Acireale✝ ‸*See ACIREALE.*

Aci Sant'Antonio

Several of the town's most important monuments are collected around Piazza Maggiore, most notably the Duomo with its imposing facade, extensively rebuilt after the terrible earthquake of 1693. Opposite stands the 16C church of San Michele Arcangelo.

At the far end of Via Vittorio Emanuele, the town's main street that leads out from the piazza, stands what remains of the Riggio family *palazzo*.

Viagrande

The centre of the village is paved with huge slabs of lava. The 18C Chiesa Madre is built from the same dark stone.

Trecastagni

According to some sources, the name of this little town (literally "three chestnuts") actually derives from *tre casti agni*, a reference to the three chaste lambs worshipped here: Alfio, Filadelfio and Cirino. A festival in their honour is annually celebrated on 9 and 10 May, the highlight coming with the **procession of the wax effigies**, some immensely heavy, borne by strong bare-chested *ignudi* through the streets to the **Santuario di Sant'Alfio** on the outskirts of town. Via Vittorio Emanuele, lined by

fine buildings, leads to **Chiesa Madre di San Nicola** with its great central campanile. The terrace at the top provides marvellous views.

Pedara

Piazza Don Diego is graced with the Duomo and its unusual spire covered in brightly-coloured maiolica tiles.

Nicolosi✷ ‸*See South side.*

For further information on the ascent to the crater, see the Address Book.

2 The Northeast Flank

60km/37mi drive starting from Linguaglossa: allow half a day to visit (excluding the ascent).

Linguaglossa✷

The name Linguaglossa derives from the ancient term for "a big tongue of lava". Perhaps this is a reference to its vulnerable "red-hot" position on the slopes of Etna down which incandescent lava has flowed on several occasions. The **Chiesa Madre**, built of sandstone and lava, looms over the central piazza. Inside, it is furnished with lovely **wooden choir stalls**★ (1728), depicting scenes from the life of Christ. The scenic **Mareneve** road leads through a wonderful larch and pine wood (effected by the eruption in 2002) to **Piano Provenzana**.

Eastern approach★

From Piano Provenzana, the Mareneve road skirts the eastern side of the summit before dropping downhill. On the lower eastern slopes, many farming villages have rallied to exploit the fertile soil, cultivating vines and citrus fruits. Near **Fornazzo**, just before the road meets the more major Linguaglossa to Zafferana Etnea road, it passes the incredible lava flow that spared the little **Cappella del Sacro Cuore** *(on the left)* in 1979. The molten stone flowed right up to one walls and even slightly penetrated the chapel. Pilgrims leave *ex-voto* offerings here, believing it was saved by sacred intervention.

▸ *From Fornazzo, a road down to the left leads to Sant'Alfio.*

Sant'Alfio
🕐 *Open Sat–Sun 10am–12.30pm, 3.30pm –6.30pm; for visits midweek, contact the tourist office ☎ 095 96 87 72.* 👣*The tourist office also organises guided tours.* 👛*Donations welcome.*

This tiny village has a monumental 17C **church**, remodelled in the 19C, with an unusual lava facade incorporating a campanile. From the terrace before the church, there is a splendid **view**★ of the Ionian Coast.

Sant'Alfio's main attraction, however, is a famous giant chestnut tree known as the **castagno dei 100 cavallia** *(on the main road to Linguaglossa)*. This fabulous specimen, over 2 000 years old, comprises three distinct trunks with a combined circumference of 60m/196ft. Its name derives from a legend relating how Queen Joan (whether it refers to Joan of Aragon, Queen of Castile, or Joan of Anjou, Queen of Naples, is not clear) sheltered under its branches one night during a storm with her entourage of 100 knights.

▶ *Go back in the direction of Fornazzo and continue towards Milo.*

Milo
This small farming community survives, against all odds, given the unpredictable, blind advances of lava. Indeed, on many occasions, its flowed within a few metres (1950, 1971, 1979) before, at the last minute, changing direction.

▶ *Continue in the direction of Zafferana Etnea as far as Trecastagni and Nicolosi, then continue along the southern slope or towards Catania.*

③ Circular Tour of Etna
155km/97mi round trip, starting in Catania – allow one day.

The road runs around the circumference of Mount Etna, providing a kaleidoscope of different views of the volcano, as it passes through a number of picturesque little villages.
This highly scenic tour is also possible by train. The directions below refer to touring by car.

Catania★ 👣 *See CATANIA.*

▶ *Leave Catania along Viale Regina Margherita or Via Vittorio Emanuele and take S 121 (6km/4mi).*

Misterbianco
🕐 *Open by prior arrangement only, 8am– noon, 3pm–8pm. ☎ 095 30 14 83.*

The imposing 18C church dedicated to **Santa Maria delle Grazie** rises tall above the rooftops, its elegant façade visible from miles away. In the south apse, nestles a *Madonna and Child* attributed to Antonello Gagini.

▶ *Continue on S 121 for 11km/7mi.*

Paternò
Via Monastero 2. ☎095 62 32 44.
In 1072, **Roger II** built a castle here atop the crag. Its square form is relieved on one side by a series of two-light windows. The black lava stone provides a strong contrast for the white stone ornamention. Clustered around the castle are the main religious buildings: the Chiesa Madre founded in Norman times and rebuilt in the 14C, and San Francesco. The town's other buildings developed below, predominantly in the 17C, and the new seat of Piccolo Teatro houses the **Galleria d'arte Moderna**.

▶ *After 7km/4mi, turn right.*

Santa Maria di Licodia
Piazza Umberto's slightly raised square stretches before a former Benedictine monastery (now the town hall) and the Chiesa del Crocifisso. Down the left side of the church stands its distinctive and attractive **bell tower** (12C–14C), built in stone of two colours.

▶ *Continue to Adrano (8km/5mi).*

Adrano
This is one of the oldest settlements on the slopes of Mount Etna (archaeological traces date to the Neolithic times). The **castle** (🕐*open Tue–Sat 9am–1pm, 3pm–6pm; Sun and public hols, 9am–1pm; ☎ 095 76 98 849)* was built during the Norman occupation and still overlooks the centrally placed Piazza Umberto.

This unmistakable square edifice of dark lava owes its form to the Swabian era; inside are three museums.

The **Museo Etnoantrolpologico** collects objects made by local craftsmen. Over three floors, the **Museo Archeologico Regionale** displays artefacts relating to the area's history. Of particular note (on the second floor) is the *banchettante* ("banqueting guest"), an early bronze figurine of Samian workmanship; the terracotta bust of a female Sicilian deity (5C BC), a clay Locrian female bust (5C BC), a figurative group of Eros and Psyche, and a splendid **Attic vase**★ with small columns (5C BC). The top floor is devoted to the **picture gallery**, showing paintings on canvas (by the so-called Zoppo di Gangi, Filippo Paladino and Vito D'Anna), glass and metal; sculptures in wood, alabaster and bronze dating from the early 17C to the early 20C; and a series of contemporary works by artists from Adrano and beyond.

The piazza extends eastwards into the delightful garden of the Villa Comunale, onto which face the imposing elevation of the **Church and Monastery of Santa Lucia**. The 18C church façade, in two colours of stone, is by Stefano Ittar.

Centrale Solare Eurelios

This power plant lies just outside Adrano. Following trial and experimentation from 1981–1987, tests were halted (it succeeded in generating 1 mW). Current attempts involve photovoltaic panels (composed of silicon cells).

▶ *The Saracen bridge is outside the town, beside the River Simeto. Leave by the road south of Adrano and follow signs for Bronte. A sign at a crossroads indicates the way to the bridge: to the right and left, the road is tarred; straight on leads to a dirt track which continues on to the river and the bridge.*

Ponte Saraceno

The Saracen bridge was first erected by the Romans, rebuilt under Roger II and altered through the successive centuries. The pointed arches spanning the water are articulated with contrasting coloured stone. A short walk north along the river leads to the amazing **Simeto Gorge**. Formed by a lava flow, it was then polished clean as water eroded great blocks of basalt. *A visitor centre is located on S 114 near Ponte Primosole, heading towards Siracusa.*

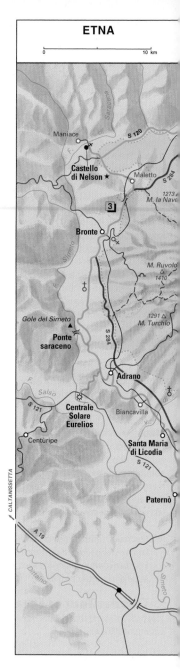

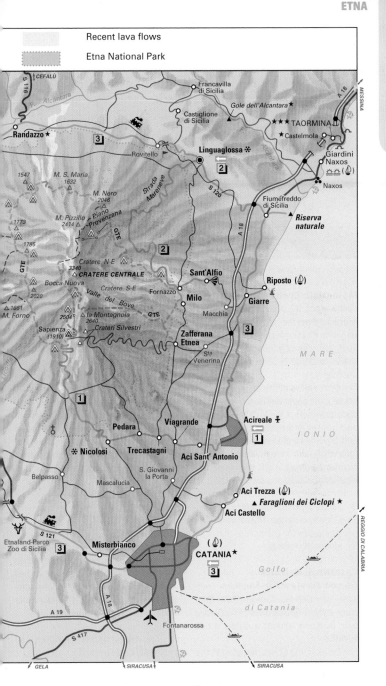

Recent lava flows

Etna National Park

▶ *Continue along S 284 for 15km/9mi to Bronte.*

Bronte

Pride of place in the centre of this town, which is famous for its pistachios, is given to the Collegio Capizzi. This prestigious 18C boarding-school is housed in a fine *palazzo.*

Adrano: Saracen bridge

M.Magni/MICHELIN

Museo della Civiltà Contadina

Follow signs to La Cascina hotel-restaurant and cross the hotel car park to the museum. ✎*Guided tours only 9.30am–1pm, 3pm–5pm.* ◷*Closed national hols.* ✆*€2.* ☎*095 69 16 35 or 328 40 08 626 (mobile).*

The centrepiece of this attractive farmhouse is the paper mill built by the Arabs sometime before the 11C. The museum also houses items relating to rural life and provides a pleasant environment for a stroll, with its many fruit trees and farmyard animals. A gift shops sells the excellent pistachios grown on-site.

▶ *Follow signs from Bronte to the Castello di Nelson. The castle is situated by the entrance to the village of Maniace.*

Castello di Nelson★

◷*Open Apr–Sept Tue–Sun 9am–1pm, 3pm–7pm; Oct–Mar Tue–Sun 9am–1pm, 2pm–4.45pm.* ◷*Closed Mon.* ✎*Guided tours available (45min).* ✆*€2.60.* ☎*095 69 00 18.*

The Benedictine Abbey, founded in the 12C at the behest of Queen Margaret, wife of William the Bad, sat on a key communication route into the Sicilian hinterland. This prosperous monastery underwent various modifications before finally being handed over to Admiral Nelson in 1799 (for his role in suppressing anti-Bourbon rebellions in Naples).

Although the British naval hero never visited the building, his descendants lived there until 1981 and transformed it into a magnificent private residence. The adjacent abbey **chapel** is graced with an elegant doorway ornamented with figurative capitals. Inside, it houses a Byzantine icon, supposedly carried by the Byzantine *condottiere* George Maniakes, who inflicted a crushing defeat on the Saracens in 1040. The main house, surrounded by a park (4ha/10 acres) and an attractive garden, has a number of beautifully furnished rooms.

▶ *Continue along S 284 for 20km/12mi.*

Randazzo★

This small town is dangerously close to the volcano. Randazzo could be called the black town for its lava paving, arches and principal monuments in its attractive historical centre, built around the main street, Corso Umberto.

▶ *The walk begins at the northeastern end of Corso Umberto.*

The 13C **Chiesa di Santa Maria** has undergone considerable modifications through the centuries. What survives from the original is the plan, the characteristic tall Norman **apses**★ ornamented with blind arcading, and the south wall pierced by its two- and three-light win-

Etna's Pistachio Industry

The pistachio tree, which exists in both masculine and feminine varieties, grows to a height of around 4–5m/13–16ft. The male trees are usually planted upwind so that they pollinate the female trees. The trees grow very slowly and produce fruit every other year. Once picked, the pistachio nuts are removed from their husks and left to dry for about a week. The nuts are used in both sweet and savoury recipes.

dows. The neo-Gothic façade and bell tower are both 19C.

▶ *Turn right into Piazza Roma.*

A street to the left leads to Piazza San Nicolò. The church after which the square is named was erected in 1594, and has a front elevation articulated by dark lava stone; the campanile dates from 1783. The other buildings overlooking the square include Palazzo Clarentano (1508), graced with decorative two-light openings, and the 14C Church of Santa Maria della Volta. To its right opens the delightful **Via degli Archi** ornamented, as its name suggests, with a series of arches. Via Polizzi, on the right, leads from the piazza to **Casa Spitaleri**, with its fine lava doorway.

▶ *Turn down Via Duca degli Abruzzi.*

An intersection from the right leads into Via Agonia, where condemned prisoners were led from their castle-prison to the Timpa, in front of San Martino, to face their executioners. Only one house conforms to the 14C archetype, with a single large open space on the ground floor and two square rooms above on the first floor.

▶ *Via Duca degli Abruzzi leads back into Corso Umberto.*

An archway on the right marks the old entrance to the **Palazzo Reale**.
Only part of the facade, a lovely two-coloured string-course and a pair of two-light windows, now remains.
Before the 1693 earthquake destroyed the *palazzo*, it accommodated guests including Joan of England, wife of the Norman King William II; Costanza of Aragon and, in 1535, Emperor Charles V.
Continue to **Chiesa di San Martino** (⏱*closed noon–4pm*), founded in the 13C and rebuilt in the 17C.
The fine **campanile**✶ (13C–14C) has an octagonal spire. Inside, there are two Madonnas by followers of the Gagini and a polyptych attributed to Antonello de Saliba.

A window made from lava stone

G. Bludzin/MICHELIN

Across from the church lie the ruins of the castle-prison. This began life in the 13C as a fortified tower set into the city walls that extended around the medieval citadel. **Porta di San Martino**, just beyond, constitutes one of the entrances to it. The tower houses an **archaeology museum** (○*Open 9am–1pm, 7pm–8pm; €1.60;* ☏*095 79 90 064)* with a collection of Sicilian puppets.

▷ *Either continue along S 120 or take the quiet road that runs parallel to it by going back towards Bronte for 4km/2.5mi and then following signs to Linguaglossa.*

Linguaglossa✷
○*See above, in the section devoted to the northeastern slope of Etna.*

▷ *Pass through Fiumefreddo di Sicilia (11km/7mi) and head for the coast, turning toward Marina di Cottone.*

Riserva Naturale di Fiumefreddo
Visitor centre near Masseria Belfiore in Via Marina, Fiumefreddo. &. ○*Open May–Sept, Tue–Sun, 9am–6pm; Oct–Apr, Tue–Sun, 8.30am–4.30pm.* ○*Closed Mon.* ☏*095 77 69 011. www.comune. fiumefreddo-di-sicilia.ct.it.*
Essentially, the River Fiumefreddo rises from two springs, both 10–12m (33–39ft) deep, known as Testa dell'Acqua and Le Quadare *(paioli* in Sicilian dialect). In full sunlight, their depth and clarity are astounding. The pH of the river – which never exceeds 10–15°C even in summer and flows remarkably slowly – provides the right conditions for an unusual range of water-loving plants (certain members of the Ranunculus family and papyrus). Other species include the white willow, aquatic iris and horsetail. The springs also attract migrating birds: herons, oystercatchers and golden orioles.
Beside the nature reserve stands the 18C **Castello degli Schiavi** (⊶*private, not open to the public),* designed by the architects Vaccarini and Ittar.

▷ *Continue for 10km/6mi along S 114 to Catania.*

Giarre
The little town was once part of the feudal estate belonging to the Mascali, having been bestowed upon the Bishop of Catania by **Roger II** in 1124. The town's main axis is Via Callipoli, lined with elegant shops and town houses, including the Liberty-style **Palazzo Bonaventura** (no 170); at no 154, **Palazzo Quattrocchi** is ornamented with Moorish designs.

▷ *From Giarre, head for the coast in the direction of Riposto.*

Riposto
The town developed around a colony of people from Messina, who established their warehouses here. In the 19C, this area became vital to wine exportation. Today vestiges of 18th C commercial buildings still survive.
The **Santuario della Madonna della Lettera** (○*open by appointment only at least three days in advance, Mon–Sat, 9.30am–11.30am, 4pm–6pm; Sun and public hols, 10am–11am;* ○*closed the week before 15 Aug;* ☏*095 93 35 27 or 095 93 11 87)* was built in 1710. Excavations beneath the sanctuary have revealed crypts containing funerary chamber from the palaeo-Christian period, coins from the Arabo-Norman era and architectural remains from Aragonese times. The choir has an interesting set of recently carved wooden stalls and a Baroque lamp set with mother-of-pearl.

▷ *Return to Giarre and head along S 114 for 13km/8mi.*

Acireale✠ ○*See ACIREALE.*

Aci Trezza ○*See ACIREALE.*

Aci Castello ○*See ACIREALE.*

GELA

POPULATION: 72 000

The surrounding plain – which assisted the disembarkation of American troops in July 1943 – is one of the more fertile zones of the island. The oil that feeds the refinery and petrochemical complex contributes to the economy, but not all aspects of the city. Still, it remains noteworthy for its illustrious past.

- **Information:** Via Bresmes Navarra 48. ☎0933 92 32 68. www.comune.gela.cl.it.
- ▶ **Orient Yourself:** Modern Gela has little in the way of tourist attractions. Head directly for the museum on the eastern side of the city.
- **Don't Miss:** The archaeological museum.
- **Also See:** AGRIGENTO; CALTAGIRONE; COMISO.

A Bit of History

The colony of Gela was founded by colonists from Rhodes and Crete towards the end of the 7C BC. The town prospered and expanded westwards, leading to the eventual foundation of Agrigentum, which soon surpassed it in importance. Gela reached its height during the rule of two tyrants: Hippocrates and Gelon. The latter decided halfway through his reign to move to Syracuse. The city gradually lost its political might, but none of its cultural importance. Indeed, Aeschylus decided to spend the last years of his life here. Legend claims the tragic poet died when an eagle dropped a tortoise on his bald head, mistaking it for a rock. Following each successive attack, the town was faithfully rebuilt; finally, in 1230, Gela was completely reconstructed by Frederick II.

The Greek City

Museo Archeologico★
At the east end of the town in Corso Vittorio Emanuele.
♿ ⏲Open 9am–1pm, 3pm–6.30pm. ⏲Closed last Mon in the month. ☎0933 91 26 26.
The collections are beautifully presented in chronological order and by category. The fine array of **antefixes** come from the acropolis area; some bear the features of gorgons, others the sneering traits of sileni or satyrs (6C–5C BC).

Recovered from a 5 BC shipwreck is a delicate *askos* with a silenus and a maenad. The last room *(on the ground floor)* gathers together a fine selection of **Archaic and Attic vases** from the necropoli at Navarra and Nocera.

Acropolis
Alongside the museum.
The *plateia* divides the town neatly: to the south lie two temples; to the north sit the residential quarters and shops.

Fortifications★★
West of the town, in the district of Capo Soprano.
♿⏲Open 9am–1hr before dusk. ⊙€2. ☎0933 93 09 75.
A stretch of Greek wall, some 300m/ 330yd long, dates from the era when Timoleon restored democracy and rebuilt the town, razed by the Carthaginians (in 405 BC).

Complesso termale
A short distance from the fortifications, near an almshouse. For information, call ☎0933 91 26 26.
The two rooms of this baths complex date from Hellenistic times. The first is divided into two areas: one containing a series of small tubs arranged in a circle, the other set in a horseshoe shape. The second room would have been the *hypocaust* (with under-floor heating), used at times as a sauna. The baths were largely destroyed by fire some time towards the end of the 3C BC.

Castelluccio

7 km north on S 117. This petite castle – in the Arab-Norman style – was erected in the 13C. Thanks to its elevation and position, the building controls access to the city.

Excursions

Riserva Naturale Orientata Biviere di Gela 🎫

8km/5mi southeast on the road to Scoglitti.
Organise a visit through the office at Venezia 91, Gela. ☎/Fax 0933 92 60 51. lipu.gela@ntv.it.

The grand lake of the Sicilian coast represents a wetland that is of extreme importance for migrating birds.

Licata

31km/19mi W.

At the heart of the little town is Piazza Progresso and from this radiate Via Roma and Corso Vittorio Emanuele, the two main streets along which the town's principal 18C monuments are aligned. On Via Roma are the church and cloisters of **San Domenico** and **Chiesa del Carmine**. Corso Vittorio Emanuele, meanwhile, claims Palazzo Frangipane with its fanciful brackets shaped like monsters, and the churches of San Francesco and the Chiesa Madre dedicated to Santa Maria la Nova.

GIARDINI NAXOS ♨♨

POPULATION: 9 000.

The beach that received the first Greek colonists to Sicily 2 700 years ago now accommodates thousands of tourists. They're drawn to the charming position, the particularly mild climate, the long gilded beach and the splendid scenery in the Taormina area. The seaside attractions only add to the archaeological lustre.

- 🛈 **Information:** Lungomare Tysandros 54. ☎0942 51 010. www.aastgiardininaxos.it
- ▶ **Orient Yourself:** Giardini Naxos stands behind a popular sandy beach, which runs from Capo Taormina to Capo Schisò. The archaeological site lies close to the Giardini Naxos exit on the A 18 motorway. The town is 5km/3mi from Taormina and is linked to the city by frequent bus services (departures every 30min).
- 🅿 **Parking:** In the centre of the small town and walk to the beach front.
- 👁 **Don't Miss:** The ruins at Naxos, Capo Schisò.
- 🕐 **Organising Your Time:** In summer, spend the morning on the beach, have lunch in the shade and visit Naxos late afternoon when the sun isn't quite as strong.
- 🧒 **Especially for Kids:** The long sandy beach is perfect for children.
- 👣 **Also See:** ACIREALE; ETNA;MESSINA; TAORMINA.

A Bit of History

Capo Schisò is a promontory formed by a great lava flow. Here the first Chalcidian colonisers founded Naxos in 735 BC, making it the oldest Greek settlement in Sicily. The name is borrowed from the Cycladic island, where, according to legend, Dionysus met and then married Ariadne after she was abandoned by Theseus.

From the 5C BC, the domination of Naxos became a prime objective for aspiring empire-builders, notably Hippocrates of Gela and, later, Hieron of Syracuse. The latter evicted the inhabitants of Naxos and deported them to Leontinoi in 476. Eventually, the support offered by Naxos to the Athenian expedition against Syracuse (415 BC) led to the city's demise. In 403 BC, Dionysius the Great razed it to the ground, leaving the exiled survivors to found Tauromenion. For a long

Address Book

For coin ranges, see the Legend on the cover flap.

WHERE TO STAY

Agriturismo Villa Antonella – *Via Fondaco d'Accorso, Trappitello, 2km/1.2mi W of Giardini on S 185. ☎0942 65 41 31. www.villantonella.com. Closed Oct–Apr (open Sat–Sun only). .10 rooms. .*

This modern family-run agriturismo guesthouse is attractively situated among fruit and citrus trees and has 10 simple, but well-maintained rooms. The service here is both friendly and efficient.

Hotel La Riva – *Via Tysandros 52, Giardini Naxos. ☎0942 51 329. www. hotellariva.com. Closed Nov. 38 rooms.* A charming family-run pensione on the seafront, with 38 rooms furnished in

original Sicilian style and a dining room on the fourth floor that offers superb sea views.

Hotel Arathena Rocks – *Via Calcide Eubea 55, Giardini Naxos. ☎0942 51 349. reservation@hotelarathena.com. Closed 27 Oct–11 Apr. 49 rooms.* Facilities at this quiet, elegant hotel in an isolated location include a beautiful garden and a swimming pool overlooking the sea.

WHERE TO EAT

Sea Sound – *Via Jannuzzo 37/A, Giardini Naxos. ☎0942 54 330. Closed Nov–Apr.* This sea-facing restaurant serves delicious fish dishes on a delightful terrace surrounded by greenery.

For more suggestions, see TAORMINA.

---

time the "garden town" merely served as a sheltered anchorage for nearby Taormina.

The epithet originated from the cotton and sugar-cane plantations, eventually replaced by citrus orchards. A popular resort since the 1950s, it's now one of Sicily's largest tourist centres.

Visit

Naxos

Access to the site is from Via Stracina, the continuation of Via Naxos, or, during opening hours, via the museum in Via Schisò. Open 9am–1hr before dusk. €2. ☎0942 51 001.

The 4 BC town followed the same boundaries as its 7C–6C BC predecessor: all but the old city walls and the **temenos** (sacred precinct) were removed and replaced by a regular orthogonal (right-angled) street plan as advocated by the 5C BC architect-urban planner Hippodamus of Miletus.

On entering the site from Via Stracina, follow the path along the boundary walls of the ancient city. On the southwest side, these incorporate the walls

Beach with the snow-capped volcano in the background

G. Bludzin/MICHELIN

of the **temenos**, enclosing the ruins of a large temple (B) from the late 6C BC. Nearby sit two kilns: the larger for firing architectural elements in terracotta, the smaller for vases and votive objects.

Leave the sacred precinct by its northern entrance (traces of which are still visible) to emerge onto plateia B.

Follow this broad avenue some distance, while surveying the urban plan of the new city.

At stenopos 6, turn left towards the museum: on the left, level with stenopos 11, are the remains of a small temple from the 7C BC.

Archaeological museum

Via Schisò. ⏱*Open 9am–1hr before dusk.* ⊙*€2.* ☎*0942 51 001.*

Situated alongside a small Bourbon keep, the museum houses artefacts from the excavations. The ground floor contains pottery that testifies to the existence of settlements on Capo Schisò from Neolithic times and the Bronze Age. A fabulous range of painted **cymae** (decorative roof ornaments) are displayed, as well as a lovely figurine of a veiled goddess (probably Hera); a delicately contrived **statuette of Aphrodite Hippias**; a collection of objects from a **surgeon's tomb**. Inside the keep are objects found at sea: anchor shafts, amphorae and grindstones.

GIBELLINA

POPULATION: 5 000

Completely destroyed by the 1968 earthquake, Gibellina has been reconstructed 18km/11mi from the original. The ruins became a museum of sort, the very streets and structures overlaid with concrete – a work of art by the Tuscan sculptor Alberto Burri. Other installations are by Arnoldo Pomodoro, Cascella, and Isgrò (to mention a few). The 50-plus works of art include the imposing "Star" at the town entrance by Pietro Consagra, Quaroni's "Piazza del Municipio" with its musical tower, and his white spherical "Chiesa Madre" that dominates the landscape.

🛈 **Information:** Piazza XV Gennaio 1968 no 1. ☎0924 67877. www.comunedigibellina.it

▶ **Orient Yourself:** Along S 119 linking Castelvetrano (11km/7mi to the south) with Alcamo, Gibellina Nuova is situated just a few kilometres from the A29 motorway, which runs from Palermo to Mazara del Vallo.

🚗 **Don't Miss:** "Crack" by Alberto Burro in Gibellina.

🕐 **Organising Your Time:** A half-day is suitable for the site.

👣 **Also See:** CASTELVETRANO; SEGESTA.

Driving Tour

The Ruins of the 1968 Earthquake

60km/38mi – allow at least half a day.

On the afternoon of 14 January 1968, an earthquake shattered eastern Sicily, tearing buildings from their foundations, opening fissures in the ground and destroying underground cavities. Many of the villages in the Belice region were completely destroyed, and Gibellina, Salaparuta and Poggioreale were subsequently all rebuilt away from their original locations.

▶ *From Gibellina, take S 188 heading south. Turn left onto S 119 and follow signs to Ruderi di Gibellina.*

Ruderi di Gibellina

The ruins are still visible, although many have been petrified into a work of art called **Cretto** *(Crack).* **Alberto Burri**, the

Tuscan sculptor, covered much of the old town in a gentle concrete blanket furrowed by cracks.

▷ *Return to Santa Ninfa and take S 188 to Partanna.*

Partanna

This small town was also badly affected by the same earthquake of 1968. Its distinguishing feature, a castle with battlements was rebuilt in the 17C by the princes of Graffeo (or Grifeo) on the foundations of an earlier, Norman, construction. The flat area behind the castle provides a splendid view★ of the valley. Unfortunately, the churches have been reduced to ghostly shells by the earthquake: all that remains of San Francesco along Via Vittorio Emanuele is a lonely bell tower (16C–17C) while, higher up, the church of the Madonna delle Grazie also preserves its original tower.

▷ *Take S 188 to Salemi.*

Salemi

The small town of Salemi enjoys a lovely position surrounded by the vineyards that are so typical of the Trapani region. The older parts bear the indelible imprint of Arab influences. Narrow cobbled streets wind up to the inevitable hilltop castle. Salemi was inadvertently blessed with a moment of unexpected glory, when it was declared the first

FESTIVAL

In summer, the Orestiadi music, film and drama festival is held in the ruins of Gibellina. *Contact the Fondazione Orestiadi, Baglio di Stefano; ☎0924 67 844; www.fondazione.orestiadi.it.*

capital of Italy, following the arrival of Garibaldi in Sicily.

Castello Normanno

The Norman castle was erected at the wishes of Roger d'Altavilla on the foundations of a fortress: the castle has two square towers and one high round one. On its right stand the remains of the **Chiesa Madre**, destroyed by the 1968 quake.

▷ *Turn down Via D'Aguirre and along past the church.*

Chiesa e Collegio dei Gesuiti

🕓 *Open Tue–Sun 9am–1pm, 3pm–6.40pm.* 🕓*Closed Mon and holidays.* ⊜*Donations welcome.* ☎*0924 98 23 76.* The rather elegant facade of the church is Baroque, complete with a portal flanked with spiral columns of tufa. The Collegio, meanwhile, accommodates the **Museo Civico**, which contains various religious works of art rescued from the churches destroyed in the earthquake in 1968: a particular highlight is the lovely *Madonna della Candelora* (Candlemas) by

Consagra's Star at the entrance of the town

B. Kaufmann/MICHELIN

Domenico Gagini. Beyond the last room of the museum sits an 18C chapel that replicates the Casa Santa of Loreto.

Further downhill, lies the picturesque **Rabato** quarter complete with all its Moorish flavour.

The outside streets provide wonderful **views**★ of the valley. Here, on 3 February each year, the residents distribute tiny, very elaborate and strangely shaped loaves of bread for the feast day of San Biago.

Bread also plays its part in the celebrations of St Joseph's day (19 March), when special large votive loaves are baked in the shape of angels, garlands, flowers, animals and work-tools.

▶ *Take S 188A north, then follow S 113 to Calatafimi.*

Calatafimi

This little town was once well defended by its **Castello Eufemio**, a Byzantine fortress that was rebuilt in the 13C and now lies in ruins. From here, a fine **view**★ stretches over the valley and town.

On the hill opposite stands the **Pianto Romano**, a monument commemorating the followers of Garibaldi who died in action (Calatafimi was the scene of an important battle). From there, a marvellous **view**★★ extends. Every five years, during the first three days of May, the Festival of the Holy Crucifix **(Festa del Santissimo Crocefisso)** is held: this important procession takes place through the streets with representations from all the various town "corporations." The Massari delegation can be distinguished by its unique float, which is decorated with bread.

▶ *From Calatafimi, it is possible to continue to Segesta (4km/2.5mi).*

CAVA D'ISPICA ★

Situated between the towns of Ispica and Modica, this crack, approximately 13km/8mi, it is studded with rooms, sanctuaries and necropoli, which date from the Neolithic era. Nature created the grottos, later modified by humans.

🛈 **Information:** Sopraintendenza ai Beni Culturali, Contrada Cava d'Ispica. ☎0932 77 16 67.

▶ **Orient Yourself:** The gorge comprises two parts: the first, between Modica and Ispica, consists of a fenced section open to the public and an area to the north, which is less accessible and best visited on a guided tour.
The second part of the gorge, known as the Parco della Forza, is located in Ispica and is mainly visited on organised tours.

🅿 **Parking:** Park at the Ufficio della Sovrintendenza for Cava d'Ispica tours.

♿ **Also See:** COMISO; MODICA; NOTO; RAGUSA.

Visit

Cava d'Ispica

From S 115 follow signs to Cava d'Ispica. Tours leave from the Ufficio della Sovrintendenza.

🕐*Open Apr–Oct, 9am–7.30pm; Nov–Mar, 9am–1.45pm.* ⊚*€2.* ▪*Guided tours available.* ☎*0932 77 16 67.*

The actual Cava d'Ispica contains the **Larderia**★ (from the word *ardeia* – with abundant water), which consists of a pal-aeo-Christian catacomb (4C–5C) lined with an impressive number of burial chambers (464).

The tour follows the contours of a rock wall. Beyond the Church of Santa Maria (high up in the cliff on the left) and the Camposanto or Holy Ground, are located the **Grotte Cadute**, which comprise a residential complex on several levels. Holes in the ceiling and cut steps enabled the residents to move around with

Larderia

the aid of poles and ropes that could be pulled up in times of danger.

Opposite the entrance to the fenced area, on the far side of the main road, another road leads to the **rock-hewn Church of San Nicola** and the **Spezieria**, a little church perched on a sharp rocky outcrop. The name, corrupted from dialect, is linked to the myth of a monk-cum-apothecary who prepared herbal remedies. The church interior is subdivided into two parts: a nave and a misaligned chancel with three apses.

▶ *Return to the car and drive up the main road to the first turning on the left.*

Baravitalla

On the plateau stand the ruins of the Byzantine Church of **San Pancrati** *(on the left, fenced off)*.

Further on, a path leads left to other points of interest *(difficult to find without a guide)*: the **Tomb with decorative pilasters** has a double front entrance, and the **Grotta dei Santi** has fresco fragments.

Back on the main road, continue towards Cava d'Ispica, seeking the **Grotta della Signora**, sheltering a spring considered sacred since ancient times. The walls bear graffiti from prehistoric or palaeo-Christian eras (swastikas and crosses).

Meanwhile, in the opposite direction, further towards Ispica, the central part of the gorge conceals the **"Castello,"** an enchanting residential complex several storeys high that was abandoned only in the 1950s *(very difficult to find: consult a local guide for detailed directions)*.

Parco della Forza

Located at Ispica, 13km/8mi SE of Cava d'Ispica.

For information on admission times, call ☎ 0932 77 16 67. Closed Sun and public hols. €2.

This site, one of the earliest areas of settlement, has been occupied since Neolithic times and was abandoned in the 1950s *(very difficult to find: consult a local guide for directions)*. During the Middle Ages, the plateau above the gorge was fortified with a citadel. This was raised around the **Palazzo Marchionale**, the layout of which may still be made out. Some rooms preserve fragments of original painted, fired lime floor tiles. The small fortress also contained several churches including the **Annunziata**, with 26 graves inlaid into its floor.

The cave known as the **Scuderia**, because it accommodated stables in medieval times, bears traces of graffiti horses. The most striking feature is the **Centoscale**, a immensely long under-

G. Bludzin/MICHELIN

ground stairway (240 steps cut into the rock), which descends 60m/200ft at an angle of 45º to emerge on a level with the valley floor, below the river bed. The passage's age is uncertain, but its function was to ensure a water supply even in times of drought. A total of 100 slaves (hence the name) collected the liquid as it filtered down from the river bed (at its deepest point, the passageway was 20m/65ft below water level).

Outside the park stands **Santa Maria della Cava**, a little rock-hewn church containing the fragments of fresco in successive layers *(apply to the custodians for access)*.

Excursions

Ispica

13km/8mi SE of Cava d'Ispica. The hub of the little town is **Piazza Regina Margherita**, where the Chiesa Madre, San Bartolomeo and Palazzo Bruno (1910) with its distinctive angular tower are situated. Corso Umberto I, running behind the church, passes between a series of fine buildings before leading to the Liberty-style jewel of the town: **Palazzo Bruno di Belmonte** (now the town hall) designed by **Ernesto Basile**. Opposite stands the lovely **covered market**. Other buildings of quality lie beyond it, notably at no 76 and no 82.

Return to Piazza Regina Margherita and turn down Via XX Settembre to the church of **Santa Maria Maggiore**. The semicircular arcade before the church was conceived by **Vincenzo Sinatra** as a **complement**★.

Inside it contains a cycle of **frescoes**★ by Catanian artist Olivio Sozzi (1763). The large central panel depicts scenes from the Old and New Testaments: Adam and Eve, Judith with the head of Holofernes, Moses *(below)*, the Apostles with St Peter *(centre)* and Christ holding the Eucharist *(above)*. The chapel in the left transept contains a canopy with an unusual carved wooden figure of Christ at the Column.

This statue is carried in procession annually during the Maundy Thursday (the Thursday before Easter) celebrations. In the opposite direction, Corso Garibaldi leads to the elegant **Chiesa dell'Annunziata**.

LAMPEDUSA★

POPULATION: 6 025

The island of Lampedusa is a limestone table that finishes to the north with an impressive **cliff**★★★, while to south it plunges into long deep capes, coves and sandy beaches. More neighbor to Africa than to Italy, it's encircled by a spectacular **sea**★★, which shades from transparent to turquoise and emerald.

- **Information:** Via Vittorio Emanuele 89. ☎0922 97 59 11. www.isoladilampedusa.it
- **Orient Yourself:** The port is in the southeastern section of Lampedusa, an area that is also home to the island's beaches and hotels. The north is mountainous; best explored by boat. Most roads are located to the east, although one heads west inland from the town of Lampedusa to Capo Ponente. The Riserva Naturale Isola di Lampedusa covers the southeastern section of the coast between Cala Greca and the Vallone dell'Acqua, and includes the Isola dei Conigli.
- **Don't Miss:** The Isola dei Conigli bay, Tabaccara bay, the view from Albero del Sole in Lampedusa, Pozzolana in Linosa.
- **Organising Your Time:** Plan three days to absorb all the beauty. Avoid July and August, when the sea turtles lay their eggs and tourism spikes.
- **Especially for Kids:** The sea turtles (apply for viewing permission)
- **Also See:** ISOLE EGADI; ISOLE EOLIE.

Address Book

GETTING THERE AND AROUND

The simplest way to get to the islands is by air: **flights** operate from Palermo (approximately 1hr), with additional services during the summer months from the main Italian cities.

There is also a **hydrofoil** service during the summer months from Lampedusa to Linosa (1hr). Ustica Lines, ☎0923 87 38 13, www.usticalines.it.

Overnight **ferry** services operate from Agrigento (Porto Empedocle) to Linosa (6hr) andLampedusa (8hr). Contact Siremar, ☎091 74 93 111 (from Italian landlines) or 081 017 1998 (from mobiles), www.siremar.iy.

For coin ranges, see the Legend on the cover flap.

WHERE TO STAY

Various types of apartments are available to rent, in addition to the usual array of expensive traditional hotels. Book well in advance for the summer months. For further information, contact the tourist office.

Campeggio La Roccia – *Via Madonna, Cala Greca, Lampedusa. ☎0922 97 00 55. www.laroccia.net.* Right on the seafront, this campsite offers a selection of accommodation: bungalows, mobile homes and caravans, as well as large shady pitches for tents. Facilities include a restaurant and supermarket.

I Dammusi di Borgo Cala Creta – *Contrada Cala Creta, Lampedusa. ☎0922 97 03 94. www. calacreta.com.* The traditional *dammusi* (white-domed buildings with stone walls) offer a picturesque alternative to staying in a hotel. The complex also includes small white villas rented out by the week.

Cavalluccio Marino – *3, Contrada Cala Croce. ☎0922 97 00 53. www.hotelcavalucciomarino. com. Closed Nov–Easter. 10 rooms, half board only.* This small, elegant family-run hotel, situated near one of the island's prettiest bays, offers 10 comfortable, well-maintained rooms. Fresh fish is caught daily by the hotel owner, Signor Pietro.

WHERE TO EAT

Lampedusa has a wide choice of small restaurants and trattorias all serving a wonderful variety of fresh fish. The *cuscus di pesce* (often made with grouper), a local speciality based on a Tunisian dish, is particularly recommended.

Al Gallo D'Oro – *Via Ludovico Ariosto 2, Lampedusa. ☎0922 97 12 97. Closed Dec–Feb.* This restaurant is renowned for its fresh fish and good value for money. The decor is rustic, with a wooden gallery, exposed beams, and numerous prints and paintings. Meals are served outside in summer.

Da Nicola – *Via Ponente, Lampedusa. ☎0922 97 12 39. Closed Thu (in winter). Booking recommended.* For excellent seafood and home cooking typical of Lampedusa, this family-run restaurant is well worth a visit. Meals are served in a simple rustic dining room full of small paintings.

Lipadusa – *Via Bonfiglio 6, Lampedusa. ☎0922 97 16 91. Closed at lunchtime, Nov–Easter.* This friendly, family-run restaurant in the centre serves regional cuisine with an understandable emphasis on fresh fish. The decor is simple.

SHOPPING

Natural **sponges** are collected from all around Lampedusa making them one of the most popular purchases available to visitors. A word of advice – the whiter sponges, although more attractive, have been treated with bleach making them less durable. The slightly brown sponges, on the other hand, last longer.

M. Magni/MICHELIN

The locally grown produce available on Linosa includes lentils and miniature tomatoes; reed baskets are also on sale in the town centre.

TURTLE CONSERVATION

The Pelagie – notably Lampedusa's bay of Isola dei Conigli with its long stretch of sand – have been chosen by the loggerhead turtles as suitable sites for laying eggs. A special conservation-cum-education centre, **Centro Recupero, Marcaggio e Tutela delle Tartarughe Marine**, has been set up on Lampedusa to monitor and protect the turtle population, with a programme involving local children under the supervision of Dr Daniela Freggi. The number to call should a turtle be found in distress, or for volunteers to participate in local monitoring, is ☎0338 219 85 33 (mobile).
On **Linosa**, the black (and therefore warm) sands of Cala Pozzolana di Ponente seem to favour the birth of female turtles. Scholars say the sex of a turtle is determined by the temperature: below 30°C males predominate, temperatures in excess of 30°C favour females. By the beach the Assocazione Hydrosphera runs its **Centro Studi sulle Tartarughe Marine**: this displays information concerning the life cycle of the turtles, complete with illustrations provided by enthusiastic volunteers. The centre also has a small "Casualty department" for turtles found sick and exhausted or brought in by fishermen who have inadvertently caught them on a hook. The two centres (on Lampedusa and Linosa) are part of an Italian project run by the Department of Animal and Human Biology of La Sapienza University in Rome. *Open mid-Jun–mid-Sept 10am–1pm, 4pm–7pm. The rest of the year only 4pm–7pm. Closed holidays.* ☎0922 97 20 76.

A Bit of History

The islands of the "high sea" – The archipelago of the **Isole Pelagie**★, approximately 200km/125mi south of Agrigento between the island of Malta and Tunisia, comprises the large island of **Lampedusa** (surface area of 33km2/12.7sq mi) and the two small islands **Linosa** and **Lampione**. The inhabitants of Lampedusa have little experience of agriculture: the interior of the island is white and yellow, stony and arid, like a miniature desert. Instead they depend on fishing for a livelihood, as the large fleet anchored offshore in the well-sheltered bays will testify. A few finds confirm that the island was inhabited as early as the Bronze Age. In 1843, the island belonged to the illustrious Lampedusa family (of which Giuseppe, author of *The Leopard*, is the most famous member). When it was acquired by King Ferdinand II, he had a prison built on the island and sent a handful of people to reside there.

Marine underworld – Snorkelling is excellent along the rocky coastline: brightly coloured rainbow wrasse, scorpion fish, blenies (lurking in small crevasses in the rock), sea stars, slender needlefish, octopus, sea cucumbers, sea hares and sponges. The sea floor is a jigsaw of rocky and white sandy patches. At intervals these are suddenly monopolised by dark green underwater meadows of *Poseidonia oceanica,* the seaweed nicknamed "the lung of the Mediterranean".
Divers will discover abundant groves of coral, sponges and madrepores populated with shoals of colourful parrot fish and, off Capo Grecale (at a depth of 50m/165ft), lobsters.

Visit

Lampedusa⌂

The town shares its name with the island land mass. Apart from the odd house scattered here and there, this is the only town as such, and it hinges on Via Roma. The main street comes to life in the morning at breakfast time, and again in the evening at sunset until late into the night. It hosts a cluster of small shops and cafés that sprawl onto the pavement. In summer, these bars proffer low-key entertainment (sessions of karaoke or live music).

Boat trip around the island★

In summer, many a boat owner will tout his or her business down in the harbour, happy to take visitors out and round the island for a reasonable sum. Excursions usually take a whole day, departing at about 10am and returning at approximately 5pm.

The low, jagged coastline is laced with little creeks and inlets including the one known as **la Tabaccara**★★: this lovely bay washed with the most stunningly turquoise sea is only accessible by boat. The next in line is the **Baia dell'Isola del Coniglio**★★★, before the headland Capo Ponente, the most westerly point of the island. Here, the landscape suddenly changes. The northern **coastline**★★ consists of a single great tall cliff plunging straight down into the sea, indented here and there by a number of intriguing caves and grottoes. Eventually, the contours open into the **Baia della Madonnin**★★ (so called because of the shape of one of the rocks above it), and various impressive rocks. These are known as the *Scogli del Sacramento* and they guard a deep cave with the same name and its neighbour **Grotta del Faraglione**.

The northeastern tip of the island, Capo Grecale, is capped with a lighthouse that swings its beam across some 60 nautical miles (110km) offshore. Immediately after Cala Pisana, by the *Grotta del Teschio* (Cave of the Skull) is a 10–15m/30–50ft long beach, accessible down a path on the right.

Exploring the island on land

▶ *The circular coast road is not asphalted all the way around the island; it is therefore recommended that mopeds or small four-wheel drive vehicles be hired for the day. From the town of Lampedusa, head east towards the airport.*

The dirt track parallel to the runway skirts round many of the creeks and small rocky bays on the south coast. Beyond Cala Pisana, it continues to the tip of Capo Grecale, where the lighthouse is situated From this lofty position, the fine **view**★ pans in either direction along the coast and down to the sea stirring dizzily below. The road then links up with another that traces the south side of the island. Turn right towards the telecommunications signalling station.

Albero del Sole

These steep cliffs are the highest point on Lampedusa (133m/436ft). The small round building contains a wooden crucifix. From the other side of the stone wall (⊙ *be careful, as it conceals a treacherous*

Isola dei Conigli

G. Bludzin/MICHELIN

drop), there is a dramatic **view**★★ of the **Faraglione** – or *Scoglio a Vela* (shrouded rock) as it is also called – and the cliffs plunging steeply down into the sea. One way of enjoying the view without fear of falling is to lie flat on the ground, not too near the edge.

Return back the same way and fork right along the partially asphalted road, that runs past a tree plantation on the right. At the far end of the enclosure wall, continue along the vague dirt track leading to a small iron cross. The headland on the right provides a glorious **view**★★ of the **Scoglio del Sacramento**★ *(right)*. In the distance on the left, can be seen the little island of Lampione.

Return to the main road and head south towards the bay around *Isola dei Conigli* (Rabbit Island).

Baia dell'Isola dei Conigli★★★

In this broad bay, with its petticoat of white cliffs and the most beautiful beach on the island, sits a little islet. It could almost be a corner of the Caribbean: the whitest sand slopes gently down to the water's edge, delicate clear tints of turquoise and emerald green stretch out to sea. Annually, a colony of loggerhead turtles makes its way up the beach to lay its eggs. Today, this exciting event is threatened by the ever larger numbers of spectators who linger here until sunset (turtles lay their eggs at night, but their extreme shyness means that the slightest disturbance will frighten them away). This is also the only place in Italy inhabited by an unusual species of stripy lizard of the Large Psammodromus *(Psammadromus algirus)* variety, more usually found in North Africa (Tunisia, Algeria and Morocco).

Madonna del Porto Salvo

This small, ancient shrine of uncertain date is surrounded by a pretty garden, bursting with colour in the summer.

Linosa★

The untamed beauty of the northernmost island, Linosa resides in the blackness of its volcanic rock, and its four great lofty cones pitched dramatically against the blue sky. This island, the tip of a submerged volcano, has evolved in different stages, and this is strikingly evident. The gaping maws of the volcano craters, now extinct, and bleak laval beaches with their crystal waters leave the visitor with a lasting, if haunting, impression.

The only town, huddled around the little harbour, consists of a collection of houses attractively painted in pastel shades with strongly accented coloured corners, doors and windows. From here,

Loggerhead Turtle (Caretta Caretta)

The Mediterranean's most common sea turtle is a docile, solitary being – other than during the mating season. They live in temperate waters, except when the females haul onto dry land to lay their eggs, every two or three years. The mother-to-be chooses a sandy beach undisturbed by lights or noise. With enormous effort, she heaves from the water (deprived of all her natural dignity, agility and grace) and, using her hind flippers, she digs a deep hole in the sand (40–75cm/16–30in deep). There she passively lays and then buries her eggs. Her task now over, she turns round and shuffles back to the sea.

Hatching takes place six to eight weeks later. The baby turtles emerge from the sand and instinctively scuttle towards the sea, a threatening and dangerous world – at least until they grow to any size. Only a few survive to adulthood. In fact, even before they hatch, the eggs easily fall prey to birds and man. As newly hatched turtles, their greatest threat comes in the shape of fish, greedy for their tender meat. This is why it is important to protect and safeguard both the nesting sites (eliminating noise, light and disturbance) and the seas the turtles inhabit. People should respect a few fundamental rules, notably disposing of their plastic bags with care. In the water, these take on the appearance of a tasty jellyfish for a turtle, and the mistake can cost it its life.

G. Bludzin/MICHELIN

Street of Linosa

there are a variety of possible excursions on foot into the mountains, or by boat around the coast. The few hundred inhabitants of this peaceful islet, who once depended on rearing cattle, now eke out a living from tourism.

The tallest peak is Monte Vulcano (186m/610ft), a volcano, as its name suggests, though now extinct.

The interior of the island is predominantly desert-like, but still supports a few areas of cultivation (notably the *Fossa del Cappellano*, which is particularly well sheltered from the wind).

Fringed with a jagged lava coastline, Linosa is considered to be a veritable paradise by scuba-divers and snorkelling enthusiasts.

The land-based fauna includes large colonies of Maltese wall lizards and **Cory's shearwaters** – the seabirds that shatter the quiet summer nights with their plaintive cries. Loggerhead turtles still lay eggs on the black beach in Cala Pozzolana.

A number of footpaths, popular among keen walkers, lead to the summits of the island's three main peaks: **Monte Rosso** – the crater of which shelters various garden allotments, **Monte Nero** and **Monte Vulcano**.

Boat trip round the island★★

Excursions by boat can be arranged down at the harbour. The boat sets out from the harbour leaving Monte Nero, Monte Bandiera and Monte Vulcano behind it.

It skirts the **Fili**, a group of rocks surrounding a sort of natural swimming-pool, enclosed on the landward side by sheer walls of **rock**★ polished and moulded by the rain and wind into wave-like forms. The restless sea and a handful of caper plants complete the landscape. Beyond the *Faraglioni* rocks that stand guard outside the "natural pool" or *Piscina Naturale (also accessible on foot)*, the lighthouse comes into view. This stretch of coastline is particularly jagged. Just before the circular trip draws to its conclusion, the boat steams across **Cala Pozzolana**★★; this shelters the only beach on the island, which is backed by an amazing wall of incredible colour that ranges from sulphur yellow through to rust red. The hydrofoils from Lampedusa moor here.

Lampione

Occupied only by a lighthouse, this small uninhabited and sparsely vegetated island rises vertically from a depth of 60m/196ft as a series of sheer cliffs. The deep and therefore relatively unpolluted sea provides ideal conditions for scuba divers to glimpse groupers, lobsters, yellow and pink coral and the occasional grey shark on the reefs around the island. Off shore fishing is also popular – ask around down at the harbour in Lampedusa town for a boat and skipper to hire to take you out there for the afternoon.

MADONIE E NEBRODI★★

With gentle green hills, extended woodlands, torrential rivers and soaring summits, the national parks of the Madonie and Nebrodi provide a spectacular and ever-changing landscape that is full of surprises.

Information: Madonie: Corso Paolo Alliata 16, Petralia Sottana, ☎0921 68 40 11, www.parcodellemadoni.it. Nebrodi: Via Cosenz 149 Sant'Agata di Militello, ☎0941 70 59 34, www.parcodeinebrodi.it, www.parchi.info.

▶ **Orient Yourself:** The gently undulating hills of the Madonie, which dominate the coast between Cefalù and Castel di Tusa, are replaced to the north by the wilder scenery of Piano Battaglia and Battaglietta, the Pizzo Carbonara (1 979m/ 6 491ft, the highest peak in the range) and the Serre di Quecella; the latter are often referred to as the "Sicilian Alps" on account of their resemblance to the Dolomites. The Nebrodi, which extend between Santo Stefano di Camastra and Capo d'Orlando, culminate in Monte Soro, near San Fratello, at a height of 1 847m/6 060ft.

P **Parking:** Car parking is available at Rifugio Sempria for the Giant Holly Trail.

Don't Miss: Outdoor sculpture at La Fiumara d'Arte, the lofty outlooks of Petralia Soprana and Polizzi Generosa, gorge walks in Le Golle di Pollina and handpainted ceramics at Santo Stefano di Camastra.

Organising Your Time: Allow one day for round-trip driving itineraries in the Madonie and Nebrodi.

Kids **Especially for Kids:** The sandy beach at Sant'Agata di Militello and Punic ship remains at Museo Archeologico di Baglio Anselmi.

Also See: CAPO D'ORLANDO, CEFALÙ, NICOSIA.

A Bit of History

The Sicilian Apennines form a natural extension in geological terms to the Calabrian Apennines. The range comprises the **Monti Peloritani** (above Messina) together with the **Nebrodi** and **Madonie** mountains: these are entirely consistent in terms of the landscape, flora and fauna.

The two latter areas have been designated national parks so as to preserve the natural heritage.

Rivers and mountain streams flow through valley gorges cut by erosion: one of the most spectacular is the **Gole di Pollina**, near Borrello. The vegetation varies with altitude: the coastal strip, up to 600–800m (2 000–2 600ft), is covered with oaks (cork, holm) and scrubby shrubs typical of the Mediterranean maquis (tree spurge, myrtle, *Pistacia lentiscus*, wild olive, strawberry tree/arbutus, juniper); above, at 1 200–1 400m (4 000–4 600ft), grow various species of oak; over 1 400m/4 600ft, the slopes are covered with glorious beech woods.

Between Vallone Madonna degli Angeli and Manca li Pini (northern side of Monte Scalone), grow 25 Nebrodi spruce, the only examples of this endemic, and now rare, species (one other stands by the ruined castle at Polizzi). One of the most interesting places for plants is Piano Pomo where the giant holly grows: a few, thought to be over 300 years old, reach over 14m/46ft in height and have a circumference of 4m/13ft.

The area has a variety of indigenous birds and animals, although the growing presence of humans (and increased hunting and poaching) has virtually annihilated many of the larger species (red and fallow deer, wolf, lammergeier and griffon vulture).

Those still found, however, include porcupines, wild cats, foxes, martens and some 150 or so species of bird such as hoopoes, buzzards, kestrels, red kites, peregrine falcons, ravens, golden eagles and grey herons.

Among the area's most interesting groups of residents are the many (some 70 or more) species of butterfly.

Driving Tours

The itineraries proposed below follow scenic routes, which, depending on the direction in which they are followed, provide a completely different set of views.

1 The Heart of the Madonie

160km/100mi round trip starting from Cefalù – allow one day.

Cefalù★★ 🐾 *See CEFALÙ.*

▸ *Take the road out of Cefalù along the coast eastwards, enjoying the views of the look out tower on the promontory. A signpost a little farther on indicates the road, right, for Castelbuono (22km/14mi).*

Castelbuono

This charming town, laid out across the lower undulations of the surrounding mountains, grew up in the 14C around the **castle** built by the **Ventimiglia** family. This massive square construction with square towers has undergone many alterations over the years; inside the small stuccoed chapel is the work of Giacomo Serpotta. The town itself is a charming jumble of winding streets, many on a steep incline, that converge on shady piazzas. The heart of the town is Piazza Margherita, overlooked by the Church of **Madrice Vecchia** and the old **Banca di Corte**. This currently accommodates the local **Museo Civico** (🕐 *open summer 9am–1pm, 4pm–8pm (4pm–7pm otherwise);* 🕐 *closed Mon;* 🎫 *€5.50;* ☎ *0921 67 34 67*) pending its relocation to the castle as soon as restoration work is completed. Its collections include treasures and furnishings from the Cappella Palatina (🐾 *See below*) and a fine selection of contemporary paintings, mainly by Italian artists.

Madrice Vecchia

Built in the 14C on the ruins of a pagan temple, the church has a 16C Renaissance portico and a splendid central portal in the Catalan style. On the left side rises a campanile with a fine Romanesque two-arched bell opening, culminating in an octagonal spire covered with maiolica tiles. The interior preserves several rare works of art, including a **polyptych**★ above the high altar depicting *The Coronation of the Virgin*, attributed to Pietro Ruzzolone (or possibly Antonello del Saliba). Note, in the bottom right, the unusual figure of a saint wearing spectacles. To the right is a statue of the *Madonna delle Grazie* by **Antonello Gagini**. Below the north aisle, the fresco of the *Sposalizio delle Vergini* (Betrothal of the Virgins) shows a strong Sienese influence in the elegant features and the pleasing symmetry of the composition.

A few of the columns separating the aisles are painted with frescoes; among these is the figure of St Catherine of Alexandria, characterised by her poise and delicate features. The crypt is entirely

Castelbuono

©durisi63/Fotolia.com

Address Book

For coin ranges, see the Legend on the cover flap.

WHERE TO STAY

SANT'AGATA DI MILITELLO

Villa Nicetta – *Contrada Nicetta, Acquedolci, 6km/4mi SW of Sant'Agata di Militello.* ☎*0941 72 61 42. www. villanicetta.it.* .*10 rooms.* . This old house dating from 1700 is surrounded by old barns, olive presses and other farm buildings, now transformed into tastefully decorated accommodation. Horse-riding and mountain biking is available.

CASTELBUONO

Hotel Milocca – *Contrada Piano Castagna, 7km/4.5mi SW of Castelbuono.* ☎*0921 67 19 44. www.albergomilocca. com. 54 rooms.* . A narrow road leads through holm oak woods to this isolated hotel with magnificent views of the Aeolian Islands and where each room has its own individual style. Local cuisine is to the fore in the restaurant.

Agriturismo Masseria Rocca di Gonato – *Località Eremo di Liccia, 8km/5mi S of Castelbuono.* ☎*0921 67 26 16. www.roccadigonato.it. Restaurant closed Tue.* . *11 rooms, half board. Restaurant* . This typical mountain agriturismo enjoys an isolated location with panoramic views within the Parco delle Madonie. The spacious rooms are furnished with basic creature comforts and the restaurant serves local cuisine, including meat produced on the farm.

CASTEL DI TUSA

Albergo Atelier sul Mare – *Via Cesare Battisti 4, Castel di Tusa.* ☎*0921 33 42 95. www.ateliersulmare.it. 40 rooms.* . This hotel-cum-museum provides a highly original approach to art, with guest rooms that are each decorated in their own unique way by artists of international renown.

GANGI

Villa Rainò – *Contrada Rainò, Gangi.* ☎*0921 64 46 80. www.villaraino. it. Closed first week of Jul. 15 rooms.* . *Restaurant* . Access to this delight-ful hotel is via an awkward descent along a narrow road. The effort is worth it, as the hotel has 15 tastefully

decorated rooms and a restaurant serving typical regional cuisine.

Tenuta Agrituristica Gangivecchio – *Contrada Gangi Vecchio, 4km/2.5mi from Gangi.* ☎*921 68 9191. www.tenutagangivecchio. com. Closed Jul. 9 rooms.* . This 14C Benedictine monastery was converted into a hotel in 1978. Guest rooms are housed in the main building, as well as in the converted stables. A delightful guesthouse with a fascinating history.

SAN MAURO CASTELVERDE

Agriturismo Flugy Ravetto – *Contrada Ogliastro, San Mauro Castelverde.* ☎*0921 67 41 28. www. aziendeflugyravetto.com. Closed Mar.* . *6 apartments, half board.* . *Restaurant* . The former fief of Ogliastro and Parrinello, now owned by Baronessa Flugy, is located on a gentle hill. The family property has six comfortable apartments for rent, with a swimming pool and play area for children. The perfect setting for a relaxing stay.

WHERE TO EAT

CASTELBUONO

Vecchio Palmento – *Via Failla 2, Castelbuono.* ☎*0921 72 099. Closed Mon.* This simple, family-run restaurant has a number of dining rooms, and a delight-ful garden (unfortunately by the road) where meals are served in the summer. The menu features typical Madonie specialities.

Nangalarruni – *Via Alberghi 5, Castelbuono.* ☎*0921 67 14 28. Closed Wed and for 2 weeks in Nov.* This typical local restaurant serves delicious region-al cuisine. The main dining room, dating from the mid-18C, is an attractive blend of exposed brickwork, old wooden beams and bottles lined up on shelves and around the chimney piece.

Romitaggio – *Loc. San Guglielmo, 5km/3mi S of Castelbuono.* ☎*0921 67 13 23. Closed Wed.* . Housed in a former 14C monastery, this restaurant has retained the simple, rustic style of its original building. Traditional local cuisine is served in a pleasant inner courtyard in the summer months.

GALATI MAMERTINO

⊜⊜⊜**Antica Filanda** – *Contrada Parrazzi, Galati Mamertino.* ☎*0941 43 47 15. Closed Wed and 15 Jan–15 Feb.* Genuine regional specialities are the order of the day in this friendly, rural style trattoria offering excellent value for money.

SAN MARCO D'ALUNZIO

⊜**La Fornace** – *Via Cappuccini 115, San Marco D'Alunzio.* ☎*0941 79 72 97. www.casemedievali.com. Closed Mon (in winter).* A popular address for gourmets who are more concerned with the quality of the cuisine than the elegance of their surroundings. This restaurant is renowned for its *maccheroni al ragù* and char-grilled meat.

SHOPPING

CASTELBUONO

Manna – Small, whitish, slightly sweet stalactites hanging from ash trees, manna is an exudation from these trees which, when dried, is collected and used as a sweetener and a laxative. Although once one of the town's sources of income, it is now more of a curiosity sought as souvenirs by tourists, who can find it at the tobacconist's at the end of Corso Umberto I (virtually in Piazza Margherita).

SAN MARCO D'ALUNZIO

La Tela di Penelope – *Via Aluntina 40.* This shop sells delightful hand-crafted woven textiles produced on old restored looms. Well worth a visit.

TAKING A BREAK

CASTELBUONO

Extra Bar Fiasconaro – *Piazza Margherita 10.* ☎*0921 67 12 31.* This bar sells the most delicious panettone (traditional Christmas cake), *colomba* (dove-shaped Easter cake) and, in summer, *ciambelle* (almond doughnuts). Also available if ordered in advance is the local speciality, *testa di turco* ("Turk's head"), made from bread dough stuffed with pork, ricotta cheese, eggs, cocoa and cinnamon.

POLIZZI GENEROSA

Pasticceria al Castello – *Piazza Castello 10.* ☎*0921 68 85 28.* This *pasticceria* produces excellent pastries and cakes including the typical *sfoglio polizzano,*

a type of local millefeuille made with *fromage frais,* sugar, chocolate and cinnamon, which is traditionally eaten during the third week of July as part of the **Sagra dello sfoglio**.

TOURS

Parco delle Madonie – The Madonie Park was founded in 1989 and encompasses 39 679ha/98 007 acres. Its roughly rectangular perimeter also contains four categories of reserve designated special, general, protected and controlled according to different guidelines. For detailed information, illustrated material and advice on excursions (by car or on foot), contact the Ente Parco at Petralia Sottana or Isnello *(see Location).*

Parco dei Nebrodi – The Nebrodi Park, designated a nature reserve in 1993, covers a large area, touching upon several local districts or *comuni.* Its 85 687ha/211 647 acres are divided into four categories consistent with the level of conservation implemented: special, general, protected and controlled. The park authority (Ente Parco) provides a number of information centres which dispense advice and guidance about footpaths and nature trails *(see Location).* The office at Cesarò organises free guided walks of different grades and duration, especially in summer: book in advance by phone.

FESTIVALS

Museo domestico – As part of the Fiumara d'arte project *(see below),* a large canvas is painted by dozens of artists and laid along the streets of participating villages, which vary from year to year. The event usually takes place in June. *For further information, contact the Atelier sul Mare,* ☎*0921 33 42 95; www.ateliersulmare.it*

Madonna della Luce – Mistretta celebrates its *Madonna of Light* festival annually, on 7 and 8 September, when a Madonna is borne aloft in solemn procession, escorted by two giant figures representing Mythia and Kronos (the legendary founders of Mistretta).

San Marco d'Alunzzio - Processione dei babbaluti – On the last Friday in March, in celebration of the Passion, the wooden cross of Ara Coeli is borne aloft through the town by hooded men singing and praying, known as the *"babbaluti."*

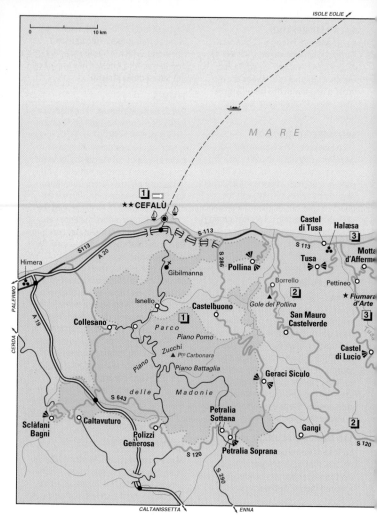

decorated with 17C frescoes depicting episodes from the Passion, Death and Resurrection of Christ.

▶ *Take Via Sant'Anna up to the castle.*

The massive form of the **castle** (🕐*open summer 9am–1pm, 5pm–8pm (rest of the year 4pm–7pm);* 🕐*closed Mon)* appears through the Gothic arch, with a square tower at each of its corners. The **Cappella Palatina**, on the second floor of the **castle**, is decorated with **stucco work**★ picked out from a gold-leaf background, attributed to Giuseppe Serpotta (1683), the brother of Giacomo.

▶ *Via Roma leads off from Piazza Margherita.*

Museo Francesco Minà-Palumbo
Via Roma.
🕐*Open summer 9am–1pm, 4pm–7.30pm.* 🕐*Closed Mon.* ✏€1.50. ☎0921 67 65 96. *www.museominapalumbo.it.*
House in a former Benedictine convent, the **museum** evolved from the botanical passion of **Francesco Minà-Palumbo**, a local 19C doctor. The result is a lifetime's systematic collection, classification and representation on paper of the botanical species, reptiles and

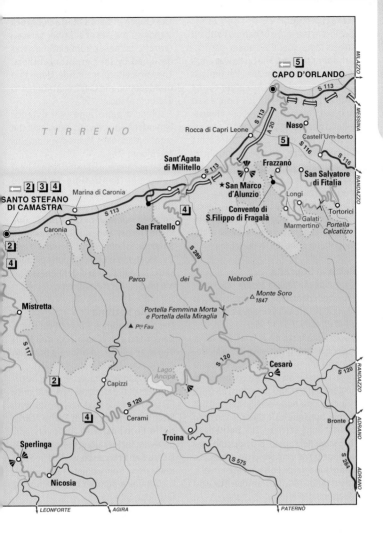

insects of the Madonie mountains, some of which are now extinct.

A little farther on is the church of **San Francesco** together with its extension, the **Mausoleo dei Ventimiglia**, a late medieval octagonal structure known as **la Madrice Nuova**, which contains a fine *Deposition from the Cross* by Giuseppe Velasco, and Baroque altars with spiral columns by Vincenzo Messina. In Corso Umberto I is the **Fontana di Venere Ciprea** (reconstructed in 1614), with Andromeda *(at the top)*, Venus and Cupid in the central niche and four bas-reliefs depicting the myth of Artemis (Diana) and Actaeon.

▶ *Leave Castelbuono and follow signs for San Guglielmo and Rifugio Sempria, where the car can be left.*

Il Sentiero degli Agrifogli giganti

3.5km/2mi – allow 2hr 30min.
This beautiful walk along the **Giant Holly Trail** leads from **Piano Sempria** through woods of holm and young oak to **Piano Pomo**. The giant holly trees here are 15m/50ft tall and some are more than 300 years old.

▶ *The road continues onwards towards Geraci Siculo 22km/14mi.*

Geraci Siculo

Get lost in the maze of narrow cobbled streets that spider this hamlet, particularly the upper part. The castle was originally built for the Marchesi Ventimiglia *(accessible by road – turn right by the entrance to the town)*: it's now a sad ruin, but from here, marvellous **views**⋆ extend out in every direction.

At the town centre stands the Gothic **Chiesa Madre**, whose highlight is the *Madonna and Child* by **Antonello Gagini** found in the second chapel of the north aisle.

The road from Geraci to Petralia *(14km/ 9mi)* proceeds through a glorious, sweeping landscape with lovely **views**⋆ of the mountains, Enna and Mount Etna.

Petralia Soprana

🕐 *To visit the Chiesa Madre and other churches, contact the local police (Polizia Municipale) a few days in advance. ☎0921 64 10 08 or 0921 64 14 96.*

Upper Petralia stands at 1 147m/3 762ft, making it the highest town in the Madonie and blessing it with spectacular views. Narrow streets weave between austere *palazzi* and churches, all built of local stone, occasionally opening out into picturesque little squares and onto breathtaking scenery. The **Belvedere** (by Piazza del Popolo) provides the best vantage point from which to survey the **panorama**⋆⋆ of Enna *(on the far left)*, Resuttano, Monte Cammarata and Madonna dall'Alto *(on the right)*.

The focal point of the town is **Piazza del Popolo** where the town hall is located, occupying the former premises of a Dominican convent. The street to the Chiesa Madre leads through the delightful Piazza Quattro Cannoli past its stone fountain. The right flank of the **Chiesa Madre**, preceded by a lovely portico, has a lovely **view** that extends over Piano Battaglia, Polizzi, Mount Etna and Enna. **Inside** look for the fine wooden crucifix by the master craftsman **Frà Umile da Petralia** *(right of the altar)*, who was born here, and a lovely wooden altar carved by Bencivinni in the Cappella del Santissimo Sacramento *(left of the main altar)*. The rear wall is taken up by an 18C organ case.

The Church of **Santa Maria di Loreto** stands on the site of a former Saracen fortress. Its convex front elevation was designed by the Serpotta brothers. The large altarpiece inside, depicting the Madonna and Child, is attributed to Giacomo Mancini (15C).

A splendid **panorama**⋆⋆⋆ extends behind the church with views over the jagged Madonie e Nebrodi mountains and Mount Etna.

Another church, dedicated to the Great Redeemer **(Santissimo Salvatore)** conforms to an elliptical plan and has an 18C decoration. It contains a wooden figure of St Joseph by Quattrocchi and, in the sacristy, two works by **Giuseppe Salerno**: *St Catherine of Alexandria* and the *Madonna with a Cat*; both pictures show an intimacy and gentleness that are unusual for this painter.

Petralia Sottana

Despite its name, Lower Petralia is perched on a rocky spur 1 000m/3 300ft above sea-level, in a lovely position overlooking the River Imera valley.

Corso Paolo Agliata, where the headquarters of the Madonie Park Authority (Ente Parco delle Madonie) are located, leads past the church of **Santa Maria della Fontana** with its lovely 15C doorway. Farther along the same street stands **San Francesco**, with its fine bell tower rising from a pointed arch; inside, it contains a number of paintings by Giuseppe Salerno.

As the street curves round to the right, the eye is drawn to the bell tower-cum-archway of the Chiesa della Misericordia, inlaid with a meridian line. A little farther on lies Piazza Umberto I and the **Chiesa Madre** (17C), an imposing building overlooking the valley, holding various paintings by **Giuseppe Salerno** including a *Triumph of the Eucharist* (first altar on the left) and *The Five Wounds of Our Lord* (once erroneously thought to be a *Deposition*). Look for the delicate rendering of the *Nativity* by **Antonello Gagini** in the chapel to the right of the high altar. The church also holds an 11C bronze Islamic candelabra in its sacristy: it is generally locked away for most of the year, but brought out for certain religious ceremonies.

G. Bludzin/MICHELIN

Petralia Sottana

Continue uphill to the 16C **Chiesa della Trinità** (la Badia) (🕐 *to visit the church, contact the parish priest*). A fine Gothic doorway leads into the church, which gives pride of place to a large 23-panel **marble altarpiece**★ by **Giandomenico Gagini**. The central section shows the Mystery of Easter; this is surrounded by the Trinity *(above)*, the Crucifixion, the Resurrection and the Ascension. The lateral panels *(top left to bottom right)* relate incidents from the life of Christ.

Excursion on foot

Allow 3hr 30min to the top.

On the northern edge of Petralia, a track worn by pilgrims leads up to the **Santuario della Madonna dell'Alto** (1 819m/5 966ft). This houses a painting of the Virgin and Child from 1471.

▸ *Proceed to Polizzi Generosa (20km/12mi).*

Polizzi Generosa

Polizzi enjoys a splendid **situation**★, sitting on a limestone spur dominating the northern and southern slopes of the Imera Valley. From here, the surrounding mountain tops appear to float on low cloud when it collects around the valley floor on crisp mornings. Despite the town's elusive origins, it seems to have played an active role in ejecting Arab invaders: **Roger II** had a castle built here against an attack from the infidels.

Later, Frederick II was so impressed by the hospitality extended to him on his visit that he bestowed the title of Generosa on the little town.

Begin a tour from the main piazza, marked by the ruins of the castle on the highest point (917m/3 008ft). Also located on the piazza is the Palazzo Notarbartolo (16C), which houses the **Museo Ambientalistico Madonita** (♿🕐 *open summer, 9am–1pm, afternoons by appointment; for admission times at other times of year, call ☎0921 64 94 78; ⊛€4; www.mam.pa.it; www.polizzi-generosa.it)*, a natural history collection presented as a series of reconstructed natural habitats (note that the preserved animals died of natural causes or were retrieved from poachers).

Via Roma leads downhill past Palazzo Gagliardo (16C–17C) and, opposite, the **Chiesa Madre** (⊶ *closed for restoration at the time of going to press)*, which contains a Flemish triptych *(presbytery)* and a lovely *Madonna of the Rosary* by **Giuseppe Salerno** – one of the two Zoppi di Gangi (⚲ *See below)*.

Piazza Umberto I lies beyond. From here, Via Garibaldi leads to San Girolamo with its fine Baroque doorway before finally terminating at Piazza XXVII Maggio. This square offers a dramatic **view**★★★ across the highest peaks of the Madonie: in the centre is the northern valley of the River Himera; to the left, sits Rocca di Caltavuturo, Monte

Calogero (right in the middle, in the far distance) and Monte Cammarata; the far right is marked by the Dolomite-like profile of Quacella, followed by Monte Mufara and Pizzo Carbonara. Almost directly opposite is the lower section of the Massicio dei Cervi, known as the *Padella* (meaning a frying pan). According to local tradition there is a secret entrance to a cave full of treasure here, the whereabouts of which may only be revealed during Easter Mass. Below lies the Valle dei Noccioleti.

▶ *Continue on down to the coast along S 643 for approximately 15km/9mi; at the fork, turn left towards Caltavuturo (25km/ 15mi from Polizzi).*

Caltavuturo

Clinging to the foot of the Rocca di Sciara, the "Fortress of the Vulture" – derived from the Arabic (*qalaat*, fortress) and the Sicilian vernacular (*vuturo*, vulture) – preserves a few prized 16C works of art in the **Chiesa Madre**★. These include an attractive *Madonna of the Rosary surrounded by the Mysteries*, executed by followers of Pietro Novelli and, at the back of the church, a fine Baroque organ by Raffaele della Valle.

▶ *Leave Caltavuturo by S 120 towards Cerda; at the fork, turn left for Sclafani Bagni (10km/6mi).*

Sclàfani Bagni

Crouched on the edge of a rocky crag in a wonderful **position**★, the entrance to this hamlet is marked by the **Porta Soprana**, a gate surmounted by the Sclàfani family coat of arms. On the left sits the *castelletto*, a defensive tower and beyond lies the **Chiesa Madre**, graced with a decorative Gothic doorway (15C). Highlights inside are *L'Agonizzante* by the Zoppo di Gangi **Giuseppe Salerno** (See below), and a sarcophagus carved with a bacchanal from the ancient city of Himera (See TERMINI IMERESE). The beautiful organ *(currently under restoration)* at the back of the church is by Raffaele della Valle (1615). Up to the right of the church the 14C tower offers a wonderful **view**★★ over

the sea below Himera and Caltavuturo and across to the Madonie mountains.

▶ *Return to S 643, following it to Collesano (30km/19mi).*

Collesano

The heart of this small holiday resort preserves its original medieval fabric, with its most interesting building, the **Chiesa Madre**, theatrically placed at the top of a great flight of steps. An enormous 16C *Crucifixion* hangs above its nave. Also look out for *St Catherine* (1596) in a bay in the south aisle, completed by Giuseppe Alvino, also known as *Il Sozzo* (literally translated as the Soak!) and for works by Zoppo di Gangi **Gaspare Vazzano**, such as the **Santa Maria degli Angelia** *(north aisle)*.

The way up to Piazza Gallo, in the oldest part of town, leads past the ruins of the castle, from where a splendid view opens out over the valley bottom and the coast.

▶ *From Collesano, turn down towards the coast signposted for Cefalù (17km/10.5mi).*

② **Between the Madonie and the Nebrodi**

180km/112mi round trip starting from Santo Stefano di Camastra – allow one full day.

Santo Stefano di Camastra

Santo Stefano is famous for its colourful **hand-painted ceramics**★★ and the streets are lined with small gift shops offering pots, vases and plates to buy. Gentle haggling for the best price is acceptable. At the **Palazzo Sergio** you will find the **Museo della Ceramica** (open 9am–1pm, 3.30pm–7.30pm; closed Mon and festivals; donations welcome; 0921 33 10 10), where pride of place is given to S Lorenzini's *Andare (Departing)* comprising of five warriors "sinking" into the ground. Upstairs several beautifully restored *palazzo* rooms have original **tiled floors**★, frescoed ceilings and 18C furnishings.

Outside the town (beyond the Ceramics Institute), lies the **Cimitero Vecchio:**

Hills of the Madonie

a cemetery, which contains graves ornamented with maiolica.

Mistretta

This small hamlet, located 950m/3 000ft above sea-level, is one of the departure points for excursions into the Nebrodi mountains. The town is a collection of simple stone houses grouped around the ruins of a feudal castle, with a clutch of striking buildings including the Church of **San Giovanni** (1530) and the 16C **Chiesa Madre**, dedicated to St Lucy (the popular saint martyred in Syracuse). Inside, a chapel dedicated to the Madonna shelters a *Madonna of Miracles* attributed to Giorgio da Milano; a larger side chapel honouring St Lucy contains a fine altarpiece by **Antonello Gagini** with statues of St Lucy, St Peter and St Paul (1552). Misretta's Saint's Day festivities are one of the biggest events of the year here, held on the 7–8 September, when the Madonna delle Luci is paraded through the streets, along with statues of the village's legendary founders, Mytia and Kronos.

At the top of the town stands the Renaissance Church of **Santa Caterina**.

▶ *From Mistretta, continue along S 117 as far as the junction with the Troina/Nicosia road, then turn right to Nicosia (30km/19mi).*

Nicosia ⓖ *See NICOSIA.*

8km/5mi farther on, the road reaches Sperlinga, a little town overlooked by its castle, backed up against a vertical cliff face.

Sperlinga

The compact hamlet stretches along a spur of rock shaped like an upturned ship's keel. It seems to have started life as a troglodyte community contemporary with the Sicani; several cave dwellings are open to view below the town. At the highest point the strategic **castle-fortress** stands rooted to the bedrock. The castle is built on several levels. The caves excavated from the rock *(to the left of the entrance)* were used for stabling animals, as prison cells and as forges. Two of the caves now house a small **anthropological museum** *(ⓒ open daily 9am–1pm, 4.30pm–7pm; ☎0935 64 31 98).* At the front of the castle is the prince's reception room. The chapel and residential quarters lie opposite: the undercrofts in this section of the castle served as granaries. Between the two wings, a steep staircase cuts up into the bedrock to the lookout tower: from here the **view**★★ pans 360° over the Gangi plateau with the Madonie range behind, the Nebrodi to the north, Mount Etna to the east and the Erei mountains to the west. To the right an undulating ridge runs from Monte Grafagna to San Martino, and links up with the Nebrodi mountain chain.

Sperlinga: the castle

A scenic road snakes its way towards Gangi, the largest of the towns in the Madonie area *(20km/12.5mi)*.

Gangi

🔎 *The Gangi Pro Loco organises guided tours of the town. Those interested should book at least a week in advance. For information, contact Corso Umberto I 1; ☎0921 50 20 17 (🕐open 9am–1pm, 3pm–7pm; 🕐closed Mon); www.comune.gangi.pa.it.*

At one time, Gangi was identified with the ancient Engyum, a Greek town founded by colonists from **Minoa**; the town that survives today has largely evolved since the 14C, scattered over the crest of Monte Marone. Best known as the birthplace of the two 17C artists both known as Zoppo di Gangi (look out for the beautifully rendered *Last Judgement* by one of them in the church of San Nicola), today's Gangi is a curious mix of modern concrete houses interwoven with picturesque narrow streets. These, lined with stone-built houses, are what preserve its medieval character to a certain extent.

Città alta

The tree-lined Viale delle Rimembranze, commemorating every soldier killed in the Second World War, leads to the entrance to the higher town. The most obvious point of reference in **Piazza San Paolo** is the simple stone front of the church (16C) dedicated to St Paul. The later Chiesa della Badia (18C) has a similar, bare stone, front elevation. **Corso Umberto I** passes a number of harmonious *palazzi*, including the 19C **Palazzo Mocciaro**, on its way into the town centre.

The imposing 18C **Palazzo Bongiorno**★ (🕐*Open 9am–1pm, 3pm–7pm;* 🕐*closed Mon;* ☎ *0921 50 20 17; www.comune. gangi.pa.it)* was built for the wealthy Bongiorno family and has elegant *trompe l'oeil* **frescoes**★ in the rooms on the piano nobile. These are by Gaspare Fumagalli, a painter from Rome active in Palermo around the mid-18C, and comprise a series of allegorical subjects, sacred and profane *(Modesty, The Triumph of Christianity, Time)*.

The town's main square is the **Piazza del Popolo**, overshadowed by the **Torre Ventimiglia**★. This watchtower was erected in the 13C and transformed into a bell tower in the 17C when the Chiesa Madre was built. It is Norman Gothic in style, with a pointed arcade portico and attractive three-light, double-arch windows above.

In a corner of the piazza is a charming grotto with a fountain, the Fontana del Leone (1931).

The **Chiesa Madrice**, the town's main church, was erected in the 17C on the foundations of an older oratory; inside, are several significant works of art including **The Last Judgement**★ (1629), on the left side of the chancel. The main masterpiece of Giuseppe Salerno, it was modelled on Michelangelo's Sistine

Guidorlando/Lara Pessina/MICHELIN

The Popular Epithet: Zoppo Di Gangi

The last work of **Gaspare Vazzano** (or Bazzano), a cycle of frescoes in the Chiesa Madre at Collesano, is clearly signed "Zoppo di Gangi". Vazzano was born in Gangi in the latter part of the 16C and, despite being trained as a painter in Palermo, always gravitated towards the towns of the Madonie mountains in search of work. The other painter with whom he shares his nickname (which translates as "The Lame Man of Gangi") was a contemporary, also from Gangi, **Giuseppe Salerno**. It remains difficult to ascertain the relationship enjoyed by the two artists, despite a recent theory suggesting that Salerno collaborated with Vazzano, at least during his early career as a painter.

The common pseudonym might possibly be explained as an act of homage by the pupil, who was a few years younger than Vazzano. The two painters fit into the same artistic movement, yet their styles are quite different. Vazzano's use of tonal colour, gentle facial expression and softer line endow his paintings with a certain sentimentality that contrasts sharply with Salerno's bolder style achieved by a strong use of line and precise draughtsmanship. His intention is to produce a cruder kind of work that dogmatically embodies a concept, a message or a doctrine. These different personalities and distinctive means of artistic expression are the hallmarks of two Sicilian painters who have each left an important legacy to their native land.

Chapel in Rome (⌖See The Green Guide Rome), among others: common elements include the standing figure of Christ, the skin of St Bartholomew, a self-portrait of the artist, and the figure of Charon, the devil's ferryman. The level beneath is divided into two: to the left, stand the Elect with the Archangel Michael; to the right, the Damned, with the jaws of Leviathan. Each of the Damned embodies one of the capital sins. The Damned include various religious figures, but there is no priest, as it was a priest who commissioned the work.

The church also contains fine wooden sculptures by Quattrocchi, among them a **San Gaetano**★ (at the far end of the south aisle).

From the church forecourt, there is a good view of the lower part of Gangi including the Torre Saracena on the left and the Capuchin Monastery.

The natural continuation of Corso Umberto I, Corso Fedele Vitale, is lined with "Roman shops" (**botteghe romane**) that date in origin from the 16C – so called because goods are sold through a small window and counter next to the doorway.

Farther up the street, Palazzo Sgadari houses the local **museum** (⌖open Tue–Sun; 9am–1pm, 3pm–7pm; ✆€1.50; ☎0921 68 99 07; www.comunedigangi.it) with archaeological artefacts from

Monte Alburchia. At the far end sits the square mass of **Castello dei Ventimiglia**.

Città bassa

Return to Piazza del Popolo and turn down Via Madrice to find the **Chiesa del Santissimo Salvatore**. This contains a wooden Crucifix by Fra' Umile da Petralia and a painting by Giuseppe Salerno entitled On the Road to Calvary, reflecting the influence of Raphael's Spasimo diSicilia in the Chiesa dello Spasimo of Palermo.

Farther downhill stands the **Chiesa di Santa Maria di Gesù**, which originally comprised a Benedictine Hospice (15C). Inside, there are several works by Quattrocchi, most notably a wooden group representing The Annunciation.

Santuario dello Spirito Santo

About 1.5km/1mi S of Gangi on the Casalgiordano road.

A local story relates how, in the 16C, a deaf mute labourer was working in the fields when he came across an image of Christ painted on a rock, and miraculously began to speak.

A sanctuary was built on the miracle site, which continues to attract pilgrims. Today, the image on the rock is masked by the painting behind the altar attributed to Vazzano.

▶ *From Gangi, it is possible to continue along S 120 to link up with itinerary ①, extending it with a drive to Petralia Sottana (15km/9mi).*

▶ *Alternatively, if proceeding with itinerary ②, make your way back for about 3km/2mi to the fork and turn left towards San Mauro Castelverde (30km/19mi from Gangi).*

San Mauro Castelverde

On a clear day, this little hamlet enjoys bird's-eye **views**★ from its hilltop across to the Aeolian Islands and the Nebrodi and Madonie mountain ranges (visible from Piano San Giorgio in the higher part of the town). The centre is typically medieval in layout. The church, **Santa Maria dei Franchi** (13C), and its 18C bell tower are surrounded by a web of narrow streets. Inside, it contains a Madonna by **Domenico Gagini** and a font by **Antonello Gagini**.

▶ *Follow the road to Borrello. After Borrello Alto, follow signs to Gangi-San Mauro (left). After approximately 1km/0.6mi, a signpost on the right indicates the Case Tiberio U' Miricu.*

Le Gole di Pollina

Follow the small road to a fork, then turn left. The asphalt peters out at this point, so park here and proceed on foot. A little farther on, follow the paved road on the right to the flight of over 400 steps leading to the gorge.

The **gorge**★★ is particularly impressive in summer when dry conditions make the river bed accessible, allowing visitors to walk between the overhanging cliff faces.

▶ *Head back to Borrello and continue down towards the coast: at the fork, turn left, following the coast road. Turn right along the road signposted for Pollina.*

Pollina

The hilltop town of Pollina is in a perfect **position**★ to enjoy picture-postcard **views**★ of the coast below. The

Chiesa Madre (16C) sitting at the heart of a complicated network of medieval streets, shelters an engaging **Nativity**★ by **Antonello Gagini**. In the Middle Ages, the top of the town was marked by a castle: today only a square tower remains. A Greco-Roman style theatre has recently been built alongside, complete with spectacular panoramic mountain and sea **views**★★; a winding road leads from the theatre all the way to the coast.

▶ *Continue back down towards the coast and Cefalù. Signs on the right indicate the way to Tusa and the archaeological site of Halaesa, lying before the village itself.*

Halaesa

🕐 *Open 9am–1hr before dusk.*
€2. ☎0921 33 45 31.

The remains of Halaesa are found just beyond the chapel of Santa Maria di Palate. The little town was originally founded by the Siculi in the 5C BC; it passed into Greek then Roman hands, before being destroyed by the Arabs. **Excavations** have revealed a Roman forum, a patrician family house and sections of bastions along the enclosure walls from the Greek era.

Tusa

8km/5mi S of Halaesa.

This little town was probably founded by the people who escaped Halaesa as it was being razed by the Arabs. Access to the medieval upper area is through the main gateway. This is where the most interesting churches are found, including the **Chiesa Madre** with its entrance set in a decorative pointed arch. Inside, a delicate marble Annunciation from the Renaissance (1525) ornaments the altar; the wooden choir stalls carved with dragons, cherubs and masks are 17C; the *Madonna and Child* is by followers of Gagini.

Nestling among the other narrow streets in the town is the little stone Church of San Nicola with its distinctive tile-topped campanile.

▶ *Return to the coast road. At this point you can either continue the tour by following the itinerary described below, or return to Santo Stefano di Camastra (9km/5.5mi).*

3 La Fiumara d'Arte ★
80km/50mi, starting at Santo Stefano di Camastra – allow at least half a day.

Fiumara d'Arte literally translates as **River of Art** ★★, and is an open-air "gallery" following the course of the River Tusa that exhibits contemporary sculpture by international artists. The brainchild of Antonio Presti, who also founded the Atelier sul Mare hotel-cum-museum (⊚*see below*), the River of Art provides an interesting symbiosis of art and landscape and an original way to explore the area off the beaten track.

▸ *From Santo Stefano di Camastra, follow S 113 towards Palermo.*

The first gigantic sculpture looms into sight on the right, standing on the beach of Villa Marigi. Tano Festa's *Monument to a Dead Poet* (1990) is as blue as the surrounding sea and sky, and was conceived as a type of window looking out to infinity.

▸ *Continue a few kilometres along S 113, then turn left to Pettineo.*

On the right, the second work stands in the middle of the almost permanently dry river bed: Pietro Consagra's *Matter could have not existed* (1986), consists of two reinforced concrete sections on two levels, one white, the other black, creating a complex line. The **scenic road** ★ climbs up into the Nebrodi mountains providing **good views** ★ over the landscape. Before long, evidence of humankind dwindles and disappears, giving way to the overriding presence of nature. All along the sides of the road, contorted olive trees eventually make way for a landscape ablaze with yellow bushes of flowering broom. **Pettineo** crouches on the top of a small hill. Beyond it on the left, just before Castel di Lucio, stands a work by Paolo Schiavocampo entitled *A Curve Thrown After Time (1990)*. At last **Castel di Lucio** comes into view; a sign on the

left points to Italo Lanfredini's *Ariadne's Labyrinth* (1990) standing lonely on a hill (*as the road turns in a hairpin bend to the left, keep straight on*). This cement and clay maze enclosed by a succession of towering mountains enjoys a fabulous **location** ★. At the Carabinieri station in Castel di Lucio, note Piero Dorazio and Graziano Marini's **Arethusa** (1990), made from a number of large polychrome ceramic panels.

Back down on the main road, follow the winding road to **Mistretta** (⊚*See above*) to view *The Ceramic Wall* (1993), the combined work of 40 artists.

After Mistretta, a road forks left towards **Motta d'Affermo**, where Antonio Di Palma's blue wave entitled *Mediterranean Energy* (1990) dominates the landscape. Head back down towards the sea to the Atelier sul Mare hotel in **Castel di Tusa**.

Atelier sul Mare
Via Cesare Battisti 4, Castel di Tusa. ⊶*Guided tours of the art rooms, 11am–noon.* ⊚€4. ☎0921 33 42 95. www.ateliersulmare.com.

In this hotel-cum-museum Antonio Presti has allowed artists to transform several rooms into works of art in their own right to create an interaction between the existing work, which with time becomes inert and part of the everyday furnishing, and the artist who during his/her stay will respond with his/her

---

The Hidden Work of Art

One other work deserves a mention: **The Room of the Golden Boat** by Hidetoshi Nagasawa takes shelter within a cave on the bed of the River Romei *(near Mistretta)*. Inside, the rock is entirely faced with plates of polished steel – most disorienting. Somewhere within the enclosed space, a pink marble tree has been "planted" in the ground, on which the shell of an overturned boat has been built, and covered in gold leaf. This work, however, is not intended to be seen: the reason for its existence lies in the fact that it exists at all. As such, we are encouraged not to go and see it, but merely to imagine it.

personal touch. *For further information, see Address Book.*

4 A Day in the Nebrodi Mountains

Approx 200km/125mi – allow one day.

This circuit may also be undertaken from Sant'Agata Militello, although it is worth doing it in an anti-clockwise direction to enjoy the best views of Mount Etna, notably from Lago Ancipa. For the first part of the tour, from SantoStefano di Camastra to Mistretta (14km/9mi), see itinerary 2 . From Mistretta follow S 117 to the Nicosia/ Troina fork, then turn left to Troina.

Troina
A medieval citadel perched high above the town's rooftops shelters Troina's main church: sadly, only the bell tower survives from the original Norman building (11C), that was built in blocks of sandstone spanning the road.

▶ *From Troina, return towards Cerami so as to turn right down to Lago Ancipa (approximately 8km/5mi from Troina).*

Lago Ancipa
This man-made lake, formed when the San Teodoro dam (120m/394ft) was built, lies in a glorious stretch of country-side. The road skirts the lake before leading on to Cesarò *(25km/16mi)*. Although narrow and badly rutted, it picks its way through woods and along valleys, providing unforgettable **views**★★ of Mount Etna.

Cesarò
The town is overshadowed by the volcano - follow signs just outside the town to Cristo sul Monte, from where a haunting **view**★★ extends across to Mount Etna, particularly impressive on a clear day. The best panorama is from the Christo Signore della Montagna, a huge bronze statue of Jesus located in the cemetery above the town.
S 289 twists and turns up to the narrow pass, Portella della Miraglia and Portella della Femmina Morta, through the mountain scenery and beech woods. At the top, a dirt track leads to the summit of **Monte Soro**, the highest peak in the Nebrodi mountains (1 847m/6 058ft).

▶ *Continue along the scenic road to San Fratello (35km/22mi from Cesarò).*

San Fratello
This town, founded by a group of Lombard settlers, was partly destroyed by a landslide in the 18C. San Fratello is linked by name to the *sanfratellani*, a fine breed of horse, that can occasionally be spotted roaming freely on the edge of town.

Herd on the Nebrodi mountains

B. Kaufmann/MICHELIN

On the north side of the hamlet, by the cemetery, there is a track to a Norman church, the 11C–12C **Chiesa Normanna dei Santi Alfio, Filadelfio e Cirino** (⏰ open 9am–1pm, weekends and public holidays on request; ☎0941 79 40 30). A marvellous **view**★★ extends over the surrounding landscape from the area behind the church.

▶ *From San Fratello, follow the road back to the coast and turn right for Sant'Agata di Militello (18km/11mi).*

Sant'Agata di Militello

This seafront resort has access to a long stretch of beach. The main buildings, the Castello dei Principi Gallego and the adjacent 18C Chiesa dell'Addolorata, are both located on Piazza Crispi. The town has a small natural history museum dedicated to the inland mountain region, the **Museo Etnoantropologico dei Nebrodi** (Via Cosenz) (⏰ open 9am–noon, 3pm–6pm; ⏰closed Sun; ☎0941 72 23 08).

Sant'Agata is a good place to stay as it is conveniently situated close enough to the mountains for short excursions to escape the summer heat, and within easy range of other coastal sights like Capo d'Orlando to the east, Halaesa and Tusa to the west.

▶ *From Sant'Agata follow S 113 to Capo d'Orlando, then turn right to San Marco d'Alunzio (10km/6mi).*

San Marco d'Alunzio★

This delightful small town, situated 550m/1 800ft above sea level and 9km/6mi from the coast, enjoys **magnificent views**★★ of Cefalù and the Aeolian Islands. Each phase in Sicilian history has left its mark here, with the site occupied by the Greeks and becoming *Municipium Aluntinorum* under the Romans. It was renamed San Marco dei Normanni in memory of the first town conquered by the Normans in Calabria. The locally quarried red marble can be seen in many of town's buildings. Just outside the town centre is the Church of **San Marco**, built on the foundations of a **temple** dedicated to Heracles (4C BC), of which a few tufa stone blocks remain.

The open-air church preserves its stone walls and a re-erected doorway.

San Teodoro (or Badia piccola)

San Teodoro was built in the 16C on the site of a Byzantine chapel. It is built on a Greek-cross plan with each square arm enclosed by a little dome. The interior is ornamented with magnificent Serpotta-style **stuccowork**★ depicting *Judith and Holofernes, Manna falling from Heaven in the Desert* (at the sides of the altar), scenes from the parable of the prodigal son; saints and the four Theological Virtues grace the pilasters that rise up to the vault. Hellenistic cisterns and the remains of 2C–3C AD paving can be seen in the churchyard.

Monastero delle Monache Benedettine

♿⏰Open 9am–1pm, 4pm–8pm (winter 3pm–6.30pm). ⏰Closed 1 Jan, Easter and 25 Dec. ☞€1.55. ☎0941 79 77 19; www.comune.sanmarcodalunzio.me.it.

Next to San Teodoro, the former 16C Benedictine convent accommodates a **museum** of Byzantine-Norman art. On the ground floor, interesting 11C **frescoes**★ have been uncovered. Those on the right are well preserved: the Madonna in the vault has beautifully delicate hands; in the tier below, the four Doctors of the Orthodox Church – St John Chrysostom, St Gregory of Nazianzus, St Basil the Great and St Athanasius – are shown against a blue background. Frescoes from other churches are also displayed on the ground floor, while objects discovered in local necropoli are on the first floor.

In the Chiesa di San Giuseppe is the Parish Museum **Museo Parrocchiale** (⏰open 10am–1pm, 4pm–7pm in summer, and by appointment for the rest of the year; ☎0941 79 70 45) with collections of sacred furnishings and wooden reliquaries.

The main street, Via Aluntina, runs through the **historical centre** of San Marco past the Chiesa Madre dedicated to **San Nicolò**.

In Piazza Sant'Agostino some way ahead stands **Santa Maria delle Grazie**, which preserves the Filangeri funeral monument by Domenico Gagini (1481) with its fine reclining figure exuding gentle serenity.

Note the 18C **Church of San Basilio** with its arcade of pointed arches on the right, and then continue on to the 17C **Church of Ara Coeli**, graced with a doorway ornamented with volutes and floral elements, whose **Cappella del Santissimo Crocefisso**, houses an expressive 17C Spanish wooden **Crucifix**★.

San Salvatore

San Salvatore, also known as the **Badia Grande**, used to adjoin an important Benedictine convent; now it stands in ruins. Its elegant Alunzio marble **doorway**★ is ornamented with columns, angels and cherubs. **Inside**, visitors are greeted by a band of serenading angels playing trumpets, allegorical figures, playful cherubs, scrolls and garlands of flowers; the exuberant **stucco decoration**★ culminates in sumptuous drapery hanging from the wooden canopy over the tabernacle.

▶ *Leave San Marco and head back to S 113. Turn left to Santo Stefano di Camastra.*

Look out for signs along the road to **Caronia** (4km/2.5mi inland) where one of the Parco dei Nebrodi visitor centres is situated (See the Address Book).

⑤ The Eastern Nebrodi

Approximately 85km/53mi – allow at least half a day.

This itinerary snakes its way inland from Capo d'Orlando located on the eastern slopes of the Nebrodi Mountains.

▶ *Leave Capo d'Orlando by the coastal road towards Sant'Agata Militello. At Rocca di Capri Leone, turn left towards Frazzano (17km/11mi S of Capo d'Orlando).*

Frazzanò

According to tradition, the town was founded in the 9C AD by people fleeing the Arab invasions. The **Chiesa Madre della Santissima Annunziata** (18C) has a fine Baroque façade ornamented with giant pilasters and an elegant portal with spiral columns, flanked by niches containing statues.

The **Chiesa di San Lorenzo** has a plainer façade relieved by a fine portal with spiral columns and a flurry of sculptural motifs including plant fronds, cherubs and volutes. Inside, there is a fine wooden statue of the church's patron, St Lawrence (1620).

▶ *Proceed to the next right turning, signposted for the Convento di San Filippo di Fragalà (4km/2.5mi S of Frazzanò towards Longi).*

Convento di San Filippo di Fragalà

This recently restored Basilian abbey was built by Roger I d'Altavilla in the 11C. The imposing building has been abandoned and is crumbling under neglect, but it is still worth viewing the exterior from below: note the three apses in the Arabo-Norman style, articulated by brick pilasters, and the octagonal drum over the intersection of the transepts. The remains of Byzantine frescoes can be seen on the walls of the church - if there's no one around to let you in, look through the windows. There are also some fine views from the ramparts The adjoining monastic buildings are open to visit by the public.

▶ *The road continues to Portella Calcatizzo. Beyond the town, turn left at the fork towards San Salvatore di Fitalia (approximately 20km/12mi from San Filippo di Fragalà).*

San Salvatore di Fitalia

Perched high among the Nebrodi Mountains, this small town has a fine church (1515) dedicated to **San Salvatore**. Recent interior restoration has uncovered the 16C structure of the building with its nave separated from the aisles by sandstone columns supporting pointed arches. The fine **capitals** are sculpted with plant and anthropomorphic motifs typical of medieval decorative schemes. The capital of the first column on the right, bearing the name of the stonemason who carved it, features an unusual mermaid with a forked tail. In the right aisle hangs Antonello Gagini's gentle *Madonna of the Snow* (1521) and, on the high altar, a **wooden statue**★ of Salvator Mundi (Saviour of the World, 1603) at the moment of the Transfiguration.

Museo Siciliano delle Tradizioni Religiose

⚷ *Closed for restoration at the time of going to press.* ☎*0941 48 60 27.*
The fascinating **museum of religious practices** documents local popular cults with displays of amulets for protection against the evil eye, votive objects including a series of anatomical replicas made of wax originally from the Santuario di San Calogero (18C-19C), *pillole* (pills), tiny squares of paper designed to be swallowed by the faithful while they recited prayers requesting divine intervention and terracotta whistles bearing figurative images sold on saints' days. The collection also includes a series of engravings and lithographs depicting sacred images (17C-20C), special dress robes worn by the confraternities in sacred processions, various examples of devotional statuary in wood, plaster and terracotta, and small figures for Nativity cribs (19C).

▷ *Return to Portella Calcatizzo and Tortorici, then head towards Castell'Umberto. From here, follow S 116 to Naso (28km/17mi from San Salvatore di Fitalia).*

Naso

This small town, translated as the "nose", is situated inland on a strategic headland at an altitude of 500m/1 640ft. As such, it enjoys superb **views**★ of the Aeolian Islands. Founded by the Normans, it was subsequently controlled by the Cardona family before becoming a lordship of the Ventimiglia family. The central Piazza Garibaldi, with its magnificent **view** of Etna, runs into Piazza Dante and Piazza Roma. The **Chiesa Madre** on Piazza Roma is notable for its *Madonna and Child* painted in the distinctive Gagini style and housed in the Baroque Cappella del Rosario *(left aisle).*

▷ *Follow the right side of the Chiesa Madre into Via degli Angeli.*

This street leads to the Chiesa di **San Cono**, founded in the 15C and restored two centuries later. An interesting crypt housing the relics of the church's patron saint can be seen in the catacombs here.

▷ *Return to Piazza Roma and take Corso Umberto.*

After Piazza Parisi, turn right into Via Belvedere to enjoy another spectacular **view**★★ of Etna and the Aeolian Islands.

Follow Via Convento past a small well to the Convento dei Minori Osservanti and the neighbouring Chiesa di **Santa Maria del Gesù**. Inside the church, note the splendid funerary monument of Artale Cardona, in Gothic-Renaissance style. The route back into town along Via Cibo passes the **Chiesa del Salvatore**, adorned with a Baroque façade, double bell tower and a splendid parvis in locally fired brick.

▷ *Continue along S 116 for another 15km/9mi as far as Capo d'Orlando.*

From Naso, visitors can continue on to Randazzo (approximately 55km/34mi) to link up with the circular tour of Etna (⬤*See ETNA).*

MARSALA

POPULATION: 79 719

Local history tells a fable that begins with "there was once an English mer-chant…" and ends with a city's name on the tables of the world. Today the city continues to produce the fortified wine for which it is famed, but the area's intoxicating charm extends beyond the glass. With its mixture of people (many Tunisian), lively port and the maze of alleys that spider the centre, Marsala has a uniquely African atmosphere.

- **Information:** Via XI Maggio 100; ☎0923 71 40 97; www.comunemarsala.it.
- ▶ **Orient Yourself:** Marsala sits on the westernmost tip of Sicily, closer to Africa than to the rest of Europe. Situated on the headland of Capo Lilibeo (also known as Capo Boeo), behind the Lungomare Boeo and Piazza Vittoria, its historical centre is a maze of narrow streets best explored on foot. From Piazza Vittoria, Via XI Maggio leads to Piazza della Repubblica *(see Walking Tour)*. Marsala is a good base for excursions to the surrounding area.
- **Don't Miss:** Sample Marsala wines at local wineries; appointments necessary.
- **Organising Your Time:** Start your walking tour from the Piazza della Repubblica, the hub of the city.
- **Especially for Kids:** Punic ship remains at the Museo Archeologico di Baglio Anselmi.
- **Also See:** ERICE; MAZARA DEL VALLO; MOZIA; TRAPANI; VIA DEL SALE.

A Bit of History

Marsala is situated on the headland that continues to bear the town's ancient name, Lilybaeum (from *Lily* meaning water and beum referring to the Eubei, its pre-Phoenician inhabitants). The settlement is presumed to have been founded in 397 BC by the Phoenicians who fled from Motya following their defeat by the Syracusans. The name 'Marsala' probably derives from the Arabic *Marsah el Ali,* meaning port of Ali, indicating its role as a important maritime town since its early history, including witnessing one of Sicily's most momentous events: the landing of Garibaldi's Thousand.

Grazie…mille – Early May 1860: accom-panied by 1000 volunteers, **Garibaldi** set sail from Quarto (near Genoa) bound for Sicily to overthrow the Bourbon government and liberate the Kingdom of the Two Sicilies. On 11 May, the two ships – the *Lombardo* and the *Piemonte* – moored at Marsala. The Mille (one thousand) made their way inland, winning their first battle at Calatafimi: opening up the way to Palermo. As the campaign progressed, the band was swollen by new volunteers so that by the time they reached the Straits of Messina, their number exceeded 20 000. In less than two months, Sicily had been lib-erated from Bourbon government. The expedition swept through the rest of the kingdom until on 21 October, following a plebiscite, the island was admitted to the northern states (Piedmont, Lom-bardy, Liguria, Emilia Romagna, Tuscany and Sardinia) that were later to form the Kingdom of Italy.

Marsala Wine

History – In 1770, a storm forced a Brit-ish ship to take shelter in Marsala har-bour. A merchant, **John Woodhouse**, disembarked and went into town to sample the Marsala wine in one of the taverns. Although more accustomed to the liqueur wines of Spain and Portugal, his palate immediately detected their similarity, prompting him to dispatch a consignment of wine (blended with alcohol so as to withstand the journey) to his native land to sound out the mar-ket. The response was positive, and the merchant set up his own company in Marsala. A little later, a second English merchant landed in Marsala: **Ben Ingham**, a connoisseur of fortified wines. With his intervention, the quality of the wine was improved using blends of different grape varieties. His business passed to his nephews, the **Whitakers**. In 1833, the entrepreneur **Vincenzo Florio**, Calabrese by birth and Palermitano by adoption, bought land between the two largest established Marsala producers and set to making his own vintage with an even more specialised range of grapes. By the end of the 19C, several more wine-growers had joined the competition, including Pellegrino (1880). After the turn of the century, Florio bought out Ingham and Woodhouse, and retained the two labels before succumbing in turn to a takeover by a conglomeration of other producers.

The wine – Marsala is registered as a DOC wine (a state-designated label of controlled quality); this means that production is restricted to an exclusive area around Trapani, and a collection of additional vineyards in the provinces of Agrigento and Palermo. Only grape varieties with a high natural sugar content are used to make Marsala: these, once pressed, are left to ferment, and/or caramelise, before being blended with ethyl alcohol to produce the different types and flavours of Marsala. Relative to the sugar content, Marsala may be categorised as dry, semi-dry or sweet. Its main denomination, however, is relative to the length of time it is left to mature: Marsala Fine (1 year), Superiore (2 years), Superiore Riserva (4 years), Vergine (5 years) and Vergine Riserva (10 years). Dry Marsala is usually served as a refreshing aperitif, while the sweeter forms are drunk as a dessert wine.

Wine Producers

Florio
Via Florio.
Guided tours by appointment only. *Closed public hols and Aug.* €5 (for tasting). ☎0923 78 11 11. www.cantine florio.com.

A tour of this **winery** and its small museum provides the opportunity of comparing old and new techniques and installations. The 19C wine cellars *(cantine),* built by Vincenzo Florio, are somewhat close and stuffy: the environment is maintained at a constant temperature by tufa walls (insulation), a tiled roof (aeration) and sand on the floor (temperature control and humidity). The most interesting part of the process, however, is the **Soleras Method** by which the wine is conditioned through a pyramid of oak barrels.

Pellegrino
Via del Fante 39.
Call for opening hours. *Closed public hols.* ☎0923 71 99 11; www.carlo pellegrino.it.

Another of the large producers, fortifying a wine that is full of tangy raisin and citrus zest flavours. This winery also produces the superlative sweet wines of Passito and Moscato di Pantelleria.

Marco De Bartoli
292 Contrada Samperi.
Open by appointment only. For information, call ☎0923 96 20 93. www.marco debartoli.com.

This producer, situated in the Samperi district, is responsible for one of the best Marsalas, a feat achieved by traditional production methods.

In addition to the numerous Marsala wine producers, the **Cantina Sperimentale Istituto Regionale della Vite e del Vino** *(Via Trapani 218, Istituto*

Marsala wine cellar

©Giovanni Rinaldi/iStockphoto.com

Tecnico Agrario A Damiani; 🕐*visits and tastings by appointment only;* ☎*091 62 78 111)* allows visitors to sample a number of experimental wines.

Walking Tour

The most impressive way to enter Marsala is through the **Porta della Vittoria**, a grand entrance that was restored in the time of Mussolini. Inside the gate, Via XI Maggio, the city's main street, leads to the **Piazza della Repubblica**. The literal and spiritual heart of Marsala, the square sits in the centre of a network of quiet narrow streets that radiate out from it. Garibaldi ignited the unification of Italy here in 1860, with a stirring nationalist speech. Today, this elegant square is defined by two 18C buildings, the Chiesa Madre (👆*See Visit)* and the arcaded Palazzo Senatorio.

Chiesa Madre

The main church, dedicated to San Tommaso di Canterbury, the patron saint of Marsala, was built during the Norman occupation. Its exterior was extensively remodelled in the 18C; inside it contains a fine icon by **Antonello Gagini** and Berrettaro *(north apse)*, and a delicate Madonna by **Domenico Gagini** from 1490 *(south transept)*. Above this, a Ren-aissance painting by Antonello Riggio depicts the Presentation of the Virgin at the Temple.

The main thoroughfare leading from Piazza della Repubblica is Corso XI Maggio, the old *Decumanus Maximus* of the Roman town, lined with splendid buildings. Perpendicular to the principal axis, **Via Garibaldi** leads southwards to **Porta Garibaldi** on the edge of town, running past the town hall, a former Spanish military barracks.

Behind the Chiesa Madre is the Museo degli Arazzi (👆*See Visit below).*

Visit

Museo degli Arazzi

Entrance in Via Giuseppe Garraffa. 🕐*Open 9am–1pm, 4pm–6pm.* 🕐*Closed Mon and public holidays.* ▧*€2.50.* ☎*0923 71 13 27.*

The collection comprises of eight enormous 16C Flemish **tapestries** *(arazzi)*⋆ depicting scenes from the war waged by Emperor Vespasian and his son, Titus against the Jews, and the capture of Jerusalem. The hand-stitched tapestries, woven in rich red, gold and green wool and silk, were originally a gift to the city from King Philip II of Spain via the Spanish ambassador, who was also the archbishop of Messina.

Porta Garibaldi

B. Kaufmann/MICHELIN

Address Book

For coin ranges, see the Legend on the cover flap

WHERE TO STAY

Tenuta Volpara – *Contrada Volpara, 9km/5.5mi E of Marsala.* ☎0923 98 45 88. www.delfinobeach.com. *18 rooms.* *Restaurant*. Situated in the countryside outside Marsala, this farm guesthouse offers genuine Sicilian hospitality. The restaurant specialises in local cuisine, including a special warm ricotta cheese with whey, known as *zabbina*, which, in accordance with centuries old Sicilian tradition, is served at breakfast.

WHERE TO EAT

Divino Rosso – *Via XI Maggio (Largo A. di Girolamo), Marsala.* ☎0923 71 17 70. *Closed Mon and in Nov. Booking recommended.* This restaurant-cum-wine bar, situated in the historical centre of Marsala, serves typical Sicilian cuisine and excellent fresh fish dishes. In summer, the tables outside on the main street are shaded beneath large parasols.

FESTIVALS

Settimana Santa – Marsala becomes progressively more animated in the period leading up to Easter: celebrations begin with a Maundy Thursday procession (the eve of Good Friday) when the Stations of the Cross are re-enacted in the streets of the town centre in front of heaving crowds, by local men and women playing the different roles involved in the Passion. In the evening, the Crucifixion and Resurrection are also re-enacted.

Marsala Doc Jazz Festival – This International Jazz Festival takes place every year in July.

Museo Archeologico di Baglio Anselmi

Lungomare Boeo (turn left at the end of Viale Vittorio Veneto and follow the road along the headland).
Open daily, 9am–6pm. *€3.* ☎0923 95 25 35; www. regione.sicilia.it/beniculturali.

Pride of place at this archaeological museum, located in a stone-vaulted warehouse, is given to the remains of a **Punic ship**★ Kids (3C BC) recovered in 1969 near the island of Motya. This was probably a *liburna*, a type of fast warship (35m/115ft long) used and lost at the end of the First Punic War, in the Battle of the Egadi (241 BC).

Today less than five percent of the ship, which was originally around 105ft, remains, but the reconstruction is nevertheless impressive. Analysis of the ship has provided detailed information on Phoenician life - including the crew's diet - and shipbuilding methods including the use of prefabricated units and remarkable metal alloy nails that show no deterioration even after 2 000 years submerged underwater. Elsewhere in the museum the displays include items found in or around the ship, such as anchors and amphorae, as well as photographs and a detailed explanation of how the ship was raised from the sea and restored.

Insula di Capo Boeo

At the end of Viale Vittorio Veneto, turn right and follow the headland.
Closed for restoration at the time of going to press. ☎0923 95 25 35.

On the tip of the headland sit the remains of three Roman *insulae* (blocks of buildings). One is taken up by a large **villa** (3C BC), complete with a set of baths. Look out for the fragments of the mosaic floors and small pillars *(suspensurae)* that were used to support the floor, and enable hot air to circulate through the cavity.

A little farther on stands the Church of **San Giovanni al Boeo**, built around the grotto of the Sibyl of Lilybaeum, one of the three legendary prophetesses of antiquity, reputed by some legends to have foreseen the coming of Christ.
Guided tours only. Contact the tourist office to make a reservation. ☎0923 71 40 97.

MAZARA DEL VALLO

POPULATION: 51 164

The first Sicilian city to be taken by the Arab conquerors, Mazara's historical demographic is reflected today in the high percentage of North African inhabitants. Many are Tunisians, drawn here by work in Mazara's fishing fleet; the city is still considered one of the main centres for the fishing industry and contributes to 20 percent of the national product.

🔢 **Information:** Piazza S. Veneranda 2; ☎0923 94 17 27; www.comune.mazara-del-vallo.tp.it.

▶ **Orient Yourself:** The town is centred on the harbour and the shipping canal of the River Mazara, where the town's fishing industry is based. The main town monuments lie to the east of the harbour, behind Lungomare Mazzini.

🅿 **Parking:** Car parking is available around the Piazza della Repubblica.

👁 **Don't Miss:** Passeggiata at Lungomare Mazzini, Museo Civico, Sala Consagra.

🕐 **Organising Your Time:** Start the day early at the harbour and watch the bustling scene as the catch comes in. As dusk falls, join the locals in their evening constitutional along Lungomare Mazzini.

👅 **Also See:** Neighbouring sights are described in the following chapters: CASTELVETRANO; MARSALA; Antica città di SELINUNTE.

Walking Tour

Harbour and shipping canal

The heart of the town is the harbour; this throbs with life early in the morning when the fishing fleet returns with its catch and the quays bustle with activity. Overlooking the scene with benign approval, set back from the actual harbour front, is the restored Norman church, San Nicolò Regale, with a simple interior that rises to a single cupola.

San Nicolò Regale

This evocative building erected under William I, has a square plan with the three apses that are contained by a bulbous dome, a characteristic of Arabo-Norman architecture.

Below the floor inside, fragments of mosaic have been discovered: these, from palaeo-Christian times, probably form part of a Roman floor.

Among the streets behind sits **Piazza Plebiscito**, with the elegant facade of **Sant'Ignazio** (18C), and the former **Jesuit College** (17C), currently accommodating the library, local **museum** and the Sala Consagra (👁 See Visit below).

Cathedral

The main building dates from the 11C although it was considerably remodelled in the 17C. The facade, completed in 1906, is ornamented with a highly decorative doorway and a 16C shallow relief panel that depicts Roger I, on horseback, felling a fleeing Saracen.

Interior★

The overall theatrical effect is achieved by interspersing gilded stucco decoration among frescoed *trompe l'oeil* stucco volutes, curlicues and cherubs. The most complex group is in the central apse where a large drape is drawn aside by angels to reveal the **Transfiguration★**. The composition of seven marble statues by Antonello Gagini sits upon a majestic Renaissance altar. Nestled in the niche to the right of the altar is a fragment of

H. Champollion/MICHELIN

Decoration on the doorway of the cathedral depicting Roger I felling a Moor

13C Byzantine fresco depicting Christ Pantocrator. In the first chapel on the right is an ancient ciborium, which was possibly used at the christening of Frederick II's son. The Chapel of the Crucifix, also right of centre, takes its name from the wooden Crucifix (13C) found in the adjoining room.

Set into the floor is a glass plate revealing ancient Norman foundations. Elsewhere, through a marble doorway on the right side of the nave are some fine Roman sarcophagi bearing interesting reliefs of a hunting scene and a battle.

Piazza della Repubblica

This piazza laid out in the Baroque period is the focal point for the old town. The statue (1771) in the centre is by **Ignazio Marabitti** and represents San Vito, the patron saint of Mazara. A harmonious collection of sandstone and white stucco *palazzi* from the 18C rise up on all sides: at the far end the cathedral is overshadowed by an elegant Baroque campanile, along the left side stands the Bishop's Palace and, to the right, extends the **Seminario dei Chierici** complete with its neo-Classical portico and round-headed arched loggia. The former seminary now houses a small **Museo Diocesano** (&*See Visit*).

Lungomare Mazzini

South of Piazza della Repubblica. The seafront is flanked by gardens shaded by magnolias and palm trees, such elegance making it a perfect for the habitual Italian *passeggiata*.

Visit

Museo Civico and Sala Consagra

Piazza Plebisicito 2.

⌾ *Closed for restoration at the time of going to press.* ☎0923 67 11 11.

This compact museum housed in the Collegio dei Gesuiti contains a small selection of artefacts predominantly representing the Neolithic, Roman and late Byzantine Eras. The **Sala Consagra** is devoted to the etchings, acquatints and relief panels of Pietro Consagra, a contemporary artist born in Mazara.

Museo Diocesano

Entrance at Via dell'Orologio 3. &⌾*Open Tue–Sat, 9am–1pm.* ⌾*Closed Mon and Sun, public hols.* ⌾*€2.* ☎0923 94 17 27.

The most important section of this collection, comprising silverware, church furnishings and vestments (14C-19C), is a display containing items belonging to the cathedral treasury.

MESSINA

POPULATION: 248 616

Historically a major stop in the Mediterranean trade routes, Messina was also a crossroads of cultural and artistic exchange, providing a dynamic and stimulating environment for important artists, most notably Antonello da Messina. In more recent times the city has endured several natural catastrophes, most notably two earthquakes in 1783 and 1908, as well as intensive bombing raids during the Second World War.

- **Information:** Via Calabria isol. 301 bis, ☎090 64 02 21; Piazza Cairoli 45, ☎090 29 35 292, www.aptmessina.it.
- ▶ **Orient Yourself:** Messina is a modern city that grew up behind the sickle-shaped port that gave the town its name in ancient times. Most of the monuments that survived the terrible earthquake of 1908 and the bombing raids of the Second World War are grouped behind the central port area. To reach the historical centre from the motorway, take the Messina-Boccetta Porto exit and follow Viale Boccetta to Corso Garibaldi, which runs parallel to the seafront.
- **Don't Miss:** Panoramas from Monte Antennammare and Casalvecchio, glorious beaches at the tip of Capo Peloro and the macabre fascination of the crypt of the Capuchin monastery at Savoca.
- **Organising Your Time:** Allow half a day for driving tours around Capo Peloro, and a full day for a tour from Messina to Taormina.
- Kids **Especially for Kids:** The lively mechanical show of the Orologio astronomico on the Duomo belltower as it strikes midday.
- **Also See:** Isole EOLIE; GIARDINI NAXOS; MILAZZO; TAORMINA.

A Bit of History

Founded as a Greek colony in the 8C BC, Messina was originally called **Zancle** after the sickle-like shape of its harbour. The history of the town is inextricably linked to the sea and to the straits that bear its name. According to tradition, sailors have long claimed that the straits are guarded by two monsters, Scylla and Charybdis. **Scylla** was the daughter of Phorcys and Hecate (Greek goddess associated with the underworld) and loved by Poseidon. This aroused the jealousy of his wife Amphitrite who used herbs to turn her into a monster

Aerial view of Messina port

G. Bludzin/MICHELIN

Address Book

For coin ranges, see the Legend on the cover flap.

GETTING THERE

From mainland Italy – Messina handles the principal ferry services from mainland Italy. Ferries run from Reggio Calabria (45min, Stazione Ferrovie Stato, ☎0965 75 60 99) and Villa SanGiovanni (20min, Caronte Shipping, Via Marina 30, ☎0965 79 31 31 and Ferrovie dello Stato, Piazza Stazione, ☎0965 75 60 99). For hydrofoil services (20min), contact SNAV, Reggio Calabria, ☎0965 29 568.
For visitors arriving by air, the nearest airports are in Reggio di Calabria and Catania.

From within Sicily – Messina is linked by train with Palermo (3hr), Taormina (1hr), Catania (approximately 2hr) and Siracusa (3hr). A number of bus companies operate services to Palermo, Taormina, Catania, Capo d'Orlando, Patti and Tindari.

Connections with the Aeolian islands – Trains (approximately 40min) and buses run from Messina to Milazzo, from where ferries cross to the Aeolian islands. Alternatively, hydrofoil services are operated by Aliscafi SNAV from Messina (1hr 20min), Via San Raineri 22, ☎090 3621 14, Fax 090 71 73 58.

WHERE TO STAY

Villa Morgana – *Via C. Pompea 237, Ganzirri, 5km/3mi N of Messina along the coast road. ☎090 32 55 75. www.villamorgana.it. 14 rooms.* ⌁.
Guests will immediately feel at home in this hotel housed in a private villa, surrounded by a large, well-tended garden. Situated on the coast road a few kilometres from Messina, the hotel has an attractive lounge and comfortable rooms.

WHERE TO EAT

Don Nino – *Viale Europa 39, Isolato 59, Messina. ☎090 69 42 95.* Take some dried cod, tomatoes, potatoes, olives, capers, pine nuts, sultanas, onion, garlic, oil, celery and carrot, mix them all together and you have *ghiotta di pesce stocco,* one of the specialities of Messina cuisine and of Don Nino in particular. *Buon appetito!*

Casa Savoia – *Via XXVII Luglio 36/38, Messina. ☎090 29 34 865. www.ristorantecasasavoia.it.* Built on the spot where the "Regio Teatro Savoia" once stood, this family-run restaurant comes highly recommended for those visitors wanting to sample local Messina cuisine.

Le Due Sorelle – *Piazza Municipio 4, Messina. ☎090 44 720. Closed Sat–Sun at lunchtime and in Aug. Booking recommended.*
This restaurant in the heart of the historical centre serves a range of local home-made dishes. Fish takes centre stage in the evening, although you will still find other traditional Messina dishes on the menu.

TAKING A BREAK

Pasticceria Irrera – *Piazza Cairoli 12, Messina. ☎090 67 38 23. www.irrera.it.* Founded in 1910, this pastry shop is one of the best in Messina. Local delicacies include *pignolata* (a typical Messina speciality made with twists of fried puff pastry with lemon or chocolate icing) and *torrone fondente* (a sweet delicacy stuffed with candied fruit and almonds).

Pasticceria F. Gordelli – *Via Ghibellina 86 (the road running parallel to Via Cesare Battisti), Messina. ☎090 66 29 22.* Another excellent pasticceria in which to sample some of the city's renowned cakes and pastries.

FESTIVALS

Venerdì Santo – The *Processione delle Barette,* a procession of wooden sculptures that follow the Stations of the Cross, takes place on Good Friday.

Passeggiata dei Giganti – On 14 August, the Moor Grifone and Mata, the legendary founder of the city, are borne aloft in procession through the streets.

Processione della Vara – The image of the Assumption of the Virgin is carried through the town on 15 August.

A. Picone/Lara Pessina/MICHELIN

Orologio astronomico

that devoured mariners sailing too close to her cave on the Calabrian side of the strait. Her victims included six sailors on Odysseus's ship. Under another rock on the Sicilian side of the strait lived **Charybdis**, who used to drink and regurgitate sea water three times every day; when trapped by this whirlpool, the sailors often fell prey to Scylla (Odyssey, Book XII, v 234–259).

Strategically situated commercially, Messina acted as a trading post for goods and people, and also artistic trends and ideas. From this dynamic context figures such as the 15C painter **Antonello da Messina** emerged.

In more recent times, the town has suffered the effects of devastating earthquakes, most notably in 1783 and in 1908, when 90 per cent of the town was destroyed, leaving more than 60 000 victims. During the Second World War, the town was subjected to several intensive bombing raids.

Piazza Duomo Area

Duomo

After the 1908 earthquake, the **cathedral** was almost completely rebuilt in the style of the Norman original. The façade rises in tiers and is relieved with single-light windows and a small central rose window. The **central doorway**★, one of three, was re-erected using elements of the original fabric (15C). It is flanked by small columns supported by lions, and surmounted by a lunette with a *Madonna and Child* from the 16C. Projecting from the right is a building lit by two-light Catalan Gothic windows. The beamed, painted **ceiling** replaces the older one, which was destroyed by WWII bombing raids. The carved rosettes on the central beams betray Eastern design influences.

Treasury

Access from inside the Duomo.

🕑*Open Apr–Oct 9am–1pm, 3pm–7pm; rest of the year 9am–1pm (Sat, Sun and public holidays 10am–1pm, 4pm–6.30pm).* ⊚€5 *with belltower access.* ☎090 67 51 75.

On display are a number of religious objects and vestments. The oldest exhibit (from the Middle Ages) is the Pigna, a lamp made of rock crystal. Much of the silver plate was made in Messina, including the arm-shaped reliquaries (the one of San Marziano is inscribed with Moorish and Byzantine patterns), candlesticks, chalices and a fine 17C **monstrance** (containing a host) with two angels and a pelican on top presiding over the rays of divine light.

Orologio astronomico★

The **astronomical clock** is the most interesting component of the 60m/200ft high bell tower to the left of the cathedral. The mechanism dates from 1933 and was built in Strasbourg. It comprises several tiers, each bearing a different display with a separate movement. At the bottom, a two-horse chariot driven by a deity indicates the day of the week; above, the central figure of Death waves his scythe threateningly at the child, youth, soldier or old man – the four ages of man – that pass before him. At the third stage, the Sanctuary of Montalto *(turn left to compare it with the real one)* sets the scene for a group of figures which, according to the time of year, represent the Nativity, Epiphany, Resurrection and Pentecost. At the top, the tableau enacts a scene relating to a local legend whereby the Madonna delivers a letter to the ambassadors of Messina in which she thanks and agrees to protect the inhabitants of the town, who were converted to Christianity by St Paul the Apostle: the same **Madonna della Lettera** (Madonna of the Letter), is patron saint of the city. The two young female bell-strikers are the local heroines Dina and Clarenza, who were alive during the period of resistance against the Angevins (1282). The summit is capped with a lion.

The south side of the bell tower *(starting from the bottom)* shows a perpetual calendar, the astronomical cycle marked by the signs of the zodiac, and the various phases of the moon.

When the clock strikes midday, all the mechanical figures come to life accompanied by a musical air: the lion, the symbol of the vitality of the town, roars three times while the cockerel crows from between the two girls.

Fontana di Orione

In the centre of Piazza del Duomo, is a **fountain**, designed by the sculptor Montorsoli to commemorate the inau-guration of an aqueduct. Sculpted in a pre-Baroque style (16C), it incorporates allegories of four rivers: the Tiber, Nile, Ebro and Camaro – the River Messina was diverted into the new aqueduct.

Santissima Annunziata dei Catalani

A short way from the cathedral, nestling among fine *palazzi* in Via Garibaldi, sits the Catalan Church. Built in the 12C when the Normans were in power, it is named after the Catalan merchants who patronised it later.

The **apse**★ is a fine example of the Norman composite style, incorporating Romanesque elements (small blind arches on slender columns), Moorish influences (geometrical motifs in polychrome stone) and Byzantine features (dome on a drum).

Walking Tour

The walk described below can either start in Via Garibaldi, Messina's main street, linking Piazza Cairoli in the south (close to the railway station and port)

Antonello Da Messina

Antonello "of Messina" was born around 1430 at a time when Sicily was under Spanish rule, and while the town was particularly prosperous. He transferred to the Spanish domain on the mainland, settling in Naples so as to study, possibly in the renowned studio of Colantonio. This proved to be a highly dynamic and stimulating environment. Spain also ruled Flanders at that time and so the artistic currents of Flemish, Spanish and Provençal schools merged here in Naples; Antonello assimilated them all to formulate his own highly personal style of painting. From the Flemish masters, he learnt to paint with oils (becoming the first in the southern part of Italy to practise the new technique; Piero being among the first in northern Italy), aped their realism and copied the way they portrayed textures in exquisite detail. These stylistic elements, however, did not affect the formal – and distinctly Italian – way in which he constructed his compositions and unified his picture space with light. The unified harmony of his paintings is achieved by his use of a rich and warm palette, clear and rational perspective and soft lighting effects. In a different domain, Antonello painted several portraits showing a three-quarter view of his sitter as was common among Flemish artists of the time, rather than the more common Tuscan and Umbrian side profile. His ability to reproduce the different effects of light, in contrast with a plain dark background, concentrates the impact of the picture on the noble yet serene facial features of his sitters. Certainly, his style is further enriched by the influences exchanged with other contemporary artists. During his sojourn in Venice, Antonello met Giovanni Bellini; the encounter made a lasting impression on both artists. Antonello began to use colour tonally and more gently as in the Annunciation in Palermo, perhaps the most famous of his Annunciations.

with Piazza Castronuovo, or directly from Piazza del Duomo.

Santa Maria Alemanna

In Via S. Maria dell'Alemagna, which runs across Via Garibaldi.

The sad ruin (there is no roof or façade) still manages to convey something of the original Gothic style, so rare in Sicily, with its graceful pointed arches supported on pilasters and column clusters.

▶ *From Piazza Duomo take Via Oratorio S. Francesco and turn right into Via XXIV Maggio.*

Monte di Pietà

Corner of Via XXIV Maggio and Piazza Crisafulli. The front elevation of this late Mannerist building is ornamented with a massive rusticated doorway framed between solid columns and a broken pediment; above, the balcony rests on brackets carved with volutes. The upper storey, destroyed by the earthquake, has not been rebuilt, giving the building an unfinished air. Today it is used for concerts and recitals.

▶ *Continue as far as Viale Boccetta.*

Chiesa di San Francesco d'Assisi o dell'Immacolata

This monumental church was almost entirely rebuilt following the 1908 earthquake, and retains original features such as the three austere 13C stone **apses** and the fine rose window on the façade.

▶ *Continue as far as Via S. Giovanni di Malta, parallel to Viale Boccetta to the north, then turn right.*

Chiesa di San Giovanni di Malta

The west front of this square late-16C building, overlooking Via Placida, is articulated with white stone pilasters, niches and windows and, in the upper tier, a gallery.

Museo Regionale

Via della Libertà 465. &🕐*Open 9am–1.30pm, May, Jun and Sat 4pm–6.30pm (winter 3pm–5.30pm).* ◐*Closed Wed.*

€2.50. ☎090 36 12 94; *www.regione. sicilia.it/beniculturali.*

The chronological arrangement of the displays begins with the history of the area and the artistic climate that prevailed through the Byzantine and Norman eras. The first rooms are dedicated to paintings and sculpture: shallow reliefs and capitals. Among the most notable examples, there is a fine early-15C polychrome wooden Crucifix *(third room on the right)* and a glazed terracotta medallion from the Della Robbia workshops of a sweet-faced Madonna gazing down at her Child.

The works in the next room betray the strong influence exerted by the Flemish style: a strong sense of realism and an astute attention to detail characterise the edge of the mantle and intricate cuffs of the garments in the **Madonna and Child** attributed to a follower of Petrus Christus (15C).

Other pictures hanging in the same room include the striking *Deposition* by Colijn de Coter: in this the drama of the scene is heightened by the anguished expressions of the mourners supporting the weight of the dead Christ, and in the predominant use of a palette of burnt, dull colours.

The adjacent room is devoted to the Messina painter Girolamo Alibrandi. The most striking paintings include the huge *Presentation at the Temple* of 1519 (note the noble expression and gentle features of the woman in the foreground) and St Paul. The elegant statue of the *Madonna and Child* nearby is by Antonello **Gagini**.

The Roman painter Polidoro da Caravaggio and the Florentine sculptor and architect Montorsoli introduced Mannerism to Messina. Their work, together with that of their followers, is displayed in the next galleries.

Michelangelo Merisi, better known as **Caravaggio**, spent a year in Messina (1608–1609); during this time he painted the Adoration of the Shepherds and the *Resurrection of Lazarus (Room 10)*. The short time he spent here was sufficient to influence contemporary artists living in the city.

The splendid **Senator's Coach**★ *(Room 12)*, dated 1742, incorporates a number of exquisite furnishings, including gilded wooden carvings and painted panels. The top floor of the museum is devoted to displaying decorative and applied arts.

Driving Tours

Capo Peloro
70km/44mi – allow half a day.

This excursion starts from Messina and follows a panoramic road around the headland, past the glorious beaches that skirt the tip, continuing along the Tyrrhenian shore.

The houses that make up the lively little fishing village of **Ganzirri** *(5km/3mi N of Messina along the coast road)* are clustered around two wide saltwater lagoons used for farming shellfish. The road along the "lakeside" hums with restaurants, pizzerias and activity late into the summer evenings.
Continuing north for 3.5 km/2mi beyond the Straits of Messina lies **Torre Faro**, a small fishing village overlooked by a lighthouse.
Drive through **Lidi di Mortelle** and on to Divieto, before turning inland towardsGesso. The road that forks right 6km/4mi past the town leads up to Antennammare.

Monte Antennammare
The road winds up to the San Rizzo pass where a second road forks right for the **Santuario di Maria Santissima di Dinnammare**, situated right on the top of Mount Antennammare (1 130m/706ft). From here, a spectacular view spans the **panorama**★★ of Messina, Capo Peloro and Calabria to the east, the Ionian coastline with the sickle-shaped promontory of Milazzo, and Rometta on a hill to the west.

▶ *On the way back, continue down to the crossroads and then turn right. This road coasts its way down the wooded slopes of Colle San Rizzo.*

Santa Maria della Valle o Badiazza
The Benedictine abbey of **Santa Maria della Valle**, known also as Santa Maria della Scala, was probably built in the 12C and restored in the 14C. The actual church is not open to the public. The exterior, however, has windows set into pointed arches finished in volcanic stone. Through these, the interior can be glimpsed with its two-coloured ribbed vault and sculpted truncated pyramid capitals.

▶ *Return to Messina.*

Ionian Coast: Messina to Taormina

Approximately 70km/44mi from Messina – allow one day.

This trip follows the coast and can be undertaken in reverse, starting from Taormina.

Monastero di San Placido Calonerò
On the road to Pezzolo, a short distance before Galati Marina.
⚷ *Closed for restoration at the time of going to press.* ☎090 68 58 00.
The **Benedictine monastery**, now a technical institute for agriculture, has attractive 17C cloisters with columns with high dosserets and Ionic capitals. A fine little Durazzo Gothic portal to the right of the atrium leading into the first cloisters, provides access to a vaulted chapel articulated with clustered columns.

Scaletta Zanclea
Scaletta Superiore *(2km/1.2mi inland)* boasts a **castle** that was built originally to serve as a Swabian military outpost (13C); it was eventually acquired by the Ruffo family who used it as a hunting lodge until the 17C. The massive fortress now houses the **Museo Civico** (🕐*open Mar–Oct 9am–1pm, 4pm–8pm; for more information call ☎090 95 967*) and its collections of weaponry and historic documents.

▶ *At Itàla Marina turn right, heading inland. Itàla is 2.5km/1.5mi from Itàla Marina.*

Itàla

The little hamlet of Croce jostles around the Basilian Church of **San Pietro e San Paolo**, which was rebuilt in 1093. Continuing back along the coast, the road passes **Capo Alì**, which is topped by a round watchtower probably from the Norman period. It continues through the seaside resorts of **Alì Terme**, **Nizza di Sicilia** and **Roccalumera**.

Sàvoca

Approx 3km/1.8mi inland.

This medieval town is divided into two hilltop ridges, interconnecting with three spurs on which the districts of San Rocco, San Giovanni and Pentefur are built.

Beyond the town hall, but still outside the old town sits the **Convento dei Cappuccini** (⏱*open summer, 9am–1pm, 4pm–7pm;* ☏*0942 76 12 45*), a Capuchin monastery with a **crypt** that contains the mummified bodies of 32 former town dignitaries and friars from the 17C and 18C. Several of these are displayed in niches, others in wooden sarcophagi. From the sacred area before the church there is a wonderful view of the town, the ruined castle and il Calvario or hill of "Calvary" in the distance.

▶ *Go back the same way and turn up Via Borgo and then immediately left on to Via San Michele.*

This leads to the gateway to the old town centre. Beyond the archway stands the 15C Church of **San Michele**. As the same street continues, wonderful **views**★ extend over the rooftops and the valley or up to the Norman **castle** ruins and the Church of San Nicola (or Santa Lucia). At last, the **Chiesa Madre** comes into view with its 16C portal surmounted by the Savoca coat of arms, bearing the elderberry (sambuco) branch from which the town's name is supposedly derived.

▶ *The road continues to meander its way (2km/1.2mi) inland to Casalvecchio.*

Casalvecchio

This little town enjoys a fabulous panorama: from the terrace before the

Chiesa Madre di Sant'Onofrio this **view**★ takes in the Ionian Sea lying off Capo Sant'Alessio and Forza d'Agrò and, to the south, Mount Etna.

In a neighbouring former church house is the eclectic **Museo Parrocchiale** (*contact Signore Carmelo Crisafulli at the town hall for information;* ☏*0942 76 10 30, or 339 62 68 248*), which displays a silver life-size statue of Sant'Onofrio (1745), liturgical furnishings and sacred vestments.

▶ *Follow directions for Antillo and, after 500m/550yd, fork left along a minor road that winds to its destination.*

Chiesa di Santi Pietro e Paolo d'Agrò

The **church**, founded by Basilian monks, is striking not only on account of its unusual use of brick, volcanic stone, limestone and sandstone, but also as a synthesis of Byzantine, Arab and Norman influences. The **exterior** is ornamented with decorative banding, interlaced arcading and herringbone patterns. The **interior** space is divided into nave and aisles by Corinthian columns.

▶ *Turn back down towards the coast to Capo Sant'Alessio.*

Capo Sant'Alessioa

This headland is crowned with a round fortress and a polygonal castle on the eastern tip (⚬ *closed to the public*).

On the south side is the wonderful **beach** of Sant'Alessio Siculoe.

▶ *A road extends from the fortresses to Forza d'Agrò.*

Forza d'Agrò

This medieval hamlet caps the furthermost spurs of the Monti Peloritani, enjoying a splendid **prospect**★ of the coast. The best viewpoint is the terrace of Piazza del Municipio.

Behind this steps climb up to the sacred area before the **Chiesa della Triade**.

Taormina★★★
🎧*See TAORMINA.*

MILAZZO

POPULATION: 32 327

This ancient city of the sea is the natural gateway to the Aeolian islands, which can be seen crowning the horizon some miles away. This part of Sicily is threaded with myth: it was considered to be the grazing pasture for the herds of the God of the Sun and the dwelling place of Eolo, God of the Wind, as well as the legendary nymphs and satyrs, who danced and drank wine here.

- **Information:** Piazza Caio Duilio 20. ☎090 92 22 865. www.comune.milazzo.me.it.
- ▶ **Orient Yourself:** Milazzo sits at the base of a promontory jutting into the Tyrrhenian Sea. Despite its modern, industrial appearance, the town has a number of important historical and artistic monuments.
  The oldest part is the medieval centre, perched on a hill leading to the castle, to the north of the city. The lower town, built to a regular grid plan in the 18C, is situated to the south, along the eastern coast. Milazzo is the main port for the Aeolian Islands.
- **Don't Miss**: A stroll in the medieval quarter of The Borgo, the views from delightful inland hilltop towns Cristina and Rometta, the beach at the Baia del Tonno and the quirky apothecary's pharmacy in Roccavaldina.
- ⏱ **Organising Your Time:** Allow one day for inland tours from Milazzo. An antiques fair is held in The Borgo on the first weekend of every month.
- **Especially for Kids:** Myth and legend at the Grotta di Polifermo cave.
- **Also See:** CAPO D'ORLANDO; Isole EOLIE; MESSINA; Golfo di PATTI.

Citadel and Castle★

⏱ *Open daily, 10am–noon, 3pm–5pm.* *Closed Mon.* ◉€3.10. *For information on admission times, call ☎090 92 21 291; www.comune.milazzo.me.it.*

The town's main fortification was initiated by the Arabs (10C) on the site of a former Ancient Greek acropolis. On the left, through the **Spanish walls**, the **Duomo Vecchio** (1608), is a good example of Sicilian Mannerism. The **Aragonese city walls** (15C) are punctuated by five truncated-cone towers: two flank a gateway bearing the coat of arms of the Spanish monarchs, Ferdinand and Isabella – a shield divided into four sections (representing the monarchs under

Port and the citadel of Milazzo

H. Champollion/MICHELIN

which Spain was unified), supported by the eagle of St John. Within, stands Frederick II's **castle**. It was here that representatives from the five *campate* (regions of Sicily) met to constitute the Sicilian Parliament of 1295. The castle provides breathtaking views of the Aeolian Islands (from left: Vulcano, Lipari, Panarea and, on clear days, Stromboli) and the Bay of Tono.

Walking Tour

The Borgo

The *borgo* is the oldest part of the town: a medieval quarter, overlooked by the citadel. The entrance to this district coincides with the beginning of Via Impallomeni (from Piazza Roma), lined on both sides by the Spanish Military Barracks (1585–95). There are many religious buildings within the *borgo*: on the right, in the steep street with the same name, is the **Santuario di San Francesco di Paola**. **Inside**, in the Gesù e Maria chapel, there is an unusual carved wooden altar decorated with gilt and mirrors, set with a *Madonna and Child* panel by Domenico Gagini (1465).

A little farther on, up Salita San Francesco, is the Viceroy's residence (*Palazzo* **dei Vicerè**), built in the 16C and altered in the 18C when the balconies with Baroque brackets were added. Beyond, on the other side of the road, is the **Chiesa del Santissimo Salvatore**, whose 18C façade was designed by Giovan Battista Vaccarini.

Continuing along Via San Domenico, on the right, is the **Chiesa della Madonna del Rosario**, which until 1782 served as the main seat of the Inquisition Tribunal. Erected in the 16C, it was radically altered during the 18C when the interior was given its stucco decoration and frescoed by the Messina painter Domenico Giordano. Salita Castello, on the left, leads up to the Spanish city walls.

Città bassa

The lower part of town is the more modern section of Milazzo, built in the 18C. At the heart is the Piazza Caio Duilio. Facing onto the Piazza's west side is *Palazzo* Marchese Proto (once Garibaldi's

headquarters); on the eastern side is the **Chiesa del Carmine's** elegant **façade**★, composed of a doorway (1620), with a niche containing the statue of the Madonna della Consolazione (1632).

Continue along the old Strada Reale, now Via Umberto I, and on the parallel street, Via Cumbo Borgia is the **Duomo Nuovo**, built in the 1930s. Its interior is hung with a few prized paintings: on the high altar, figures of St Peter and St Paul (1531) frame the wooden effigy of St Stephen; these panels are from a dismantled polyptych by Antonello de Saliba, who also painted the *Adoration of the Shepherds*. The luminous *Annunciation* painted with vibrant colours typical of the Venetian School and the *St Nicholas Enthroned with Scenes from his Life* are both attributed to Antonio Guffrè, a painter of the Antonelli School (end of the 15C).

Posted at the crossroads with Via Cristoforo Colombo is the Liberty-style **Villino Greco**, with its fine friezes of stylised flowers and organic decoration.

Driving Tours

Capo Di Milazzo

Approximately 8km/5mi by car

Take the **Lungomare Garibaldi** along the seafront, overlooked by the elegant proportions of the 18C façade of *Palazzo* dei Marchesi D'Amico, and cross the waterfront district of Vaccarella, which begins with the piazza before the Church of Santa Maria Maggiore; follow the **panoramic road**★ that runs along the eastern side of the Milazzo promontory to the end. Arriving at **Capo dì Milazzo**★, pause to take in the wonderful **view**★★ of the Mediterranean *maquis* extending over the rocky spur to blend with the dazzling blue sea beyond.

From the left side of Piazza Sant'Antonio, steps drop down to the **Santuario di Sant'Antonio di Padova** and the bay. It is said that St Antony of Padua sought refuge in a cave here during a storm in 1221. Since then, it has been a place of pilgrimage; it was transformed into a sanctuary in 1575 under the patronage

Address Book

🪙 *For coin ranges, see the Legend on the cover flap.*

GETTING THERE

Milazzo is linked to Messina by train (40min) and by bus, operated by the Giuntabus company (Via Terranova 8, Messina, ☎090 67 37 82; www.giunta bus.com). Palermo, approximately 200km/125mi away, can be reached by train (approximately 2hr 30min). Milazzo's railway station is situated in Piazza Marconi, approximately 3km/1.8mi from the historical centre of the town.

BOATS TO THE AEOLIAN ISLANDS

Ferries and hydrofoils operated by SNAV and NGI depart daily from Milazzo to the Aeolian Islands. Taranto Navigazione runs mini-cruises, both during the day and in the evening. 🪙 *For further information, see Isole EOLIE.*

WHERE TO STAY

🍽️ ⊜**Jack's Hotel** – *Via Colonnello Magistri 47, Milazzo.* ☎090 92 83 300. *www.jackshotel.it. 14 rooms.* This small hotel, conveniently located for both the port and the town centre, is simple and well maintained, with well-furnished rooms. Good value for money.

WHERE TO EAT

⊜**Il Covo del Pirata** – *Via San Francesco 1, Milazzo.* ☎090 92 84 437. *www.ilcovodelpirata.it. Closed Wed (except Aug).* Situated on the seafront, this rustic, ground-floor pizzeria serves excellent pizzas, baked in a wood-fired oven. Popular with locals.

⊜⊜⊜**L'Ugghiularu** – *Via Acquaviole 137 Milazzo.* ☎090 92 84 384. *Closed Wed.* The cuisine at this trattoria housed in an attractive old olive oil store is simple and based on seasonal ingredients. Well worth a visit.

⊜⊜**Al Castello** – *Via Federico di Svevia 20, Milazzo.* ☎090 92 82 175. *Closed Wed.* This pleasant, attractive restaurant enjoys an atmospheric location at the foot of the castle. Outdoor dining by candlelight during the summer months.

TAKING A BREAK

Bar Washington – *Lungomare Garibaldi 95, Milazzo.* ☎090 92 23 813. A perfect place for a lunchtime snack, this bar also serves pignolate (a local speciality made with twists of fried puff pastry with lemon or chocolate icing), a selection of pastries and ice cream.

---

of a nobleman, Andrea Guerrera; in the 18C it was further endowed with altars and decoration of polychrome marble, and panels depicting scenes from the saint's life.

To return a different route, take the road along the ridge of the little peninsula and fork right along the road to **Monte Trino**, the highest point on this tongue of land, unfortunately blighted by telecommunications transmitters. From the little piazza before the **Chiesetta della Santissima Trinità**, there are wonderful **views**★ over Milazzo, its citadel and the sickle-shaped promontory.

To the west, the coastal road leads to the **Grotta di Polifemo**, mythical meeting place of Odysseus and the Cyclops. In front of the cave is a broad beach that lines the glorious **Baia del Tono** (known locally as *Ngonia*, from the Greek word for bay).

A Day Trip Inland

180km/112mi round trip from Milazzo – allow one day.

This excursion follows S 113, occasionally heading inland up the slopes of the **Monti Peloritani**, *the Sicilian extension of the Calabrian Apennines.*

▶ *Follow S 113 to Patti as far as San Biagio (for information on the Villa Romana di Terme Vigliatore, see Golfo di PATTI), then take S 185 to Novara di Sicilia. After 5km/3mi, turn right to Montalbano Elicona (44km/27mi from Milazzo).*

Montalbano Elicona

Perched at 900m/3 000ft on the eastern spur of the Nebrodi mountains, this town offers excellent opportunities for woodland walking (Bosco di Malabotta) and rambling among the crags of Argimosco. The town's most impressive feature is the great **castle** (o⊸ *closed for restoration at the time of going to press;* ☎0941 67 80 19; www.comune.montalbanoelicona.me.it, or www.montalbano.info), erected by Frederick II of Swabia, and destroyed by him following the Guelph uprising in 1232. It was rebuilt by Frederick II of Aragon in the early 14C and is surrounded by atmospheric, sloping medieval streets.

It is worth walking around the ramparts, although this may be awkward in parts. (♿*special care required climbing up*), so as to take full advantage of the views in every direction.

▶ *Return to S 185 and turn right to Novara di Sicilia (36km/22mi from Montalbano).*

This scenic road winds through pine forests and Mediterranean vegetation.

Novara di Sicilia

This small mountain town, between the Peloritani and Nebrodi mountain ranges, is laid out on medieval lines, complete with a towering Saracen castle, now in ruins. In the centre, the **Duomo** shelters a carved wooden altar and lecterns, sculpted with unusual figures with primitive features.

The road continues inland on S 185 to a mountain pass, **Portella Mandrazzi** (1 125m/3 690ft), with wonderful views over the Alcantara valley to Mt Etna. From here, it is possible to carry on to Francavilla di Sicilia and explore the Valle dell'Alcantara (Ⓒ *See TAORMINA*).

▶ *Continue inland and return to S 113, head towards Milazzo and after 5km/3mi, turn right to Castroreale (33km/21mi from Novara diSicilia).*

Castroreale

The ancient town of Cristina, perched upon spurs among the Monti Peloritani, became a dominion of considerable jurisdiction, following Frederick II of Aragon's concession of sovereignty in exchange for loyalty during the war against the Angevins. Re-Christened Castroreale, it retains many medieval features; interconnecting streets that open onto delightful little piazzas, and many churches, several containing art that testifies the town's glorious past.

▶ *The visit starts in Piazza del Duomo.*

Chiesa Madre

An elegant Baroque portal graces the façade of the main church in stark contrast with the massive 16C campanile. **Inside** hang a charming **St Catherine of Alexandria** (1534) and *Mother and Child* (1501) by Antonello Gagini and, in the north aisle, Andrea Calamech's *St James the Great (St James the Apostle)*.

From the east terrace outside there is a fine **view**★ over the plain of Milazzo.

Continue along Corso Umberto I, and turn left towards the 15C **Chiesa della Candelora** – a church dedicated to Candlemas, the feast commemorating the purification of the Virgin Mary and the presentation of Christ in the Temple.

Proceed along Salita Federico II to a round **tower**, all that survives of the castle built by Frederick II of Aragon in 1324. From the top there is a fine **view**★ over Castroreale, the little Moorish dome of the Church of the Candelora, and the countryside beyond.

Head down to Piazza Peculio, flanked by the 15C Church of the Holy Saviour (**San Salvatore**), damaged in the 1978 earthquake. Its semi-collapsed bell tower (1560) once formed part of a chain of watchtowers with those of the cathedral and castle.

Pinacoteca di Santa Maria degli Angeli

🕐*Open by appointment only. For further information, contact Signore Bilardo at least two days in advance.* ☎090 97 46 036 or 090 97 46 514. ⊕€2.

This art gallery houses rare paintings and sculptures, including a panel of St Agatha (c. 1420) in the Byzantine style, a Flemish triptych depicting *The Adoration of the Magi* with St Marina and St Barbara, a fine polyptych of The Nativity from the Neapolitan studio of GF Criscuolo, a marble statue of St John the

Baptist by Calamech (1568) and a silver altar-frontal by Filippo Juvarra (18C).

Museo Civico
Via G. Siracusa.

🕐*Open Jul–Aug 9am–noon, 3pm–6pm.* 🕐*Closed Wed afternoon, public hols.* ☞*€1.03.* ☎*090 97 46 444; www.castro reale.it.*

The municipal museum, in a former oratory dedicated to St Philip Neri, contains sculptures in wood and marble, including the splendid **funeral monument**★ of Geronimo Rosso (1506–08) and a fine work by **Antonello Gagini**.

Along the same street is **Sant'Agata**, containing an Annunciation by Antonello Gagini (1519), a statue of St Agatha (1554) by the Florentine sculptor Montorsoli, and a 17C plaster and papier-mache image, the **"Cristo Lungo,"** carried in procession on a 12-metre pole to be visible from every corner of the town.

▷ *Return once again to S 113 and continue along the road as far as Olivarella, then turn right to Santa Lucia del Mela (20km/12.5mi from Castroreale).*

Santa Lucia del Mela
The little town is overshadowed by the **castle**, built in the 9C by the Arabs and altered during the Swabian and Aragonese occupations. Little survives other than a massive round tower fortifying the main gateway, part of a triangular bastion, and sections of defensive walls sheltering the **Santuario della Madonna della Neve** (1673). Take a look at the *Madonna of the Snow* by **Antonello Gagini** (1529) inside.

On the way down into the town, there is an elegant Renaissance **doorway**★ in the façade of the **Chiesa Madre di Santa Lucia** (17C): note the lunette containing a relief of the Madonna attended by St Agatha and St Lucy, with the royal eagle, symbol of regal patronage. To the left of the church is Piazza del Duomo and the Bishop's Palace.

▷ *From Santa Lucia, return to Olivarella and then turn right onto S 113. Follow the road as far as Scala, then turn right to*

Roccavaldina (20km/12.5mi from Santa Lucia).

Roccavaldina
The main attraction of this little town is the extraordinary apothecary's **pharmacy**★ (🕐*for admission times* ☎*090 99 77 741, or 090 99 77 736*).

The shopfront consists of a 16C Tuscan-style doorway flanked by a stone counter from which members of the public were served. Inside is a rare **collection**★★ of maiolica drug jars *(albarelli)*. All the pieces come from the famous Patanazzi family workshop in Urbino, having been commissioned by the Messina herbalist Cesare Candia (whose coat of arms, consisting of a dove and three stars, is found on each of the 238 jars). The collection has been in the town since 1628; it includes typical long-necked vases, jugs and *albarelli* (pharmacy jars) bearing scenes from the Bible, Classical mythology or Ancient Rome.

Overlooking the same piazza is the 16C **castle**, an imposing transitional building that is at once both a fortress and an aristocratic residence.

On the edge of the town, in the tranquil gardens of the former Capuchin monastery, stands a **municipal villa**, enjoying a panoramic **view**★ over the Milazzo promontory.

▷ *Follow the scenic road for a further 6km/4mi.*

Rometta
Strategically positioned at 600m/2 000ft, Rometta earned its place in history by courageously resisting the Arab invaders: it was the last town to fall into their hands in 965. Little remains of the city walls other than the gateways, Porta Milazzo and Porta Messina.

From the ruins of Frederick II's **castle**, there is a wonderful **view**★ of Capo Milazzo and the Aeolian Islands.

▷ *From Rometta, either return to Milazzo (22km/14mi) or head towards Villafranca and follow the tour around Capo Peloro (see MESSINA).*

MODICA★

POPULATION: 53 070

In medieval times Modica was a powerful base for the Chiaramonte family. Since then history has not been kind to it; an earthquake in 1693 badly damaged the town, followed by a flood in 1902. However, each time it has rallied to adapt itself to the aftermath and make the best of its new circumstances. Today the city is a small jewel set with Baroque churches and palazzi in its upper and lower towns.

- **Information:** Etnos, Via Castello 21; ☎0932 75 28 97; www.etnosmodica.it.
- **Orient Yourself:** Modica is divided into two parts: the upper town, dominated by the castle, to the north; the lower town, hemmed in by high ground, extends along the two main streets Via Marchesa Tedeschi and Corso Umberto I that converge to form a Y. The Scalinata di San Giorgio links the two sections.
- **Don't Miss**: Climb the staircase at San Giorgio, enjoy contemporary paintings at Palazzo Polara and head off the beaten track to the elegant town of Scicli.
- **Organising Your Time:** Visit churches and museums first thing in the morning, or late afternoon, most are closed for 2–3 hours in the middle of the day.
- **Especially for Kids:** The caves of Colle di San Matteo at Scicli.
- **Also See:** COMISO; Cava d'ISPICA; NOTO; RAGUSA.

A Bit of History

Before the earthquake of 1693, a large proportion of the population lived in troglodyte dwellings cut into the limestone cliffs surrounding the modern town. In the centre, stood the castle, isolated on its rocky spur and enclosed on the north side by walls. Two rivers flowed through the valley, converging midway to form the River Scicli (or Motucano). As the threat of attack dwindled, the people moved down into the valley; but it was not until the terrible earthquake of 1693 that the cave dwellings were finally abandoned. The town clustered naturally into a Y-shape around the confluence of the two rivers, linked by a succession of 20 bridges between banks and earning it the epithet "Venice of the South." Then, in 1902 a series of freak storms raised the water level to a terrifying height of 9m/29ft at the confluence, after which the waterways were sealed off and transformed into wide streets that became the main thoroughfares of present-day Modica.

San Giorgio

©Antonio Brundo/Fotolia.com

Walking Tour

Since the 19C, the upper and lower sections of the town have been dramatically linked by a fabulous stairway leading up from Corso Umberto I to San Giorgio, Modica's most beautiful church.

San Giorgio★★

The flight of almost 300 steps was completed in 19C and complements the elegant façade, merging with it to produce a dramatic **composition**★★. Its conception has been attributed to Rosario Gagliardi, although some claim

Address Book

For coin ranges, see the Legend on the cover flap.

GETTING THERE

The most convenient way of reaching the town is by car, although train (20min from Ragusa and approximately 2hr from Siracusa) and bus services are also available (for information contact the tourist office).

WHERE TO STAY

Hotel Bristol – *Via Risorgimento 8/B, Modica. 0932 76 28 90. www. hotelbristol.it. 27 rooms.* . Situated in a quiet, residential area in the modern part of the town, this simple, well-kept hotel is ideal for both business visitors and tourists. The rooms here are comfortable and well-appointed, and the staff are friendly and welcoming.

WHERE TO EAT

L'Arco – *Piazza Corrado Rizzone 11, Modica. 0932 94 27 27. Closed Mon.* A typical rustic trattoria serving generous portions of home-made, regional cuisine. Good value for money.

Fattoria delle Torri – *Vico Napolitano 14, Modica. 0932 75 12 86. Closed Mon. Booking recommended.* This traditional restaurant, located in an elegant old *palazzo* in the town centre, serves a range of interesting and creative dishes based on local specialities. Meals can also be taken under the shade of the lemon trees in the attractive outdoor courtyard.

TAKING A BREAK

Antica Dolceria Bonajuto – *Corso Umberto I 159, Modica. 0932 94 12 25. Closed Mon.* This confectioner's, founded in 1880, offers delicacies such as *mpanatigghi* (sweet pastries with an unusual filling of minced meat and chocolate); *liccumie* (aubergine and vanilla- and cinnamon-flavoured chocolate made according to the original

Aztec recipe); and *riposti* (delicately decorated almond sweets, originally produced for weddings). Also worth sampling are the *aranciate* and *cedrate* (sweets made with orange and lemon peel) and the *nucatoli* (made with dried figs, almonds, quince and honey).

Caffè dell'Arte – *Corso Umberto I 114, Modica. 0932 94 58 95. www. caffedellarte.it. Closed Wed.* This café is renowned for its granite (crushed ice drinks), its excellent *cannoli* and its *cassate*.

FESTIVALS

EXCURSION, SCICLI

Three festivals are honoured and celebrated by Scicli. The first, the Cavalcata di San Giuseppe, takes place on 18 (evening preparations) and 19 March. This essentially commemorates the flight of Joseph and Mary into Egypt, although it also celebrates the rite of spring after the passage of winter with all the affiliated pagan rituals required. Colour is the festival's dominant element as flowers are used to bedeck the horses' harnesses and great wood bonfires are lit along the route followed by the fugitives, lighting up the garish costumes of the onlookers who throng the streets. Meanwhile the air rings with jingling horse bells and people's voices animated with merriment after the procession, gathering for great feasts partaken in each other's houses. At Easter, the **Festa dell'Uomo Vivo** celebrates life itself with a lively procession of a statue representing the Resurrected Christ, raced along by young men, through the town's streets. At the end of May, the **Battaglia delle Milizie** takes place: this consists of a statue of the Madonna on horseback being carried in procession, defeating and trampling over Saracen soldiers (long ago, this festival took place on the Saturday before Easter).

---

the design resulted from a collaboration of architects, notably Paolo Labisi. The lofty front elevation rises through three levels to a single bell tower; a sense of sweeping movement is imparted by the projecting convex central bay, flanked by twin bays that accommodate the double aisles. Inside, St George's contains a chased silver altar front upon which sits a fine **polyptych** (1513) by

©Antonio Zimbone/Tips Images

San Pietro with statues of Apostles

Bernardino Niger. The three tiers show the Holy Family between St George and St Martin with, above, the Joyful Mysteries and the Glorious Mysteries. The transept floor is inlaid with a 19C meridian line by A Perini. The third chapel on the right contains an Assumption altarpiece by Francesco Paladini.

Beside the church stands **Palazzo Polara**, which houses the **Pinacoteca Comunale** (◐*open daily except Sun, 9am–1pm*), and its collection of contemporary paintings.

On Via Posteria is the **Casa Natale di Salvatore Quasimodo** (◐*open daily. 10am–1pm, 4.30pm–7.30pm;* ◐*closed Mon;* ⊛€2; ☏0932 75 27 47), the house where the 20C poet was born, containing furniture and possessions from the writer's study in Milan.

Bird's-Eye Views

Two spots provide a good overview of the town's rooftops: one is **Colle della Croce** in front of the 16C17C Church of Santa Maria della Croce; the other, offering the marginally better prospect, is **Colle di San Matteo** set before a church of the same name, now sadly abandoned.

Behind it rise the ruins of a castle that was possibly constructed during the Arab occupation.

Continue on down to Corso Umberto I, the main thoroughfare of the Città Bassa (lower town), lined with elegant 18C *palazzi* and religious institutions. As the street approaches the centre, it passes the undulating façade of **Santa Maria del Soccorso** and, a little farther on, the Church of San Pietro.

San Pietro

St Peter's was rebuilt after the earthquake: the front **façade**★ is ornamented with statues of the twelve Apostles.

Museo Civico Archeologico

Tribunale in Corso Umberto, opposite San Pietro.

◐*Contact Ragusa Tourism for information:* ☏0932621421 *or visit www.modica. it/turismo_museo.htm.*

This museum offers everything the visitor could need to learn about the history, people and culture of Modica.

Chiesa Rupestre di San Nicola Inferiore

◐*Open 10am–1pm, 5pm–7.30pm.* ⊛€2. ☏0932 75 27 47.

In the apse of the rock-hewn church are a series of Byzantine-style frescoes dating from the Norman era. Pride of place is given to Christ Pantocrator (in the centre); at His sides, stand the Madonna and Child and the Archangel Michael.

At the intersection with the other branch of the Y (Via Marchesa Tedeschi) stands **San Domenico**, beyond, the town hall. This provides a good view of the castle above. Almost opposite, the Via De Leva leads through to the *palazzo* that shares its name and a fine **Chiaramonte Gothic** entrance. Before the end of the street stands the Baroque **Chiesa del Carmine**. Continue to the junction with Via Mercé and turn right: ahead is the **Convento dei Padre Mercedari** housing the Museo Civico and Museo delle Arti e Tradizioni Popolari (⬧*opposite*).

Behind the castle in Via Crispi, sits **Palazzo Tomasi Rosso** with its limestone doorway and balconies; note the stone-carved grimacing masks, acanthus leaves and wrought iron railings.

Via Marchesa Tedeschi, the other arm of the Y, climbs steadily to *Modica Alta* (upper Modica).

Santa Maria di Betlem

This church is notable for the elaborate 19C Nativity scene, comprising 60 terracotta figures modelled by G Papale. The street continues uphill past the 19C Baroque-fronted Church of **San Giovanni Evangelista**. At the top (Belvedere del Pizzo), a splendid **view**✶ extends over the town encompassing the Jewish quarter known as il Cartellone *(on the right, beyond Corso Umberto I)*, and the Francavilla district *(the near side of Corso Umberto I)*, the oldest part of town dominated by San Giorgio.

Museo delle Arti e Tradizioni Popolari✶

In the Convento dei Padri Mercedari. ♿◷*Open Tue–Fri 9am–6pm, Sat–Sun 9am–8pm.* ◷*Closed 1 Jan, 1 Mar, 25 Dec. 4€.* ☎*0932 75 27 47. www.popolari.arti. beniculturali.it.*
This museum, dedicated to the rural arts, crafts and practices, presents objects in their "natural context": alongside the reconstructed farmstead, are the beekeeper, blacksmith, cobbler, cartwright and the barber's shop.

Excursions

Scicli

10km/6mi SE. The tour starts in Piazza Italia.
◷*For information on opening times of the churches, contact the local tourist office (Pro Loco) at Via Castellana 2,* ☎*0932 93 27 82.*
Scicli is tucked away high up in the hinterland, off the beaten track. Affected by the 1693 earthquake, it has risen, phoenix-like, from the ashes.
The **Chiesa Madre** shelters the **wooden statue of the Madonna on horseback**. Originally, the figure was kept in its own sanctuary 6km/4mi west of the town.

Opposite the church stands **Palazzo Fava;** its corbels carved with emblems of chivalry. The balcony overlooking San Bartolomeo is especially fine.
On the corner of the piazza, a narrow staircase to the right of the church leads up to Via Duca d'Aosta and **Palazzo Beneventano**. This building, an elegant example of secular late Baroque architecture (18C), is flamboyantly ornamented with fantastical figures, decorative pilasters, masks of Moors and Muslims, and wild tiger-like animals.

▷ *Head down to Piazza Italia, follow Via San Bartolomeo to the end of the street.*

The façade of **Chiesa di San Bartolomeo** rises through three tiers of columns to a bell tower. Inside, it contains an 18C **Nativity scene**✶ by the Neapolitan craftsman Pietro Padula. All 29 carved wooden figures (originally there were 65) are especially finely crafted. To the rear of the church is the **Colle di San Matteo**. The caves that punctuate the side of the hill form part of the **Chiafura troglodyte settlement**, inhabited until the 1960s.

Via Mormino Penna

This elegant street passes between the fine Baroque exteriors of several *palazzi* and three churches. The first is **San Giovanni Evangelista**, a church with a **façade**✶ fronting a convex central section. Farther up is a second church, **San Michele** laid out to the same oval plan. The 19C building opposite, **Palazzo Spadaro**, preserves its original decoration inside and out. The street ends before **Santa Teresa**, a church with a late Baroque interior.
Walk back along Via Mormino Penna and turn down Via Nazionale to Piazza Busaccasu. Buildings facing onto the square include a Rococo church, **Chiesa del Carmine** and its adjacent convent, and **Palazzo Busacca**.

MONREALE★★★

POPULATION: 33 879

In a scenic position, commanding spectacular views down the Conca d' Oro valley, the small hill-town of Monreale grew up around its majestic cathedral, which is till the town's hub today. Piazza Monreale is dominated by this extraordinary building and from this square a maze of narrow lanes spider off, lined with cafes and small restaurants.

- **Information:** Piazza Duomo. ☎091 54 01 22. www.comune.monreale.cres.it.
- **Orient Yourself:** The historical centre of the town stretches across the slopes of Monte Reale, with the cathedral visible to the east.
- **Parking:** Visitors are advised to park in the lower town car parks.
- **Don't Miss:** Mosaics and cloisters at the Duomo, views over the town from Colle della Croce and Colle di San Matteo.
- **Organising Your Time:** Head for the cool climate of San Martino delle Scale in the hot summer months.
- **Also See:** BAGHERIA; CARINI; PALERMO; SOLUNTO.

A Bit of History

In Norman times, Monte Reale was a royal hunting ground and hunting lodge.

In addition to the cathedral, this splendid complex of a Benedictine abbey and a royal palace (converted in the late 16C into the Archbishop's Seminary), was initiated by the grandson of Roger II, **William II**, around 1172. Legend relates how the Madonna appeared to him in a dream to suggest that he build a church with money concealed by his father in a hiding place that she would reveal. The building should be so grandiose as to rival the greatest cathedrals of other European cities and should outshine the beauty of the Palatine Chapel in Palermo built by his grandfather, Roger. And so the most highly skilled craftsmen were employed to work on the project, with no expense spared. The church was flanked by the royal palace and the Benedictine monastery, whose magnificent cloisters can still be admired today.

Mosaics in the main aisle of the Duomo

G. Bludzin/MICHELIN

Duomo ★★★
(Santa Maria La Nuova)

Duomo is open 8am–6.30pm; 9am–1pm, 2pm–5.30pm (treasury in the Cappella del Crocifisso), €1.50; ascent to the terraces 8.30am–noon, 3.30pm–6pm, €1.50. 091 64 04 413.

The left side of the Duomo overlooks Piazza Vittorio Emanuele with its Fontana del Tritone. The main front overlooks a smaller piazza that provides access to the cloisters and a small **public garden** *(last doorway on the right facing the cloisters entrance and across a large courtyard)*, offering a magnificent **view**★★ over the Conca d'Oro.

Exterior

The impressive church is the product of a blend of various artistic styles implemented by a combination of craftsmen. The two great towers on either side of the main front are quintessentially Norman in concept, as are the apses, the basilica plan and, therefore, the fundamental arrangement of the cathedral. The superficial decoration applied to the **apses**, on the other hand, is clearly Arab in origin: this can best be **viewed**★★ from Via dell'Arcivescovado. Also from the same street, it is possible to make out the vestiges of the original royal palace which is now incorporated within the Archbishop's Palace.

The apses are articulated with three tiers of intersecting blind arcading: the pointed arches, of varying heights, rise from tall bases through slender columns. The decorative effect is heightened by the use of two different kinds of stone (gold-coloured limestone and black lava). The same elements are repeated on the façade, although the full impact is marred by the portico, rebuilt in the 18C. This shelters the magnificent bronze **doors**★★**(D)**, designed in 1185 by **Bonanno Pisano** – the architect and sculptor responsible for the Leaning Tower of Pisa. It comprises 46 panels illustrating scenes from the Old and New Testaments. The two doors are hung within an elaborately moulded stone door frame in which panels of geometric motifs alternate with animals and human figures in shallow relief and narrow strips of mosaic. The entrance from Piazza Vittorio Emanuele, beneath a 16C portico, also consists of bronze **doors**★**(E)** with several narrative panels, this time by Barisano da Trani.

Interior

Entrance from the west end.

Take coins for the coin-operated lighting of the mosaics.

The wide nave is separated from the two much smaller side aisles by columns with splendid capitals, some Corinthian, others of a composite order with acanthus leaves below and representations of Demeter and Persephone (Ceres and Proserpine) above. The capitals and the intrados (curved inner surface of the springer arches) sandwich dosserets decorated with Arab mosaics. Just beyond the halfway mark, the nave is interrupted by a monumental triumphal arch preceding the spacious area contained by the transept and apses, that rise up and above the level of the nave and aisles. This section of the floor is of inlaid marble, as are the skirting and lower part of the walls, echoing Byzantine influences. The wooden ceiling above the choir is 19C.

The church contains the tombs of William I (**F**) and William II (**G**); the altar in the north transept (**H**) encloses the heart of Louis IX (St Louis), King of France, who died in Tunis in 1270 while his brother Charles I ruled Sicily.

The **Cappella del Crocifisso**★**(K)**, situated in the north apse, is elaborately decked with marble Baroque decoration; inlay work, shallow-and high-relief carving, figurative statues and volutes. The wooden Crucifix dates from the 1400s. The **treasury** (**L**), set to one side of the chapel, houses various reliquaries and other cult objects.

Mosaics★★★

Against a gold background, the characters of the Bible re-enact their stories. The colours are not as bright as those of the contemporary mosaics in the Palatine Chapel, but the figures are represented with greater realism and are more expressive personality. These mosaics were completed during the late 12C and early 13C by craftsmen from

Address Book

For coin ranges see the cover flap.

GETTING THERE

If arriving in Monreale by car from Palermo on Viale Regione Siciliana, take the Calatafimi-Monreale exit and then follow N 186. For visitors without their own transport, bus nos 309 and 389 connect Piazza dell'Indipendenza with Monreale. For information contact AMAT, ☎*091 69 02 690* or *848 800 817*; *www.amat.pa.it*

WHERE TO EAT

Taverna del Pavone – *Vicolo Pensato 18, Monreale.* ☎*091 64 06 209.*

www.tavernadelpavone.it. Closed Mon. This informal restaurant has a friendly, easygoing atmosphere and serves a menu of typical Sicilian dishes all at reasonable prices.

FESTIVAL

Settimana di musica sacra – This Festival of Sacred Music takes place between September and December, with concerts of sacred, spiritual and liturgical music held in the town's church. For further information, contact the tourist office.

Venice and Sicily and tell the story of Divine Redemption, beginning with the Creation of the Earth and Man.

The individual scenes are full of realistically portrayed incidental detail: the ropes that bind the scaffolding erected around the Tower of Babel (**29**); the knives on the table at the Wedding at Cana *(high up on the left-hand side of the crossing)*; the coins falling from the table upset by Christ when He chased the moneylenders from the temple *(about halfway along the north aisle)*; the astonishing variety of fish depicted in the Creation (**6**) and caught in the fishermen's nets illustrating the Miraculous Draft of Fishes *(north transept)*. Many iconographic symbols are used, such as the cloud *(to denote transportation to another world)* that wraps itself around the figures that have fallen asleep as in the scene of the angel appearing to Joseph *(crossing, on the right)*, or the little dark figure that appears in several scenes, representing the devil. Note also how the soul of Abel is depicted as a small red figure of spilt blood (**20**).

Christ Pantocrator majestically fills the **central apse**, with the Virgin and Child below, pictured among angels and Apostles. The lowest tier is populated with saints. Below the arch, in the middle, is the Throne of Judgement.

The vaults of the **lateral apses** accommodate the figures of St Peter *(right)* and St Paul *(left)* with scenes from their lives.

The life of Christ is depicted in the **chancel**, starting at the crossing where a series of stories from His childhood are related. Christ's adult life is represented in the transept *(starting south side)* until the descent of the Holy Spirit. The aisles illustrate Christ's miracles.

Below the **triumphal arch**, across the far side of the transept, sit two thrones with mosaic scenes above: the one on the right, above the archbishop's throne, shows William II's symbolic tribute to the church (the king offers up a model of the cathedral to the Madonna); on the left, the royal throne stands as confirmation of the Divine Protection conferred upon the king (Christ Himself is depicted crowning William).

The **nave** is devoted entirely to the Old Testament: (**1**) The spirit of God moving upon the face of the waters. (**2**) God dividing the light from the darkness in the presence of seven angels (one designated for each day of the Creation). (**3**) The making of the firmament (Heaven) to divide the waters above the heavens from those below.

(**4**) Separation of the waters into the seas from the land that was Earth. (**5**) Creation of the sun, the moon and the stars. (**6**) Creation of the birds of the air and the fish of the oceans. (**7**) Creation of Man. (**8**) God resting. (**9**) God leads Adam into the Garden of Eden. (**10**) Adam in the Garden of Eden. (**11**) Creation of Eve. (**12**) Eve is presented to Adam. (**13**) Eve is tempted by the Serpent. (**14**) Original Sin. (**15**) God discovers that Adam and Eve are ashamed of their nudity. (**16**) Adam and Eve are expelled from Earthly Paradise. (**17**) Adam working. Eve is seated with a spindle in her hand. (**18**) Sacrifice of Cain and Abel. *Only the sacrifice of Abel pleases God, symbolised by the ray of light shining straight from the Lord's hand.* (**19**) Cain slays Abel. (**20**) God discovers Cain's crime and curses him. (**21**) Cain is slain by Lamech *(a story from the Jewish tradition and not mentioned in Genesis).* (**22**) God commands Noah to build an Ark. (**23**) Noah builds the Ark. (**24**) The animals board the Ark. (**25**) Noah welcomes the dove carrying the olive sprig, the sign that the waters have abated. (**26**) The animals come out of the Ark.

(**27**) Noah's sacrifice as a sign of thanks to God. Behind him is the rainbow, the symbol of God's covenant with Man. (**28**) The grape harvest *(on the left).* On the right, Noah, drunk and half-naked, is discovered by his son, Ham, who calls his brothers to deride him. They are more respectful of their father's dignity and cover his nudity. *Hence the reason for Noah to curse Ham and his descendants, the Canaanites. This is why, henceforth, fathers often express the hope that their sons should not take a Canaanite wife.* (**29**) Noah's descendants unite and build the Tower of Babel in an attempt to reach heaven; this results in chaos. *God, fear-*

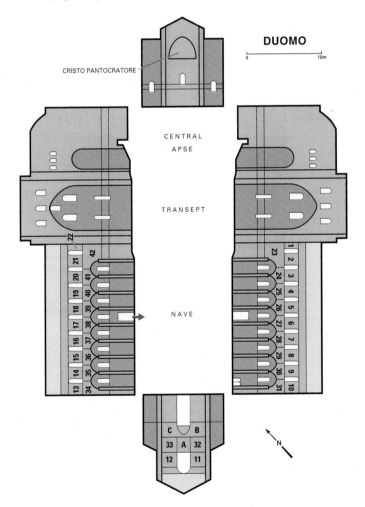

DUOMO

0   10m

CRISTO PANTOCRATORE

CENTRAL APSE

TRANSEPT

NAVE

CENTRAL APSE

C   B
33 A 32
12   11

N

ing that the force of Man might overthrow Him, caused the people to quarrel with each other, to confound their language and scatter them abroad: this story is often taken to be a parable for upholding Church authority in the face of Man's litigiousness. (**30**) Abraham, *having settled in the land of Sodom and Gomorrah, encounters three angels sent by God and invites them to his house. The angels represent the Trinity.*

(**31**) The hospitality of Abraham. (**32**) *God sends two angels to destroy Sodom. Lot, Abraham's nephew, shows them hospitality. Lot tries to prevent the inhabitants of Sodom from entering the house where the two angels are.*

The three following scenes do not come from the Old Testament but relate to the story of St Cassius, St Castus and St Castrense (patron saint of Monreale).

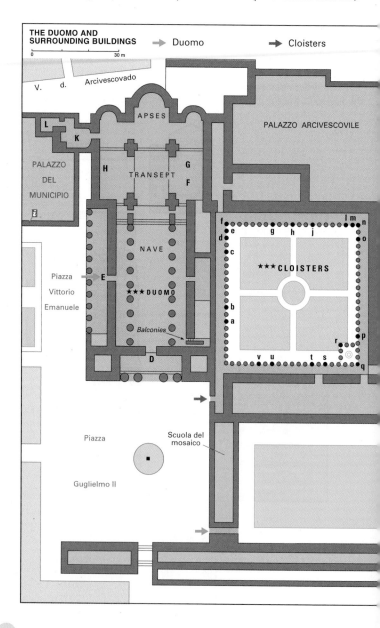

(**A**) Cassius and Castus, condemned to being thrown to the lions because they refused to renounce their faith in Christ, are saved when the lions are suddenly tamed and lick their feet. (**B**) Cassius and Castus are taken to a pagan temple causing it to collapse onto the infidels. (**C**) St Castrense cures a man possessed of the Devil who throws himself into the sea and causes a storm.

(**33**) Sodom in flames while Lot flees with his daughters; his wife, turning round to look back, is transformed into a pillar of salt. (**34**) God appears to Abraham and bids him to sacrifice his only son, Isaac. (**35**) The angel of the Lord stops Abraham from sacrificing his son. (**36**) *Abraham sends a servant to seek a wife for Isaac.* At the well, Rebecca offers up water to Abraham's servant and his camels to drink. (**37**) Rebecca sets out on the journey to her chosen bridegroom, Isaac. (**38**) Isaac with his favourite son Esau, and his second son Jacob. (**39**) Isaac blesses Jacob, believing mistakenly that he is Esau *(depicted on the right, as he returns from hunting)*. Isaac, who is almost blind in his old age, is deceived by the goatskins covering the arms of Jacob who, unlike his brother, is smooth-skinned. (**40**) Jacob

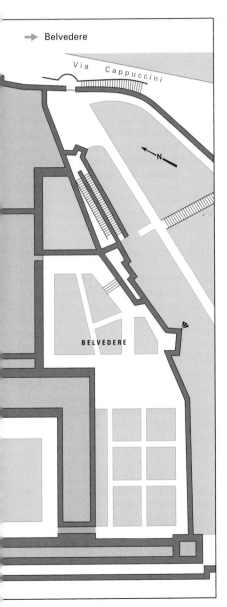

Belvedere

Via Cappuccini

N

BELVEDERE

CLOISTERS

a	The parable of dives and lazarus
b	Corinthian capital with windswept leaves
c	The story of Samson
d	The Massacre of the Innocents
e	The Four Evangelists dominated by a mermaid
f	The Annunciation
g	Owls, symbols of vigilance formerly placed above a monk's cell
h	Birds pecking the volutes of the capital
j	Joseph sold into slavery in Egypt
l	The Resurrection
m	Telamons
n	Constatine and Helen present the cross of Christ rediscovered on Calvary, symbol of the Church's victory over the Synagogue
o	Acrobat
p	The cult of Mithras
q	The Apostles' mission to evangelise the world: they are depicted in groups of three, in tabernacles protected by a flying angle
r	The 12 months of the year
s	William II offering Monreale cathedral to the Virgin
t	Men of oriental appearance
u	Cherubs feeding animals
v	The story of Noah

Cloisters of the Duomo

flees from the vengeful anger of his brother, from whom he has stolen his father Isaac's blessing. (**41**) On his journey, Jacob dreams of a ladder leading from earth up to heaven being ascended by angels. God, at the top, grants him the land on which he has fallen asleep; on awaking, Jacob takes the stones he had been using as pillows and lays them down as a foundation for his city. (**42**) Jacob wrestles with the angel. On his journey back to his brother Esau's, Jacob sent forth his sheep and goats as offerings to him. That night, having made his family ford the stream, an angel approached and wrestled with him until dawn, when the angel blessed Jacob and bestowed upon him a new name: Israel *(meaning the one who has fought with God and with Man, and has prevailed)*.

Ascent to the terraces★★★
Access from the end of the south aisle: but it involves an arduous climb.
The first outlook provides a view down over the cloisters. Farther round, there is a wonderful view of the **apses★★**. The highest section has magnificent **views★★**of the Conca d'Oro.

Cloisters★★★
♿🕐*Open Mon–Sat, 9am–7.30pm (7pm rest of the year); Sun and public hols, 9am–2pm (1.30pm rest of the year).* ✆€6. *For more information ☎091 64 04 403.*
The huge cloisters present a series of pointed arches supported by sets of splendid small paired columns, many

decorated with polychrome mosaic that is Eastern in inspiration. Those columns are sculpted with animals and human figures interwoven among luxuriant vegetation. The highlights though are the fabulous **Romanesque capitals★★**, each distinctively and imaginatively carved. The subject matter is drawn from both medieval and Classical iconography. Scenes from the Gospels alternate with stories from the Old Testament, each possessing an originality of its own. Even the Classical subjects betray a certain inventiveness: the acanthus leaves of the Corinthian capitals, for example, appear ruffled by the wind (**b**). To these are added a variety of other subjects: birds stretching down to peck the plant volutes of the capital (**h**), Atlas figures reaching up to support the weight of the arch (**m**), cherubs feeding animals (**u**), exotic characters wearing turbans with snakes (**t**). Perhaps the most remarkable capital is the one (**s**) in which William II offers up the church to the Madonna: note the detail with which the south side of the church has been carved. One capital depicts a man killing a bull, the sacred symbol of the cult of Mithras (**p**). Another features an acrobat (**o**): his position, his weight supported by his arms, his back arched so that his feet rest on the back of his head *(his head in the centre)*, recalls the Trinacria, the ancient symbol of Sicily.
The tiny cloisters in the southwest corner, include a **fountain**. The column in the circular bowl is sculpted with banding and crested with a animals.

Excursions

Castellaccio
3km/1.8mi W.
The ruins of the Norman castle perch on **Monte Caputo**, a popular picnic spot in spring and summer.

San Martino delle Scale
10km/6mi W of Monreale.
Situated at a height of 548m/1 797ft, this retreat has long been prized for its cool climate during the burning summer months endured by the coast. The town has assumed the name of the Benedictine monastery that was founded in the 6C by St Gregory the Great, and which was rebuilt and enlarged in the 16C. The **church** preserves a wonderful 16th **wooden intarsia choir stall**★.

The road leading up to the town affords spectacular **views**★★over the roofs of Monreale, the cathedral, the Conca d'Oro and Palermo.

MOZIA★

One of the four islands of the Stagnone Lagoon, Motya was once a prosperous Phoenician colony. The Carthaginians laid siege to it in the 6C BC and after its inhabitants fled to the mainland, the colony was soon forgotten. Its renaissance came in the 1800s when Englishman, Joseph Whitaker, a member of a family of Marsala wine exporters, built a house here. Today the island greets its visitors with a profusion of scents and colour: the Mediterranean vegetation is especially beautiful in spring, and worth a visit in itself.

- **Information:** Via G Garibaldi, Marsala. ☎0923 99 3111. www.comune.marsala.tp.it.
- **Orient Yourself:** Ferries from the Ettore Infersa saltpans (saline) link Mozia with mainland Sicily. For visitors without their own transport, the easiest way to reach the ferry dock is by bus from Marsala. There are no restaurants on the island, so visitors are advised to bring their own provisions.
- **Don't Miss:** Visit the museum and walk the causeway from Mozia to Birgi on the mainland (bring waterproof shoes with grip).
- **Organising Your Time:** Ferries to the island run from 9am to one hour before dusk. Watch out for reduced hours in winter.
- **Also See:** VIA DEL SALE.

A Bit of History

The Island– The ancient Phoenician colony was founded in the 8C BC on one of the four islands of the Stagnone Lagoon, now known as the **island of San Pantaleo**. Motya, the Phoenician name by which it was known before, is said to translate loosely as "spinning centre," after the wool carding and spinning cottage industries on the island. Like most other Phoenician colonies, the island became a commercial trade centre and staging post for Phoenician ships plying the Mediterranean. The 8C BC also saw the beginning of the Greek colonisation of Sicily, concentrated mainly on the east side of the island.

The Phoenicians consolidated their activities in the west, enabling Motya to grow in importance. In the 6C BC, the struggle for Greek or Carthaginian supremacy over Sicily gained momentum, and Motya was forced into taking sides. In 397 BC, the tyrant of Syracuse, Dionysius the Elder, laid siege to the town until it capitulated. Its surviving inhabitants sought refuge on the mainland, and integrated themselves among the people of Lilybaeum, corresponding to present day Marsala.

The rediscovery of *Motya* is associated with the name of **Joseph Whitaker**, an English nobleman living in the 1880s related to the family that owned a well-established and flourishing busi-

G. Bludzin/MICHELIN

Cothon - small man-made harbour

ness producing and exporting Marsala wines. The house on the island built for Whitaker now accommodates a small museum.

The Lagoon – Since 1984, the **Laguna dello Stagnone**, Sicily's largest lagoon (2 000ha/5 000 acres), has been designated a nature reserve of special interest – **Riserva Naturale Orientata**. This area extends into the sea, and includes the coastline between Punta Alga and Capo San Teodoro. The water here is shallow and very salty, the ideal conditions for salt works to be set up all along the coast and on Isola Grande, where it soon became the main industry; many of these have since dwindled into disuse.

The lagoon harbours four islands: Isola Grande - the largest, Santa Maria, San Pantaleo is and Schola - a tiny islet with a the roofless houses that give it an eerie air.

The most common plant species to thrive here include the Aleppo pine, dwarf palm, bamboo (Isola Grande), **sea marigold** *(Calendula maritima)* which, in Europe, grows only here and in Spain, glasswort or sea samphire (with fleshy branches), sea scilla with its star-like white flowers, the sea lily and the sea rush. The islands are also populated with a multitude of bird species, including the lark, goldfinch, Kentish plover, tawny pipit and Sardinian warbler. The waters of the Stagnone ('large pool') provide

fertile habitats for underwater flora and fauna: sea anemones, murex – collected by the Phoenicians for a valuable purple dye – and over 40 kinds of fish, including sea bass, white bream and sole. The seabed also supports the **Poseidonia oceanica**, a ribbon-leafed seaweed that produces a flower like an ear of wheat from its centre. This plant is fast becoming a menace to others, spreading itself through the Mediterranean like wildfire: its contribution, however, is to thrive in polluted and stagnant conditions; it stabilises the sea bed, oxygenates the water and provides nutrients for other species, thereby playing a role similar to that of the forests on land.

Visit

&.*Access to the island and museum, 9am –1hr before dusk (reduced hours in winter).* €3 *(ferry);* €6 *(museum).* ☎0923 71 25 98.

As recently as 1971, it was possible to take a horse-drawn cart across the old Phoenician causeway linking the island to the mainland. With the causeway just below the water's surface, passengers had the impression that they were "walking on water" (*See Porta Nord below*). This was also how Grillo grapes, used for making Marsala, were transported. In the centre the 19C house built by the Whitakers, is now a museum.

Excavations

Footpaths run along the island perimeter among the remains of the Phoenician town (allow 90min; visitors are advised to follow the path in an anti-clockwise direction).

Fortifications

The island lies in the lee of what was once a peninsula – modern day Isola Grande – naturally protected from attack by the mainland and the lagoon's shallow waters. Motya was also enveloped by a 6C BC wall with watchtowers. The footpath skirts the remains, notably those of the **east tower** with its staircase up to the ramparts.

Porta Nord

The North Gate is the better preserved of the town's two entrances. Inside, a section of the original main street shows wear, its surface deeply rutted by ancient cart wheels.

On the seaward side, just below the surface of the water, a paved causeway once linked Motya to Birgi on the mainland 7km/4.5mi away. Today, it is marked above the surface allowing visitors to walk the causeway (⊙*wear flip-flops or plastic sandals as the surface is rough*).

▶ *Enter through the gate and proceed along the main street.*

Cappiddazzu

This alludes to the areas just inside the North Gate: among the buildings, the one divided into three aisles may have had once served some sort of a religious function for the area.

▶ *Make your way back towards the shore.*

Necropolis

A series of stelae and urns indicate the area used for Archaic cremations and burials. A second necropolis was located on the mainland at Birgi, at the far end of the submerged causeway directly opposite.

Tophet

The sacred area consists of an open-air sanctuary where urns containing the remains from human sacrifices to the goddess Tanit and the god Baal Hammon were deposited. At that time, the immolation of first born male children was widespread. Farther along the track, Schola is recognisable by its three pink, houses without roofs.

Cothon

The rectangular man-made harbour is linked to the sea by a narrow channel. The **Porta Sud** (South Gate) is situated immediately beyond the harbour: like the North Gate, it too is framed by towers. A little farther on, the **Casermetta** was reserved for the military: with typical Phoenician vertical stone shafts. The last monument is the **Casa dei Mosaici**, with two fine black and white pebble panels that depict a winged griffin chasing a deer, and a lion attacking a bull.

Museum

The museum is devoted to artefacts recovered from the island itself, from Lilybaeum (Marsala) and from the necropolis at Birgi, on the shore opposite Motya. In the front courtyard, are arranged a series of stelae from the Tophet. The Phoenician and Punic pottery is simple in shape and devoid of decoration; the imported Corinthian, Attic and Italiot vases are decorated with black or red figures. The sculpture collection includes allegorical statuettes of motherhood, such as the figurine of the *Great Mother;* terracotta heads betraying a Greek influence and the **Ephebus of Motya**★★.

Casa delle Anfore

The House of the Amphorae is behind the museum. Its name derives from the considerable number of amphorae found here.

NICOLA

POPULATION: 15 000

Around the castle ruins in the upper part of Nicosia, the city's stone roads rise and fall in an irregular pattern, revealing churches, palaces and dwellings cut into the cliff. These caves are the residues of a troglodyte movement once prevalent in Southeastern Sicily. Today they are commonly used as warehouses or garages.

- 🛈 **Information:** Piazza Garibaldi. ☎0935 63 81 39. www.proloconicosia.it.
- ▶ **Orient Yourself:** Situated at an altitude of 700m/2 300ft, the mountain town of Nicosia is perched on four rocky spurs across the southern slopes of the Nebrodi mountains. Signs to the town centre lead visitors to the elegant Piazza Garibaldi, the starting-point for visits to the town.
- ☺ **Don't Miss:** Fine paintings and intricate choir stalls in Cattedrale di San Nicolo, wonderful views from the ruined castle behind Santa Maria Maggiore.
- 🕒 **Organising Your Time:** Take a stroll through Piazza Garibaldi at dusk, when it is especially atmospheric.
- 🕙 **Also See:** MADONIE E NEBRODI.

A Bit of History

Founded during the Byzantine era when it acquired its name (possibly a corruption of "Città di San Nicolò"), Nicosia shared the same fate as the rest of Sicily, having passed from Norman hands into Swabian, Aragonese, Castilian and then Bourbon control.

However, Nicosia managed to resist subordination with each successive occupier, largely as a result of the rivalry between the upper and lower parts of the town, with each faction clinging fiercely to its respective church (San Nicolò and Santa Maria). This predicament also faced other towns in Sicily (Ragusa and Modica being two examples), but here it assumed an unusual level of determination. Scuffles would break out during religious processions until, finally, a gate was set up to mark the official division of the town into two. Even as recently as 1957, two crucifixes were borne through the town in separate Good Friday processions.

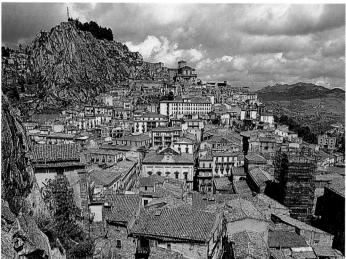

Nicosia

B. Kaufmann/MICHELIN

Walking Tour

Piazza Garibaldi

The piazza is especially atmospheric in the evening when it is suffused with artificial light. It is lined with distinguished buildings, including the 19C **Palazzo di Città**, which encloses an elegant courtyard and wrought-iron lamp.

Cattedrale di San Nicolò

The cathedral was originally built in the Gothic style, but has undergone several remodellings. Evidence of its original splendour, however, is found in the main **doorway**★ decorated with flowers, acanthus leaves and palmettes. The ceiling, completed in the 19C, is crowned in the dome by an unusual statue of St Nicholas "suspended" from on high. This 17C figure is by Giovan Battista Li Volsi who also built the decorated walnut **choir stalls**★ (1622). The first stalls show four scenes depicting *Christ entering Jerusalem (first on the left)* and, opposite, the *Coronation of the Virgin* (note, in the lower section, a carving of Nicosia before the 1757 landslide), while the *Martyrdom of St Bartholomew (second on the left)* has the *Miracle of St Nicholas* as its pennant.

The roof of the church, however, holds a secret: above the vault spans another earlier trussed and painted wooden ceiling from the 14C-15C. Attached to the inside wall of the main façade is an organ by Raffaele della Valle. The church preserves examples of Gagini workmanship in the font and pulpit, and a sculptural arrangement of *Christ in Glory between the Virgin and John the Baptist* attributed to Antonello Gagini *(second chapel on the left)*. The **chapter house** is hung with three fine 17C paintings: *Madonna and Child between John the Baptist and Santa Rosalia* by **Pietro Novelli**, a **St Bartholomew**★ by *Lo Spagnoletto* (José de Ribera), in which the flogger and onlookers are animated by intense realism, and a *Martyrdom of St Sebastian* by **Salvator Rosa**. Turn up Salita Salomone and continue along Via Ansaldi to **Chiesa di San Vincenzo Ferreri**, frescoed by Guglielmo Borremans, and then on to Santa Maria Maggiore, strategically situated with glorious views of the hills.

Santa Maria Maggiore

In 1757, a landslide swept away the upper part of the town including Santa Maria Maggiore. Soon after, work was initiated on a replacement church, while all the local residents set about meeting the cost. The noble La Via family gave a lovely 17C doorway from their *palazzo*; this now adorns the main front. Inside, the **Cona**, a large marble composition in six tiers, illustrates scenes from the life of the Virgin, crowned with a figure of St Michael: a work by **Antonello Gagini** and his pupils.

Atop the steep rocks behind the church stood the **castle** *(accessible by car along Via San Simone, leading uphill from just outside the town centre, thus saving a long walk)*. From the ruins, a wonderful **view**★ extends over the mountains.

▷ *Returning towards Piazza Garibaldi, take Via Fratelli Testa. On a rise off to the right sits the Chiesa del Santissimo Salvatore.*

The church of **Santissimo Salvatore** enjoys a fine **view**★ over the town.

▷ *Continue along Via Fratelli Testa, then Via G.B. Li Volsi; at the intersection with Via Umberto I, turn left uphill.*

Chiesa dei Cappuccini

Inside is a fine 18C wooden tabernacle attributed to **Bencivinni**.

Legend of Santa Claus

St Nicholas, or Santa Claus to Anglo-Saxons, was a bishop at Myra in Lycia (southwest Turkey) in the 4C. According to legend, he is reputed to be the mysterious benefactor of three eligible young girls whose father, unable to provide dowries for them, proposed to send them out as prostitutes until the necessary funds were raised. One night, the saint slipped unseen into their house to leave three full bags of coins, thus preserving their moral integrity. And so was born the figure of Santa Claus (or Father Christmas) who bestows gifts on well-behaved children.

NOTO★★

POPULATION: 23 225

Noto, which dates from the time of the Siculi, was completely destroyed by the terrible earthquake of 1693 and was rebuilt on a new site 10km/6mi away from the original town. It streets, laid out on a grid plan, are lined with handsome palaces, churches and other Baroque monuments in the local white limestone, which has mellowed with time to a golden hue. Several Sicilian architects worked together on this project; the most inventive was probably Rosario Gagliardi.

- **Information:** Via Gioberti 13; ☎0931 57 21 456; www.pronoto.it.
- **Orient Yourself:** The main monuments in the historical centre are grouped between the central Corso Vittorio Emanuele, which runs through the town from east to west, and Via Cavour, its counterpart to the north.
- **Parking:** Take a right turn past the town of Avola Antica to a viewpoint where you can park for the Cava Grande Gorge.
- **Don't Miss:** A walk through the Baroque city centre, or the eerie atmosphere of Noto Antica. Descend into the Cava Grande Gorge, and take a refreshing swim in the natural rock pools at the bottom.
- **Organising Your Time:** Allow one day for a tour of the surrounding area. Allow half an hour to descend into the Cava Grande Gorge, but double to walk back up. Early morning and late evening are the best times for bird watching at the Vendicari Nature Reserve.
- **Especially for Kids:** Swimming in the natural rock pools at the Cava Grande.
- **Also See:** COMISO; Cava d'ISPICA; MODICA; RAGUSA; SIRACUSA.

A Bit of History

Prior to 1693, Noto stood some 10km/6mi away from its present site (see below, Noto Antica). The earthquake destroyed the old town, and a less vulnerable site was chosen for the new town, one that might accommodate a straightforward linear town plan in accordance with the new Baroque taste. Three of the main streets run on an east to west axis, so that they might always be bathed in sunshine. Three social categories were catered for: the highest part was reserved for the nobility, the centre for the clergy, while ordinary people were left to fill the rest of the town. Many Sicilian artists cooperated in Noto's reconstruction, conducted under the supervision of the Duke of Camastra, the acting representative of the Spanish viceroy; these included **Paolo Labisi**, **Vincenzo Sinatra** and **Rosario Gagliardi**.

The new town was built like a stage set: its perspectives were enhanced with curvaceous forms and curvilinear accents in façades, decorated brackets and keystones, curlicues and volutes, masks, cherubs, and balconies with wrought-iron railings. Although Noto was rebuilt by local craftsmen, it fits into a much larger picture, as Italian hands modelled, fashioned and realised expressions of the Baroque movement all over Europe.

Walking Tour

Baroque City Centre★★

The main axis is provided by **Corso Vittorio Emanuele**, which runs through three piazzas, each with its own church. The street extends from **Porta Reale**, a monumental gateway modelled on a triumphal arch, erected in the 19C. Above the entrance is a pelican, the symbol of self-denial – a reference to King Ferdinand II, who visited the town in 1838 – flanked by a tower (a symbol for strength) and a *cirneco* (an old Sicilian breed of dog and symbol of loyalty). Beyond, to one side the elegant public gardens (Giardino Pubblico) are dotted with bougainvillea, palm trees, and marble busts. This is a common place for townspeople to congregate for the daily social ritual of the *passeggiata*.

Piazza Immacolata

The square is overlooked by the Baroque façade of *San Francesco all'Immacolata* (designed by Sinatra). An impressive stairway leads up to a terrace, with a statue of the Virgin in the centre. The church contains notable works of art removed from the Franciscan church abandoned in the old town of Noto. These include a painted wooden *Virgin and Child* attributed to Antonio Monachello (1564) on the altar and the tombstone of a Franciscan priest (1575) set into the floor of the nave on the right.

To the left of the church, by the entrance to Via San Francesco d'Assisi, sits the **Monastero del Santissimo Salvatore** marked by an elegant tower rising above the curved frontage. The windows have wonderful pot-bellied wrought-iron balconies, which are echoed across the street at the **Convento di Santa Chiara**, by Gagliardi.

Piazza Municipio★

This is the busiest and most majestic of the three squares, overlooked on the left by the eye-catching elevation of the Palazzo Ducezio, and on the right by the flight of steps to the cathedral entrance, flanked by two horseshoe-shaped hedges.

Cathedral★★

The broad façade with its two bell towers do not completely obscure the remains of the dome which collapsed in 1996 destroying a large section of the nave.

The wide stairway appears to sweep up from the piazza, accentuated by the two tall exedra side hedges, each with a paved area above, emphasising their serpentine line. Alongside the cathedral, on the same level, stand the 19C **Palazzo Vescovile** (Bishop's Palace) and **Palazzo Landolina di Sant'Alfano**, both sober in appearance in contrast with the exuberant style of the other buildings in the square.

On the opposite side of the square sits the **Palazzo Ducezio** enclosed by a classical type of portico designed by Sinatra. The upper section was added in the 1950s.

On the east side of the square is the **Basilica del Santissimo Salvatore**.

Via Nicolaci★

Right off Corso Vittorio Emanuele.

The eye is naturally drawn along the street as it gently rises up to the **Chiesa di Montevergine** with its concave frontage framed between bell towers. Both sides of the street are lined with Baroque buildings: on the left, note **Palazzo Nicolaci di Villadorata** (⊶ *closed for restoration at the time of going to press;* ☎ *0931 83 50 05*) with

Piazza Municipio

its fabulous **balconies★★★**. The richly carved brackets are ornamented with fantastical cherubs, horses, mermaids and lions, grotesque figures among which is a figure with distinctly Middle-Eastern features.

Returning to Corso Vittorio Emanuele, on the left stands the imposing complex of the **Jesuit Church and College** attributed to Gagliardi.

Piazza XVI Maggio

The most striking feature on the square is Gagliardi's elegant convex façade for the **Chiesa di San Domenico★**, designed with an emphatic use of line and contained by two tiers of columns separated by a high cornice. The interior is predominantly white and encrusted with stucco and is graced with polychrome marble altars.

In front of the church lies the delightful **Villetta d'Ercole ★**, a public garden with an 18C fountain named after the mythological hero Heracles. Opposite, stands the 19C Teatro Comunale.

The second street on the left off Corso Vittorio Emanuele, Via Ruggero Settimo, leads to the **Chiesa del Carmine** with its concave frontage and charming Baroque doorway.

▶ *Return to Piazza XVI Maggio so as to turn up Via Bovio, which passes, on the right, the former Carmine convent known as Casa dei Padri Crociferi.*

Via Cavour

This noble street runs parallel to, but on a level above, Corso Vittorio Emanuele, between a series of interesting buildings: **Palazzo Astuto** (n° 54), with its bulging wrought-iron balconies; and **Palazzo Trigona Cannicarao** (n° 93).

▶ *Beyond the palazzo turn left onto Via Coffa, then left again at the end so as to pass before the late Baroque* **Palazzo Impellizzeri**; *and turn right onto Via Sallicano.*

Via Sallicano leads right up to the **Chiesa del Santissimo Crocefisso** in Piazza Mazzini. Designed by Gagliard, the church was never completed. Inside, though, it contains a few works of note, including a splendid pair of Romanesque lions and, behind the altar to the right, **Francesco Laurana's** sensitive *Madonna della Neve* (Madonna of the Snow), the only statue in Sicily that was actually signed by the artist.

Excursion

Noto Antica
10km/6mi NW.

Along the road to the site of the original Noto there is a sign for **Eremo di San Corrado fuori le Mura:** this 18C sanctuary was built beside the cave where St Corrado lived in the 14C. The main road then continues past the **Santuario di Santa Maria della Scala**, to the site where the town of Noto stood before the 1693 earthquake. Stretched along the Monte Alveria ridge, between two deep gorges, the site was easily defensible and had been a significant historical stronghold on a number of occasions. Most notably as the last bastion of Arab Sicily to fall before the Normans conquered the island. Beyond Porta Aurea, the gateway to the now deserted city, the street system remains eerily intact. Archaeological finds and pieces of wall

Palazzo Astuto

B. Juge/MICHELIN

Address Book

For coin ranges, see the Legend on the cover flap.

GETTING THERE

Noto is 55km/34mi from Ragusa and 30km/19mi from Siracusa, from where there are train (90min and 40min respectively) and bus (1hr to Ragusa and 40min to Siracusa) services. The bus station is situated in Piazzale Marconi, behind the park (giardino pubblico), while the railway station is in Viale Principe di Piemonte, a 10min walk from the historical centre of the town. Bus services run between Noto and Fontanarossa airport in Catania (approximately 80km/50mi).

SIGHTSEEING

Through the streets – Throughout the 18C rectilinear town centre layout, popular districts have sprung up (Agliastrello, Mannarazze, Macchina Ghiaccio, Carmine) among the tightly knit and often maze-like streets more usually associated with medieval towns. The Allakatalla association not only provides guided tours of the historic quarters, but also organises "alternative" routes coloured with local stories and popular legend. These veritable leaps into the past are even more captivating in the evening, when the subdued light creates an almost magical atmosphere. For further information, contact **Allakatalla**, Corso Vittorio Emanuele 47; ☎0931 83 50 05; Fax 0931 83 60 21; www.allakatalla.it.

WHERE TO STAY

⊜⊜⊜**Hotel Al Canisello** – *Via Pavese 1, Noto. ☎0931 83 57 93. www.villacanisello.it.* 🛏🏊. *6 rooms.* This typical 19C farmhouse has thick, whitewashed walls and simple, rustic decor. The old-world atmosphere here is enhanced by plain, elegant furnishings.

⊜⊜⊜⊜**Villa Mediterranea** – *Viale Lido, Noto Marina, 7.5km/4.5mi SE of Noto. ☎0931 81 23 30. www.villamediterranea.it. Closed Nov–Easter. 15 rooms.* 🏊. This attractive Mediterranean-style villa, located on the seafront at Noto Marina, has recently extended its number of guest rooms, while still managing to retain its friendly, family-run atmosphere. Direct access to the beach.

WHERE TO EAT

⊖**Trattoria del Carmine** – *Via Ducezio 1/A, Noto. ☎0931 83 87 05. Closed Mon.* A good option after a hard day's sightseeing, this trattoria serves good, home-made cooking in a small dining room with tables covered with paper tablecloths.

⊖⊖**Trattoria del Crocifisso Da Baglieri** – *Via Principe Umberto 46/48, Noto. ☎0931 57 11 51. Closed Wed, one week after Easter and two weeks at the end of Sept.* 🍴. This simple trattoria takes visitors on an enjoyable trip back in time with its traditional Sicilian atmosphere, regional dishes and reasonable prices.

FESTIVAL

Primavera barocca – This spring festival, held during the third weekend in May, culminates in the famous **Infiorata**, a flower festival which takes place in Via Nicolaci. Towards the middle of May, the local inhabitants recreate brilliantly coloured tableaux of flowers composed entirely of petals inside the doorways of the *palazzi*. The cobbles of the street are transformed into a gigantic canvas of petals to form designs which vary from year to year.

G. Iacono/MICHELIN

Infiorata festival

are preserved in the small museum at the **Eremo della Madonna della Providenza** nearby (*ask the caretaker on duty to let you in*).

Driving Tour

Ruins and Beautiful Natural Landscapes

85km/53mi – allow at least one day, including the excursion to Cava Grande and the tour of the Riserva di Vendicari.

▶ *Head to Avola and follow signs to Avola Antica (10km/6mi along a winding road). After the town, turn right to a viewpoint where you can park the car.*

Cava Grande del Cassibile★★

An excursion to Cava Grande provides the opportunity of exploring a forgotten corner of the Iblei mountain landscape, dominating southeast Sicily - of particular interest to nature lovers. From the viewpoint, there is a magnificent **view**★ over the **Cava Grande Gorge**★ plunging down between sheer limestone cliffs. The river winds along the valley bottom, opening out intermittently to make a succession of tiny lakes, which are accessible by a path leading down into the gorge. To the left is the **Grotta dei Briganti** (Bandits' Cave), one of the many rock-hewn dwellings in this small settlement.

Descent

It takes half an hour to walk down to the river, or *cava* as it is known locally – allow twice that time to climb back to the top. The track, which at times is quite difficult to follow, cuts its way along the river through luxuriant vegetation. After a few hundred metres, the bush gives way to an open clearing around a series of **natural rock pools**★★ created by the river, complete with flat, rounded slabs of rock ideal for whiling away an hour in the sunshine. In summer, the cool water is very tempting. Furthermore, the rock pools are surrounded by idyllic scenery, providing an unusual and highly recommended alternative to a swim in the sea off the Syracuse coast.

▶ *Return to Avola. Take S 115 to Noto and then S 19 to Capo Passero. A road to the left leads to Eloro.*

Eloro

Ancient Helorus was probably founded by the Syracusans in the 7C BC. It enjoys a splendid **situation**★ on a hill overlooking the sea.

Excavations

On entering the site, to the east you see the ruin of a great stoà (portico) once the entrance to the sacred precinct where the **sanctuary** dedicated to Demeter and Kore was located. The sanctuary is now buried below remains of Byzantine buildings that were later erected.

Down to the river lie the remains of a **theatre** *cavea*, badly scarred after a drainage channel was dug under Fascist rule. Westwards is the base of a **temple** thought to have been dedicated to Asclepius (Aesculapius), the son of Apollo and god of medicine and healing. Beyond, northern and western sections of the **enclosure walls** are still in evidence, as is the **north gate** marking the beginning of the main street, running on a north to south axis, rutted by cartwheels. In an area east of the principal thoroughfare lies a large open space that was most likely used as the agora (market place).

▶ *Return to S 19. After 3km/2mi, turn right towards the Villa Romana del Tellaro.*

Villa Romana del Tellaro

Closed for restoration at the time of going to press, due to reopen in 2008. For information call ☎0931 48 11 11.

The remains of a Roman villa dating from the second half of the 4C AD have been recovered beside the River Tellaro, west of the main Noto-Pachino road. These fragments, found in the 1970s, suggest that the internal decoration of this villa must have been at least as sumptuous as that of the Roman Villa del Casale, near Piazza Armerina.

Tour

The residence is planned around a square peristyle: excavations of the north wing have revealed mosaic floors with geometric designs of diamonds and spirals.

Before leaving, note on the right, the traces of buildings annexed to the main complex – possibly servants' quarters – and the remains of a wall from the Greek period.

▷ *Return to S 19, continue south for a further 4.5km/3mi and then turn left to the Riserva Naturale di Vendicari.*

Riserva Naturale di Vendicaria

🕐*Open Apr–Nov 8am–8pm, Nov–Mar 7am –5.30pm. For information, call ☎0931 46 24 52.*
The reserve is open throughout the year; the best time of day for bird watching is early morning or late afternoon.
👓*Bring your binoculars!*

The Vendicari Nature Reserve was created in 1984 and consists of a strip of marshy coastline covering 574ha/1 418 acres. It provides a rare, and now completely protected, habitat for migratory species and a variety of sand-loving Mediterranean vegetation.

In autumn, it is common to see a variety of waders: grey heron, little egret, black stork, greater flamingo. Later lesser black-backed, slender-billed and Audouin's gulls regularly winter in the area. Between November and March, the swamp attracts many species of wintering duck, including teal, shoveler, pintail, mallard and red-crested pochard. Among the species that breed here are black-winged stilt – the emblem of Vendicari – Kentish plover, little tern, reed warbler and little bittern.

Tour

The track skirts the edge of the **Pantano Grande** before leading off towards the **Torre Sveva** (Swabian Tower) and the ruins of the **tonnara** (tuna fishery), which functioned until the Second World War. Nearby, lie the remains of a Hellenistic **fish-processing plant:** the tanks were used to steep the excess fish

---

Go Fish!

During the catch, the fishermen used to signal the number of tuna netted in the various chambers: a white and red flag was flown when there were 10; a red flag meant there were 20; a white one meant 30; a red and white one was flown with a white one to signal 40, and so on. If they were unable to estimate the number of fish, they used to wave a sailor's jacket on top of an oar, a gesture known as **u' cappottu**, which meant "we can't count them any more, there are too many".

---

before salting them (*tarichos*) or using the by-products to make *garum* or fish paste – a highly lucrative commodity that was traded across the Mediterranean from Phoenician to Roman times.

▷ *Follow S 19 for 18km/11mi.*

Capo Passero

The Ionian Sea meets the Canale di Sicilia at this southeastern headland.

Here, the local *tuna fishery* flourished during the 20th century and the now unused complex comprises a canning works, a house for the *Rais* – the quartermaster overseeing the cruel practice of *mattanza* (the ritual killing of the tuna) – and the owner's house.

A natural channel separates the *islet of Capo Passero* from the mainland, a strategic place to lay nets when the tuna are running. The islet, meanwhile, has been subject to a compulsory purchase to protect the rare dwarf palms that grow there, and decimating the once-dominant tuna industry. As a result the area is no longer the bustling centre of activity that it once was.

Portapalo di Capo Passero

This harbour is the hub of activity in this picturesque, archetypal fishing village. Its sleepy air is disrupted daily between noon and 2pm, when the fishing boats return and the quays suddenly throng with inquisitive old men and busy housewives come to purchase the fresh catch of the day.

PALERMO ★★★

POPULATION: 679 730

Palermo, the capital and chief seaport of Sicily, is nestled in a delightful setting★★, at the head of a wide bay enclosed to the north by Monte Pellegrino and to the south by Capo Zafferano. It lies on the edge of a wonderfully fertile plain, bounded by hills and nicknamed the Conca d'Oro (Golden Basin or horn of plenty), where lush citrus plantations, palm trees and olive groves flourish.

🛈 **Information:** Piazza Castelnuovo 35. ☎091 60 58 111. www.aapit.pa.it.

▶ **Orient Yourself:** The Viale Regione Siciliana, an extension of the A19 motorway, runs through the outskirts of the city. The historical centre is clustered around the crossroads of the two main streets, Corso Vittorio Emanuele and Via Maqueda; from the Viale Regione Siciliana, take the Corso Calatafimi exit (this street runs into Corso Vittorio Emanuele). To get to Via Lincoln from Viale Regione Siciliana, take the Via Basile exit, which is also the junction with S 624 from Sciacca. Ferries and hydrofoils depart from Palermo for Ustica.

🅿 **Parking:** Parking is problematic in Palermo. Visitors are advised to park their car in one of the car parks on the outskirts of the city (marked by a P on the map).

🚫 **Don't Miss:** The vibrant renaissance of the La Kalsa district, Baroque splendour at the Oratorio del Rosario di Santa Cita, fine frescoes at the Galleria Regionale di Sicilia and Sicilian artefacts at the Museo Archeologico Regionale. Outside the city, take in the macabre Catacombe dei Cappuccini with its 8 000 interred friars and the sulphurous Turkish baths at Cefala Diana.

🕐 **Organising Your Time:** Most churches are open in the morning and late afternoon. Allow one day for an inland driving tour from Palermo, taking in Monreale, Bosco della Ficuzza and Cefala Diana.

👶 **Especially for Kids:** International Puppet Museum (Museo Internazionale delle Marionette) and puppet collections and theatres at Teatro di Mimmo Cuticchio, Teatro Ippogrifo and Teatroarte-Cuticchio.

👣 **Also See:** BAGHERIA; CARINI; CEFALÙ; SOLUNTO; USTICA.

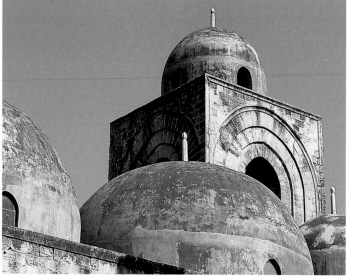

Red domes of San Giovanni degli Eremiti

B. Kaufmann/MICHELIN

Death by tongue-twister

Sicilian Vespers - Charles of Anjou arrived in Palermo in 1266, supported by the Pope. The French were held in scorn by the people, to such an extent that, given their inability to pronounce Italian properly, they were nicknamed *tartaglioni* (stutterers). In 1282, on Easter Monday, in front of the Church of Santo Spirito, just as the bell was calling the faithful to Vespers, a French soldier directed an insult at a Sicilian woman, thereby sparking off a reaction of indignation in the crowd. The situation deteriorated and, with the help of the local aristocracy, the quarrel was transformed into a revolt which then spread throughout Sicily. Any Frenchmen unable to pronounce the word *cicero* correctly were massacred, while the others were driven out. Eventually, Peter of Aragon, husband of Costanza d'Altavilla, the daughter of Manfred (the Swabian king ousted by the Angevins), was called upon to rule the island.

A Bit of History

The Phoenicians, who laid the foundations of the city in the 7C BC, called it Ziz, meaning flower. In time, it was conquered by the Romans who gave it the name Panormus (from the Greek meaning "large port or rock") from which "Palermo" (corrupted by the introduction of the Arabic name *Balharm*) was eventually derived. The city's golden age began under Arab domination (9C), when it was established as one of the main Islamic centres in the West. The town expanded as new quarters were developed beyond the old centre, known as the Cassaro (from the Arabic Qasr meaning castle); the Kalsa (from *al Halisah* – the chosen one), in particular, flourished down by the seafront and provided a residence for the Emir.

In 1072, the city fell into the hands of the Norman **Count Roger**, but the transfer was peaceful as merchants, artisans and Muslims were permitted to continue to live and practise their chosen professions. Indeed, it was precisely this magnanimity that made it possible for the Arabo-Norman decorative and structural style to develop in architecture. **Roger II**, son of Count Roger, harbouring a predilection for luxury, built Oriental-style gardens to complement his palaces (La Zisa and La Cuba). After a short period of disorder and decadence, Palermo and Sicily passed into the hands of Frederick II of Swabia (1212), under whom the city regained its importance and vigour. The Swabians were succeeded by the Angevins, in turn driven out by the Spaniards at the end of the War of the Sicilian Vespers. In the 18C, the city fell to the Bourbons of Naples, who embellished it with Baroque palaces.

The 19C heralded the opening of the city to trade and relations with Europe. The entrepreneurial bourgeoisie became the new economic driving force. The city outgrew its boundaries. The Viale della Libertà, an extension of Via Maqueda, was inaugurated; the surrounding district mushroomed, populated with elegant Liberty-style buildings. Sadly, this was to be the final flurry before a period of stagnation. The bombing raids of 1943 badly damaged the historical centre, destruction that was followed by an earthquake in 1968. The construction of large, modern, now crumbling buildings in the suburbs did nothing to improve the city's image. Today, this trend is being reversed as a new sense of determination prompts a re-evaluation and restoration of the city's magnificent monuments in an attempt to stir this wonderful giant of the East from its protracted slumber.

The Mandamenti – Palermo's urban plan is centred on the intersection of two main streets: Corso Vittorio Emanuele and Via Maqueda. Corso Vittorio Emanuele corresponds roughly to the historical **Cassaro** (from the Arabic *al-Qasr*), the city's main artery, which once linked the Emirate's palace to the sea and was enclosed at either end by Porta Nuova and Porta Felice. In time the district around the street gradually

PALERMO

C   D

0   300 m

X

GOLFO

DI

PALERMO

Y

STAZIONE
MARITTIMA

PORTO

MOLO
SUD

F. Patti

ORRE MASTRA

Castellammare

LA CALA

Porta Felice

S ³

Passeggiata delle Cattive

M ³

**Palazzo
Branciforti-Butera**

Pza Marina

**Giardino
Garibaldi**

**PALAZZO
CHIARAMONTE**

85

S ⁴

147

N 5

**PAL.
MIRTO**

G

**S. FRANCESCO
D'ASSISI**

Alloro

**La
Gancia**

S ⁷

Porta dei Greci

Pza
d. Kalsa

136

**S. Maria Della Vittoria
e Oratorio dei Bianchi**

34

Via

Pza
Magione

141

117

**Pal.
Ajutamicristo**

Pza
di Spasimo

**S. Maria
d. Spasimo**

VILLA GIULIA

**La
Magione**

P

Via

Lincoln

Pza
Tumminello

**ORTO
BOTANICO**

Corso

Lincoln

V.

Via

**GIARDINO
TROPICALE**

Via

Z

AIR TERMINAL

Pza
iulio Cesare

Via dei

Via G. F. Ingressia

CENTRALE

Via

V. S. Boccone

Archirafi

Cipolla

Mille

Ponte dell' Ammiraglio

C   D

S. Caterina	BY S 1	S. Ignazio all'Olivella	BY S 2	S. Teresa alla Kalsa	CY S 7
S. Cita	BY	S. Maria della Catena	CY S 3	SS. Salvatore	BZ
S. Domenico	BY	S. Maria della Pietà	CY S 4	Teatro Massimo	AY
S. Francesco d'Assisi	CY	S. Maria dello Spasimo	CYZ	Villa Bonanno	AZ
S. Giorgio dei Genovesi	BY	S. Maria di Valverde	BY S 5	Vucciria	BY
S. Giovanni degli Eremiti	AZ	S. Matteo	BY		
S. Giuseppe ai Teatini	BY	S. Orsola	BZ S 6		

assumed the same name. Via Maqueda was created at the end of the 16C, when the medieval quarters were demolished and the city was divided into four areas, known as *mandamenti*.

Mandamento Palazzo Reale or Alberghería, to the southwest, coincides with the oldest part of the city: it was here that the Phoenicians settled, followed by the Romans, Arabs and Normans, who built their most important civic buildings in the western section of the district. The eastern part of the *mandamento*, towards Via Maqueda, was originally an irregular and densely populated urban centre, which grew up around Via Alberghería, and included firstly a Muslim quarter (hence *meschita* – mosque – in Via Meschita and Piazza Meschita) and later a Jewish quarter.

Mandamento Monte di Pietà or Capo, to the northwest, was the area mostly inhabited by the Islamic population, and where much of the city's artisanal and commercial activity took place. This is still the case today, as shown by the lively Capo market which takes place in this district.

Mandamento Castellammare or Loggia, to the northeast, changed by the creation of Via Roma at the end of the 19C and badly damaged by bombing raids in 1943, included the port area, which brought mercantile activity to the district, and merchants from Amalfi, Pisa, Lucca, Genoa and Catalonia.

Mandamento Tribunali or Kalsa, to the southeast takes its name from the Court of the Inquisition whose headquarters were in the Palazzo Chiaramonte. It grew up around the Kalsa, the fortified citadel, and Via Alloro, along which noble mansions were built in the 15C. From the 18C onwards, *palazzi* were built along the seafront, with terraces overlooking the

Passeggiata della Marina (the present Foro Italico).

Palazzo Dei Normanni, Cappella Palatina★★★

The **Norman Palace** is located at the heart of the original town, probably on a site occupied in Punic times by a fortress. The earliest documents, however, date from the Arab occupation; these confirm this to be where the Emir's palace was once situated. The castle was eventually abandoned and the Emir's residence transferred to the Kalsa. The area returned to favour when the Normans re-established a royal seat there, having extended and embellished the palace. Life in the palace revolved around the green hall, in which regal ceremonies, assemblies and banquets were held. The building comprised various wings, assigned to different people and functions, interconnected by a terrace or garden ornamented with fountains. Four towers punctuated the corners: the Greek, the Pisan, the Joaria (from the Arabic for airy) and the Kirimbi. Sadly, only the central part of the original complex survives today, together with the Pisan Tower. The palace then endured abandonment and decline until the 17C when, under the Spanish viceroys, it was restored and the impressive south front and the beautiful courtyard with its loggias were inserted.

Today, the *palazzo* serves as the seat of the Sicilian Parliament.

Cappella Palatina

⊘*Open Mon–Fri 9am–11.45am, 3pm–4pm; Sat 9am–noon; Sun 9am–10am, noon–1pm. ⊗€6. ☎091 70 56 001, or 54 096; www.ars.sicilia.it. Partly under restoration until the end of 2008. On the first floor (take the staircase on the left).*

Before entering the Palatine Chapel, take a moment to admire the superb **court-**

Address Book

GETTING THERE

BY AIR

This is certainly the easiest and quickest way to get to Palermo. **Falcone-Borsellino** airport (once known as Punta-Raisi airport; www.gesap.it) is situated 30km/19mi north of Palermo, on the A29 motorway. It is served by a number of airlines operating both domestic and international flights. There are a number of **car rental** agencies at the airport:

Avis	☎091 59 16 84
Europcar	☎091 59 16 88
Hertz	☎091 21 31 12
Holiday Car	☎091 59 16 87
Maggiore	☎091 59 16 81
Sicily by Car	☎091 59 12 50

Connections with the city centre – A bus links the airport with the city centre every 30min from 5am until the arrival of the last flight of the day, stopping in Viale Lazio, Piazza Ruggero Settimo (in front of Politeama Hotel), and at the main railway station. The journey takes 50 minutes and costs €5. For information, contact Prestia and Commandè, Stazione Centrale; ☎091 58 04 57.

The cost of a **taxi** from the airport to the city is approximately €40. Beware of individuals who offer transport at considerably lower prices.

BY CAR

Close to Palermo the motorway joins the ring road around the city (the Viale Regione Siciliana), from where various exits lead to most of the major sites of interest. The Corso Calatafimi exit is the most convenient for the historical centre, as this road eventually continues into Corso Vittorio Emanuele, one of the main streets through the old town.

Car Parks – The difficulty of finding somewhere to park in Palermo discourages many visitors from driving in the city. Large car parks are found on the outskirts of the city (marked by a P on the map); it is also sometimes possible to park in Via Lincoln, next to the Botanical Gardens, which is a short walk from Piazza della Kalsa

The following guarded car parks are situated in the old town: Piazza Giulio Cesare 43 (railway station); Via Guardione 81 (running parallel with Via Cavour to the north, in the port area); Via Archimede 88 (north of Politeama); Via Sammartino 24 (northwest of Teatro Massimo).

These car parks cost about €20 for 24hr but often have special arrangements with hotels nearby. Do not leave luggage or valuables in their car.

BY BOAT

Ferries leave for Palermo from Genova (Grandi Navi Veloci, 20hr); Livorno (Grandi Navi Veloci, three times a week, 19hr); Naples (Tirrenia, 10hr and SNAV, 11hr, plus a fast service, Apr–Oct, 5hr 30min); Cagliari (Tirrenia, once a week, 13hr 30min).

For information and reservations, contact: **Grandi Navi Veloci** ☎010 55 091 or 899 199 069; www1.gnv.it.

SNAV, Stazione Marittima, Napoli; ☎081 42 85 555; www.snav.it.

Tirrenia, Molo Angioino, Napoli; ☎199 123 199 (from Italy), or 081 31 72 999 (from mobile phones and from abroad); www.gruppotirrenia.it.

BY BUS

There is a direct daily service between Rome (Stazione Tiburtina), Palermo (Via P. Balsamo 26 and Piazza Politeama) and Trapani, operated by Segesta Internazionale. The service departs Rome at 9pm and Palermo at 6.30pm; journey time 12hr (☎091 30 05 56; www.segesta.it). Palermo can also be reached from all other major towns in Sicily. The main bus companies are: SAIS ☎091 61 66 028. www.saisautolinee.it, Cuffaro ☎091 61 61 510 and Segesta ☎091 61 67 919; www.segesta.it.

BY TRAIN

Travelling to Sicily by train from mainland Italy involves crossing the Straits of Messina; the train drives directly onto the ferry; the crossing is included in the price of the train ticket. For information, contact the Italian State Railways (*Ferrovie dello Stato*), www.trenitalia.com). For visitors travelling from within Sicily, Palermo has train connections with Messina (approximately 3hr), Caltanissetta (approximately 2hr) and Catania (just over 3hr, but the service is infrequent). Palermo's main railway station is situated in Piazza Giulio Cesare.

GETTING AROUND

It is best to avoid driving in Palermo because of the traffic congestion and the difficulty of finding somewhere to park. By far the best way to see the city is by public transport and taxi for longer distances. Exploring the narrow streets of the old town is best done on foot.

A slower, yet nonetheless enjoyable way of soaking up the atmosphere is to take one of the horse-drawn carriages available for hire outside the central station or elsewhere in the city. It is advisable, however, to agree a price before setting off.

Buses – Palermo's city bus services are operated by AMAT, Via Stabile, on the corner of Via Ruggero Settimo; ☎091 35 01 11 or 848 800 817; www.amat. pa.it/. There are two types of bus ticket: one valid for up to two hours (€1) or one for a full day (€3.50); the latter is worth purchasing if public transport is likely to be used several times in the course of the day.

Radio Taxis – two main taxi firms are Autoradio Taxi ☎091 51 27 27; Radio Taxi Trinacria ☎091 22 54 55.

SIGHTSEEING

The tourist office publishes a monthly magazine with information on events taking place in the city, plus all the opening times for museums, churches and various *palazzi*.

Combined tickets – There are combined tickets for the Galleria Regionale di Palazzo Abatellis, Museo Archeologico Regionale and Palazzo Mirto (€12; valid for two days); the Chiostro di Monreale, Cuba, Zisa and Chiostro di San Giovanni degli Eremiti (€12; valid for two days); the Galleria di Palazzo Abatellis and Palazzo Mirto (€7; valid for one day); and the Museo Archeologico and Palazzo Mirto (€7; valid for one day).

Guided tours – The **CST** (Compania Siciliana Turismo) organises visits to several of the main sights in combination with a visit to the Duomo at Monreale every Saturday morning. On other days of the week, it also arranges accompanied day trips to Segesta, Erice and Trapani; Mount Etna and Taormina; Agrigento and Piazza Armerina; Il Capo market; Mondello and the Capuchin Catacombs in Palermo (half-day visits only). The CST office can be found at Via Resuttana 360; ☎091 74 87 234; www. compagniasicilianaturismo.it

The **AMAT** (Azienda Municipale dei Trasporti) organises various bus tours around the sights of the city and Monreale. Tours leave at 9am and last approximately 4hr. €10.33 (transport only). Via Stabile, on the corner of Via Ruggero Settimo; ☎091 35 01 11 and 848 800 817.

The **Cooperativa Solidarietà** offers tours to the historical *mandamenti* and a themed tour entitled *"I Beati Paoli."*. For further information, call ☎091 58 32 18 or 091 33 42 77. It was in the Capo district that a large number of the *Beati Paoli* stories were set. This massively popular novel by Luigi Natoli was published in instalments between 1909 and 1910, capturing the imagination of large numbers of Palermitani who read it avidly and who spent hours speculating on the suspense maintained with each new edition. Its vivid style succeeds in painting a uncompromising yet faithful picture of Palermo in times past.

"Palermo sottosopra" – The **qanat** are artificial underground canals, built on an almost imperceptible slope, which absorb moisture from the water table and transport it for miles underground. First built in Persia around the 7C-6C BC, these canals were adopted in Europe after the fall of the Roman Empire. The *qanat* were built by the

M. Magni/MICHELIN

muqanni or water masters, who passed on their skills from father to son and spent their short lives building these miraculous masterpieces. The *qanat* in Palermo *(open to the public)* date from the Norman period. The tour *(approximately 2hr, €10)* is an experience not to be missed, in which visitors are taken underground dressed in overalls and equipped with a speleologist's helmet, and are then led along the narrow canals by a CAI guide. It is advisable to wear a bathing suit underneath the waterproof overalls as you are higly unlikely to keep dry, and to bring a towel for after the walk. *For further information, contact the Cooperativa Solidarietà a few days in advance; ☎091 58 04 33 or 349 54 31 848.*

100 open churches – The aim of this excellent initiative is to provide access to a number of buildings hitherto closed to the public. The idea is to appoint groups of volunteers to administrate and oversee opening times (ideally 9am–5pm) and provide guided tours. Those buildings to have benefited from the scheme so far include a number of churches: Sant'Eulalia dei Catalani, Santa Maria dei Miracoli, Madonna della Mercè, Madonna dei Rimedi, San Carlo, Santa Caterina, dell'Itria or dei Cocchieri, Santa Ninfa dei Crociferi, Sant'Orsola, Santa Teresa alla Kalsa, the Convento di Santa Maria del Gesù and Stand Florio. For information and reservations, ☎ 091 740 60 35.

For coin ranges, see the Legend on the cover flap.

WHERE TO STAY

Hotel Cavour – *Via A. Manzoni 11 (5th floor with a lift), Palermo. ☎091 61 62 759. www.albergocavour.com.* 10 *rooms.* This recently renovated hotel on the fifth floor of an old *palazzo* is conveniently located near the railway station. It has light, airy rooms with high ceilings and functional furnishings.

Hotel Moderno – *Via Roma 276 (3rd and 4th floor with a lift), Palermo. ☎091 58 86 83. www.hotelmodernopa. com.* 38 *rooms.* A friendly, family-run hotel, where the staff go out of their way to make guests feel welcome. The fair-sized rooms are complemented by simple, functional furnishings.

Hotel Gardenia – *Via M. Stabile 136 (7th floor with a lift), Palermo. ☎091 32 27 61. www.gardeniahotel. com.* 16 *rooms.* A small family-run hotel on the seventh floor of a building in the old town. Some of the simply furnished rooms have private balconies overlooking the city centre. Good value for money.

Hotel Posta – *Via A. Gagini 77, Palermo. ☎091 58 73 38. www.hotel postapalermo.it.* 27 *rooms.* Behind the busy Via Roma, this family-run hotel with 27 simple, but comfortable rooms is popular with actors performing in the nearby Teatro Massimo.

Massimo Plaza Hotel – *Via Maqueda 437, Palermo. ☎091 32 56 57. www.massimoplazahotel.com.* 15 *rooms.* This elegant hotel, situated right opposite the neo-Classical Teatro Massimo, offers excellent service and comfortable rooms with parquet floors and tasteful furnishings.

Hotel Principe di Villafranca – *Via G. Turrisi Colonna 4, Palermo. ☎091 61 18 523. www.principe divillafranca.it.* 34 *rooms.* The hotel's small, bright and tastefully decorated reception area comes as a pleasant surprise. Comfortable lounges, antique furniture, attractive paintings, a small library and high quality bedrooms.

Centrale Palace Hotel – *Corso Vittorio Emanuele 327, Palermo. ☎091 33 66 66. www.centralepalaceho- tel.it.* 63 *rooms.* The elegant and tasteful Centrale Palace is located in a 17C mansion and offers excellent hospitality. This hotel has pleasant lounges, including a superb panoramic restaurant located on the top floor.

Hilton Villa Igiea – *Salita Belmonte 43. ☎091 63 12 111. www. hilton.com/italy.* 108 *rooms.* Housed in a 15C building, this "Grand Hotel" was restored in the early 20C and decorated in magnificent art nouveau style. Now a Hilton property, excellent service and charming rooms with private balconies still make for a very comfortable stay.

WHERE TO EAT

SICILIAN FAST FOOD

Local specialities include snacks such as *u sfinciuni* or *sfincione* (a type of pizza topped with tomato, anchovies, onion and breadcrumbs), *pani ca' meusa* or *panino con la milza* (roll filled with charcoal-grilled pork offal), *panelle* (fried chickpea flour pancakes) and *babbaluci* (tiny marinated snails sold in paper cornets), which are often sold from stalls in the local markets.

Antica Focacceria San Francesco – *Via A. Paternostro 58, Palermo.* ☎*091 32 02 64. www.afsf.it.* Situated in the heart of the old town opposite San Francesco church, this old-style café has marble tables and an original counter made from a cast-iron stove. It has an excellent selection of *focaccia farcita* (flat, heavy pizza dough baked with various fillings) as well as *arancini di riso* (deliciously moist, deep-fried rice balls sometimes with tomatoes and peas stuffed with meat sauce, otherwise filled with melted mozzarella), *torte salate* (Sicilian savoury "cakes"), fried ricotta cheese and *sfincione*.

Di Martino – *Via Mazzini 54, Palermo.* 📷. This café is a perfect retreat after visiting 19C Palermo or the Museo d'Arte Moderna. A good selection of delicious *panini* (rolls) which can be eaten at the tables outside.

Focacceria Basile – *Via Bara all'Olivella 76, Quartiere Massimo, Palermo.* ☎*091 33 56 28. Closed Sun and evenings (except Sat).* This attractive trattoria-cum-rosticceria has a long counter displaying takeaway pizza and *focacce*, an open-view kitchen which prepares fast cooked meals and two somewhat plain dining rooms.

Focacceria Basile 2 – *Piazza Nasce 5, Quartiere Politeama, Palermo.* ☎*091 61 10 203. Closed Sun.* Run by the same family as the Focacceria Basile in Via Bara all'Olivella, this pleasant rosticceria prepares a range of snacks and Sicilian-style fast food, such as *arancini*, *caponate* (a tomato and aubergine mixture) and *panini con la milza*.

Giannettino – *Piazza R. Settimo 8/11, Palermo.* ☎*091 61 14 560.* One of the best addresses in the city for pizzas, calzoni, rolls and other typical Sicilian snacks. The café has a pleasant sitting area for those who want to eat in, as well as offering a takeaway service.

I Cuochini – *Via R. Settimo 68, Palermo.* ☎*091 58 11 58. www.icuochini.it. Open 8.30am–2.30pm, 4.30pm–7.30pm. Closed Sun.* This tiny shop, located for the past 170 years in the inner courtyard of the Palazzo del Barone di Stefano, sells an irresistible range of Sicilian specialities, such as pizza, *panzerotti* (fried pastries) and *arancini*. Not to be missed!

RESTAURANTS

🍽️🍽️**Villa Cicara** – *Via G. Filangeri 10 (Piazza Magione), Palermo.* ☎*091 61 77 777. Closed Tue (Jan–Mar).* The dining room of this restaurant is decorated in rustic style, with old tools on the wall and a large wrought-iron chandelier. Guests can also dine in the beautiful garden, surrounded by orange and pomegranate trees, a large palm tree and a host of other plants.

🍽️🍽️**Hostaria da Ciccio** – *Via Firenze 6 (at the intersection with Via Roma 178), Palermo.* ☎*091 32 91 43. Closed Sun.* This trattoria, founded towards the end of the 1930s, has two small dining rooms and a very pleasant outdoor summer dining area. The restaurant still specialises in a traditional menu of Sicilian dishes and fresh fish and neither the authentic atmosphere nor the excellent quality of the cuisine has changed since it first opened.

🍽️🍽️**Casa del Brodo** – *Corso Vittorio Emanuele 175, Palermo.* ☎*091 32 16 55.* Founded over 100 years ago, this restaurant once had a rustic feel, which has been replaced by a more elegant ambience. With its attractive blue tablecloths, copious antipasti buffet laid out in the corridor between the two dining rooms, and excellent Sicilian cuisine focusing on fish specialities, this restaurant offers good value for money.

🍽️🍽️🍽️**Ai vecchietti di Minchiapititto** – *Piazza San Oliva 10, Palermo.* ☎*091 58 56 06. www.aivecchiettidiminchiapititto. com.* This restaurant, housed in a 19C building, has two small atmospheric, rustic-style dining rooms with vaulted ceilings and brick arches. In summer, meals are served outside in a small garden.

🍽️🍽️🍽️**La Cambusa** – *Piazza Marina 16, Palermo.* ☎*091 58 45 74. www. lacambusa.it. Closed Mon and in Dec.* Overlooking Piazza Marina, this elegant, quiet restaurant specialises in fish dishes. Excellent antipasti buffet.

◯◯◯**Capricci di Sicilia** – *Via Istituto Pignatelli 6 (on the corner of Piazza Sturzo), Palermo. ☎091 32 77 77. Closed Mon (except Jul and Aug).* Mime artists and street vendors occasionally make an appearance at this lively restaurant, which has simple decor and informal service. The food here is excellent; the menu has strong emphasis on regional specialities.

◯◯◯**Trattoria Biondo** – *Via Carducci 15 (N of Piazza Castelnuovo), Palermo. ☎091 58 36 62. Closed Wed and 30 Jul– 15 Sept.* Situated near Teatro Politeama in the historical centre of Palermo, this restaurant specialises in Mediterranean cuisine. The ambience is rustic and friendly, with bottles, old wine and tomato crates, gourds and other small objects brightening the decor. Note that a 10% service charge is added to your bill.

◯◯◯**Al Genio** – *Piazza S. Carlo 9 (near Piazza Rivoluzione), Palermo. ☎091 61 66 642. Closed Mon and at lunchtime (Jun–Sept).* This restaurant in Palermo's old quarter has two dining rooms with vaulted ceilings, one with exposed stonework. Run by the same family for generations, the Al Genio specialises in genuine Sicilian cuisine.

◯◯◯◯**Santandrea** – *Piazza Sant'Andrea 4 (Vucciria), Palermo. ☎091 33 49 99. Closed Tue and Wed lunchtimes; Mon and Sun (Jul–Aug) and Jan. Booking recommended.* This pleasant restaurant, situated in the heart of the Vucciria district, serves traditional Sicilian cuisine.

TAKING A BREAK

POLITEAMA DISTRICT

Antico Caffè – *Via Principe di Belmonte 107–115, Palermo.* One of the oldest cafés in Palermo, the traditional Antico Caffè enjoys a splendid setting on Via Principe Belmonte. Since 1860 it has served excellent cakes and pastries on its attractive terrace.

Bar-Pasticceria Mazzara – *Via Magliocco 15, Palermo. ☎091 32 14 43.* This bar was where Giuseppe Tomasi di Lampedusa, author of The Leopard, used to stop for breakfast. The bar started out as a *pasticceria* (the cas-

sata, *cannoli*, typical Sicilian cakes and pastries, and ice cream are excellent), then extended to include a rosticceria, self-service restaurant and pizzeria.

Enoteca Picone – *Via G. Marconi 36, Palermo. ☎091 33 13 00. Closed Sun.* This traditional, family-run wine bar, founded in 1946, has one of the best cellars in Palermo, with a choice of over 4 000 different wines. Wine tasting has developed into an art form in these rustic, elegant surroundings, where the wine is accompanied by cold meats, cheeses and other local specialities.

I Quaderni di Mamma Andrea – *Via Principe di Scordia 67, Palermo. ☎091 33 48 35. Open Mon–Fri 8.30am–1pm, 4pm–7.30pm; Sat 8.30am–1pm.* Since 1990, Mamma Andrea specialises in fruity jams, cakes, liqueurs, honey and other delicacies, with the emphasis on high quality and sophistication.

NEAR THE GIARDINO INGLESE

Bar Costa – *Via Gabriele d'Annunzio 15 (N of the Giardino), Palermo. ☎091 34 56 52. Closed Tue.* This friendly bar specialises in all kinds of cakes and pastries, including its delicious orange and lemon mousses.

Pasticceria-Caffetteria Castiglione – *Via Catania 96, Palermo. ☎091 30 49 19. Closed Mon.* A perfect setting for a cup of coffee accompanied by a delicious cake or pastry, this café is situated away from the more famous tourist areas, not far from the English Garden.

Stancampiano – *Via E. Notarbartolo 51, Palermo. ☎091 62 54 099.* This gelateria has the largest selection of ice creams in Palermo. Take your pick from a choice of cones or tubs, or do as the Sicilians do and enjoy your scoops of ice cream accompanied by a brioche.

OTHER DISTRICTS

Gelateria di Ciccio – *Corso dei Mille 73, Palermo. ☎091 61 61 537.* Only a few hundred metres from the railway station, this ice cream parlour, dating from 1940, offers a range of over 50 different flavours of ice cream. A welcome oasis in the summer months.

Oscar – *Via Mariano Migliaccio 39, Palermo. ☎091 68 22 381. Open 8am–9pm. Closed Tue.* Sicilian cassata, torta Devil (Devil's Cake, the house speciality), almond pastries and a whole range of other delicacies can be sampled at this *pasticceria*, considered by many to be the best in Palermo. Slightly off the beaten track, but well worth the effort.

SHOWS

Cantieri culturali alla Zisa – *Via Gili 4, Palermo.* ☎091 65 24 942. *www.comune. palermo.it.* The old Ducrot warehouses, near Castello della Zisa, were once home to a well-known furniture factory. Nowadays, they have been transformed into public rooms which host a broad range of different exhibitions, concerts and plays.

Lo Spasimo – *Via Spasimo (Piazza Magione), Palermo.* ☎091 61 61 486. *www.comune.palermo.it.* The Santa Maria dello Spasimo complex, home to the Scuola Europea di Musica Jazz, provides an atmospheric setting for a range of cultural events.

IL TEATRO DEI PUPI Kids

The name synonymous with the ancient tradition of the puppet theatre in Palermo, is that of the Cuticchio family. For generations not only have these highly skilled puppeteers put on performances, they have themselves made the actual puppets. Sadly, puppet shows no longer attract the same large crowds they used to. At one time they were the talk of the day, followed by everyone and, as such, provided work not only for puppeteers (of which there were many companies in business), but also for many a skilled craftsman who specialised in giving form to their fabulous creations. A simple suit of armour, for example, might comprise some 35–36 individual parts before being assembled by hand.

Teatro di Mimmo Cuticchio – *Via Bara all'Olivella 95, Palermo.* ☎091 32 34 00. *www.figlidartecuticchio.com* This theatre is the setting for performances by the Mimmo Cuticchio puppet company. The workshop opposite *(open to the public)* is used to store the company's puppets, as well as the theatre's stage machinery.

Teatro Ippogrifo – *Vicolo Ragusi 6 (near the Quattro Canti), Palermo.* ☎091 32 91 94; 347 06 76 368 (mobile). *Performances at 6pm (for a minimum audience of 20 people).* This theatre company belongs to Nino Cuticchio, from Sicily's most famous puppet-making families. The puppet workshop is located at Via Bara all'Olivella 38.

Teatroarte-Cuticchio – *Via dei Benedettini 9, Palermo.* ☎47 45 47 613 or 091 32 34 00; *www.teatroarte-cuticchio. com.* Founded by Girolamo Cuticchio in 1946, this renowned company is now run by his sons. The puppet workshop is situated on the same premises.

SHOPPING

LOCAL MARKETS

The most colourful and picturesque markets are, without doubt, those selling food, with their multicoloured awnings, their brightly painted stalls decked with assortments of fruit, vegetables or fish, lit with bare light bulbs.

La Vucciria – This historic market is certainly Palermo's most famous, always bustling with colour and noise, and is the most important food market in the city. It takes place set back from the waterfront in Via Cassari-Argenteria and the surrounding area (stretching as far as Piazza San Domenico). The origin of the name is controversial: some maintain that it comes from the French term *boucherie* (meat), others are of the opinion that it refers to the deafening clamour of the traders' voices drawing attention to their wares.

Ballarò – Ballarò market is held in the area stretching from Piazza Casa Professa to Corso Tukory. The food stalls cluster around Piazza del Carmine, while clothing and second-hand items

Colourful scale in La Vucciria

are near **Casa Professa**. A lively atmosphere, especially in the morning.

Il Capo – The first, more picturesque, food section is along Via Carini and Via Beati Paoli; the clothing and shoe stalls congregate in Via Sant'Agostino and Via Bandiera. In addition to the brightly coloured stalls, it is worth noting the interestingly named streets in this area, such as Sedie Volanti (flying chairs) and Gioia Mia (my love).

Mercato delle Pulci – A range of antique and modern bric-a-brac can be found in the lively fleamarket (located between Piazza Peranni and Corso Amedeo), where intense haggling over prices is mandatory!

I Lattarini – The name of this market derives from the Arabic *suk-el-attarin* (grocery market). Once a food market, its stalls now sell an array of clothing, work tools and ironmongery.

SHOPS

The city's most elegant shops are concentrated in the new development along Via della Libertà, Via Roma and Via Maqueda. The pedestrianised **Via Principe di Belmonte** is also lined with elegant shops; the central section of the street has been planted with trees to provide shade for tables spilling onto the pavement from its many bars. In the bustling **Via Calderai** (*which crosses Via Maqueda south of Piazza Bellini*) there are a number of arts and crafts shops selling firedogs for fireplaces, chairs, china and crockery. The small Via **Bara all'Olivella** (*opposite Teatro Massimo*) is lined with handicraft shops specialising in ceramics, woodwork and puppets.

Enoteca Picone – *Via G. Marconi 36, Palermo.* ☎*091 33 13 00. www.entocapi cone.it. Closed Sun. See Taking a Break.*

Enoteca Sicilia – *Via Maqueda 92, Palermo.* ☎*091 61 62 288. www.entoca sicilia.it. Open 9am–12pm. Closed Sun and public hols.* €*5.* This permanent exhibition of Sicilian wine labels is housed in the beautiful Palazzo Ramacca. A wine tasting is included in the price of the guided tour (two wines, which change daily).

Franco Bertolino – *Salita Ramires 8, Palermo.* ☎*0347 05 76 923. Closed Sun.* Bertolino is one of the last remaining artists to specialise in the production of the traditional, colourful Sicilian carts. His workshop, boutique and small museum are housed in an old building near the cathedral.

Il Laboratorio Italiano – *Via Principe di Villafranca 2, Palermo.* ☎*091 62 69 785. www.lboratorioitaliano.it. Closed Sun.* A range of fine, hand-crafted ceramics are exhibited and sold in the three rooms of this small workshop. A reputable address that is renowned for its unusual and original items.

La Bottega d'Arte di Angela Tripi – *Corso Vittorio Emanuele 450, Palermo.* ☎*091 65 12 787. www.angela-tripi.it. Open Mon–Sat, 9.30am–7.30pm.* Situated near the cathedral in Palazzo Santa Ninfa, this workshop specialising in small terracotta statues for cribs is famous throughout the world. A superb showcase of high-quality craftwork.

Vincenzo Argento e Figli – *Corso Vittorio Emanuele 445, Palermo.* ☎*091 61 13 680. Open Mon–Sat from 10am (shop); performance at 6pm.* The old artistic tradition of making puppets has been handed down through the generations in this long-established family business, founded in 1893. Today, the shop continues to sell an incredible variety of puppets.

Opening hours – Most shops are closed on Monday morning (food shops close on Wednesday afternoon). Shops generally open between 9am and 1pm and from 3.30pm–7.30pm (4pm–8pm on Saturday afternoon).

FESTIVALS

U' Fistino – This festival, held in honour of the city's patron saint, Santa Rosalia, takes place on 14 and 15 July, with processions, costumed parades and some grand firework displays.

Festa dei Morti – On 2 November, in celebration of All Souls' Day, children receive gifts and sweets from their departed loved ones.

Festival di Morgana – This gathering of puppeteers and performers from around the world isheld at the Museo Internazionale delle Marionette (*end of Nov–mid-Dec*).

yard enclosed by three superimposed loggias. The chapel was built by the king between 1130 – the year of his coronation – and 1140. In the beginning it stood alone, gradually becoming incorporated into a complex of other buildings that now conceal it completely. What can still be seen is the exterior of the side wall (corresponding to the north aisle) with its two-tier decoration. The lower section echoes the decorative arrangement at the same level inside: slabs of white marble surrounded by *pietra dura* decoration (inlay of semi-precious stones). The upper tier comprises 19C composite panels depicting scenes from the life of David. At the rear, Roger II is depicted handing a decree to the *ciantro* (literally a singer, but, in this case, the person in charge of the chapel).

The Arabo-Norman interior decor of blazing gold offset by the marble is notable.

Structure – The internal space, with a rectangular ground plan, is divided into two parts: the first section is divided into three aisles by 10 granite columns; the second comprises the chancel, contained within a marble balustrade. On the right, near the division of the two halves, is the double **ambo**, supported by four columns and two small pilasters, with integrated lecterns borne by the eagle of St John and the lion of St Mark. To one side is the richly-decorated Paschal **candlestick** (12C). Above, Christ sits in a mandorla supported by angels, holding the Gospels in his hand while, below, a figure in bishop's clothing kneels before him (possibly Roger II himself). Two tiers of birds (vultures pecking the tails of slender storks) support three figures representing the three ages of man.

Set against the back wall of the chapel is the majestic **royal throne**, which also forms an integral part of the mosaic above depicting Christ seated, attended by the Archangels St Michael and St Gabriel (representing death and birth respectively) and by the Apostles St Peter and St Paul. The actual throne is inlaid with mosaic and porphyry; the coat of arms in the centre is that of the House of Aragon.

The remarkable **wooden muqarnas ceiling**★★in the central nave, is a masterpiece by North African artists and depicts a number of scenes from daily life (unfortunately not visible to the naked eye): courtly and hunting scenes, drinking, dancing, games of chess, animals etc. This exceptional work of art comprises the most extensive cycle of Fatimid painting to have survived to the present day.

Mosaics – The exquisite mosaics comprise tesserae of coloured paste (cement and pigment) and glass with delicate gold leaf application. They recount the story of the Old Testament (nave) and the lives of Christ (chancel), St Peter and St Paul (aisles).

The mosaics were executed in two different phases: the oldest ones date from the 1140s, the ones in the nave date from the 1160s and 1170, and the sequence of scenes in the nave is didactic. Of particular note is the illustration of the earth being separated from the sea: the terrestrial globe is shown as a sphere of water in which there are three areas of land (America and Oceania had not yet been discovered). These are divided by sea, which takes the form of a Y – the symbol of the Holy Trinity; the firmament is not yet illuminated by stars. Look out also for the **Creation of Adam:** note the striking resemblance in the face of Adam with that of God, thereby underlining the inscription in Latin: *"creavit ds ominem at imaginem sua"* (And God created Man in His own image). The scene recounting the story of **Original Sin** is unusual, for both Adam and Eve are shown with the forbidden fruit in their mouths. The section that follows on from the second half of the panel illustrating the **Sacrifice of Cain and Abel** up to the scene showing Noah and his family was substantially remodelled in the 19C: this is evident from the radical change in style.

To read the Old Testament scenes in the nave, begin from the top of the right-hand side of the nave and follow the length of the top register along the left-hand side of the nave; continue with the second register, starting again on the right-hand side of the nave (⏱ *for an explanation of the lesser-known biblical*

Dreams of Palermo the Red

Many writers have dipped their pen into an inkwell with the intention of encapsulating the elusive spirit of Palermo or of using the city as the backdrop to their stories. Here is an excerpt from a Sicilian text by a writer who transforms Sicily into a dream, evoking images, smells and sounds through words that are sometimes lyrical, sometimes nostalgic and sometimes crude. "To Palermo the red, Palermo the child… Red, Palermo, which we might imagine the likes of Tyre or Sidon, perhaps Carthage, like the purple of the Phoenicians; of rich red earth, with springs of water where the palm grove rises tall and slender, creating sweet shade, bending with the wind, vibrant with the echo and nostalgia of an oasis, a green mosque, a carpet of comfort and prayer, image of the eternal garden of the Koran. A child because she is sleeping and still, content with her own beauty, having always had to be subservient to foreigners, obedient in particular to her mother, her own natural mother who locks her children in an eternal adolescence.

She settles down, relaxed and happy, in the gentle hollow of a shell…"

From *La Sicilia Passeggiata* (Strolling through Sicily) by Vincenzo Consolo.

stories, see the description of the mosaics in MONREALE).

In contrast, the iconography of the scenes in the **chancel** is modified for contemplation by the clergy and is therefore conducive to reflection. Thus scenes from the life of Christ are not arranged sequentially but in order of importance (note especially above the right-hand apse). The **cupola** above the choir contains the figure of Christ Pantocrator, flanked by the three Archangels (St Gabriel, St Michael and St Raphael) and Tobit, and four angels.

The Annunciation is represented above the graceful arch of the apse, placed there as a reminder of the Word of God that foretold Christ in Benediction (in the vault) and the enthroned Madonna, the Queen of Heaven.

In the **south transept**, pride of place is given to the figure of St Paul (apse vault) surrounded by scenes from the life of Christ. The story of the *Nativity* is particularly well related: the three kings are represented on their journey towards Bethlehem and the Christ Child. The Magi on the left wear Phrygian caps, a pointed hat with the top folded forward, to denote the fact that they come from the East.

Dominating the **north transept** is St Andrew (apse vault), who replaced the original mosaics of St Peter in the 14C; beside him is the Hodegetria Madonna and Child (Guide or Instructress pointing to the Way of Redemption based on an icon said to have been painted by St Luke). To one side, St John the Baptist preaches in the desert.

Royal Apartments★★

Guided tours only (30min), Mon, Fri and Sat, 8.30am–5pm, Sun and public holidays 8.30am–12.30pm. Groups by appointment only. ☎091 70 51 11 or 091 62 62 833; www.ars.sicilia.it.

The visit begins in the Salone d'Ercole (1560), now the chamber of the Sicilian Parliament, so called after the large frescoes by Giuseppe Velasquez (19C) depicting the *Twelve Labours of Heracles*. Today, only six panels are visible, namely (starting from the far end of the hall) Heracles and the giants, the slaying of the many-headed Hydra of Lerna, the capture of the Ceryneian hind, the taming of the three-headed dog Cerberus, the capture of the Erymanthean boar, and the Cretan Bull. The frescoed ceiling illustrates the birth, triumph and death of the hero.

Across the hall of the viceroys is a small entrance room that once constituted the heart of the **Joaria**, one of the Norman palace's original towers, now incorporated into other buildings. On the left is the **Sala di Ruggero II**, with decoration reminiscent of the Palatine Chapel. From the marble panelling, framed within friezes of mosaic, springs the golden mantle that covers the upper sections

CAPPELLA PALATINA

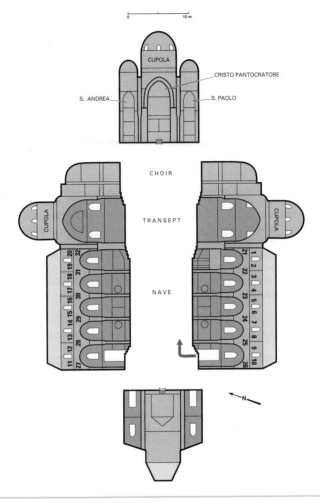

1 The creation of light and of the seas
2 The dry land separated from the waters
3 The creation of plants and trees
4 The creation of the sun, moon and stars
5 The creation of fish and birds
6 The creation of land animals
7 The creation of Adam
8 God resting from his labours
9 God pointing out the tree to Adam
10 The creation of Eve
11 Original sin
12 The shame of Adam and Eve
13 Paradise lost
14 Adam and Eve at work
15 The sacrifice of Cain and Abel
16 Cain kills Abel and lies to God
17 Lamech confesses to his two wives that he has killed two men
18 Enoch taken up to heaven on account of his deep faith
19 Noah with his wife and three sons
20 Building the Ark
21 Return of the dove
22 God tells Noah to leave the Ark
23 Noah planting a vineyard and getting drunk
24 Noah's descendants build the city of Babel
25 Abraham meets three angels and offers them hospitality
26 Lot on the threshold of his house tries to restrain the Sodomites
27 Destruction of Sodom, and Lot leaving the city
28 God tells Abraham to sacrifice Isaac, but an angel intervenes
29 Rebecca at the well and departure for Canaan
30 Isaac blessing Jacob
31 Jacob's dream
32 Jacob wrestling with the angel

of the wall and ceiling. Hunting scenes alternate with symbolic animals such as the peacock (for eternity, as it was alleged that its flesh didn't decompose) and the lion (for royalty and strength); all are portrayed in pairs, in accordance with an Eastern iconography. A number of other 18C and 19C rooms follow, including the Yellow Hall (or Hall of Mirrors).

Osservatorio Astronomico

Top floor of the Pisan Tower. Guided *tours daily 9.30am–11.30pm.* Closed *Sat–Sun, public hols and in Aug.* €3.50. *☎091 23 34 43; www.astropa.unipa.it.*
The **astronomical observatory** houses a museum of old instruments used in astronomy, meteorology, seismology and topography; visitors are able to relive the discovery of the first asteroid, on this spot, on 1 January 1801, by Father Piazzi. From the top, there is a fabulous bird's-eye **view**★★★ over Palermo.

Walking Tours

Unless otherwise stated, churches are open in the morning and late afternoon.

1 The Historic Quarter

For the Palazzo dei Normanni, see above.

Porta Nuova

Built under the Emperor Charles V, the gateway is topped by a Renaissance-style loggia. Beyond the gate, **Corso Vittorio Emanuele** stretches to **Porta Felice**.

Palazzo e Parco d'Orléans

This elegant house and garden, with its magnificent banyan tree, is where Louis Philippe d'Orléans, the future King of France, lived in exile from 1810–1814. Today, it is used as a municipal building by the Sicilian regional authorities.

San Giovanni degli Eremiti★★

Open 9am–7pm; Sun and public hols, *9am–1.30pm (last admission 30min before closing).* €6. *Cloisters open, but church closed for a programme of*

restoration in some of 2008. ☎091 65 15 019 ; *www.regione.sicilia.it/beniculturali/sopripa.*
The Church of **St John of the Hermits** and its garden are close to Palazzo dei Normanni, providing a haven of peace from the Palermo traffic.
In a luxuriant garden of palm trees, agaves, bougainvillea and orange trees stands the church that was built around the middle of the 12C at the request of King **Roger II**. This is one of the most famous Arabo-Norman monuments in Palermo. Its simple, square forms enclose spaces consisting of perfect cubes and rise to a red roof with five squat domes (echoing the profile of San Cataldo not far away), all clearly the work of Moorish craftsmen. The simple interior is shaped into a Latin-cross plan.
At one time, the church was flanked by its monastery. Today, only the delightful delicate 13C **cloisters**★ with their paired columns remain.

Villa Bonanno★

These lovely public gardens lie behind the Palazzo Reale (Norman Palace). Extensive excavations have revealed the **remains of Roman patrician houses** containing colourful mosaics that feature the seasons and Orpheus, now housed in the Museo Archeologico Regionale (see Histroic Centre, below).

Palazzo Sclafani

The front of the building (1330) overlooking Piazzetta San Giovanni Decollato is ornamented with fine Gothic two-light windows within interlacing arches, and an elegant cusped doorway. It is from this *palazzo* that the famous fresco *The Triumph of Death* was transferred to the Galleria Regionale di Sicilia.

Cattedrale★

Palermo's cathedral is an imposing edifice, built in the late 12C in the Sicilian-Norman style, with considerable alteration over the centuries. A notable addition from the 15C is the Catalan Gothic south porch with, on the outermost wall, the symbols of the four Evangelists (St Mark's lion and St Matthew's angel on the right, St Luke's ox and St John's eagle on the left). The neo-

Classical dome was added in the 18C, when the interior was also completely refurbished. The original fabric of the building, however, can still be seen in the **apses**★, which retain their distinctive geometric decoration. **Inside**, the first chapel on the right contains the tombs of members of the Swabian and Norman royal families: Frederick II, his wife Costanza of Aragon, Henry VI and, at the rear, Roger II and his daughter Costanza d'Altavilla.

Treasury and crypt
Access from the south transept.
🕐*Open Mon–Sat 7.30am–6.30pm; Sun and public hols 8am–1.30pm, 4pm–7pm.* ⊛*€2.* ☎*091 33 43 76; www.cattedrale. palermo.it.*
The **treasury** contains a fine carved ivory staff made in Sicily in the 17C, and jewels belonging to Queen Costanza of Aragon, including the magnificent **Imperial gold crown**★ set with precious stones, pearls and enamels. A number of tombs from different periods are preserved in the crypt, a large proportion belonging to former bishops. Note the Classical Roman sarcophagus decorated with the figures of the nine Muses, Apollo, and a seated man wearing a toga.

Chiesa del Santissimo Salvatore
The present oval-shaped Church of the Holy Saviour was designed in the late 17C by **Paolo Amato**. The interior is richly decorated in the Baroque style, and contains fragments of a fresco of the *Triumph of St Basil* (1763). Today, the church is used as an auditorium.
Farther along Corso Vittorio Emanuele is **Piazza Bologni:** among a series of fine 18C buildings sits the lovely **Palazzo Alliata di Villafranca**.

2 The Quattro Canti to the Alberghria

I "Quattro Canti"★★ (Piazza Vigliena)
The intersection of Palermo's two main thoroughfares, Via Vittorio Emanuele and Via Maqueda, is marked by a spacious octagon: the infilled corners of the square are furnished by four elegant 18C

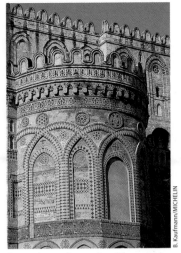

Decoration on the exterior of the apse of the cathedral

B. Kaufmann/MICHELIN

Baroque *palazzo* façades, their elevations subdivided into sections with Classical columns (Doric, Ionic and Corinthian). At the centre of each there is an elaborate fountain dedicated to the four seasons. The niches of the middle storey contain statues of the four Spanish kings of Sicily, those in the upper level contain effigies representing the patron saints of Palermo, who protected the districts lying behind them: St Christina, St Ninfa, St Oliva and St Agatha (who was subsequently replaced by St Rosalia).

San Matteo
The Church of St Matthew was built in the mid-17C. Its façade consists of three orders, the niches and projecting surfaces of which contrast to produce striking *chiaroscuro* effects. The richly decorated interior reflects the church's ties with the Unione dei Miseremini, founded with the aim of hearing masses for souls suffering in Purgatory. Works of art here include two canvases by P Novelli *(The Presentation at the Temple* and *The Marriage of the Virgin,* fourth chapel in the side aisle), the 18C frescoes in the vault and dome by Vito d'Anna, and the statue of *Faith and Justice* to the side of the presbytery and the lunette portraying *Christ Freeing Souls from the Flames of Purgatory* opposite, by Giacomo Serpotta. Serpotta himself is

One of the "Quattro Canti" in Piazza Vigliena

buried in the crypt of the church (access from the left aisle).

Piazza Pretoria★★

At the centre of this lovely piazza is a spectacular **fountain**★★ by the 16C Florentine sculptor Francesco Camilliani, originally intended as a garden ornament for some Tuscan villa and comprising concentric circles of gods and goddesses, nymphs, monsters, animals' heads, allegories, ornamental staircases and balustrades.

The top basin is divided into four sections; below each is a smaller bowl which, in turn, is overlooked by one of the four allegories of the rivers of Palermo: Gabriele, Maredolce, Papireto and Oreto. Among the statuettes guarding the ramps is Ceres, the Classical patroness of Sicily, who holds a sheaf of wheat and a horn of plenty.

The piazza is bounded by fine buildings: to one side the dome of **Santa Caterina;** on the south axis the **Palazzo Pretorio** (Palazzo Senatorio or Palazzo delle Aquile), the city hall. Across the road is the church of San Giuseppe ai Teatini.

Palazzo Pretorio

🕐*Open Mon–Sat, 9am–12pm.*
🚫*Closed Sun.* ☏*091 74 01 111.*

Concealed by the present austere exterior, the result of 19C renovations, lie the vestiges of a succession of earlier façades in various styles, the oldest of

which dates from the 1300s. Since then, it has been the seat of the City Council. Rooms open to the public include the **Sala dei Lapidi** lined with marble tablets bearing inscriptions and now used for Council meetings (note the magnificent central 17C chandelier carved from a single piece of wood), and **Sala Garibaldi**, named after the Italian hero who addressed the assembled crowds from the balcony in 1860. A glass case on the right contains a collection of weapons and scabbards inlaid with gold and mother-of-pearl that once belonged to Napoleon Bonaparte.

San Giuseppe ai Teatini

Piazza Pretoria is bordered by the side of this striking Baroque church. The most eye-catching element is the original campanile which rises to an octagonal section with spiral columns at the top. The theatrical **interior**★ in the form of a Latin cross is endowed with a majestic ceiling, white and gold stucco decoration and frescoes.

To either side of the entrance is one of a pair of impressive 18C **stoups**★ each consisting of an angel in flight with a basin in its arms.

Piazza Bellinia

This small square is contained by three churches: Santa Caterina (dating from the end of the 16C, with an 18C dome), la Martorana and San Cataldo which, with

G. Bludzin/MICHELIN

Fountain on Piazza Pretoria

its three red domes, endows the square with an Eastern flavour.

La Martorana★★

This church is named after Eloisa Martorana who founded the nearby Benedictine convent in 1194, to which the church served as a chapel.

The church, dedicated to **Santa Maria dell'Ammiraglio** (St Mary of the Admiral), was founded in 1143 at the request of George of Antioch, an admiral in

the fleet of Roger II. Mass is celebrated here according to the Greek Orthodox liturgy.

Interior

The building is divided into two parts. The first two bays, added in the 16C, were frescoed in the 17C; the older church shelters glorious **mosaics★★** of Byzantine iconography. The wall, which once constituted the main façade, has two mosaic panels representing George

La Martorana's Fruitful Nuns

Frutta martorana, also known as *pasta reale* (one of the most typical kinds of Sicilian *pasticcerie*), is named after the church of the same name. According to tradition, the origins of this delicacy can be traced back to medieval times when every convent specialised in making a different kind of confectionery. The ones made by the Benedictine convent of la Martorana in

early November for the feast day of All Saints, were of marzipan, shaped and coloured to resemble various fruits. The tradition continues today: during the Fiera dei Morti at the beginning of November the district between Via Spicuzza and Piazza Olivella is invaded by brightly coloured stalls selling *frutta martorana*, fruit made from sugar, along with children's toys.

Marzipan is also of medieval origin: the term is derived from the Arabic *mauthaban* which originally denoted a coin, then a unit of measurement and, finally, the container used to store the paste, made of almonds, sugar and white of egg.

Occultist and Traveller

Giuseppe Balsamo was born in Palermo in 1743. He became fascinated by occult science and founded a Masonic lodge; assuming the name **Count of Cagliostro**, he embarked upon his travels around Europe practising the "arts" of healing and magic with his miraculous "water of eternal youth." In France, he became involved in court intrigues which led to him being imprisoned in the Bastille. Following his return to Italy, fortune still refused to smile upon him and he was again arrested. This time, accused of belonging to the sect of the *Illuminati*, he was incarcerated in the fortress of San Leo, in the Montefeltro near Urbino. Here, he died in poverty, and his body was taken to the cemetery in Palermo. His house is located off Piazza Ballarò, in Via Cagliostro.

of Antioch at the feet of the Virgin *(on the left)* and Roger II receiving the crown from Christ *(on the right)*. Filling the nave dome is Christ Pantocrator surrounded by four Archangels. In the register below are eight Prophets and, in the pendentives, the four Evangelists. The nave vault holds the Nativity (on the left) and the Death (Dormition) of the Virgin (on the right).

San Cataldo★★

⏱ *Open 9.30am–1pm, 3.30pm–6.30pm; Sun 9.30am–1pm.* ⏱ *Closed public hols.* 💶 *€1.*

The church, the main seat of the Knights of the Holy Sepulchre, was built during the Norman period (12C). A distinctive Moorish quality is imparted by the combination of its severe square forms, crenellated walls, perforated window screens and characteristic bulbous red domes (likened by the Italians to a eunuch's hat).

Chiesa del Gesù di Casa Professa

When the Jesuits arrived in Sicily in the mid-16C, the Spanish government gave them its generous support. They founded their first church here, which was later sadly damaged during the Allied bombing of 1943.

Its sober façade contrasts with the Baroque exuberance of the interior, which is encrusted with stucco and *pietra dura* decoration. The **chancel decor**★ shows a euphoric display of cherubs holding flowers, torches, musical instruments, set squares, and lances with which they pierce devils.

The second chapel on the right has two paintings by **Pietro Novelli**: *St Philip of Agira* and **St Paul the Hermit**★; the last figure on the left is a self-portrait of the artist.

Next to the church stands **Casa Professa**; this houses the **municipal library** which contains a large number of incunabula and manuscripts.

Chiesa del Carmine

Piazza del Carmine, in front of the Church of Our Lady of Mount Carmel, is brought to life each day by the picturesque **Ballarò food market**. Before entering the church, admire the splendid tile-covered **dome** supported by four giant Atlas figures.

Inside the church, the most interesting features are the two sumptuous **altars**★ in the transepts, decorated with pairs of golden twisting columns on which spirals of stucco tell the story of the life of the Virgin Mary *(on the left)* and of Christ *(on the right)*. They are the work of Giacomo and Giuseppe Serpotta. Above the left-hand altar is a 15C canvas of *La Madonna del Carmine* (Our Lady of Mount Carmel).

▸ *Return to Via Maqueda. Palazzo Comitini stands on the left at the corner of the street (see Visit, below).*

Sant'Orsola

This 17C church was once the headquarters of the Compagnia dell'Orazione della Morte, an organisation that was responsible for burying the deceased of the district.

In the last chapel to the right, decorated by Serpotta, the usual rejoicing *putti* are replaced by skeletons and dangling bones.

Camera dello Scirocco di Palazzo Marchesi

From Piazzetta SS Quaranta Martiri, go into passageway no 14 (to the left of the tower), and from the courtyard take the staircase on the left. Ring the bell if the door is closed.
For information, call ☎091 58 45 65 (Assessorato al Centro Storico).
Donations welcome.

One of the oldest of the Palermo *scirocco* rooms is under the cloisters of the 15C **Palazzo Marchesi**, at a depth of 8m/26ft. An enormous Arabic cistern, once used for the city's water supply, has been found next to this room.

③ La Kalsa and Via Alloro

The Kalsa district, behind the port, was razed by Allied bombing raids in 1943, during which a large number of lives were lost and countless buildings destroyed. The ruins were thrown into the sea and, as a result, the Foro Italico now stands a little way from the seafront. This fascinating district is currently under major reconstruction, with the creation of new squares such as **Piazza Magione**, *palazzi* and monuments, and the opening of cultural centres such as the Chiesa dello Spasimo and Teatro Garibaldi breathing new life into the historic heart of Arabo-Norman Palermo. The focal point is Piazza della Kalsa, although the district itself stretches all the way to Corso Vittorio Emanuele, and contains a high proportion of the city's most interesting monuments.

The main entrance to the quarter is the **Porta dei Greci** beyond which lies the piazza and the church of **Santa Teresa alla Kalsa**, a monumental Baroque church built between 1686 and 1706 by **Paolo Amato**.

Turning onto Via Torremuzza, note the beautiful stone-framed Noviziato dei Crociferi at number 20 and, farther along on the opposite side of the street, **Santa Maria della Pietà** designed by Giacomo Amata.

Via Alloro

Throughout the Middle Ages, this served as the quarter's main street. Today, most of the elegant *palazzi* that once lined the thoroughfare have either been destroyed or have fallen into disrepair. The few surviving buildings include Palazzo Abatellis and, next to it, the lovely Chiesa della Gancia.

Palazzo Abatellis ★

This magnificent *palazzo*, built in Catalan-Gothic style with some Renaissance features, was designed by Matteo Carnelivari, who worked in Palermo towards the end of the 15C. Its elegant front has a great square central doorway ornamented with fasces (bundles of rods, an Ancient symbol of authority), and a series of two-and three-light windows. The *palazzo* is arranged around an attractive square courtyard and now houses the Galleria Regionale di Sicilia (see Historic Centre).

La Gancia

The church dedicated to **Santa Maria degli Angeli** was originally built by the Franciscans in the late 15C. The exterior retains from the original its square profile and rustication. On the side of the church flanking Via Alloro, note the *Buca della Salvezza:* this "Hole of Salvation" was made by two patriots who had hidden in the crypt of the church during the anti-Bourbon rebellion of 1860.

The **interior** ★ gives the impression of being Baroque although elements date from several different periods. The wooden ceiling painted with stars, the magnificent **organ** ★★ by Raffaele della Valle, the marble **pulpit** and Antonello Gagini's relief tondi of the *Annunciation (on either side of the altar)* date from the 16C. Most of the superficial decoration dates from the 17C and fine original details survive, including a **novice monk** ★ peeping out over a cornice in the chapel to the left of the altar.

▶ *Cross Piazza della Magione.*

Santa Maria dello Spasimo ★

The church and convent were built inside the walls of the Kalsa in 1506 and to mark the occasion **Raphael** was commissioned to paint a picture of the anguish of the Madonna before the Cross (now in the Prado in Madrid).

Building work on the church was not yet completed when the Turkish threat made it necessary to build a new bastion just behind the church. In turn the complex was transformed into a fortress, a theatre, a hospice for plague victims (1624) then, later, for the poor (1835) and finally a hospital; it was eventually abandoned in 1986. The church and old hospital have been transformed into venues for cultural events (the church houses the Scuola Europea di Music Jazz). The section around the 16C cloisters is accessible to the public. The **church**★ beyond is the only example of Northern Gothic architecture in Sicily; the slender nave reaches up towards the open sky without a roof and ends with a lovely polygonal **apse**, while the original entrance is given prominence by a *pronaos* with two side chapels. This, in turn, provides access to the old Spanish bastion, now laid out as a garden. The complex is particularly evocative as the sun sets.

La Magione

An attractive little avenue of palm trees leads up to the Romanesque church, which was founded in the 12C by Matteo d'Ajello, a prominent official in the service of the Norman sovereigns. In 1193, it was given to the Order of Teutonic Knights by Emperor Henry VI, in whose hands it remained for more than 300 years. The **front elevation**★ rises through three tiers of pointed arches, elegantly ornamented at the lower levels. The church has fine **cloisters** from the original Cistercian monastery. Vestiges of pre-existing constructions, including a 10C Arab tower, are visible from the cloisters.

Via della Magione runs along the side of **Palazzo Ajutamicristo**, an imposing building that was designed by **Matteo Carnelivari** in the 15C.

Piazza della Rivoluzione

This little square is where the anti-Bourbon rebellion of 1848 was ignited. In the centre is a fountain depicting a king feeding a serpent and symbolising the city.

▶ *Head back to Via Alloro. The walk continues with the monuments located to the north of Via Alloro.*

San Francesco d'Assisi★

Little of the original 13C church survives and its appearance owes much to delicate restoration respecting the original design. The front elevation includes the rose window and Gothic **portal**★ from the original 13C structure. Of note are eight statues by Giovanni Serpotta, and the entrance **doorway**★ to the Mastrantonio Chapel, by **Francesco Laurana** and **Pietro di Bonitate** *(fourth chapel on the left)*.

Oratorio di San Lorenzo★★★

⏰*Open Mon–Sat 9am–5pm.* ⏰*Closed Sun.* 💶€2.

This masterpiece created by a mature **Giacomo Serpotta** has been described as a "cave of white coral." On the walls, paintings alternating with statues of the Virtues illustrate scenes from the life of St Francis (to the right) and St Lawrence (to the left); the martyrdom of the latter is depicted opposite these works. Nude thinkers on the upper sections of the walls recall figures by Michelangelo. The lofty detachment of the Virtues and the veiled sadness of the nudes contrast with the triumph of the delightful rejoicing *putti*, depicted in the most imaginative poses (note the figure making a soap

Rich interior of Oratorio di San Lorenzo

© Andrea Jemolo/CORBIS

bubble and the two characters kissing each other tenderly). However, the innocent vitality of these figures is in contrast to the church's most notorious event, the 1969 theft of Caravaggio's *Nativity*, which above the altar of the church.

▶ *Keeping the Chiesa di San Francesco to your left, continue to Palazzo Mirto (see Visit, below).*

Piazza Marina

In the centre of this piazza at the heart of medieval Palermo, is an attractive garden, the **Giardino Garibaldi**, planted with magnificent **banyan trees**★★.

The piazza is enclosed by fine buildings: Palazzo Galletti (n° 46), Palazzo Notarbartolo (n° 51) and Palazzo Chiaramonte. Diametrically opposite this sits the lovely **Fontana del Garraffo**, (from the Arabic *gharraf*, meaning abundant water) which was constructed at the close of the 17C by G Vitaliano, to designs by Paolo Amato.

Palazzo Chiaramonte★

This splendid *palazzo* was built in 1307 for the Chiaramonte family, one of the wealthiest and most powerful dynasties of the Aragonese period. The building also came to be called **Lo Steri** from *Hosterium*, a fortified residence. It passed into the hands of the Spanish viceroys, and served as the headquarters of the Court of the Inquisition from the 17C until 1782, when the institution was abolished in Sicily.

The main front is ornamented by elegant two- and three-light **windows**★★ (note the fabulous stone inlays on the underside of the arches on the first floor). The style is so distinctive as to be described simply as Chiaramonte; this may be discerned in many other Sicilian civic buildings of the same period.

The Museo Internazionale delle Marionette is nearby (ⓘ *see Historic Centre*). Close by stands the monumental **Porta Felice** (1582), marking the eastern end of Via Vittorio Emanuele. The 17C **Loggiato di San Bartolomeo** can be seen close to the gate and is now a venue for exhibitions and cultural events.

The Foro Italica, the old **Passeggiata alla Marina**, starts at Porta Felice. From the 16C onwards this promenade, with its esplanade overlooking the sea, was a popular area for Palermo's elegant aristocracy to stroll, as well as the site of festivals and parades. A number of fine *palazzi* were built here, including the 18C **Palazzo Branciforti-Butera**. Nostalgia is evoked by the natural beauty of the setting and the neo-Classical bandstand (*immediately after the crossroads with Via Alloro*).

Passeggiata delle Cattive

Built in 1823 along the wall which marked the end of the Passeggiata alla Marina, this promenade owes its unusual name to the popular expression *"mura di li cattivi,"* which translates as the "wall of the wayward women." The walkway provided widows with more privacy (as well as a better view) than the promenade below. The splendid seafront façade of the Palazzo Branciforti-Butera can be admired from here.

④ **The Old Harbour to the Vucciria**

The *cala*, the city's ancient harbour, was once protected by the **Castellammare**, built by the Arabs, and later transformed into a fortress, prison and private residence. The massive construction was, however, damaged in 1922 when the jetty was extended. A description of the Cala quarter, which extends behind the old harbour, must begin with the church as this was where the chains that were used to close off the area were kept through the centuries, hence its dedication to Santa Maria della Catena.

Santa Maria della Catena★

⛔ *Closed for restoration.*

The design of the church is attributed to Matteo Carnelivari. Its elevation is dominated by the broad square portico with three arches; behind these are doorways set with low reliefs by Vincenzo Gagini. The overall style is transitional Gothic-Renaissance (1490) with a lovely interior articulated by blind arcading into square bays with pointed cross-arches. The second chapel on the right contains fragments of a frescoed Madonna and, on the altar, symbolic chains. The church is especially evocative at sunset, when the façade is dramatically set alight by the glowing colours of the setting sun.

Farther along the curve of the harbour lies Piazza Fonderia, with the historic **Vucciria** market (between Via Cassari and Piazza San Domenico) behind it.

San Domenico

🕐*Call ahead for admission times.* ☎*091 58 48 72; www.domenicani-palermo.it.*
An attractive **piazza** stretches before the church with a statue of the Madonna raised on a column at the centre of it.

The church was initiated in the 17C and completed a century later. The Baroque front elevation rises in three ordered tiers of Doric and Corinthian columns and square pilasters framing a statue of St Dominic. The spacious interior is divided into nave and aisles, with a side chapel off each bay.

A fine scheme of inlaid *pietra dura* decoration ornaments the fourth chapel on the right and the Chapel of the Rosary in the north transept. Adjacent to the church are lovely 14C **cloisters** with paired columns.

The neighbouring buildings accommodate the **Sicilian Historical Society** (Società Siciliana per la Storia Patria) which, in turn, has its own small **Museo del Risorgimento** containing mementoes of Garibaldi. From the windows of the museum, there is a splendid view of the cloisters of San Domenico.

Oratorio del Rosario di San Domenico★★★

🕐*Open 9am–1pm.* 🕐*Closed Sundays.* ☞*€2.50. For information call ☎091 60 90 308; www.campodivolo.it.*
The oratory is a treasury of stucco decoration by **Giacomo Serpotta**, who conferred a spontaneous playfulness to the antics of his sculptured cherubs.

The stucco provides frames for a series of paintings relating to the Joyful Mysteries of the Rosary *(left and rear walls)*, some of which are by **Pietro Novelli**, and the Sorrowful Mysteries of the Rosary *(right wall)*, which include a *Flagellation* by Matthias Stomer. Niches alternate with the paintings, containing allegories of the Virtues, a series of female figures remarkable for their poise. In some instances they are attended by *putti*; the statue of Meekness, for example, holding a dove, is flanked by a *putto* dressed in a monk's attire stretching a podgy little hand towards her.

In the large ovals above the paintings, Serpotta has depicted scenes from the Apocalypse of St John: note how the figure of the Devil writhes as he falls from heaven.

Above the altar dome, more cherubs hold up a great sheet. On the high altar itself, sits the splendid painting of the *Madonna of the Rosary* (1628) by Anthony Van Dyck. The ceiling, frescoed by Pietro Novelli, illustrates the *Coronation of the Virgin*.

© Francesco Tomasinelli/Tips Images

San Domenico with a statue of Madonna on a column

Stucco decoration in Oratorio del Rosario di Santa Cita: cherubs and the Battle of Lepanto

Santa Maria di Valverde
🕙*Open 9am–1pm.* ☎*091 33 27 79 (Parrocchia di San Mamiliano).*
An elegant marble portal by Pietro Amato (1691) leads into this small church. The **interior** is extravagantly decorated in the Baroque style using different types of marble, sculpted into soft drapery on the side altars.

Santa Cita
🕙*Open 9am–1pm. For afternoon admission times, call* ☎*091 33 27 79 and 091 60 90 308. If the chapel crypt is closed, contact the nuns in the nearby Istituto del Sacro Cuore.*
This church was badly damaged by the bombing raids in 1943, which destroyed its side aisles. Note the beautiful **marble chancel arch**★by Antonello Gagini in the presbytery: the Nativity and Dormition of the Virgin are represented inside the arch; Dominican saints can be seen in the pilaster panels on the arch, and portraits of St Thomas Aquinas and St Peter the Martyr grace the two medallion tondi, on the corners. In the eight coffers of the arch intrados are episodes of the life of St Zita. Also worthy of note is the beautiful **Cappella del Rosario** to the right of the presbytery, with its

delicate stuccowork and polychrome marquetry. Access to the **crypt** *(cripta della Cappella Lanza)*, decorated with different types of marble, is from the chapel to the left of the presbytery.

Oratorio del Rosario di Santa Cita★★★
Access from Via Valverde or Via da S. Cita.
🕙*Open Mon–Sat, 9am–1pm, Sundays on request to the Sisters of the Instituto del Sacro Cuore.* ☎*091 60 90 308 and 091 33 27 79; www.campodivolo.it.*
The oratory is a remarkable work by the leading Baroque decorator **Giacomo Serpotta**, who worked here between 1686 and 1718. A host of angels and cherubs are endowed with carefree expressions and realistic attitudes, intent on playing among themselves, climbing up onto the window frames, larking about with garlands of flowers, crying, sleeping, and hugging their knees deep in thought.
On the wall at the back of the nave a great drape hangs across the entire wall, supported by a struggling crowd of cherubs. A central panel depicts in relief the Battle of Lepanto; this is flanked by two emaciated youths, symbolising the horrors of war. All around the oratory,

even below the side windows, are panels depicting the Mysteries of the Rosary. On the left wall begin the series relating to the Joyful Mysteries: the Annunciation, Visitation, Nativity and Presentation at the Temple. On the right are the Sorrowful Mysteries: Jesus in the Garden at Gethsemane, the Flagellation, Crowning of Thorns, and Calvary. At the far end are a second series of Joyful Mysteries (*starting bottom left*): the Resurrection, Ascension, Descent of the Holy Spirit, and the Assumption of Mary. At the top, in the centre, the Crowning of Mary.

A little farther on, sits **San Giorgio dei Genovesi** (🕐*open during exhibitions only*) overlooking its own piazza: this is one of the rare expressions of the late Renaissance. Now de-consecrated, the former church now houses various temporary exhibitions.

In Via Cavour, is the **Prefettura**: a Venetian neo-Gothic building that was once known as the Villa Whitaker, having been erected by one of the 12 grandchildren of Ingham, the British Marsala magnate.

5 From Via Roma to the Capo Quarter

Via dell'Orologio, on the right just before Teatro Massimo on Via Maqueda, provides an unexpected view of one of Sant'Ignazio's two bell towers.

Sant'Ignazio all'Olivella

This fine Baroque church was initiated in the late 16C on the site where, according to tradition, the villa of the family of Santa Rosalia once stood. An interpretation of Olivella would confirm this: *Olim villa,* once a villa (was here).

Inside, an eye-catching inscription in bright red proclaims *jahvé* in the centre of the Gloria behind the altar. The first chapel on the right contains a great wealth of decorative inlay in the form of polychrome *pietra dura.*

Access to the Oratorio di San Filippo Neri (or Sant'Ignazio) is from the south transept only.

The small Museo Archeologico Regionale stands next door to the church (*see Visit below*).

Oratorio di San Filippo Neri

Access from the piazza or from Sant'Ignazio.

🕐*Open 9am–10am.* 🕐*Closed Sun and public holidays.* ☎*091 58 68 67.*

This was designed by the architect **Venanzio Marvuglia**. Inside, the stuccowork illustrates the Gloria: the attractive composition with the angel surrounded by groups of joyful cherubs in twos and threes, is recognised as the work of **Ignazio Marabitti**.

Liberty-Style – The Città Nuova and Beyond

Besides the ones described under Città Nuova (📖*opposite*), Palermo's best Liberty-style residences include **Palazzo Dato** with its pink external detailing on the corner of Via XX Settembre and Via XII Gennaio; Ernesto Basile's Villa **Favaloro Di Stefano** in Piazza Virgilio and the **Villino Ida** at 15 Via Siracusa, with its fine wrought-iron balcony and tiled frieze.

Another must, albeit in a completely different part of the city, is the **Villa Igiea** (*Salita Belmonte 43,* ☎*091 63 12 111*). This very large building is scenically positioned on the slopes of Monte Pellegrino. It began life as a nursing home for Igiea Florio (who suffered from tuberculosis), adapted from a preexisting neo-Gothic building to designs by Ernesto Basile for an exotically luxurious home. The dining room in particular, now the **Sala Basile** ★(*accessible by request and subsequent permission from the hotel staff, who are always very helpful*), was completely renovated: lovely wooden panelling was installed, and the interior decoration with beautiful female figures surrounded by delicate, long-stalked flowers was commissioned from Ettore de Maria Bergler, a well-known Liberty-style painter. On the walls of the corridor are photographs depicting illustrious guests who stayed here in the past, including many European kings and queens.

Grand Dame of Fame, Aristocracy and Intrigue

Grand Hotel et Des Palmes - This building came to prominence in the mid-1800s when used as a residence by Ben Ingham, the Englishman who played a key role in the history of Marsala. Soon converted into a hotel *(Via Roma 398, ☎091 58 39 33)*, it has provided hospitality to all the persons of note passing through the city: musicians (Wagner finished *Parsifal* here – his stool remains), painters (sketches by Guttuso and Fiume furnish one of the salons), writers, politicians past and present (President Andreotti for one), great names from the theatre world and countless numbers of aristocrats have silently passed through its corridors over the years. It has provided an objective context for important political occasions, newsworthy events, mysterious incidents linked to the world of *omertà* (tacit complicity demanded by the Mafia) and intrigues. It was here, in 1957, that a secret dinner was held for the top henchmen of the Italian and American Mafia; that a secret agent disappeared in mysterious circumstances, having fallen from the seventh floor straight through the skylight of the great hall of mirrors (before being immediately rushed "to hospital" by two equally mysterious figures on standby); it was here that, in 1933, the French writer Raymond Roussel ended his dissolute and tragic life by committing suicide (or overdosing on hallucinogenic drugs). Another strange story involves the Baron of Castelvetrano who lived hidden away in his suite on the first floor for more than half a century. This enforced exile was allegedly levied upon him for having killed a boy guilty of petty theft; the sentence was pronounced by the father of the unfortunate victim.

Oratorio di Santa Caterina d'Alessandria★

Via Monteleone 50.

Closed for restoration at the time of going to press. ☎091 87 28 047.

Although more static and less vigorous than work by his father Giacomo, this stuccowork by **Procopio Serpotta** elegantly portrays various scenes from the life of St Catherine, the protector of scholars, alongside allegories of the sciences: Rhetoric, Ethics, Geography and Astrology to the right; Dialectics, Physics, Geometry and Theology to the left and, under the beautiful triple-arched tribune of the entrance wall, Knowledge and Science. The ceiling is decorated with delicate foliage patterns.

▶ *Continue along Via Monteleone as far as the crossroads with Via Roma.*

Chiesa di Sant'Agostino

The splendid 13C St Augustine's was built at the request of the Chiaramonte and Sclafani families. The **front**★ is graced with an entrance decorated with duotone geometric and flower motifs, and a lovely rose window. The Gaginesque side entrance in Via Sant'Agostino is also worthy of note. The interior is dominated by Baroque alterations, including stuccoes by followers of the Serpotta School, signed on the shelf under the second statue on the right with Serpotta's mark, a lizard.

The heart of the quarter which lies farther along Via Sant'Agostino, is brought to life every morning by the busy market, the **mercato di Capo**.

▶ *To continue with the walk described below, take Via Porta Carini and then turn right into Via Mura di San Vito to Piazza Verdi.*

Città Nuova

At the beginning of the 19C, the city underwent a period of expansion. The wealthy merchant bourgeoisie chose the northwest side of the city to build fine residences lavishly decorated with wrought-iron work, glass and floral panels. The hub of high society shifted from Via Maqueda to its extension, which took the name of Via Ruggero Settimo and, a little farther on, **Via della Libertà**. Here they built the great temples of opera, two theatres – the Massimo and the Politeama – and a large number of modern *palazzi* scattered through the neighbouring streets. Even today, a walk along Via XX Settembre, Via Dante and Via Siracusa reveals a flavour of the splendour promoted by the wealthy upper-middle classes in the late 19C.

Teatro Massimo★

Guided tours of the theatre are available from 10am–3.30pm. ⓧClosed Mondays. ☞€3. ☎091 60 53 111; www.teatromassimo.it.

This opera house is one of the largest in Europe. The front of this imposing neo-Classical structure is composed of six columns and a broad triangular pediment, modelled on the *pronaos* of an ancient temple. Set back, a great dome rises from its high drum.

The initial design was completed by Giovan Battista Basile in 1875; building work was concluded by his son Ernesto, who took it upon himself to add the two small, distinctive Liberty-style kiosks in front of the theatre (the one on the right, built of wood and wrought iron, is known as the Vicari al Massimo Kiosk, while the one on the left, made of iron, is the Ribaudo Kiosk).

The **interior** is highly elegant. The ceiling of the auditorium is adorned with a magnificent gilded wheel, decorated with a representation of the Triumph of Opera.

Teatro Politeama

The Politeama Theatre, built in the same neo-Classical style, faces onto the Piazza Castelnuovo. Its façade is dominated by a quadriga of bronze horses.

Inside, it houses the Galleria d'Arte Moderna Empedocle Restivo (*See Modern City, below*).

The delightful Villa Malfitano (*See Modern City, below*) stands right at the end of Via Dante, which heads west starting from Piazza Castelnuovo.

At no 36 Viale Regina Margherita (*the street running across Via Dante near Villa Malfitano*) stands **Villino Florio**★, a magnificent house built for one of the most powerful families in 19C Sicily: the Florio. One of the finest examples of the Palermo Liberty style, it was designed by Ernesto Basile and originally surrounded by a garden.

Historic Centre

Galleria Regionale di Sicilia★★
Via Alloro 4.
ⓧ*Open Mon–Sat, 9am–1pm, also 2.30pm –7.30pm Tue–Fri. ☞€6. ☎091 62 30 011.*

The gallery's internal layout was completed in the 1950s by Carlo Scarpa, one of Italy's foremost contemporary interior designers. For each important work of art, the designer has created a

Teatro Politeama

G. Bludzin/MICHELIN

tailor-made solution in terms of support and background, using different materials and colours to display it in the best possible manner.

The gallery collects together sculptures and paintings from the medieval period. The first exhibit to draw attention on the ground floor is the magnificent fresco of the **Triumph of Death**★★★**(Room II)**, from the Palazzo Sclafani. The title probably refers to the 13th Tarot card as the cards, which were popular in the Middle Ages, were also known as *Trionfi* (Triumphs). The painting shows Death, astride a skeletal horse and armed with a bow and arrows, in the act of striking down men and women in the full flush of youth. On the left, a figure *(top)* gazes out from the picture; the brush in his right hand denoting a self-portrait of the unknown author of the picture.

The admirable **bust of Eleonora of Aragon**★★*(Room IV)*, with its gentle expression and delicate features, together with the bust of a young woman, are by the sculptor **Francesco Laurana** who worked in Sicily in the 15C. The gallery also has a fine **Madonna and Child**★ by **Antonello da Messina**. The first floor is entirely devoted to painting (with many works from the Sicilian School). Note the lovely portable Byzantine icon *(first room opposite the entrance)* with scenes from the life of Christ, and Antonello da Messina's gloriously peaceful **Annunciation**★★. In the room devoted to Flemish painting is the **Malvagna Triptych**★★(1510) by **Mabuse**, which shows the Virgin and Child surrounded by angels singing and playing instruments in a lavishly decorated frame, set against an equally fabulous landscape background.

Museo Archeologico Regionale★★

Piazza Olivella.

♿ ⏱ *Open daily 8.30am–1.45pm Tue–Fri also 3pm–6.45pm.* ⬤ *€6 (ticket with Palazzo Abatellis and Palazzo Mirto).* ☎ *091 61 16 805.*

The Regional Archaeological Museum is situated in the Olivella monastery which, with the adjoining Baroque church of **Sant'Ignazio all'Olivella** (⏺ *See above*) was founded in the 17C by the fathers

Bust of Eleonora of Aragon

of St Philip Neri. The museum contains a magnificent collection of artefacts recovered from Sicilian sites, in particular those from Selinunte.

Ground floor

The visit begins in **small cloisters**★ with a hexagonal fountain in the centre. At the back is a beautiful single-light window with a decorative surround. The portico shelters an assortment of Punic and Roman anchors. One small room, devoted to Phoenician art, displays two sarcophagi from 6C BC; another is dedicated to Egyptian and Punic finds, including the hieroglyphic inscription known as the **Palermo Stone** (the other three parts are in Cairo and London), which narrates 700 years of Egyptian history, and a Punic one recovered near Marsala harbour, bearing the figure of a priest before a perfume burner, worshipping the god Tanit.

Beyond are a series of rooms devoted to artefacts from **Selinunte**. The first displays the twin stelae formed by pairs of busts representing the gods of the Underworld, both in shallow relief and in the round. This leads into the Sala Gabrici *(interactive information terminals)* which contains a reconstruction of the front elevation of Temple C and a selection of the original triglyphs. Sala Marconi has various lion masks with waterspouts from the Temple of Victory at Himera. The exhibits in the following larger room are principally from Selinunte, including the range of marvellous **metopes**★★ dating from

575 BC. As these are the only sculptures of their kind to have been discovered in the region, experts believe that there may have been a sculpture school in the city. Some of the metopes represent the gods worshipped in Selinunte, such as the Apollonian triad (Apollo, Artemis and their mother Latona), Demeter and Persephone. The oldest (smaller) artefacts, notably from a 6C BC Archaic temple, are displayed below the window on the right: one fragment depicts the Rape of Europa by Zeus in the guise of a bull.

On the left are three more marvellous metopes from Temple C (6C BC), brightened by traces of colour on the bodies and clothes. The high relief, which in places verges on being in the round, shows Perseus severing the head of Medusa while Pegasus, the winged horse, springs form her breast; above is Athena with the four-horse chariot of the sun god Apollo to the left and Heracles capturing the Cercopi.

Against the back wall are four metopes from Temple E: these are considered to be the finest in terms of their expressiveness. Starting from the left, they show Heracles fighting with an Amazon, Hera before Zeus, Actaeon being transformed into a stag and Athena fighting the giant Enceladus. The four rooms filled with Etruscan finds contain some fine cinerary urns and *bucchero* ware.

First floor

Among the various **bronzes** from the Greek, Roman and Punic periods, are a couple of superb ones: **Heracles catching the stag**★ and the lifelike bronze **Ram**★★, a Hellenistic work from Syracuse. This masterpiece, dating from the 3C BC, was originally part of a pair that adorned the tyrants' palace on the island of Ortygia.

The following room displays a number of small marble statues that include a fine **Satyr**★, a Roman copy of an original by the sculptor, Praxiteles.

Second floor

On this floor are the museum's prehistoric collections and a selection of its finest Greek vases, Roman mosaics and frescoes. The room with the mosaics

includes panels illustrating **Orpheus with the animals**★ (3C AD), the seasons, and representations of allegories and myths associated with the cult of Dionysus found in Palermo.

Museo Internazionale delle Marionette★★

Via Nixcemi 1.

🕐 *Open daily 9am–1pm, Mon–Fri 3.30pm–6.30pm also.* 🕐 *Closed public hols.* ✆€5. ☎091 32 80 60; www.museo marionettepalermo.it.

The International Puppet Museum contains a rich collection of pupi (Sicilian puppets based on characters from the French *chansons de geste*), marionettes (articulated puppets operated with strings), shadow puppets, scenery and panels from all over the world. The first rooms are devoted to Sicilian puppets, many presented "on stage." Notice, in particular, the delicate facial features of Gaspare Canino's theatre puppets (19C). The second section presents the European tradition, including such renowned figures as the English *Punch and Judy,* and a vast Oriental collection: Chinese glove-puppets; string-puppets from India, Burma, Vietnam, Thailand and Africa; shadow puppets from Turkey, India and Malaysia (made of leather). All the caricatures are evocatively displayed in semi-darkness (for preservation purposes) as if to suggest the remoteness of their origins. The final section is dedicated to special puppets destined for a violent, spectacular death. The museum also has a theatre (*performance details available from the museum*). The walls are hung with decorative puppeteers' posters, used by storytellers to illustrate their stories.

Palazzo Mirto★

Via Merlo 2.

🕐*Open 9am–6.30pm (1pm Sun and public hols).* ✆€3. ☎091 61 67 541; www. regionesiciliana.it.

The *palazzo* that provides the princes of Lanzi Filangeri with a residence has been altered several times to meet the family's needs. Its current form dates from the late 18C. Just inside, on the left, are the magnificent **stables**★(19C) complete with stalls and ornamen-

Gardens at Villa Malfitano

tal bronze horse-heads. A red marble staircase leads up to the first floor which is still furnished in the main with original pieces. Among the rooms open to the public there is the **Chinese sitting room**★ with its leather-covered floor, painted silk walls depicting scenes from everyday life, and fine *trompe l'oeil* ceiling: this was used as an intimate smoking room or for playing cards. The next room, a small vestibule, contains a good set of 19C Neapolitan plates decorated with people in costume; it is said that the service was used for masked balls and that each guest would sit in front of the plate featuring their particular costume. Another unusual **smoking room**★ leads from the vestibule, panelled with painted and embossed leather, a suitable material as it does not become impregnated with smoke.

The most striking elements of the **Pompadour sitting room**★ are the beautiful wall silks embroidered with flowers. The mosaic floor is the only original one.

The dining room contains a Meissen service (18C) exquisitely painted with flowers and birds.

Palazzo Comitini

Via Maqueda 100.

&. Open 9.30am–1.30pm (also 3pm–5pm Thu). Closed Sat–Sun and public hols. ☎091 66 28 260; Fax 091 66 28 254. The *palazzo* (1768–71), built for the Prince of Gravina, incorporates two older ones belonging to the Roccafiorita-Bon-

anno and Gravina di Palagonia families. The front has two large entrances and nine openings (now windows) on the ground floor, and a series of bulbous balconies (evocatively described in Italian as a *petto d'oca*, which translates as "goose breasted"), on the first floor. The building was radically altered in 1931 with the addition of another floor for use as the administrative offices for the Province of Palermo. A wide staircase leads up from the internal courtyard to the loggia on the first floor and the Sala delle Armi (Armoury), now the Salone dei Commessi: the two masks flanking the doorway served as torch extinguishers. Off to the left is the Green Room, furnished with a fine 18C Murano glass lamp. **Sala Martorana**★, now the seat of the Provincial Council, is lined throughout with 18C wood panelling inlayed with mirrors; these add luminosity to the room and enhance the impact of the ceiling which is frescoed with *The Triumph of True Love*.

Modern City

Villa Malfitano★★

Via Dante.

Guided tours tours only (30min), 9am–1pm. Closed Sun, public hols. €3. ☎091 68 20 522.

The Liberty-style Villa Malfitano, contained within its glorious **garden**★★, was begun in 1886 by **Joseph Whitaker**,

Green Havens of Palermo

The parks around Palermo in the time of the Arabs and the Normans covered great areas of land. The one lying west of the city, known as the **Genoard** or the Paradise on Earth, was chosen by the sovereigns as an apt place for a summer residence or a pleasure palace in the Oriental sense of the word: a peaceful haven set among gardens of exotic plants, with pools containing fish, watercourses and even wild animals from distant lands. Such were the dreams that inspired the building of the city's many parks, which included **la Zisa** and the much-restored **Scibene Castle**, which is still visible from Viale Tasca Lanza *(from Via Pitrè, the continuation of Via Cappuccini, turn right after passing Viale Regione Siciliana)*. Also of importance were the **Cuba Sottana** and **Cuba Soprana**, now part of the crumbling Villa Napoli complex (a few arches are just visible; *entrance at Corso Calatafimi 575)*. In the latter stands **la Cubola**, a small, square pavilion surmounted by the characteristic bulbous red dome, which is accessible from Via Zancla *(heading towards the centre, cross Corso Calatafimi to your left, and Viale Regione Siciliana shortly after)*.

This passion for gardens has continued over the centuries, so that the city now has many havens of peace, planted with a host of exotic plants and trees. These veritable corners of paradise are ideal for relaxing or strolling amid the greenery: the exotic garden of San Giovanni degli Eremiti, Villa Bonanno, Villa Giulia, the Botanical Gardens, Villa Malfitano, Villa Trabia, Giardino Garibaldi in Piazza Marina, or the beautiful **English Garden**, extremely well kept, with an enormous number of palms, cactuses, parasol (maritime) pines and banyans, where walking is a sheer delight.

a grandson of **Ingham**, the English gentleman-cum-wine-merchant who came to live in Sicily in 1806 and built himself a commercial empire out of a Marsala wine business. In contrast to his grandfather, Joseph was fascinated by ornithology and archaeology: to satisfy his interests he travelled to Tunisia, where he studied the birds, and initiated a programme of excavation on the island of Mozia which he had purchased *(see MOZIA)*. Another of his passions was botany: he arranged to have trees sent from all over the world to plant them around his villa; these gardens soon comprised of rare and exotic species: palm trees, Dragon's Blood trees, the only example in Europe of *Araucaria Rouler* and an enormous banyan tree. The villa soon became one of the main points of reference for high society at that time. Lavish parties were held there and important guests, such as the reigning monarchs of Great Britain and Italy, were received and entertained.

The internal furnishings are exquisite: a profusion of Oriental items include a pair of *cloisonné* elephants from the Royal Palace in Beijing, and a pair of wading-birds riding on the back of a turtle, symbolising the four elements. Also notable is the *Safari in Tunisia* by Lo Jacono and the pastel portrait of Joseph's daughters by Ettore de Maria Bergler above the lovely spiral staircase leading up to the first floor.

The real highlight of the Whitaker house, however, is the **decoration** conceived by the same artist for the **Sala d'Estate** (Summer Room): this consists of a *trompe l'oeil* composition covering the entire room (walls and ceiling), transforming the enclosed space into a cool veranda surrounded by vegetation.

Galleria d'Arte Moderna Empedocle Restivo ★

Via Turati 10.

🕐*Open 9am–8pm (1pm Sun and public hols).* 🎫€5. ☎*091 58 89 51; www.comune palermo.it.*

The Empedocle Restivo Gallery of Modern Art is contained within an elegant Liberty-style interior. The collection comprises a prized selection of 19C and 20C paintings and sculptures by Sicilian artists and a few foreign artists.

The sculptures include a delightful *Faun* by **Trentacoste**, a marble figurine of Classical proportions, coiled upon itself like a spiral ready to burst free.

Sicilian 19C art developed in different directions while simultaneously giving rise to a new generation of concepts.

The great themes tackled often revolved around psychological introspection, interspersed with neo-Classical composure, history and landscape.

This period gave rise to portraits by Patania, such as his *Study of a Sick Priest* in which the man's suffering is rendered with piercing realism, and those by Salvatore Lo Forte, who imparted such strength of character to his subjects. This was also the age of patriotism, encapsulated by Erulo Eruli in *The Sicilian Vespers*.

Different trends may also be detected in the style and expression of the various landscape painters represented: Lo Jacono's realism *(Wind in the Mountains)* becomes loaded with feeling in the works of A Leto who painted "impressions" by dabbing strong, warm colours onto his canvas (three studies for *The Rope-makers)*; Michele Catti absorbed all the tenets of Impressionism before painting his hazy landscapes with horizons lost in infinity, as in *Last Leaves*. Onofrio Tomaselli *(The Carusi)* adds a note of compassion (in the sense of the Latin word, implying a sharing of pain) with his bold use of warm colours. A few works both from the Italian and other foreign schools exemplify the new trends that emerged at the close of the 19C and the beginning of the 20C: Expressionism in the *Nativity* by Lienz, Symbolism in the works of Von Stuck (The Sin), and Pointillism in Terzi's *Summer Morning*.

The last few rooms show paintings and sculptures from the 1930s and a selection from the years following the Second World War.

Albero di Falcone

At the beginning of Via Notarbartolo (which intersects with Viale della Libertà just beyond the English Garden), on the right heading towards the ring road.

"Falcone's Tree" stands outside the house of Giovanni Falcone, the judge who was killed by a Mafia bomb in 1992. Since his death, the tree appears to have become a shrine in its own right: messages, photographs and offerings bear witness to the people's esteem and affection for Falcone and for Borsellino, another Mafia victim.

Museo della Fondazione Mormino

Viale della Libertà 52.
🕐 *Open daily, 9am–1pm, 3pm–5pm.*
🕐 *Closed Sun and public hols.* 🎟€4.
☎ *091 60 85 972; www.fondazioneban codisicilia.it.*

The Mormino Foundation Museum is housed on the first floor of the Banco di Sicilia (Villa Zito) and displays art work, original creations and recovered artefacts acquired over the years by the Banco di Sicilia. The first rooms are devoted to artefacts recovered during the excavations of Selinunte, Himera, Solunto and Terravecchia di Cuti, a small town farther inland where a village from the 6C-5C BC was unearthed. A second section displays maiolica from Sicily and from the rest of Italy (with a few examples from Turkey and China). The third section is devoted to 13C-19C coins and medals.

On the ground floor is the bank's philatelic collection with stamps dating from the era of the Kingdom of the Two Sicilies.

Villa Trabia

Via Salinas. Take Via Latini, which then becomes Via Cusmano, as far as Piazza D. Siculo; Via Salinas is one of the streets leading off this square.

A wonderful garden surrounds the villa, built in the 18C and bought the following year by Giuseppe Lanza Branciforte, prince of Trabia and Butera. The building, now used as municipal offices, has a splendid entrance reached by a monumental staircase.

Beyond the City Gates

Catacombe dei Cappuccini ★★
Via Cappuccini.
🕐 *Open 9am–12pm, 3pm–5pm (5pm winter).* 🎟€1.50. ☎*091 21 21 17.*

The Capuchin Catacombs consist of a maze of corridors containing thousands of mummified bodies, contorted in expression and posture, perfectly dressed, appended (as if they had been hanged, with a rope around the neck) to the walls, in niches or propped up against the wall. The overwhelming

La Zisa

sense of tragedy, which never fails to touch visitors, is heightened by the fact that these figures are shut away behind railings. The catacombs contain the remains of almost 8 000 Capuchin friars (the oldest corpses date from the late 16C), as well as those of illustrious or wealthy Palermitani, children and virgins, each category having been allotted its own special area. What is extraordinary is the condition of the corpses, preserved intact by the special environmental conditions causing gradual desiccation. In especially good condition is the body of a little two-year old girl who died in 1920; she is so well preserved that she seems merely asleep; her body was injected with a concoction of chemicals (the doctor who administered them died without revealing his secret potion).

In the cemetery adjacent to the Capuchin monastery is the tomb of Giuseppe Tomasi di Lampedusa, author of *The Leopard,* who died in 1957 *(third avenue on the left).*

La Cuba★

Corso Calatafimi 100.

&. ⏱ *Open summer, 9am–7pm; otherwise, 9am–6.30pm; Sun and public hols, 9am–1pm.* ✆€2. ☎091 52 02 99.

The Cuba Sottana, now incorporated into military barracks, was probably surrounded by a vast artificial lake known as the Pescheria (fishpond). In the old stables, just inside the entrance on the

right, is a model reconstruction of how the palace must have looked originally. On the wall, the Kufic inscription celebrates the completion of the building, confirming that it was erected in 1180 at the request of William II. The decoration of the building is exquisitely simple: above a series of tall pointed arches of differing widths are various other smaller openings. The internal space was divided into three parts; in the central section there is a star-shaped pool from which water would trickle gently into the Pescheria without breaking the surface and disturbing the reflections of the building and garden.

La Zisa★

Piazza Guglielmo il Buono.

&.⏱*Open Mar–Oct, 9am–7.30pm (2pm Sun and public hols).* ✆€3. ☎091 65 20 269; www.regione.sicilia.it/beniculturali/ The name is derived from El Aziz, meaning the splendid or noble one. Today, sadly, only the shell of the palace remains, yet this retains an undeniable aura. It was initiated by William I and completed by his son William II between 1166 and 1175; work on the building was entrusted entirely to Moorish craftsmen. In the 14C, after a period of neglect, it was transformed into a fortress, then into a depository for objects contaminated by the plague (16C), before being converted into a *palazzo* for a noble family; recent restoration has endeavoured to return it to its original state.

Tour

The main attraction on the ground floor is the room with the fountain: built on a cruciform plan, the room has two square pools that collect water from the main channel in the centre of the room, fed from a waterspout. The upper section of the walls has a mosaic frieze of peacocks and arches. From here there is a succession of rooms, each with a ventilation system so cool air could circulate through gaps in the walls.

The niches and windows have *muqarnas*, a honeycomb of miniature vaults and stalactite pendants characteristic of Islamic architecture.

The *palazzo* houses a collection of objects, mainly from Egypt (from the Mameluke and Ottoman periods), that typify the style of furnishings that might once have adorned the original palace. The 15C *mushrabiyya*, a perforated wooden screen placed in front of doors and windows as protection against excessive heat and light, is particularly fine.

Albergo delle Povere

Corso Calatafimi 217.
🕐*Open to the public during exhibitions and conferences.*

This complex was originally intended at the end of the 18C as a hospice for the poor of the city; in the 19C, it was reserved for spinsters who set up a weaving workshop there; it is now used for temporary exhibitions and conferences.

The left wing still shelters Opera Pia, a charity providing assistance to the poor; the right wing serves as operational headquarters for the exclusive carabinieri hit-squad unit charged with protecting Sicily's artistic heritage.

If you get the chance, take up position at one end of the semicircular wall enclosing the fountain and get someone else to stand at the other end; a mere whisper will carry from one side to the other. Who needs a mobile phone?

Orto Botanico★

Via Lincoln 38.
🕐*Open Jun–Aug 9am–8pm, May and Sept 9am–7pm, Oct–Apr 9am–6pm.*
🕐*Closed public hols.* ✏€4. ☎091 62 38 111; www.ortobotanico.palermo.it.

The Botanical Gardens have occupied their present site since 1789 and contain a huge range of species, including Oriental and exotic plants, such as the majestic Dendrocalamus giganteus or the incredible **banyan tree**★★*(Ficus magnoloides).* There are various South American plants such as *Chorisias* and *Bombacaceae*, brought to Palermo in the 19C, whose thick, hairy seed covering was once used like horsehair.

Ponte dell'Ammiraglio

Corso dei Mille.
The picturesque medieval bridge once straddled the River Oreto. It was built in 1113 by George of Antioch, an admiral serving under **Roger II**.

San Giovanni dei Lebbrosi★

Via Cappello (a road left off Corso dei Mille, beyond the Ponte dell'Ammiraglio).
St John of the Lepers may be the oldest Norman church in Sicily. The church was supposedly founded in 1070 (although some say it may have been a century later).

Chiesa di Santo Spirito or dei Vespri

Inside the cemetery of Santa Orsola, in Piazza di Santa Orsola (from Piazzetta Montalto take Via Colomba and then turn right into Via dei Vespri).
The Church of the Holy Spirit or of the Vespers was built in 1178 during the reign of Roger II. It came to fame on 31 March 1282 when, during Evensong (Vespers), a French soldier insulted a Sicilian woman, provoking the bystanders to jump to her defence and so providing a pretext for an outburst of growing resentment towards the invaders from beyond the Alps. The incident sparked off the War of the Sicilian Vespers which, in turn, led to the eviction of the French from the island.

Santuario di Santa Maria di Gesù

Follow Viale della Regione Siciliana to the intersection with Via Oreto (the southern extension of Via Maqueda). Turn right along Via Santa Maria di Gesù (look out for the green sign above the shoe shop on the corner). *Open daily, 8am–12.30pm.* ☎*091 44 51 95.*

The 15C Sanctuary of St Mary of Jesus occupies a serene and cool spot on the slopes of Monte Grifone. The way to it leads through a cemetery where, traditionally, aristocratic families kept their mausoleums. The area in front of the church is surrounded by fine patrician tombs mainly from the 19C or the beginning of the 20C, including the Liberty-style chapel belonging to the princes of Lanza di Scalea. **Inside**, the chancel has two bays articulated by pointed arches; Antonio Alliata's marble sarcophagus is attributed to Antonello Gagini (in the chancel, high up on the right); there is a rare **wooden statue of the Virgin**★(1470); and a fine coffered wooden **ceiling**, painted with flowers and angels (early 16C), spans the church entrance and the organ above it, painted with scenes from the life of St Francis (1932).

Parco della Favorita
3km/1.8mi N. Follow Viale della Libertà to Piazza Vittorio Veneto. Turn right into Piazza dei Leoni; Viale del Fante runs by the park as far as the Chinese palace.

The parkland at the foot of Monte Pellegrino was created in 1799 by Ferdinand III of Bourbon, when the Napoleonic troops drove him out of Naples (where he had reigned as Ferdinand IV). It was donated to the king by noble Palermo families and became his private hunting estate; he had a house built there, the **Chinese palace**. The servants' quarters lay in the building next door, arranged around a courtyard facing the kitchens (connected to the palace by an underground passageway); now the Museo Etnografico G Pitré.

Museo Etnografico Pitré
Viale Duca degli Abruzzi 1, Parco della Favorita.
♿*Open 9am–8pm.* *Closed Fridays, 1 Jan and 25 Dec.* *€5.* ☎*091 74 04 890.*
The Pité Ethnographic Museum houses artefacts associated with local folklore; reconstructions of houses containing tools, needlework and embroidery, fabrics, a 17C wrought-iron bedhead, pottery, "Sunday-best" clothes, splen-

did engraved horn goblets and gourd containers for water or wine. Amulets and trinkets linked with magic and superstition, together with handmade votive objects, testify to the strong faith of the country people. The museum also has a library (*Open mornings only*) of books about popular traditions in Sicily and beyond.

Villa Niscemi★
Piazza Niscemi, at the end of Viale del Fante.
Open 9am–dusk (gardens); Sun only, 9am–1pm (villa). *Donations welcome.* ☎*091 74 04 801.*
Next to the Parco della Favorita stand the gardens and beautiful country villa that once belonged to the princes Valguarnera di Niscemi. Bought by the local authorities in 1987 and now used as their headquarters, the villa has several frescoed rooms decorated with 18C furnishings. One of the most attractive is the Salone delle Quattro Stagioni with a fresco of Charlemagne depicted on the Valguarnera coat of arms.

Driving Tour

Inland From Palermo
120km/75mi – allow one day.

This day trip combining archaeology, art and natural landscapes passes through verdant scenery that is almost Alpine in places.

▶ *From Viale Regione Siciliana, take the Calatafimi-Monreale exit and follow S 186 to Monreale (8km/5mi).*

Monreale★★★ See MONREALE

▶ *Return to S 186.*

After Pioppo and the turn off to San Giuseppe Jato, there is a magnificent **view**★of Palermo and the sea.

▶ *After Giacalone, turn left onto S 624 (the Palermo-Sciacca road). Turn off this road at San Cipirello (25km/16mi) and take the road to*

Corleone and Tagliavia. A turning on the left farther on is marked with yellow signs for Scavi del Monte Jato. The road winds uphill for 5km/3mi. The final dirt track section must be undertaken on foot.

Scavi del Monte Jato

🕐*Open 9am–dusk, Sun and public holidays 9am–12pm.* 🕐*Closed Mon.* ☎091 85 72 976.

Founded by the Elimi (or the Sicani) as early as the 1st millennium BC, Jetae enjoyed its period of greatest splendour in the 3C BC.

On the west side of the **agora** or market place (300 BC) stand a portico and a *bouleuterion*, a council chamber where the orator would stand between the two doorways to address the assembly. West of the agora is the **theatre** (late 4C-early 3C BC), which was able to accommodate an audience of 4 400. The **house** with the peristyle was built over two storeys, around a porticoed courtyard; the north side is distinctively arranged with three reception rooms. The position of the doorways, offset from the central axis (so as to accommodate the couches they used when eating), implies they were banqueting rooms. One preserves its original *opus signinum* floor with the inlaid inscription of thanks and farewell that a departing guest might give after a meal or a banquet. The **Temple of Aphrodite** *(opposite the south side of the house, on the far side of the paved street)*, erected in about 550 BC in Greek style, bears witness to the earliest cultural exchanges between the indigenous population and the Greek world.

Museo Civico di San Cipirello

San Cipirello, Via Roma 320.

♿🕐*Open daily, 9am–1pm, Tue, Thu and Sat 3pm–7pm also.* 🕐*Closed 25 Dec.* ☎091 85 73 083.

This municipal museum displays the artefacts recovered from the archaeological excavations at Monte Jato, including sculptures from the theatre: maenads and satyrs, followers of Diony-

The Albanian Community in Sicily

Towards the middle of the 15C, the area occupied by the Balkans was invaded by the Turks. Many inhabitants emigrated, some settled in Molise and Apulia. A century later, an Albanian *condottiere* (mercenary) was summoned by Alfonso of Aragon to contain a spate of revolts thereabouts: the soldiers then stayed in southern Italy, particularly in Calabria, before trickling through into Sicily over the ensuing years, and arriving at **Piana degli Albanesi**. Here they were welcomed with open arms and obtained permission to continue practising their faith in accordance with the Greek Orthodox Church. The Church granted them ever-greater administrative and religious autonomy, enabling them to maintain their traditions, language and literature. One of their most important communities is centred around Piana degli Albanesi and, although completely integrated within the local population, the Albanians retain their own ancient traditions, especially during religious festivals. Two of the most important festivals are Epiphany (12 days after Christmas) and Easter, when the locals don their most splendid costumes, typically embroidered with gold and silver, before pouring out onto the main street, Corso Giorgio Kastriota, and rallying before the churches of Santa Maria Odigitria, nearby San Giorgio (actually in Via Barbato) and San Demetrio, the town's main church. Outward signs of their heritage are evident at all times in the local dialect they speak and in the Greek Orthodox masses they celebrate; even the road signs and street names are inscribed in two languages. The town itself has another name, *Hora*, meaning the town.

Although there are no actual Albanian specialities as such to have gained popularity in Sicily, at least one typical Palermo sweetmeat is said to be of Albanian origin. It is the *gelu i muluni* which consists of watermelon sweetened with sugar and thickened, pieces of chocolate, candied pumpkin, pistachio nuts, cinnamon and vanilla, and served with ice cream.

G. Iacono/MICHELIN

Palazzo Reale with Rocca Busambra in the background

sus, god of the theatre (and wine), and a crouching lion.

▶ *Follow S 624 towards Palermo and take the turn-off to Piana degli Albanesi.*

The road affords magnificent views of the valley as it climbs up to **Portella della Ginestra**, where a monument marks a massacre perpetrated by the bandit Salvatore Giuliano in 1947, before descending to **Piana degli Albanesi** *(12km/7.5mi).*

▶ *From Piana degli Albanesi follow signs to Ficuzza (20km/12.5mi S). The winding road leads upwards and offers splendid views of the town and man-made lake.*

Palazzo Reale and Bosco della Ficuzza

For information on opening times, call ☎091 84 60 108. For information on trips into the forest, contact the Centro di Recupero della Fauna Selvatica (same opening times as the palace), ☎091 84 60 107.

The village of Ficuzza is arranged around the piazza in front of this **hunting lodge** built for Ferdinando III of Bourbon in the 19C. The limestone walls of Rocca Busambra (1 613m/5 290ft) are an impressive backdrop to the striking neo-Classical building.

To the right, the **Centro di Recupero della Fauna selvatica di Ficuzza**

(Ficuzza Wildlife Protection Centre) provides information on local fauna.

▶ *A road to the left of the palace leads into the woods and is the starting-point for a number of excursions.*

The **Bosco della Ficuzza**, once a royal hunting ground, is a plateau covering approximately 7 000ha/17 300 acres of land dominated by Rocca Busambra. The forest comprises mainly holm oak, maple, oak and cork oak, while its rich fauna includes porcupines, martens, hedgehogs, tortoises, golden eagles and peregrine falcons.

▶ *From Ficuzza, return to the main road and head towards Godrano and Cefala Diana (17km/10.5mi E).*

Cefalà Diana

The town deserves a visit even if solely on account of its 10C **Turkish baths**, the only example of its kind in Sicily. The expressive bronze sculptures in the main piazza are by a contemporary artist from Corleone, Biagio Governali and are also notable.

The baths

Open daily, 9.30am–1pm. Closed public holidays. ☎091 82 01 184.
The baths are located just over 1km/0.6mi outside the town, by the River Cefala within a restored complex. The original complex of baths, built sometime pre-1570, was used to relieve

Palermo Outskirts Address Book

🔥 *For coin ranges, see the cover flap.*

WHERE TO EAT

BEYOND THE CITY GATES

🍽 **Pizzeria Tonnara Florio** – *Discesa Tonnara 4, Arenella district – ☎091 63 75 611 – www.tonnaraflorio.it – Closed Mon evening –* 🖼.
This attractive Liberty-style building, unfortunately in need of restoration, has a beautiful garden and a number of rooms once used for processing tuna

and repairing fishing boats. The building now houses a nightclub and a pizzeria.

MONDELLO

🍽🍽 **Bye bye blues** – *Via del Garofalo 23, Mondello. ☎091 68 41 415. Closed Tue, at lunchtime on weekdays and Nov. Booking recommended.* This restaurant is well worth a visit for its original atmosphere and inventive cuisine, with a good balance of meat and fish dishes. It also has an excellent wine list.

rheumatism by locals who bathed in the hot sulphurous springs.

▶ *Return to the main road and continue as far as the junction with S 121. Follow signs back to Palermo (87km/54mi).*

Excursions

Monte Pellegrino

14km/9mi N. From Viale della Libertà, turn right into Via Imperatore Federico and then head along Via Bonanno.
The road up Monte Pellegrino offers magnificent **views**★★★ over Palermo and the Conca d'Oro; in places it is crossed by a much steeper, paved path dating from the 17C.
As the road climbs, it passes **Castello Utveggio**, a massive pink construction that can also be seen from the city, then continues on to the **Santuario di Santa Rosalia** (17C), a sanctuary built around the cave where, legend has it, St Rosalia lived, and where her bones were found in 1624.
They were carried through the streets and credited with freeing the city from the Plague. Following this St Rosalia became the patron saint of Palermo. The cave has guttering to collect the dripping water from the walls, which is considered by locals to possess miraculous properties.
Farther on up, the road comes to a lookout point with breathtaking sea **views**★.

Grotte dell'Addaura★

Between Mondello and Arenella. Take Via Crispi and follow the Lungomare Cristoforo Colombo to Punta di Priola. From Monte Pellegrino, go along Via Bonanno, turn right into Viale Regina Margherita, then right along the seafront. 🔒*Closed for renovation. For information ☎091 70 71 315.*
A series of caves among the lower slopes of Monte Pellegrino were inhabited during Palaeolithic times (5th millennium BC) and **rock engravings**, possibly associated with some initiation ceremony or a ritual, have been found in one of them.

Mondello 🏖

11km/7mi N of Palermo. Continue along the seafront.
The road passes below the slopes of Monte Pellegrino. This area, now an elegant holiday resort, was "discovered" at the beginning of the century by rich Palermitani who were looking for a short break to enjoy the health and wellbeing benefits of the sea air.
There's little to see in this quiet town, other than the ruins of a medieval tower and a small harbour, with a lively jetty populated by amateur fishermen in summer.
Mondello's main attraction, its 2km sweep of sandy beach, runs between nearby Valdesi to the resort. In the evenings, join locals and visitors alike in Piazza Mondello for the *passeggiata*, and enjoy a relaxed drink at one of the many bars in the square.

PANTALICA★

Once the site of ancient Hybla, the fascinating and evocative landscape of Pantalica combines the honeycombed archaeological remains of the necropoli with the dramatic natural surroundings of the Anapo Valley.

🛈 **Information:** Via San Sebastiano 43. ☎0931 48 12 00. www.apt-siracusa.it.

▶ **Orient Yourself:** The archaeological site is accessible from both Ferla and Sortino; the former provides better views of the necropolis and avoids having to climb down to the river bed, cross the river and climb up the other side. The protected natural area can be reached either from the Floridia-Sortino road or from Cassaro, to the south of Ferla *(see below for details)*.

🅿 **Parking:** Park at the point where the tarred road ends, 7mi before Ferla, to take the steep path down to the gorge of Calcinara and the northern necropolis.

👁 **Don't Miss:** Cavetta, southern, northern and Filiporto necropoli, walking tours among the gorges and cliffs of the protected area around the Anapo Valley,

🧒 **Especially for Kids:** Puppet theatre at Museo dell'Opera dei Pupi, horse-drawn carriage rides from Pantalica to the Case Specchi refuge.

👤 **Also See:** CALTAGIRONE; SIRACUSA.

A Bit of History

Pantalica, identified as the ancient Hybla (founded, it is alleged, like Megara Hyblaea, in 728 BC by a group of colonists from Megara with the blessing of their last king Hyblon), has been inhabited since the Bronze Age. Towards the middle of the 13C BC, the Sicani moved inland from their original settlements in the coastal regions to a chosen site at Pantalica, as the coast at this time was subjected to attack and regular waves of settlers, therefore no longer secure. The narrow valley through which the River Anapo ran, together with the Cavagrande (which becomes the Calcinara in its final section) were naturally defensible, with two deep gorges and one means of access (the saddle of Filiporto, to the west); furthermore, the area had two rivers considered to be of inestimable value. Today, little survives of the original town, which was probably destroyed by the Syracusans before the foundation of Akrai in 664 BC, save for a number of tombs in the limestone cliffs (which must have been excavated with huge effort using bronze or stone axes, given that iron had not yet been discovered). New life was breathed into Pantalica by the Byzantines, who installed small communities in rock-hewn dwellings there. The site prob-

ably continued to be occupied during the Arab and Norman periods before being abandoned until the beginning of the 20C, when the archaeologist Paolo Orsi began excavations.

Visit

Archaeological site★

🕐*Always open.* 👛*Donations welcome.* ☎*0931 48 11 11.*

More than 5 000 burial chambers honeycomb the walls of this quarry to make five necropoli that run through successive periods. The earliest tombs in the north and northwest necropoli (13C–11C BC) are elliptical in shape, the most recent (850–730 BC) are rectangular. The most distinctive element of these tombs are the intriguing way in which they are organised into compact family units, rather than into extended groups, which was a more common practice.

Follow the signs for Pantalica from Ferla; after 9km, stop and park at Sella di Filiporto *(yellow sign)*, the ancient gateway to the town, where the remains of the fortification trench can still be seen. From here, a path runs along the southern edge of the upland plateau; looking back, the **Filiporto necropolis** can be seen within a broad amphitheatre of rock. Farther along there are splendid **views**★★ over the Anapo gorge below; the path then continues down to a Byzantine settlement and to the Oratory of San Micidiario. Follow the path and, after about 1km/0.6mi, turn left for the **anaktoron** or Prince's Palace; this is also accessible by car, by continuing along the main road some 1.5km/0.9mi (note in passing the **northwest necropolis** on the left) and then taking a short path *(indicated by a yellow sign)*. This megalithic construction is thought by Orsi to have been built by Mycenean workmen in the service of the prince.

Return to the car. 11km/7mi before Ferla the tarred road peters out (note the Byzantine village of Cavetta just before this). Leave the car here 🅿 and take the steep path down, enjoying the marvellous **views**★★ of the gorge of Calcinara on the way. The vast **northern necropolis** enclosed by the wall, opens out before the path on the opposite side *(the walk takes approximately 20min to the river)*.

Protected Natural Area★

There are two entrances to the Anapo Valley, via the Fusco gate (off the Floridia-Sortino road, turn left after about 12km/7mi at the fork marked with a sign for Valle dell'Anapo; 700m/770yd farther along, continue left), or via the Cassaro gate (from Ferla, follow signs for Cassaro; at the first fork, turn left and continue to the bridge over the river; the

Address Book

HORSE-DRAWN TRANSPORT

The section from Pantalica to the Case Specchi refuge can be taken by horse-drawn carriage (maximum 14 people). This service must be booked in writing, two weeks in advance, by contacting the Ispettorato Dipartimentale delle Foreste, Via S. Giovanni alle Catacombe 7, Siracusa. For further information, call ☎0931 46 24 52. If taking the walking tour (highly recommended), visitors are advised to bring a torch for the tunnel sections.

Ponte Diga gate is located thereabouts – 4km/2.5mi from Ferla).
🕐*Open May–Oct, 8am–7.30pm; Nov–Apr, 8am–5pm.* 💶*Donations welcome.* ☎*0931 46 24 52.*

An expedition through the protected area (soon set to become a nature reserve) around the Anapo Valley reveals an extraordinary **landscape** that comprises of a succession of gorges defined by cliffs, along which the old Syracuse-Ragusa-Vizzini railway ran.

For those who don't wish to walk the whole route (13km/8mi), there is an alternative, shorter and clearly marked track that combines natural and archaeological points of interest along the way, leading to the **Cavetta necropolis**

Flora and Fauna

The geological formation known as the **cave iblee** (or Hyblaean quarries), a series of deep canyons cutting through the landscape, harbours a broad range of plants in a concentrated area. The tree varieties that make up the thickly wooded section up the rocky slopes include white and black poplars, and willows; there is also a profusion of tamarisks, oleanders, wild orchids and the nettle *Urtica rupestris*, a relic from the Ice Age. Clinging to the slopes elsewhere are patches of Mediterranean maquis: forest of holm and cork oaks interspersed with, in the more arid parts exposed to the sun, an aromatic scrub of sage, thyme, giant fennel, euphorbia and thorny broom. The Oriental plane tree deserves a special mention as it only grows wild in a very few places in Italy; the threat of a spreading fungus, a pathogenic canker, seems to have been checked here for the time being, thanks to appropriate measures.

As regards fauna, the Anapo Valley also accommodates a large number of different species: foxes, pine martens, porcupines, hares and hedgehogs; painted frogs and other amphibians; dippers, stonechats, kingfishers, partridges and a pair of peregrine falcons.

©Peeter Viisimaa/iStockphoto.com

Burial chambers made of honeycombed rocks

(on the right after the first tunnel), the **southern necropolis** *(on both sides after the second tunnel)* and the **Fili-porto necropolis** *(after 4km/2.5mi in the wall on the right).* At the start of the alternative route, immediately on the right, are vents associated with the Galermi aqueduct.

These were originally built by the tyrant Gelon as part of a system to convey water from the river to Syracuse, and they continue to be used for irrigation purposes today.

Excursions

Ferla

Isolated on the limestone upland plateau crossed by the River Anapo, the town boasts several attractive 18C religious buildings. These include the **Church of San Sebastiano**, whose three naves house various chapels and works of art including a 17C painting depicting the Martyrdom of St Sebastian, and **Sant'Antonio**, which overlooks an attractive square cobbled with geometric designs.

The elegant frontage of this church comprises of five convex panels that are articulated with columns, while inside there are some lovely Baroque details. The road from Ferla to Sortino provides panoramic views over the surrounding plateau and the deep cleft hewn by water erosion.

Sortino

Completely rebuilt in the 18C on the top of a hill, the town is laid out on a rectilinear grid-like plan.

The **Chiesa Madre** (open 5.30pm–7.30pm; ☎0931 95 21 73) is fronted by a forecourt cobbled with lozenge-shaped stones and has a fine façade of warm golden stone. The elevation comprises a doorway flanked by spiral columns ornamented with organic decoration; a level above with statues; and, along the top, an open balustrade. The interior ceiling and apse are charmingly frescoed (1777–78) by Crestadoro.

The **Museo dell'Opera dei Pupi** (Kids open Mon–Fri, 10am–noon; Sat –Sun and public hols, by appointment only; Closed 10 Sept; donations welcome; ☎0931 95 207) is housed in the former monastery of St Francis.

This museum contains the puppet theatre and puppets that once belonged to the renowned puppeteer Ignazio Puglisi (1904–86). This fascinating collection is organised by theme, with rooms dedicated to grotesque monsters (devils, skeletons and giants), Paladins and Saracens and to the *cartoni*, large sections of cardboard portraying the puppets that were used as a background.

One of the last rooms in the museum is dedicated to the characters of farce, which spoke in Sicilian dialect and traditionally brought the puppet shows to a rousing end.

PANTELLERIA★★

POPULATION 7 624

Known as the 'Black Pearl of the Mediterranean', the island of Pantelleria is full of character with its indented coastline, steep slopes covered with terraces under cultivation and its Moorish-looking cubic houses (dammusi). The highest point of this volcanic island is Montagna Grande (836m/2743ft); around it, vineyards produce wines such as the sparklng Solimano and the muscat Tanit. Capers are also grown here. Pantelleria has remains of prehistoric settlements and, like Sicily, later suffered invasions by the Phoenicians, Carthaginians, Greeks, Romans, Vandals, Byzantines, Moors and Normans, the latter uniting the island with Sicily in 1123.

- **Information:** Piazza Cavour 1. ☎0923 69 50 11. www.pantelleria.it.
- **Orient Yourself:** Pantelleria is the largest of Sicily's satellite islands (83km2/ 32sq mi); it is also the most westerly, lying 84km/52mi from the African continent, at the same latitude as Tunisia. Its warm climate, however, is constantly tempered by strong winds blowing in from the sea, hence the island's Arabic name Qawsarah or Bent el Rion, meaning Daughter of the Wind.
- **Parking:** Parking is available near the official picnic sites at La Montagna Grande, and on the outskirts of Nika (walk into the town).
- **Don't Miss:** Dramatic views at Scauri, Nika and La Montagna Grande, boat tours of the island, Pantelleria gardens at Rekhale and the Grotta Benikula.
- **Organising Your Time:** A round trip of the island by car is just 25 miles. Leave half a day to a day to explore, depending on your schedule.
- **Especially for Kids:** Island boat trips, picnics at La Montagna Grande.

A Bit of History

Volcanic land – The highest point on the island is Montagna Grande (836m/2 742ft), an ancient crater. The rocky black lava coastline is riddled with caves and small headlands projecting into the sea. The land mass, being volcanic, is extremely fertile and well drained, and therefore suited to the cultivation of the vine.

Solimano, a sparkling wine with a delicate bouquet, together with the Passito di Pantelleria, made with *zibibbo* grapes, are the island's principal specialities.

Salted capers are another local delicacy, harvested from plants abundant with exquisitely delicate flowers.

Various phenomena provoked by volcanic activity are still much in evidence on Pantelleria: hot springs emerge from the sea floor just off the coast, sulphuric vapour emanates from natural caves, and jets of steam (known locally as *favare*) intermittently escape from the rock, especially in the vicinity of the craters (⟐*see below*).

Evolution of a house style – The first residents of Pantelleria may have come from Africa in Neolithic times to extract its black gold, namely obsidian which, at that time, was highly sought after. Near to a village dating from this period, with fortifications of a type found elsewhere only at Los Millares in Spain (near Almera), are a number of megalithic funerary structures that are distinctive to the island, known locally as **sesi** (⟐*See below*), yet reminiscent in shape of the *nuraghi* of Sardinia.

Next came the Phoenicians: they called the island Kossura and provided it with a large harbour on the spot occupied by the modern main port. Waves of Carthaginians, Romans, Vandals, Byzantines and Arabs followed, who boosted the local agriculture by introducing cotton, olives and figs, and improving the cultivation of the vine. Many of the island's farming communities still preserve their original Arab names: Khamma, Gadir, Rakhali, Bukkuram, Bugeber and Mursia.

During the Second World War, Pantelleria's key strategic position right in the

Address Book

For coin ranges, see the Legend on the cover flap.

GETTING THERE

The quickest and easiest way of getting to the island from mainland Italy is by **air**. There are direct flights from Trapani and Palermo; during the summer, services also operate from Rome and Milan. A shuttle bus links the airport, situated 5km/3mi south of Pantelleria town, to Piazza Cavour in Pantelleria.

Those already in Sicily, ideally in the area of Trapani, might like to consider the **ferry** travelling overnight on the outward journey (6hr) and returning by day (5hr). For information and reservations, contact **Siremar** ☎091 74 93 111 (from Italy) or 081 01 71 998 (from abroad and mobile phones); www.siremar.it **Ustica Lines** (Via Amm. Staiti 23, Trapani; ☎0923 87 38 13, www.usticalines.it) operates a **hydrofoil** service (2hr 30min) from June to September.

SIGHTSEEING

The best way of exploring the island is by car, enabling visitors to discover the island's many surprises at a leisurely pace. The road running around the island is asphalted but very narrow. Bus services from Piazza Cavour link Pantelleria with other parts of the island. Several tour operators, some private, are able to provide information on the types of accommodation and facilities available. Most can also arrange holiday packages, car and boat rentals. **Pro Loco** ☎0923 91 29 48; **Associazione Turistica Pantelleria** ☎0923 91 29 48; **Promozione**

Turistica di Pantelleria ☎0923 91 22 57. To explore the coast from the sea, rubber dinghies may be hired; organised boat trips are also provided.

WHERE TO STAY

If you are planning to stay one or more nights on the island, it is well worth renting a *dammuso*, one of the typical local Arab-style square houses. Tourist information providers will be happy to give information on terms and conditions and where to find houses to rent.

Port Hotel – *Via Borgo Italia 71, Pantelleria.* ☎0923 91 12 99. *43 rooms.* This simple white building on the seafront near the port is both comfortable and well maintained. Although the rooms are quite small, their attractive blue and white decor is both pleasant and refreshing.

Albergo Papuscia – *Contrada Sopra Portella 28, Tracino.* ☎0923 91 54 63. *www.papuscia.it. Closed Dec–Easter 11 double rooms.* This small, friendly hotel in the upper part of the town has rooms in traditional *dammusi* with typical walls of lava rock. Guest areas include a bar and a simple restaurant, with a pleasant veranda for the summer months.

WHERE TO EAT

La Favarotta – *Località Khamma Fuori, Khamma.* ☎0923 91 53 47. This restaurant offers welcome respite during the heat of summer. Located inland at an altitude of 400m/1 300ft, the menu here nevertheless includes a number of excellent fish dishes on its hearty menu.

La Nicchia – *Scauri Basso, Scauri.* ☎0923 91 63 42. *Open Sat–Sun only. Closed at lunchtime and Jan–Feb.* At La Nicchia, guests can choose between dining on an outdoor terrace with tables and wooden chairs, in the indoor dining room where the pizza kitchen is open to view, or beneath a delightful pergola at the end of the garden, surrounded by colourful flowers and plants.

S. Sauvignier/MICHELIN

Capers

⊜⊜⊜⊜**l Mulini** – *Kania 12, Tracino.*
☎0923 91 53 98. Closed Nov–Easter. This
picturesque restaurant housed in an old
mill has been tastefully restored in traditional style. The restaurant specialises
in simple, local cuisine.

SHOPPING

Visitors should not leave the island
without buying some capers and a
bottle of the excellent dessert wine,
the Passito di Pantelleria, for which
the island is renowned. These can be
bought from shops in the built-up areas
or from local farms.

middle of the Canale di Sicilia separating North Africa from Italy, earned it the
attentions of the Fascist government,
which began to fortify the place. As a
result, it was subjected to systematic
bombing raids in 1943 by the Allies
based on the Tunisian coast.

The traditional type of house found on
Pantelleria is the **dammuso**; Arab in
origin. Built with square stones and a
undulating roof that doubles as a terrace, many of these charming houses
have been bought up and converted
into summer homes.

The inhabitants of Pantelleria, who traditionally tend to be farmers rather than
sailors, have tried to resolve the problem
posed by the area's strong winds and
restrict tree heights (even the olive trees
have been adapted to grow at ground
level by pruning them into a circular fan
of low-lying espaliers). The **Pantelleria
garden**, a circular or square enclosure
with high stone walls, is a sanctuary in
which citrus trees might grow, protected
from the wind. Sometimes these gardens
are attached to a house, others might be
situated in the centre of a field.

Driving Tours

Island Circuit★★
Approx 40km/25mi round trip.

A scenic road winds its way around the
coast providing glorious views of the
landscape at every turn.

Pantelleria

The houses of the island's main built-up
area are clustered around the harbour.
As one of the main German bases in
the Mediterranean during the Second
World War, Pantelleria Town was subsequently flattened by Allied bombs.
Post-war reconstruction done without
any formal planning, replaced the idyllic original layout with a mish-mash of
charmless concrete cubes. As a result

Traditional sesi

G. Iacono/MICHELIN

the town is a slightly disappointing introduction to this beautiful island. The main landmark is the brooding black **Castello Barbacane;** probably founded in Roman times. Since then it has been demolished and rebuilt on a number of occasions. Its partially restored interior is sometimes open to visit, and sometimes not (*check at the tourist office for the current access*).

Look out for the plaque on the wall facing the harbour, dedicated to the anti-Mafia judge Paolo Borsellino who was assassinated by a car bomb in Palermo in 1992.

▶ *Follow the west coast,
   heading south.*

Neolithic Village

The archaeological site is situated some 3km/1.8mi beyond Mursia and the **Kuddie Rosse**, ancient craters of a reddish colour. The only discernible feature among the low stone field boundary walls and scattered piles of rubble is the **Sese Grande**★ just beyond the

quarry, which rises from an elliptical base of large blocks of lava into a kind of tower. It is surrounded by an ornamental ledge that spirals its way up to the top. The base has 12 entrances serving passages that interconnect the same number of funerary chambers. Here, the dead were entombed in the foetal position, with the head pointing towards the west, surrounded by their personal grave goods.

A little farther on, the rocky black **Punta Fram** points out to sea. Past the tip of the headland, a flight of steps leads down from the right side of the road, to the **Grotta di Sataria**, which contains pools of water fed by hot springs.

Scauri★

High on the cliff edge, enjoying a spectacular **position**★, the tiny village of Scauri sits above its picturesque harbour (*a twenty minute walk*), and is fed by hot springs. The village itself is little more than a clutch of houses and a couple of small shops, but the cemetery is worth visiting for the marvellous sweeping

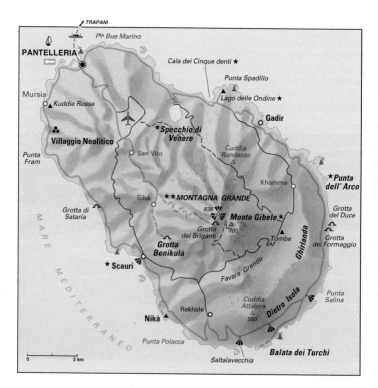

views★ it offers that even extend out to Cape Mustafa in Tunisia on a clear day.

▶ *After continuing some way along the coast, park the car and walk into Nikà.*

Nikà

30min on foot there and back. The minuscule fishing village is situated in a lava gorge, with a number of hot springs emerging from the nearby rocks.

Back on the coastal road, turn left at the junction for **Rekhale**, one of the few villages that preserve *dammusi* and Pantelleria gardens in their original state. Return to the coast, which at this point drops steeply down to the sea. There is a notable sea cave along this stretch, best reached by boat, called the **Grotta di Nika**, where a hot spring rises up.

Saltalavecchia (literally translated as the "old lady's leap") appears after a bend in the road.

The village, perched on the cliff at one of the highest points, has a dramatic **view**★★ down a sheer face to the sea, 150m/500ft below (☺*be careful here as the ground can give way*).

Balata dei Turchi

This wild and remote beach was reputedly where the Saracens used to land on the island unseen. It is one of the few sheltered coves that has access to the sea, and as it is protected from the wind it is handily overgrown with tall vegetation to hide in, notably wild juniper and sweet-smelling pines.

Dietro Isola

The road around the southeastern part of the island provides some splendid coastline **views**★★ dominated here by the jutting headland.

Punto dell'Arco★

At the far end of the promontory sits the **Arco dell'Elefante**★, a spectacular natural archway of grey lava which resembles the head and trunk of an elephant lying down to take a drink from the sea.

Gadir

The small, picture-perfect harbour bubbles with thermal spring water (in the harbour hollow). It's a favourite spot for sunbathers who take it turns to wade in small thermal pools and recline and relax on the concrete harbour side when the weather is balmy.

A short way beyond, a path leads off to the right of the road to the lighthouse on **Punta Spadillo**. When the lighthouse comes into view, branch left along a second track towards a collection of abandoned houses, then climb up to the batteries.

Follow the path behind the white one downhill between low lava walls; it eventually opens out by the tiny **Lago delle Ondine**★(lake of waves). Almost completely surrounded by cliffs and volcanic rock boulders, this lava hollow collects water from the breaking waves to form a small emerald-green pool of stillness.

After the **Cala dei Cinque Denti**★ (the inlet with five teeth), where the craggy lava rock formations look as if they are about to bite a chunk out of the scenery, take a left hand turn at the fork in the road.

Specchio di Venere★

Venus' looking glass is a delicious lake of aquamarine water in a former volcanic crater, fed by a sulphur-rich spring on its western flank. Its name comes from the myth that tells how Venus studied her reflection in this lake when comparing her beauty with that of her rival Psyche. Modern visitors in search of aesthetic satisfaction apply the rich muddy mineral deposits found round the edges of the lake to their bodies and then leave the covering to dry in the sun. When it is baked to a shell, the home made mud wrap is then washed off with a final dip in the warm waters.

Inland★★

▶ *Leave the town of Pantelleria by the airport road and continue to Sibà. Beyond the village is the Benikulà Cave or Bagno Asciutto (natural sauna).*

Grotta Benikulà

Coming from the direction of Sibà, there are no signs: access to the cave is down a road on the left (signposted from the other direction). Leave the car and proceed on foot. It takes 10min to walk there and back. ⊙*Take a swimming costume and a towel for the sauna.* ⊙*Don't spend too long inside the cave, where the heat can be intense. Ten minutes is long enough for a first visit.*

Looking down over the valley from above, two pretty Pantelleria gardens may be seen. Inside the cave, entered through what looks like a crack in the rock face, is a powerful natural sauna. Here, the temperature of the steam rises the deeper in that one goes - and the ceiling becomes so hot that it's impossible to keep your hand pressed against it for longer than a couple of seconds. It is worth pausing at the cave entrance to acclimatize yourself, entering only once you are accustomed to the heat. The intense subterranean temperature and darkness of the cave can be a little overwhelming for some visitors.

La Montagna Grande★★

The road up to the Montagna Grande offers magnificent **views**★★ over the surrounding landscape. The mountain's sides are pitted by volcanic vents (*Stufe de Khazen*), which can be spotted by the escaping vapour trails, and the terrain is covered with pine forest *(there are a number of designated picnic sites here).* Leave the car by the building at the end of the road 🅿 and continue on foot past two other buildings (a *dammuso* and a chapel); on to the left, a gentle walk up a series of stone steps leads to the **Grotta dei Briganti**, a large cave where the temperature is constantly warm. The cave once served as a refuge for outlaws (hence its name).

Ghirlanda

Costa Ghirlanda, on the east side of the island, conceals a number of tombs of indeterminable age. Access to them is by a bumpy dirt track for which a four-wheel drive vehicle (or a horse) is recommended. In a tranquil oak wood *(on the left)* lies a notable collection of rock-hewn **tombs**, which local tradition

claims as Byzantine. The exceptional beauty of this mysterious place alone makes the excursion worthwhile.

Monte Gibele★

This old volcano, now extinct, is a lovely walk to take. From Rakhali, head inland and, at the junction, fork right along the road until a path appears on the left. Continue from here on foot. The path leads to the crater, now covered in vegetation. On the way, the track skirts past the dramatic **Favara Grande**, a powerful geyser that issues great jets of steam into the air.

Tour of the Island by Boat★★

The perfect complement to an exploration of the island, is to go off and discover her other splendid attributes by sea. The opaque blackness of the lava rocks contrasts sharply with the deep blue sea, which, in places, appears emerald green. The coastline is interrupted by secluded creeks, ravines and intriguing caves, many of which can only be reached by boat. Starting out from Pantelleria, a clockwise tour of the island reveals the jagged and low-lying north coast; in the area of Cuddia Randazzo, the rocks assume strange black profiles resembling animals or other worldly creatures. A series of inlets and caves follows, many of which are perfect spots for swimming. Then comes the **Arco dell'Elefante**★ (⊙*see above*) and a further succession of caves and hollows divided by pillars of lava. The most dramatic of the grottoes are situated in the coastline between Punta Duca and Punta Polacca, however **Grotta del Duce**, **Grotta del Formaggio** and **Grotta della Pila dell'Acqua** can only be fully explored by the smallest craft. This is the most spectacular stretch of the island's shore. Here, towering great cliffs reach far into the sky and large monolithic rocks point sharply out of the sea until, at last, the drama culminates in a view of **Saltalavecchia**. Increasingly taller rocky outcrops follow (following the sections of coastline around Scauri), before the coast flattens again in the vicinity of Cala dell'Alga.

GOLFO DI PATTI ⌣

From Capo Calva to Capo Milazzo, the sweeping Golfo di Patti is a ribbon of undulating scenery, pretty beaches, charming towns and archeological interest.

🛈 **Information:** Piazza Marconi 11, Patti. ☎0941 24 11 36. www.pattietindari.it.

▶ **Orient Yourself:** The bay stretches for 30km/19mi from Capo Calavà to Capo Milazzo, which juts out into the sea like a sickle. The beach, stretching along the bay, is dotted with seaside resorts, such as Gioiosa Marea, Marina di Patti, Oliveri and Falcone. It is interrupted halfway by Capo Tindari.

⊘ **Don't Miss:** Well preserved ruins at the archaeological site and Villa Romana di Terme Vigliatore, views from the hills behind Tindari. Tindari is also well-known for the cultural Tindari Estate Festival, late-July to the third week in August.

🕐 **Organising Your Time:** Allow half a day to drive the coast road.

🧒 **Especially for Kids:** Rock pools and the sandy beach at Laghetti di Marinello.

👣 **Also See:** CAPO D'ORLANDO; MILAZZO.

Driving Tour

40km/25mi – allow half a day.

Patti

This small town in the hinterland extends down to the sea at Marina di Patti, where the remains of a Roman villa were recently discovered (👣 *See below*). The old town centre still retains its medieval network of narrow streets, spanned by arches.

Elevated to a bishopric by Roger II in 1131, then nominated a royal town by Frederick III of Aragon in 1312, Patti received the title of *magnanima* (generous) from Charles V for a generous tribute to the crown.

Little remains of this glorious period, Patti having succumbed to repeated earthquakes.

The present **cathedral** (🕐 *for admission times* ☎ *0941 84 08 13*) building dates from the 18C, its 15C **portal** having been restored to the main façade. The small clusters of columns flanking the main entrance have magnificent capitals, carved with fantastical monsters.

Inside, the **sarcophagus of Queen Adelasia** *(in the right transept)* – wife of Roger I – is a 16C restoration of the 1118 original.

On the northern side of the town, beside the River Montagnareale, is Porta San Michele, the only fragment of the Aragonese defensive town walls to survive. Beyond the gate sits the church of **San Michele**, with a marble ciborium by Antonello Gagini (1538) and a triptych featuring angels flanked by St Agatha and Mary Magdalene.

Address Book

👣 *For coin ranges, see the cover flap.*

WHERE TO EAT

🍽🍷 **Il Casaro** – *Via Luca della Robbia 3, Marina di Patti.* ☎*0941 36 74 75. Closed Mon, Dec and Jan. Booking recommended*. This popular eatery, a former pub converted to a restaurant by the new, dynamic owner, enjoys a good reputation in the area.
Facilities here include a dining room with an attractive bar-counter, a delightful wooden veranda, and a small garden for summer dining. Good-quality cuisine at reasonable prices.

FESTIVAL

The Tindari Estate festival is held in the theatre at Tindari from the last week in July to the third week in August. The festival's programme includes prose readings, dance performances and classical and contemporary music concerts.

City of Castor and Pollux

The Greek colony of **Tyndaris** was founded by the tyrant of Syracuse, Dionysius the Elder, in 396 BC to accommodate refugees from Sparta at the end of the Peloponnese War (404 BC). The name refers to the Dioscuri, **Castor** and Polydeuces/**Pollux**, sons of Leda and Zeus and brothers of Helen (whose abduction was the catalyst for the Trojan War) and Clytaemnestra. Leda was the wife of the mythical hero Tyndareus of Sparta, who was said to have fathered Castor, while Pollux was believed to have been fathered by Zeus. Consequently, the Dioscuri are also known as the Tyndaridi. The link between the town and the heavenly twins is taken up on coins and mosaics.

The new town, occupying a raised, yet naturally defensible position, developed its strategic importance in policing the sea between Messina and the Aeolian Islands. Despite its impressively solid defensive fortifications on the landward side, the town fell into the hands of the Carthaginians. Later, under Roman dominion, it flourished through a period of great prosperity, prompting a range of public buildings such as schools, markets and public baths to be constructed or redeveloped. The theatre, which was built by the Greeks, was modified so as to accommodate the demands of its new audience.

Thereafter, Tyndaris progressively declined: a landslide destroyed part of the city including its most important features, and further damage was then incurred by the Arab conquest in the 9C.

Villa Romana di Patti

In Patti Marina, near the underpass
of the motorway on the right.
🕐Open 9am–2hr before dusk. ⬤€2.
☎0941 36 15 93.

The Imperial Roman villa was discovered during motorway construction work. The complex is arranged around a peristyle with a portico from which lead various rooms, including one paved with mosaics featuring geometric motifs and depictions of domestic and wild animals.

▶ *Follow S 113 for 9km/6mi,*
then turn left to Tyndaris.

Tindari★

From the east, **Tyndaris** sits against a succession of hills that emerge from the sea and rise to form a land mass resembling a dragon slumbering peacefully; perched high upon its head stands the sanctuary, a discernible landmark from afar. As the road winds down the dragon's back, wonderful **views**★ open out over the bay of Patti and the beaches that sweep round to Capo Milazzo.

The **sanctuary**, a relatively recent addition to the landscape, shelters a Byzantine Black Virgin, which attracts large bands of pilgrims around the Marian feasts of the Visitation (31 May) and the Birth of the Virgin (8 September).

At the foot of the rock face are the **Laghetti di Marinello**. (◔*See below*).

Archaeological Site★

🕐Open 9am–2hr before dusk. ⬤€2.
☎0941 36 90 23; www.regione.sicilia.it.

The path up to the top of Capo Tindari passes alongside sections of the defensive **walls** built during the reign of Dionysius.

The walls were only built around the vulnerable parts of the town, laid out on a grid system with three wide *decumani* (main thoroughfares) interconnected by *cardini* at right angles.

An **antiquarium**, beyond the entrance to the site on the left, displays artefacts recovered from the excavations.

The **Insula romana** comprises an entire block to the south of the main axis or *decumanus superiore*, with baths, taverns and houses, including a patrician house with fragments of mosaic.

The arcaded remains of the **basilica** give some suggestion of the scale and elegance of the original building. Even though the ruin has been classified as a basilica or public meeting house, its true function is still uncertain: it may possibly be a part of some monumental *propy-*

Laghetti di Marinello

laeum (gateway) for the agora or main square of the city.

▷ *Turn left onto decumanus superiore.*

The **theatre** was built by the Greeks (late 4C BC) to take advantage of the lie of the land, with the *cavea* (auditorium) facing the sea and the Aeolian Islands. It was adapted in Imperial times for staging gladiator fights.

▷ *Follow S 113 for 3.5km/2mi, then turn left to Oliveri.*

Laghetti di Marinello   Kids

This is the name given to the pools of water left by the tide on the wide sandy strip below Capo Tindari, some of which contain a rich variety of aquatic plants. The area also attracts a selection of birds: gulls, grebes, coots and little egrets. According to legend, these rock pools appeared to save a little girl who otherwise would have fallen to her death from the headland; she was saved when the sea miraculously withdrew to leave a soft landing pad of sand. In 1982, one of the rock pools assumed the profile of a veiled woman, identified by local people as the Madonna of the sanctuary.

The pools can be reached on foot *(about 30min)* from Oliveri. The beach tails off into a glorious **bay**★★. In summer this is a paradise for bathers although the

beach is rarely crowded *(swimmers are strongly recommended not to bathe in the pools, as the water is stagnant: it is preferable to swim in the bay).*

▷ *Return to the main road, continuing along it for 6.5km/4mi to the district of SanBiagio.*

Villa Romana di Terme Vigliatore★

Open 9am–2hr before dusk. ☎090 97 40 488.

The 1C AD suburban residence has not been fully excavated. The villa comprises the residential quarters *(on the left)* and a small baths complex *(on the right)*.

To the left is a square **peristyle** with eight columns down each side. Ahead is a **tablinum** (archive room) with an *opus sectile* floor of geometric patterns.

The most interesting part of the complex, however, is the private baths *(to the right of the entrance to the site)*. To the left of the semicircular bath is the **frigidariu**. The baths' heating system is visible. Hot air from a furnace circulated by convection through the wall cavities and between the ground and the floor, raised by brick columns *(suspensurae)*.

▷ *From Terme Vigliatore either continue to Milazzo (See MILAZZO).*

PIAZZA ARMERINA

POPULATION: 20 760

Overshadowed by the Villa Imperiale del Casale, Piazza Armerina is a pleasant stop in its own right. The pretty town is dominated by its grand Baroque cathedral, which commands its own Piazza in the historic centre. Every August, the streets of Piazza Armerina come alive with medieval re-enactments of the historic arrival of the Norman Count Roger to liberate the town from the Saracens.

- **Information:** Viale Generale Muscarà 13. ☎0935 68 48 14. www.comune.piazzaarmerina.en.it.
- ▶ **Orient Yourself:** The town sits in rolling countryside at an altitude of 700m/ 2 300ft. Behind a mass of modern constructions, the narrow streets of the historic centre wind uphill to the cathedral at the town's highest point. Piazza Armerina is the closest settlement to Villa del Casale and visitors travelling from Enna or Caltagirone must first drive through Piazza Armerina to reach the villa.
- **Don't Miss:** Fine art in the Duomo, excursions to Villa Imperiale del Casale.
- **Organising Your Time:** Piazza Armerina's sights can been seen in a couple of hours, and it makes a nice short stop on the way to Villa Imperiale del Casale.
- **Also See:** CALTAGIRONE; CALTANISSETTA; ENNA; VILLA IMPERIALE DEL CASALE.

Majestic dome of the cathedral

R. Mattes/MICHELIN

Walking Tours

Medieval Quarter★

The little town, threaded by narrow medieval streets, is visible from a good distance away, dominated by the Duomo at the highest point (721m/2 364ft), overlooking Piazza del Duomo. At the heart of the old town, Piazza Garibaldi is lined with elegant palazzi.

Duomo

This monumental Baroque building, crowned with a great dome, towers over its own **piazza**. Commissioned and built with funds donated by Baron Marco Trigona, who is commemorated in the statue that crowns the square, the front elevation of the cathedral contains an elegant central doorway surmounted by a square window. Above it sits the eagle, the heraldic emblem of the Trigona family. Inside, notable works of art include the baptismal font and the **Madonna delle Vittorie**★, above the main altar, at the far end of the nave. This Byzantine image is popularly linked to the banner given at the Council of Melfi, the capital of the Norman kingdom of Puglia, where several councils were held, by Pope Nicholas II to his legate Roger I "to go before him and inspire his army in its future campaigns". In the chapel to the left of the chancel is a **painted wooden cross**★ from 1455. Overlooking the nave there are two wooden organ cases; one ornamented with the Trinacria, the ancient symbol of Sicily (on the left), the other showing Count Roger on horseback (on the right).

A walk through the streets

In Via Cavour, behind the Duomo, stands a 17C **Franciscan complex** (now a hospital); its sandstone and brick church is marked by a bell tower with a conical spire covered in maiolica tiles. The south face of the convent buildings includes an elegant **balcony** supported by Baroque brackets, designed by GV Gagini. Continue on down the street to Slargo Santa Rosalia and **Palazzo Canicarao**, which now comprise commercial offices (Azienda di Promozione Turistica).Turn down Via Vittorio Emanuele,

The Palio and Its Legend

The Palio festival (see Address Book) stems from the people's huge admiration for the great Count Roger: in those days, the town was held by the Saracens, the infidels, so the Norman advance in Sicily was considered a kind of holy war. Very soon, the inhabitants of Piazza rose in revolt, acclaiming Roger Guiscard de Hauteville (known in Italy as Ruggero d'Altavilla) as their leader. On arrival, the paid mercenary/condottiere gave the town a banner which earned great admiration from the faithful. The banner was then furled and put away until the mid-1300s, when it was recovered and borne with great ceremony to the town church. As if by a miracle, the plague which was then decimating the town, suddenly died out and the banner became a cult object. According to tradition, the standard in question is the one bearing the Madonna delle Vittorie, now in the cathedral.

which opens out before two church façades situated face to face: **Chiesa di Sant'Ignazio di Loyola** is preceded by a staircase that divides into two above the first flight; **Chiesa di Sant'Anna** has a convex façade. Above, the solid profile of the **Aragonese castle** (1392–96), once the home of Martin I of Aragon, towers protectively.

Return to Piazza Duomo and take the Via Monte down to the **Chiesa di San Martino di Tours**, founded in 1163.

Outskirts

On the western side of town, at the far end of Via Sant'Andrea, stands a 12C hermitage, l'Eremo di Sant'Andrea and, farther on, the precincts of **Santa Maria del Gesù** (17C). These are now abandoned but preserve a fine portico with a loggia above.

Excursions

Villa Imperiale del Casale★★★
5km/3mi SW.

 See VILLA IMPERIALE DEL CASALE.

Address Book

🪙 *For coin ranges, see the Legend on the cover flap.*

WHERE TO STAY

🛏️🛏️**Mosaici–da Battiato Hotel** – *Contrada Paratore Casale 11, 3.5km/2mi W of Piazza Armerina.* ☎*0935 68 54 53. Closed 20 Nov–25 Dec. 23 rooms.* 🍽️. A simple, well-maintained hotel in an ideal location for visitors wishing to explore Piazza Armerina and admire the mosaics at the Villa Casale.

🛏️🛏️**Ostello del Borgo** – *Piazza San Giovanni 6, Piazza Armerina.* ☎*0935 68 70 19. www.ostellodelborgo.it.* 🍽️🛏️. Don't be deceived by the name –this is not a hostel in the normal sense of the word, but accommodation provided in a wing of the former monastery of St John. Some of the monks' cells have been converted into spacious, comfortable guest rooms.

WHERE TO EAT

🍴🍴🍴🍴**Al Fogher** – *S 117 bis, 3km/1.8mi N of Piazza Armerina.* ☎*0935 68 41 23. Closed Sun evening and Mon. Booking recommended.* Efficiently run by an enthusiastic, entrepreneurial couple (he runs the kitchen, while she takes care of the dining room), the Al Fogher is one of the best-known restaurants in Sicily. Traditional, authentic Sicilian fare with a contemporary twist.

FESTIVALS

Palio dei Normanni – From 12–14 August, the town of Piazza Armerina puts on a re-enactment of the legendary arrival of Roger de Hauteville (Ruggero d'Altavilla) in the town.

This is followed by jousting and a procession in which the statue of the Madonna and Child with two angels, kept in the cathedral, is carried through the streets to be presented to the town by the Count (🪙 *See infobox, 'The Palio and its Legend'*).

Aidone

From Piazza Armerina take the S 228 (7km/4mi NE).

The small town, a few kilometres from the ruins of Morgantina, accommodates the small **Museo Archeologico Regionale** (🕐*open 9am–7pm;* 💶*€3;* ☎*0935 87 307*), housed in a former Capuchin monastery it displays prehistoric and protohistoric artefacts found in the immediate area.

Access to the museum is through the Church of San Francesco. The exhibits include some fine antefixes from the mid-6C BC, bearing masks of gorgons, lions and maenads, the female worshippers of Dionysus, Greek god of wine and mystery.

Scavi di Morgantina

From Aidone follow signs for Scavi di Morgantina (approx 7km/4mi NE of Aidone). 🕐*Open Apr–Sept, 8am–6.30pm; Oct–Mar, 8am–5pm.* 💶*€3.* ☎*0935 87 955.*

The area of **Serra Orlando** has been inhabited since the Bronze Age. During the Iron Age, one particular settlement became the focal point of the area, growing to become Morgantina (probably named after the king of the Morgeti, an Italic tribe from central-southern Italy). In the 5C BC, the town was refounded a short distance beyond the original, at Serra Orlando. Excavations have uncovered remains of the Siculi centre colonised by the Greeks, which grew to prominence in the 1C AD, and was then abandoned.

The **site** extends from one hill, into a small valley and up the next rise.

Excavations here include a large **agora**, a small **theatre**, a marketplace and a trapezoidal stairway with an adjacent senate chamber (*bouleuterion*). Remains of a gymnasium, and a sanctuary to the deities Demeter and Kore, as well as the foundations of a number of Hellenistic houses, have also been found. On the northern hill, there are a number of fragments of mosaics visible under protective roofing.

Other finds from the site were relocated to the Museo Archeologico Regionale in nearby Aidone.

RAGUSA★★

POPULATION: 71 222

Ragusa, partly rebuilt following the 1693 earthquake, boasts a splendid setting on a plateau between deep ravines. The modern town lies to the west, while the old town, Ragusa Ibla, clusters on an outlier of the hills of Monti Ibei, to the east. The Syracuse road offers magnificent views of the old town.

- **Information:** Palazzo La Rocca, Via Capitano Bocchieri 33, Ibla.
  ☎0932 62 41 21. www.comune.ragusa.it.
- ▶ **Orient Yourself:** Ragusa is actually two cities in one: the less interesting upper, more modern town, built to a regular street plan, and the charming lower town situated to the east.
- **Parking:** Park in the upper town, as the narrow medieval layout of the lower town is most suited to exploration on foot.
- **Don't Miss:** Ragusa Ibla, fine collections of Antiquity at Museo Archeologico Regionale di Camarina and the elegant gardens at Castello di Donnafugata.
- **Also See:** CALTAGIRONE; COMISO; Cava d'ISPICA; MODICA; NOTO.

Walking Tours

Ragusa Ibla★★

A visit to the old town will logically begin from the long stairway of Santa Maria delle Scale, which leads down from the new (higher) part of town to Ragusa Ibla. At certain points, it provides splendid **views**★★ of the town's rooftops, notably the dome of Santa Maria dell'Itria *(left)* and the neo-Classical dome of the cathedral.

Santa Maria delle Scale was rebuilt in the 18C; the Gothic south aisle, with its elegant **pointed arches**★, remains from the earlier fabric. Below the second archway is a lovely Gagini School terracotta panel depicting the Dormition of the Virgin.

In Ibla itself, as if guarding the entrance to the Salita Commendatore *(on the right),* stands the statue of San Francesco di Paola set against a corner of **Palazzo Cosentini**, which has beautiful **balconies**★★ and brackets carved

Santa Maria dell'Itria

San Giorgio

with caricatured figures and masks. This is one of the most secluded corners of town, with a warren of intersecting stepped alleyways hiding some interesting buildings.

The Church of **Santa Maria dell'Itria** is notable outside for its campanile ornamented at the top with lovely floral panels of maiolica from Caltagirone.

Just beyond the church is **Palazzo Nicastro**★★ or Vecchia Cancelleria (1760) – the old prison: note its lovely doorway and balcony. The steep slope downhill on the left emerges in front of the steps leading up to the elegant convex front of the **Chiesa del Purgatorio**.

▷ *To get to Via Bocchieri, follow Via del Mercato, turn right into Via Solarino and then left into Via S. Agnese, which leads into Via Tenente di Stefano.*

Palazzo La Rocca

Azienda Autonoma Provinciale del Turismo headquarters.

This Baroque *palazzo* still bears traces of the original medieval building that preceded it.

An elegant double staircase leads from the main entrance on the first floor where the tourist office is located. The six **balconies**★★ along the main façade

are ornamented with portrait heads depicting real people of the day.

Duomo di San Giorgio★★

The most striking feature from a distance is the 19C neo-Classical dome with its blue lantern articulated with Corinthian columns. From the piazza, on the other hand, the eye is drawn up the imposing flight of steps to the wonderful pink façade. The elegant and harmoniously proportioned front elevation comprises a central, slightly convex bay contained by three tiers of columns, flanked by a side bay surmounted by a volute. Delicately carved decoration ornaments the doorway and cornice. The figure of St George on horseback driving a spear into the dragon, is incorporated into the façade (above the left volute), and as the centrepiece of the beautiful railings at the bottom of the steps. The building was erected in the 18C by **Rosario Gagliardi**.

The interior, divided into nave and aisles, has the same frieze along the nave as the one on the exterior, thereby linking the two into an ideal whole.

Piazza

The rectangular space before the Duomo is set at a slight angle to the church, on a slope. The other buildings enclosing it include **Palazzo Arezzi**, with a wonderful balcony projecting over an archway through to the street beyond; farther on, across on the opposite side of the square, is **Palazzo Donnafugata**.

San Giuseppe★

Silence and modest dress should be observed in the church which is part of the Benedictine monastery.

The elegant front elevation bears a remarkable resemblance to that of San Giorgio, and for this reason has been attributed to Gagliardi. It rises through three tiers of Corinthian columns and figurative statues. The oval **interior** is enclosed below a dome; the floor is a combination of maiolica tiles and black pitchstone. Note the gratings that enabled the enclosed nuns to follow mass out of sight of the congregation.

▷ *Follow Via XXV Aprile.*

Address Book

For coin ranges, see the Legend on the cover flap.

GETTING THERE

There are daily bus services from Agrigento (2hr 30min), Catania airport (2hr), Palermo (4hr) and Siracusa (approximately 2hr), as well as a train service from Siracusa. Both trains and buses arrive in the modern town. For further information and timetables, contact the tourist office.

WHERE TO STAY

Hotel Montreal – *Via S. Giuseppe 6 (on the corner of Corso Italia), Ragusa. ☎0932 62 11 33. www.montreal hotel.it. 50 rooms. ☐.*
Despite its lack of frills, this old-fashioned hotel is friendly, impeccably clean and in a good central location.

Eremo della Giubiliana – *Contrada Giubiliana, 7.5km/4.5mi SW of Ragusa. ☎0932 66 91 19. www.eremo dellagiubiliana.it. Closed 7 Jan–1 Apr. 9 rooms. ☐.* This attractive and unusual hotel is housed in a beautifully restored old monastery in the heart of Ibla's upper town. High levels of comfort and the facilities expected of a hotel of this category.

WHERE TO EAT

Il Barocco – *Via Orfanotrofio 29, Ibla. ☎0932 65 23 97. www.ilbarocco. it. Closed Wed and Jan.* This restaurant/pizzeria in the town centre has bright, colourful decor and an informal and homely atmosphere.

Baglio la Pergola – *Contrada Selvaggio (in the stadium district), Ragusa. ☎0932 68 64 30. Closed Tue.* A varied selection of main courses and pizzas are on the menu in this restaurant in a typical country baglio or stronghold. The traditional Sicilian specialities are particularly recommended.

Locanda Don Serafino – *Via Orfanotrofio 39, Ibla. ☎0932 24 87 78. www.locandadonserafino.it. Closed Tue.* The main features of this pleasant restaurant are a piano bar, perfect for an after-dinner drink, and a dining room housed in the converted stables of an aristocratic mansion. The culinary emphasis here is distinctly Sicilian.

SEASIDE RESORTS

Ragusa is situated close to some of the most popular seaside resorts in southern Sicily, characterised by fine sandy beaches, sand dunes and rocky cliffs. Sampieri, Donnalucata and Scoglitti are perfect for a relaxing holiday, while Marina di Ragusa and Marina di Modica, both of which are exposed to the wind and therefore very popular with surfers and windsurfers, are more suited to outdoor enthusiasts and night owls.

FESTIVALS

I Misteri – This parade and torchlit procession takes place on Good Friday.
Festa di San Giorgio – A re-enactment of the martyrdom of St George is held in Ragusa on the last Sunday in May, ending with a grand firework display.

Giardino Ibleo

For information on admission times, call ☎0932 62 14 21.

These public gardens containing several religious buildings are laid out at the far end of Ragusa Ibla. Just outside the entrance, on the right, stands the elaborate Catalan Gothic portal of **San Giorgio Vecchio** (15C).

The church just inside the gardens, on the left, is **San Giacomo**, better known as Chiesa del Crocefisso because of the wooden effigy contained within, left of the main altar. It dates in the main from the 14C (the 1693 earthquake caused the lateral aisles to collapse; these were never rebuilt), and encloses a ceiling painted with historical panels from 1754 – unfortunately several are missing. The *trompe l'oeil* dome is especially effective.

To the side of the garden stands the **Chiesa dei Cappuccini**. This contains a lovely **triptych**★ by **Pietro Novelli** showing the Virgin Mary, St Agatha and St Lucy. The figure left of the central panel looking out of the picture is a self-portrait.

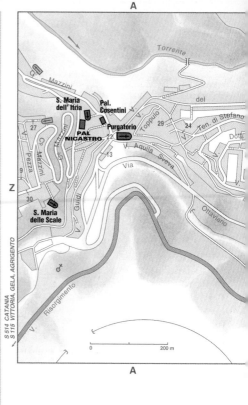

A wonderful **view** from the gardens extends over the Irminio Valley.

Archaeological excavations conducted on a site just beyond the garden have unearthed a street and a residential quarter dating from the Classical period, on top there are layers of various medieval constructions.

Farther along Via Pescheria, on the right-hand side, note the **Chiesa di San Francesco all'Immacolata**. The church, rebuilt in the 17C, preserves a 13C Chiaramonte doorway *(west flank)*.

New Town

The "modern" town has been developed on a framework of straight, parallel streets intersecting at right angles to each other, to form a grid-like pattern up the side of the Patro hill. The elegant **Via** Roma bisects the town on a parallel axis to the side of the hill; the perpendicular **Corso Italia** runs down towards Ibla. On the right is Piazza San Giovanni, overlooked by the church with which it shares its name.

Cattedrale di San Giovanni

The cathedral dates from the early 18C. Its imposing Baroque front elevation, flanked by its campanile, has a broad, raised terrace.

Farther along Corso Italia, on the left, is the 19C Chiesa del Collegio di Maria Addolorata, with **Palazzo Lupis** beyond. Via San Vito *(right)* follows: no 156 is **Palazzo Zacco**, marked by a great coat of arms supported on decorative brackets on the corner. Note the balcony **brackets** projecting from the lateral façade carved with figures and grotesques. Back in Corso Italia, a short distance

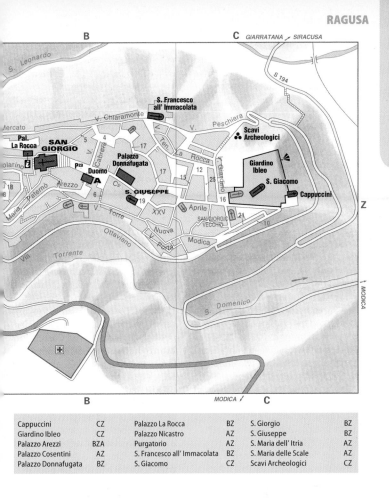

B   C GIARRATANA SIRACUSA

MODICA / C

Cappuccini	CZ	Palazzo La Rocca	BZ	S. Giorgio	BZ
Giardino Ibleo	CZ	Palazzo Nicastro	AZ	S. Giuseppe	BZ
Palazzo Arezzi	BZA	Purgatorio	AZ	S. Maria dell' Itria	AZ
Palazzo Cosentini	AZ	S. Francesco all' Immacolata	BZ	S. Maria delle Scale	AZ
Palazzo Donnafugata	BZ	S. Giacomo	CZ	Scavi Archeologici	CZ

farther along on the left, rises the 18C **Palazzo Bertini**. Three **masks**★ peer down from the carved window keystones to watch the pedestrian traffic. According to tradition, these personify a hungry and toothless pauper *(left)*; a nobleman, serene in assured social status; and a prosperous merchant with a self-satisfied expression, a result of the money in his pocket.

Museo Archeologico Ibleo
Via Natalelli; under the Ponte Nuovo, on the first floor of a building, above a garage.
🕑 Open 9am–1.30pm, 4pm–7.30pm. €2. ☎0932 62 29 63.
The local archaeological museum displays artefacts recovered from the surrounding area. Among the most interesting exhibits is a reconstruction of the

Classical necropoli at Camarina and Rito, and one of the kiln at Scornavacche.

Coastal Driving Tour

110km/69mi from Ragusa, finishing in Comiso – allow one day.

▸ *From Ragusa take S 194 to Modica (12km/7.5mi SE).*

Modica 🕭 *See MODICA*

▸ *Take S 115 to Pozzallo (20km/12.5mi SE).*

Pozzallo
This sleepy hamlet lies on the edge of a long beach. Its most characteristic landmark is the **Torre dei Conti Cabrera**,

355

which was originally built by the local count as a watchtower at a time when pirates frequently assaulted the community. Destroyed by the 1693 earthquake, it has since been rebuilt.

▸ *Continue along the coast road.*

This coast road passes the resorts of **Marina di Modica** and **Sampieri**.

▸ *Turn right at the junction to Scicli and continue 10km/6mi to the town (⟳ See MODICA).*

After 6km/4mi the coast road passes through the **Riserva Naturale della Foce dell'Irpinio**, before arriving at **Marina di Ragusa**⌂, a popular seaside resort.
The **Parco Archeologico di Kaucana** (✆ *closed for restoration at the time of going to press; ☎ 0932 91 61 42*) is located nearby, between Punta Secca and Casuzze. There are two entrances to the archaeological site: one along the coastal road, the other on the road from Punta Secca to Marina di Ragusa. It encloses the ruins of a residential area and a small palaeo-Christian church.

▸ *Continue along the coast road.*

Rovine di Camarina
⟳*Open 9am–2pm, 3pm–7pm.*
👓€3. ☎0932 82 60 04.
Camarina was founded in 598 BC as an Greek town at the behest of Syracuse; an important commercial town, it suf-

fered assaults on many occasions, only to be rebuilt and then finally destroyed by the Romans in 258 BC. **Excavation** has revealed part of the walls, as well as the remains of a 5C temple dedicated to Athena and a residential quarter built on a grid street pattern, dating from Hellenistic times *(marked by the fence on the other side of the road).*

Museo Archeologico Regionale di Camarina
♿⟳*Open daily, 9am–2pm, 3pm–7pm.*
👓€3. ☎0932 82 60 04.
In the first room the most recent finds recovered as a result of ongoing work are displayed; these are gradually replaced and transferred to the permanent collection. The layout is therefore subject to reorganisation.
The sea off Camarina has proved to conceal a wealth of treasures lost in numerous wrecks: a wonderful **Corinthian bronze helmet**★ (6C-5C BC), an Attic-Etruscan helmet (4C BC), an elegant bronze and enamel perfume container (2C AD), and a hoard of more than 1 000 bronze coins (AD 275). There is also an unusual set of **lead weights** recovered from the seabed. The museum possesses a vast collection of well-preserved Corinthian (older and therefore more crudely made) and Attic **amphorae**★. The Etruscan and Punic amphorae are distinguished by their elongation. The section devoted to the Archaic period contains a number of interesting pieces, including a fine aryballos (a small bucket-like vessel used for drawing water from a well) decorated with two lions facing each other (T 2281), from the necropolis at Rifriscolaro.

▸ *From Camarina head inland to Donnafugata (12km/7.5mi).*

Castello di Donnafugata★
♿⟳*Open daily 9.30am–1pm (also afternoon visits in summer 3pm–7pm).*
⟳*Closed Mon.* 👓€5. ☎0932 61 93 33.
The oldest part of the castle (which includes the square tower) dates back to the mid-17C when the Donnafugata fiefdom was acquired by Vincenzo Arezzo La Rocca.

Origins of 'Donnafugata'

The name, which is Arabic in origin, is misleading. It does not, in fact, refer, as first appearances might suggest, to a woman fleeing some tyrannical husband or father (*fuga* in Italian means "escape" or "flight"), nor to one of the legends that linger in some popular memory, but is a free interpretation and transcription of *Ayn as Jafât* (meaning Fountain of Health), which in Sicilian dialect became Ronnafuata and so was corrupted to its modern form.

The building was then continuously altered until the early 20C, when Corrado Arezzo transformed the façade into the one that can be seen today.

What is striking about the castle's exterior is the elegant Venetian Gothic loggia that dominates the centre of the façade. The trefoil arches are a recurrent motif here, and are repeated in the two-light windows throughout the building.

Gardens

The large garden, shaded first by large banyan trees (Ficus magnolioides), then by other Mediterranean and exotic species (succulents and cluster pines), conceals various follies intended to charm and bemuse its visitors, like the round temple and a coffee house (where refreshments could be taken), the stone maze and several artificial caves encrusted with fake stalactites (below the temple).

Villa

The first floor is open to the public. At the top of the black stone (pietra pece in Italian) staircase, ornamented with neo-Classical statues, is the **Salone degli Stemmi**, named after the armorial crests of great Sicilian noble families painted on the walls. Among the suites of rooms are some with delicately painted trompe l'oeil ceilings.

These include the stucco-decorated **Salone degli Specchi** (the Hall of Mirrors), the **Billiard Room** and **Music Room**, each with painted landscapes projecting out beyond the walls, and the bedroom of the Princess of Navarre, paved in black pietra pece (a bitumous limestone mined locally, from which pitch is made) and white limestone where, it is said, Princess Bianca was kept segregated from Count Cabrera (an anachronistic legend, given that the princess lived in the 14C).

The **Stanza del Signore** and the **Fumoir** are beautifully furnished; the decoration of the latter, a smoking room, is perfectly appropriate to its function. It is papered with pipe motifs and the ceiling is painted with medallions filled with playing cards and beautiful peacocks fanning their tails at the corners.

This beautiful castle has a history of inspiration for writers and artists. Giuseppe di Lampedusa used the name Donnafugata in his famous 1960 novel *The Leopard*, as the title of the country house inhabited by main protagonists, the Salina family. It has also been featured in the making of many well-known films including the *La Giara* scene in the film *Chaos* by the Taviani brothers.

> ▶ *From here, continue to Comiso (16km/10mi N, ⌖See COMISO).*

Excursion

Carmelo Cappello Sculpture Collection

The collection is housed in the industrial estate (ASI) south of Ragusa, in Contrada Mugno (the junction at Km 321.700 on S 115).
⊙*Open Mon–Thu 9am–12.30pm, 3.30pm–5pm; Fri 9am–12.30pm.*
⊘*Closed Sat–Sun.*

Carmelo Cappello, a native of Ragusa (b. 1912), began to work in the 1930s. His style, which evolved from being highly figurative in the early years to becoming pure abstraction in his latest creations, is well represented in this small, but interesting collection. *Il freddoloso (Shivering with Cold* – 1938), one of his most famous works, is a realistic figure charged with great expression. In the later works, facial features become abstracted by being reduced to a minimum: compare the expressive faces of the two women with well-defined noses and eyes (though no hair or mouth) in *Le prime stelle (The First Stars)* to the faces of the two athletes in Acrobati (1953–54). In this latter work, individual personality and detail has been distilled, abstracted and replaced by a concentration on rhythm and movement of line. Cappello's latest works are austere studies of pure line, clinically cold (an impression imparted by the polished steel) yet which twist and merge, attempting to encapsulate in form the fluid dynamics of the universe.

SCIACCA

POPULATION: 40 758

Perched on a flank of Monte Kronio on the edge of the sea, pretty Sciacca rises up from its port, replete with colourful houses and fishing boats. An important thermal region notable for its sulphurous waters, it is also famous for the production of remarkable malioca ceramic work, which can be admired and acquired in numerous local workshops.

- **Information:** Corso Vittorio Emanuele 94. ☎0925 20 478. www.comune.sciacca.ag.it.
- **Orient Yourself:** Physical stamina is required for a visit to Sciacca; natural terracing divides the town into three sections: the narrow, winding streets of the medieval district of Terravecchia lie to the north of Via Licata; the town's major monuments lie between Via Licata and Piazza Scandaliato; while the port area extends beyond Piazza Scandaliato.
- **Parking:** Sciacca has countless flights of steps and narrow alleyways, so visitors are advised to park their car and explore the town on foot.
- **Don't Miss:** A thermal bath at Valle dei Bagni and a sauna at the Stufe di San Calogero natural steam caves, a walk in the sculpture gardens at Castello Incantato and views from the hilltop towns of Prizzi and Bisacquino.
- **Organising Your Time:** Have thermal treatments after you have finished sightseeing, as they can have a very soporific effect.
- **Also See:** AGRIGENTO; CASTELVETRANO; Antica città di SELINUNTE.

Historic Centre

The perfect kernel at the heart of Sciacca is **Piazza Scandaliato** with its broad terrace overlooking the multi-coloured harbour packed with boats, and the open sea beyond. Dominating the west side of the square is the 18C Church of **San Domenico;** the longer flank accommodates the former **Jesuit College** (complete with fine 17C cloisters), now used as the town hall. Behind lies Piazza del Duomo.

Duomo

The cathedral was founded by the Normans and rebuilt in the 1600s. The Baroque *façade* remains unfinished. The **interior** nave and side aisles preserve various works of interest. The barrel-vaulted nave is frescoed (1829) by the local artist Tommaso Rossi with the Apocalypse and episodes from the life of Mary Magdelene. The chapel to the right of the chancel contains a lovely Renaissance marble altarpiece (1581) by Antonio Gagini; its walls are hung with evocative paintings of scenes from Christ's Passion.

The central thoroughfare, **Corso Vittorio Emanuele**, runs to the right of the Duomo, past the 15C-17C **Palazzo Arone Tagliavia** *(on the right)*, its fine castellated frontage accommodating three pointed entrances and, above the central arch, a three-light Gothic window. Farther on sits the 19C Imperial-style **Palazzo San Giacomo** (or Tagliavia), with its south-facing façade graced with four sphinx-like herms. The Venetian neo-Gothic building overlooks Piazza Friscia.

In **Viale della Vittoria**, which leads off the piazza to the right, stands the **Convento di San Francesco** (*for opening times, call ☎0925 96 1111; www.termesciacca.it*). This has been transformed into a conference and exhibition centre. The monastery cloisters display sculptures by contemporary artists, including three large *Bathers* by Bergomi (1989). At the far end of Viale della Vittoria, **Santa Maria delle Giummare** (entrance in Via Valverde) rises above the surrounding buildings. This was founded by the Normans and rebuilt in the 16C. The actual church is contained within the main body of the building; the two square "tow-

M. Magni/MICHELIN

Colourful carnival decorations

ers" provide residential quarters for the dependent monastery.

A little farther on the right lie the ruins of **Castello della Luna**. This was built in the late 14C, rebuilt in the 16C and almost completely destroyed in the 19C. Today, only the perimeter walls and an imposing cylindrical tower remain.

San Nicolò la Latina

Open summer, 6.30pm–7pm; otherwise 5.30pm–6pm. ☎*0925 21 315.*

This church was founded in the early part of the 12C by Giulietta, the daughter of Roger I. Its simple façade has a doorway with a heavily moulded surround, and three similarly accented single openings above (the two side ones are blind). The interior comprises a Latin-cross plan, complete with nave, short transepts and three semicircular apses typical of transitional Arabo-Norman prototypes.

Climb back up to the castle ruins and follow Via Giglio to the town gate, **Porta di San Calogero**, where remains of the medieval walls may be seen. On Piazza Noceto is **Santa Maria dell'Itria**, an annexe to the larger Chiesa Madre with a fine Baroque façade, **San Michele Arcangelo** (17C-18C). Inside there is a lovely 18C gallery and a carved, painted wooden organ case against the back wall; on the right look for the Catalan Gothic cross and, in the south aisle, a 15C altarpiece of St Jerome.

Continue down towards Corso Vittorio Emanuele to the junction with Via Licata which accommodates two fine 18C buildings: Palazzo Inveges, and farther up on the right, Palazzo Ragusa. At the next intersection with Via Gerardi, turn left: on the corner with Corso Vittorio Emanuele is the **Palazzo Steripinto**, a Catalan-style *palazzo* dating from the 15C whose facade is articulated with diamond-cut rustication,

Via Gerardi opens out into Piazza del Carmine, named after the Carmine church that stands there before the 16C town gateway, **Porta San Salvatore**,

Visitor from the Deep

July 1831: at the time, anyone looking out to sea from Sciacca was unlikely to imagine what was about to happen. For, in a very short space of time, a great land mass emerged from the water. Rather than a monster rising from the underworld, this apparition was a volcanic outcrop that gently settled back into a truncated cone. This precipitated a huge stir and prompted a host of heatedly contested theories. The island was christened **Ferdinandea**, in honour of the reigning Spanish monarch. But it was short lived: after a mere five months, the island disappeared into oblivion.

ornamented by two lions facing each other.

Santa Margherita

🕐 *Open Mon–Fri 8am–2pm, 4.30pm–7pm; Sat 8am–2pm only; Sun and public hols by appointment only.* ☎*0925 20 478; www.comune.sciacca.it.*

The original church fabric dates from the 13C; the alterations were implemented in the late 16C. The main front has a lovely Catalan Gothic doorway, although the Renaissance-Gothic side door on the left side with *St Margaret and the Dragon* by Pietro da Bonitate and Francesco Laurana (apparently only the figure of Mary Magdalene on the left jamb is his) is more famous. Inside, the coffered ceiling is painted to suggest a starry sky. A monumental 19C organ takes up most of the back wall, and a splendid marble altarpiece in the right chapel relates scenes from the life of St Margaret.

The other church nearby is **Chiesa di San Gerlando**. A little farther on the left stands the 15C **Palazzo Perollo**: its façade has three late Gothic three-light windows and an inner courtyard furnished with a lovely, although dilapidated, Catalan staircase.

Palace and Baths

Palazzo Scaglione★

Piazza Don Minzoni (near the Duomo). 🕐*Open daily, 9am–1pm.* ☎*0925 20 111.* This 18C residence, now a museum, displays the objets d'art and works of art collected in the 19C by Francesco Scaglione. All the rooms are crowded with pictures – the majority by Sicilian painters – engravings, coins, archaeological artefacts, bronze sculptures and ceramics in a clear demonstration of the eclecticism and collecting mania typical of the period. The last room contains an 18C ivory and mother-of-pearl crucifix.

Thermal baths

Viale delle Terme, SE of the town. 🕐*Open daily, 9am–1pm.* 🕐*Closed Sun and national holidays.* ☎*0925 96 11 11; www.termesciacca.it.*

The thermal treatments in the region surrounding Sciacca have been famous since Antiquity, yet it was only in the mid-19C that a spa was opened outside the town centre in the **Valle dei Bagni** (☛*this has still to be restored and reopened*). The most modern thermal facilities at the **Nuovo Stabilimento Termale** date from 1938: this extensive, Liberty-style complex lies southeast of the town, in private gardens by the edge of the sea. Here, the natural sulphurous waters are used in mud therapy (for relieving arthritis), balneotherapy (for osteo-arthritis and skin conditions) and inhalation treatments. Other degenerative conditions are treated with various therapies also available from the Stufe di San Calogero on Monte Kronio, and at the thermal pools at Molinelli. These baths are supplemented by mineral-rich waters that issue from the ground at a constant temperature of 34°C.

Excursions

Monte Kronio

Leave Sciacca along Via Porta S. Calogero. 7km/4mi.

The haul to the summit provides ample opportunity to survey the broad **panorama**★★ panning over the coast, the plain of Sciacca and the bare mountains inland. At the top sits the **Santuario di San Calogero**, built by the Franciscans. The natural occurrence of caves in which hot vapours are caught has been exploited to provide steam baths since Antiquity. The largest and most well known is the Stufe di San Calogero. The rational explanation for the phenomenon is that a vein of hot water runs deep within the mountain; when it comes into contact with direct heat the water evaporates and escapes upwards, mingling with the air as it rises through fissures and cracks in the rock, to break through into the open at a temperature of 40°C.

Italians consider the vapours to have therapeutic powers for rheumatism, skin disease and gynaecological problems.

Stufe di San Calogero

🕐*Open daily, 8am–1pm.* 🕐*Closed Sun and national hols.* ☞*€1.* ☎*0925 96 11 11; www.termesciacca.it.*

Son of the Earth and the Sky

Monte Kronio - The name of this isolated peak (386m/1 266ft), set in a deserted landscape, suggests an immediate association with Cronus (Greek Kronos), the god of time and one of the oldest figures of the pantheon, born out of a union between Mother Earth (Gaea) and her son, the god of heaven (Uranus).

Banished to Tartarus along with his other siblings (the Titans) by his father, Cronus was assisted by his mother in rising up against Uranus and castrating him; there followed a Golden Age on earth that lasted until his youngest (oldest in Homer) son Zeus, assisted by the Cyclops and the Hundred-handed Giants, declared war on Mount Olympus and the other Titans: at this point the myths vary in detail. According to some, the gods were defeated by thunderbolts and falling stones before being imprisoned in Tartarus; other accounts prevalent in Sicily relate how Zeus inveigled the gods by inebriating them with ambrosia and honeyed mead, chaining them up as they slept, and relegating them to a group of islands called the Isole dei Beati (Islands of the Blessed).

The other legendary hero associated with this place is Daedalus who, being an expert on labyrinths, as is well known, decided to redirect the boiling vapours that emanated from cracks in the rock in order to harness their power: and so the origins of the stufe vaporose – the steamy caves – are explained.

The caves were either inhabited or regularly used for religious practices until the Bronze Age; they were finally abandoned some time around 2000 BC when steam began to pour into them, possibly as a result of a landslide, making permanent occupation impossible. The caves began to be used again some time during the Greek occupation, possibly as a result of steam emanating from the mountain side being interpreted as a mysterious (and hence divine) phenomenon. Numerous artefacts have been recovered from the caves, especially vases and votive figurines *(some are displayed in the archaeological museum at Agrigento)*. The names of the caves were bestowed by a monk who came here in the 4C; having realised the therapeutic potential of the vapours, he set about dividing the caves into rooms with stone benches for his patients. The largest caves include l'Antro di Dedalo and the Grotta degli Animali. The Grotta del Santo nearby, probably provided living quarters for St Calogero, depicted in the maiolica icon above the altar (15C).

Today, the caves are part of the modern spa complex Grande Albergo delle Stufe.

Next to the Stufe, a small **antiquarium** (open Tue–Sat 9am–1pm, 3pm–7pm; Mon, Sun and public hols 9am–1pm; donations welcome; ☎0925 28 989) displays artefacts.

Castello Incantato

2km/1.2mi W: take Via Figuli out of Sciacca and follow signs for Agrigento (S 115).

Open Apr–Sept (except Mon) 10am–noon, 4pm–8pm; Oct–Mar, daily except Mon 9am–1pm, 3pm–5pm. Donations welcome. ☎0925 99 30 44; www.comune.sciacca.it.

This incredible garden, dotted with sculpted stone heads, was conceived in 1913 by Filippo Bentivegna (1888–1967). Over half a century, *Filippu delli Testi* – as he is called here – sculpted these faces out of the rock in every corner of his extensive estate, with expressions that range from the worried to the serene.

Driving Tour

Valle del Belice and Valle del Sosio

160km/100mi – allow 1 day.

▸ Take S 115 towards Castelvetrano and then S 188 as far as Portella Misilbesi. From here turn right to Sambuca di Sicilia, still following S 188.

The road skirts around **Lago Arancio**, a man-made protected lake of major environmental importance due to the storks that inhabit the area.

Address Book

🪙 *For coin ranges, see the cover flap.*

WHERE TO STAY

🪙 *Also see CATANIA: Address Book.*

SCIACCA

🍴🍴🛏️**Verdetecnica** – *Via Monte Kronio 22, Sciacca.* ☎*0925 81 133. www.verdetecnica.it.* 🖂*. 6 apartments.* A small gem of a hotel situated on a hill overlooking Sciacca and comprising six apartments, all equipped with bathroom and kitchen of varying sizes. Simple decor, in tune with the surrounding countryside. Minimum stay of five days is required in August.

SAMBUCA DI SICILIA

🍴**Lago Arancio Vacanze** – *Contrada Arancio, Sambuca di Sicilia.* ☎*0923 94 60 03. www.agriturismoed-intorni.com.* 🖂*.* This small rural hotel has just a handful of rooms giving it an intimate air. It enjoys a panoramic and peaceful location on the lake edge, where there are a number of activities on offer. These include canoeing, water-skiing, swimming and fishing.

WHERE TO EAT

🍴🍴**Porto San Paolo** – *Largo San Paolo 1, Sciacca.* ☎*0925 27 982. Closed Wed, Oct and second week in Apr.* The Porto San Paolo specialises in fish dishes. Choose between the rustic ambience and wooden decor of the dining room and the summer veranda overlooking the port.

🍴🍴🛏️**Villa Palocla** – *Contrada Raganella, 4km/2.5mi W of Sciacca.* ☎*0925 90 28 12. www.villapalocla.it.* This villa has a truly Sicilian flavour, with its garden planted with fragrant citrus trees surrounding a mid-18C, late Baroque style building. Offering both accommodation and a restaurant, the Villa Palocla's menu is dominated by an excellent range of fish dishes.

🍴🍴🛏️**Hostaria del Vicolo** – *Vicolo Sammaritano 10, Sciacca.* ☎*0925 23 071. Closed Mon and 14 Oct–1 Nov.* This small, elegant restaurant in the heart of Sciacca serves typical, traditional Sicilian cuisine enlivened with contemporary touches. Good wine list.

TAKING A BREAK

Bar Roma – *Piazza Dogana 12, Sciacca.* ☎*0925 21 239.* Aurelio Licata, the owner of this bar, is famous for his lemon *granita* (crushed ice drink), which, served with a delicious brioche, is considered a typical Sicilian breakfast.

FESTIVALS

Carnevale – Sciacca's extravagant carnival is one of the most famous in Sicily, with its magnificent procession of allegorical carts.

Sambuca di Sicilia

The town reclines on a gentle slope. Noble palazzi run along the central street Corso Umberto I: at the far end, a stairway climbs to a viewing terrace.

▸ *From Sambuca, follow signs for Scavi di Monte Adranone (7km/4mi).*

Scavi di Monte Adranone

🕐*Open Tue–Sat 9am–1pm, 3pm–7pm.* 🕐*Closed Mon and Sun.* ☎*0925 28 989.* The Ancient Greek settlement (6C BC) overlies another earlier, indigenous, one. The site, perched high on a mountain top, overlooking the surrounding countryside, is naturally defended on one side and reinforced by strong defensive walls on the other two. The town, loosely identified with Adranon, a place documented by the Classical historian Diodorus Siculus, was probably destroyed during the First Punic War.

Tour

Outside the walls, the **necropolis** includes the **Tomba della Regina**. **Views**★★ from the hilltop **acropolis** take in Sambuca and **Lago Arancio** and continue out along the entire length of the valley.

▸ *Continue along the road for a few kilometres and then turn right to Bisacquino.*

The road runs through a **landscape**★ of rolling hills and steep mountains, passing the abbey of **Santa Maria del Bosco** (16C-17C) on the right.

Bisacquino

The birthplace of Frank Capra (1897–1991), the director of the film *It's A Wonderful Life,* Bisacquino is a small town attractively perched on the slopes of Monte Triona. Dominated by the impressive dome of the 18C Chiesa Madre, the town has an intricate Arab-influenced layout. The majolica bell tower of Santa Maria delle Grazie stands on the same square as the church.

The town's other monument of note is the unusual triangular-shaped bell tower of San Francesco, also decorated with majolica.

A number of typical scenes relating to rural life and traditional trades have been recreated in the interesting **Museo Etnologico** (◷*open Mon–Fri 8am–2pm (also 3pm–6pm Tue), Sat–Sun by appointment only;* ✍*donations welcome;* ✆*091 83 08 047; www.comune.bisacquino.pa.it*) in Via Orsini.

From Bisacquino follow S 188c towards Palermo and take the exit to the 17C sanctuary of the **Madonna del Balzo**. A stunning **view**★★ of the surrounding area can be enjoyed 900m/2 950ft above the clearing opposite the sanctuary.

▸ *Return to S 188. From Bisacquino, head towards Palazzo Adriano.*

The road passes Lago Gammauta, which can be explored with a diversion.

Palazzo Adriano

www.comune.palazzoadriano.pa.it. The focal point of this village, in which Tornatore filmed part of *Nuovo Cinema Paradiso,* is the **Piazza Umberto I**★. This elegant square is paved with white stone and lined with fine buildings. From Palazzo the road continues to Prizzi, passing through mountain scenery.

Prizzi

www.comune.prizzi.pa.it. Standing at an altitude of over 1 000m/3 300ft, Prizzi enjoys a charming **site**★, framed by the Sicani mountains. An unusual measurement conversion chart, erected after the unification of Italy, can be admired in the central Corso Umberto I. Further on, the **Piazza Sparacio** is decorated with murals. The oldest part of town, with its narrow streets winding around the Chiesa Madre and the castle, is to the north of Corso Umberto. The town comes to life on Easter Sunday, with the Ballo dei Diavoli festival.

Return to S 188 and retrace your route for 30km/19mi. Turn left at the junction to **Chiusa Sclàfani**, an attractive town which has retained its historic medieval centre. The town is built around a Benedictine monastery, which has an attractive garden next door.

▸ *10km/6mi after Chiusa Sclàfani, follow signs to Caltabellotta.*

Caltabellotta

www.comune.caltabellotta.ag.it. The two roads up to the town offer wonderful **views**★; the route via **Sant'Anna** is especially scenic. Caltabellotta enjoys a fabulous **position**★★, 900m/2 950ft above sea level and was consequently turned into a military post. Here, the Angevins signed the peace treaty ending the War of the Sicilian Vespers (1302). The tallest point is the chapel, hermitage of San Pellegrino, and the ruins of the Norman castle.

The Arabo-Norman **Chiesa Matrice** and **Chiesa del Salvatore** stand at the foot of the castle. The road heading down to Sciacca offers splendid **views**★★ of the valley below.

SEGESTA★★★

Splendidly situated against the hillside, its ochre colours in pleasant contrast to the vast expanse of green, Segesta archaeological park is dominated by a fine Doric temple standing in an isolated site. Probably founded like Erice by the Elimi, Segesta soon became one of the main cities in the Mediterranean basin under Greek influence, rivalling Selinus in importance. Segesta was probably destroyed by the Vandals.

- **Information:** Calatafimi Segesta Tourist Office. ☎924 95 46 80.
- **Orient Yourself:** Segesta occupies a splendid **position**★★, among gently sloping hills of yellow ochre and ruddy brown. This timeless landscape is presided over by the majestic silhouette of the Doric temple, one of the most perfectly preserved monuments to survive from Antiquity, standing on a hill surrounded by a deep valley, framed by Monte Bernardo and Monte Barbaro where the theatre is situated.
- **Parking:** Park at the site's car park and take the shuttle bus to the theatre.
- **Organising Your Time:** There is no shade at the site of Segesta, so visit early morning, preferably when it opens at 9am, or late afternoon in summer, when the soulful solitude and the light of the site is at its most evocative.
- **Also See:** ERICE; GIBELLINA.

A Bit of History

Ancient Segesta was probably founded in 12C BC on the slopes of Monte Barbaro by the Elimi; under Greek sponsorship. Like Erice (Eryx) it soon ranked among the leading towns of the Mediterranean basin. In the 5C BC, it was pitched against its great rival Selinunte (Selinus). In an attempt to rally its defences against this threat, Segesta appealed for help from Athens in 415 BC, but these reinforcements were subsequently defeated by Syracuse whose forces were allied to Selinunte. In 409 BC, Segesta turned to Carthage for support; on landing in Sicily, these troops destroyed both Selinus and Himera in vast and bloody battles. In turn, Segesta was destroyed by the Syracusan tyrant Agathocles in 307 BC but rose again to power under the Romans. Subsequent developments are not well documented, although it is thought that the city probably succumbed to further damage at the hand of the Vandals in the 5C AD.

What is certain is that the area was inhabited in medieval times, as the excavated ruins of a Norman castle and a small three-apsed basilica situated in the northern part of the ancient acropolis, testify. This part of the site extended over two areas separated by a hollow. The southeastern section was predominantly residential, whereas the north was populated by public buildings, including the theatre.

Archaeological Site

Temple open in summer, 9am–1 hour before sunset. €6. A regular shuttle bus service operates to the theatre (€1.50). Bar and restaurant. ☎0924 95 23 56.

Tempio★★★

Built in 430 BC (although scholars are divided about its exact date), this amazingly well preserved temple is a Doric building with the 36 limestone columns of its peristyle, plus entablature and pediment almost completely intact. The shafts are unfluted, no holes were left in the architrave for roof beams and coupled with the absence of a *cella*, this arrangement has prompted the suggestion that the temple was abandoned before completion. Some scholars dismiss this theory, claiming that the lack of a *cella* (usually the first part of the sanctuary to be undertaken) might indicate that the building was intended to consist merely of a peristyle, making it a pseudo-temple. Other recent academic theories and exploration suggest that the

B. Kaufmann/MICHELIN

Temple of Segesta

Egestans stopped work around 420 BC, which would put pay to the idea of the structure serving as some sort of outdoor temple for a Elymian cult. The mystery of whether the temple was used for worship or not is compounded by the lack of any indication as to which, if any, deity it might have been dedicated to.

The road up to the theatre *(approx 2km/1.2mi: take the regular minibus service from the car park)* winds through overgrown wild fennel and provides fabulous **views**★★ back over the temple. Before the theatre, on the right, other layers of history have been peeled back, which further illustrate the importance of this strategic site. These include the remains of the Hermitage of San Leone, with a single apse, built over the foundation of an earlier three-apsed church and, behind it, the ruins of the Norman castle.

Teatro★

The white stone theatre was built in the 3C BC during the Hellenistic period, while the area was under Roman domination. It consists of a perfect semicircle with a diameter of 63m/207ft slotted into a rocky slope. The 20 tiers of seats face west towards the hills, beyond which, to the right, may be glimpsed the broad Bay of Castellammare. The true purpose of the theatre can still be experienced on odd-numbered years when performances of Greek tragedies, Roman plays and Shakespearean dramas are held here *(see box below)*.

Sanctuary of the Elymians

The third of Segesta's sites is only accessible by a strenuous hike eastwards uphill toward Contrado Magno. Now just a large, overgrown and partially excavated area, probably dating from around the 6C BC, it was once a site of some religious significance to the Elymians. There's not much to see here compared with the impressively intact remains of the temple and theatre, but it is still of interest if only to appreciate the poetic loneliness and natural splendour of the site with few or no other visitors.

Address Book

FESTIVALS

In July and August, the theatre hosts a programme of concerts and contemporary and classical plays. The atmosphere at the theatre is particularly moving during performances of music, poetry and literature, known as *albe* (dawn), which take place at 5am. For further information, contact the Calatafimi Segesta tourist office on ☎0924 95 46 80.

ANTICA CITTÀ DI SELINUNTE★★

Selinus was founded in the mid-7C BC by people from the east coast city of Megara Hyblaea and was destroyed twice, in 409 and 250 BC, by the Carthaginians. The huge ruins of its temples, with their enormous platforms probably wrecked by earthquakes, are impressive.

- **Information:** A.P.T. ☎0924 46251. www.selinute.com.
- ▶ **Orient Yourself:** Take the Castelvetrano motorway exit and follow S 115d to Marinella. Buses run from Agrigento, Castelvetrano, Marsala, Mazara del Vallo and Trapani. It's possible to drive from the eastern temples to the acropolis.
- **Don't Miss:** The Cave di Cusa where the temple's stone blocks were quarried.
- **Organising Your Time:** The ruins are scattered over a deserted area with little shade, therefore sightseeing in summer is best done in the early morning or later afternoon when the sun is not so fierce.
- **Parking:** Parking is available by the Visitors Centre at the eastern temples.
- **Where to Stay:** For accommodation in the area, see CASTELVETRANO.
- **Also See:** CASTELVETRANO; MAZARA DEL VALLO; SCIACCA.

A Bit of History

The most westerly, and one of the most important of all the Greek colonies, ancient Selinus was founded by settlers from Megara Hyblaea during the 7C BC. Situated on a fertile plain, carpeted in wild celery (the city's name is derived from the Greek name - *selinon*) it occupied a much coveted stretch of land, that unsurprisingly drew constant territorial attention from bitter rivals, the Segestans and the Carthaginians in the west and north west of the island. Despite this, from the 6C BC, Selinute itself enjoyed a short but intensive period of prosperity over two centuries thanks to prudent government by the line of successive tyrants.

However, in 409 BC Segesta allied itself to Carthage, in the hope of its support in the conflict with its rival. As a result,

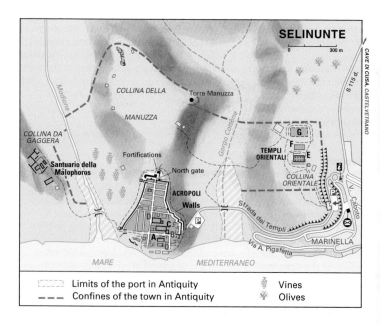

SELINUNTE

0   300 m

CAVE DI CUSA, CASTELVETRANO

Modione

COLLINA DELLA MANUZZA

Torre Manuzza

COLLINA DA GAGGERA

Santuario della Malophoros

Fortifications

Gorgo Cottone

S 115 d

North gate

TEMPLI ORIENTALI

G

F

E

COLLINA ORIENTALE

ACROPOLI

Walls

Strada dei Templi

Cabolo

Via A. Pigafetta

MARINELLA

MARE   MEDITERRANEO

Limits of the port in Antiquity   Vines

Confines of the town in Antiquity   Olives

Temple C towers over the other ruins

Selinute was destroyed by the Carthaginian general Hannibal in a surprise attack that sent 100 000 men into the city to capture it over a bloody period of nine days. His ferocious methods to win supremacy resulted in the death of 16000 Selinuntini and the capture of 5000 as prisoners, most of whom were sold into slavery.

The survivors begged him to spare the city's many temples in return for a substantial payment, Hannibal consented, but once he had the money, he sacked the temples and pulled down the walls.

Selinute invested every last effort in repairing the damage, but the city never managed to regain its former prosperity, and eventually reverted to Carthaginian rule once more, serving as a garrison town until the First Punic War. Against all the odds, it survived largely intact until the Second Punic War, when it was razed to the ground by earthquakes.

Parts of the city that remained, however, were still occupied all the way up to 250BC, when the last inhabitants moved to Marsala prior to the Roman invasion. Fleetingly occupied by the Arabs and then again in the 13th century, Selinute fell into decay and lay forgotten until it was rediscovered in the 16C BC and painstakingly excavated in the 18C BC by two Englishmen, Samuel Angeli and Walter Harris.

Archaeological Site

&🕐*Open 9am–7pm, last entry 1hr before dusk.* €6. ☎0924 46 251.

The archaeological site is divided into four areas: the first, spread across the hill on the eastern side, contains three large temples, one having been re-erected in 1957; the second, on the hill to the west and surrounded by walls, comprises the acropolis, south of the third area, where the ancient town ruins can be seen; the fourth, west of the acropolis also consisted of a sacred precinct of temples and sanctuaries.

The ruins are scattered over a deserted area, abandoned since Selinunte's downfall: the ruined temples continue to point great columns to the sky; other buildings, reduced to monumental rubble, probably by an earthquake, inspire a tragic air of desolation.

The nearby quarries that provided the tufa stone used in the temples' construction lie a short distance away and are also worth a visit if you have time. The huge, roughly hewn blocks that still litter the quarries put the incredible architectural feats of the Selinute temples into perspective.

Templi orientali

The first of the eastern temples to come into view is **Temple E**, dedicated to Hera and the only reconstruction on the site,

Breaking Stone with Wood and Water

Once the dimensions and profile of a stone building block had been marked out in the quarry, a double groove about half a metre deep was dug around it to enable the stonemasons to work and cut the block *in situ*. The tools used included picks, bronze saws and wedges. To split the harder layers, wooden wedges were inserted into cracks and then dampened with water so that, as they swelled, the stone would crack open. The block was then severed at the base and removed by means of winches or slid down ramps. The deep U-shaped grooves visible in some of the square blocks were made so that a rope could be fed through them for lifting. Many blocks have a square hole at either end. Into these sockets were fitted special shafts that enabled the blocks to be moved and set in place. The blocks were transported on wooden frames with wheels, and pulled by oxen and slaves. A wide rocky track led from the quarries to Selinunte.

having been re-erected in 1957. A fine example of Doric peripteral elegance, it dates from the 5C BC and is built on a complex ground plan. The entrance to the *pronaos* was from the east-facing side, through the colonnade. Only the capitals remain from doorway remain, lying on the ground. Beyond lay the *cella* with a secret chamber (the *adytum*) where the statue of the deity was kept. Behind that lay the *opisthodomus*, which was identical to the pronaos. On the right, lie the ruins of **Temple F**, on a smaller scale than Temple E and belonging to the mid-6C BC. This graceful temple is made up of unusually slender columns topped by widely protruding capitals, arranged in a pattern of six at the end and fourteen along the sides. The temple is comparable in size to Temple C, and was probably dedicated to the goddess Athena.

Lastly, **Temple G**, one of the four largest Greek temples in the world –and the second largest Greek temple in Sicily, after the Temple of Olympian Zeus at Agrigento – would have been the most impressive. Conceived on gigantic proportions – 17 columns long and 8 wide, each with a diameter of almost 3.5m and a height of more than 16m/53ft – it was probably dedicated to the god Apollo. The temple, the only octastyle one found on the site (the rest are all hexastyle) was never finished: work on it was interrupted by the attack on the city by Carthage, led by Hannibal in 409BC. In the nearby quarries of Cusa, huge columns intended for it can still be seen, gouged from the tufa rock.

Acropoli

Drive from the eastern temples car park to the next one.

The acropolis stretched across a hill on the far side of the dip called Gorgo di Cottone, through which the River Cottone flowed down to the sea where the town's **harbour** (now overgrown) was situated. The site was levelled off by the first settlers here, allowing them to build on it: sacred buildings initially, followed by residential and commercial structures later. The acropoli itself was enclosed within defensive walls built in the 6C-5C BC. The streets were laid out according to the Classical town plan proposed by Hippodamus of Miletus, with three main arteries bisected by a grid of smaller streets. This area contained public and religious buildings and houses that accommodated all the highest ranking members of society. Today, the agora, or "marketplace" and two main streets have been fully excavated and help provide a picture of ancient life here.

The path skirts the graduated **walls** that run all the way around the eastern side of the acropolis.

Temples

As the track climbs uphill you will see the ruin of **Temple A**. Within the wall are two spiral staircases, the most ancient examples known to date. This precinct, however, is dominated by 14 of the 17 monolithic columns of **Temple C**, which were re-erected in 1925. This, the earliest surviving temple at Selinus (initiated early 6C BC), was probably dedicated to Apollo or Heracles, and would have originally been decorated with terracotta and polychrome elements.

It is hard to imagine the impact of the pediment (an imposing Gorgon's head in shallow relief, whose function was to look over and protect the city) as it lies broken on the ground. The finest metopes, depicting scenes from Greek mythology recovered from this site are now displayed in pride of place at the archaeological museum in Palermo. Also found in the museum is a reconstruction of the pediment.

Fortifications

At the far end of the *decumanus maximus* rises a curtain wall, which once surrounded the acropolis. What may now be seen consists of the fortifications that were built using recycled building stone after the site was destroyed in 409 BC. A second, smaller circle of walls was built around 305 BC. Beyond the north gate, the grand **Porta Nord** is a three-storey structure of two superimposed galleries surmounted by arches, allowing soldiers and equipment to move quickly and easily through them.

Ancient town

The residential part of the town was situated on the hill of Manuzza: over the period following the 4C BC, this area was gradually abandoned and used as a necropolis for burials.

Santuario della Malophoros

The sanctuary may be reached by following the track that extends from the first cardo to the left of the decumanus maximus (from the acropolis); allow 20min there and back.

The sanctuary was built in honour of Demeter, also known as Malophoros (she who bears the pomegranate), the goddess of plants and the protector of farmers and growers. It was built around 575 BC inside a sacred precinct *(temenos)* on the opposite side of the River Modione. Beyond the propylaeum is a sacrificial altar. A channel bearing water from the Gaggera mountain spring separates it from the temple. The latter, without

columns, comprised a *pronaos*, a *cella* and an *adytum* containing a statue of the deity. Over 12 000 votive statues of Demeter were found outside the sanctuary, giving some indication as to the importance and power of the cult of Demeter at the time of Selinute's power. Around the sanctuary also lies a large necropolis, with tombs that stretch up the nearby coastline.

Excursion

Cave di Cusa★

20km/12mi NW of Selinunte.
Head towards Campobello di Mazara, then follow signs to Cave di Cusa.
🕐*Open 9am–dusk.*

The Cusa quarries were the main source of building stone for the temples of Selinunte. The stone, a fine-grained and resistant tufa, was quarried for more than 150 years, from the first half of the 6C BC. The huge blocks were hewn straight from the base rock, worked here *in situ* and moved from the quarry to the site on wooden frames with wheels on, pulled by oxen and slaves. However, work at the quarry ground to a halt in 409 BC following the outbreak of war when Selinunte was forced to confront the Carthaginian onslaught (resulting in the town's eventual destruction). The quarries and the houses of those who worked here were abandoned suddenly, as shown by the enormous blocks of rock that remain here, half-quarried.

From the considerable number of such unfinished blocks, scholars have calculated that there may have been anything up to 150 stone masons working at the Cave Di Cusa, using a lengthy and complex technique to work the stone to make it fit for construction (*see opposite page*).

In the first section of the quarry, blocks sit cut and ready for transporting; others barely sketched out, are ready for the stonecutter. At the far end of the quarry is a capital in the making. Its cylindrical mass tapers from a square base; the cracks still show pick marks.

SIRACUSA★★★

POPULATION: 123 022

A city of the sea, and also in the sea thanks to the island of Ortygia, Siracusa is set along one harmonious bay. The name evokes the historical struggles endured by the town; its Greek past, the tyrants and the rivalry with Athens and Carthage. A lesser- known period of its history, but no less evocative, is relived in the narrow lanes of the Ortygia, where time seems to have stopped somewhere between the Middle Ages and Baroque. The area's pleasant and dreamy atmosphere is accented by dusty palaces set between characteristic dead ends. Restoration of many Ortiygian buildings is now finally being undertaken, revealing even more of the island's original beauty.

- **Information:** Via San Sebastiano 43; ☎0931 48 12 00. Maestranza 33, Ortygia; ☎0931 46 42 55. www.apt-siracusa.it. www.comune.siracusa.it.
- **Orient Yourself:** The historical centre of Siracusa is situated on the island of Ortygia, linked to the mainland by the Ponte Nuovo, the only road access to the island. Just behind Ortygia lies the district of Akradina, the modern and commercial part of town crossed by Corso Gelone. The Neapolis quarter, literally meaning "new town", contains the archaeological area and can be seen to the northwest of Akradina, while to the east of Neapolis lies Tyche, a residential area in Ancient times and so called because a temple here was dedicated to the goddess of fortune (from the Greek *Tyche* – fortune or luck). Dominating the remainder of the city is the area known as Epipolae (meaning "upper town"); this section of the city was guarded by the castle of Euryalus, built in the most strategic position in Siracusa.
- **Parking:** Leave your car in the Ponte Nuovo area and use the bridge to Ortygia.
- **Don't Miss:** The charm of the historic island of Ortygia, going back in time at Teatro Greco, the acoustics at Orecchio di Dionisio and the collections at the Museo Archeologico Regionale Paolo Orsi.
- **Organising Your Time:** Allow one full day to tour the surrounding archaeological sites, including Thapsos and Megara Hyblaea.
- **Especially for Kids:** Testing the echoes at the Orecchio di Dionisio.
- **Also See:** CATANIA; NOTO; PANTALICA.

A Bit of History

Syracuse was colonised in the 8C BC by Greeks from Corinth, who settled on the island of **Ortygia**. Soon this power base was seized by a succession of tyrants. Under their rule the city enjoyed success and great splendour (5C-4C BC), establishing its supremacy over the rest of Sicily. Between 416 BC and 413 BC a furious conflict developed between Syracuse and Athens, the Athenian warriors being led by the great general Alcibiades. The city then fell to the Romans, and so to subsequent invaders – barbarians, Byzantines, Arabs and Normans.

Tyrants of Syracuse – The tyrant in Antiquity corresponds with the modern dictator, and several such figures populate late Sicily's history during the Hellenistic period, particularly in Syracuse.

Gelon, already tyrant of Gela, extended his dominion to Syracuse in 485 BC. His expansionist ambitions provoked open conflict with the hostile Carthaginians. Gelon, in alliance with **Theron**, the tyrant of Akragas (Agrigento), succeeded in defeating them at the battle of Himera in 480 BC. He was succeeded by his brother **Hieron I** (478–467 BC), and it was during his reign that Cumae was assisted in averting the Etruscan threat (474 BC).

After a brief period of democracy, punctuated by battles against Athens, **Dionysius the Elder** acceded to the throne (405–367 BC). He refused the discred-

D. Boggini/MICHELIN

Ortygia

ited title of tyrant and adopted instead that of **stregòs autokrátor**, meaning absolute general. This shrewd strategist underpinned his government with popular consensus, which he secured with gifts and favours, and by his reputation as the defender against the Punic threat, which he did not, however, succeed in eliminating. During his tyrannical rule, Syracuse became an independent and mighty force in its own right. On a more personal level, Dionysius I appears to have been haunted with suspicions, ever fearful that someone might be plotting against him. His fears developed into manias of persecution and culminated in his decision to retreat with his court to the castle of Ortygia. Writers such as Valerius Maximus, Cicero and Plutarch describe how the tyrant was so distrustful of the barbarians that he entrusted the task of shaving to his daughters but, fearing that even they might murder him, he insisted that walnut shells be used rather than razors; he had a ditch dug around his marital bed with a bridge that he could remove when he retired for the night and a sword suspended from a horsehair above the head of an envious member of his court called Damocles (hence the expression "the sword of Damocles" to allude to a looming threat).

Upon his death, he was succeeded on the throne by his son **Dionysius (II) the Younger**, who lacked the political astuteness of his father; he was briefly toppled by his uncle **Dion** in 357 BC

who, in turn, was assassinated four years later. Dionysius II was expelled a second time following a desperate plea from the Syracusans to the mother-city Corinth; in 344 BC **Timoleon**, a general, was sent to the rescue; as a wise and moderate statesman he restored peace to Sicily. There followed **Agathocles**, who in order to secure power harboured no qualms in murdering members of the aristocracy; his attempts to rout the Carthaginians from Sicily were unsuccessful (culminating in his defeat at Himera in 310 BC).

The last tyrant to govern Syracuse was **Hieron II** (269–216 BC), a mild and just ruler celebrated by Theocritus *(Idyll xvi)*, who oversaw the last golden age of Syracuse and signed an alliance with Rome against the Carthaginians in the First Punic War. In 212 BC, despite the clever devices designed by Archimedes, the town fell to Roman rule and became the capital of the Roman Province of Sicily.

Archimedes – No reliable source of information exists for details on the life of Archimedes, the mathematician, born in Syracuse in 287 BC. It is said that he was so absorbed by his research that he even forgot to eat and drink; his servants were forced to drag him to the public baths, where he continued to draw geometric shapes in the ash. It was while he was soaking in his bath that he came upon the principle that ensured his fame: a body immersed in a liquid is subject to a force equal to the weight of

H. Champollion/MICHELIN

Spectacular Teatro Greco

the volume of the liquid that has been displaced. Thrilled with his discovery, he stood up suddenly and rushed from the house shouting "Eureka!" (I've got it!).

Besides his contributions to the study of arithmetic, geometry, physics, astronomy and engineering, Archimedes is credited with several significant mechanical inventions, notably the Archimedes Screw – a cylinder containing a spiral screw for moving liquid uphill, like a pump; the cogwheel; celestial spheres; and burning glasses – a combination of lenses and mirrors with which he succeeded in setting fire to the Roman fleet.

According to tradition, Archimedes was so deeply involved in his calculations when the Romans succeeded in penetrating the city, that he died from a sword wound inflicted by a Roman soldier, oblivious to what was happening.

Poetic muses – Syracuse played its own part in developing its artistic prominence in Antiquity. Several of its rulers became so taken with the power of patronage that, before long, established foreign poets and writers were being welcomed to their court. Some, like Dionysius the Elder, tried to establish themselves as writers but without success. The first to take an effective interest was Hieron I, who proclaimed himself protector of poets and invited illustrious figures such as Bacchylides, Xenophon and Simonides, and competitive rival poets **Pindar** and **Aeschylus** to his court.

By contrast, **Plato** endured difficult relations with Syracuse, particularly with its rulers. Dionysius the Elder welcomed him reluctantly, only to expel him shortly afterwards; after his demise, the philosopher returned (under protection of the regent Dion), only to be expelled a second time – by Dionysius II – after failing to persuade the tyrant to accept the principles of his Utopian state (outlined later in his *Republic*).

Theocritus, the protagonist of a kind of bucolic poetry at which Virgil was later to excel, was probably a native of Syracuse.

More recently, **Salvatore Quasimodo** (1901–68) was born in Siracusa. A terse poet obsessed with the malaise of life, he won the Nobel Prize for literature in 1959.

Parco Archeologico della Neapolis★★★

&⏱Open daily, 6am–6pm.
€6. ☎0931 66 206.
There are two different entrances: one is in Via Rizzo and the other in Viale Paradiso. To follow the itinerary prescribed below, begin from the entrance in Via Rizzo.

Teatro Greco★★★
This is one of the most impressive theatres to survive from Antiquity. The *cavea*, cut out from the bedrock, took full dramatic advantage of the natural slope of Colle Temenite.

Address Book

For coin ranges, see the Legend on the cover flap.

GETTING THERE AND AROUND

The nearest airport is Fontanarossa airport in Catania, which is linked to Siracusa by buses that run daily (1hr). Buses leave from Piazzale San Antonio to Catania (approximately 1hr), Palermo (4hr), Ragusa (2hr) and a number of other destinations. For further information, contact the following two bus companies: AST, ☎0931 46 27 11; www. aziendasicilianatrasporti.it and Interbus, ☎0931 66 710; www.interbus.it. A train service also operates from Siracusa to Catania (1hr 30min), Messina (3hr), Ragusa (approximately 2hr) and Taormina (2hr 15min).

SIGHTSEEING

Antico mercato d'Ortigia – Siracusa's old covered market (Via Trento 2), built at the beginning of the 20C but abandoned in the mid-1980s, is now home to a number of tourist agencies selling excursions, guided tours, tickets for local transport and cultural events, and audioguides. For information, call ☎0931 44 92 01; www.anticomercato.it

Combined tickets – All tickets are valid for two days. €12: Museo Archeologico Regionale Paolo Orsi, Galleria Regionale di Palazzo Bellomo and Zona archeologica della Neapolis; €7: Museo Archeologico Regionale Paolo Orsi and Galleria Regionale di Palazzo Bellomo; €10: Museo Archeologico Regionale Paolo Orsi and Zona archeologica della Neapolis.

Siracusa by sea – Boat trips around the **Porto Grande and Ortygia**★ by motor launch are operated by **Motonave Selene**. Excursions along the coast provide a different perspective on the town. Outings last on average 35min, but can be extended on request; they can also include lunch or dinner by prior arrangement. Those timed around sunset and nightfall, when monuments are floodlit, are especially enjoyable.

This is also the only means of seeing Castello Maniace. Trips run Mar–Nov (and at other times of year, depending on sea and weather conditions) by

appointment only. ☎0931 79 10 33, or 340 05 58 769.

WHERE TO STAY

Casa Mia – *Corso Umberto 112.* ☎*0931 46 33 49. www.bbcasamia.it.* *10 rooms.* Elegant and simple, the rooms at this family-run B&B are filled with antiques and period quirks. There's a charming courtyard where breakfasts of hot rolls, fruit tarts and home made jams are served in the summer. Bicycles are available for guests at the B&B to use on request.

Bed & Breakfast Dolce Casa – *Via Lido Sacramento 4, Loc. Isola (take S 115 towards Noto, then turn left to Loc. Isola).* ☎*0931 72 11 35. www.bbdol cecasa.it. 10 rooms.* Situated halfway between Siracusa and the sea, this private villa has been converted into a friendly B&B. The light, spacious rooms, furnished in rustic style with the occasional romantic touch, and the beautiful garden adorned with palm and pine trees, ensure a relaxed and pleasant stay.

Agriturismo La Perciata – *Via Spinagallo 77, 14km/9mi SW of Siracusa on P 14 (from Maremonti, head to Canicattini, then take the turn-off to Floridia).* ☎*0931 71 73 66. www.perciata. it. 11 rooms. Restaurant.* This Mediterranean-style villa amid an oasis of greenery is ideal for a relaxing holiday. Activities on offer here include tennis, horse-riding and hydro-massage. Comfortable rooms and apartments with elegant, rustic decor.

Hotel Gutkowski – *Lungomare Vittorini 26, Siracusa.* ☎*0931 46 58 61. www.guthotel.it. 13 rooms.* Careful attention to detail is evident throughout this hotel, with its elegant entrance on the ground floor, delightful panoramic sun-terrace and tastefully decorated rooms.

Albergo Domus Mariae – *Via Vittorio Veneto 76, Siracusa.* ☎*0931 24 854. www.sistemia.it/domusmariae. 13 rooms.* The spacious guest rooms in this traditional hotel run by Ursuline nuns are furnished with both elegance and taste. The pleasant sun-terrace offers attractive views of the Mediterranean.

WHERE TO EAT

Giardino di Epicuro – *Largo della Gancia 5 (at the end of Via Nizza), Siracusa. ☎0931 46 89 96. Closed Wed. Booking recommended.* This pleasant, relaxed restaurant in the heart of the historical centre serves a selection of fish dishes and a good choice of pizzas.

Darsena da Jannuzzo – *Riva Garibaldi 6 (turn right as soon as you arrive in the Ortygia district), Siracusa. ☎0931 61 522. Closed Wed.* The main reason for visiting the Darsena da Jannuzzo can be seen at the restaurant entrance where a splendid display of fish is on display. The simple but delicious cuisine here is served either in the unassuming dining room or on the veranda, with its view of the canal, both of which have a pleasant atmosphere.

TAKING A BREAK

Enoteca "Capriccio" – *Via dell' Amalfitania 11, Siracusa. ☎0931 46 49 18. Open 10am–10pm.* This wine bar serves a selection of Sicilian wines, including the more unusual *Rosolio al mandarino* and *Rosolio alla cannella*.

Gelateria Bianca Salvatore – *Corso Umberto I, Siracusa.* Customers are spoilt for choice at this reasonably priced gelateria, which has a selection of 30 different flavours of ice cream served either in a cup or cone and a pleasant shady terrace from which you can watch the world go by.

Pasticceria-Gelateria Dolcidea – *Viale Regina Margherita 23, Siracusa. ☎0931 22 920.* Enjoy a range of typical Sicilian ice cream and *granite* on the small, shady terrace outside this *gelateria* close to the Porto Piccolo.

Istituto Nazionale del Dramma Antico, Siracusa

SHOWS

Teatro dei Pupi del Fratelli Mauceri – *Via della Giudecca 17, Siracusa. ☎0931 46 55 40. www.pupari.com. Open Tue–Sat 10am–1pm, 4pm–7pm; Sun 10.30am–1pm.* This small theatre in the heart of the Ortygia district is run by the Mauceri brothers, whose puppet performances offer an entertaining insight into traditional Sicilian culture. Make sure you also visit the nearby Alfredo Mauceri workshop, where the puppets are made.

SHOPPING

Galleria Bellomo – *Via Capodieci 15, Siracusa. ☎0931 61 340. www.bellomo gallery.com* This workshop-cum-gallery, opened in 1980, displays a fascinating collection of papyrus items made by the owner, Signora Massara, who inherited her love for papyrus from her father-in-law.

Galleria del Papiro – *Via Ruggero, Settimo 35, Siracusa. ☎339 15 02 337 (mobile). Open Mon–Sat 9.30am–1pm, 3.30pm–7pm.* The artist Alessandro Romano uses papyrus as the raw material for his works of art, many of which are exhibited and on sale in this gallery.

SEASIDE RESORTS

The coast to the south of Siracusa has a number of attractive sandy beaches, such as **Arenella**, with its stretches of rocky coastline and picturesque creeks, including Ognina, a paradise for diving enthusiasts. The most beautiful beach in the area is Fontane Bianche, 20km/12mi south of the city.

FESTIVALS

Classical theatre – In May and June, the Greek theatre provides a wonderful setting for performances of famous Classical Greek and Latin plays. For information on dates and performances, contact: *Istituto Nazionale del DrammaAntico, Corso Matteotti 29, Siracusa; ☎0931 48 72 00; Fax 0931 48 7210; www.indafondazione.org.*

Festa di Santa Lucia – The festival of the patron saint of Siracusa, St Lucy, is celebrated on 13 December.

The theatre was modified by Hieron II in the 3C BC, when it was divided into nine wedge-shaped sections, and a passageway was inserted around the *cavea* about halfway up. The wall in front of each section is inscribed with the name of a famous person or deity. Today, certain letters may still be distinguished, including those spelling out Olympian Zeus in the central section; to the right, facing the stage, appear the letters naming Hieron II, his wife and his daughter-in-law. It was altered in Roman times possibly to host gladiatorial combats before the amphitheatre (♨ *See below*) was completed. Later the Spaniards installed water-driven millstones in it: the furrows left by mill-wheels in the *cavea* can still be seen, as can the drainage channel.

Behind the cavea is a large open area with the **Grotta del Ninfeo** (Nymph's Cave) in the centre. The rectangular tank set before it was filled with water drawn from the aqueduct that was built by the Greeks. Having fallen into disuse during the Middle Ages, the aqueduct was restored in the 16C by the Marchese di Sortinoto in order to power the watermills erected in the theatre.

To the left extends the **Via dei Sepolcri** (Street of Tombs). Pockmarking the rock face on each side are a series of Byzantine tombs and votive niches.

Orecchio di Dionisio★★★

The haunting cave known as the Ear of Dionysius is situated in one of the most striking former limestone quarries (*latomie*) in Siracusa: the aptly named **Latomia del Paradiso**★★ **Kids** , now a delightful garden shaded with orange trees, palm trees and magnolias. As its name suggests, the cave resembles an auricle (cavity inside the ear), both in the shape of the entrance and the winding internal space beyond. It was the artist Caravaggio who gave the cave its name during his visit to Sicily in the early 1600s on hearing the intriguing explanation of how Dionysius the Elder was able to hear his enemies without seeing them, thanks to the cave's extraordinary echo. The cave has amazing acoustics which guides or visitors will occasionally test by suddenly bursting into song.

Orecchio di Dionisio

Vito Arcomano/Fototeca ENIT

The neighbouring **Grotta dei Cordari** earned its name from its use until fairly recently as a cool place where ropemakers would work, twisting stretches of twine.

Ara di Ierone II

This enormous altar, 200m/650ft partly carved out of the rock, was commissioned by the tyrant Hieron II in the 3C BC for public sacrifices. Originally, a large rectangular area may have stretched out in front, probably with a portico and a central pool.

Anfiteatro Romano★

The Roman amphitheatre was built during the Imperial era. The rectangular pit in the centre of the arena is connected to the southern entrance by a ditch. This "technical" area was reserved for the stage machinery that provided special effects during performances.

Opposite the amphitheatre entrance stands the pre-Romanesque Church of **San Nicolò dei Cordari** (11C). To its right, sits a Roman water tank used to flood the amphitheatre for performances of *naumachiae* (re-enactments of sea battles) and for cleaning the arena after the gory fights between gladiators and wild animals.

Ortyga

*"Sicanio praetenta sinu
iacet insula contra*

*Plemyrium undosum;
nomen dixere priores*

*Ortygiam. Alpheum fama
est huc Elidis amnem*

*occultas egisse vias subter
mare, qui nunc ore,*

*Arethusa, tuo Siculis
confunditur undis."*

"Stretched in front of a Sicanian bay lies an island, over against wave-beaten Plemyrium; men of old called it Ortygia. Hither, so runs the tale, Alpheus, river of Elis, forced a secret course beneath the sea, and now at thy fountain, Arethusa, mingles with the Sicilian waves."

Virgil, *The Aeneid*, Book III
(lines 692–695).

Tomba di Archimede

Visible from the outside only from the corner of Via Romagnoli and Via Teracati.

At the eastern end of Latomia Intagliatella are the **Grotticelli Necropolis**. Among the cavities hollowed out of the rock, one is ornamented with Doric columns (now badly damaged), pediment and tympanum. This "Tomb of Archimedes" actually conceals a Roman *columbarium* (a chamber lined with niches for funerary urns).

Walking Tour

With so many wonderful buildings and outlooks, it is impossible to set an itinerary including all that might be worth seeing. The descriptions below therefore mention only the most interesting streets, leaving a large section of the historical city without commentary for visitors to explore according to inclination. Raise your gaze as often as possible so as not to miss any secret lurking in the narrow streets among the splendid buildings.

The island, the most ancient area of settlement, is linked to the mainland by the Ponte Nuovo, a natural extension of one of the main thoroughfares of Siracusa, Corso Umberto I.

A powerful awareness of the sea pervades this area: the harbour, filled with colourful boats, stretches to the right and to the left.

Along the seafront, lies a lovely neo-Gothic red-plastered *palazzo*, once the home of poet and writer **Antonio Cardile** (b. Messina 1883, d. Siracusa 1951). The linearity of the **Porta Marina** is interrupted by a Catalan aedicule framing the entrance to Passeggio Adorno, a 19C walltop walkway.

The view also includes the Porto Grande, where several major historical naval battles were fought.

Fonte Aretusa★

The Fountain of Arethusa played a significant part in persuading the first group of colonists to settle here in Antiquity. Legend relates how Arethusa, one of Artemis' nymphs, tormented by the demonstrations of love from a hunter named Alpheus, turned to the goddess for help.

Artemis turned Arethusa into a stream so that she might escape underground and re-emerge on the island of Ortygia as a freshwater spring or fountain. Alpheus, meanwhile, changed himself into an underground river, crossed the Ionian Sea and came up in Ortygia having mingled his waters with those of Arethusa.

Today, the fountain sustains palm trees and clumps of papyrus, ducks and drakes. Looming on the horizon on the far side, sits the **Castello Maniace** (the castle is generally open to visit from 8.30am–1pm; €2; for more information call ☎0931 46 42 20), a sandstone fortress built by Frederick II of Swabia in the first half of the 13C. Its name honours the Byzantine general, George Maniakes who, in 1038, tried to rescue Ortygia from the Arabs, and then fortified the island. The massive square structure is a typical example of Swabian building: the architectural features are both functional and cosmetic, suggesting that the castle was conceived to function as a defensive stronghold and also as a bold visual reminder of Swabian authority.

Cross the tip of the island to reach the eastern shore, from where a series of wonderful views extend over the castle (the best view, however, is from the sea); pass before the Church of **Santo Spirito**, with its three-tiered white façade unified by volutes and decorative pilasters. Farther along, in Via **S. Martino**, the Church of **San Martino**, whose origins date back to the 6C, is fronted by a Catalan-Gothic style doorway.

Continue along Via S. Martino to the Church of **San Benedetto**, with its fine coffered ceiling, and the adjacent Galleria Regionale di Palazzo Bellomo (⌂ *see Ortygia*).

▶ *Take Via Capodieci, then turn right into Via Vergini.*

Piazza Duomo★★

The attractive irregular square precedes the cathedral, curving at one end to accommodate its majestic front elevation. The open space becomes especially dramatic when the cathedral façade is caught by the setting sun or floodlit after nightfall. The other fine Baroque buildings enclosing the square include the **Palazzo Beneventano del Bosco**, which conceals a lovely courtyard, and opposite, **Palazzo del Senato**, whose inner courtyard displays an 18C senator's carriage; at the far end stands the Church of **Santa Lucia**.

Next to Santa Lucia, the former convent and Church of Montevergini houses the Galleria Civica di Arte Contemporanea (⌂ *see Ortygia*).

Duomo★

The area now occupied by the cathedral has been a place of worship since early Antiquity. A temple erected in the 6C BC was replaced by a temple dedicated to Athena, honouring the goddess with profits from the fateful defeat of the Carthaginians at Himera (480 BC). In the 7C AD, the temple was incorporated into a Christian church: wall.

It was then possibly converted into a mosque during the Arab domination, before being restored for Christian use by the Normans. The 1693 earthquake caused the front façade to collapse; it was rebuilt in the Baroque style (18C)

Duomo façade

by the Palermo architect Andrea Palma. The entrance is preceded by an atrium screening a fine doorway flanked by a pair of twisted columns, the spirals of which are decorated with vines and grapes (a symbol of the Passion).

Inside, the right side of the south aisle incorporates the temple columns; today these frame the entrance into the lateral chapels. The first bay on the right contains a Greek marble krater font, supported protectively by seven small 13C wrought-iron lions.

Greek columns of the Duomo

SIRACUSA			Bengasi (Via)	BZ		Crispi (Via F.)	BY	9
			Cadorna (Viale L.)	BY		Diaz (Viale A.)	BY	10
Agatocle (Via)	BCY		Capodieci (Via)	CZ	4	Dionisio il Grande Riviera	CY	12
Agrigento (Via)	BCY	2	Cappuccini (Piazza)	CY		Duomo (Piazza)	CZ	13
Archimede (Piazza)	CZ	3	Castello Maniace (Via)	CZ	6	Elorina (Via)	ABZ	
Arsenale (Via d.)	BCY		Catania (Via)	BY	7	Ermocrate (Via)	AY	
Bainsizza (Via)	BY		Columba (Via)	AYZ		Euripide (Piazza)	BY	

SIRACUSA

0 ——— 300 m

A VALLETTA (MALTA) / CATANIA   B Fonte Ciane

The next **chapel**, dedicated to **St Lucy**, has an 18C silver altar front. The silver figure of the saint in the niche is by Pietro Rizzo (1599). Elsewhere, the cathedral is furnished with statues by the various **Gagini**: the *Virgin* is by **Domenico**; *St Lucy* (north aisle and the *Madonna della Neve* in the north apse are by **Antonello Gagini**. Via Landolina, north of the piazza, accommodates the **Chiesa dei Gesuiti**.

From the church, make your way to the nearby **Piazza Archimede**. This square was constructed more recently. Presiding over the central space, overlooked by fine buildings, is the 19C fountain of Artemis.

Palazzo Mergulese-Montalto★
Via Montalto.

This superb, although rather dilapidated, *palazzo* dates from the 14C. The upper section is ornamented with wonderful highly elaborate **windows★★**, set into richly carved arched settings subdivided by slender twisted columns.

▶ *Return to Piazza Archimede.*

Via della Maestranza★

Via della Maestranza is one of Ortygia's main thoroughfares, and one of the oldest. It threads its way between a succession of aristocratic residences, predominantly Baroque in style. Among the most interesting are: **Palazzo Interlandi Pizzuti** (n° 10) and, a little farther on, **Palazzo Impellizzeri** (n° 17) with its sinuously linear arrangement of curved windows and balconies. **Palazzo Bonanno** (n° 33), which now accommodates the headquarters of the tourist office, is an austere medieval building sheltering a lovely inner courtyard and a first floor loggia. At no 72 stands the **Palazzo Romeo Bufardeci**, with its exuberant frontage and Rococo balconies.

The street opens out into a small square before the Church of **San Francesco all'Immacolata** flanked by a 19C bell tower. The elegant front elevation is gracefully articulated with columns and pilasters. At one time the church used to host a ritual rooted in Antiquity: on the 28 November the *Svelata* (literally, the unveiling) took place, during which an image of the Madonna was unveiled. This event occurred in the early hours before dawn (so that people could go to work, in an era when the working day started very early) after a long vigil accompanied by local bands. Almost at the end of the street the curved façade of **Palazzo Rizza** (n° 110). **Palazzo Impellizzeri** (n° 99) dominates the view, rising to its full height through a sumptuous frieze ornamented with human faces, grotesque masks and organic decorations.

The **Quartiere della Giudecca**, extends behind this section of the street. During the 16C a community of Jews settled and thrived in this quarter until expelled. Today the quarter retains its medieval street plan, threaded by atmospheric narrow streets.

At the end of the street the **Belvedere S. Giacomo**, once a defensive bastion, offers a splendid **view★** of Siracusa. The nearby **Forte Vigliena** can be seen on the right.

Mastrarua

Renamed Via Vittorio Veneto, this street was once the main thoroughfare of Ortygia. It was the route followed by official parades and royal processions and is lined with fine *palazzi*. **Palazzo Blanco** (n° 41) is graced outside with a niche in which stands a statue of St Anthony; it has a lovely courtyard and staircase within. **Casa Mezia** (n° 47) has a doorway surmounted by a griffin. Beyond the Church of **San Filippo Neri** there follows **Palazzo Interlandi** and the badly damaged **Palazzo Monforte**. This last *palazzo* marks the corner with Via Mirabella, which also contains yet more fine buildings. Note, right opposite Palazzo Monforte, the elegant **Palazzo Bongiovanni**: the doorway is surmounted by a mask and, above, a lion holding a scroll bearing the date 1772 which, in turn, acts as a central support for a balcony.

▶ *Continue along Via Mirabella.*

A small diversion to the right allows for a detour past the neo-Gothic **Palazzo Gargallo** (Archivio Distrettuale Notarile – Records Office). Via Mirabella heralds the beginning of the Arab quarter, characterised by extremely narrow streets known as *ronchi*. One of these streets conceals the palaeo-Christian Church of **San Pietro**, which is now used for concerts. A little farther along Via Mirabella stands the Church of **San Tommaso**, which was founded in Norman times (12C). Turn back along the Mastrarua; no 111 has a lovely doorway decorated with monstrous creatures. No 136, is the birthplace of the celebrated writer, **Elio Vittorini** (1908–66).

Tempio di Apollo

This temple of Apollo, built in the 6C BC, is the oldest peripteral Doric temple (that is, enclosed by columns) in Sicily. According to one inscription it was dedicated to Apollo; according to Cicero it was dedicated to Artemis – before being transformed into a Byzantine church, then a mosque, and back again into a church by the Normans. The remains of the peristyle columns and the sacred precinct wall are still in evidence.

Corso Matteotti, described as the drawing room of Ortygia, leads off the piazza, flanked on either side by elegant shops.

Museo Archeologico Regionale Paolo Orsi★★

&♿🕐*Open 8am–6pm, Sundays and public holidays 9am–2pm.* 🚫*Closed Mon.* ✎€6. ☎*0931 46 40 22; www.regione.sicilia.it.*

The Paolo Orsi Museum nestles in the garden of **Villa Landolina**, detailing Sicily's prehistory up to the period of the sub-colonies of Syracuse.
The inception and development of the various cultural phases are presented chronologically in three main sections. There is also a basement auditorium where audio-visual presentations are given (🕐*See programme schedule at the entrance*).

Section A: Prehistory and protohistory

Displays open with a collection of fossils and minerals, skeletons and prehistoric animal remains along with informa-

Mother-goddess, Megara Hyblaea (6C BC)

Museo Archeologico, Siracusa/SCALA

tion about the fauna of the island. The models of two dwarf elephants found in the Grotta di Spinagallo in Siracusa (the originals are in Rome's Museo di Paleontologia) are of particular interest; these were thought to have been at the root of the Cyclops myth, through a mistaken interpretation of the hole created by the elephant's trunk. Human artefacts representing the Palaeolithic and Neolithic eras, are followed by specimens dating from successive phases. The majority of artefacts comprise pottery fragments, including a large red-burnished **vase**★ from Pantalica – a simple, yet highly sophisticated tall-footed shape.
Finally, a number of hoards recovered from concealed or hidden underground containers are shown alongside bronze objects (spearheads, belts and buckles).

Section B: Greek colonisation

These objects mark and illustrate the foundation and development of Greek colonies in eastern Sicily. The three Ionic colonies were Naxos, Katane and Leontinoi, from where the beautiful headless marble **kouros** (Archaic male figure) came. The two Doric colonies were Megara Hyblaea and Syracuse, both of which are extremely well represented. The singular limestone figure of the **Mother-goddess**★ nursing twins (6C BC) was recovered from the necropolis at Megara Hyblaea. Seated and headless, the figure powerfully embodies maternity, extending her arms to embrace and contain two babies that seem to melt into her, as if all three were all one.

The Syracuse collection is vast and includes two famous exhibits which are often reproduced: a polychrome shallow-relief clay panel with a **gorgon**, and the bronze statuette of a horse, the symbol of the museum, found in the necropolis at Fusco. At the entrance to this section devoted to Syracuse, is temporarily displayed the splendid headless statue of **Venus Anadyomene**★or Landolina Venus (after the man who discovered her). This Roman copy of an original by Praxiteles is one of many made in Antiquity (others include the Medici Venus, the Capitoline Venus) characterised by sinuous lines. The poise with which she holds the drapery is underlined by the delicate way in which the fabric falls into folds that echo the perfect shape of a shell.

Section C: Sub-colonies and Hellenised centres

The first part, devoted to the sub-colonies of Syracuse, contains a selection of various anthropomorphic figures, including a clay *acroterion* representing a **rider on horseback**. The second part details the history of minor centres. Note the tall clay sculpted enthroned figure of **Demeter** or **Kore** dating from the latter half of the 6C BC.

The third and last part of this section is devoted to Agrigento and Gela. The striking painted **Gorgon's mask**, part of a decorative temple frieze, comes from Gela as does the fine Attic red-figure *pelike* (two-handled vase) by the painter Polygnotos. Three wooden **Archaic statuettes** are rare examples of votive art: although these were probably widespread, in most cases the wood will have perished with time.

Catacombe di San Giovanni★★

⏲*Open daily, 10am–1pm, 2.30pm–5.30pm.* ⊘*Closed Mon.* ☞€5. ☎0931 64 694; www.kairos-web.com.

The catacombs are situated in the Akradina area which, until Roman times,

was reserved for the cult of the dead. Unlike the Roman catacombs elsewhere in mainland Italy that are excavated from fragile tufa, which restricted their size (lest they collapse), these in Siracusa are cut out from a layer of hard limestone. This meant that they could therefore be safely extended into considerably larger underground chambers.

This complex system of catacombs was developed around the tomb of St Marcian, one of the early Christian martyrs (4C-5C). The extensive network of rectilinear tunnels depends upon a central axis that probably followed the lines of an abandoned Greek aqueduct.

At right angles to this principal artery lead a series of minor vein-like passageways. The chambers vary in size according to whether they accommodated a single person or several (maximum 20 people). Interspersed among these large cavities are a number of smaller and shallower hollows for children.

At intervals, there appear round or square areas used by the Christians for interring martyrs and saints. The most significant of these is the *Rotonda di Adelfia,* in which a wonderful sarcophagus was found intact, carved with biblical scenes *(awaiting to be displayed, possibly on the second floor of the archaeological museum).* Note also, beside the main gallery, the Greco-Roman conical cisterns, later used as burial chambers.

Cripta di San Marciano

The Crypt of St Marcian, situated near the necropolis, marks the place where the martyr is alleged to have met his death.

The Greek-cross chamber lies 5m/16ft below ground level. The far wall accommodates three semicircular apses: the right one is the altar where St Paul is supposed to have preached on his return from Malta in AD 60 *(Acts of the Apostles,* Ch 28 v12); against the right wall sits the tomb that is popularly believed to be that of the martyr.

The peep-hole inserted on one side was to enable the pilgrims to see the body of the saint and to allow a cloth to be passed over it that might then be considered a special relic-cum-keepsake.

Basilica di San Giovanni Evangelista

Basilica di San Giovanni Evangelista

The church stands over the crypt of St Marcian. This picturesque ruin, open to the sky, is one of the most atmospheric spots in Siracusa, especially at sunset, and even more intensely on saints' days and holidays when Mass is celebrated. The basilica was founded in association with the martyr's crypt, for it was usual to mark a sacred burial place with a shrine of some kind. The basilica was destroyed by the Arabs, and restored by the Normans. The main frontage of the Norman church, ornamented with a lovely rose-window, is still visible on the left flank. The main damage was incurred during an earthquake when the roof collapsed, never to be rebuilt.

The interior, now partly taken over by clumps of tree spurge *(Euphorbia dendroides)*, preserves its original Byzantine main altar.

Additional Sights

Museo del Papiro

○*Open daily, 9am–2pm.* ○*Closed Mon.* ☜*Donations welcome.* ☎*0931 61 616; www.sistemia.it/museopapiro.*

The rediscovery of papyrus in Syracuse can be attributed to Saverio Landolina who, in the 18C, reassessed the value of the plant, which was being used by the local population at that time for decoration. He also succeeded in reinventing the means of making paper (several examples can be seen in the museum).

Santuario della Madonna delle Lacrime

○*Open 7am–1pm, 3pm–8pm.* ☎*0931 21 446; www.madonnadellelacrime.it.*

This modern conical structure in reinforced concrete (80m/262ft in diameter and 74m/243ft high) dominates the skyline. Its construction was prompted by a miraculous event that occurred in 1953, when a painting of the Madonna shed tears. Since then the shrine has attracted large numbers of pilgrims.

Santa Lucia

St Lucy, the patron saint of Siracusa, lived here in the 4C, hence the reason why so many local churches are dedicated to her, including the Duomo. The date of 13 December (her *dies natalis*, when the saint's earthly life came to end and her spiritual life began) is celebrated with a procession headed by the silver statue of the saint from the Duomo to the place where she was entombed.

Papyrus and the Origins of Paper

Cyperus papyrus is a plant which grows vigorously in Egypt; it has also been known to man in Siracusa, along the banks of the River Ciane *(see Excursions)*, since Antiquity. It consists of a perennial marsh plant which grows in various forms and sizes, and produces a profusion of tall stems ending with ruffs of bracts (inflorescence). In Ancient Egypt, it was used in all kinds of different ways that exploited its amazing versatility: stems were bundled together to build lightweight boats; it was used for making ropes, baskets and trays, for weaving fabric for clothes and wigs, even for making shoes (such as sandals). The ruff at the top was used to make fans and parasols for civil or religious ceremonies and funeral rites. It has even been suggested that the most tender spongy part of the stalk might have been eaten.

The most famous product made from papyrus is paper, although this involves a fairly complex process. The variable factors include the age of the plant and the stabilising treatment following the bleaching process. Strips are laid in two perpendicular layers one on top of the other, pressed and dried. The resulting sheet has a flat surface (with horizontal fibres) suitable for writing, backed and supported by the vertical fibres. It is interesting to note that in many languages the word for paper actually comes from the word "papyrus" (French *papier*, German *Papier*, Spanish *papel*, Welsh *papur* and so on).

The material displayed in the museum covers all the possible applications of papyrus. This includes documents from the time of the pharaohs (fragments of the *Book of the Dead*); objects made of rope; fans all made from the same variety of plant; featherweight boats with slightly raised prows and sterns adept for navigating through shallow waters and marshy areas, and still very much in use by hunters and fishermen in Africa. The last section is dedicated to paper, its actual production (reconstruction of a workbench) as well as the pigments and instruments used by scribes.

Luxuriant clumps of papyrus

Lara Pessina/MICHELIN

Basilica di Santa Lucia extra Mœnia

This basilica faces onto its own piazza. According to tradition, it was erected to mark the spot where the saint was martyred in 303, as Caravaggio suggests in his painting of the subject *(now in Palazzo Bellomo)*. The original Byzantine church underwent considerable changes over the years to arrive at its present form in the 15C-16C.

The oldest extant parts are the front entrance, the three semicircular apses and the two lower tiers of the bell tower (12C). The painted wooden ceiling is 17C. Below the church lie the **Catacombs of Santa Lucia** (👁‍🗨*Closed to the public*).

Still in the same square, the small octagonal building contains the tomb of the saint. Her actual relics, however, were transported to Constantinople in the 11C by the Byzantine general George Maniakes, and then to The Duomo in Venice following the fall of Constantinople during the Fourth Crusade.

Ginnasio Romano

The Roman Gymnsasium, situated on Via Elorina just beyond the **Foro Siracusano**, formed part of the market place of ancient Akradina, along with the Forum. It was part of a complex that comprised a *quadroporticus*, with a small theatre – seating is still visible in the cave – and a small marble temple, which served as a stage set.

Ortygia

Galleria Regionale di Palazzo Bellomo★

☞ *Closed for restoration at time of going to press. For information* ☎*0931 69 511.*
Palazzo Bellomo, first built under Swabian rule (13C), was extended and raised in the 15C, giving it two different styles: at ground level it has the appearance of a fortress; the first floor has elegant three-light windows separated with columns. The *palazzo* was built as a private residence before being acquired by the nuns from the adjoining convent of St Benedict in the 18C. Today it is all part of the same museum.

Museum

The museum is dedicated in the main to Sicilian art. However, Byzantine influences pervade a series of paintings *(Room IV)* by Venetian artists working in Crete (at a time when it formed part of the Venetian Empire). These show *The Creation* (six panels), *Original Sin* and *Earthly Paradise*. The upper floor is largely devoted to painting: the most striking, despite damage, is the **Annunciation★** by **Antonello da Messina**. There is an inherent Flemish quality to this picture in its minute attention to detail; the overall formality, spacious composition and precise definition of perspective is more typically Italian.

in The **Entombment of St Lucy**★ by **Caravaggio**, the artist's characteristically dramatic and provocative style is evident in the arrangement of the crowd: the main figures jostling around the dead saint are the gravediggers, including one in the foreground turning his back to the onlooker.

The museum also displays an eclectic collection of objects: furnishings, holy vestments, Nativity figures, furniture and ceramics.

Galleria Civica d'Arte Contemporanea

♿ ⊙*Open 9am–1pm, 5pm–9pm.* ⊙*Closed Mon.* ☎*0931 24 902.*
The former convent and Church of Montevergini *(entrance in Via delle Vergini)* houses the municipal collection of contemporary art. This consists mainly of paintings by Italian artists (Sergio Fermariello, Marco Cingolani, Aldo Damioli, Enrico de Paris).

Excursions

Castello Eurialo★

9km/5.5mi NW along Via Epipoli, in the Belvedere district.
⊙*Open daily, 9am– 6pm.* ≈*€2.* ☎*0931 71 17 73.*
The road up to the fortress gives an idea of the scale of the defensive reinforcements imposed on the city by Dionysius the Elder. In addition to fortifying Ortygia, the strategist built a wall around the entire settlement, encompassing the districts of Tyche and Neapolis which, until then, had stood outside the city limits. With this in mind, he ordered the construction of the imposing **Walls of Dionysius** *(mura dionigiane – 27km/17mi)* across the Epipolae high plateau enclosing the north side of the town; one section of the wall is still visible along the road leading up to Belvedere *(on the left)*.

The ridge provided a strategic position for the castle. Its name, Euryalus, is derived from its headland position, which resembles the head of a nail (Greek: *euryelos*). The fortress is one of the most impressive Greek defences to have survived from Antiquity. Its heart

©ordus/Fotolia.com

Castello Eurialo

is ringed with a series of three consecutive ditches linked by a warren of underground passages. The entrance to the archaeological area coincides with the first of these ditches. A little farther on, the second deep trench lined with vertical walls may be discerned before, finally, arriving at the third, making this a veritable Chinese-puzzle masterpiece of defensive design.

Behind stood the square keep, preceded by an impressive series of defensive towers. The far corner provides a fine **view**★ down to Siracusa *(opposite)* and the plain stretching away to the left.

Tempio di Giove Olimpico

3km/1.8mi out of town along Via Elorina, signposted right.

The 6C BC Temple of Olympian Zeus occupies a suitably commanding position, raised high above the surrounding landscape.

Fiume Ciane★★

8km/5mi SE.

In high season, visitors should turn up and wait until enough people arrive to form a group. Booking is recommended out of season. Visitors are advised to contact Signore Vella for further information, ☎0931 39 889.

The River Ciane, which almost merges with the River Anapo, is the main link with the internal area of Pantalica (*See PANTALICA*). Its mouth is a favourite starting-point for **boat trips**★★. Shortly after

setting off, a splendid view of the Grand Harbour of Siracusa opens out before you. The boat then continues through lush vegetation: reeds, ancient ash trees, and eucalyptus, before entering a narrow gorge and emerging in a papyrus grove. Here, according to the myth transcribed by Ovid *(Metamorphoses: The Rape of Proserpine,* Book 5, l 409–437), Cyane the water nymph tried to obstruct Pluto from abducting Persephone and was transformed into a spring.

Driving Tour

Archaeological Sites

80km/50mi – allow one day.
From Siracusa, take the S 114 towards Catania.

Thapsos

Open daily, 9am–1pm. Closed Sun and public hols. For information and reservations, contact the Soprintendenza a few days in advance. ☎0931 48 11 42.

The Magnisi peninsula, which separates the Bay of Augusta from the Bay of Siracusa, is tenuously connected to the mainland by a isthmus of sand.

Thapsos grew to be one of the most important prehistoric cultures in the Middle Bronze Age (15C-13C BC), and the recovery of Mycenaean and Maltese ceramics from this area suggest that Thapsos continued to be a trading emporium of considerable importance.

Archaeological site

Excavation has revealed substantial remains from a settlement, including round huts from the 15C–14C BC. More sophisticated residential complexes survive from a subsequent phase (13C–12C BC); rectangular chambers arranged around a cobbled courtyard; these concur with Mycenaean prototypes.

Farther south along the dirt track there are some fragments of Early Bronze Age fortifications if you look carefully.

A few hundred metres beyond this extends a vast **necropolis** containing 450 burial chambers. These consist of man-made hollows preceded by a vestibule, which in most cases consists of a small shaft, *dromos* passageway or tunnel (these are more evident along the seashore where the sea has eroded the external wall). The burial chambers are round with conical ceilings; in some, the walls have shallow niches (visible in one tomb where the ceiling has collapsed) where grave goods were deposited. These chambers were used for complete families and dependants, and designed to serve several generations. Entombment was by inhumation.

▷ *Return to the coast road and continue in the direction of Augusta.*

Megara Hyblaea

♿ ◷ *Open Apr–Oct, 9am–6pm; Nov–Mar, 9am–3pm.* ✉*Donations welcome.* ☎*0931 48 11 11.*

The Greek colony of Megara Hyblaea, founded by the Megarians of Greece in 728 BC, was twice razed to the ground: once in 483 BC by Gelon, the tyrant of Gela, and again by the Romans in 213 BC. The archaeological site is situated in a strange landscape, stranded between the sea and the chimneys of the Augusta oil refinery.

Excavations

The **necropolis** lies outside the town walls, alongside the older enclosure walls *(before crossing the railway bridge, by the bend, take the dirt track off to the right).* Beyond the entrance extends one of the *decumani* that once led to the **agora** (market-place).

The site shows clear evidence of successive building phases as Archaic constructions give way to Hellenistic ones above. On the left of the piazza sits a sanctuary, recognisable by the semicircular north end wall. Follow D 1, a street on the left, which passes alongside a large **Hellenistic house** from the 4C–2C BC (entrance marked by iron steps): comprising of 20 rooms arranged around two courtyards. Some rooms preserve remains of *opus signinum* floors (an amalgam of clay particles mixed with minute pieces of rubble, bound with lime).

To the left of the agora, lie the **Hellenistic baths**. Farther along C is a *Pritaneo* (where magistrates would meet) from the Archaic period (6C BC). The *decumanus* continues beyond the square, as far as the **West Gate** and fortifications from the Hellenistic period.

▷ *Continue north for 15km/9mi.*

Augusta

Augusta today is an important Italian commercial port. The axis of the old town is Corso Principe Umberto, the commercial thoroughfare which runs north to south.

Brucoli

This small and charming fishing village is clustered around its picturesque little **harbour**, which lies at the mouth of the River Porcaria.

▷ *Head towards Lentini (25km/15mi W of Brucoli).*

Lentini

The centre of this small town dependent on citrus fruit farming, is marked by the **Chiesa Madre** dedicated to Sant'Alfio (a popular saint in the hamlets around Etna); preserved in its palaeo-Christian vault are the alleged relics of St Alfio, St Filadelfio and St Cirino.

A small **archaeological museum** (◷*open 9am–7pm;* ◷*closed Mon;* ✉*€2;* ☎*095 78 32 962*) displays artefacts recovered from the Leotinol excavations.

Leontinoi

Access is easiest via Carlentini.
For information, call ☎095 78 32 962.

This area has been inhabited since protohistoric times (as the bases of huts on Collina di Metapiccola testify: these are found to the right of the entrance to the archaeological zone). In 729 BC it was targeted by the Chalcidians of Naxos as a good place to found a colony. It was here that the philosopher **Gorgias** was born.

Excavation has revealed remains of pyramidal tombs and walling beyond. The Syracusan gate serves as the main town entrance. The way leads on towards the vestiges of a temple. From the top, a wonderful view extends over Lentini and the **Biviere**. The mound to the left is Colle di Sant'Egidio where the town's necropolis was located.

Case del Biviere★

In the Contrada Biviere: from Lentini railway station, turn right and follow the sign for SP 67 to Valsavoia. By the fork in the road, on the right, stands a villa with a large green entrance.
The garden is open by appointment only; to make a reservation, phone or send a fax at least two weeks in advance. Brunch, drinks, lunch or tea can be booked for groups. €10. 095 78 31 449; Fax 095 78 35 575.

According to legend, when Heracles came to these parts intending to present the skin of the Nemean lion to Ceres, he fell in love with the area and created a lake that would bear his name; this was subsequently changed to Biviere (drinking trough or fish-farm) during the time of Arab occupation.

The gardens were initiated in 1967 at the behest of the Borghese princes. They comprise Mediterranean species and exotics such as *Encefaloartus horridus* – the blue prickly cycad, thought to exist only in fossil form before botanists discovered the plant in Tanzania.

ROVINE DI SOLUNTO ★

Solunto, one of three Punic cities on Sicily together with Mozia and Palermo, occupies a beautiful position on the promontory formed by Monte Catalfano. Today, the magnificent ruins include a frescoed patrician house and an agora.

▶ **Orient Yourself:** Starting from Bagheria, cross the level crossing near the station and turn down S 113 towards Porticello. A minor road forks left towards the hill. Open Mar–Oct, 9am–6pm, rest of the year 9am–4.30pm, Sun and public hols, 9am–1pm. €2. 091 90 45 57.

Organising Your Time: Because of Solunto's hilly location much of the walk around the ruins is uphill and the site is best avoided during the hottest part of the day.

Also See: BAGHERIA; CEFALÙ; MONREALE; PALERMO; TERMINI.

Visit

Solunto was founded by the Carthaginians in the 4C BC and succumbed to Roman rule in the 5C BC.

The name has two origins: one legendary and linked to the evil creature **Soluntus**; the other finds its origin in the Carthaginian word *Selaim*, meaning crag.

The urban layout conforms with the Classical principles upheld by Hippodamus of Miletus, arranged orthogonally with a *decumanus maximus* and perpendicular side streets enclosing *insulae* (blocks). The precipitous site required terraces to be built, and for additional living space to be accommodated in tall houses.

The way up to the ruins passes the Antiquarium, just inside the gate, which displays artefacts recovered from the site, including a fresco fragment of a tragic mask.

Baths

The thermal baths preserve the underfloor brick supports that enabled hot air heat the rooms from below, and a

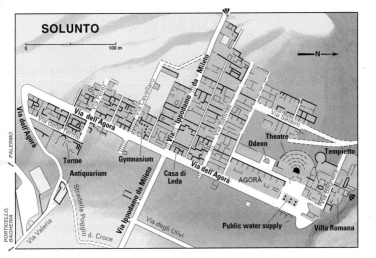

room with a mosaic floor which served as a bath.

Via dell'Agorà

The *decumanus maximus* is partly paved in stone and, unusually, in terracotta. It bisects the town on a south-west to north-east axis, extending to the forum, here designated with the Greek name agora.

Gymnasium

This is the name commonly given to the patrician house with an atrium and a peristyle, from which there remain three Doric columns and part of the entablature, complete with architrave, frieze of metopes and triglyphs and cornice.

Via Ippodamo da Mileto

This is a *cardo*: from the bottom, a magnificent **view**★★ extends over the bay of Palermo and Monte Pellegrino.

Casa di Leda

This large patrician house is so called because it contains a wall frescoed with Leda and the Swan.

The house is arranged around a peristyle (as indicated by the stump of a corner column and cavities for the other columns) with an *impluvium* for rainwater collection. One of the rooms facing onto the peristyle is frescoed in Pompeiian style.

Agora

The square, was originally enclosed on all sides by public buildings and lined with shops *(at the far end)*. On the east side, there was a large **public cistern:** note the bases of the 26 columns that supported the roof.

Odeon

The small theatre was intended for musical performances or council meetings: the orchestra and a few rows of *cavea* seating are still visible.

Villa Romana

From the villa, there is a good view of Capo Zafferano and **Sant'Elia**. At the far end of the bay on the headland what is left of the **medieval castle of Solunto** sits looking out to sea.

TAORMINA★★★

POPULATION: 10 858

From its location on a rock plateau, 200m above sea level, Taormina occupies one of the best seats in the house, looking out from its balcony over the sea to Mt Etna. The breathtaking beauty of the landscape and its artistic history (the Greek Theatre in particular stands testament to its creative past) have rendered Taormina famous all over the world.

A popular destination for travellers since the 1700's, Taormina's popularity soared in the last thirty years of the 19C, prompting a period of tourist development. Many foreigners, in particular English and German tourists, constructed villas in the city; luminaries drawn here included magnates such as the Rothschilds and the Krupps, and writers such as DH Lawrence. In more recent times, Taormina has become a favourite with the international jet set. From April to September the countless tourists who pour into the town slightly dim the sublime fascination of Taormina. However, even with crowds, the locality remains a must-see on any modern Grand Tour of Sicily.

- **Information:** Piazza S. Caterina (Palazzo Corvaja).
  ☎0942 23 243. www.gate2taormina.com.
- ▶ **Orient Yourself:** The historical centre is best explored on foot, and the reward for tackling the many flights of steps and steep slopes (avoid the hottest part of the day) is the magnificent view from the top of the town.
- **Parking:** As it is extremely difficult to find parking in the historical centre, visitors are advised to leave their cars in one of the well signposted car parks along the road leading into the town and to walk into the centre.
- **Don't Miss:** Magnificent panoramas of Mt Etna from the Greek Theatre, the atmosphere of the Old Town with its splendid palazzi, coffee and a stroll along Porta Catania and a tour of the Alcantara Valley, including the Gole dell'Alcantar.
- **Especially for Kids:** Cable car rides from Taormina to Mazzaro, and boat rides to grottoes and caves at Mazzaro and Capo Sant'Andrea.
- **Also See:** ACIREALE; ETNA;GIARDINI NAXOS; MESSINA.

Greek theatre with Mount Etna in the background

B. Morandi/MICHELIN

A Bit of History

Legend relates how the crew aboard a Greek vessel that was sailing along the eastern coast of Sicily were distracted while making a sacrifice to Neptune, the god of the sea. The god, outraged, sent forth such a strong wind that the boat was shipwrecked. Just one of the sailors, Theocles, succeeded in reaching a local beach. Fascinated by the area, he returned to Greece to persuade a band of compatriots to come to Sicily and found a colony.

This was **Nasso**, modern-day Naxos (see GIARDINI NAXOS). There is a seed of truth in the legend: for a Greek colony was indeed founded here in the 8C BC, and its people prospered quietly until 403 BC when Dionysius, the tyrant of Syracuse, decided to extend his territory by including this part of the island; following their defeat, the colonists were allowed to settle on the plateau of Monte Tauro (200m/650ft above sea level) which hitherto had been occupied by the Siculi. From that time, records begin to refer to the settlement of *Tauromenion*, modern Taormina. At first the town was allied with Rome, and was then conquered by Octavian; when the Roman Empire fell, it became the capital of Byzantine Sicily. Shortly after the arrival of the Arabs it was destroyed, only to be immediately rebuilt and, in 1079, conquered by the Norman Count Roger d'Altavilla, under whom it enjoyed a long period of prosperity.

In the centuries that followed, it became a Spanish dominion before succumbing to French and then Bourbon rule, until the Unification of Italy.

Theatre★★★

 Open 9am–2hr before dusk. €6. ☎0942 23 220; www.regione.sicilia.it. The theatre was built by the Ancient Greeks (Hellenistic period), and then transformed and enlarged by the Romans. What survives today dates from the 2C AD. The amphitheatre exploits the natural lie of the land: several of the *cavea* steps are cut directly from the bedrock. The Greek theatre conformed with the correct application of the Classical orders; it included a semicircular *orchestra* section reserved for musicians, chorus and dancers. The Romans removed the lower tier of steps when converting the orchestra into a circular arena, a shape better suited to hosting circus games; they also added a corridor to provide access for gladiators and wild animals. From the top of the *cavea* (auditorium), visitors and spectators can absorb the full impact of the **panoramic view**★★★ spread before the majestic presence of Mount Etna. The magical prospect is extended all along the top of the *cavea* as far as the opposite left-hand corner where the outlook encompasses Taormina itself.

The theatre, which continues to be used, has hosted the *David di Donatello* prize, a prestigious event in the Italian film industry. It now hosts *Taormina Arte,* an international festival of cinema, theatre, ballet and music, during summer.

Walking Tour

The centre of Taormina radiates from the main thoroughfare Corso Umberto I.

Corso Umberto I★

Stroll along this peaceful thoroughfare beginning at **Porta Messina** as it gently climbs up to **Porta Catania**, past its elegant shops, restaurants and cafés. Behind this front, an intricate network of side streets extends, full of unexpected sights and smells (like the scent of almond paste wafting from back-street sweet-shop kitchens). Just beyond Porta Messina, at the entrance to the street, stands the 17C **Chiesa di San Pancrazio**. This is dedicated to St Pancras who, according to legend, was the first Bishop of Taormina. The church, meanwhile, sits among the foundations of a temple dedicated to Zeus Serapis (notice the remains of the Ancient wall which are now incorporated into the building's left flank). Along the street there are three lovely piazzas.

Piazza Vittorio Emanuele

This square occupies the site of the Roman Forum. Behind the **Chiesa di**

Address Book

⟡ For coin ranges, see the Legend on the cover flap.

GETTING THERE

Trains and buses run to and from Catania (approximately 1hr), Messina (1hr) and Siracusa (2hr 30min). There is also a daily bus service from the town to Fontanarossa airport at Catania. Taormina-Giardini train station is situated in Villagonia, 3km/1.8mi from the centre. The bus station is on Via Pirandello.

EXCURSIONS FROM TAORMINA

The CST (Compagnia Siciliana Turismo) bus company offers a number of excursions to places of interest, including Siracusa, Agrigento, Piazza Armerina, Palermo, the Aeolian Islands, the Alcantara gorge and Etna. For further information, contact CST, Corso Umberto 101; ☎0942 62 60 88; www.compagniasicilianaturismo.it

WHERE TO STAY

⟡ For further accommodation options, see GIARDINI NAXOS.

⊖⊖**Bed & Breakfast Villa Regina** – *Punta San Giorgio, Castelmola, 5km/3mi NE of Taormina.* ☎0942 28 228. *www.villareginataormina.com. Closed Nov–Feb. 10 rooms.* This simple guesthouse has a cool, shady garden and a delightful view of Taormina and the coast. Ideal for those in need of a peaceful break.

⊖⊖⊟**Hotel Villa Schuler** – *Piazzetta Bastione, Via Roma, Taormina.* ☎0942 23 481. *www.hotel-villaschuler.com. Closed Dec–Feb. 26 rooms.* ⊏⊐. Converted into a hotel in 1905, this old house in the historical centre is surrounded by a Mediterranean garden full of tropical flowers and plants. The hotel retains some of its late-19C atmosphere and has old-fashioned, comfortable rooms.

⊖⊖⊟⊟**Andromaco Palace Hotel** – *Via Fontana Vecchia, Taormina.* ☎0942 23 834. *www.andromaco.it. 20 rooms.* ⊏⊐. Despite its rather grand name, this elegant family-run hotel close to the town centre is both cosy and romantic, with simple, yet comfortable furnishings and panoramic views.

⊖⊖⊟**Hotel Del Corso** – *Corso Umberto 238, Taormina.* ☎0942 62 86 98. *www.hoteldelcorsotaormina.com. Closed Jan and Feb. 15 rooms.* ⊏⊐. This well-known, recently restored Taormina hotel has been under new management since 2000. Although the reception area is small, the rooms are tastefully decorated and comfortable.

⊖⊖⊟⊟**Hotel Isabella** – *Corso Umberto 58, Taormina* – ☎0942 23 153. *www.gaishotels.com/isabella. 32 rooms.* ⊏⊐. The perfect destination for those who prefer the town to the beach. This top-quality hotel is elegant, efficiently run and enjoys an excellent location in the town centre. Breakfast is taken on a delightful terrace with views of the Greek theatre.

⊖⊖⊟⊟**Hotel Villa Sonia** – *Via Porta Mola 9, Castelmola, 5km/3mi NW of Taormina.* ☎0942 28 082. *www.hotelvillasonia.com. Closed Nov–Feb. 35 rooms.* ⊏⊐. Situated at the entrance to the charming village of Castelmola, this attractive villa is tastefully decorated with period items and Sicilian handicrafts.

⊖⊖⊟⊟**Grand Hotel Timeo** – *Via Teatro Greco 59, Taormina.* ☎0942 23 801. *www.framonhotels.com. 87 rooms.* ⊏⊐. This superbly located hotel helped to establish Taormina's reputation. Recently restored to its former period splendour, the hotel offers all the modern creature comforts expected of a high-quality establishment.

WHERE TO EAT

⟡ For further restaurant options, see GIARDINI NAXOS.

In addition to the restaurants listed below, the district to the west of Corso Umberto I teems with typical outdoor Sicilian restaurants set out on discreet terraces or in secluded gardens.

⊖**Porta Messina** – *Largo Giove Serapide 4, Taormina.* ☎0942 23 205. The list of pizzas in this friendly restaurant is endless, with more unusual options for those who are ready to experiment.

La Piazzetta – *Vicolo F. Paladini 5/7, Taormina.* ☎*0942 62 63 17. www.paginegialle.it/ristorantelapiazzetta. Closed Mon (except Jul and Aug), Nov and Jan.* The cuisine at this friendly, family-run establishment with a typical village-restaurant atmosphere is distinctly Mediterranean, with an emphasis on fish. Pleasant terrace.

Il Baccanale – *Porta Filea 1, Taormina.* ☎*0942 62 53 90. Closed Thu (except Apr–Sept).* This restaurant serving fine Sicilian cuisine is popular with foreign tourists and enjoys a rustic atmosphere with outdoor tables on a small piazza.

Al Duomo – *Vico Ebrei 11, Taormina.* ☎*0942 62 56 56. www.ristorantealduomo.it. Closed Mon, Jan and Nov. Booking recommended.* The highlights of Al Duomo are its delightful terrace with a view of the cathedral and its excellent local cuisine.

Al Saraceno – *Via Madonna della Rocca 18, Taormina.* ☎*0942 63 20 15. www.alsaraceno.it. Closed Mon (except Jul and Aug) and Nov.* This recently restored restaurant is situated along the street running from the Castello Saraceno. On fine days the splendid view from the spacious terrace on the first floor extends as far as the Straits of Messina. Fresh fish and pizza are the house specialities.

Il Delfino–da Angelo – *Via Nazionale, Mazzarò, 5.5km/3.5mi S of Taormina on S 114.* ☎*0942 23 004. Closed Nov–15 Mar.* Combine lunch with a dip in the sea at this attractive restaurant situated right on the beach.

TAKING A BREAK

TAORMINA

Caffè Wunderbar – *Piazza IX Aprile 7, Taormina.* ☎*0942 62 53 02.* Greta Garbo and Tennessee Williams enjoyed meeting for cocktails in this famous cafe at the foot of the Torre dell'Orologio, in one of the most attractive corners of Taormina. The interior is elegant in style, while the terrace enjoys magnificent views of the Bay of Naxos.

Mocambo Bar – *Piazza IX Aprile 8, Taormina.* ☎*0942 23 350.* "Take a seat at the Mocambo and watch the world go by…" is the advice given by the owners of this bar-pasticceria, which enjoys a superb location overlooking the beautiful Piazza IX Aprile. Open from breakfast to after dinner, this bar has a pleasant atmosphere throughout the day and into the evening.

Pasticceria Saint Honoré – *Corso Umberto I 208, Taormina.* ☎*094 22 48 77. Open 7am–midnight.* You're spoiled for choice in this pasticceria with its wide selection of cakes, ice creams, pastries and *torroni* (a type of nougat). Alternatively, enjoy a cooling glass of granita on the Saint Honoré's terrace.

CASTELMOLA

Bar San Giorgio – *Piazza S. Antonio 1, 98030 Castelmola, 5km/3mi NW of Taormina.* ☎*0942 28 228.* Established at the beginning of the 20C, this traditional café enjoys a wonderful location in the quiet Piazza S. Antonio, with superb views of Taormina and the sea. Past customers have included Charles Rolls and Henry Royce as well as John D Rockefeller, and the café continues to be popular with celebrities. Specialities include *vino alla mandorla* (almond liqueur).

SHOPPING

La Bottega del Buongustaio – *Via G. di Giovanni 17, Taormina.* ☎*094 26 25 769.* Set back from the hustle and bustle of Corso Umberto, this shop specialises in DOC-label Sicilian produce, including wines, liqueurs, sauces, preserves, honey, pasta and olive oil. An excellent address for those wishing to take home some of the island's gastronomic specialities.

FESTIVALS

Festa del costume e del carretto siciliani – In April and May, this festival celebrates the Sicilian cart and local costume, hosting traditional folk shows.

Taormina arte – This international music, theatre and film festival takes place from Jul–Sept.
For information, call ☎*0942 21 142; www.taormina-arte.com*

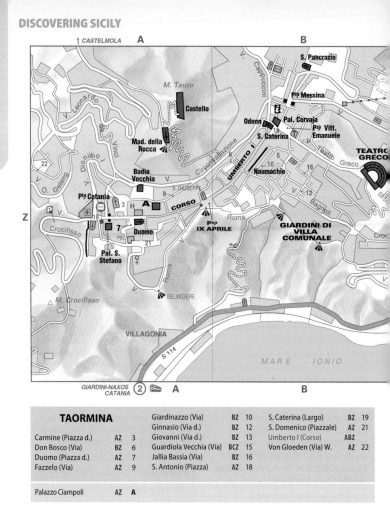

TAORMINA		Giardinazzo (Via)	BZ	10	S. Caterina (Largo)	BZ	19
		Ginnasio (Via d.)	BZ	12	S. Domenico (Piazzale)	AZ	21
Carmine (Piazza d.)	AZ 3	Giovanni (Via d.)	BZ	13	Umberto I (Corso)	ABZ	
Don Bosco (Via)	BZ 6	Guardiola Vecchia (Via)	BCZ	15	Von Gloeden (Via) W.	AZ	22
Duomo (Piazza d.)	AZ 7	Jallia Bassia (Via)	BZ	16			
Fazzelo (Via)	AZ 9	S. Antonio (Piazza)	AZ	18			
Palazzo Ciampoli	AZ A						

Santa Caterina with its Baroque pink marble and Taormina stone doorway, there are red-brick ruins of an **Odeon**, a small covered theatre from the Roman period (1C AD).

Palazzo Corvaja

The heart of the building, which includes the square tower and the central section overlooking the courtyard, dates from the period of Arab domination. The left wing and the staircase up to the first floor were added in the 13C; the right wing dates from the 15C. Having been abandoned and left to become dilapidated over the years, it was restored after the Second World War. A succession of styles is discernible: the top of the tower is Arab, the windows of the state room (13C) and the front entrance are Catalan

Gothic and the Sala del Parlamento *(in the right wing)* is Norman.

The offices located off the courtyard, are in part occupied by APT, the Sicilian Tourist Authorities; they also display typical Sicilian puppets and a number of ornate Sicilian carts.

On the first floor of the *palazzo* is the **Museo Siciliano di Arte e Tradizioni Popolari** (☉ *open daily 9am–1pm, 4pm–8pm;* ☉ *closed Mon;* ◎ *€2.60;* ☎ *0942 61 02 74)*, housing a collection of carts, puppets, costumes, embroidery, cribs and a series of ex-votos.

Naumachie

In a side-street off to the left.

The name technically refers to the simulated naval battles that the Romans so enjoyed watching. In this case, it

trough at one time. Elevated in the centre, it bears the symbol of the town; a female centaur, with two legs and two arms, who holds an orb and a sceptre, the attributes of power.

Duomo
The 13C cathedral is dedicated in honour of St Nicholas of Bari. The front elevation has a starkly simple façade, relieved only by a Renaissance doorway flanked by single-light windows, surmounted by a rose window. The crenellations along the roof line have earned it the name of "cathedral-fortress".

Interior
The fabric of the building is Gothic; the ground plan is a Latin cross. The nave is separated from the side aisles by an arcade of pointed arches, which spring from column shafts of pink marble. The clerestory above comprises of simple single-light windows that illuminate the nave. A fine 16C polyptych by Antonello de Saliba sits over the second altar in the south aisle.

Taormina's Palazzi★

The old town centre is dotted with fine *palazzi*: most are Gothic in style with Arabo-Norman touches and built of black lava stone and white Syracuse stone, set into geometric patterning.

Palazzo di Santo Stefano
Via del Ghetto (left), before Porta Catania.
This fine building was built for the Dukes of Santo Stefano, part of the De Spuches family, in the 15C. The bold rustication gives it the appearance of a fortified residence.
The most effective decorative element is the two-tone (black lava and white Syracuse stone) geometric frieze, which runs the length of the upper storey. The *palazzo* accommodates the **Fondazione Mazzullo** (☉*open daily 9am–12.30pm,*

relates to a red-brick wall dating from the Roman period, which has been reinforced by a system of blind arcading.

Piazza IX Aprile★
This delightful little square overlooks the sea, offering wonderful **views**★★ over the bay and across to Mount Etna. It is enclosed on the other three sides by the bare façade of San Giuseppe (17C), San Agostino (now a library) and the Torre dell'Orologio, which sits on an open loggia that provides a through way to the 15C part of the town. The extant building dates from the late 17C, when the clock was added, although the foundations appear to date as far back as the 6C AD, when the tower formed an integral part of the town's defences. The piazza is a popular meeting place, crowded with people sitting at the outside tables of its many bars.

Piazza Duomo
A splendid Baroque **fountain** in Taormina stone rises from a circular base at the centre of the square. The largest basin, facing eastwards, served as a drinking

4pm–7.30pm; ☏0942 61 02 73), which hosts exhibitions of sculpture and drawings by the artist Graniti (and the occasional temporary show, notably during Advent when a display of terracotta Nativity scenes is arranged). A recurrent theme among the works in lava, granite and bronze, is the expression of pain: this is especially notable in the series of *Executions by Firing Squad*; and in the *Wounded Cat*.

Badia Vecchia
Via Dionisio 1.
A pleasant building that currently houses the **Museo Archeologico** (🕐 *open 9am–1pm, 4pm–6.30pm;* 🚫 *closed Mon and public holidays;* ☏*0942 62 37 00*).

Palazzo Ciampoli
Providing a backdrop to the steps of Salita Palazzo Ciampoli, to the right of Corso Umberto I, just before Piazza Duomo.
Despite its poor condition and an unsightly old discotheque sign, the façade of this *palazzo* is a fine one, composed of two levels separated by a decoratively engraved stone panel. The entrance is set into an elegantly pointed arch, surmounted by a shield bearing the date when the palace was built: 1412.

I giardini di Villa Comunale★★
Via Roma.
The gardens are planted with flowering plants and shrubs ranging from the common to the exotic. When the gardens were under private ownership, a series of eclectic follies were erected; the most unusual consists of arches and arcades reminiscent of a beehive, hence the name *(the Beehives)* given to it by its owner, Lady Florence Trevelyan, who used it for bird-watching.
The little road that runs along the seaward edge provides a fine view of Mount Etna and the south coast.

Excursions

Beaches
A cable car links Taormina with Mazzarò on the coast. From Mazzarò a bus service operates to the other beaches (🚌*€3.50 there and back for the cable car + bus; ask for a Funibus ticket). The cable car runs every 15min and the bus every 30min.*
The little bay of **Mazzarò** is enclosed on the south side by **Capo Sant'Andrea**, which is riddled with caves and grottoes, including the Blue Grotto (Grotta Azzurra). The sound of fishermen calling for people to join a boat trip echoes the lengths of all the beaches.
Beyond the headland is the delightful bay★★ that sweeps round to **Isola Bella**, linked to the main shore by a narrow strip of land. The island is part of the WWF Isola Bella Regional Reserve *(entrance at Km 47.2 on S 114; for further information, contact Viale S. Pancrazio 25, Taormina;* ☏*0942 62 83 88*). The longest beaches, **Spisone** and **Mazzeo**, extend north of Mazzarò.

Castello
4km/2.5mi along the road to Castelmola; a track turns up to the right.
The castle can also be reached on foot by following the signs for "Salita Castello", up a series of broad steps, from Via Circonvallazione (about 1km/ 0.6mi there and back) in Taormina, or by taking Salita Branco, which starts in Via Dietro i Cappuccini.
🚷*Avoid taking this walk in the midday sun or at the height of summer!*
The **castle** stands isolated on the summit of Monte Tauro (398m/1 305ft). Just below it stands the **Santuario della Madonna della Rocca:** the little terrace before the church offers a fine **view**★★ of Taormina's ancient theatre and town. A footpath continues up to the castle, a medieval fortress built on the foundations of a former acropolis from Antiquity. Little survives other than the old walls and tower fragments. From here, another splendid **view**★★ extends over the theatre and Taormina.

Castelmola★
5km/3mi NW.
This village, occupying a strategic **position**★ behind Taormina, centres on the picturesque Piazzetta del Duomo, from which a network of tiny streets extends outwards. Magnificent glimpses of the landscape may be

Rivers of Water and Lava

Alcantara Gorge - Lost in the mists of time, a small volcano north of Mount Etna woke and poured forth enormous quantities of lava which flowed down to the sea and beyond, to form Capo Schisò. The tortuous route taken by the river of lava was followed by a torrent of water which ploughed a channel through it, smoothing the lava and clearing away the aggregate. Towards the end of its journey, the water encountered more friable ground and, sweeping onwards, exposed two sheer cliffs of very hard basalt that had cooled and hardened into fascinating prism-like shapes. This is the gorge, only part of which is now accessible.

The name of the river, and of its valley, *Al Qantarah,* dates back to the period of Arab occupation and refers to the arched bridge built by the Romans to withstand the force of the river in full spate, an impressive sight even today.

snatched from various points, especially from Piazzetta di Sant'Antonino, where the **view**★ opens out towards Mount Etna, the north coast and the beaches below Taormina.

Very little remains of the ruined **castle** other than sections of the 16C walls and a good view of Monte Venere (beyond the cemetery) and the lesser Monte Ziretto. The **Chiesa dell'Annunziata** next to the cemetery, preserves an attractive doorway sculpted in white stone.

Try the regional speciality, a potent almond liqueur that was invented by Castelmola locals.

rest of the year 8am–5pm. 🎫*€2.50. Rental of boots and waders €7.50 Prices are subject to change. For more information call,* ☎*0942 98 50 10.*

The gorge is accessible when the water level is low, for a stretch of 50m/55yd to 200m/220yd.

Waders can be hired at the entrance to the gorge to keep out the freezing cold river waters.

Under normal conditions it is possible to walk upriver May–Sept. There is also a lift to take visitors back up to the top of the gorge. Special camping facilities are available nearby.

Driving Tour

The Alcantara Valley

60km/37mi – allow one day (including the visit to the gorges and riverbed walk).

Etna looms over the Alcantara Valley, appearing and disappearing between the hills as the road winds its way in an ever-changing kaleidoscope of **views**★.

Giardini Naxos ♨♨
🛇*See GIARDINI NAXOS.*

Along the road, you will see olive-wood sculptures by Francesco Lo Giudice, known as *Il Mago* (the magician) on the left hand side.

Gole dell'Alcantara★
Contact the Ente Parco Fluviale dell'Alcantara, ☎*0942 98 10 38; www.parcoalcantara.it.* 🕓*Open May–Sept, 7am–8pm,*

M. Magni/MICHELIN

Walking in the Alcantara Gorge

Legend of the Alcantara Gorge

At one time the Alcantara River flowed calmly along its course without crags, rapids or sheer drops, making the valley fertile. The people who lived there, however, were evil: they hurt each other and had no respect for nature.

Two brothers lived in the valley and cultivated a field of wheat. One was blind. When the time came to divide up the harvest, the sighted farmer took the grain measure and began to share out the wheat. One measure for himself and one for his brother. Then, overtaken by greed, he decided to keep most of the harvest for himself. An eagle, happening to fly overhead, witnessed what was happening and reported the incident to God, who hurled a thunderbolt at the cheat, killing him outright. The thunderbolt also struck the heap of grain that had unjustly been set aside, turning it into a mountain of red earth from which poured a river of lava which flowed down to the sea.

Legend from the book entitled *Al Qantarah* by L Danzuso and E Zinna.

The gorge

The descent on foot affords a spectacular **view**★ of the entrance to the gorge. Once level with the river bed, the salt cliffs tower some 50m/165ft above the narrow tongue of water. Their massive bulk, exaggerated by shadow, seems accentuated farther up the gorge, where the world suddenly seems to be composed of three elements: rock, water and sky. As you walk, the sun casts bright light into the darkness; occasionally refracted into a thousand tiny mirrors by droplets of water ejected by the waterfalls and collected into rivulets that stream down the sheer rock face.

Motta Camastra

A road off to the right leads to this small town at an altitude of 453m/1 486ft.

Francavilla di Sicilia

On 21 June 1719 a battle took place here between Spaniards and Austrians, an event recorded for posterity by prints preserved in the Capuchin monastery on top of the hill nearby. Founded in the 16C, the monastery has a few original cells and a small museum about life in this offshoot of the Franciscan Order. In the church there is an 18C wooden aumbry (small cupboard) for Eucharist vessels bearing a pelican plucking the flesh from its breast to feed its young; a symbol of the sacrifice of Christ.

Castiglione di Sicilia

Castel Leone (now reduced to a ruin) dominates the town from on high, set as it is on its rocky spur of tufa. The **site**★ of the castle has been a lookout point since ancient times. From here magnificent **views**★★ stretch over the town and Etna. To the east lie the ruins of a fortress dating from 750 BC.

The main monuments are clustered around the highest part of the town. The 18C church, **San Antonio**, has a concave façade and a campanile built of lava with an onion-shaped dome. The interior, decked with polychrome marble, has a triumphal arch (1796) and a fine wooden organ in the chancel.

San Pietro preserves some of the primitive Norman original tower in its campanile. **Santa Maria della Catena** has a fine doorway with spiral columns.

A right fork off the road to Mojo Alcantara leads to the remains of a **Byzantine chapel** (or *cuba*) dating from the 7C-9C.

Mojo Alcantara

The name of this little town comes from a small volcano, which erupted and gave rise to the creation of the gorge. Today, it is a green, innocuous-looking cone.

Randazzo★ See ETNA.

From Randazzo it is possible to join the Circumtenea (See ETNA) or continue on towards the Nebrodi Mountains (See MADONIE E NEBRODI).

TERMINI IMERESE

POPULATION: 26 760

Termini has been famous since Antiquity for the hot, sulphurous thermal waters that gush from its rocks, held to have therapeutic properties. Modern Termini is also an important port with a large and bustling industrial area. The town is further energised by an annual carnival, during which a procession of allegorical floats and events fill the streets with spectacle.

- **Information:** Palazzo Civico, Piazza Duomo; ☎091 81 28 111; www.comune.termini-imerese.pa.it.
- ▶ **Orient Yourself:** Termini comprises an old upper town and a modern, industrial lower town, linked by a series of narrow streets and flights of steps. Most of the monuments in Termini are in the upper town, which is best explored on foot.
- **Also See:** BAGHERIA; CEFALÙ; SOLUNTO.

Walking Tour

A good place to start exploring the town is Piazza Duomo, overlooked by the Palazzo del Comune containing a former Council Chamber decorated with frescoes by Vincenzo La Barbera (1610) depicting the history of the town.

Duomo

🕐 *Open daily 9am–noon, 3.30pm–8.30pm.* 🕐*Closed Fri.* ☎*091 81 41 291.*
The cathedral was largely rebuilt in the 17C. Inside, it has a fine marble relief Madonna del Ponte *(fourth chapel on the right)* by Ignazio Marabitti (1842). A lovely wooden statue of the Immacolata by Quattrocchi (1799) adorns the chapel dedicated to the Immaculate Conception, and the chapel of San Bartolomeo is furnished with a Venetian-style Rococo sedan chair once used for taking communion to the sick.
The Museo Civico can be seen in Via Museo Civico on the opposite side of the piazza to the Duomo *(see Visit)*.
From behind the Duomo, Via Belvedere leads up to a terrace with **views** of the coast. A little farther on, to the left, is an attractive little church dedicated to **Santa Caterina d'Alessandria** (14C); above the fine pointed arch doorway is a shallow relief of the saint. Just beyond lie the shaded gardens of **Villa Palmeri**, where the remains of the **Roman Curia** can still be seen. From the park, follow Via Anfiteatro down to the ruined **Roman amphitheatre** (1C AD).

Return to Piazza Duomo and follow Via Mazzini; on the right stands the 17C **Chiesa del Monte**, long used as the town's Pantheon (mausoleum for dignitaries).

Città bassa

Return to the car and drive down to the lower part of town along the Serpentina Balsamo. A lane leading off a left bend provides a perfect opportunity to stop and take in the lovely view of the pale blue tiled dome of the **Chiesa dell'Annunziata**.

Piazza delle Terme, at the bottom, is dominated by the Grande Albergo delle Terme, built in the 19C to designs by the architect Damiani Almeyda.

Visit

Museo Civico

In Via Museo Civico, on the opposite side of the piazza to the Duomo.
♿🕐*Open daily 9am–1pm, 4pm–7pm; Sundays 9am–12.30pm.* 🕐*Closed Mon and public hols.* ☎*091 81 28 550.*
The museum is well laid out with helpful information boards; it comprises an archaeological collection and a section dedicated to art. The first rooms display material from Palaeolithic and Neolithic times recovered from local caves; excavated artefacts from Himera, including two fine red-figure Attic craters (5C BC); coinage from the Ancient Greek, Roman

and Punic periods. Finally, a large room is dedicated to Hellenistic and Roman pottery: grave goods such as oil lamps, small receptacles and ointment jars; figurines dressed in togas found in the forum and the House of Stenius (1C AD); portraits, including one of Agrippina (the mother of Caligula), which still bears traces of paint; terracotta pipe from the aqueduct of Cornelius; and Roman inscriptions.

The chapel of San Michele Arcangelo frescoed by Nicolò da Pettineo leads off the archaeology department. It also contains a *Madonna and Saints* triptych by **Gaspare da Pesaro** (1453) and an interesting 15C wooden composition, unusual in its depiction of the Trinity as a *Pietà* (with the Holy Spirit personified). On the floor above, the **art gallery** is hung with paintings from the 17C-19C. Notable works include a Flemish *Annunciation* (16C), several pieces by the local painter Vittorio La Barbera (*Crucifixion*, 17C), a *St Sebastian* by Solimena and, in a small room at the far end, a tiny portable Byzantine-style 18C panel triptych.

Excursions

Caccamo
9km/5.5mi S.

Clinging to a rocky precipice among the lower spurs of Monte San Calogero, this pretty little town is overlooked by its impressive castle.

Castle★
Entrance from Via Termitana. ○*Open in Aug 9am–12.15pm, 4pm–6.15pm.* ○*Closed on public hols.* ∞€1. *For information, call* ☎091 81 03 111.
This is one of Sicily's best preserved castles, arranged over several levels as a result of spiralling 14C, 15C and 17C extensions. The main unit probably dates from the 11C. The defensive elements of the castle were reinforced by the Chiaramonte, while in the 17C, under Amato ownership, these were relaxed as it was transformed into a noble residence.
Beyond the first gate, a 17C ramp leads up to a second gate. The broad, paved courtyard provides access to the Torre

Mastra, where magnificent **views**★ include Termini Imerese, Mongerbina, Capo Zafferano, Rocca Busambra and the Vicari Castle. An 18C doorway leads through to the Sala delle Armi or Salone della Congiura where the rebellious barons gathered before confronting William the Bad. The apartments to the left of the Weapons Hall give access to the Torre Gibellina; the rooms to the right include the Salotto dei Nobili, before leading onto a terrace with a panoramic view.

▷ *Return to Corso Umberto I and turn right to Piazza Duomo.*

Piazza Duomo★
The square provides an attractive open space split between two levels. The elevated northern side is fronted by a harmonious group of buildings, namely the **Palazzo del Monte di Pietà** (17C) flanked on the left by the **Oratorio del Santissimo Sacramento** and the **Chiesa delle Anime Sante del Purgatorio** on the right. This very special arrangement constitutes a sort of theatrical stage from which to survey the lower part of the square. The balustrade, which separates and links the two levels, is surmounted by four statues representing the Blessed Giovanni Liccio, Santa Rosalia, San Nicasio and San Teotista.

Chiesa Madre
The main church, dedicated to St George, is on the west side of the piazza. **Inside** hangs a dramatic painting of *The Miracle of Sant'Isidoro Agricola* (1641) by Mattia Stomer, while in the chapel of the Holy Sacrament, a ciborium sits above the inlaid marble altar with reliefs by the Gagini School (15C).
Down Corso Umberto I, and off to the right, is Piazza San Marco lined with the buildings of a former Franciscan monastery, the Church of the Annunciation with its twin bell towers, the Chiesa della Badia, and what was the 14C church of **San Marco** (the doorway with its pointed arch is still visible).

San Benedetto alla Badia
The single-nave church has a superb majolica **floor** attributed to Nicolò

Sarzana from Palermo (18C), although this is badly damaged in places and mostly covered by carpets. When possible, it is worth climbing up to the women's gallery, once the preserve of nuns of a closed order from the convent that stood adjacent to the church. From the gallery there is an excellent view of the whole church, and, in particular, of the fine wrought-iron railings (18C) at the far end. Admire the **stuccoes** in the apse by Bartolomeo Sanseverino (18C): the lunette, above, depicts *The Supper at Emmaus;* the statues on either side of the altar are allegories of *Chastity* and *Obedience*.

▷ *Return to Corso Umberto I.*
Just before Piazza Torina turn
left uphill.

Santa Maria degli Angeli (or San Domenico)

The two-aisled church has a trussed **wooden ceiling** with paintings of Dominican saints (damaged by humidity). In the chapel dedicated to Santa Maria degli Angeli *(on the right)* is a lovely *Madonna and Child* by Antonello Gagini (1516), and, on the underside of the main arch, a series of small paintings by Vincenzo La Barbera depicting *The Mysteries of the Rosary* (17C).

Before leaving Caccamo, it is worth walking to the far side of town and turning right (signposted "Centro Storico"): at a certain point along this almost circular route, there is a wonderful **view**★ over the whole town.

Acquedotto Cornelio

Take the road to Caccamo, and turn left *(yellow sign)*; after 300m/330yd, on a bend, the Roman aqueduct can be seen on the left, spanning the width of the River Barratina valley.

Scavi di Himera
18km/11mi E.

◷*Open Mon–Sat, 9am–dusk; Sun and public hols, 9am–1pm. ⊗€2. ☎091 81 40 128.*

Himera was founded in 648 BC by colonists from Zancle (modern Messina).

The Carthaginians suffered a crushing defeat here in 480 BC at the hands of the allied forces of Agrigento and Syracuse. Its demise came in 408 BC, however, when a second wave of invading Carthaginians first conquered and then razed the town to the ground.

The ancient town is sited at the top of a hill south of the Messina-Palermo road. Here, sections of wall and part of the sacred area with three temples have been excavated. Farther along the road is the **antiquarium**, displaying artefacts found on site.

The most significant and best-preserved structure, however, is the **Temple of Victory** (5C BC), which stands at the bottom of the hill. It seems probable that the Greeks forced the Carthaginians to build this temple to celebrate their victory in 480 BC. Stumpy vestiges of columns, the *cella*, the *pronaos* and the *opisthodomus* are clearly visible.

The eaves were once marvellously decorated with sculpted lions' heads, now to be found in the archaeological museum in Palermo.

San Nicola l'Arena
13km/8mi W.

A **castle** with three round towers overlooks the picturesque harbour of this seaside resort.

An old harbour-front shed still preserves tuna fishing boats. In the distance (westwards) stands a lookout tower, situated in a strategic position on Capo Grosso.

TRAPANI

POPULATION: 68 335

Situated within sight of the Egadi Islands, Trapani has a sheltered port that is important to the salt trade.

Information: Piazza Saturno. ☎0923 29 000.
www.comune.trapani.it. www.apt.trapani.it.

▶ **Orient Yourself:** Most visitors arriving in Trapani will drive along the central Via Fardella, which crosses the modern town and leads to the medieval district at the end of the headland. Trapani is the main port for the Egadi Islands and Pantelleria.

Parking: Most of the town's monuments of interest are located in the old town, which is best explored on foot.

Don't Miss: Sculpture by the Gagni family and malioca ceramics at the Museo Pepoli; an exploraiton of the Old Town medieval district, Centro Storico.

Also See: Isole EGADI; ERICE; MARSALA; MOZIA; PANTELLERIA; VIA DEL SALE.

Walking Tour

Centro Storico ★

The medieval districts of the old town are situated on the headland and the tip was developed by the Spanish in the 14C (quartiere Palazzo). The oldest section, built in Moorish fashion around a network of interconnecting narrow streets, stretches back along the peninsula; this would originally have been enclosed by walls.

Rua Nova

Now named Via Garibaldi, the "New Road" was laid in the 13C by the Aragonese. Today, it is lined with fine 18C *palazzi* and churches, including the statue-crested **Palazzo Riccio di Morana**, **Palazzo Milo** and **Badia Nuova** (Santa Maria del Soccorso; ⏱open 8.15am–1pm; ☎0923 43 21 11), the flamboyant interior of which is decorated with Baroque polychrome marble and two elaborate **galleries★**, which are supported by angels.

Trapani harbour

B. Kaufmann/MICHELIN

Easter procession in Trapani

Palazzo Burgio opposite is graced with a fine 16C doorway.

Via Torrearsa is lined with elegant shops to the left and leads down to the Pescheria (fish market) on the right. Beyond the intersection, Via Garibaldi continues as Via Libertà, past **Palazzo Fardello di Mokarta** and Palazzo Melilli with its 16C doorway.

▷ *Turn left into Corso Vittorio Emanuele.*

Rua Grande

The second principal thoroughfare constructed in the 13C (the modern Corso Vittorio Emanuele) stretches between elegant Baroque buildings such as the Palazzo Berardo Ferro (n86) and the Sede del Vescovado (Bishop's Palace).

Cattedrale

Ⓒ *Open Mon–Fri 9am–noon, 5pm–6pm; Sat, 9am–noon; Sun and public hols, 10.30am–11.30am, 5.30pm–6.30pm.* ☎ *0923 23 362; www.parrocchie.org. trapani/cattedrale.*

The cathedral dedicated to St Lawrence was erected in the 17C on the site of an earlier 14C building.

Inside, it contains a number of paintings by Flemish artists: a *Nativity (third chapel on the right)*, a crucifixion and a **Deposition** *(fourth chapel on the left)*.

Chiesa del Collegio dei Gesuiti

Ⓒ *Open 9am–1pm, 4pm–7pm.*

The 17C church has an imposing Mannerist façade, ornamented by pediments, columns, pilasters, grotesque masks and caryatid figures.

Palazzo Senatorio (Cavaretta)

This elaborate facade of this lovely *palazzo* rises through two orders of columns and statues up to a pair of large clocks. Alongside stands a 13C bell tower.

Sant'Agostino

This church, built in the 14C, was badly damaged during the Second World War. Built by the Knights Templar, it is one of the only buildings associated with the order still in existence on the island. The **rose window**★ with its Islamic geometric arabesque pattern and Gothic doorway are memorable. The Fountain of Saturn in front of the church commemorates the building of an aqueduct.

Nearby, the **Biblioteca Fardelliana** (Ⓒ *open 9am–1.30pm;* Ⓒ *closed Sun, public hols and 7 Aug;* ☎ *0923 21 06*) displays engravings from the Gatto collection.

Santa Maria del Gesù

Ⓒ *Open Mon–Fri 7.30am–10am (5pm–6pm Thu).* Ⓒ *Closed public hols.* ☎ *0923 87 20 21.*

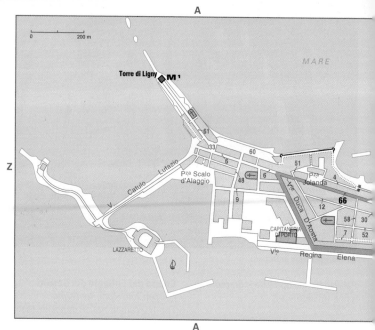

This church, founded by Emperor Charles V, dates from the 16C. Inside, through its lovely Catalan Renaissance doorway, the Cappella Staiti (in the right aisle at the back of the church) houses the terracotta **Madonna degli Angeli**★ by Andrea della Robbia, underneath a magnificent marble tribune by Antonello Gagini (1521).

▶ *Head along Corso Italia.*
Turn left by the church of San Pietro, then immediately right.

Palazzo Ciambra (della Giudecca)

This fine example of the Plateresque (Spanish renaissance) style (16C) has

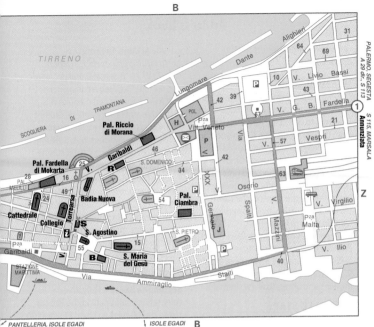

heavy rustication to emphasise the doors and windows, as well as the front of the tower.

Visit

L'Annunziata

In Via Pepoli at the far eastern end of town (in the direction of Palermo) stands the large Carmelite institution known as the Annunziata. The actual church adjoins the former convent, which now houses the town's main museum, the Museo Pepoli.

Santuario dell'Annunziata★

For information on admission times, contact the parish priest several days in advance on ☎0923 53 91 84. Donations welcome.

The church, built in the early 14C, was transformed and enlarged during the 18C. The original front elevation is ornamented with a Chiaramonte Gothic portal, surmounted by an elaborate *rose window* above.

The **Cappella dei Marinai** (16C) is a lovely Renaissance tufa building sur-

mounted by a dome. Inside, a fusion of styles are drawn from Eastern and Renaissance sources.

The **Cappella della Madonna** extends from behind the main altar of the church. Access is through a Renaissance arch with bronze gates dating from 1591. On the altar is the delicate marble figure of the **Madonna of Trapani** (14C), attributed to Nino Pisano.

Museo Pepoli★

Open Mon–Sat, 9am–1.30pm; Sun and public hols, 9am–12.30pm. €2.50. ☎0923 55 32 69. Poor lighting in the museum means that it is best to visit early in the day.

The ex-Carmelite convent beside the Santuario dell'Annunziata is entered through the Villa Pepoli. Inside, the museum, which is named after benefactor and obsessive collector Count Pepoli, houses a wide ranging collection of artefacts and art work from prehistoric times to the 19C.

The ground floor is devoted to sculpture, and the Gagini family is well represented here, the star exhibit being four statues of saints, including *St James the Greater* by **Antonello Gagini**.

Address Book

⌖*For coin ranges, see the Legend on the cover flap.*

GETTING THERE AND AROUND

Trapani is approximately 150km/95mi from Agrigento and 100km/60mi from Palermo, to which it is connected by both bus and train (3hr 30min and 2hr respectively). The bus and train stations are both situated in Piazza Umberto I. For further information and timetables contact the tourist office. Birgi airport, 15km/9mi to the south of the town (☎0923 84 25 02), operates services from Trapani to Pantelleria.

Ferry services to the Egadi Islands and Pantelleria leave from Trapani, with sailings operated by **Siremar** ☎091 74 93 11 (from Italy) or 081 17 19 98 (from mobiles and abroad); www.siremar.it

WHERE TO STAY

⌖ *See ERICE: ADDRESS BOOK.*

WHERE TO EAT

One of Trapani's more typical dishes is *cuscus di pesce,* which originates from North Africa and has been adapted by the addition of locally caught fish.

◌◌◌**Ai Lumi Tavernetta** –
Corso Vittorio Emanuele 75, Trapani.
☎*0923 87 24 18. www.ailumi.it. Closed Sun and Jul. Booking recommended.*
The reasonably priced menu at this attractive and fashionable restaurant in the centre of town includes a menu of fish and meat dishes with a strong emphasis on traditional local cuisine and ingredients.

◌◌◌**Taverna Paradiso** –
Lungomare Dante Alighieri 22, Trapani.
☎*0923 22 303. Closed Sun. Booking recommended.* Situated right on the seafront, this friendly, attractive restaurant specialises in fish dishes, especially those using tuna.

FESTIVAL

Settimana Santa – Holy Week celebrations culminate in the **Processione dei Misteri** on Good Friday as 20 groups of sculpted figures are carried through the streets all day and the following night. At other times, the statues are kept in the **Church of the Purgatorio** (in the town centre, in Via San Francesco); made of wood, cloth and glue by local craftsmen, they date from between 1650 and 1720.

A sumptuous polychrome marble staircase leads up to the first-floor **art gallery**: the most arresting paintings are the **Trapani polyptych**★(15C), and a **Pietà**★by the Neapolitan Roberto di Oderisio (14C). Also notable are a *St Francis Receiving the Stigmata* by Titian and *Madonna and Child with Angels* by Pastura (1478–1509). Works from the Neapolitan School include *St Bartholomew* by Ribera.

The medium favoured above all others by local artists and craftsmen of the 16C–19C was the Mediterranean red coral, found on the reefs off the Trapani and San Vito Lo Capo coasts. The coral is now virtually extinct in the region - the spread of liturgical objects and jewellery represented here give an indication as to why. Elsewhere in the museum is a wonderful series of 16 small wooden figurative groups depicting the *Slaughter of the Innocents* (17C).

The local **pottery "industry"** is represented by a pair of lovely maiolica panels depicting the bloody practice of the **mattanza** (the ritual killing of the tuna fish) and a view of Trapani (17C).

Tip of the Headland

Museo della Preistoria e di Archeologia Marina

🕒*Open daily, 9am–12.30pm (and 3.30pm–6.30pm Mon–Fri).* ☎*0923 22 300.*

The **Torre di Ligny**, built in 1671 as a defensive bastion, houses archaeological artefacts, fossils and palaeontological finds. Most of the medieval objects were recovered from nearby shipwrecks, including a display of well-preserved Spanish amphorae. At the top of the tower, a fine view extends out over the town and over to the Egadi islands.

USTICA★★

POPULATION: 1335

This small volcanic island, characterised by its inky rock and arid landscape, was named Ustica by the Romans, after the Latin word for 'burnt'. Its dramatic coastline hides beautiful coves and inlets, while the waters around it, including a Marine National Park, are popular scuba diving areas. The island's main economy is tourism, although specialist agricultural cultivation of vegetables, cereals and particularly lentils, is increasingly important.

- **Information:** Piazza V. Longo. ☎091 84 49 190. www.comune.ustica.pa.it.
- ▶ **Orient Yourself:** Situated 60km/37mi from Palermo, this tiny island is dotted with rocky inlets and is best discovered by boat. A road and several footpaths allow visitors to explore the island's interior. The western coast is now part of a marine national park.
- **Don't Miss:** Sea-watching boat trips and scuba diving in the Marine National Park and views all along the beautiful path from Torre di Santa Maria.
- **Especially for Kids:** Boat trips to explore the Marine National Park and swimming in the Piscina Naturale natural pool.
- **Also See:** PALERMO.

A Bit of History

Ustica was inhabited continuously from the late Neolithic until the end of the Classical period, when it was left to serve as a pirate refuge. Until the 1950s, it was used as a penal colony, the most famous prisoner here being Antonio Gramsci, the prominent Italian Communist. A new identity for the island began to develop in earnest with tourism, a result of international divers who came to explore the surrounding limpid waters. In 1987 the waters around Ustica were designated a marine national park.

Marine National Park

The nature reserve, Italy's first, was created in 1987 to preserve and protect the natural diversity of flora and fauna off Ustica's coastline. The National Park comprises three zones. **Zone A**, classified as **riserva integrale**, extends along the island's west flank from Cala Sidotti to Caletta and as far as 350m/1148ft offshore (marked with special yellow buoys): swimming is permitted, fishing and boating are prohibited.

©Roberto Rinaldi/Tips Images

Admiring the beauty of Ustica from onboard a boat

Address Book

For coin ranges, see the Legend on the cover flap.

GETTING THERE

Direct services operate out of Palermo. Crossings by ferry (2hr 30min) and hydrofoil (1hr 10min)are provided by **Siremar**, (Gruppo Tirrenia), ☎091 74 93 111 (from Italy) or 081 01 71 998 (from mobiles and abroad); www.gruppotirrenia.it During the summer season, a hydrofoil service calling at Trapani-Favignana-Levanzo-Ustica-Naples is operated by Ustica Lines. The Ustica-Naples leg takes approximately 4hr. Contact **Ustica Lines**, Via. Amm. Staiti 23, Trapani; ☎0923 87 3813; www.usticalines.it

SIGHTSEEING

The standard means of transport available include hired mopeds and a regular minibus service around the island in both directions on the one circular road. Extremely good value bus passes, valid for a week, two weeks or a month, are available from the town hall.

Walking is one of the most popular ways to cover the sights. The island is small enough (9km) to circumnavigate by foot in around four hours. If you are keen to explore the coastline and marine reserve then pick up boats at the quay or buy a ticket for the glass bottomed boat tours, run by Centro Accoglienza (ask at the tourist office for more details).

WHERE TO STAY

Stella Marina – *Via C. Colombo 33, Ustica.* ☎091 84 48 121. www.stellamarinaustica.it. The ambience is chic and modern at this boutique hotel, one of the most high-end on the island. Rooms and suites are both available, and there's also a wellness centre onsite offering massage, including Shiatsu treatment.

Hotel Clelia – *Via Sindaco I° 29, Ustica.* ☎091 84 49 039. www.hotelclelia.it. 26 rooms. Once a small pensione, this hotel has recently been renovated and now offers much higher levels of comfort and better facilities for guests The rooms are pleasant and airy and offer all the necessary creature comforts.

Grotta Azzurra – *San Ferlicchio, Ustica.* ☎091 844 9048. www.framonhotelgroup.com. Closed Oct–May. Luxury hotel with a splendid situation, overlooking its own private bay. A swimming pool and restaurant on the cliff edge and air conditioned rooms add to the draw.

Punta Spalmatore – *Spalmatore, Ustica.* ☎091 844 9388. Closed mid-Sept–mid-Jun. Large tourist village for those who want a wide selection of sports facilities on site. Huge range of cottage-style accommodation to choose from, with over 4000 rooms.

Hotel Diana – *Contrada San Paolo.* ☎091 84 49 109. www.hoteldiana-ustica.com. Closed Nov–Feb. 30 rooms. This circular hotel enjoys a quiet location outside Ustica town, with impressive panoramic views. The only disadvantage to the irregularly shaped rooms is the space taken up by the beds. Accommodation is complemented by a good restaurant.

Ariston – *Via della Vittoria 5, Ustica.* ☎091 84 49 0 42. www.usticahotels.it. 11 rooms. Simplicity is the style of this small and unassuming inn. The comfortable rooms are well appointed, the best have small private terraces some with sea views. Diving trips can be arranged by the hotel.

WHERE TO EAT

La Luna sul Porto – *Corso Vittorio Emanuele II 11, Ustica.* ☎091 84 49 799. Closed Sun (in winter). Booking recommended. This pleasant restaurant is run by an Italian woman from Piedmont who fell in love with Ustica over 10 years ago. Simple service, reasonable prices and a lovely view of the port from the outdoor terrace.

Mario – *Piazza Umberto I 21, Ustica.* ☎091 84 49 505. Closed Mon (in winter) and Jan. Dine outdoors in summer and in the restaurant's cosy dining room in winter. A firm favourite for genuine, simple Sicilian cuisine in this delightful corner of the Mediterranean.

Al Cielia– *ia Sindaco I° 29, Ustica.* ☎*091 84 49 039. www.hotelclelia.it.* 🍴. Set on the top floor of the Hotel Clelia, this excellent restaurant also welcomes those not staying there. The menu is typical Sicilian, with a confident modern twist. The fish cous cous and Ustican lentils are specialities.

Le Terrazze – *Via Cristoforo Colombo 3, Ustica.* 🍴. The sea views are showstopping from the terrace of this pizzeria-ristorante, with its simple menu of Sicilian favourites.

Giulia – *Via San Francesco 13, Ustica.* ☎*091 844 90 39.* 🍴. *Booking recommended.* Friendly restaurant that's extremely popular with locals. The menu is simple and hearty - the couscous is recommended.

SPORT AND LEISURE

Those who love the sea and enjoy swimming should not forget to bring a mask, snorkel and fins: snorkelling and diving will introduce the visitor to a spectacular underwater world, considered by divers to be one of the top spots in the world, and add a new perspective to their appreciation of the natural beauty of Ustica. As well as the natural wonders of the marine reserve, the area is also rich in subterranean archaeological wonders, with anchors, amphorae and ancient objects resting *in situ* at many dive sites.

Every year, a special week-long subaqua course is organised, including theoretical and practical diving lessons (marine archaeology, marine biology, modern recovery techniques for lifting artefacts from the sea bed) and guided tours. For further information, apply to the Riserva Marina or to Archeologia Viva, ☎055 50 62 303.

FESTIVALS

Rassegna Internazionale delle Attività subacquee – An International Review of Underwater Activities is organised annually during the summer (usually in May, June or September). This gathering includes a range of different events, such as exhibitions, tastings of local seafood and other activities. There are also special organised dives and courses for divers of all levels – from beginners to advanced – who come from around the world to explore the depths around this tiny island. For detailed information, contact the Azienda di Promozione Turistica in Palermo, ☎091 60 58 111.

Zone B, classified as **riserva generale**, extends beyond Zone A from Punta Cavazzi to Punta Omo Morto: here swimming is permitted, as is underwater photography, hook-and-line fishing and commercial fishing (with a permit from the Commune).

Zone C, classified as a **riserva parziale**, applies to the rest of the coast: here national fishing regulations apply and speargun fishing is permitted.

The submerged world

The sea around Ustica is especially clean and pollution free (lying in the middle of an inward current from the Atlantic Ocean). It provides ideal conditions for different species of aquatic flora and fauna to proliferate. One striking sight is the vast meadow of *Poseidonia oceanica,* a beneficial seaweed, nicknamed the "lungs of the Mediterranean" (because it oxygenates the water), found up to a depth of 40m/131ft. Just below the surface, the water shimmers with shoals of white bream, two-banded bream, voracious-looking grey mullet (at the worst they only tickle), saddled bream, salpas, and rainbow wrasse. The patches shaded by overhanging rock attract cardinal fish; the rock face itself shelters colonies of beautiful orange "flowered" madrepore, which sometimes cover vast sections at a time with colourful sponges.

At greater depths lurk larger fish – notably grey mullet. Here the underwater landscape also harbours moray eels, lobsters, mantis prawns and shrimps.

Guided tours

The west coast, designated *riserva integrale* (highly restricted), harbours two secret, pink-hued grottoes, **Grotta Segreta** and **Grotta Rosata**, coloured by algae.

©Roberto Rinaldi/Tips Images

Exploring the underwater world of Ustica

The reserve authorities also lay on **sea-watching** trips (with commentary) in the *riserva integrale:* a guide will point out specific organisms and fish as they appear (accustomed to the presence of man, they appear almost tame).

Scuba-diving

Highlights for any scuba-diving enthusiast include the **Grotta dei Gamberi**, near Punta Gavazzi, where delicate fan-like red gorgonians thrive (at a depth of approx 42m/138ft), and the **sub-aqua archaeological trail** off the lighthouse-topped headland Punta Gavazzi (depths of 9m/30ft-17m/56ft, marked by an orange buoy), where many artefacts – anchors and Roman amphorae – can be admired *in situ.*

Another popular haunt is the **Scoglio del Medico**: an outcrop of basalt riddled with caves and gorges that plunge to great depths and whose crystal clear water provides a spectacular underwater **seascape**★★ of sponges, shoals of colourful fish and weed. **Secca di Colombara** (40m/131ft below) is spectacular in a different way, populated as it is by rainbow-coloured spreads of sponges and gorgonians.

Town★

A single road and various flights of steps, flanked with magnificent hibiscus bushes, lead up from the harbour to the main town above. A characteristic feature of the houses peculiar to Ustica is the practice of painting their exteriors with artistic murals: bright landscape scenes, *trompe l'oeils,* portraits, still-life paintings and any other fanciful compositions that might spring to mind. The most eye-catching building is the **Torre di Santa Maria**, which houses the **Museo Archeologico** (🕐*open 9am–1pm, 3pm–8pm in summer;* 🎫*€2.50; for information on opening times for the rest of the year call ☎091 66 28 452*) and its collections of artefacts recovered from shipwrecks, the prehistoric village at I Faraglioni and Hellenistic and Roman tombs found on Capo Falconiera.

Capo Falconiera

At the far end of the central piazza where the Chiesa Madre is situated, turn right past the Stations of the Cross. From here, a stepped path on the left climbs to the top and the ruins of a Bourbon fortress and a 3C BC settlement. Naturally restricted by space and inaccessibility, the area was extended by cutting terraces into the rock: as a result, three tiers of housing are stacked one above the other.

At the foot of the fortress, remnants of a contemporary hypogeum necropolis have been discovered together with a second necropolis dating from palaeo-Christian times (5C-6C AD). From here, a **view**★ stretches from the harbour to the centre of the island, marked with the profiles of Monte Costa del Fallo and Monte Guardia dei Turchi.

Villaggio Preistorico★

This settlement can still be seen through a fence.

An extensive Bronze Age settlement has been discovered at Colombaia, in the vicinity of **I Faraglioni**. This comprises a collection of foundations for circular huts that were re-used later for square-based constructions of a type similar to prehistoric houses found on the Island of Panarea.

Coast

The jagged coastline has a number of caves that can be explored either by boat (fishermen in the harbour will volunteer their services to visitors for a small fee) or by land. Small beaches (Cala Sidoti, Punta dello Spalmatore, al Faro) succeed lovely rocky bays – including one beneath the lighthouse that encloses the **piscina naturale**★ (a natural pool immensely popular with swimmers and sunbathers) along the island's west coast. Conversely, the east coast shelters magnificent caves such as the **Grotta Azzurr**a, **Grotta Verde** and **Grotta delle Barche**, which are best explored with a snorkel; the G**rotta delle Barche** can also be reached by a lovely **path**★ that threads its way through forests of fragrant pine trees from Torre di Santa Maria, providing marvellous **views**★ of the sea and the coast along it's length.

LA VIA DEL SALE★

The road that leads from Trapani to Marsala along the coast of the lagoon offers a beautiful vista : the mirrors of water on the salt flats are subdivided by thin strips of earth to form one irregular multi-coloured chessboard. At times the shape of a windmill appears on the horizon, a memory of the time when their powerful sails were the main method of drawing water and milling salt in the area.

- **Information:** Piazza Saturno. ☎0923 29 000. www.comune.trapani.it. www.apt.trapani.it.
- ▶ **Orient Yourself:** The white saltpans lie south of Trapani and extend along the coast almost as far as Marsala. They offer a striking sight in summer when the salt is ready to be collected: then, the pink hues of the concentrated saline in the outer pans contrast with those towards the centre of a deeper colour, while the innermost, now dry, sparkle in the sunshine.
- **Don't Miss:** Find out about salt production at Museo del Sale di Nubia and watch a working windmill at the Ettore e Infersa saltworks.
- **Organising Your Time:** Allow one day to explore the area between Trapani and Marsala, including a visit to the Island of Mozia.
- **Also See:** ERICE; MARSALA; MOZIA; TRAPANI.

A Bit of History

Ancient origins – The Phoenicians began exploiting the coastal area between Trapani and Marsala when, upon realising the favourable conditions of shallow water, searing temperatures and arid winds, they set about building basins in which to collect salt. This valuable commodity was then exported all over the Mediterranean to treat perishable food for the lean winter months. After the Phoenicians, however, there are no reliable references to the saltpans around Trapani until the Norman era, when Frederick II himself alludes to

G. Bludzin/MICHELIN

Man working in the saltworks

them in the Constitutions of Melfi. From this date on, the rise in status of the port of Trapani can be tracked fairly easily. The economic success of the saltpans shows that major fluctuations in output shadowed the rise and fall in fortunes of the territory as it succumbed to wars, epidemics and transitions of government. On the whole, the area and its commercial activity were profitable, and that is why it has continued, albeit with fits and starts, until the present day. The salt is still being extracted, although the methods used have changed with mechanism and the windmills that characterise the landscape are no longer employed.

Automating the saltworks

Mechanisation – The most important individual pieces of machinery used in the cultivation and processing of salt, in the past at least, were the classic Dutch windmill, the American windmill, introduced in the early 1950s, and the Archimedes screw.

The **Dutch windmill** comprises a conical building and roof, and six trapezoidal vanes consisting of cloth sails attached to wooden frames that catch the wind and propel a system of mechanical gears. Inside the building, a complex system of interconnected cogs and wheels, shafts and stays allow the circular roof (and, hence, the sails) to be orientated according to the wind direction and so exploit the natural resource to grind the salt or to pump water.

Should the mill be required to pump water, the gearing is harnessed to an Archimedes screw.

The main difference between the **American windmill** and its smaller Dutch counterpart is its sophistication: it has a greater degree of automation (including a gearing system allowing the roof to regulate itself automatically to catch the wind).

The **Archimedes screw** can be activated in a few centimetres of liquid and is powered by hand or by means of a windmill. It consists of a rotating shaft with small wooden blades attached to form a continuous spiral.

Manpower – Few people were fully employed to work the saltpans all year round other than the curatolo, the overseer, and the miller. In July, a team of seasonal labourers would begin breaking up the crust of salt. Next, the salt was shovelled into piles in rows, thereby allowing any damp residue to dry out. A band of 20 men or *venna* were charged with filling baskets with the salt and emptying them on the dike in larger piles. In the autumn, the heaps were covered with tiles by the curatolo.

Driving Tour

30km/19mi excursion between Trapani and Marsala along SP 21 – allow one day, including a visit to the Island of Mozia.

Trapani ⟲ *See TRAPANI.*

From Trapani, follow the coast road (SP 21) to Marsala, with a succession of fine **views**★★ over the saltpans of Trapani, Paceco and Stagnone. The first stop is **Nubia**, the headquarters of the WWF, formerly the World Wide Fund for Nature *(Via Garibaldi 138)*, which manages the **Riserva Naturale Salina di Trapani e Paceco** (♿ ⟲ *guided tours only; ☎0923 86 77 00)*, a saltwater nature reserve habitat.

M. Magni/MICHELI

Windmills in the saltworks

Museo del Sale di Nubia

Open summer 9.30am–7pm; rest of the year 9.30am–1pm, 3pm–6pm. Guided tours available (30 minutes). €2. 0923 86 74 42.

A small salt museum has been set up in a 300-year-old salt worker's house: it recounts the different stages involved in collecting salt from the saltpans and displays tools adapted for its extraction and harvest.

Le Saline

The saltworks in front of the museum show how and why the different salt-pans interact, and the phases in the "cultivation" and extraction of the crystallised salt.

A canal supplements the two large basins on the outer edge of the complex known as the *fridde* (a corruption of *freddo* meaning cold because of the temperature of the incoming water). The *Mulino Americano* (literally the American mill) located between these two basins uses an Archimedes screw contraption to transfer water into the *vasu cultivu*, where it blends with the yeast-like residue of the previous crop. The greater the saline concentration (measured in Baum), the warmer the water. From here, the water is drained to the *ruffiana*, an intermediary stage between the vasu and the caure, where the water temperature is considerably warmer and the salinity attains 23 Baum. Next in line comes the *sintine*, where the high concentration of salt and the high temperature combine to

lend a pinkish tinge to the solution, and so begin the last stages in the process. The water now passes into the salting pans or *caseddri*, where layers of pure salt crystals are allowed to form (27–28 Baum) in preparation for harvest twice a year, usually around mid-July and mid-August. The conical piles of sand, aligned the length of the *arione*, are left open to the elements to be rinsed through by the rain, before being covered with "Roman" tiles for protection from heavy downpours and dirt.

▶ *From Nubia, return to the main road and continue towards the Stagnone lagoon, where the most spectacular saltpans are located. A sign indicates the way to the Ettore e Infersa saltworks.*

Working windmill

Wind permitting, the mill operates in summer. Open 9am–6.30pm, by appointment only. €3.50. 0923 96 69 36.

This 16C windmill, once indispensable for grinding salt, survives today in working order because of the loving attention from its owners (Saline Ettore e Infersa). The sails can rotate at 20kph/12.5mph and generate a up to 120 horsepower.

Mozia★ *See MOZIA.*

The coast road winds to Marsala along a particularly spectacular route at sunset.

Marsala *See MARSALA.*

VILLA IMPERIALE
DEL CASALE ★★★

This splendid and imposing Roman villa, built between the end of the 3C and the beginning of the 4C AD, owes its reputation to the extraordinary and well-preserved mosaic floors that cover much of the site.

- **Information:** ☎339 265 7640. www.romanadelcasale.it.
- ▶ **Orient Yourself:** To get to the villa from Caltagirone or Enna, cross Piazza Armerina and take the Caltanissetta road (no direct links to this road from S 117b).
- **Don't Miss:** The fascinating thermal complex and the amazing attention to detail in the Corridor of the Great Hunt and the Room of the Small Hunt.
- **Organising Your Time:** Visit the villa early in the morning, especially in summer when conditions can be unpleasant due to the large number of tour groups and the heat generated by the plexiglass roofs.
- ✕ **Where to Stay/Eat:** For hotels and restaurants, see PIAZZA ARMERINA.
- **Also See:** CALTAGIRONE; CALTANISSETTA; ENNA; PIAZZA ARMERINA.

A Bit of History

This country villa was built between the end of the 3C and the beginning of the 4C AD, possibly by a member of the Imperial family: one of the most likely candidates is Maximian, one of the tetrarchs who jointly ruled the Empire

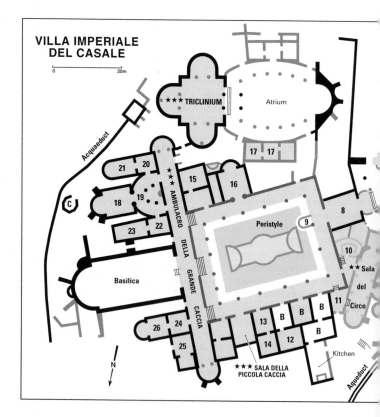

VILLA IMPERIALE
DEL CASALE

from AD 286–305. Surrounded by large estates, the villa was occupied occasionally until the 12C. It was destroyed by a fire, then buried in mud following floods and a subsequent landslide in 1161. it was only partially rediscovered at the end of the 19C.

The large complex (c. 3 500m2/37 600sq ft) was built on different levels. The main entrance (**A**) led into a polygonal courtyard, which provided access to the large peristyle overlooked by guest rooms (to the north – note: the map given has north pointing downwards) and the owner's private apartments (to the east). Beyond the guest rooms were the servants' quarters (**B**), complete with kitchen. The private apartments used by the members of the household were divided into two by a large basilica for meetings and official receptions. At the rear of these buildings stands a separate octagonal latrine reserved for the family (**C**). The living area was situated to the south of the complex and consisted of an elliptical atrium which gave onto an apsed triclinium (dining room) (**24**), six small rooms and service amenities (**D**). The western part of the complex housed the baths. The water was supplied by two aqueducts connected to a third which, in turn, was fed by the River Gela.

Mosaics – What makes the villa unique is its floors, which consist almost entirely of mosaics that survive in excellent condition. The majority of panels are polychrome and feature mythological scenes, incidents from daily life, special occasions such as a hunt, circus games, feast days honouring the gods and a grape harvest – alternated with geometric decorations. The evocative portrayal of movement is remarkable and has been interpreted as the work of North African craftsmen.

Visit

Open Apr–Sept 8am–6pm, rest of the year 8am–5pm. €6. 0935 68 00 36 or 0935 85 605.

Terme

Information on the villa's baths can also be found under Introduction: Art.

Just inside the entrance to the steam baths, on the left, is a section of the **aqueduct** that supplied the villa with water. Immediately beyond is the suite of rooms that makes up the thermal complex. In the first are the great furnaces (*praefurnia*) (**1**) which heated the water in order to generate the steam then circulated through cavities below the floors and in the walls, to heat the rooms. The underfloor heating is visible in the **Tepidarium** (**3**): small brick columns support the floor, leaving a large cavity between the floor and the ground through which hot air could circulate. This room was maintained at a moderate temperature for use immediately after the **Caldaria** (**2**) where saunas and the hot baths were taken.

Sala delle Unzioni (4)

The function of the small square anointing room is reflected in the mosaic deco-

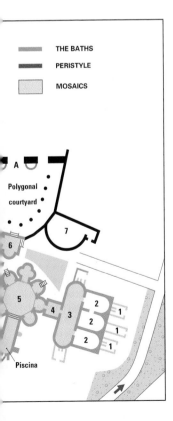

THE BATHS

PERISTYLE

MOSAICS

A

Polygonal courtyard

7

6

5

4 3

2
2

2

1

1

1

Piscina

ration. Slaves are shown preparing oil and unguents for application and massaging the bodies of the bathers *(the figures at the top left)*, with some of the tools of their trade: the *strigile*, a sort of curved spatula with a handle used for scraping and cleaning the skin, and a jar of oil *(the figure at the top right)*.

Frigidarium (5)

The octagonal room set aside for cold baths has a central mosaic with a marine theme: cherub fishermen surrounded by tritons, nereids (sea nymphs) and dolphins. From the *frigidarium*, the **piscina** and the end of the aqueduct can be seen. Beyond the **shrine of Venus (6)** is the **polygonal courtyard** articulated by a colonnade. In the centre are the remains of the impluvium – a cistern in which rainwater is collected from surrounding roofs and then channelled towards the great **latrina (7)**.

The main villa entrance was from the courtyard: on the south side you can see the remains of the entrance (**A**) comprising a central door flanked by two side doors.

Peristilium

Pass through the **vestibule (8)**. The mosaic features figures bearing a candlestick, a branch of laurel and, below, a figure with a diptych (a book consisting of two panels) from which he might address the master of the house and any guests. Opposite is the **lararium (9)**, where statues of the household gods, the *lares*, were kept.

The imposing rectangular portico (eight columns on the short sides, 10 on the longer sides) is dominated by a great fountain with a small statue as its centrepiece. **Peristilium mosaic**★★ – running along all four sides of the portico is a beautiful mosaic ornamented with round medallions that feature the heads of both wild and domestic animals (bears, tigers, wild boars and panthers; horses and cows).

Piccola latrina (10)

The floor mosaic depicts animals, including an ass, cheetah, hare and partridge.

Sala del Circo★★

The long room, apsed at both ends, represents a circus, identified as the Circus Maximus in Rome. The decoration illustrates a chariot race, the final event in the festival honouring Ceres, the goddess of plenty and the harvest, whose cult was particularly popular in nearby Enna (◖*see ENNA: Mythology*). Above the *spina*, the central line around which the horses are racing, the winner receives his prize, the victory palm, while another character blows a horn to signal the end of the race.

Along the south side of the peristyle are rooms reserved for guests. Access to these was via a second **vestibule (11)**, decorated with beautiful mosaics showing the lady of the house with her children and her servants as they hold lengths of cloth and a box containing oils. Other rooms (**B**) comprised the servants' quarters and kitchen.

Sala della Danza (12)

The mosaic, unfortunately incomplete, shows women and men dancing.

Sala delle Quattro Stagioni (13)

The four seasons, after which this room is named, are personified here by two women (spring and autumn), and two men (summer and winter).

Sala degli Amorini Pescatori★★ (14)

A few cupid-like cherubs aboard six boats concentrate on fishing with lines, tridents and nets, while in the centre of the composition two others play in the water with dolphins. In the upper section a large building stands on the shore, fronted by a columned portico, among palm trees and umbrella pines.

Sala della Piccola Caccia★★★

Here, in the **Room of the Small Hunt**, five panels depict the heat of the hunt. In the top left corner, a hunter releases his dogs to chase after a fox *(on the right)*. To give thanks for favourable conditions and a successful day, a sacrifice is offered to Diana, the goddess of hunting. Two high-ranking officials burn incense on the altar while, behind them, a wild boar is seen in a net *(on the left)* and another

Detail of the mosaic from the Corridor of the Great Hunt

hunter *(on the right)* holds up a hare. The central part of the mosaic is dominated by a banqueting scene. Shaded by an awning, game is being cooked over a fire. There is a pause in the day's activity: the horses are tethered, the nets are hung up, the huntsmen relax around the fire. All around are hunting scenes: at the top left, two falconers seek out birds hidden among tree branches; on the right a man encourages his dogs to follow a hare. The last panel depicts the netting of deer and a boar being speared.

Ambulacro della Grande Caccia★★★

The fabulous **Corridor of the Great Hunt**, 60m/200ft long with a recess at each end, is the most engaging and monumental part of the whole villa. The floor mosaic depicts an elaborate hunting scene. Panthers, lions, antelopes, boar, dromedaries, elephants, hippopotamuses and rhinoceroses are caught prior to being shipping to Roman amphitheatres.

Just beyond the midway point are three figures: the central one is presumed to be the Emperor Maximian, protected by the shields of two soldiers. Farther on, another scene shows a tiger pouncing on a crystal ball in which his image is reflected. Nearby, a controversial scene illustrates a griffin holding a box from which a boy's peeps out. Some maintain that the boy is bait to attract the animal, while others interpret the scene as a stark warning against the cruelty of hunting.

In the right recess, Africa is depicted as a female figure with an tusk, flanked by an elephant, a tiger and a phoenix *(for a description of these rooms, see below).*

Sala delle Dieci Ragazze in Bikini★★ (15)

In the **Room of the Ten Girls**, the mosaic shows two rows of girls pictured in their underwear, which was also commonly worn when doing gymnastic exercises. The upper part was called the *fascia pectoralis* and the lower part *subligatur*. The young women perform their various exercises: weightlifting, discus throwing, running and ball games. In the bottom row, the girl wearing a toga is about to crown and award the palm of victory to a girl who has been performing exercises with a hoop.

Diaeta di Orfeo★ (16)

The Chamber of Orpheus was reserved for playing music.

At the centre is Orpheus, seated on a rock, playing the lyre and enchanting the animals that surround him with his

Mosaic showing girls in "bikinis" in the Room of the Ten Girls,

R. Mattes/MICHELIN

music. In the apse behind is a statue of the god Apollo.

The south wing of the villa accommodated the principal reception rooms: a central atrium is flanked by a apsed *triclinium* where meals were served. Two rooms on the north side (**17**) contain mosaics of cherubs harvesting grapes from the vines.

Triclinium★★★

The large central square space extends into three broad apses.

Central area

The main mosaic is dedicated to the **Twelve Labours of Heracles** (Hercules to the Romans). On the left is the Cretan Bull (or Bull of Minos), the powerful animal sent by Poseidon to Minos, which was eventually sacrificed to Athene by Theseus at Marathon, after he was captured by Heracles. Beside it is the Hydra of Lerna, whose many heads were chopped off by the hero. The Hydra, the younger sister of Cerberus, acted as guardian of the Underworld, her realm being the deep waters near Lerna on the border with Argos. In this Labour, Heracles is assisted by his nephew and friend Iolaus. At the top, in the centre, is the great Nemean Lion, which terrorised a mountainous area. Having killed the monster, Heracles wore its pelt as a cloak and its head as a helmet. In honour of

this great deed, Zeus brought the lion to the heavens, making it into one of the zodiac constellations.

Left apse

This mosaic represents the **glorification of Heracles**, depicted in the centre, holding the hand of Iolaus *(on the left)*, while Zeus bestows a laurel wreath on his head.

The panel below illustrates the metamorphoses of **Daphne** into a laurel *(on the left)* and of Cyparissus into a cypress *(on the right)*, a reminder of why laurel is twisted into crowns honouring the heads of brave warriors, emperors and poets: Daphne was the nymph loved by Apollo; to escape him she prayed to her father, a river god, and her mother, Earth, to be turned into a laurel tree. In consolation Apollo made himself a laurel wreath, which was awarded as a prize at the Pythian Games from then on.

Central apse

The scene represents a **battle of the giants:** five huge creatures have been struck by Heracles' poisoned arrows. One of the Labours consisted of Heracles stealing the Oxen of Geryon and carrying them back to Greece; as he crossed Italy he encountered the giants, one of whom was called Alcyoneus, and fought them by the Flegraean Fields (near Naples).

In the mosaic below, **Hesione**, the daughter of Laomedon, king of Troy, is threatened by a sea monster sent by Poseidon, an incident resulting from Laomedon's failure to honour his agreement to pay Poseidon and Apollo for their assistance in building the walls of Troy. The only way to safeguard the city from the sea monster was to sacrifice Hesione. Heracles undertook to slay the monster on condition Laomedon should give him his famous horses; when the king again reneged on his promise, Heracles raised an army against Troy and gave Hesione to Telamon.

Right apse

On the left, three maenads (literally *mad women)* are depicted attacking Lycurgus, king of Thrace.

Continue along the wall of the aqueduct. Just before a small hexagonal latrine (**C**), some steps on the left lead into room 18.

Diaeta di Arione (18)

The chamber of Arion was probably dedicated to making music and reading poetry, judging by the mosaic decoration which depicts the poet and musician Arion sitting on the back of a dolphin in the middle of the sea, holding a lyre and surrounded by sea nymphs, tritons and cherubs astride wild beasts and sea monsters.

Atrio degli Amorini Pescatori★★(19)

The mosaic illustrates various fishing scenes, running all the way around the semicircular portico.

Vestibolo del Piccolo Circo★★ (20)

The Vestibule of the Small Circus in the larger private apartment of the villa, takes its name from another circus scene in the thermal baths, this time with children as the protagonists. Racing around the posts are chariots drawn *(working anti-clockwise from top right)* by flamingos, geese, waders and wood pigeons. Each chariot team also has a child on foot beside it, carrying an amphora and chasing the birds to make them run.

Cubicolo dei Musici e degli Attori (21)

This particular *cubiculum* probably served as a bedroom for the owner's daughter. In the apse, two girls sit at the foot of a tree making crowns out of flowers.

Vestibolo di Eros e Pan (22)

Dominating the antechamber is the horned figure of Pan, the god of the woodlands fighting Eros, the god of love. Next to Pan is the judge, bearded and wearing a purple toga and laurel wreath. Behind are satyrs and maenads who are supporting Pan, and the family of the house who are supporting Eros. Above the wrestling match is a table carrying prizes for the winner. On another level, the fight symbolises the difficulty for the ugly (Pan) to vanquish love.

Cubicolo dei Fanciulli Cacciatori★ (23)

This *cubiculum* was probably the bedroom of the son of the house-owner. At the top of the mosaic, girls collect flowers; a boy carries two rose-filled baskets on his shoulders. Lower down, a group of children kill a hare, a small antelope and capture a duck.

Walk around the large **basilica**, noting the marble-tiled floor fragments.

Vestibolo di Ulisse e Polifemo★ (24)

These mosaics illustrate the story of Odysseus (known as Ulysses to the Romans) outwitting the Cyclops Polyphemus, who has eaten some of his men, by enticing him with a cup of wine intended to send him to sleep.

Cubicolo della Scena Erotica★ (25)

Surrounded by images of the four seasons, a polygonal medallion enclosed within a laurel wreath shows a man embracing a loosely clad girl. In his left hand he also holds a situla, or jar.

In the room behind the vestibule (**26**) is a luscious fruit **mosaic**★ rendered with an exquisite delicacy.

CALABRIA

MICHELIN MAP 564 G-N 28-33.

Greeks colonized the southernmost tip of Italy over 2 800 years ago. The coast rivalled Athens as a cosmopolitan centre in 8 BC; the mystic philosopher Pythagoras preached vegetarianism there alongside the decadent Sybarites and Homer set part of *The Odyssey* on the Strait of Messina. Invaders plundered this land throughout history; Byzantines, Germanic warriors, Saracens, Normans, Turks and Bourbons. But although infamous for bandits and Mafia bloodshed, Calabria also has a gentle side. The sea– often purple-hued–between Gioia Tauro and Villa San Giovanni– washes the base of this craggy coast. Ionian ruins and Roman mosaics dot the farmland, rich with agritourism B&Bs. High in the crumbling mountains, five villages retain a bilingual Greek-Italian culture, while in season, mushroom hunters search the slopes here among the ski chalets. The backbone of Calabria is formed by the Pollino Massif (Pollino Mountain has an altitude of 2248m/7375ft), which is a national park, and by the Sila and Aspromonte massifs. Here, the olive groves produce excellent oil – Rossano's has a very low level of acidity – and the citrus harvest includes clementines, blond and bergamot oranges.

- **Information:** Parco Nazionale del Pollino: Via delle Freece Tricolori 6, 85048 Rotonda (Potenza), ☎0973 66 93 11, www.parcopollino.it; Parco Nazionale dell'Aspromonte: Via Aurora, 89050 Gambarie di Santo Stefano, ☎0965 74 30 60, www.parcoaspromonte.it.

- ▶ **Orient Yourself:** Calabria is in the extreme south of the Italian peninsula, covering the narrow stretch of land between the Gulf of Policastro and the Gulf of Taranto. The main access road is A 3, the Salerno-Reggio Calabria motorway.

- **Don't Miss:** The Bronzi di Riace at Reggio's archaeological museum, La Cattolica near Stilo, the ghost town of Pentedattilo and the natural wonders of the national parks, such as the Montalto in the Aspromonte and ancient forests of La Sila.

- **Organising Your Time:** Allow half a day to explore the Tyrrhenian Coast and two days for the "Toe" and along the Ionian Coast. Take 1–2 days for each of the national parks, including their villages and towns.

Tropea - aquamarine waters of the Tyrrhenian Coast

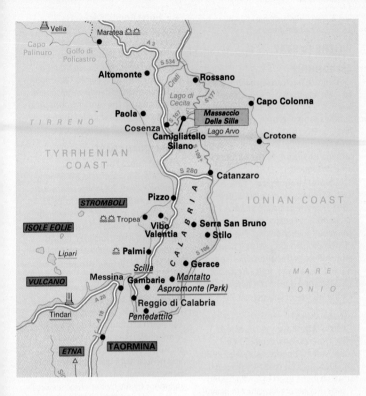

A Bit of History

Archaeological finds from Italy's boot indicate that Calabria was settled as far back as the Neanderthal, Palaeolithic and Neolithic ages. However, the first notable colonies on the Ionian coast were settled by the Greeks in the 8C BC, starting with Reggio di Calabria, and progressing to the important Magna Graecia cities of Locri, Crotone and Sibari during the 6C and 5C BC. The Greeks, together with the Byzantines and Basilian monks (St Basil, the father of the Greek Church, lived in Calabria from c, AD 330–379) shaped the early art and history of this region. In the 3C BC, Rome set out to conquer southern Italy, decimating the region's natural resources as they swept through, including Calabria's magnificent forests. However, they did not establish a complete and peaceful domination until Sulla reorganised the administration of these provinces in the 1C BC. After the fall of the Roman Empire, Calabria and the neighbouring regions fell under the sway of the Lombards, Saracens and Byzantines, before being reunited with the Norman kingdom of the Two Sicilies. The administrative divisions, Calabria Citeriore (Latin Calaria) in the north and Calabria Ulteriore (Greek Calabria) in the south, created in the late medieval times, were maintained right up until the region became part of a unified Italy in 1860.

Natural disasters, such as the powerful earthquakes that struck the area in 1783 and 1908, famine, malaria, grinding poverty, banditry,

Mafia activity (organised crime syndicates in Calabria are known as 'ndrangheta), social and emigration problems, have plagued 'the boot'. But thanks to agrarian reform and an increasing commitment to tourism and cultural activities, modern Calabria finally has occasion for real hope of a rebirth.

Calabria Address Book

For coin ranges see the Legend at the back of the guide.

WHERE TO STAY

ASPROMONTE

Azienda Agrituristica il Bergamotto – *Via Amendolea -89030 Condofuri.* ☎*0963 72 72 13. www.agriturismo.it.* Simple rooms and basic creature comforts, but this rustic retreat is comfortable and friendly. The owner is happy to arrange excursions to the surrounding area on request.

Hotel Lungomare – *Viale Zerbi 13/b, 89100 Reggio di Calabria.* ☎*0963 66 31 39. www.hotellungomare.rc.it.* *32 rooms.* ☞. Located in an elegant white balconied building, overlooking the promenade, there's a friendly atmosphere and comfortable, if plain rooms. The a panoramic terrace has sea views and guests can borrow beach umbrellas free of charge.

IONIAN COAST

Hotel Annibale – *Via Duomo 35, 88841 Isola di Caporizzuto, 10 km southwest of Caporizzuto.* ☎*0962 79 50 04. 20 rooms.* This rustic-style hotel is situated in the heart of an old fishing village. Rooms are furnished in heavy-duty pine. The dining room boasts a large fireplace and a profusion of pans and meats hanging from the wooden ceiling.

La Casa Di Gianna – *Via Paola Frasca, 89040 Gerace. www.lacasadigianna.it.* ☎*0963 66 31 39. 11 rooms.* ☞. Decorated in a clean and elegant style, the ten rooms and one suite at this small hotel offer a peaceful oasis. In winter there is a fireplace in the salon to sit and read a book by. Dinner is served on the small restaurant terrace in summer, on request.

MASSACCIO DELLA SILA

B&B Calabria – *Via Roma 7, Scigliano.* ☎*0984 966150. www.bedandbreakfast calabria.it. 4 rooms.* ☞.Exceptionally warm greeting at this small B&B, where nothing is too much trouble for the owners, from local recommendations to lending out mountain bikes. Rooms have character and forest views.

Hotel Aquila-Edelweiss – *Via Stazione 11, 87052 Camigliatello Silano, 31km/19mi northeast of Cosenza on S 107.* ☎*0984 57 80 44. www.hotel aquilaedelweiss.com. Closed Nov and Dec. 48 rooms.* ☞. A comfortable hotel, with a warm and friendly atmosphere, tucked away in the conifer woods up in the Sita. Worth a detour for the restaurant's regional specialities.

TYRRENHIAN COAST

Hotel Punta Faro – *Località Grotticelle, Capo Vaticano, 89685 San Nicolò di Ricardi, 10km/6mi southwest of Tropea.* ☎*0963 66 31 39. Closed 23 Sept–May. 19 rooms.* ☞. This well-situated hotel is a stone's throw from the sea. Good parking facilities. Rooms are modern and functional. Lovely balcony with views of the Aeolian Islands and Sicily. Free umbrellas.

Residence il Barone – *Largo Barone, 89861 Tropea.* ☎*0963 660 7181. www.residenziailbarone.it. 6 suites.* ☞. Top notch accommodation in this former palazzo-now-boutique hotel's six suites. Room decor is calm, cool and neutral, with low lighting and big beds. Minimalism is brightened up with paintings by the owner's brother. Facilities include LCD TVs, and there's a great roof terrace for breakfast, with sea and rooftop views.

WHERE TO EAT

ASPROMONTE

Le Rose al Bicchiere – *Via Demetrio Tripepi 118, 89125 Reggio di Calabria.* ☎*0965 229 56. Closed Sun (winter).* Associated with the Slow Food movement, this wine bar has a huge wine cellar of local and national wines to try, all accompanied by a menu of dishes using locally-sourced organic food, including fabulous cheeses, fresh meats and vegetables.

IONIAN COAST

Trattoria del Sole – *Via Piave 14 bis, 87075 Trebisacce, 15km/9mi north of Sibari on S 106.* ☎*0981 51 797. Closed Sun (except 15 Jun–15 Sept).* This simple eatery is tucked away in the maze of little streets at the heart of the historic centre. Warm and friendly atmosphere.

Mouthwatering selection of fish (and a few meat) dishes prepared with the freshest ingredients. Ask the proprietor for his recommendations. In summer meals are served on the terrace.

Ristorante a Squella– *Viale Della Resistenza 8, 89040 Gerace.* ☎*0964 35 60 86. Closed Mon (dinner).* Modest surroundings but the friendly atmosphere at this simple, family-run restaurant ensure customers come back time and again to fill up on classic Calabrian cooking in hearty proportions.

Gambero Rosso – *Via Montezemolo 65, 89046 Marina di Gioiosa Ionica, 10km/6mi north of Locri on S 106.* ☎*0964 41 58 06. www.gamberorosso. rc.it. Closed Mon.* A traditional restaurant located on the main thoroughfare. Good selection of antipasti, laid out on a large table in the entrance of the main dining room. Variety of delicious fish dishes, prepared with super fresh ingredients.

Da Annibale – *Via Duomo 35, 88841 Isola di Caporizzuto, 10 km southwest of Caporizzuto.* ☎*0962 79 50 04.* Attached to the Hotel Annibale, this restaurant offers a real seafood treat. The fish is exceptionally fresh and simply, but deliciously cooked. Meals are also served in the garden in summer, under the pergola.

MASSACCIO DELLA SILA

Hostaria de Mendoza – *Piazza degli Eroi 3 – 87036 Rende – 10km/6mi northwest of Cosenza –* ☎*0984 44 40 22 – Closed Wed, Sun (Jul and Aug), 10–18 Aug – – Booking advisable.* An unpretentious restaurant with rustic ambience and heavy wooden furnishings. Genuine home cooking. During the summer, meals are served under a large wooden gazebo.

TYRRENHIAN COAST

Il Normanno – *Via Duomo 12, 89852 Mileto, 30km/18mi southeast of Tropea on S18.* ☎*0963 33 63 98. www.ilnormanno.com. Closed Mon (except Aug), 1–20 Sept.* Attractive trattoria in the town centre. Rustic-style interior with wood panelled walls. Small terraced area for dining in summer. Good, traditional home cooking.

Pizzeria Ruota – *Via Piave 14 bis, 87075 Trebisacce, 15km/9mi north of Sibari on S 106.* ☎*0981 51 797. Closed Sun (except 15 Jun–15 Sept).* This simple eatery is tucked away in the maze of little streets it the heart of the historic centre. Warm and friendly atmosphere and huge, wood fired pizzas.

L'Approdo – *Via Roma 22. 89811Vibo Valentina.* ☎*0963 57 2940. www.lapprodo.com.* Elegant ristorante with a slightly more formal air, and a menu of Mediterranean influences with a contemporary twist. Fish dishes are one of the specialities.

SIGHTSEEING

The geographical backbone of Calabria is the epic and rugged scenic sweep of its three national parks; the northern **Pollino massif**, on the Basilicata boundary, the vast plain of **La Sila** in the centre of Calabria and in the south, with views across Calabria and out to Sicily from Montealto, the highest peak, the **Aspromonte massif**. Each national park offers small towns and villages, to explore, as well as numerous opportunities for summer and winter outdoor activities, such as hiking, climbing, horse riding and skiing. For more information contact the parks authorities:

Parco Nazionale del Pollino, ☎*0973 66 93 11, www.parcopollino.it*
Parco Nazionale dell'Aspromonte, ☎*0965 74 30 60, www.parcoaspromonte.it.*
Parco Nazionale La Sila, ☎*0984 57 95 57, www.parcosila.it*

Parco Nazionale del Pollino

©Alberto Nardi/Tips Images

ASPROMONTE★

The Aspromonte Massif forms Calabria's southern tip and culminates in a peak of 1 955m/6 414ft. Fabled mushrooms sprout on this misty crag, known as "the Cloud Gatherer" or the "harsh mountain" and celebrated by Homer: "piercing the sky, with storm cloud round the peak dissolving never… No mortal man could scale it, nor as much land there, not with twenty hands and feet, so sheer are the cliffs." Italy's most recently established national park protects chestnut trees, oaks and beeches. The massif serves as a catchment area from which radiate deep valleys eroded by fast-flowing torrents (fiumare). The wide riverbeds are dry in summer, but can fill up rapidly and the waters become destructive.

- **Information:** Parco Nazionale dell'Aspromonte.
  ☎0965 74 30 60, www.parcoaspromonte.it.
- **Orient Yourself:** S 183 between S 112 and Melito di Porto Salvo runs through attractive scenery and affords numerous spectacular **panoramas**★★★.
- **Parking:** Park in Montalto for hikes into the mountains, and up to the peak of Montalto.
- **Organising Your Time:** Allow 1–2 days.
- **Don't Miss:** Views from the top of Montalto and a pilgrimage to the Sanctuary di Santa Maria di Polsi.
- **Especially for Kids:** A gentle lesson on the ski slope at Gambarie.
- **Also See:** MASSICCIO DELLA SILA.

Parco Nazionale dell'Aspromonte

A Bit of History

Beautiful, wildly dramatic and uncompromising, the Aspromonte massif has inspired everyone from artists to storytellers throughout history. The first settlers were Greeks, moving inland from the coast to spread Magna Graecia to small mountain villages. Later, the mountains were immortalised by the painter Edward Lear in the 19C.

To many Italians though, it is synonymous with the Calabrian mafia, the 'Ndrangheta, who used its harsh geography to hide organized crime, especially kidnap victims in the 1970s and 80s. The area is now a designated national park.

Gambarie

Gambarie at the westernmost point of the Aspromonte national park is the main town in the area and a popular place for reggini (from Reggio) to escape to and avoid the scorching coastal heat in summer. Set in the heart of the mountains, it's an excellent base for walking (P; *for Montalto, head along the SS183 toward Melito, and turn left after 4km to the road that takes you 16km to the top*), In winter, when the mountains are spectacularly covered in snow, it turns into a small ski resort. A family oriented **ski slope** from the top of Monte Scirocco connects with the town, served by a small chair lift.

Montalto★

The highest peak in the Aspromonte massif, Montalto rises up 1995m, with the town of Gambarie nestling in its shadow.

Spectacular views are available from the top (via a 16km walk) all the way out to Sicily – look carefully and you can see the cone of Etna, piercing the low cloud cover. The mountain is crowned with a large bronze statue of Christ the Redeemer gazing out over the Straits of Messina; the first was put here in 1901, and subsequently destroyed by lightening twice since, each time being rebuilt. Beside the statue is a granite compass pointing to key cities in the world.

Sanctuary di Santa Maria di Polsi

From the top of Montalto, a steep track leads 10km down the east side of the mountain to the Sanctuary di Santa Maria di Polsi (also known as Our Lady of the Mountain), founded by Ruggero the Norman in 1144. Protected in a gorge and surrounded by high mountains, visitors could only reach it on foot until fairly recently.

This Basilian convent has been an important centre of faith for the people of the Aspromonte for centuries, and even today most devout Calabrians consider at least one pilgrimage here to be an important religious rite of passage.

The sanctuary is also infamous for a rather more secular use, as an annual meeting place for the 'Ndrangheta, the Calabrian Mafia.

Walking Tour

Sentieros

The Aspromonte massif has an excellent network of marked hiking trails (Sentieros), many of which are circular routes.

▶ *Start from Gambarie at the SS 183 on the Sentiero Verde. The walk to Monte Basilicò takes five hours there and back.*

The path (green trail markers) leads up on the right to the slopes of Monte Scirocco and on to Monte Nardello, beyond the youth hostel. The walk cuts through the fir and beech woods of Monte Basilicò before dropping back down into the valley below.

▶ *At the bottom of the valley the hiking trail ends on a non-asphalt road leading back to Gambarie.*

IONIAN COAST

Calabria's Ionian coastline to the east is flatter than its Tyrrhenian counterpart to the west, offering miles of wide sandy beaches and warm, blue Ionian sea. It's a magnet for holidaymakers and as a result, development has been more sustained here than anywhere else in the region, resulting in an almost uninterrupted string of resorts, and leaving little of the wild flavour that infuses the rest of Calabria's scenery.

▶ **Orient Yourself:** The Ionian coasts runs roughly 500km/300mi up the east side of Calabria.

🅿 **Parking:** Outdoor parking is available close to most of the bigger beaches. Shady covered car parks are also common, usually near the seafronts.

🕐 **Organising Your Time:** Allow 2 days. The Ionian Coast is a seasonal area, and many facilities may be closed in winter.

🚫 **Don't Miss:** The Graecanico mountain villages, as their ancient Greek-Italian culture is fading quickly.

👁 **Also See:** TYRRENHIAN COAST.

A Bit of History

The first colonies on the Ionian coast were founded in the 8C BC by the Greeks, whose influence can still be seen today in the Graecanico cultures that still exist in small inland mountain villages. Magna Graecia, together with Byzantine colonies and Basilian monks who came to the area (including St Basil, father of the Greek Church, who lived from c. AD 330–379) shaped the early art and history along the coast. Today it is a popular beach holiday destination, particularly for Italians who descend on it in droves to enjoy broad, sandy beaches and warm waters, between June and September.

Pentedattilo★

Pentedattilo is a striking and evocative ghost town, crouching on the slopes of Mount Calvary and now totally abandoned by its inhabitants. Once the site of a grisly 17th century ambush (a *misfatto*) between two noble families, the Alberti and the Abenavoli, the bloody hand prints of the slaughtered Alberti family are said to be visible, pressed into the stone. Legends abound concern-

Striking location of Pentedattilo ghost town

ing the menacing rock that resembles a hand and stands above the town (in Greek pentedaktylos signifies 'five fingers', although due to erosion and collapse of parts of the mountain the hand is not as complete as it once was). One version holds that the fingers represent the hand of Baron Abenavoli, the reason that it was referred to locally as the Hand of the Devil (the eerie sounds of the winter wind howling through the gorges was also said to echo the screams of his victim, the Marquis Lorenzo Alberti). Another is that the craggy digits eventually put an end to men's violence and thirst for blood. There is some truth to this: no voices have echoed in the narrow alleyways of the town since it was abandoned in the mid-1960s, mainly as a result of the crumbling rock being deemed unsafe.

Gerace

www.comune.gerace.rc.it.
Gerace rises up on a hill of 480m/1 575ft, composed in the main of compacted sea fossils over 60 million years old. Worth a visit for the stunning and lofty views from its highest points, the Graecanico town has a more commercial veneer – the vast 11C Romanesque cathedral – crowned by Greek domes, courtyards and ornate pillars (pirated from ancient buildings) charges admission, which destroys the remote aura. The town's symbol is a hawk, reflected in its Greek name, hierax. Byzantines and Normans lived there together, and it was subjected to invasions by the Swabians, French and Aragonese. It was also an illustrious episcopal seat. At one time Gerace had so many churches (around 120 in total) it was known both as "the city of a hundred bells" and "the city of saints".

Duomo

One of the largest religious buildings in Calabria, this imposing cathedral includes the **Prison of the Five Martyrs of Gerace**. Damaged by numerous earthquakes throughout the centuries, it has been painstakingly rebuilt each time and has lost none of its impressive pres-

ence. Inside, the ceiling soars above a nave and two aisles, divided by 13 Corinthian columns, whose stone originated from the ancient temples at the nearby coastal area of Locri. Visits to the crypt are also possible, and the cathedral also has a small Diocesan museum in the lower chapel of St Joseph, with displays of statues, silver and gold crowns and other church relics.

Close to the cathedral is an interesting archway, crowned by a lovely sundial.

Church of San Francesco

In the Largo delle Tre Chiese (square of three churches) the **Church of San Francesco** (☎0964 35 61 40; www.locride.net/gerace.htm) has a polychrome marble **high altar**★.

Stilo

The native town of philosopher **Tommaso Campanella** (1568–1639), filled with hermitages and Basilian monasteries, clings to a mountain at an altitude of 400m/1 312ft. Further up, almost camouflaged, sits the Byzantine jewel of a church, **La Cattolica**★.

La Cattolica

♿◷*Open daily, 21 Mar–21 Oct, 8am–8pm, rest of the year 8am–6pm.* ✉*Donations welcome.* ☎0964 77 60 06; www.comune.stilo.rc.it.

Cattolica church in Stilo, a delicate expression of 10C Greek-Byzantine art

T. Zane/MICHELIN

Built in the 10C, this mid-Byzantine structure is one of the most important examples of its kind in Italy. Built to a square plan, it is roofed with five cylindrical domes. The elegant external decoration consists of brickwork, a traced central dome and roof tiles. Inside, the Greek cross is composed of nine domed and barrel-vaulted sections, each supported by four marble columns. In the left apse there is a bell, added in the 16th century when the church was converted to the Latin rite. The interior was once covered with exquisite frescoes and mosaics, but unfortunately these cannot be admired in their full glory now, due to earthquake damage over the years.

Catanzaro

The regional capital of Calabria, is a lively town, if not particularly physically attractive, thanks to numerous earthquakes and hasty rebuilding efforts. The centre has the most charm, with a whisper of its Byzantine and Medieval past if you look carefully. The shady park of the **Villa Trieste** (*open daily, 7am–9pm in summer, rest of the year 6pm*) contains the **Museo Provinciale.**

Museo Provinciale
Via Margherita.
Open Tue–Fri 10am–1.30pm, 3.30pm–5pm; Sat 10am–1.30pm; Sun 9am–12.30pm. Closed Mon. Donations welcome. 0961 72 00 19.

A small, but interesting collection of artefacts recovered from the surrounding area, and artwork from Calabrian artists. The highlight is a selection of work by Mimmo Rotella, a native to Catanzaro, who was famous for his iconic 1950s film-poster collages.

Capo Colonna

In Antiquity, this cape, crowned by the ruins of the temple of **Hera Lacinia**, was known as Capo Lacinio or Promunturium Lacinium.

Hera Lacinia
From the last decades of the 8C BC, one of Magna Graecia's most famous temples stood here, that of of **Hera Lacinia**★★. It had a golden age in the 5C BC, but began to decline in 173 BC, when the Consul Fulvio Flacco removed part of the marble roof. The rennovation failed due to the complexity of the original design. It was then plundered by pirates and became a quarry for the Aragonese foundations of Crotone in the 16C. The temple was finally destroyed by an earthquake in 1683. Now only 48 columns remain at the ruins of this Doric temple, which was dedicated to Hera, the wife of Zeus and the most important goddess on Mount Olympus (*see Museo Archeologico at Crotone*).

Ruins of the Hera Lacinia temple

©Marcella Pedone/Tips Images

In 1964, italian film maker Pier Paolo Pasolini (1922–75) shot some of the scenes of his film *The Gospel According to St Matthew* here.

Crotone

The ancient town of Croton was an Achaean colony of Magna Graecia, founded in 710 BC. It was celebrated in Antiquity for its riches, the beauty of its women and the prowess of athletes such as Milo of Croton, so admired by Virgil. Around 532 BC Pythagoras founded several religious communities devoted to the study of mathematics. When they became too powerful, these scholars were expelled northwards toward Metapontum (present-day Metaponto). The rival city of Locari defeated Croton in the mid-6C BC, which in turn defeated its other rival, Sybaris.

The city welcomed Hannibal during the Second Punic War, before being conquered by Rome. A succession of rulers followed, including the Byzantines, Saracens and the Normans. It became part of the Kingdorm of Sardinia in 1860, and was incorporated into the newly formed Kingdom of Italy in 1861. Today, Crotone is a prosperous seaport, located between the ports of Taormina and Messina, and industrial centre, as well as a popular holiday resort.

Museo Archeologico
Via Risorgimento.
Open daily, 9am–9pm (last admission 7.30pm). Closed first and third Mon of the month, 1 Jan and 25 Dec. €2. 0962 23 082.

Arguably the best collection of finds from along the Ionian Coast, there's a wealth of Magna Graecia artefacts and information at this modern museum (and some blissfully cool rooms to retreat to during the fierce summer heat). Collections include Greek and Roman coins, fragments and details of the excavations at Crotone including maps of the digs, and lists of Olympic winners from Antiquity.

The most arresting displays are a rare nuraghic boat from Sardinia, dated between 5–7C BC that was raised from

a tomb at Capo Colonna in 1987, and the **Treasure of Hera**★★, a collection of bronze votive statues that include a gorgon, a horse, a winged siren and a sphinx, as well as an delicate gold diadem, garlanded with leaves and myrtle springs, found at the temple of Hera Lacinia.

Duomo
Corso Vittorio Emanuele.
Dating from 9–11C BC, Crotone's cathedral has been rebuilt with a neo-classical façade. The interior consists of a nave with two aisles and is decorated with Baroque details. Of note inside is a pretty 12C baptismal font and the statue of the Madonna di Capo Colonna, an icon of the Black Madonna.
Tradition holds that it was brought from the East in the early years of Christianity. The statue is usually locked away in the cathedral, but at midnight on the third Saturday in May it is brought out and paraded through the town on a pilgrimage to Capo Colonna, and returned to the Duomo by boat the following day, as part of a week of festivities.

Rossano

The town spreads liberally over a hillside clad in rows of olive groves. In the Middle Ages Rossano was the capital of Greek monasticism in the west, and a place where expelled or persecuted Basilian monks came for refuge. The monks lived in the cells, which can still be seen today.
The perfect little church of San Marco dates from this period. The flat east end has three projecting semi-circular apses, all with graceful openings. To the right of the cathedral, is the **Museo Diocesano**.

Museo Diocesano
Open Tue–Sat 9.30am–12.30pm, 4.30pm–7pm; Sun and public holidays 10am–noon, 5pm–7pm. Closed Mon. €3.10. 0983 52 52 63.
The highlight of this eclectic collection of liturgical artefacts is a valuable **Purpureus Codex**★, a 6C evangelistary with brightly coloured illumination.

MASSICCIO DELLA SILA★★

Sila has an ancient name that translates as "primordial forest": the Greek version of the word is *hyla*, the Latin *silva*. This plateau measures 1 700km2/656sq mi, alternating prairies and forests of larch pine and beech trees. On the Sila Grande are the two towns of Camigliatello and Lorica. About ten kilometres away from Camigliatello is the visitors' centre of the **Parco Nazionale della Calabria**, which offers botanical and geological walks for visitors. The wooden houses that dot the landscape contribute to the northern-country atmosphere, particularly along the lakes Cecita, **Arvo**★ and Ampolino.

- 🛈 **Information:** www.paarcosila.it; www.portalesila.it.
- ▶ **Orient Yourself:** Cosenza is the gateway to La Sila and a the most convenient base for mountain activities in the area.
- 🅿 **Parking:** Parking is available at the visitors' centre.
- 🕘 **Organising Your Time:** Allow plenty of time here if you're a hiker - the area has some of the best, and most underused, walking trails in Southern Italy.
- 😊 **Don't Miss:** The pretty, winding Medieval centre of Consenza.
- 🧒 **Especially for Kids:** Enclosures at the Parco Nazionale della Calabria visitors' centre display deer and wolves in their natural habitat, viewed from wood hideouts.
- 🕯 **Also See:** ASPROMONTE; TYRRHENIAN COAST.

A Bit of History

Europe's largest high altitude plain, the Sila, sits deep in the interior of Calabria. Exploited for centuries by feudal landlords for its natural wealth, the Sila was the site of a large logging industry, as well as extensive ancient royal forests, some of which were bequeathed intact by their landowners to the state following the unification of Italy. Today the area is part of the non-contiguous Parco Nazionale della Calabria, along with the Aspromonte to the south.

Driving Tour

Approx 110km/70mi round trip.
Allow half a day.

Camigliatello Silano

🅿🕘*Call ahead for opening hours.*
Walking tours available. ☎*0984 57 97 57.*

The main visitors centre for the Parco Nazionale della Calabria is located in the town of Camigliatello Silano, also a key ski centre in winter.

Cosenza

© Giuseppe Bevacqua/Fotolia.com

▶ *Head west from Camigliatello to Consenza on the main Silana-Crotonese road SS 107.*

Cosenza

Town plan in the Michelin Atlas Italy.

The jumble of flyovers and faceless streets that greet visitors to this modern town cradle a welcome surprise in the old town, where medieval streets and palaces recall the prosperity of the Angevin and Aragonese periods. Sitting proudly above the Crati and Busento rivers, Consenza was then considered the artistic and religious capital of Calabria. The 12C-13C **cathedral** (Duomo) on the *Corso Telesio* has recently been restored to its original Baroque aspect. Among the treasures inside are a lovely 13C Byzantine Madonna in a chapel off the north aisle, and a **mausoleum**★ that contains the heart of Isabella of Aragon, wife of Philip III, King of France. Isabella died in 1271 outside Consenza on the way back from Tunis with the sainted king's body and was buried in France's St-Denis Basilica.

▶ *Head north on the A3 out of Consenza. Exit on to the SS 105 after approx 35km and head west to Altomonte.*

Altomonte

The large market town is dominated by an imposing 14C Angevin cathedral dedicated to **Santa Maria della Consolazione**, which boasts a fine rose window. Inside there are no aisles and the east end is flat. The fine **tomb**★ is that of Filippa Sangineto. The small **museo civico** (🔊 *tours available;* 🕐 *open daily;* 💶€3; ☎0981 94 80 4116; *www.altomonte.com*) beside the church has several precious works of art in addition to a statue of **St Ladislas**★ attributed to Simone Martini.

Market Town

Serra San Bruno

Set between the Sila and Aspromonte Massifs, amid the imposing Calabrian

mountains covered with oak and pine forests★, this small market town grew up around a hermitage founded by St Bruno of Cologne, who died in 1101. The confraternity of San Bruno still lives in The Priory, whose library and a small adjacent museum are open to the public.

Santa Maria della Consolazione

TYRRHENIAN COAST

The western side of the vast Calabrian seaboard, the Tyrrhenian coastline runs from Scilla to Capo Scalea. The southern stretch has the most ruggedly beautiful stretches, bitten into by pretty sandy bays and small resorts. Further north, the natural beauty is challenged periodically by cheap hotel developments, a result of the popularity of this coastline in the summer months.

▶ **Orient Yourself:** The A3 road north of Reggio up to Pizzo is one of Italy's most scenic coastal drives.

🅿 **Parking:** Most beaches around Tropea have car parking space on the roads behind them.

🕐 **Organising Your Time:** Allow two days to explore the coast.

🐾 **Don't Miss:** The Bronzi di Riace at the Museo Archaeologico of Reggio di Calabria, underground tufa statues at the Chiesa di Piedigrotta and mythological Scilla.

Especially for Kids: Sandy beaches at Palmi, beaches around Tropea and tartufo at Pizzo.

👣 **Also See:** IONIAN COAST.

A Bit of History

Like the Ionian coast, the history of the Tyrrhenian coast is bound up with Magna Graecia, whose Greek citizens settled along here in the 6C BC. With its dramatic jagged look, the Tyrrenhian coastline was the perfect foil for classical mythological heroes, the greatest being Ulysses, who fought the Scilla off along the southern stretch and was immortalised in the writings of Homer. Byzantine and Roman Empires arrived in succession, followed by Normans, Swabians, Aragonese, Arabs and Anjous, all of whom left their marks in the small clifftop villages along the stretch. Today, the invaders are holidaymakers, who fill the beaches, particularly around Tropea, in high season.

Paola

St Francis of Paola was born here around 1416. A **monastery** (santuario) stands 2km/1mi away up the hillside.

Santuario di San Francesco di Paola

🕐 *Open daily, summer 6am–1pm, 2pm –8pm; winter 6am–1pm, 2pm–5pm.* ☎ *0982 58 25 18; www.sanfrancescodi paolalamezia.it.*

Visited by numerous pilgrims, this large group of sacred buildings includes the basilica with a lovely Baroque exterior that enshrines the relics of the saint, tranquil cloisters and a hermitage that is hewn out of the rock, and contains a number of striking votive offerings.

Tropea ♨♨

www.tropea.biz.

Tropea has a dramatic setting, perched on a sandy clifftop on the Promontorio di Tropea, which stretches from Pizzo in the north to Nicotera in the south. Set in the middle of one of the most beautiful, and holiday-friendly stretches of coastline in Calabria, Tropea is the jewel in the Tyrrhenian coastal crown and heaves with tourists in the summer months. The influx is primarily those heading for the broad white-sand beaches fringed with aquamarine sea nearby.

However, the town itself offers a shady break from scorching heat, and is a pleasant place to wander, made up of pretty, winding lanes and genteel piazzas. Look out for the renowned local onions on sale on the grocery shops; grown in villages around Tropea, these vegetables are so highly regarded that *Cipolla di Tropea* (Tropea's onions) has become a synonym for all generic red onions in Italy.

©Danin Tulic/iStockphoto.com

Santa Maria dell'Isola, Tropea

Santa Maria dell'Isola

The solitary church of **Santa Maria dell'Isola**, stands opposite the town, clinging as it has done for centuries to an unforgiving rock. Medieval in origin, it has undergone a significant Renaissance facelift. The church was originally built in isolated sacred splendour on its own island. However, centuries of silt deposits have now joined the remote hermitage to the mainland.

Cathedral

The most evocative reference to Tropea's past is its beautiful Romanesque-Norman **cathedral**, complete with its original façade. The Swabian portico, grafted onto it, links the church to the bishop's residence.

Close to the doorway, two unexploded WWII bombs still in situ are regarded as a modern miracle, a result of divine protection by Our Lady of Romania, the town's patron saint.

Palmi ⚓

This town perched high above the sea on a terrace overlooking Punta Peloro, has a small fishing harbour and a lovely **sandy beach** (*la Marinella*)★ Kids.
Aside from its undeniable charm, the town's other great attraction is the **Museo Comunale**, which contains an unparalleled collection of Calabrian enthnographic material.

Museo Comunale

Casa della Cultura, Via San Giorgio.
🕐*Open daily, 8am–2pm (Thu also 3pm–6pm).* 🕐*Closed Sat, Sun and public holidays.* ✆€1.55. ☎0966 26 22 50.
The museum might not look much from the outside, but inside it houses a superlative **ethnographic section**★ evoking the life and traditions of Calabria, from local costumes to handicrafts, masks and ceramics. Its varied displays also include a casts gallery of the work of sculptor Michele Guerrisi. The library of Calabrian History is for scholars and visitors to use on request.

Scilla★

This town, like a perfect cameo carved from the rock, has a bloody mythology. Here Ulysses confronted the monster Scilla, a woman with dog-headed tentacles, who ate six of his sailors, as well as the Sirens "on their sweet meadow lolling… bones of dead men rotting in a pile beside them and flayed skins shrivel around the spot." Opposite Scilla, near Messina, lurked Charybdis, whom Jupiter turned into a sea monster for her voracity. Three times daily she engulfed the surrounding waves. Subsequently Charybdis spurted the water out, creating a strong current. Ulysses vessel rowed past her once. During their second encounter, the epic narrowly escaped her clutches by grabbing

©Giuseppe Masci/Tips Images

Chiesa di Santa Maria di Piedigrotta

a fig tree at the entrance of the monster's grotto.

The fisherman's district, the Chinalèa, is comprised of an intricate maze of houses and alleys going down to the water's edge. A short way along, the town's beach is a nice place to swim and fish. Higher up, Ruffo Castle (1255) gazes nobly over the town, while the waters around Scilla, like the waters of Bagnara Calabra, contain numerous swordfish.

Pizzo

Hanging on to the side of a steep sea cliff, Pizzo is a pleasant collection of small houses and shady alleys that occasionally open out to great views of the sea. A popular place in summer, this small village can get rather crowded with tourists enjoying its relaxed atmosphere and searching out the perfect tartufo, a local rich chocolate ice-cream desert, at one of its many small gelateria.

Chiesa di Santa Maria di Piedigrotta
Piazza Sannazzaro.
Open daily 9am–1pm, 3pm–7.30pm.
€3. www.chiesadi piedigrotta.it.
Completely excavated from the tufa rock, this quirky underground cave-church is part place of worship and part sculptural gallery. The cavern was

initially carved as a small votive church by 17th century Neopolitan shipwreck survivors. Over subsequent centuries, local sculptors have enlarged and modified the space into two lateral vaults and a central vault, adding statues and sculptural groups inspired by the Holy Scriptures; the most recent additions have included Pope John Paul II and more secular figures such as JFK and Fidel Castro.

Chiesa Matrice di San Giorgio
Via Marconi.
This 16C church houses the tomb of Napoleon's brother-in-law, Joachim Murat, who was married to his younger sister, Caroline. A former King of Naples and Sicily, Murat was an enlightened ruler, but failed to make much of an impact in Calabria.

He was eventually imprisoned here in Pizzo, at the Castello di Pizzo (now renamed **Castello Murat**), just south of Piazza della Repubblica, and executed by firing squad on the orders of his arch rival, Ferdinand IV of Naples.

Vibo Valentia

This small settlement, first colonised by the Greeks, and then by the Romans lies 8km/5mi south of Pizzo and is a pleasant pit stop on the way down the coast.

There's not a huge amount to see here, but the Norman castle, later subject to fortification by the Angevins, is worth visiting for the splendid panoramas over the coastline and the small, but interesting and well laid-out **museum**, (◐open Tue–Sun, 9am–7.30m; ◐closed Mon and national hols; ☞€2; ☎0963 433 50) with its displays of antiquities from the Greek settlement Hipponion, including piece of 6C bronze armour.

Reggio di Calabria

Once the capital city of Calabria, this gritty port on the toe of the Italian peninsula boot is the oldest and largest city in the region. Founded by Greek settlers in 720 BC, it was known as Rhegion, later to become Rhegium Julium under Roman rule. With the lure of its strategic position, the city was claimed by successive rulers; through Byzantine rule it then fell under the sovereignty of the Kingdom of Sicily, followed by the Kingdom of Naples. Reggio's most trying hour, however, came in 1908, when an earthquake, still the most intense on record in modern western European history, razed practically all of the city to the ground. The subsequent rebuilding has a charmless, hurried feel to it. The island of gentility in its utilitarian solidity is the long and charming seafront parade, which is the site for most of the city's evening passeggiata.

Modern Reggio is now best known for two things; the beautiful **Bronzi di Raice** in the Museo Nazionale, and being the annual producer of half the world's supply of bergamot (a citrus flower, made into oil). It is also the main ferry port for passage to Sicily, whose lights can be seen twinkling in the distance at night from the port.

Museo Nazionale

▱✗♿ *Piazza de Nava.* ◐*Open daily 9am–7pm.* ☞*€6.* ☎*0965 812 255; www. museonazionaleerc.it.* ◐*With so much in this densely packed museum, it's worth investing in an audioguide. www.turismo. regione.calabria.it.*

This splendid museum evokes all the grandeur of Reggio in Antiquity, as room after room of exhibits from Magna Graecia greet the visitor. Pride of place is given to the **Bronzi di Riace**★★★ on the lower floor, two larger than life-size bronze statues found in the sea near Riace in 1972. Thought to have been forged around 450BC, these statues are an intriguing mix of physical beauty and mystery, their provenance unknown, indeed even whether they represent mortals or Gods.

Elsewhere in the museum there are other wonderful exhibits to seek out, including the oldest known Greek portrait, a 5C BC bronze called the *Philosopher's Head*, a superlative collection of art, primarily by southern Italian artists and the **pinakes**★, terracotta low reliefs used in Locri as ex-votos in the 5C BC. These were dedicated to Persephone, bride of Hades who carried her off to the Underworld while she was picking flowers.

©World Illustrated/Photoshot

Statue B of Bronzi di Riace (c. 450BC), Museo Nazionale

A

B

C

INDEX

INDEX

WHERE TO STAY

># INDEX

WHERE TO EAT

MAPS AND PLANS

LIST OF MAPS

THEMATIC MAPS

TOWN PLANS

TOURING MAPS

PLANS OF ARCHAEOLOGICAL SITES

PLANS OF CHURCHES

COMPANION PUBLICATIONS

- Michelin map 565 Sicilia, which covers the island of Sicily and includes an alphabetical index of towns, as well as maps of Agrigento, Catania, Messina, Palermo and Siracusa. Scale 1:400 000.
- Michelin map 735 Italia, a practical map which provides the visitor with a complete picture of Italy's road network. Scale 1:1 000 000.

- Michelin Road Atlas Italia, a useful, spiral-bound atlas with an alphabetical index of 70 towns and cities. Scale 1:300 000.

Internet users can access personalised route plans, Michelin maps and town plans, and addresses of hotels and restaurants featured in the Michelin Guide Italia through the website at: **www.ViaMichelin.com**

Abbreviations

H   Town hall (Municipio)

J   Law courts (Palazzo di Giustizia)

M   Museum (Museo)

P   Local authority offices (Prefettura)

POL.   Police station (Polizia)
(in large towns: Questura)

T   Theatre (Teatro)

U   University (Università)

Selected monuments and sights

Tour - Departure point

Catholic church

Protestant church, other temple

Synagogue - Mosque

Building

Statue, small building

Calvary, wayside cross

Fountain

Rampart - Tower - Gate

Château, castle, historic house

Ruins

Dam

Factory, power plant

Fort

Cave

Troglodyte dwelling

Prehistoric site

Viewing table

Viewpoint

Other place of interest

Special symbols

Gendarmerie (Carabinieri)

Temple, Greek and Roman ruins

Beach

LEGEND

	Sight	Seaside resort	Winter sports resort	Spa
Highly recommended ★★★		☆☆☆	✳✳✳	‡‡‡
Recommended ★★		☆☆	✳✳	‡‡
Interesting	★	☆	✳	‡

Additional symbols

🛈	Tourist information
═══ ═══	Motorway or other primary route
❶ ❶	Junction: complete, limited
⊞═══ ═══	Pedestrian street
ɪ═════ɪ	Unsuitable for traffic, street subject to restrictions
▭▭▭▭ ----	Steps – Footpath
🚆 🚉	Train station – Auto-train station
🚌 S.N.C.F	Coach (bus) station
──	Tram
Ⓜ	Metro, underground
🅿	Park-and-Ride
♿	Access for the disabled
✉	Post office
☎	Telephone
✉	Covered market
⨯×⨯	Barracks
⚠	Drawbridge
ᴗ	Quarry
✕	Mine
🅱 🅵	Car ferry (river or lake)
⛴	Ferry service: cars and passengers
⛵	Foot passengers only
③	Access route number common to Michelin maps and town plans
Bert (R.)...	Main shopping street
AZ B	Map co-ordinates

Sports and recreation

🏇	Racecourse
⛸	Skating rink
≋ ▱	Outdoor, indoor swimming pool
🎥	Multiplex Cinema
⛵	Marina, sailing centre
⌂	Trail refuge hut
◻▪◼▪◻	Cable cars, gondolas
◻++++◻	Funicular, rack railway
🚂	Tourist train
◇	Recreation area, park
🐎	Theme, amusement park
ⵘ	Wildlife park, zoo
❀	Gardens, park, arboretum
⬡	Bird sanctuary, aviary
🚶	Walking tour, footpath
☺	Of special interest to children

447

Michelin Apa Publications Ltd

A joint venture between Michelin and Langenscheidt

Suite 6, Tulip House, 70 Borough High Street, London SE1 1XF, United Kingdom

© 2009 Michelin Apa Publications Ltd
ISBN 978-1-906261-41-2
Printed: September 2008
Printed and bound: Himmer, Germany